P9-EEQ-888

JOHN JAY

THE WINNING OF THE PEACE

1780–1784

A 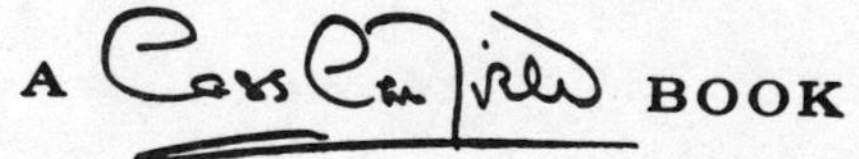 BOOK

BOOKS BY RICHARD B. MORRIS

John Jay: The Winning of the Peace 1780–1784 (*editor,* 1980)
The U.S. Department of Labor Bicentennial History of The American Worker (*editor,* 1976)
John Jay: The Making of a Revolutionary 1745–1780 (*editor,* 1975)
Seven Who Shaped Our Destiny (1973)
Harper Encyclopedia of the Modern World *(with Graham W. Irwin)* (1970)
The Emerging Nations and the American Revolution (1970)
John Jay, the Nation, and the Court (1967)
The American Revolution Reconsidered (1967)
The Peacemakers (1965)
(Volumes I and II of THE LIFE HISTORY OF THE UNITED STATES)
The New World (1963)
The Making of the Nation (1963)
Great Presidential Decisions (1960)
The Spirit of 'Seventy-Six *(with Henry Steele Commager)* (1958, 1967)
Alexander Hamilton and the Founding of the Nation (1957)
The American Revolution: A Brief History (1955)
Encyclopedia of American History (*first edition,* 1953; *Bicentennial edition,* 1976)
Fair Trial (1953)
A Treasury of Great Reporting *(with Louis L. Snyder)* (1949)
Government and Labor in Early America (1946)
The Era of the American Revolution (*editor,* 1939)
Studies in the History of American Law (1930)
A Guide to the Principal Sources for Early American History *(with Evarts Boutell Greene)* (1929)

John Jay

THE WINNING OF THE PEACE

Unpublished Papers 1780–1784

EDITED BY

RICHARD B. MORRIS

ASSOCIATE EDITOR: ENE SIRVET

II

HARPER & ROW, PUBLISHERS
NEW YORK
Cambridge
Hagerstown
Philadelphia
San Francisco

1817

London
Mexico City
São Paulo
Sydney

The preparation of this volume of the Papers of John Jay was made possible by grants from two independent Federal agencies: the National Historical Publications and Records Commission and the Program for Editions of the National Endowment for the Humanities.

 For information address Harper & Row, Publishers, Inc., 10 East 53rd Street, New York, N.Y. 10022. Published simultaneously in Canada by Fitzhenry & Whiteside Limited, Toronto.

FIRST EDITION

Designed by Sidney Feinberg

Library of Congress Cataloging in Publication Data

Jay, John, 1745-1829.
John Jay.
(A Cass Canfield book)
Consists chiefly of previously unpublished papers in the collections of Columbia University Libraries.
Includes bibliographical references and index.
CONTENTS: v. 1. The making of a revolutionary: unpublished papers, 1745-1780.—v. 2. The winning of the peace: unpublished papers, 1780–1784.
1. United States—Politics and government—Revolution, 1775–1783—Sources. 2. United States—Politics and government—1783-1809—Sources. 3. New York (State)—Politics and government—1775–1865—Sources. 4. Jay, John, 1745–1829. 5. Statesmen—United States—Correspondence. I. Morris, Richard Brandon, 1904– ed.
E302.J425 973.3´092´4 [B] 74–28793
ISBN 0–06–013080–6 vol. 1
ISBN 0–06–013048–2 vol. 2

---

80 81 82 83 84 10 9 8 7 6 5 4 3 2 1

CONTENTS

INTRODUCTION

I

IMPASSE IN SPAIN

II

PARIS AND THE CHALLENGE OF PEACEMAKING

III

AMERICA AND THE GENERAL PEACE

IV

CLOSING MONTHS ABROAD

ILLUSTRATIONS AND MAPS

JOHN JAY

THE WINNING OF THE PEACE

1780–1784

INTRODUCTION

Let Posterity Judge

"Let posterity have all means of judging and let them judge," John Adams declared, in an appeal to all parties and to all nations concerned in the peacemaking of the American Revolution to open up their papers.[1] In the present volume Adams' plea has been heeded, and an effort has been made to make as fully available as possible the unpublished documents, correspondence, journals, and diaries bearing on John Jay, a principal figure in the negotiations by which the United States secured its independence.

From the start Jay's role proved to be a subject of intense and protracted controversy. Convinced that France, though an esteemed ally, opposed America's claims in matters other than independence, Jay declined to accept the constrictions laid down both by the American Congress and Versailles and opened direct and even secret negotiations with the British ministry. Jay "glories in being independent,"[2] was how France's minister to the United States, the Chevalier de La Luzerne, characterized the American's diplomatic posture, while Luzerne's chief, the Comte de Vergennes, found John Jay and John Adams principled but unmanageable, or, as he put it more diplomatically, "too cosmopolitan for France to figure in their calculations."[3] Both French observers hit the mark.

For making the first, and what was to prove the most durable, peace treaty in the history of American diplomacy, the American Commissioners in Paris, Jay included, were privately criticized by their own Secretary for Foreign Affairs, Robert R. Livingston, and narrowly missed censure by Congress. The issue was not permitted to die down. Party divisions in the 1790s revived it, and the nineteenth-century editors of pertinent diplomatic documents exercised their judgments on the basis of partial documentation.

John Jay's own prompt documented defense is included in this

[1]*Boston Patriot,* 24 July 1811.
[2]Luzerne to Vergennes, 26 Sept. 1783, CP EU 25: 317.
[3]Vergennes to Luzerne, 24 Dec. 1783, *ibid.,* pp. 224–29.

volume,[4] but he did not see fit to release his fragmentary, but highly significant diary of the negotiations hereinafter published. His colleagues were less reticent. John Adams hastened to forward his "Peace Journal," a diary which by some route came into the hands of Secretary Livingston and was read to Congress, some of whose members finding its comments "ungenerous" if not "ridiculous."[5] Not to be outdistanced in any literary contest, Franklin had already taken up his pen to record his own version of the negotiations in a journal which did not see the light of day for many years.[6] The matter was not permitted to rest. Years later Adams took to the public prints to defend with his customary vigor his and Jay's actions as peacemakers,[7] while their sons and grandsons entered the lists as champions of their respective forbears' joint and separate roles.[8]

Even before the Definitive Treaty was completed Jay evidenced concern about the need for a correct historical account of the great events in which he and his colleagues had participated. If anyone could write it, in Jay's opinion, it was Charles Thomson, the permanent Secretary of Congress. Jay appealed to Thomson to "devote one Hour in the four and twenty to giving posterity a true account" of the "Rise, Conduct, and Conclusion of the American Revolution." Such a history need not be cluttered with battles and sieges, advances and retreats, Jay felt, but should concentrate on "the political story of the Revolution," the one aspect which, in his judgment, would be the most

[4]JJ to Robert R. Livingston, 19 July 1783, below, preceded by editorial note, "The Commissioners Defend the Treaty."

[5]See *AP,* III, 41–43.

[6]For JJ's comment on the so-called "Journals" of Adams and himself, found in William Temple Franklin, ed., *Memoirs of the Life and Writings of Benjamin Franklin* (6 vols., Philadelphia, 1808–18) IV, 293, see JJ to John Adams, 27 Feb. 1821, and Adams' reply, 8 March 1821, MHi: Adams, and JP (both ALS). JJ followed up with a request to William Duane, the printer of the W. T. Franklin edition, for copies of Benjamin Franklin's alleged "Journal" prior to any publication; JJ to William Duane, 22 May 1821, Dft in JP. (Illness had forced Franklin to suspend continuing his "Journal" after 1 July 1782.) It is printed in W. T. Franklin, *loc. cit.,* pp. 203–97, and in a number of later editions of Franklin's writings.

[7]See, *e.g., Boston Patriot,* 9 May 1809–10 Feb. 1810; 4 Jan., 7 Sept. 1811.

[8]See William Jay, "The Treaty of Peace, 1783; Correspondence Between William Jay and John Quincy Adams," *Magazine of American History,* III (1871), 39–44; John Jay II, *On the Peace Negotiations of 1782–83, As Illustrated by the Secret Correspondence of France and England* (New York, 1888), reprinted in American Historical Association, *Papers,* III, no. 1 (1888). *Cf.* also Justin Winsor, ed., *Narrative and Critical History of America* (8 vols., Boston, 1884–89), VII, 89–214. *Cf.* also review article by JJ's son-in-law, William McVickar, in *New York Review* (October 1841), pp. 303–07, and Charles Francis Adams, *The Life of John Adams* (2 vols., Philadelphia, 1871), II, 7–72.

subject to "misrepresentation." At the same time Jay doubted the propriety of Thomson's publishing such a work in his lifetime, and, considering the Secretary's official position, cautioned against letting people know what he was about. Regrettably, Thomson did not take the "Hint",[9] for no one had a fuller command of the central role of Congress in the Revolution.

In later years John Jay's friends sought to draw him out, but he declined to enter the arena of public debate, convinced that his own official reports and letterbook contained "a correct statement of the facts" despite historical writings inspired by partisan rancor.[10] On reflection, even Jay came to doubt the adequacy of the available documentation. "Time is daily obscuring and diminishing the material" for a history of the "late war," he conceded to one correspondent, and the task was becoming "more and more difficult." Recollection testimony of events that had transpired almost a half century earlier could prove treacherous, as the fallible accounts written in their declining years by Thomas Jefferson and John Adams attest. Jay, however, would give a high priority to interviews with surviving participants—to what we now call "oral history."[11] By 1821 Jay no longer felt competent to advise George A. Otis, who had recently translated the Piedmontese Charles W. Botta's *History of the War of Independence of the United States of America*, as to "the most authentic documents" relating to the controversial Paris peace negotiations of 1782–83. Years had elapsed since he had looked at the available documents, Jay confessed, and "others have been published which I have not seen."[12]

Like other principal actors in the drama of war and peace, John Jay had long been concerned with preserving a full record of those events. He had been meticulous in keeping letterbooks of his correspondence while on diplomatic missions abroad. Returning to America and entering upon his duties as Secretary for Foreign Affairs, he gave close attention to assembling the diplomatic archives. In 1787 he informed John Adams that he was collecting the latter's public letters and dispatches. "It is common, you know," he wrote, "in the course of time for loose and detached papers to be lost, or mislaid, or misplaced.

[9]JJ to Charles Thomson, 10 July 1782, Dft in JP; *HPJ*, III, 51–52.

[10]Judge Richard Peters to JJ, 12 Dec. 1818, ALS in JP. JJ to Peters, 25 Jan. 1819, ALS in PHi: Peters, XI, 102; Dft in JP; 25 Nov. 1820, ALS in JP; and 12 March 1821, ALS in PHi: Peters, XII, 3; *HPJ*, III, 423–25, 432–33, 444–46.

[11]JJ to Rev. Dr. Jedidiah Morse, 14 Feb. 1815, ALS in PHi: Gratz, Case 1, box VII; *HPJ*, IV, 383–85.

[12]JJ to George A. Otis, 13 Jan. 1821, Dft in JP; *HPJ*, III, 443.

It is to papers in this office that future historians must recur for accurate accounts of many interesting affairs respecting the late revolution."[13] Writing the history of that epoch would entail "much time, patient perseverance, and research," Jay counseled Jedidiah Morse, while calling his attention to the need to examine the *"public* and *private* journals of Congress," along with those of the state conventions and committees of safety, in addition to diaries, memoirs, and private correspondence. However, he cautioned that, in using personal papers, "great circumspection" must be exercised.[14]

Lacking full documentation and infected by continuing partisanship, America's scholarly editors mishandled the relevant archives in a manner that would have dismayed the principal actors in the negotiation of the peace. Two editions of the diplomatic correspondence of the American Revolution were published in the nineteenth century, both under the sponsorship of Congress. The first, a twelve-volume set, was issued in 1829–30 under the prestigious editorship of Jared Sparks. His was a bowdlerized version, and his judgment on men and motives often proved ill-founded. A much more comprehensive and better annotated edition of the diplomatic correspondence in six substantial volumes was issued under the editorship of Francis Wharton in 1889. Like Sparks, Wharton was critical of the American peace commissioners for entering into separate negotiations, and like Sparks, Wharton criticized John Jay for entertaining suspicions of French intentions which these editors, insulated in time from the events, deemed unwarranted.[15] What undermines the documentation of Wharton's edition is the editor's failure to publish the ciphered portion of diplomatic dispatches. These are customarily omitted, and often the very fact of omission is not mentioned. It need hardly be necessary to point out that what was committed to cipher represented the gist of the message, much of the remainder being innocuous. In the present volume the ciphered portion of dispatches to or from John Jay are published in full.

Absent a fully comprehensive edition of the diplomatic correspondence of the American Revolution, we must turn to other sources, published or unpublished. Among the former one should consult the ongoing series of editions of the papers of early American statesmen

[13]JJ to John Adams, 25 July 1787, Dft in JP; *JAW,* VIII, 446. For a tribute to JJ's custody of the public papers during his term as Secretary for Foreign Affairs, see *SDC,* I, x.

[14]JJ to Jedidiah Morse, 28 Feb. 1787, *HPJ,* IV, 224–25.

[15]See, *e.g., RDC,* I, 471.

currently being issued under the sponsorship of the National Historical Publications and Records Commission and edited according to the canons of modern scholarship. We must examine, too, the published *Journals of the Continental Congress,* edited by Worthington C. Ford and Gaillard Hunt,[16] as well as the invaluable microfilm edition of the papers of Congress completed in 1960 by the National Archives. The *Journals* report motions, votes, some resolves, the proceedings of Congress, and some notes of debates; on the sentiment of the delegates, we must turn for illumination to Edmund C. Burnett's edition of the *Letters of Members of the Continental Congress,* and to the ongoing more comprehensive edition being currently issued under the sponsorship of the Library of Congress.[17]

It will not suffice to confine our documentation of Jay's role in the peacemaking to the American side. To comprehend the complex negotiations which terminated the world war touched off by the American Revolution, one must supplement the lines of research that Jay himself had recommended with an investigation of the archives of the European nations involved in the peacemaking. Failure to do so would lead to drawing conclusions comparable to those drawn by diplomatic historians of the Cold War who, lacking access to the counterpart Soviet archives, have ventured judgments on Western, primarily American, policymaking without confident knowledge of the intentions and secret moves of the Soviet leadership.

In the fall of 1782, at the height of the preliminary negotiations, Vergennes cautioned Luzerne: "Our way of thinking must be an impenetrable secret from the Americans."[18] The Americans, despite Vergennes' precautions, were not completely baffled, but they could only surmise, not *know,* what went on behind the scenes and behind their backs. They were not, of course, privy to the oral instructions and private conversations engaged in by their ally and the other belligerents. What was said often substantially modified what was written down, as written instructions were at times indubitably prepared for the record. The diplomatic correspondence of foreign nations was not open to inspection by the American negotiators then or in their lifetimes. Fortunately, in our own day the extant foreign archives of the years of the American Revolution are now public, and the present

[16] 34 vols., Washington, D.C., 1904–37.

[17] 8 vols., Washington, D.C., 1921–36, and, currently, Paul H. Smith *et al.,* eds., *Letters of Delegates to Congress, 1774–1789,* to date vols. I–IV, 1774–76 (Washington, D.C., 1976–79).

[18] Vergennes to Luzerne, 14 Oct. 1782, in CP EU 22: 369.

volume draws heavily upon such sources, as did the editor in preparing his monograph, *The Peacemakers: The Great Powers and American Independence,*[19] to which the reader is referred for relevant background.

This volume seeks to pierce the "impenetrable" veil which enshrouded the diplomacy of John Jay, his colleagues, and counterparts by including herein not only Jay's own correspondence and diary but such relevant documentation from other principals and their aides as will contribute to an understanding of the bases for Jay's initiatives, suspicions, surmises, and countermoves. The volume draws upon the archives in the Quai d'Orsay, upon the dispatches to and from Vergennes, his undersecretaries, and ambassadors involved in the negotiations of the peace and specifically dealing with France's reactions to American pretensions. It reports the conversations between Jay and his Spanish counterpart, the Conde de Aranda, which the latter recorded in his "Diario," now housed in Madrid's Archivo Histórico Nacional. It includes essential portions of the meticulous record kept by Richard Oswald, Britain's negotiator with the Americans, detailing for the eyes of his superiors across the Channel his protracted talks with Jay. This prime historical source is now preserved partly among the Lansdowne and Sydney Papers at the William L. Clements Library, Ann Arbor, Michigan; partly among the papers of the Marquess of Lansdowne, Bowood, Calnes, Wiltshire; and partly in the Foreign Office series in the British Public Record Office. What gives special significance to the foreign archival material hereinafter included is that so very much of the extant documentation remains largely unpublished even today.[20]

[19]New York, 1965.

[20]An exception is the massive multivolume work of Henri Doniol, whose *Histoire de la participation de la France à l'établissement des États-Unis d'Amérique* (6 vols., Paris, 1886–92) is a subjectively selective publication of the dispatches to and from the Comte de Vergennes. Useful material in print may also be found in Manuel Danvila y Collado, *Reinado de Carlos III* (5 vols., Madrid, 1893–94); in Juan F. Yela Utrilla, ed., *España ante la Independencia de los Estados Unidos* (2d ed., 2 vols., Lérida, 1925); and in the published correspondence of George III, edited by Sir John Fortescue (6 vols., London, 1928), a work marred by numerous errors of transcription, and to be supplemented by the *Later Correspondence,* edited by A. Aspinall (2 vols., Cambridge, 1962–63). Important background material, especially on the secret service side, will be found in B. F. Stevens, comp., *Facsimiles of Manuscripts in European Archives Relating to America, 1773–83* (25 vols., London, 1889–95), but this series is regrettably brief for the years 1782–83.

Publication Objectives

The aim of this volume, as of its predecessor, is the publication of hitherto unpublished significant correspondence and papers of John Jay, as well as relevant papers of Jay's associates reporting his conversations, views, and actions. Some items printed elsewhere are included in this volume because of substantial errors of omission or transliteration or of significant variances between the published versions and the originals in the Papers of John Jay housed in the Rare Book and Manuscript Library of the Columbia University Libraries or in other depositories.[21] Often in his original draft John Jay expressed his true feelings, then, like the prudent lawyer he was, he would tone them down in the addressee's version.[22] Accordingly, where a draft of a letter contains a significant variance from the published ALS, the former is included herein and the reader duly cautioned. On other occasions Jay would bury his strong sentiments in cipher, as when he criticized William Carmichael, Secretary to the Spanish Mission, as "the most deceitful, insidious Man I ever met with in my life," which, on second thought, he changed to "the most faithless and dangerous" person he had ever encountered.[23]

Normally Jay's previous editors, whether William Jay, Francis Wharton, or Henry P. Johnston, omitted the ciphered portions of his letters and usually without noting the omission. This is also true of their handling of Jay's correspondents. A typical example was the indirect criticism of France and Spain found in a communication of Robert R. Livingston, then Secretary for Foreign Affairs. Livingston complained that France was curbing America's war aims and denounced Spain for procrastinating on the issue of the navigation of the Mississippi.[24] A distinctly filiopietistic attitude on the part of previous editors impelled them to omit Jay's comments about his errant brother Sir James and to delete references to discreditable actions attributed to the latter.[25] Thus, we are denied Jay's remarks disowning his older brother or Gouverneur Morris' characterization of Sir James' conduct as "ridiculous" and "contemptible."[26] At other times what previous

[21]For the problem of collecting and organizing the Jay Papers, see *JJ*, I, 1–10.

[22]Examples: JJ to Charles Thomson, 25 April 1781; to Floridablanca, n.d. [8–16 Sept. 1781]; to David Hartley, 17 July 1783, all below.

[23]JJ to Gouverneur Morris, 28 Sept. 1781, below.

[24]Robert R. Livingston to JJ, 13 Dec. 1781, below.

[25]See, *e.g.*, JJ to Peter Van Schaack, 17 Sept. 1782, below.

[26]Gouverneur Morris to JJ, 17 June 1781, below.

editors have seen fit to omit, even when not in code, constitutes the central point of the correspondent.[27] This volume also includes a few documents of immense historical significance, because, although previously published, they have not hitherto been adequately annotated or because their reproduction is deemed essential for comprehending the events covered herein.

The editorial notes and annotations aim to furnish the reader with the background needed to identify persons, subjects, and events treated in the correspondence, references often elusive to anyone but the recipient, and to provide such other data essential to understanding its contents or to clarify the relationship to previously published correspondence of items hereinafter printed for the first time. Persons and subjects identified in Volume I are not further identified unless their status or circumstances have changed during the years covered by the present volume.

John Jay: The Seasoning of a Diplomat

When we took leave of John Jay in the previous volume the unaccredited American minister plenipotentiary to Spain was reporting to Congress his frustrations in negotiating an alliance with and obtaining financial aid from the Spanish Court. "In my Opinion," he is therein quoted, "we should endeavor to be as Independent on the Charity of our friends, as on the Mercy of our Enemies."[28] That spirit of stiff-necked independence did not desert Mr. Jay. His difficulties were compounded both by the implacable detestation in which the Spanish monarchy held rebellions, especially rebellions threatening to succeed, and by the financial embarrassments of his position. Unrealistically anticipating that Jay would turn up a cornucopia of Spanish dollars, Congress in desperation continued to pile up fiscal obligations which it expected Jay to satisfy. Jay was thereby placed in the awkward position of having to petition the Spanish Court for funds to satisfy the claims of the creditors of the rebel Congress, which Spain adamantly refused to recognize, and to assert his countrymen's right to the free navigation of the Mississippi, which Spain vigorously contested.

Jay's difficulties as a negotiator were enormously enhanced by the

[27]See, *e.g.*, below, Robert Morris to JJ, 3 Jan. 1783, concerning the problem of educating the former's sons abroad.

[28]*JJ*, I, 834.

timelag between Philadelphia and Madrid and by the routine interception by Spanish officials of dispatches to him. He had no way of knowing that Congress on 15 February 1781 had altered his original instructions and permitted him to recede from his demands for the free navigation of the Mississippi in order "to remove every obstacle to the accession of Spain to the alliance with the United States."[29] The Spanish Court, being apprised of the revised instructions long before the American plenipotentiary had learned of them even informally, kept hinting that Jay should be more conciliatory. In this sensitive situation Jay showed much better judgment than did Congress. At the San Ildefonso Conference of September 1781 he made the relinquishment of the Mississippi contingent on Spain's acceptance of his counter-offer as well as on an alliance with the United States. Shortsightedly, Spain declined Jay's terms, and the issue of the Mississippi would remain for long years a major source of contention between the parties. Finally, as a result of Spanish procrastination, American credit in Spain went from bad to worse, and in the end Jay was reduced to protesting a batch of bills payable in March of 1782 for the comparatively trivial amount of $25,000. With this gesture of protest Jay wrote off further Spanish aid or the possibility of quick recognition. He was rescued from his intolerable situation by a timely call to Paris to take part in the peace negotiations. Yet the Spanish experience stung this prideful man. We see the consequences in his tough negotiating stance toward the Conde de Aranda in Paris and in his inclusion in the Preliminaries of the separate secret clause regarding the boundaries of Florida, a highly controversial provision reflecting the concern of both Jay and Franklin that future control of the west bank of the Mississippi be shared with a friendly power.

How Jay would conduct himself in Paris was clearly forecast by his having protested to Congress the terms of his commission to negotiate the peace, terms which subordinated the American commissioners to the King of France. Thus, he would not yield to Vergennes and make the kind of territorial concessions to Spain that the French Court desired, nor would he bow to the pressures exerted by France's foreign minister that he forego his insistence on recognition of independence as a prerequisite to entering into formal negotiations with the British. Finally, fearing a deal between France and Great Britain at America's expense, Jay made secret contacts with Lord Shelburne, worked out a formula of recognition acceptable to the British, and continued there-

[29]See below, Samuel Huntington to JJ, 15 Feb. 1781.

after to play a central role in the negotiations. Suffice to say, Benjamin Franklin's positive role in initiating the preliminary talks and John Adams' assertive stand toward the latter part of the negotiations contributed enormously to the successful issue. The three negotiators, in the last minute assisted by Henry Laurens, had secured for the United States independence and a vast continental domain, while yielding only minor concessions. The fact that Congress should have even considered rebuking the Commissioners for their tactics does in retrospect tell us more about the insistent pressures exerted on the delegates in Philadelphia and the Secretary for Foreign Affairs than about the conduct of their agents abroad, who had more backbone and greater vision.

John Jay: The Human Side

This volume is considerably more than a record of a diplomatic mission. It is concerned not only with notes and bills, with boundaries and navigation rights, with claims and counterclaims, with lands and fish. It reveals in full measure the personal problems of an American diplomat and his family living abroad in wartime and their ability to surmount them. The Jays shared moments of sadness and tragedy. An infant child born in Spain to Jay's wife, Sarah Livingston Jay, lived but a few weeks. From America came news that Sarah's brother John Lawrence Livingston was lost in the disappearance of the Continental sloop-of-war *Saratoga.* Nor were their families at home spared the terrors of warfare. Sarah's brother, Henry Brockholst Livingston, on returning to America was captured by the British and for a brief time imprisoned in New York City. The Livingston home in Elizabethtown, New Jersey, was twice raided and plundered by British troops, while a lawless band robbed the Fishkill, New York, farmhouse occupied by John Jay's aged and infirm father. Jay arrived in Paris only to learn that his father had passed away some months before. Jay, as was his wont, continued to bear a heavy responsibility for his family back in the States. His blind brother and sister, Peter and Anna Maricka, and his retarded brother Augustus needed constant attention. His younger brother Frederick, a poor manager of household and business matters, could barely keep his head above water, while Frederick's wife, Margaret Barclay Jay, embarrassed the family by insisting on going behind enemy lines to visit her relatives. John Jay's sister, Eve Jay Munro, remained a family burden. Deserted by her Tory husband, the irresponsible Reverend Harry Munro, who could not abide her scolding, she fell into a deep depression and left the family home in 1782. The Munros' son, Peter Jay Munro, became the special responsibility of John and Sarah Jay, who had taken him with them to Spain and France to direct his upbringing and education. The Jays had left their young son Peter Augustus in the joint custody of the Livingstons and the Jays and they needed constant reassurance of the well-being of their offspring, responsibility for whose rearing was divided between the two families residing in two adjacent states, neither of which was completely freed from enemy occupation.

Lastly, there was the oldest brother, the ubiquitous Sir James Jay, who managed somehow to show up at the wrong time, at the wrong place, and on the wrong side. Ever contrary and ever a source of embarrassment to his very proper younger brother, Sir James, after joining a faction in the New York State Senate which took the hard line toward Loyalists that John Jay deplored, managed to get himself captured by the British and to be shipped to England. At the very time when John Jay was engaged in sensitive peace negotiations for his country, Sir James was trying to sell a naval invention to the British and to score a triumph over his brother in the role of rival peacemaker by pressing his own unauthorized peace plan. Failing to persuade the British, who kept him in pocket money as long as it suited their purposes, Sir James crossed the Channel, and the winter of 1782–83 found him in Paris, still attempting to peddle his naval device, but advancing a grand plan for a commercial agreement with the French, in which he was to be a central figure. To John Jay, his brother's behavior was unforgivable, and they were never reconciled.

Compounding the loneliness and frustrations of Jay's stay in Spain were the difficulties John Jay encountered in dealing with his subordinates—with his brother-in-law Henry Brockholst Livingston, his personal secretary, who proved captious, sulky, ill-mannered, and thoroughly spoiled, and with William Carmichael, the Secretary of the Spanish mission, whom Jay ever suspected of being engaged in systematic intrigue to undermine his authority and of irresponsibility in financial matters. Vain, unbending, and touchy, Jay relished controversy where his self-esteem was involved, but lacked that measure of tolerance necessary to deal with the handsome, foppish, eighteen-year-old Virginian named Lewis Littlepage, a thorough stranger whom he had agreed in a generous moment to sponsor in Spain. Jay was rewarded by Littlepage's colossal insolence and by what proved to be a disgraceful public display of ingratitude on Littlepage's part. Indeed, Jay's disillusionment about the benefits of educating young

Americans abroad may have been prompted in part by his own observations of the impact of the European scene upon his brother-in-law and Littlepage. Suffice to say, his views[30] were shared by such contemporary observers as John Adams and Thomas Jefferson.

In short, the John Jay disclosed herein proves to be a complex personality, beloved and admired by family, friends, and colleagues of the standing of Franklin, John Adams, and Lafayette, and dreaded, if not detested, by others, including certain diplomats of the Spanish and French courts. He could be affectionate, compassionate, eloquent, fun-loving, and even ribald on occasion and in the appropriate surroundings; but to those less favored by this side of his nature, he seemed irritable, obstinate, and a stickler for the letter of the law. In dealing with foreign diplomats he scrupulously perused their formal written powers and, for himself, acted only on receipt of authenticated official instructions from Congress. Nevertheless, when in his judgment the national interest dictated violating explicit instructions of his government, he could display an initiative, not to say audacity, in the conduct of his negotiations belied by his circumspect lawyer-like exterior.

For the Jays Paris provided many moments of conviviality. There they enjoyed the close friendship of the Lafayettes, Alice De Lancey Izard, Matthew Ridley, and the Penns, not to mention the warm comradeship of Jay's associates in the peacemaking. Jay was heartened by John Adams' approval and support, and both John and Sarah Jay found the witty and genial Doctor Franklin an entertaining and charming companion. Despite some differences over tactics in the negotiation, relations between Franklin and Jay remained cordial. Jay was so captivated by Franklin's reminiscences that he made a point of recording some of them in a notebook, whose entries are included herein as a concluding piece.

The rigors of living and traveling abroad, combined with the state of medical knowledge in those days, could prove exceedingly taxing. Jay suffered the "heats" of Spain. Both Jays contracted influenza during the epidemic that swept Paris in the summer of '82. John, in addition, ran a gamut of illnesses, ranging from quincy sore throat to digestive disorders, dysentery, an undiagnosed "pain in the breast," fits of sleeplessness, and bouts of rheumatism. The wear-and-tear of the peace negotiations took its toll on Jay's health and induced him to go on two comparatively brief vacations, one to Normandy in the winter of 1782–83, and a somewhat lengthier stay the following winter

[30]See below, JJ to Robert Morris, 13 Oct. 1782.

in England, where he took the waters of Bath with results to his health that were not observable, saw compatriots, Loyalists, and British political figures, and sought to settle an estate left to the Jays by the Bristol branch of the Jay family. In despair over his ailments Jay once wrote his sister-in-law Catharine W. Livingston that if his health failed to improve he feared he might suffer "premature old age, if old age at all must be my lott."[31] Since Jay had forty-six more years of life ahead of him, it is apparent that he shared the hypochondriacal anxieties fashionable to his age.

John Jay nurtured a deep-rooted hostility to slavery, evidence of which is exhibited early in his public career and corroborated by documents in this volume. At the New York State Convention he had advocated inserting in the state's Constitution of 1777 a provision ending slavery,[32] and, though unsuccessful at that time, he continued to advocate emancipation legislation even when abroad. "Till America comes into this Measure," he exhorted, "her prayers to Heaven for Liberty will be impious."[33] Nonetheless, like many families of substance in New York, the Jays held household slaves, and Peter Jay, who held on to his slaves out of consideration for their age even though their maintenance proved a taxing economic burden to the family,[34] carefully provided upon his death for the disposition of those he personally owned.[35] In turn, John Jay made certain that his brothers and sisters would "not permit the Evening" of the freed slaves' lives "to be resolved in Distress."[36] In Europe the Jay household was served by two blacks—Abigail, who had been in the Livingstons' service in America, and Benoit, whom Jay had purchased as a fifteen-year-old male slave in Martinique.[37] After an harmonious start relations between Abigail and her mistress deteriorated and came to a tragic end in Paris.[38] Benoit, on the other hand, was conditionally manumitted by John Jay prior to his departure for America. Jay's instrument of manumission bespeaks his abhorrence of the institution of slavery. "Whereas," he writes, "the children of men are by nature equally free, and cannot without injustice be either reduced to

[31]JJ to Catharine W. Livingston, 1 July 1783, below.

[32]*JJ,* I, 401.

[33]*Ibid.,* p. 823.

[34]Frederick Jay to JJ, 10 April 1781, below.

[35]See below, editorial note, "The Estate of Peter Jay," 27 May 1782.

[36]JJ to Frederick Jay, 3 Oct. 1782, below.

[37]*JJ,* I, 702, 711, 712.

[38]See below, SLJ to JJ, 23 Nov., 7 Dec. 1783; Peter Jay Munro to JJ, 7 Dec. 1783, 4 Jan. 1784.

or held in slavery," and then proceeds to provide for his slave's freedom after three years.[39] Indeed, Jay was never pennypinching toward those who worked for him or his family, whether black or white. For the overseer, pay "liberal wages," he advised his brother Frederick. "The only way to get a good Man will be to pay him well."[40]

During the course of the peace negotiations Jay, without being so instructed by Congress, ventured to propose a provision in the trade treaty that would have barred British subjects from importing slaves into America, and justified his proposal on the ground that it was the intention of the "States intirely to prohibit the Introduction thereof."[41] Jay's confidence in the States' intentions would be belied by the heated struggle at the Federal Convention in 1787 to bar the slave trade. While Jay felt obliged to join with his fellow Peace Commissioners in protesting British violations of the Preliminary Treaty, among them the removal by the British army of Negro slaves belonging to American owners, he did tone down the wording of a formal protest.[42] These early anti-slavery pronouncements and efforts take on added significance in view of Jay's prominence in the Confederation years in the movement to end slavery, and the repugnance to that institution he manifested throughout his life. One should not be surprised, then, that Jay, as special envoy to Great Britain in 1794, charged by his government with demanding the return of slaves removed contrary to the Treaty of 1783, would decline to press the claim on humanitarian grounds. As governor he would sign the New York State law providing for gradual emancipation of the blacks, really the culmination of efforts he and a few intimates had initiated more than two decades earlier, efforts which in their own time were to be vigorously pressed by his son William Jay, a renowned anti-slavery leader, and, in turn, by his grandson, John Jay II.

Jay's letters, written in what Gouverneur Morris termed his "Laconick Style,"[43] while never revealing the breadth of literary scholarship one finds in the correspondence of a John Adams or a Thomas Jefferson, were heavily tinctured with Biblical allusions, as one would expect from a man of his deep religiosity. Befitting an educated man of his day, Jay drew analogies to antiquity and incorporated the standard

[39]See below, JJ's Conditional Manumission of Benoit, 21 March 1784.

[40]JJ to Frederick Jay, 6 April 1783, below.

[41]See below, JJ's Draft of a Treaty of Commerce with Great Britain [c. 1 June 1783].

[42]See below, American Commissioners to David Hartley, 17 July 1783.

[43]Gouverneur Morris to JJ, 7–9 May 1781, below.

classical phrases from Cicero, Vergil, Horace, Suetonius, Seneca, and the poet Ennius. His letters also disclose a familiarity with Cervantes and Shakespeare and with various writers on international law and military history, while his wife seems to have kept abreast of the contemporary English novel and, as a parent, made a point of reading children's books, then in vogue in both English and French.

Many of the letters included herein are first drafts by Jay or his correspondents, generally chosen by the editors in the absence of the addressee's copy or because of significant variances from the versions hitherto published. These drafts, ranging from run-of-the-mill correspondence to his five *Federalist* letters (to be published in a succeeding volume), reveal how this prudent lawyer labored over his phrases. Such literary re-working could be rewarding, but occasionally a forthright and eloquent phrase is replaced by a blander and more inhibited version. Thus, in the first draft of a letter to Elbridge Gerry, Jay wrote: "I shall always think myself a gainer when I find my civil Rights secure at the Expence of my Property." On second thought he changed this to read: "I shall never cease to prefer a little with Freedom to oppulence without it."[44] This volume is replete with examples of Jay's careful re-statement, often masking the true sentiments of which his earlier versions are more indicative.

Living abroad for more than four years and observing at close range the operations of European politics and diplomacy, along with the extreme contrasts of wealth and poverty, Jay gained a better perspective about America, its values and its future. "I never loved or admired America so much as since I left it," he wrote his friend Egbert Benson after a little more than a year in Spain.[45] Gnawing doubts about European morals convinced him that the best place for a young American to be educated was America, while confirming his conviction "that the Ideas which my Countrymen in general conceive of Europe are in many respects too high."[46] These strong impressions served to shape Jay's burgeoning nationalism, which was to give a special cast to his constitutional thinking in the Era of the Confederation, and is echoed in his insistent advice that the new nation, by "Wise Regulation and Establishments," put its house in order.[47] One of the very first American continentalists, Jay had little patience with state and regional parochialism. Few Americans other than Jay would, for

[44]JJ to Elbridge Gerry, 9 Jan. 1782, below.
[45]JJ to Egbert Benson, 19 March 1781, ALS in JP; *WJ*, II, 74–75; *HPJ*, II, 6–7.
[46]JJ to Robert Morris, 13 Oct. 1782, below.
[47]JJ to William Livingston, 21 May 1783, below.

example, have objected, as early as January, 1782, to the description of Massachusetts contained in her Constitution of 1780 as being "in *New England* as well as America." "Perhaps it would be better," he wrote a Bay State correspondent, "if these Distinctions were permitted to die away."[48]

This volume concludes as the Jays embark for America. John Adams appropriately recorded the event: "Our worthy friend, Mr. Jay, returns to his country like a bee to his hive, with both legs loaded with merit and honor."[49] Perhaps John Jay would have preferred a different metaphor, but his New England associate indubitably voiced the sentiments of his countrymen, who were to reward John Jay with one prominent post after another in the years ahead.

EDITORIAL GUIDELINES

For the details of the aim and policy of transcription, the reader is referred to the first volume, *John Jay: The Making of a Revolutionary—Unpublished Papers 1745–1780,* pp. 16–18. As therein, spelling, with all its oddities and inconsistencies, follows the original manuscripts, and the reader's attention is also called to the indifference of writers of that period to the use of accent marks in foreign language material. As in the previous volume, cipher passages have been deciphered and are printed in small capital letters, and the following textual symbols are used:

[———]	words missing
[roman]	insertion or conjectural reading
<roman>	canceled matter
<<roman>>	deletions within canceled matter.

ABBREVIATIONS FOR MANUSCRIPT DESIGNATIONS

A	Autograph
C	Copy (contemporary)
D	Document
Dft	Draft (in author's hand unless otherwise noted)
E	Extract
L	Letter

[48] JJ to Elbridge Gerry, 9 Jan. 1782, below.

[49] John Adams to Thomas Barclay, 24 May 1784, *Historical Magazine* (December 1869), p. 358.

LbkC	Letterbook copy (not in author's hand unless so stated)
RC	Retained copy
S	Signed
Tr	Transcript (made at a much later date)

SOURCES

Unless otherwise noted, thc original material drawn on for this publication is in the Papers of John Jay, Rare Book and Manuscript Library, Columbia University. When reference is made to manuscripts in the Papers of John Jay which are not being published herein, the designation JP is used. The remainder of the material comes from public collections here and abroad.

Public collections in the United States, with abbreviations as in the National Union Catalog of the Library of Congress:

CSmH	Henry E. Huntington Library and Art Gallery; reference is to the John Jay Letterbook unless otherwise noted
CtHi	Connecticut Historical Society
CtY	Yale University
DeWint	Henry Francis du Pont Winterthur Museum
DLC	Library of Congress
DNA	National Archives
FU	University of Florida, Gainesville
MHi	Massachusetts Historical Society
MiU-C	University of Michigan, William L. Clements Library
NHi	New-York Historical Society
NN	New York Public Library
NNC-RBML	Columbia University, Rare Book and Manuscript Library
NNMus	Museum of the City of New York
PCC	Papers of the Continental Congress, National Archives
PHi	Historical Society of Pennsylvania
PPAmP	American Philosophical Society
PPInd	Independence National Historical Park
PU	University of Pennsylvania

Foreign collections:

AHN Estado	Archivo Histórico Nacional, Estado Series, Madrid
BM	British Museum, London
CO	Colonial Office, Public Record Office, London
CP	Correspondance politique, Ministère des Affaires Étrangères, Paris
CP A	Angleterre
CP E	Espagne
CP EU	États-Unis
CP H	Hollande
FO	Foreign Office, Public Record Office, London
PRO	Public Record Office, London
RAWC	Royal Archives, Windsor Castle

Abbreviations and Short Titles of Works Frequently Cited

AP
Lyman H. Butterfield *et al.*, eds., *Diary and Autobiography of John Adams* (4 vols., Cambridge, Mass., 1961)

BFB
John Bigelow, comp. and ed., *The Works of Benjamin Franklin* (12 vols., New York and London, 1904)

BFS
Albert Henry Smyth, ed., *The Writings of Benjamin Franklin* (10 vols., New York, 1905–07)

Deane Papers
Charles Isham, ed., "The Deane Papers," in The New-York Historical Society, *Collections,* XIX–XXIII (1887–91), 5 vols.

GWF
John C. Fitzpatrick, ed., *The Writings of George Washington from the Original Manuscript Sources, 1745–1799* (39 vols., Washington, 1931–44)

HP
Harold C. Syrett *et al.,* eds., *The Papers of Alexander Hamilton* (26 vols., New York, 1961–79)

HPJ
Henry P. Johnston, ed., *The Correspondence and Public Papers of John Jay* (4 vols., New York, 1890–93)

JAW
Charles Francis Adams, ed., *The Works of John Adams, Second*

President of the United States: With a Life of the Author (10 vols., Boston, 1850–56)

JCC

Worthington C. Ford *et al.*, eds., *Journals of the Continental Congress, 1774–1789* (34 vols., Washington, 1904–37)

JJ, I

Richard B. Morris *et al.*, eds., *John Jay: The Making of a Revolutionary; Unpublished Papers, 1745–1780* (New York, 1975)

LMCC

Edmund C. Burnett, ed., *Letters of Members of the Continental Congress* (8 vols., Washington, 1921–36)

MP

William T. Hutchinson, William M. E. Rachal, Robert A. Rutland *et al.*, eds., *The Papers of James Madison* (Chicago, 1962–   )

Miller, *Treaties*

David Hunter Miller, ed., *Treaties and Other International Acts of the United States of America, 1776–1863* (8 vols., Washington, 1931–48)

Peacemakers

Richard B. Morris, *The Peacemakers: The Great Powers and American Independence* (New York, 1965)

PPGC

Hugh Hastings, ed., *Public Papers of George Clinton* (10 vols., New York and Albany, 1899-1914)

RDC

Francis Wharton, ed., *The Revolutionary Diplomatic Correspondence of the United States* (6 vols., Washington, 1889)

RMP

E. James Ferguson *et al.*, eds., *The Papers of Robert Morris, 1781–1784* (Pittsburgh, 1973–   )

SDC

Jared Sparks, ed., *The Diplomatic Correspondence of the American Revolution* (12 vols., Boston, 1829–30)

TJP

Julian P. Boyd *et al.*, eds., *The Papers of Thomas Jefferson* (Princeton, 1952–   )

WJ

William Jay, ed., *The Life of John Jay: With Selections from His Correspondence and Miscellaneous Papers* (2 vols., New York, 1833)

WMQ

The William and Mary Quarterly, Third Series (1944–   )

YU

Juan F. Yela Utrilla, *España ante la Independencia de los Estados Unidos* (2d ed., 2 vols., Lérida, 1925)

JOHN JAY CHRONOLOGY 1780–1784

1780	4 October	Congressional instructions to Jay
	8 November	Escorial Conference
	23 December	Spain promises Jay $150,000 in aids
1781	15 February	Congressional resolution on the Mississippi River
	15 June	Congress appoints Jay one of five peace Commissioners and adopts instructions
	19 September	The second San Ildefonso Conference
	22 September	Jay drafts proposed treaty with Spain
1782	20 February	Maria, the Jays' third child, is born in Madrid
	16 March	The United States defaults
	12 April	Franklin begins peace talks in Paris
	30 April	Congressional resolution approving Jay's conduct in Spain
	21 May	The Jays leave Madrid
	23 June	The Jays arrive in Paris
	23 June–22 December	Jay's diary of the peacemaking
	3–30 August	Jay-Aranda negotiations for a Spanish-American treaty
	7 August	Congressional instructions to Jay on the Spanish-American treaty
	7–17 August	Jay and Franklin negotiate with Oswald
	16 August	Jay drafts a revised commission for Oswald

	7–20 September	French Undersecretary Rayneval's secret mission to England
	9 September	Jay drafts a new recognition clause for Oswald's revised commission
	10 September	Jay dispatches Vaughan to Shelburne to persuade the British to adopt a more acceptable commission for Oswald
	1–8 October	Jay draws up the first draft of the Preliminary Articles of Peace
	4–7 November	Second draft of the Preliminary Articles is agreed upon
	7 November	American Commissioners' proposal on boundaries and fisheries
	17 November	Vaughan's second mission to England
	30 November	Preliminary Articles of Peace are signed in Paris by Oswald and Adams, Franklin, Jay, and Laurens
	13 December	American Commissioners inform the American Secretary for Foreign Affairs of the signing of the Preliminaries
1783	7–23 January	Jay's holiday in Normandy
	20 January	The British Declaration relative to a Suspension of Arms is signed by Fitzherbert and Adams and Franklin in Versailles
	20 February	The American Commissioners' Declaration of the Cessation of Arms is signed by Adams, Franklin, and Jay in Paris
	12–25 March	Congress debates the Commissioners' conduct

	15 April	Congress ratifies the Preliminary Articles of Peace
	1 June	Jay drafts a treaty of commerce with Great Britain
	18 July	American Commissioners defend their negotiating stance in a dispatch to the Secretary for Foreign Affairs
	19 July–17 April 1784	Jay's recorded conversations with Franklin
	6 August	Great Britain ratifies the Preliminaries
	13 August	Ann, the Jays' fourth child, is born in Paris
	3 September	The Definitive Treaty of Peace is signed in Paris by Hartley and Adams, Franklin, and Jay
	9 October–22 January 1784	Jay visits England
1784	14 January	Congress ratifies the Definitive Treaty
	9 April	Great Britain ratifies the Definitive Treaty
	15 May	Jay submits the Spanish mission accounts to Barclay
	16 May	The Jays leave Paris
	1 June	The Jays sail for America from Dover, England

I

IMPASSE
IN
SPAIN

Issues in Negotiation

The attainment of JJ's objectives in Spain—diplomatic recognition of and financial aid for America and a treaty of alliance and commerce—had been brought to a standstill in mid-1780 due to the insistence of Spain's principal minister, the Conde de Floridablanca,[1] that there would be neither a treaty nor substantial financial help unless the United States waived its insistence on sharing the navigation of the Mississippi River. On this point JJ could not yield, as he was bound by contrary Congressional instructions, which were reaffirmed on 4 October 1780.[2] Not only did JJ approve Congress' reaffirmation, but he became convinced that yielding on the Mississippi was too great a price to pay for an alliance with a monarchy inimical to American independence and on terms which, as he later stated, would "render a future war with Spain unavoidable."[3] However, on 15 February 1781, a Congress, under pressures diplomatic and military, revised its instructions[4]: now, JJ was authorized to relinquish the free navigation of and a free port on the Mississippi below 31° N. Lat., provided Spain should "unalterably" insist upon the concession while at the same time acknowledging and guaranteeing the free navigation of the river north thereof.

By late March 1781 Floridablanca knew of the reversal in instructions by Congress but JJ did not.[5] Now more obdurate than ever, Floridablanca insisted on the exclusive navigation of the Gulf of Mexico. When on 18 May JJ heard from James Lovell, the ranking member of the Congressional Committee for Foreign Affairs, who sent him a copy of the revised instructions,[6] JJ did not deem this an "official" notification, as the instructions were not "authenticated."[7] The next day Floridablanca advised JJ that the latter could count on the principal minister's "being explicit and candid" whenever JJ should declare his "having authority to yield" on the Mississippi.[8] Not receiving the authenticated instructions, JJ finally on 2 July wrote both Floridablanca and the French minister to Spain, the Comte de Montmorin,[9] formally notifying them of the changed instructions and adding the hope to Floridablanca that, since the "difficulties" had been removed, "his Majesty will now be pleased to become an ally of the United States."

During the long summer of '81 Floridablanca repeatedly delayed conferring with the American, with JJ regularly turning to Montmorin to act as a friend at Court. On 13 July JJ prodded Floridablanca for a meeting, on that occasion sending him a copy of the instructions binding the American to disavow any secret understanding or negotiations between the United States and Great Britain. The Spanish minister pleaded the pressure of other business, the same excuse being used in answer to a further request of 18 August.[10] It was not until September 1781 that Floridablanca agreed to a second San Ildefonso Conference with JJ, documented below.

JJ had previously, at the first San Ildefonso Conference on 23 September 1780, learned from Floridablanca that Spain was disinclined to furnish the loans that JJ urgently needed to meet the bills that had been drawn on him by Congress, but would guarantee repayment of a $150,000 loan made by someone else.[11] A week before that Conference, JJ had requested the President of Congress to draw no further bills on him, as those on hand and unpaid totaled $50,000.[12] At the Escorial Conference on 8 November 1780, described in JJ's notes, below, the Spanish minister intimated that a way might be found to help JJ pay the bills. As JJ's financial situation rapidly worsened,[13] he renewed his request to Floridablanca for direct aid and on 23 December he received the promise of a $150,000 loan, beyond the $17,892 that Spain had already advanced, payable as needed.[14]

Now, by the spring of 1781, Floridablanca counted on winning new concessions from JJ as a result of Congress' revised instructions. He requested James Gardoqui, a member of a family banking firm, to inform JJ in writing that Spain would not be able to advance JJ the money necessary to pay the bills coming due in April.[15] This action—"the constant inconsistency" that JJ "experienced between the Minister's promises and conduct"—was, as JJ put it, "really cruel," as bills worth $89,083 were coming due in April and JJ was in imminent danger of defaulting.[16] JJ turned for help to Montmorin, who persuaded Floridablanca to underwrite the April bills in six equal monthly payments beginning in May[17] and got the Marquis d'Yranda, a member of the Royal Council of Finance, to advance the sum of the April bills at once.[18]

At Montmorin's request, d'Yranda furthermore agreed to supply an additional $142,220—the amount of JJ's bills due May–September 1781—"provided Mr. Grand will accept his drafts to that amount."[19] This JJ immediately wrote Franklin, asking whether such an arrangement could be made with Grand, America's banker in Paris. Franklin was able to come to the rescue: on 12 April the American minister in Paris informed JJ that the latter was authorized to draw up to $142,220 as required, an amount to be diverted from a six-million livre French gift intended for supplies.[20]

Additional bills vastly increased JJ's needs, however. By the beginning of September JJ's bills totaled roughly seventy thousand dollars in excess of his April estimates.[21] On 10 September he had to write to Franklin requesting $12,567 for October bills and another $3,600 for bills payable in November.[22] Indeed, JJ's freedom from anxiety about money proved of the briefest duration. It was not until the end of October that word came back from France that the credit had been arranged.[23] Meantime JJ resorted to a loan from a Madrid banker named Francisco Cabarrús[24] to cover the bills that had matured in the interim.[25] The amount of $31,809 was required for December, and for this sum JJ turned to Floridablanca on 16 November.[26] The Spanish minister proving unresponsive, JJ wrote Franklin, apologizing in his letter of 21 November for his "incessant solicitations."[27] Again, Cabarrús came to his aid, even indicating a readiness to do business on a much grander scale.[28]

Promises did not equal performance, however. By March of '82 JJ was forced to default on obligations of a mere £25,000 sterling,[29] doubtless his most humiliating moment in his two years in Spain.

[1]See *JJ,* I, 717, 772, *et seq.*

[2]Below. These instructions were received 30 Jan. 1781, as mentioned in JJ to Thomas McKean, 3 Oct. 1781, see n. 3.

[3]JJ to Samuel Huntington, 6 Nov. 1780, C in James Madison's hand in DLC: Madison, I, 10429a–61a; LbkCs in PCC 110, I and in CSmH; *RDC,* IV, 112–50; *SDC,* VII, 306–89. JJ to McKean, 3 Oct. 1781, LS, body of letter in Carmichael's hand, in PCC 89, I, 379–440; LbkCs in PCC 110, I, 298–320, JP, and in CSmH; *RDC,* IV, 738–65, at p. 743; *HPJ,* II, 75–132, at pp. 86–87.

[4]Below.

[5]JJ to McKean, 3 Oct. 1781.

[6]Lovell to JJ, 20 Feb. 1781, ALS in JP; *RDC,* IV, 261.

[7]JJ to McKean, 3 Oct. 1781.

[8]*Ibid.*

[9]JJ to Floridablanca, 2 July 1781, ALS and Spanish trans. in AHN Estado, leg. 3884, exp. 4, docs. 132, 133; C in French in CP E 605: 304; LbkCs in JP, PCC 89, I, 397–98 and 110, I, and in CSmH; C in JJ to McKean, 3 Oct. 1781; *HPJ,* II, 93; *RDC,* IV, 747. JJ to Montmorin, 2 July 1781, below.

[10]JJ to Floridablanca, 13 July 1781, ALS and Spanish trans. in AHN Estado, leg. 3884, exp. 4, docs. 134, 135; LbkCs in PCC 110, I and CSmH; C in Carmichael's hand in JJ to McKean, 3 Oct. 1781; *RDC,* IV, 749; *HPJ,* II, 97–99. JJ to Floridablanca, 18 Aug. 1781, AL in third person in AHN Estado, leg. 3884, exp. 4, doc. 138; Dft in JP. JJ's 13 July letter to Floridablanca begins: "I have now the Honor of communicating to your Excellency a Copy of certain Instructions I have recd. from Congress dated the 28 May 1781; and which were included in the Dispatches which your Excellency was so obliging as to deliver to me the Evening before the last." Huntington to JJ, 28 May 1781, Duplicate LS in NHi: Jay, endorsed by JJ: "Congress, 28 May 1781, via Cadiz, Recd. 11 July 1781." LS in NHi: Jay, also endorsed by JJ; C of Duplicate LS in JP; *HPJ,* II, 32–35; *RDC,* IV, 451–53.

[11]See *JJ,* I, 825n. For JJ's continued fiscal problems, see Vergennes to JJ, 27 Nov. 1780, below.

[12]*Ibid.,* and JJ to Huntington, 28 Jan. 1781, below.

[13]On 2 October he learned from Franklin that the latter could divert $25,000 to JJ out of a French gift. LS in JP; LbkC in DLC: Franklin III, 72–74; *HPJ,* I, 432–34; *BFS,* VIII, 142–45.

[14]JJ to Franklin, 28 March 1781, Dft in JP; ALS in RAWC. JJ to Huntington, 25 April 1781, see below in JJ to Huntington, 21 April 1781, and n. 3.

[15]James Gardoqui to JJ, 25 March 1781, RC in English in AHN Estado, leg. 3884, exp. 4, doc. 110; C in English in JJ's hand in CP E 603: 409. JJ to McKean, 3 Oct. 1781.

[16]JJ to Huntington, 25 April 1781.

[17]See Spanish loans obtained by JJ and advanced to James Gardoqui, [1 Jan. 1781–21 March 1782], below.

[18]JJ to Huntington, 25 April 1781; JJ to McKean, 3 Oct. 1781; JJ to Yranda, 13 April 1781, Dft in JP. See *JJ,* I, 748 for Yranda.

[19]JJ to Franklin, 1 April 1781, Dft in JP; LbkC in DLC: Franklin VI, 11–13; *HPJ,* II, 10–13; *RDC,* IV, 346–47. In this letter JJ outlined the bills due for the period April through September 1781, amounting to $231,303.

[20]Franklin to JJ, 12 April 1781, ALS in PPAmP: Feinstone; LbkCs in DLC: Franklin V, 49–52, VI, 75–77; *RDC,* IV, 357–59; *BFS,* VIII, 238–41.

[21]JJ to Robert Morris, 1–8 Sept. 1781, below.

[22]See editorial note, "When the United States Defaulted," below.

[23]Franklin to JJ, 29 Sept. 1781, ALS in JP; LbkC in DLC: Franklin V, 188–89; *RDC,* IV, 736.

[24]Francisco Cabarrús (1752–1810), later Conde de Cabarrús. Born in Bayonne, he became a businessman, banker, and economist in Madrid.

[25]JJ to Franklin, 10 Sept. 1781, Dft in JP; LbkC in PCC 110, I and in CSmH; *RDC,* V, 336–37.

[26]JJ to Livingston, 28 April 1782, LbkCs in JP, PCC 110, II, and in CSmH; *RDC,* V, 336–77; *HPJ,* III, 211–96. Franklin to JJ, 29 Sept. 1781. JJ to Franklin, 29 Oct. 1781, Dft in JP.

[27]See under editorial note, "When the United States Defaulted," below.

[28]JJ to Floridablanca, 16 Nov. 1781, Dft in JP; LbkCs in PCC 110, II and in CSmH; ALS and Spanish trans. in AHN Estado, leg. 3884, exp. 4, docs. 144, 145; *HPJ,* II, 145–46. JJ to Franklin, 21 Nov. 1781, Dft in JP; LbkCs in PCC 110, II and in CSmH; *RDC,* V, 345, 346. C of both in JJ to McKean, 3 Oct. 1781.

[29]JJ to Livingston, 28 April 1782; Carmichael to the Committee for Foreign Affairs, 17 Nov. 1781, *RDC,* IV, 843.

From The Continental Congress: Instructions

[Philadelphia, 4 October 1780]

Instructions to the Honorable John Jay, Minister plenipotentiary of the United States of America at the Court of Madrid agreed to unanimously in Congress October 4th, 1780.[1]

That the said Minister adhere to his former instructions respecting the right of the United States of America to the free navigation of the river Mississipi into and from the sea, which right if an express acknowledgement of it cannot be obtained from Spain is not by any Stipulations on the part of *America* to be relinquished.[2]

To render the treaty to be concluded between the two nations permanent, nothing can more effectually contribute than a proper attention not only to the present but the future reciprocal interests of the contracting powers. The river Mississipi being the boundary of several States in the union and their citizens while connected with Great Britain and since the revolution having been accustomed to the free use thereof in common with the subjects of Spain and no instance of complaint or dispute having resulted from it, there is no reason to fear that the future mutual use of the river by the subjects of the two Nations actuated by friendly dispositions will occasion any interruption to that harmony, which it is the desire of America as well as of Spain should be perpetual.

That if the unlimited freedom of the navigation of the river Missisipi with a free port or ports below 31 degrees north latitude,[3] accessible to merchant ships cannot be obtained from Spain, the said minister in that case be at Liberty to enter into such equitable regulations as may appear a necessary security against contraband, provided the right of the United States to the free navigation of the river be not relinquished and a free port or ports as above described be stipulated to them.

With respect to the boundary alluded to in his Letter of 26 May last, that the said Minister be and hereby is instructed to adhere strictly to the boundaries of the United States as already fixed by Congress.[4]

Spain having by the treaty of Paris ceded to great Britain all the country to the north eastward of the Mississipi,[5] the people inhabiting these States while connected with Great Britain and also since the revolution have settled themselves at divers places to the westward near the Mississipi, are friendly to the revolution and being citizens of these United States and subject to the laws of those to which they respectively belong, Congress cannot assign them over as subjects to any other power.

That the said minister be farther informed that in case Spain shall eventually be in possession of East and West Florida at the termination of the war it is of the greatest importance to these United States to have the use of the waters running out of Georgia through West Florida into the bay of mexico[6] for the purpose of navigation and that he be instructed to endeavour to obtain the same, subject to such regulations as may be agreed on between the contracting parties, and that as a compensation for this he be and hereby is empowered to guaranty the possessions of the said Floridas to the Crown of Spain.

By Order of Congress.

(signed) SAML. HUNTINGTON, PRESDT.
(attest) CHARLES THOMSON, SECY.[7]

LbkC in PPAmP: Franklin LIV, 87. *JCC,* XVIII, 900–02; *RDC,* IV, 78–79; *HPJ,* I, 434–36; *SDC,* VII, 300–02.

[1]A copy of the instructions to JJ was also sent to Benjamin Franklin. *JCC,* XVIII, 935.

[2]Congress' original instructions, 28 Sept., 15 Oct. 1779 (*JCC,* XV, 1118–20, 1179–80), dated 16 Oct. 1779, LbkC in JP, *HPJ,* I, 248–50, were reaffirmed herein in reply to JJ's of 26 May 1780 to the President of Congress and in conjunction with Virginia delegates' instructions. In his letter JJ reported on his 11 May Aranjuez Conference with Floridablanca at which the latter saw as an "obstacle" to finalizing a Spanish-American treaty the "pretensions of America to the navigation of the Mississippi," noting that America "at one time relinquished that object." JJ did not "doubt" that Congress would remain "firm." But "determined to adhere strictly" to Congress' "sentiments and directions," he wished to be "favoured with them fully, and in season." JJ to Huntington, LbkCs in PCC 110, I and in CSmH; *RDC,* III, 707–34; *HPJ,* I, 316–24, 337–43; *SDC,* VII, 220–82. See also *MP,* II, 114–17 and 127–36 for Madison's 17 October draft letter to JJ explaining the instructions.

[3]The northern boundary of West Florida as set forth in the Royal Proclamation of 1763.

[4]This concerned the western boundary at the Mississippi and the southern boundaries with East and West Florida.

[5]By the Treaty of Paris, 10 Feb. 1763, Spain relinquished East and West Florida to England in exchange for Cuba.

[6]The Chattahoochee and Flint flow from Georgia southwest to form the Apalachicola; the Etowah joins the Oostanaula to form the Coosa River.

[7]For Huntington and Thomson, see *JJ,* I, 519, 675.

To Robert R. Livingston

Madrid, 6 October 1780

Dear Robert,

Your Favor of the 6 July[1] came to Hand Yesterday. This and two others viz. of the 6 October and 22 December[2] are all the Letters I have had from you since I left America. How could you discontinue writing because you recieved no Letter from me while at Martinico?[3] I am almost tempted to say it was unkind. You have seen my Letters to Congress from that Island,[4] and can easily guess at the Number of those I was obliged to write to others.[5] I was there but a little better than a Week, in Company most part of the Day. Judge then whether much more could have been written in the same Time, and under similar Circumstances. I knew you would hear the History of our Disasters,[6] and hoped you would consider my not writing to you as being rather a presumption on than a Neglect of, your Friendship.

We had heard that your Family was about to increase, and rejoiced at it.[7] Nay a congratulatory Letter from me to your Mother on that and a similar Event in her Family,[8] is now on the Water. I did not write to you at the same Time, because I was a little sorry and a little vexed at your not giving me a Hint of a Circumstance that you knew would have given me so much pleasure. Perhaps indeed you might have been too prudent to have "reckoned [———]."[9] I did not think of this before, or you would probably have been my Debtor for a Letter extraordinary. But be this as it may, I most cordially congratulate you on this Event, and sincerely join in all the good wishes which you may find applicable to it in the Book of Psalms. Not many Weeks ago we had also a fine hearty Girl, but a violent Fever has since carried her to Heaven,[10] where I expect one Day or other to see her much more charming and accomplished than if she had been educated either in Europe or America. You see, I have not left my Philosophy or rather my Christianity behind me.

I find my little Boy was well and healthy and thank you for telling me so.[11] If he should turn out good for any thing, the Circumstance you allude to, will probably with many others be among my Objects for his Happiness. Your Idea was in my Mind before I recieved your Letter, for Caty had written us the News. Imagine then how pleasing it was to find it had also a place in yours.

A Year or two ago I heard the House at Eliz[abethtown] had been burnt, and told Mrs. Jay I was glad of it.[12] Perhaps before the War ends, still stronger Reasons may arise for wishing the same Thing. But perhaps Grandmama is a Predestinarian in the Latitude of Laidly.[13] If so there is no human Reason or Wisdom in or out of the Case.

The Nephew I brought with me turns out a very fine Boy, indeed just such a one as I would wish him, or any other Boy of his age to be. My only Fear is that one of these Days some of his Blood may breake out and spoil all.[14] In that Case all my Hopes after all my Pains will be blasted.

Why do you never <tell me any thing> say a word to me of Edward? Where is he? What are you doing with him? That Boy ought to be to you as a Son, for it must be great good Luck if you or any body else have so clever a one.[15]

Mrs. Jay has a tolerable Degree of Health, better than usual. I have much Reason to pray God that it may continue and increase.

Thus much for Family Matters. As to Politics, you are or ought to be in Congress, and my Letter to the President[16] is long enough and particular enough to gratify your Curiosity. I therefore wont say a Word on that Subject now.

THE KING WANT[S] WISDOM, ATTENTION, MONEY. THE MINISTRY WANTS SYSTEM AND DECISION. THE TWO COURT[S] NOT CORDIAL. PEOPLE AVERSE TO WAR. THESE ARE JOLTS. NOTWITHSTANDING, CONGRESS SATISFIED WITH ME.

The observation that as our Years encrease, our social Attachments wear away, is untrue. Mine never were warmer than at present.

The more we know of the World, the more we prize the few good Plants we find among the many Weeds in it. Here I never enjoy the Pleasure of thinking loud. Prudence forbids it. My Heart is in America, and I am impatient for the Time when the Rest of my Body will be there also. Tell Benson I am not pleased with him. He is a bad correspondent, and you may say the same thing to your Governor[17] too. We hear R. Morris is Chief Justice.[18] I am glad of it. I lament Gouv[erneu]rs Misfortune.[19] There are many Things good as well as great in him.

The enclosed are Seeds of the best Melon I have eaten in Spain. Give half of them at least, to your Mother, for you have not Care enough to be trusted with them all. Remember me to all my Friends. You know who they are, and dont forget that you have an old one in, Dear Robert, Your affectionate

JOHN JAY

P.S. When you decypher, do it on a separate paper, and not on the Letter. And as you are sometimes a little careless, destroy the paper *immediately*.

ALS, partly in code, undeciphered, in NHi: Robert R. Livingston. Endorsed. Duplicate ALS, undeciphered, endorsed "March 1779," in *ibid.* The code is based on Abel Boyer's *The Royal Dictionary Abridged. The Second Part, Containing the English Before the French* (2 vols., 13th ed., London, 1771). For Livingston, see *JJ*, I, 71, 138–39, 668–69 *et seq.*

[1]Livingston to JJ, 6 July 1780, in *JJ*, I, 787–89.

[2]Livingston to JJ, 6 Oct. 1779, ALS in JP, *HPJ*, I, 245–46, *WJ*, II, 50–51; 22 Dec. 1779, *JJ*, I, 669–72.

[3]JJ in fact wrote to Livingston from Martinique on 24 December, the copy of which Livingston acknowledged on 26 Aug. 1780 to JJ; see *JJ*, I, 672, 809–10.

[4]JJ wrote seven letters from Martinique to President of Congress Samuel Huntington: for 20, 22, 24, and 27 Dec. 1779, see *JJ*, I, 672n., 673, 675. LbkCs of 25 Dec. (2 letters) and 26 Dec. 1779 are in PCC 110, Appendix, and in *RDC*, III, 446–49; one of 25 December is in *HPJ*, I, 253, and *WJ*, I 105.

[5]Of the thirteen extant letters JJ wrote during the stay on that island, from the 19th to the 28th December, all except the Livingston letter and one to Catharine W. Livingston, for which see *JJ*, I, 689, 691, were official: see *JJ*, I, 673–75 for his letters to Terrier de Laiske and to Captain Seth Harding. On the 27th JJ drew on Benjamin Franklin for part of his salary as minister to Spain, having provided out of pocket a sum to the strapped officers of the *Confederacy*. JJ to Franklin, 27 Dec. 1779, LbkC in DLC: Franklin III; *RDC*, III, 450. Enclosure: C of Congressional instructions to JJ, 16 Oct. 1779, see n. 2 of preceding letter.

[6]For the events necessitating the stopover in Martinique, see *JJ*, I, 666–68, 674–75.

[7]The birth of the Livingstons' first child, Elizabeth Stevens Livingston. Catharine W. Livingston to SLJ, 13 Feb. 1780, *JJ*, I, 689–91, and Robert R. Livingston to JJ, 6 July 1780.

[8]No letters to or from Margaret Beekman Livingston prior to 1782 are located. Her daughter, Gertrude Livingston (Mrs. Morgan) Lewis, had given birth to a daughter, Margaret, on 5 Feb. 1780. See also *JJ*, I, 558, 584.

[9]Blank in manuscript.

[10]The Jays' second child, Susan; see *JJ,* I, 710.

[11]Peter Augustus Jay, the Jays' first child, who was left in the care of SLJ's family. See *JJ,* I, 223 and n., 683–84. Mentioned by Livingston in his 6 July letter.

[12]For the two raids on Liberty Hall, see *JJ,* I, 572–73, 788, 789. See also JJ to Catharine W. Livingston, 27 Feb. 1779, ALS in MHi: Ridley; Dft in JP; partly in *HPJ,* I, 190–91. JJ's views are consistent with his earlier advocacy of a scorched earth policy. See JJ to Robert Morris, 6 Oct. 1777, *American Book Prices Current,* 16 Jan. 1917.

[13]A reference to the Calvinist Reverend Dr. Archibald Laidlie (1727–79), the first English-language, and therefore controversial, preacher of the New York City Dutch Reformed Church, from 1763 until the British occupation of New York. As a Calvinist, Laidlie was an expositor of the doctrine of predestination. Charles E. Corwin, *A Manual of the Reformed Church in America, 1628–1922* (5th ed., rev., New York, 1922), pp. 390–91; Hugh Hastings, ed., *Ecclesiastical Records, State of New York* (7 vols., Albany, 1901–17), VI, 3889 *et seq.*

[14]Thirteen-year-old Peter Jay Munro. His mother, JJ's sister Eve, had emotional problems, and his father, the Reverend Dr. Harry Munro, had deserted his family and joined the Loyalist cause. See *JJ,* I, 31, 32, 33, 651.

[15]Livingston's brother Edward had entered the College of New Jersey (Princeton) in 1779 as a junior, graduating in 1781. See also *JJ,* I, 558.

[16]For JJ to Huntington, 6 Nov. 1780, see editorial note, "Issues in Negotiation," above, n. 3.

[17]While from abroad JJ had written five letters to New York's Governor Clinton and three to the State's Attorney-General Benson; the latter first wrote to JJ on 30 [Sept.] 1781, below. Clinton to JJ, on 6 April 1781, ALS in JP, *PPGC,* VI, 746–49, mentions having written three letters, 1 June 1780 being the latest and the only one dated, none of which were received by JJ nor are located; see JJ to Clinton, 16 Nov. 1781, below. JJ to Clinton, 25 Oct. 1779, 1 Feb. and 14 July 1780 in *JJ,* I, 659–60, 723–25, 791–92; 6 May 1780, Dft in JP, *HPJ,* I, 314–15, *WJ,* I, 111–13, *PPGC,* V, 684–86; [20] June 1780, Dft in JP, *PPGC,* V, 861–62. JJ to Benson, [n.d.] June 1780, DftS in JP, *HPJ,* I, 363–64, *WJ,* I, 55–56; 18 Sept. 1780, DftS in JP, *HPJ,* I, 406–07, erroneously dates the letter 17 September.

[18]Richard Morris had been appointed on 23 Oct. 1779 to succeed JJ as New York State's Chief Justice. See *JJ,* I, 403, 823.

[19]For Gouverneur Morris's loss of his leg, see *JJ,* I, 788, 789, and below, JJ to Gouverneur Morris, 5 Nov. 1780.

To Samuel Huntington

Madrid, <5> [29] October 1780
(private)

Dear Sir,

Your Letter of the 5 November last never reached me. The Duplicate of it together with your Favor of the 12 July <were delivered to me this Day> are now before me.[1] I thank you for them both.

I am happy to hear that none of my Transactions mentioned in the Letters you allude to "met with the least Disapprobation in Congress."[2] While they continue satisfied with my Conduct my utmost Ambition will be gratified. My public Letter[3] will be so long and so particular as to render it unnecessary for me to say any thing on the Subjects of it in this. I know your want of Liezure and therefore cannot expect Intelligence in Detail from you, nor indeed can I expect a very accurate Correspondence with the Committee.[4] You know my Opinion of all standing Com[mittee]s and I shall be much disappointed if these affairs should ever be properly managed till committed to some able industrious responsible Person to be appointed and paid by Congress for the Purpose.[5] The Gent[lemen] of whom this Com[mitte]e is composed[6] merit Esteem and Confidence, but I do not believe that any three Members of Congress either can or will be found adequate to this Business, the offices being in my opinion utterly incompatible.

I shall never forget how much I owe to your Delicacy and Politeness nor shall I omit any opportunity of convincing you of the Esteem and Regard with which I am, Dear Sir, Your most obedient Servant.

Mrs. Jay and Col. Livingston[7] desire to be particularly remembered to you.

Dft. Endorsed by JJ: ". . . 29 Oct. 1780."

[1]Huntington to JJ, 5 Nov. 1779, Duplicate ALS in JP; 12 July 1780, ALS in JP.

[2]A reference to JJ's decisions concerning the *Confederacy* and his conduct on Martinique, in Huntington to JJ, 12 July 1780; see nn. 5 and 6 of preceding letter.

JJ's thirteen letters which Huntington referred to are: 19 and 20 Oct. 1779, not located. For 24, 25 (2 letters), 26, and 27 December, see n. 4 of preceding letter. For 27 Jan., 20 and 29 (not 28) Feb., and 3 March (3 letters) 1780, all, except one of 3 March, LbkCs in PCC 110, I and in CSmH; Dft of 27 January in JP; all, excluding one of 3 March, in *RDC,* III, 436–45, 474–75, 509–10, 526–27, 529–31; 27 January and one of 3 March in *HPJ,* I, 263–64, 274–75. All but 19 and 20 October are noted as read in Congress; *JCC,* XVI, 400 (1 May); XVII, 435 (18 May). The missing 3 March letter, "relative to seamen," and that of 29 February were referred to the Board of Admiralty; *JCC,* XVII, 435.

[3]For JJ's official dispatch of 6 Nov. 1780 to Huntington, see editorial note, "Issues in Negotiation," above, n. 3.

[4]The chief function of the Committee for Foreign Affairs was to keep Congressional representatives abroad informed of events in America. Up to 29 Oct. 1780 JJ had been the recipient of only one letter from the Committee, dated 11 Dec. 1779, in *JJ,* I, 668–69.

[5]JJ held strong views on the Congressional committee system, which he also expressed in a letter at this time to James Lovell, the ranking member of the Committee for Foreign Affairs. His draft included this: "I would throw Stones too with all my Heart if I thought they would hit only the Committee without injuring the Members of it. . . . <If Congress are determined to have Standing Com[mitte]es> <in wh[ich]> <by the bye I have very little Faith> One good private Correspondent <is> would be worth Twenty standing Committees made of the wisest Heads in America for the Purpose of Intelligence." JJ to Lovell, 27 Oct. 1780, Dft in JP; ALS in NjMoHP: Lloyd Smith; LbkCs in PCC 110, I and in CSmH; *RDC,* IV, 105–06; *HPJ,* I, 440–41; *WJ,* II, 57–58; *LMCC,* V, 430–31. This was in reply to Lovell's of 11 July 1780, in *JJ,* I, 789–91. See also JJ to Huntington,

18 Dec. 1780, n. 2, below and JJ to Charles Thomson, 23 April 1781, below.

[6]The Committee for Foreign Affairs comprised Lovell, William Churchill Houston, and Robert R. Livingston, the two last-named being "added" on 24 Nov. 1779. *JCC*, XV, 1302. See also *JJ*, I, 668–69.

[7]SLJ's brother Henry Brockholst Livingston was JJ's private secretary in Spain. *JJ*, I, 145, 651.

To Gouverneur Morris

Madrid, 5 November 1780

Dear Morris,

Three of your Letters have reached me. The last was of the 12 July.[1] Some of mine to you were worth little, and their miscarriage was of <little other> no Consequence. There was one <however> from Madrid which I wish may come to your Hands. It was interesting.[2]

I had heard of your misfortune and felt it. A Gentleman in France wrote[3] me that Mrs. PLATE[R][4] after <having made> much use of YOUR LEGS HAD <been the> OCCASIONED YOUR LOSING ONE <of them>. Susan informs Mrs. Jay that you behaved properly on the occasion, that is, with Fortitude.[5] This was a Consolation. I could write <you twenty consolatory> several common place things on the <Occasion> Subject, but you know what I feel for and think of you.

Where are you? What are you <knowing> doing? Achilles made no Figure at the spinning Wheel. Dont bury your Talents under a PETTICOAT.[6] The State of New York I take to be your Field. If prudently cultivated it will yield <you> much. Letters tho the best are poor Substitutes for Conversation, but we must be content. I wish to hear many things of and from you.

Mrs. Jay is in tolerable Health. She has had a fine little Daughter, but she is gone Home, and I am resigned. I have it in Charge from Mrs. Jay to say many friendly Things to you.

DRAWING BILLS ON ME WAS IMPOLITIC in <twenty> Respects.[7] <Mississippi> THE NAVIGATION ETC. IS STRONGLY INSISTED <up> on. <I have> FAIR PROMISES OF AIDS <but no Performances>. MANY DELAYS <in Abundance either> UNAVOIDABLE OR DESIGNED. <Spain seems> THE COURT UNDECIDED AND WAITING <the Results of> EVENTS. <Britain is> THE BRITISH COURTING THEM. <The Views of France are not altogether so clear to me.> WHY WAS NOT Ternay <reinforced> SUPPORTED?[8] DEPEND ON YOURSELVES PRINCIPALLY. <Be silent about these Matters.> THE FRENCH EMBASSADOR[9] HERE HAS EXCELLENT INTELLIGENCE FROM <Ph[iladelphia]> YOUR CITY. <I suspect Livingston and Schuyler are Favorites at the great House.> [10] I know <very> but little of what passes among you and shall be obliged to you for such Facts of publick and private Matters as you may think interesting.

WHAT <are> IS A. LEE <and Izard> ABOUT?[11] I have had some Letters from DEANE.[12] He is much displeased with what he <calls> thinks the DUPLICITY of certain Persons <in America>. Who in particular I dont know. <Neither he or Bankroft write to Carmichael, why I cannot yet discover.> <Deane> HE is endeavouring to establish HERE a BARGAIN <he made> WITH Miralles ABOUT MASTS, and talks of COMING <here the best to promote that Object> HERE.[13] How did you and HE PART?[14]

Should this find you at Philadelphia remember me to my <old> Friends there, <I promise> in particular <to ratify all the> assurances of Esteem and Regard you may make for me to Mr. and Mrs. Morris[15] <in particular>.

<God bless you Morris,> Adieu. I know you and therefore am and will be cordially your Friend

J. J.

P.S. <My> I have recieved no Letter from my Brother tho I hear he was at Philadelphia this Summer.[16]

DftS in JP. ALS and duplicate ALS not located. E in *Deane Papers,* IV, 250–51. Omissions, including paragraph two, in *HPJ,* I, 444–45, and in *WJ,* I, 113–14.

[1]Morris to JJ, 3 Jan. 1780, ALS, deciphered by JJ, in JP; DftS in FU: P. K. Yonge Library. Morris to JJ, 2 March 1780, in *JJ,* I, 746; 12 July 1780 not located.

[2]JJ is probably referring to his letter of 27 May 1780, DftS in JP, inquiring whether Morris received JJ's new cipher. In the cipher portion of that letter JJ states that he mistrusts Carmichael. The other extant letter to Morris is 2 March 1780, Dft in JP.

[3]Not located. Morris supposed it was Silas Deane; see Morris' reply to JJ, 7–9 May 1781, below.

[4]Morris convalesced in the home of George and Elizabeth Rousby Plater (d. 1789). Max M. Mintz, in his *Gouverneur Morris and the American Revolution* (New York, 1970), states that Elizabeth Plater "nursed Morris with more than ordinary kindness." See pp. 141–42. For Plater, see *JJ,* I, 671.

[5]Susannah Livingston to SLJ, not located. In Catharine W. Livingston to JJ and SLJ, 23 May 1780, AL in JP, the Jays were informed of Morris' accident.

[6]See Morris' reply, 7–9 May 1781, below.

[7]See n. 2 in Huntington to JJ, 18 Dec. 1780, below.

[8]General Washington could not move to Ternay's support since the latter's fleet was bottled up off the coast of Newport, R.I., by the British under Admiral Thomas Graves. See *JJ,* I, 760, 813.

[9]The Comte de Montmorin. See *JJ,* I, 723.

[10]This is a reference to the John Dickinson house in Philadelphia, where the Chevalier de La Luzerne had set up the French legation. See *JJ,* I, 600, for Luzerne; p. 160 *et seq.* for Schuyler.

[11]For Arthur Lee, see below, Deane to JJ, 16 Oct. 1780 and n. 5. Ralph Izard

arrived in Philadelphia in August 1780 and immediately notified Congress of his presence. He had been recalled on 8 June 1779, and now, on 9 Aug. 1780, Congress resolved that: "convinced of the faithful endeavours of Mr. Izard to fulfill the objects of the commission to which he was appointed by them on the 7th of May, 1777," they approved "of the reasons which determined him not to proceed to the court of Tuscany." *JCC,* XIV, 700–01; XVII, 701, 714–15; for Izard, see also *JJ,* I, 631.

[12]Deane to JJ, see below, 9 and 16 Oct. 1780 and n.

[13]See JJ to Deane, 2 Oct. 1780, and n. 4, below.

[14]In Morris' 7–9 May 1781 reply, below.

[15]Robert and Mary White Morris (1749–1827). See *JJ,* I, 140.

[16]For Sir James Jay, see Morris to JJ, 7–9 May and 17 June 1781, both below. See also *JJ,* I, 32, 73, 488.

John Jay: Notes of a Conference with Floridablanca

Escurial, 8 November 1780

Notes of a Conference between Mr. Jay and his Ex[cellenc]y the Count D Florida Blanca at the Escurial on <the> Wednesday the 8 November 1780 agreable to an appointment made the Day before thro Mr. James Gardoqui.[1]

After the usual Civilities the Count asked Mr. Jay if he had any thing *particular* to offer. To which the latter replied that among the first things he had to offer to his Ex[cellenc]y were his thanks for the assurances he had been pleased to make him of his Intention to give further aids to America, thro Mr. Gardoqui on his Return to Madrid from St. Ildefonso, and also for Directing Mr. Cabarrus to converse with him on that Subject and in particular on the Manner which those aids should be supplied. That he begged Leave to repeat to his Ex[cellenc]y what he had said to Mr. Cabarrus viz that the manner most convenient to his Majesty would always prefer that mode of recieving aids which they should have Reason to believe most eligible to Spain. Mr. Jay further informed the Count that as there were several Vessels soon to sail for am[erica] he wished to be enabled to give Congress certain Intelligence as to these Supplies[2] and for that Purpose also had requested the present Interview.

The Count <replied> answered that he would take an early opportunity of sending for Mr. Carbarrus who was devising Means for enabling the Court to furnish Supplies and would acquaint Mr. Jay of the Result. Mr. Jay then told the Count that from the Inquiries made by Mr. Gardoqui as well as from Letters he had recieved from France it appeared that the kind Intentions of his Majesty in offering his Responsibility to facilitate a Loan for America[3] would not be attended with the desired Success, as such a Loan had for various Reasons become impracticable. The Count replied that we must wait the Issue of Mr. Cabarrus's Endeavours of which he would inform Mr. Jay.

Mr. Jay further acquainted the Count that the Holders of the Bills which by his Ex[cellenc]ys Direction he had accepted payable at Bilboa,[4] had applied to him to be informed by what House there, they should be paid, alledging that those Bills <could not otherwise> for want of such Information could not be negociated. The Count replied that the House of Gardoqui at Bilboa would pay them.

Dft. Endorsed by JJ.

[1]James Gardoqui, brother of the English-educated Don Diego Maria de Gardoqui, of Joseph Gardoqui & Sons of Bilbao, the Spanish mercantile firm which paid bills drawn on JJ. James Gardoqui operated his own firm in Madrid. See also *JJ,* I, 717–18, 733.

[2]This concerns the supply of clothing for the military purchased by Richard Harrison, the Congressional agent in Cádiz, at JJ's authorization and with Floridablanca's concurrence. The shipment from Cádiz to the U.S. required action by Floridablanca. See *JJ,* I, 827, and JJ's note of 1 November in JJ to Huntington, 6 Nov. 1780; see *JJ,* I, 732 for Harrison.

[3]After the San Ildefonso Conference of 23 Sept. 1780, Don Diego had informed JJ that Spanish ministers in France and Holland had been instructed to procure for the U.S. loans which the King of Spain would undertake to guarantee. By November 1 JJ himself had heard from Ferdinand Grand that there was little hope of a French loan for JJ. See JJ to Huntington, 6 Nov. 1780; Grand to JJ, 21 Oct. 1780, ALS in JP; Tr in NN: Bancroft: American III, 87; and *JJ,* I, 748, for Grand.

[4]At a conference four months earlier in Madrid, Floridablanca had suggested that "if an immediate acceptance" of bills "was insisted on," JJ "might accept them payable at Bilbao," by a firm to be designated by the Minister. Now, JJ was especially concerned about the bills he had accepted under those conditions from the firm Patrick Joyce (Joyes) & Sons. Notes of 5 July 1780 conference in JJ to Huntington, 6 Nov. 1780, which also includes the 28 June and 11 July letters. JJ to Floridablanca, 28 June 1780, AL and Spanish trans. in AHN Estado, leg. 3884, exp. 4, doc. 54; LbkCs in PCC 110, I and in CSmH. Floridablanca to JJ, 11 July 1780, L in Spanish and English trans. by Carmichael in JP; RC in Spanish in AHN Estado, leg. 3884, exp. 4, doc. 61; LbkCs in PCC 110, I and in CSmH.

To Elbridge Gerry

Madrid, 18 November 1780

Dear Sir

I have had the pleasure of recieving your Favor of the 10th of July[1] and am much obliged to you for informing us of the Situation of our Friends in Jersey when you passed thro it.

Should Mr. Warren visit Madrid you may rely on his recieving from me every Mark of Attention due to an American and to the Son of a General whose Posterity and Memory have strong Claims to the Attachment and Regard of our Country.[2]

From the Letter written by your Convention to their Constituents on the Publication of your Constitution I have been led to entertain high Expectations of your Form of Government, and <shall> therefore request the Favor of you to send me a Copy[3] by some Vessel bound to Spain. I lately recieved some News papers and Journals by the Way of France and had 46 mexican Dollars to pay for the Postage, tho they came by post only as far as Bilboa, and were brought from thence by a private Hand.

My Letter to the President[4] will tell you more of Politics than you may perhaps be pleased to hear. I shall therefore avoid that Subject at present.

Mrs. Jay desires me to <make> present her Compliments to you, and permit me to assure you of the Regard and Esteem with which I am Dear Sir Your most obedient Servant.

Dft. ALS sold at Sotheby Parke Bernet, 26 April 1978. Elbridge Gerry (1744–1814) was a prominent Massachusetts Signer, merchant, and businessman, serving in the Continental Congress since 1776.

[1]Not located.

[2]This was young Joseph Warren (1768–90), son of the Major General (1741–75) who fell at Bunker Hill. Warren left four children and virtually no estate. As a memorial to the Patriot hero, Congress on 8 April 1777 resolved that "the eldest son of General Warren . . . be educated, from this time, at the expence of the United States." *JCC,* VII, 243.

[3]JJ is inquiring about *An Address of the Convention* of March 1780 urging ratification, accomplished within three months, of the Massachusetts Constitution of 1780, for which see Oscar and Mary Handlin, eds., *The Popular Sources of Political Authority: Documents on the Massachusetts Constitution of 1780* (Cambridge, Mass., 1966), pp. 434–72. See Gerry's reply, 20 Sept.–9 Oct. 1781, below.

[4]JJ is referring to his public letter to President Huntington of 30 Nov. 1780, ALS in PCC 98, pp. 235–38; LbkCs in PCC 110, I, JP, and in CSmH; *RDC,* IV, 169–70; *HPJ,* I, 450–53; *SDC,* VII, 389–91. For JJ's private letter to Huntington of the same date, see below.

From Vergennes

Versailles, 27 November 1780

Dear Sir,

I have received in good order, Sir, the letter of the 22d September last which you have done me the honor to write.[1]

You have, Sir, too many proofs of the interest which the King takes in your country's cause not to be persuaded that he would have considered the demand that you make, had that been possible; but the considerable expenses of the war that His Majesty is undertaking, in addition to the extraordinary aids that I have procured, and continue to procure, for Mr. Franklin, render His Majesty incapable of taking upon himself the drafts that Congress has judged appropriate to draw upon you. It is with the greatest regret, Sir, that I transmit to you so unfavorable a decision, and I am extremely desirous of finding other occasions in which I shall be able to convince you of my zeal in the interests of the United States, and of my willingness to oblige you personally.

I have the honor to be absolutely, Sir, your very humble and very obedient servant,

DE VERGENNES

LS in French, trans. by the editors. Tr in French in NN: Bancroft: American III, 160.

[1]The day before the scheduled San Ildefonso Conference with Floridablanca, JJ reluctantly wrote Vergennes asking for assistance on bills amounting to "about fifty thousand dollars." JJ sent a copy of this letter with a covering note to Franklin on the same day, noting that "Almost anything will be better than a protest"; see *JJ,* I, 824n. For Vergennes, see *ibid.,* p. 330.

To Samuel Huntington

Madrid, [30 November 1780]

<Dear Colonel> Sir,

It would give me great pleasure to have an opportunity of writing <to converse with you> to Congress without Reserve. But Prudence too often forbids it. Every Letter I recieve from abroad bears marks of Inspection, and I have <too much> Reason to believe that all Letters to and from America that pass thro the Post offices of France or Spain are read by the Ministry of both kingdoms or by Persons appointed by them for that Purpose.[1] Nay some of my Letters from hence to France by the Post have miscarried.[2] I am happy however in reflecting that <many Years have elapsed since I have this> none of my Letters contain any thing which it would give me uneasiness to see published.

Is It not Time for America like other Nations to provide against these Inconveniences by proper Regulations and Establishments. They ought in my opinion to have an american Consul or agent in some Port here and in France.[3] Their public Dispatches should be sent by Packet Boats to these Agents, and should on no Account be delivered to any other Person. The agents should be ordered to send them to the Courts to which they might be directed by a trusty *American*—one of the Officers of the Packet Boat for Instance, and he should be ordered to wait for and return with the Dispatches of the Minister. Till something like this be done their Correspondence will be subject to many Inconveniences and be necessarily very unsatisfactory. Would it not also be proper to provide for the safe Conduct of Letters to Congress after their arrival in america.

I have very good Reason to suspect that the french Consuls in america[4] are very watchful and attentive to these Matters, and good Care should be taken to keep american Letters out of their Way. This is really a very important Subject, and I cannot forbear being more importunate about it than Congress may perhaps think proper.

Tho many Vessels have arrived and are daily arriving from America I have recieved but one Letter from the Com[mitte]e for foreign affairs,[5] one from the Governor of Maryland,[6] and four private ones of old Dates since I came to Spain.[7] I am certain that others have reached Europe but have been detained. It is really mortifying that every body here should know more of American affairs than I do, when perhaps they are indebted for their Intelligence to the Contents of Letters directed to me. The Ministry here lately recieved from Mr. Mirallis[8] very particular Information on those Subjects by a Vessel which arrived after a short passage at Cadiz directly from Philadelphia. By this Vessel I recieved <only a short one> not a single Letter from any body except a few Lines from Miss Livingston to her Sister,[9] which came enclosed from Philadelphia in a Letter from Mr. Mallet there to his Brother here.[10]

I entreat the Attention of Congress to this Subject, and have the Honor to be with great Respect and Esteem, your Excellencys most obedient and most humble Servant.

On the 29th <Inst.> Ult. I wrote to your Excellency by Mr. Harrison who went from here to Cadiz. It is very uncertain when such another Opportunity may offer, and consequently when Congress will again hear any thing from me worth knowing.

Dft.

[1] JJ became aware of the interception of his mail at the start of his Spanish mission. See, for example, *JJ,* I, 734, 737. He noted to Lovell on 27 Oct. 1780 that posted letters "would be all inspected and many suppressed." On the 30th Nov. 1780 he wrote to the Committee for Foreign Affairs: "I recieve no Letters by the Posts but with Marks of Inspection and after much Delay. Some that I write never come to Hand, and I know of Letters having arrived from America for me which I have never seen and never expect to see." Dft in JP, LbkCs in PCC 110, I, JP, and in CSmH; *RDC,* IV, 174–75; *HPJ,* I, 453–55.

[2] Delays were considerable in JJ's letters reaching Franklin, but only one, dated 16 Aug. 1780, seems to have gone astray; Dft in JP; E in NN: Bancroft: American II, 206.

[3] On this same day, JJ wrote officially to the Committee for Foreign Affairs recommending the establishment of "American agents or Consuls in one or more of the ports of France and Spain" due to the "Necessity of putting your

Correspondence with the public Servants in Europe on a better Footing."

[4]French Consuls serving in America in the period 1779–81 included: Martin Oster, Vice Consul of France in the Port of Philadelphia, appointed in 1778 by Gérard, the French Minister to the U.S. (*JJ,* I, 475); see *JCC,* XII, 948 (24 Sept. 1778); Chevalier d'Annemours (d'Anmours) provisionally appointed French Consul in North Carolina on 24 Jan. 1780, *JCC,* XVI, 79; *RDC,* III, 468; *TJP,* III, 198n.; and Philippe de L'Étombe, Consul General of France in the four New England states, whose credentials were accepted by Congress on 31 Aug. 1781; see *JCC,* XXI, 925–26.

[5]See n. 4 in JJ to Huntington, 29 Oct. 1780, above. By 30 November, JJ had received two others, dated 16 June and 12 July 1780, as he noted on that day to the Committee for Foreign Affairs. LS and C, in JJ's hand, of 16 June in JP and *RDC,* III, 793–94; LbkCs of both in JP and in PCC 79, I and Appendix.

[6]Governor of Maryland Thomas Sim Lee (1745–1819) was authorized by the Maryland General Assembly to inform JJ that, in case Benjamin Franklin should decline appointment or die, JJ was delegated to choose a Trustee from among the Assembly's five nominees to implement abroad the Assembly's Act to have "certain Bills of Credit" withdrawn from circulation, with instructions thereto. Lee to JJ, 4 Jan. 1780, Duplicate LS in JP; LbkC in MdAA: Council Lbks. Enclosure (not located): abstract in ch. 38 of laws of 1779 in *Laws of Maryland* (Annapolis, 1787).

[7]The four private letters are: Benjamin Lewis to JJ, 20 Nov. 1779, see editorial note, "Lewis Littlepage: An Insubordinate Protégé" and n. 3, below; Robert R. Livingston to JJ, 6 Oct. and 22 Dec. 1779, see n. 2 in JJ to Livingston, 6 Oct. 1780, above; Catharine W. Livingston to SLJ and JJ, [26 Dec. 1779], AL in JP; E in NN: Bancroft: American V, 300.

[8]The dispatches of the unofficial agent of Spain in America, Don Juan de Miralles (*JJ,* I, 713), prior to 28 April 1780, the date of his death. The information no doubt concerned the January–February 1780 Congressional discussions and committee reports on Spain, including reports of and resolutions on two conferences with Luzerne; 28, 31 Jan. 1780, LbkCs of both in PCC 25, I; *JCC,* XVI, 106–09, 111–16; *RDC,* III, 481–86; 2 Feb. 1780, *RDC,* III, 488–90.

[9]Catharine W. Livingston to SLJ, 26 April 1780, AL in JP.

[10]The Mallets were associated with the Cádiz mercantile firm Mercy & Lacaze & Sons, which had established a branch in Philadelphia by 1779. See *RMP,* III, 94–95.

To Floridablanca

Madrid, 11 December 1780

Sir,

Some of the Bills drawn on me will probably become due, before Mr. Cabarrus's operations can be brought to an Issue.[1] So far as their Failure would injure the Credit and relax the operations of a People actually at war with the Enemies of his Catholic majesty, and opposing those Enemies in the very neighbourhood of his Dominions; it may certainly be considered as a matter interesting to Spain. This Consideration, together with the Proofs and assurances which America has recieved of his majesty's friendly Disposition towards her, induce me, to take the Liberty of proposing to your Excellency's Consideration, a method for preventing an Event so prejudicial to both.

If his majesty would be pleased to lend the united States the amount of these Bills, to be paid at the Havana or porto Rico, I have Reason to think it would not be difficult immediately to obtain an equal Sum for it in Europe.

I have the Honor to be with great Respect, Your Excellency's most obedient and most humble Servant,

JOHN JAY

ALS and Spanish trans. in AHN Estado, leg. 3884, exp. 4, doc. 89. Endorsed (trans. from the Spanish): "For the 23d December a conference was ordered with the American diplomats and the interpreter Don Diego de Gardoqui, in which it appears that they dealt with this and other points." For the conference, see editorial note above, "Issues in Negotiation," and n. 14.

[1]See JJ's notes of a conference, 8 Nov. 1780, above. On 20 Sept. 1780, Charles III had approved Cabarrús' proposal for the issuance of *vales reales*, the first paper money in Spanish history, to help finance the war.

FROM SAMUEL HUNTINGTON

Philadelphia, 18 December 1780

Sir,

Since writing my Letter of the 6th of October last[1] (a copy of which is enclosed) I have been honored with yours of July 10th and September 16th; by the latter I am happy to find that we may expect soon to receive further and more particular Intelligence from you.[2]

Congress, it is probable, will soon establish an Office for foreign Affairs, to be managed by an Officer stiled *Secretary for foreign Affairs,*[3] who will be constantly devoted to the Business of that Department; which it is to be hoped will remedy many Disadvantages we have hitherto laboured under, and give our Ministers at foreign Courts more frequent, better and earlier Intelligence than they have hitherto received from us.

In the Course of the last Campaign the Enemy at New York have been pretty much confined under the Protection of their Ships and Fortifications. The Particulars of their Eruption into the Jerseys under Kniphausen, and the repulse they met with, you must have been informed of before this.[4]

The Enemy from Canada have repeatedly attacked the western and northern Frontiers of New York, by the Way of the Mohawk River and Lake Champlain, marking their Route with their usual Devastation, but were soon compelled to retreat with Precipitation.[5]

Since the unfortunate Action near Camden and the Retreat of General Gates,[6] our People principally Militia of the Southern States, have been frequently skirmishing successfully with the Enemy, and have driven in most of their out Posts. The brilliant success of the Militia over Colonel Ferguson at Kings Mountain,[7] you must have learnt from the Papers. The Enemy from the last Intelligence were in Possession of Camden and some other inland Posts in South Carolina. Should they not be reinforced soon, it is probable they must have Recourse to their old Practice of retiring to the Sea Coast under the Protection of their Shipping. General Greene by Order of Congress hath taken Command of the Southern Army, which will be reinforced so as to make a respectable Army in the Course of the Winter.[8] We are waiting and wishing for a naval Force to command the American Seas; and with the Smiles of Providence might soon expect in that Case to expell the Enemy from the United States.

Necessity obliges me to confide in the Committee for foreign Affairs to give you the needful and more particular Intelligence.[9]

Please to make my Compliments acceptable to your Lady and believe me to be with sincere Esteem and regard, Sir, Your most obedient and humble servant,

SAM. HUNTINGTON

ALS. Endorsed: "Recd. 18 March 1781, priv. ansd. 21 Apr. 1781." Enclosure: Duplicate LS of 6 Oct. 1780.

[1]Not located.

[2]JJ to Huntington, 10 July Dft and 16 Sept. 1780 RC, in Carmichael's hand, both in JP; LbkCs of both in PCC 110, I and in CSmH; 16 Sept. in *RDC*, IV, 59, *HPJ*, I, 405, in which JJ stated: ". . . it is necessary immediately to cease drawing bills upon me for the Present. Your Excellency may soon expect a full detail of Particulars from me [6 Nov. 1780], you will then receive an answer to *every* question that may be raised upon this letter." The 16 September letter was read in Congress on 4 December but no action was taken on it. *JCC*, XVIII, 1120.

[3]Upon New York delegate James Duane's resolution of 15 May 1780, a committee was appointed (Lovell, Houston, and Duane) to "report a proper arrangement for the department of foreign affairs." Their report was discussed on 12 June and 15 Dec. 1780, but it was not until 10 Jan. 1781 when Congress resolved to establish the Department to be headed by a Secretary, who was to be elected on 10 Aug. 1781. See Robert R. Livingston to JJ, 20 Oct. 1781, below. *JCC*, XVII, 428, 505; XVIII, 1156; XIX, 43–44 (resolution); XXI, 851–52. For Duane, see *JJ*, I, 107.

[4]JJ received information about the Springfield raid and other military and naval events from William Churchill Houston, 7 February, and Robert R. Livingston, 26 Aug. 1780; *JJ*, I, 725–27, 809–13; see p. 727 for Knyphausen.

[5]For attacks by the Indians supported by British regulars, and for the 1780 raids under the Loyalist Sir John Johnson (1742–1830), commanding Tories and Indians, routed on 19 October, see Howard Swiggett, *War Out of Niagara: Walter Butler and the Tory Rangers* (New York, 1933), pp. 212 *et seq.*

[6]General Horatio Gates, the Commander of the Southern Department, lost the

Battle of Camden, S.C., on 16 August to Cornwallis, with Patriot losses estimated at 800 to 900 killed and 1,000 captured. Gates ordered a retreat to Hillsboro, N.C., which he himself reached in three days. See *JJ*, I, 811.

[7]On 7 Oct. 1780, Major Patrick Ferguson (1744–80) of the 71st Highlanders, Inspector of Militia in the Southern Provinces, was killed and his Tory troops defeated by a mixed force of Patriot militia and irregulars at the Battle of Kings Mountain, S.C., the turning point in the Southern theater of operations for the Patriots.

[8]Major-General Nathanael Greene was appointed Commander of the Southern Department by General Washington on 14 Oct. 1780. *GWF*, XX, 181–83; George Washington Greene, *The Life of Nathanael Greene, Major General in the Army of the Revolution* (3 vols., New York, 1878).

[9]There is no record of a letter from the Committee to JJ at this time, but an extract in Charles Thomson's hand from the minutes of Congress concerning efforts for the release and exchange of Henry Laurens, dated three days hence, is in JP. Resolution of Congress to JJ and Benjamin Franklin, 21 Dec. 1780, *JCC*, XVIII, 1179.

To Robert Morris

Madrid, 18 December 1780

Dear Sir,

As I have lately written by different vessels to Congress, and my Friends,[1] among whom I always reckon you. My chief Inducement at present is to commit the inclosed[2] to your Care and to request the Favor of you to forward them.

No Letters from America of later date than July have reached me, indeed I have had the Pleasure of receiving only one from you since we parted.[3] Some were probably carried with Mr. Laurens to England. It is generally said and believed that all his papers were taken,[4] and I presume several letters for me were among them.

Arnold's Plot was as unexpected as its Discovery was fortunate. His wife is much to be pitied. It is painful to see so charming a woman so sacrificed.[5] Some of the wise ones predict much ill from this Mans Treason. They ascribe it to the gloomy aspect of our Affairs, and impute his desertion to a Desire of Escaping the Ruin into which he saw his Country was falling. In short the Resistance of America looks so miraculous in European Eyes; that they are ready to embrace every Opinion, however erroneous, that tends to reduce the Estimate of our Power and Virtue more to a Level with that which they had formed themselves.

The Rank we hold on the Scale of Prosperity generally determines the Degree of Friendship we may expect from the Mass of Mankind. This Reflection will explain the Importance which every fortunate Event in America is of in Europe.

I hope you are preparing vigourously for another Campaign for I much doubt whether a Peace will soon take Place. The Empress Queen of Hungary is dead, and the Ambitions of the Emperor[6] will of course be less fettered. What Consequences will follow this Event is a Question much discussed at present. Time only can determine it.

When you see Col. Moyland tell him his Brother[7] is here, and very well. We see each other often. He formerly lived at Cadiz, but as Government ordered all Irish to remove from the Seaports he was obliged with many others to quit it. It is said that their too great Attachment to Britain occasioned this Ordinance.

Be pleased to present our Compliments to our Friends, and particularly to Mrs. Morris. I am Dear Sir your affectionate Friend and Servant,

JOHN JAY

Tr. ALS in collection of Mrs. Henry M. Sage, Albany. New-York Hist. Soc., *Collections,* I (1879), 453–54.

[1]JJ to Elbridge Gerry, 18 Nov. 1780, above. JJ to Egbert Benson, [20] November, Dft in JP; *HPJ,* I, 447; *WJ,* II, 68. JJ to Philip Schuyler, 25 November, Dft in JP; E in NN: Bancroft: American III, 159 and Schuyler, 1776–88.

[2]See below, under the editorial note "Keeping in Touch," SLJ to Catharine W. Livingston, 1 December, and JJ to Catharine W. Livingston, 17 December.

[3]Robert Morris to JJ, 6 July 1780, ALS in JP.

[4]Although named Commissioner to the United Provinces by Congress on 21 Oct. 1779, it was not until 13 Aug. 1780 that Henry Laurens sailed for Europe, only to be captured by the British and imprisoned in the Tower of London on 6 Oct. 1780 on suspicion of treason. *JCC,* XV, 1198; "A Narrative of the Capture of Laurens," South Carolina Hist. Soc., *Collections,* I (1857), 18–68; for the papers and documents that Laurens was carrying, see also *Peacemakers,* pp. 24–26.

[5]Benedict Arnold's plot to deliver West Point to the British was exposed on 25 Sept. 1780, and the professed innocence of his second wife, Margaret Shippen Arnold (c. 1751–1834) is, in the light of the evidence, highly dubious. Carl Van Doren, *Secret History of the American Revolution* (New York, 1941); *JJ,* I, 185.

[6]The Empress Maria Theresa (1717–29 Nov. 1780) was succeeded by her son, Joseph II (1741–90), who had served as co-regent since 1765.

[7]Arthur Moylan was a merchant in Spain and the brother of Colonel Stephen Moylan (*JJ,* I, 709). The latter was married to SLJ's cousin, Mary Ricketts Van Horne (b. 1754). JJ, *Ledger,* p. 40, in JP.

To Benjamin Franklin

Madrid, 25 December 1780

Dear Sir,

It was not till the Day before Yesterday, that I received Mr. Grand's Letter, informing me of the Credit you had lodged for me, through him with the Marquis d'Yranda, for £26459.2.[1] Your favour of the 2nd October is the last I have had the pleasure of receiving from you.[2]

Presuming that the Marquis had been apprized of the Arrangements taken with Mr. Grand[3] for furnishing me with the first of the sixty Day Bills became due, He informed me that no such Arrangement had been communicated to him. I shewed him the Paragraph of your Letter relative to it. After several Days had elapsed he desired a *Certified* Copy of that Paragraph, with a List of the Bills. From the Hesitation and these Requisitions I feared it might be inconvenient or not very agreable to the Marquis to advance the Money, and as it was easy to get a full Price for Bills on you, I forbore to press him.

On the 23d instant I signed a Bill (and Duplicate) on you for thirteen thousand seven hundred and seventy livres at ninety Days sight in favor of Don Francisco De Gorbes and Nephews.[4] This Money I will either consider as part of the before mentioned Credit with the Marquis D'Yranda, or as part of the 25000 Dollars as may be most agreable to you. Your repeated Attentions and Civilities demand from me the highest Delicacy, and be assured that Inclinations as well as duty will always prompt me to acknowledge the one and observe the other.

Tell Mr. Deane, if you please, that I confess myself indebted to him for two very acceptable Letters[5]; that I have not hitherto been able to repay him, but that he may shortly expect it with such Interest as I hope will attone for my Want of Punctuality.

Mrs. Jay charges me to present to you in the most cordial Manner the Compliments of the Season. If her Wishes would avail, I believe the Duration of your Life would not be very disproportionate to that of its Importance.

I am, Dear Sir, with sincere Esteem and Regard Your obliged and affectionate Friend and Servant,

(signed) JOHN JAY

LbkC in DLC: Franklin III, 79–80.

[1]Ferdinand Grand to JJ, *c.* 12 Dec. 1780, not located. The credit of 26,459.2 livres is entered under 10 Jan. 1781 in Grand's account of bills drawn by JJ on Franklin; D, 10 Jan. 1781–11 March 1783, endorsed by JJ, in JP.

[2]Franklin to JJ, 2 Oct. 1780, LS in JP; LbkC in DLC: Franklin III, 72–74; *RDC*, IV, 74–76; *BFS*, VIII, 142–45. LS versions herein from Benjamin Franklin are in the hand of William Temple Franklin unless otherwise noted.

[3]On 28 Dec. 1780 Yranda informed JJ in writing that he had received Grand's order dated 12 December for the 26,459.2 livres credit for JJ. LS in French in JP.

[4]The entry for 13,770 livres on the Gorbes firm is entered in JJ's accounts. D, 14 May 1784, in DNA: RG 39, Foreign Ledger of Public Agents in Europe, I, 132.

[5]These could be from among the following three letters: Silas Deane to JJ, 16 Nov. 1780, ALS in JP; LbkC in CtHi; *Deane Papers*, IV, 252–60; [November 1780], *Deane Papers*, IV, 261–63; 12 Dec. 1780, ALS in JP.

SPANISH LOANS OBTAINED BY JAY AND ADVANCED BY JAMES GARDOQUI [1 January 1781-21 March 1782]

	R.[1] V. M.	Mex. D. R. M.[2]	£. s. d.
To Loans from the Court of Spain for the following Sums paid him			
1781 January 1	357.840	17.892	
February 28)) 2 Payments March 6)	640.000	32.000	
April 28	180.705.30	9.035 5.30	
May 9	280.000	14.000	870.051.10
June 22	240.000	12.000	
August 18	240.000	12.000	
December 23	1.021.660	51.083	
1782 March 21	520.000	26.000	
To Interest Account for gain on Billets	136.28	6.16.28	34. 4
Real vellón	3.480.342.24	$174.017. 2.24	£870.085.14

D in DNA: RG 39, Foreign Ledger of Public Agents in Europe, I, 195. The total Spanish loan of $174,011 reflects the rounding off the April 28 loan to $9,036 less the interest. See the editorial note, "Settling the Spanish Accounts," below.

[1]The *moneda de vellón*, money of account in Spain of bullion, the basic unit of which was the *maravedí.*. Thirty-four *maravedís* were equivalent to one *real vellón.*

[2]A Mexican *dólar* (or dollar) was equivalent to 20 *reals vellón.*.

Silas Deane: A Worrisome Correspondent

2 October–1 November 1780

During the late summer and fall of 1780 JJ's heavy burden of diplomatic duties was hardly lightened by the receipt of a flurry of letters from a longtime friend, Silas Deane. As agent of two secret committees of Congress, Deane had been dispatched to France in April, 1776 to secure supplies and explore the possibilities of French recognition and alliance. He later was named commissioner, along with Arthur Lee and Benjamin Franklin. Accused by his enemies of lining his own pockets through his extensive operations abroad, he was recalled by Congress in 1778 to answer charges. The Deane issue rocked Congress during the very months when JJ served as its President.[1] Since JJ had proven to be a steadfast supporter of Deane, it was only natural that the latter on his return to Paris, ostensibly to straighten out his tangled accounts, should seek to reestablish contact with America's unaccredited plenipotentiary to Spain.

Unbeknown to JJ or to any of the Patriot leaders, Deane appears to have operated as the British spy "Benson" as far back as 1777, and to have allowed confidential information on his mission to be leaked to England through his salaried secretary Dr. Edward Bancroft, the "B. Edwards" of British intelligence.[2] Now, embittered by the seeming ingratitude of Congress, Deane embarked upon a course of correspondence with JJ and other prominent Patriots, which was to climax in October-December of '81 with an overt appeal to prominent Revolutionary leaders to give up the struggle,[3] a move which seems to have been prompted by an opportunity for a mere £3,000 in trade.[4] Before the open break, however, Deane was pursuing a downhill course that could only end in treason. As JJ charitably put it, and on second thought deleted the phrase, Deane's "mortifications had poisoned his Heart and turned his Brain."[5]

Not anticipating Deane's public defection, JJ continued to receive and respond to Deane's letters in 1781, the American minister seeking to reassure the latter that he was "far from being indifferent" to affairs which concerned Deane personally.[6] Subsequent to his public exposure, Deane, writing from Ghent, called on both Franklin and JJ to support his character from the charge of being a war profiteer.[7] Franklin responded affirmatively,[8] but there is no record of JJ having complied. The correspondence came to an abrupt climax with a note from JJ of 22 February 1783:

> I write thus plainly and fully, because I still indulge an idea that your head may have been more to blame than your heart, and that in some melancholy desponding hour, the disorder of your nerves infected your opinions and your pen. God grant that this may prove to have been the case, and that I may yet have reason to resume my former opinion, that you were a valuable, a virtuous, and a patriotic man. Whenever this day may happen,

I will, with great and sincere satisfaction, again become Your friend, John Jay.[9]

JJ's last letter to Deane was written on 23 February 1784,[10] and thereafter Deane does not appear again among JJ's correspondents until 1789, when the expatriate wrote on the verge of his planned return to America.

[1] *JJ,* I, 507–08, *passim,* 649.

[2] Julian P. Boyd, "Silas Deane's Death by a Kindly Teacher of Treason," *WMQ,* 3d ser., XVI (July 1959), 332–33.

[3] The letters to some eleven American public figures appear in Rivington's *Royal Gazette,* 24 Oct.–12 Dec. 1781, although they were written some months earlier.

[4] Boyd, "Deane," p. 336.

[5] JJ to Franklin, 11 Feb. 1782, below.

[6] JJ to Deane, 10 March 1781, ALS in NjP: Crosseley; and, below, JJ to Deane, 16 June 1781.

[7] In Deane to JJ, 1 Dec. 178[2], Tr in JP. Therein Deane enclosed a copy of his 17 Nov. 1782 letter to Edward Bancroft, urging him to request certificates from Franklin and JJ. ACS and C in JP, both endorsed by JJ.

[8] Certificate of Benjamin Franklin, 18 Dec. 1782, *Deane Papers,* V, 116–17.

[9] *Ibid.,* pp. 131–32; *HPJ,* III, 29–31.

[10] *Deane Papers,* V, 280–81; *HPJ,* III, 114–15.

To Silas Deane

Madrid, 2 October 1780

Dear Sir,

Since mine to you <written at> from St. Ildefonso enclosed to Doctor Franklin,[1] I have had the pleasure of recieving yours of the 4 and 13th of September a few Days ago.[2] The one you mention to have written on the 28th August I have not seen, nor do I ever expect <ever> to see.[3] Many Letters directed to me have met with the same Fate. So circumstanced It is impossible for me to give you any Opinion relative to the Success of the Business you allude to, and therefore cannot advise as to the Expediency of the JOURNEY you propose.[4] I can nevertheless <with great Sincerity assure> tell you that it will always give me pleasure to be useful to you, and that YOUR COMPANY would be a GREAT SATISFACTION TO ALL MY FAMILY.

Had <the Confederacy arrived> HARDING ARRIVED before you left Philadelphia?[5] Send your Letters under Cover to some Person here. They may then come safe. CARMICHAEL CANNOT ACCOUNT FOR B. NOT ANSWERING HIS LETTERS etc.[6] WHEN WE WRITE IN CYPHER FOR THE FUTURE ADD 20 TO EACH NUMBER.[7]

I hope your next will give me some Intelligence from America which I shall not be able to find in News Papers. There are many little Circumstances you know respecting ones Friends and indeed ones Enemies which tho not otherwise important are in a certain Degree interesting <and which we have few Opportunities of becoming acquainted>.

My <sincere good> best Wishes to the good Doctor. Mrs. Jay and the Colonel present theirs to you, and I need not add how much you possess those of, Dear Sir, <Your Friend> your obedient humble Servant,

J. J.

DftS, partly in code, decoded by JJ. Endorsed by JJ.

[1]JJ to Deane, 8 Sept. 1780, ALS (which had been enclosed in JJ to Franklin, 8 Sept. 1780, ALS not located; Dft in JP; LbkC in DLC: Franklin III, 67–68) in CtY, Dft in JP; *RDC*, IV, 49–50; *Deane Papers*, IV, 224. Therein, JJ, who was also anxious for news of America, wrote: "Your Silence is unkind. . . . [I]t would be wrong to extend to a whole Nation the Resentments excited by a few."

[2]Deane to JJ, 4 Sept. 1780, LbkC in CtHi; 13 Sept. 1780, ALS in JP; LbkC in CtHi; both in *Deane Papers*, IV, 218–19, 225–26.

[3]The actual date of the letter is 23 August. ALS in JP, enclosure not located; LbkC in CtHi; *Deane Papers*, IV, 195–97. For JJ's action on this letter, see below, 1 Nov. 1780, n. 5.

[4]In his letter of 4 September, Deane mentioned that on 23 August he had enclosed to JJ for transmittal to Floridablanca a proposed contract for masts, with an endorsement from the late Don Juan de Miralles obtained by Deane before departing from the States, on which he was anxious to have a decision. On 13 September Deane proposed that, if necessary for the acceptance of the contract, he would plan to come to Madrid.

[5]See below, Deane to JJ, 16 October.

[6]A reference to Dr. Edward Bancroft. There is no discussion of this matter in Carmichael's letters to JJ around this time, but as Carmichael, JJ's official secretary, was in Madrid on 2 October, he no doubt mentioned this to JJ orally. For the reply, see Deane to JJ, 16 October, and JJ's explanation to Deane, 1 November, below. For Bancroft and Carmichael see *JJ*, I, 330.

[7]The cipher and code agreed upon by JJ and Deane before JJ left America in 1779 is referred to and used by both in this and in their subsequent correspondence. Cipher and code, n.d. [1779], partly in JJ's hand, in JP.

FROM SILAS DEANE

Passy, 9 October 1780

Dear Sir,

This is my fifth Letter since my Arrival, and having received no Acknowledgment from you of the Receipt of any one of them I am a little uneasy for the Fate of them in particular for that which inclosed a Letter from Don Juan to the Minister. My last was of the 18th Ultimo in which I wrote you my Sentiments on political Affairs.[1] Nothing New has since occurred to induce a Change. Letters are received at L'Orient as late as the 3d of last Month when every thing remained in statu quo. A good Understanding prevailed between the American and French Troops. The latter are entrenched at Rhode Island. Admiral Arbuthnot was off the harbor with a superior Fleet, and Clinton threatned an embarkation of Ten thousand Troops at New York to attack them. The New England militia were called in to their Aid.[2] The Northern Privateers had captured and brought into Boston Nineteen shipps of the Quebec Fleet, Valued at Four Hundred Thousand pounds St[erlin]g.[3] They could not indeed have been Worth much less. This, every thing considered, is of more consequence than the Capture off Cape Finistere.[4] From the West Indies nothing New. The British Parliament meet the last of this month and it is said will be entertained with a pacific Speech from the Throne. Indeed from all I can learn, it is probable that some Overtures will be made, which I wish may lead to an honorable Peace.[5] But I dare not make any dependance on it, though I think there is a greater prospect of it at present than for some Time past. Mr. Searle[6] sets off for Holland Tomorrow, where Mr. Adams[7] has fixed himself and Family. No News of Mr. Laurens, whence Mr. Searle sets him down as lost. I beleive We are so much of the Christian and Philosopher, as to be resigned on the Occasion. His Arrival can do no good at this Time, for there is no money to be borrowed in Holland nor any where else on Our Account, and if there was, We have so many Agents of Private States bidding on one Another, and proclaiming thereby Our Wants, as well as Our Folly, that no prudent Man would venture his Money. Pray let me know your True Situation, and prospects in Spain. I wish to know them from the Interest I take in whatever affects you as well as on Account of Our Country.

In short I do not APROVE OF THE Conduct OF FRANCE OR SPAIN TO AMERICA. SPAIN evidently trifles WITH US IN THE Face OF ALL EUROPE. FRANCE does NEAR the same BUT labors to save appearances. OUR Cause HAS lost ground greatly IN FRANCE. EUROPE IS MORE AND MORE indifferent ABOUT US. The Armed Neutrality IS AT AN End, or rather WILL NEVER TAKE place. OUR Liberty AND INDEP[ENDENCE] IS AN Object WHICH becomes EVERY Day MORE OUT OF Sight. AM[ERICA] begins to grow uneasy, and this Fruitless Campaign with other Circumstances will I fear totally DISCOURAGE US. EVERY AMERICAN GOES FROM FRANCE IN disgust, though I think without Cause. The Language held BY J.A. OUR MINISTER FOR PEACE

AND HIS retiring TO HOLLAND IN disgust, has had more serious Effects than is suspected by most.[8] In short all these Circumstances laid together I fear IF A PEACE or TRUCE TAKES place, THE FIRST Object OF THE WAR ON OUR part, will have but little Weight WITH OUR FRIENDS, especially WITH SPAIN who I am convinced is very far from wishing US TO SUCCEED farther than to HER[9] her REVENGE AGAINST ENGLAND. You can doubtless set me right on this subject but if you do not think it prudent to do so I will not blame You.

My best Compliments wait on Mrs. Jay and Col. Livingston, and am with sincere Friendship, Dear Sir, Your most Obedient and Very Humble Servant,

S. DEANE

ALS, partly in code, deciphered by JJ; LbkC in CtHi; *Deane Papers,* IV, 240–42, with errors due to the incorrect rendering of the code.

[1]Deane's four previous letters were 23 August, 4 and 13 September (see above, nn. 2 and 3 of preceding letter), and 18 September: ALS, partly in code, deciphered by JJ, in JP; LbkC in CtHi; E in NN: Bancroft: American II, 301–09; *Deane Papers,* IV, 227–31.

[2]After the Charleston victory, Admiral Marriot Arbuthnot returned north with General Sir Henry Clinton's forces, anchoring his fleet off the eastern end of Long Island to block the French fleet under Guichen at Rhode Island. When, in September 1780, Admiral George Rodney assumed over-all command as the senior officer, Arbuthnot resigned in protest. For Arbuthnot, Clinton, Guichen, and Rodney, see *JJ,* I, 260, 600, 724, 799; for the battle of Charleston, see *ibid.,* pp. 776, 792, 807.

[3]As reported by General Washington to Governor William Livingston of New Jersey, 17 Aug. 1780: ". . . the greater part of the fleet of Victuallers and Merchant men bound from England to Quebec had been taken by the Eastern privateers. Sixteen of the prizes had arrived in the different ports." *GWF,* XIX, 386–88.

[4]A reference to depredations by British cruisers and privateers off Cape Finisterre, the westernmost point of Spain, for which see W. M. James, *The British Navy in Adversity* (London, 1926), p. 186.

[5]King George III addressed a joint session of Parliament on 1 Nov. 1780 requesting authorization of funds for the war, as "the whole force and faculties of the monarchies of France and Spain are drawn forth, and exerted to the utmost to support the rebellion in my colonies in North America, and, without the least provocation or cause of complaint, to attack my dominions. . . ." Parliament voted the funds. *The Parliamentary History of England from the Earliest Period to the Year 1803* (36 vols., London, 1806–20), XXI, 808–44.

[6]For James Searle, who had arrived in Paris on 10 September, carrying copies of Laurens' Congressional commissions, see *JJ,* I, 791.

[7]On 20 June 1780 Congress appointed John Adams to undertake Laurens' commission to negotiate a loan in the Low Countries. Adams left for Holland on 27 July. His formal commission and his instructions as Minister Plenipotentiary to the United Provinces were issued by Congress on 29 Dec. 1780. *JCC,* XVII, 535–37; XVIII, 1204–06. For Adams' trip on his own initiative, see *AP,* II, 442–43n.

[8]On John Adams' diplomacy in Paris, see *Peacemakers,* pp. 191–99, *passim.*

[9]A slip of the pen: the deciphered word should be "aid."

FROM SILAS DEANE

Paris, 16 October 1780[1]

My Dear Sir,

Yours of the 2d I received last Evening. Am much surprized at the miscarriage of my Letter of the 28th of August nor can I account for it as it actually went under Cover by the Courier from Court. The Contents were not secret though important to me, and containing a Letter of Don Juans to the Minister at Madrid. Its loss cannot be repaired. I trust you will yet receive it.

Capt. Harding arrived before I left Virginia but I left Philad[elphi]a soon after You. My Letters in future will come under Cover as You advise. Dr. Bancroft can best Account, for his not Answering Mr. Carmichaels Letters, though from what the Doctor has told me, I am surprized that the latter should be at any Loss at all on the subject. I do not well understand Your proposed Addition of CYPHER, and therefore must write in my former method untill You explain it more fully.[2]

I have now replyed to yours, and having made out a Letter as long and as Circumstantial as yours, might subscribe myself Yours etc., but I cannot do it without first telling you that I feel myself a little piqued at the shortness of your Letter, in reply to Two long ones of mine. I am equally desirous with you of knowing many little, and some great Circumstances, which as Your Friend, and Countryman I am Interested in. The Affair of Mr. Laurens, you are acquainted with by the public Papers, for which it is a fruitful, and seasonable Subject as that of Electioneering is exhausted in England. His Son sailed Ten Days before him for Europe but has not been heard of.[3] OUR FORCES IN SOUTH CAROLINA under GATES HAVE BEEN DEFEATED. OUR LOSS IS GREAT. Baron de Kalb killed and ABOUT 2500 KILLED AND PRISONERS. THE ACCOUNT IS I hope exaggerated.[4] J.A. IS IN HOLLAND AND HAS power to supply the place of H. LAURENS. Mr. Searle IS IN HOLLAND. You have the general American News as early probably as We have in France, but as I see almost every Week some one from thence, I must tell you OUR AFFAIRS are NOT IN A better STATE than WHEN YOU left PH[ILADELPHI]A. MANY Intrigues are on foot IN FRANCE AND IN LONDON as well as IN AM[ERICA], AND I know so much of THEM as to caution you NOT TO BE ALARMED at any thing. A REV[OLUTIO]N may happen IN 3 MONTHS AT present NOT SUSPECTED ON either PARTY. Being but a passenger, I have leisure for Observation and from my past Experience and former as well as present Connections am able to see as much of the Game as some who play the great hands. My best Wishes are for the *Peace, Safety and Liberty of America.* This was our early prayer as you must remember. A. LEE WAS AT PH[ILADELPHI]A publishing a New Edition of *COMMON SENSE* WITH Additions etc.[5] Nothing that HE can say OR CONGRESS RESOLVE can alter Facts, AND HAVING SUFFERED so much injustice and ingratitude FROM, AND seen so much practised BY CONGRESS ON others I am become indifferent in some Degree to what either of them can say or do. I know the Weakness of CONGRESS TO say no worse of IT AND THE Malignity of A. LEE AND Associates. BUT THE STATE OF AMERICA wrings my very Soul. RUINED ON THE ONE PART by weak distracted COUNCILS AND BETRAYED ON THE other by those in whom IT HAS confided IT IS TOO hard.

But Adieu to Politics. I promise to meddle no more with them in Our future Correspondance but to follow <your> the Example you have set me in your Letters and write only on indifferent Subjects. Your happiness and prosperity <will> can never be of this kind with me, and from that motive I wish to know at least the Outlines of your Situation. But perhaps you think me Gloomy, <and> if not disaffected. I can never be so to the Interests of America, and America will soon be sensible of it. But I am not cheerful, except when I am in the Company of my Friends and find them happy, or hear that they are so, and when I can cease reflecting on certain subjects. This is sometimes the Case. I hope it will soon be intirely so.

My Compliments to Mrs. Jay and Col. Livingston, and am on all Occasions, my Dear Sir, Your Affectionate Friend and Very Humble Servant,

S. DEANE

ALS. Endorsed by JJ: "... answ. 1 Nov. 1780." LbkC in CtHi; *Deane Papers,* IV, 244–46, with numerous errors due to the incorrect rendering of the code.

[1]Deane had first dated the year as 1770.

[2]See above, 2 October, n. 7.

[3]Lieutenant-Colonel John Laurens was taken prisoner on 12 May at the surrender of Charleston, S.C., but was subsequently paroled. Laurens' exchange, along with a number of high-ranking officers, was reported to Congress by General Washington on 7 Nov. 1780. LS in PCC 152, IX, 355; *JCC,* XVIII, 1049; *GWF,* XX, 311–15. Laurens did not sail for Europe until 11 Feb. 1781; for his mission, see below, p. 75.

[4]See Huntington to JJ, 18 Dec. 1780, above. For Kalb, see *JJ,* I, 813.

[5]Arthur Lee returned to the States in the fall of 1780. Evidence is lacking that Lee did issue such an edition; see Richard Gimbel, *Thomas Paine: A Bibliographical Check List of Common Sense With an Account of its Publication* (New Haven, 1956), pp. 91–92. For Lee, see also *JJ,* I, 487–88, 507 *et seq.*

To SILAS DEANE

Madrid, 26 October 1780

Dear Sir,

At length your first Letter contrary to my Expectations, has <been delivered to me> arrived, and my Attentions <to the object of it> shall not be wanting. I have also recieved your Favor of the 18th September since which more of my Letters than one have I hope reached you, this being the fourth.[1]

I have read, considered and reconsidered the Facts and reflections you communicate, and am persuaded that the Consequences you draw tho in a certain Degree just, are not quite so extensive as you seem to suppose. I am not free from similar apprehensions but they are not so strong as yours. But however well founded they may be, they ought only to increase our Prudence <and should be carefully concealed>. If I had Leisure it would give me pleasure to go largely into this Subject; at present I cannot because matters of more immediate Importance engage me.

That you have been hardly treated I know and shall never hesitate to say, but I cannot think the Cases of <Mr. Adams, Izard and Lee> the gentlemen are similar or prove the points to which you apply them.[2] You was blamed not for omitting finally to settle your accounts in France, but for not being in *capacity* to shew (when in America) what those accounts were, and I don't know that those gentlemen were or will be chargeable with the like incapacity. I mention this only to shew the Destinction between the cases. How far the Destinction is important or how far that Incapacity could justify the Treatment it occasioned are other Questions. For my own part I think it could not justify it.

It will also remain a Question of how far your Measures were prudent. I think some of them were and some not, but this Inquiry requires many Considerations and Combinations of Circumstances, which I must defer for the present. The Discoveries you allude to respecting secret practices surprize me exceedingly. I have no such Suspicions. Perhaps you may give more Weight to Circumstances than they may merit. The Inquiry nevertheless is very important and while any Doubts remain the pursuit should be continued. Justice demands that we should not, even in our opinions, injure Men who may be innocent <even in a> and prudence also demands that we permit not <the Goodness of the> a Good Heart to impose on a good Head, a Case by no means uncommon.

I wish there were twenty other Motives than those you mention for <drawing you to Spain> your passing to Spain, Exclusive of the <Pleasure> *Satisfaction it will* <always>*give me to see you.* The <Facts>Matters you mention are highly interesting *in a public and private view;* they *cannot* possibly *be so* well <discussed or understood from> *handled* in *Letters* as *Conversation.*

Whether it will be in my power *to meet you* <at either of the places you name> I cannot predict and therefore cannot promise. <The Excursion> *It would be agreable* <to me> but I have hitherto found so many Matters not to be neglected constantly demanding my attention, that I cannot flatter myself with being more disengaged till the greater objects of coming here shall be either attained or become unattainable. If I should nevertheless be able <to meet you> I will. If not I hope you will <not permit a few Days Journey to separate us, especially as your coming here would probably be a means of bringing your Business with the Minister to a more speedy and perhaps more satisfactory Conclusion, but of this <<how>> I cannot as yet be certain> *come on.*

The attachment you express for your Country notwithstanding <the Injustice> <your Measures> <in some of her Representatives which you have been used> your Complaints of her Ingratitude, does you much Honor. The Injustice of <endeavouring to> resenting on a whole People the mistakes or Transgressions of a few is obvious <yet as> but there are comparatively not many who under similar Circumstances either think right or act so. Truth is seldom so immersed in Darkness as to not be capable of being brought to Light if attempted in season, and as the Mass of the People mean well, they will finally do Justice, tho their mistakes and Passions sometimes delay it. Persevere therefore. Do good to your Country and evince <your> the Rectitude of your Conduct while in her Service. I believe you honest and I think you injured. These Considerations will always prompt me to every friendly office in my power to render.

I must again advise you to <review> collect, review and ascertain precisely the Evidence you may have or can obtain of the Duplicity of the Persons you allude to, whoever they may be. I see this Business in many important Lights and the Time may come when you may rejoice in all the Trouble you may now be at about it. Nay all this Evidence provided it <should prove conclusive> should appear material ought to be committed to Paper and not permitted to diminish or die in or with your memory. Put it in the power of your Friends to vindicate your Reputation when you may be no more. It will be of particular Importance to your Son,[3] to whom you cannot leave a better Inheritance than a good, nor a worse one than a bad <Name> or doubtful Reputation. Remember too that time <elapses> is spending, Men forgetting or dieing, Papers wasting, etc., and therefore the sooner you reduce these Matters to certainty the better.

Mrs. Jay and the Colonel desire to be particularly remembered to You. This will go under Cover to Dr. Franklin.[4] Be pleased to assure him of my Regard and Esteem, of which also believe you have no little share.

I am dear Sir very sincerely yours, etc.,

J. J.

DftS. (the intended cipher passages were underscored by JJ and are rendered in italics) Endorsed by JJ: "... In answ. to 18 Sepr. 80." *HPJ,* I, 455–58 (misdated 26 December); *Deane Papers,* IV, 248–50.

[1] JJ's first letter to Deane in Paris is dated 8 September; see n. 1 in JJ to Deane, 2 October (JJ's second letter), above. JJ's third letter, written some time between 2 and 26 October, has not been located.

[2]In a long postscript on 18 September, Deane noted that John Adams, Ralph Izard, and Arthur and William Lee had not settled their private or public accounts upon return to America, stating also that: "These men have . . . as appears by the accounts, received more than twice the amount of public monies which I ever received, and have literally done worse than nothing." For William Lee, see *JJ,* I, 588.

[3]Jesse Deane (1765–1830), Silas Deane's only offspring.

[4]Deane had moved into his former lodgings with Franklin, as he informed JJ on 23 August. Franklin resided at the Hôtel de Valentinois in Passy, owned by Jacques-Donatien Le Ray de Chaumont, an early supporter of the American cause. The letter was probably dispatched in JJ to Franklin, 30 Oct. 1780, Dft in JP; LbkC in DLC: Franklin III, 76–77; *HPJ,* I, 442–44; *RDC,* IV, 108–09. For Chaumont, see *JJ,* I, 631.

To Silas Deane

Madrid, 1 November 1780

Dear Deane,

I have just recieved your Letter of the 16th October. How happens it that you do not yet KNOW ME? Time and opportunity have not been wanting <nor HAVE I BEEN NEUTRAL.> I suspect YOU sometimes SEE DOUBLE.

<Your having left Philadelphia when you did accounts for your not knowing certain Matters which you otherwise would have done and which would have explained my Remark relative to DOCTOR BANCROFT AND WILLIAM CARMICHAEL.>

If my Regard for my Friends be measured by the Length of the

Letters I write them, I confess they have often Reason to complain, especially as a constant Attention to Matters of public Concern leaves me little Leizure for that pleasing Method of employing one's vacant Hours. Not many Days have passed since I wrote you a Letter of more than moderate Length and if I could indulge my Inclination you would read much of my writing.[1] There are many Subjects both interesting and otherwise on which I should be glad to converse with you either on paper or in person, but the former is seldom in my Power for the Reason I have mentioned. MY QUESTION ABOUT DR. BANCROFT AND WILLIAM CARMICHAEL was not with HIS PERMIT OR BY HIS REQUEST. Nor shall I make the least Mention of your Remark on that Head. It is a matter about which I have little Curiosity and could if explained be no further useful to me than as the Circumstances which gave Rise to it, might explain Characters.

Could I transport myself for a few Hours to Passy we should soon find ourselves in a Situation similar to those we were often in at Mrs. Houses in 1775.[2] LETTERS cannot effect this. A multiplicity of Circumstances must necessarily be stated and combined; besides I percieve that YOU neither KNOW MY Situation respecting certain PEOPLE NOR I YOURS. I am convinced that we have the same REGARD FOR EACH other AS BEFORE. You will be of the same opinion if Providence should again GIVE US AN OCCASION OF CONVERSING. These are not Times to bid adieu to Politics. While you can be useful in them don't restrain your Pen from those Subjects. If ever you and I should talk these Matters over, you will think my Letters less reprehensible. In my last I told you that SPAIN WANTED MISSISSIPPI. A Sheet could not convey more to a Person so well acquainted with the Subject as you are. I could tell you that SPAIN DELAYS, DOES LITTLE <EXPECTS THE RESULT OF EVENTS,> etc. etc. but this would be only useless Comments on the Text.

The Captain of a Vessel lately arrived at Cadiz from North Carolina says our Paper was appreciating there. The King of Spain has offered us his Responsibility to facilitate a Loan, and I am in a fair way of <getting> having some Cloathing for our Army. These Circumstances will give you Pleasure I am sure.

If I am not much mistaken the Enemy will attempt to INCLINE HENRY LAURENS TO THEIR VIEWS.[3] The REVOLUTION you <mention I don't well understand> mention or rather intimate would have great Consequences. Instances of the like have happened. This Matter deserves much thought. As to the Editions etc. of ARTHUR LEE no very great Effects will follow them in my opinion. But though Facts cannot be altered, they may be misrepresented and sometimes sunk, unless care be taken to do them Justice. THE STATE OF AMERICA I admit to be a serious Matter, but I still think it will terminate well though it may be <a little> scorched by the ordeal through which it is to pass. Of this you know more than I do, and therefore can better judge. FRANCE had better be cautious. I believe firmly the old adage nil utile nisi quod honestum,[4] and therefore before <People> Politicians or others deviate from Integrity they should well consider the Consequences. I see very clearly that in the Instance alluded to Repentance would soon follow, and not only prove ineffectual but severe. In a word my Friend as to all these Affairs, I believe that a wise and good <God> Being governs this World, that he has ordered <me> us to travel through it to a better, and that We have nothing but our Duty to do on <my> the Journey which will not be a long one. Let <what will happen> us therefore <I shall> travel on with Spirits and Chearfulness without grumbling much at the Bad Roads, bad Inns or bad Company we may be obliged to put up with on the Way. Let us enjoy Prosperity <while> when We have it, and in adversity <succeed> endeavour to be patient and resigned without being lazy or insensible.

I cannot approve of your ceasing to reflect on certain Subjects. The more you reflect on them the better in my opinion, upon the same principle that it is better to meet and reduce <your> one's Enemies than submit to their Bondage or remain exposed to repeated <attacks and> Injuries. <Your Country has been ungrateful you say, admit it. I have done nothing but constantly serve my Country for these six years past and shall most faithfully, but I confess that I did it and am still doing it as much and more for my own Sake as for theirs, that is because I thought and think it my Duty, without doing which I know I cannot please my Maker and get to Heaven, provided he is satisfied with my Conduct. <<I care very little>> The mistaken Opinions of others cannot deprive me of Happiness. I ought to wish and do wish to stand well in the opinion of Mankind and therefore>

Mrs. Jay and the Colonel desire me to make their Compliments to you. I am Dear Sir your Friend and very humble Servant,

J. J.

P.S. <The Beginning of> next Week I shall be at the Escurial, and from thence shall <now> write you particularly relative to Your affairs.[5]

DftS, partly in code. Endorsed by JJ: "... In answ. to 16 Octr." ALS in MB; *WJ*, I, 117–19.

[1]Preceding letter.

[2]The boarding house at Fifth and Market streets in Philadelphia of Mrs. Mary House, where Deane, and JJ, while a member of the New York delegation to Congress, had resided. See also *JJ,* I, 330.

[3]Laurens steadfastly resisted pressures by the British government to defect. "A Narrative of the Capture of Laurens," South Carolina Hist. Soc., *Collections,* I (1857), 18–68.

[4]"Nothing is useful except what is honorable." Cicero, *Letters to Friends* 5.19.1.

[5]In his subsequent letter to Deane on 20 November from Madrid, JJ stated that: "The long lost Letter was delivered by me at the Escurial on the 9th Inst. and I was promised an answer with all convenient Expedition. More could not be desired. As yet I am not enabled to say any thing further on the Subject. The Court will soon be here, and then I shall have more frequent opportunities of expediting this Business." Dft in JP.

To Samuel Huntington

Madrid, 28 January 1781

Sir,

Is it possible that my Letter <from S. Ildefonso> OF SEPTEMBER <last> REQUESTING CONGRESS TO FORBEAR DRAWING should not have arrived?[1] Many Copies were sent by various Vessels from different ports and yet <Shoals of> BILLS DAILY ARRIVE. I have been PROMISED 150 THOUSAND DOLLARS, WHEN it will be PAID IS UNCERTAIN.[2] It is hard to make BRICK WITHOUT STRAW. Col. Livingston left this the Beginning of last Month with <very> LONG LETTERS <for you, which>. He is with his OWN HANDS TO DELIVER THEM TO <american> one of our COUNTRY CAPTAINS. <He is now at nantz.[3] No Letter from Philadelphia from Congress of later> Let me beseech you to KEEP THE CONTENTS SECRET. The Letters brought for me by the La Luzerne <tho put in the Post Office> have not reached me.[4] My Intelligence for many Months past has been by GAZETTES ONLY. I refer to my last Letters and have the Honor to be with great Respect and Regard, Your Excellencys most obedient and most humble Servant.

P.S. Four Copies of this Letter will be sent Tomorrow Evening by the Post to my Correspondents at different posts here and in France.

Dft. The code is based on Boyer's *Royal Dictionary.* ALS in PCC 89, I, 361; duplicate, triplicate, and quadruplicate ALS in Misc. PCC 5, two endorsed as received on 27 April and the third on 28 May; LbkCs in JP, PCC 110, I and in CSmH; Tr in NN: Bancroft: American I, 104. Congress ordered on 27 April "That no more of the bills drawn on the honble John Jay or the honble Henry Laurens be sold until the farther order of Congress, and that the Board of Treasury take immediate steps for stopping the sale." *JCC,* XX, 451.

[1]JJ to Huntington, 16 Sept. 1780, cited in 18 Dec. 1780, n. 2, above.

[2]See editorial note, "Issues in Negotiation," above.

L'Orient with JJ's 6 and 30 Nov. 1780 letters to the President of Congress and the Committee for Foreign Affairs as well as private letters. See JJ to Livingston, 21 Feb. 1781, DftS in JP.

[4]The October 1780 letters to JJ, among others, from Congress were sent by the Pennsylvania ship, the *Chevalier de la Luzerne* and the letter of marque, the *Lady Washington.* The accompanying instructions of 28 October from James Lovell to the captains were that "They are of much importance and should be put into faithful hands for conveyance upon your arrival in Port." LbkC in PCC 79, I, 274; *LMCC,* V, 431.

From Samuel Huntington

[Philadelphia], 15 February 1781

Sir,

Congress having since their Instructions to you of the 29th of September 1779 and the 4th of October 1780, relative to the Claim of the United States to the free Navigation of the river Mississippi, and to a free Port or Ports below the 31st Degree of North Latitude, resumed the Consideration of that Subject, and being desirous to manifest to all the World, and particularly to his Catholic Majesty, the Moderation of their Views, the high Value they place on the Friendship of his Catholic Majesty and their Disposition to remove every resonable Obstacle to his Accession to the Alliance subsisting between his most Christian Majesty and these United States, in order to unite the more closely in their Measures and Operations three Powers who have so great an Unity of Interests, and thereby compel the common Enemy to a speedy, just and honorable Peace, have *resolved,* and you are hereby instructed to recede from the Instructions above referred to, so far as they insist on the free Navigation of that Part of the River Mississippi which lies below the 31st Degree of North Latitude, and on a free Port or Ports below the same, provided such Cession shall be unalterably insisted upon by Spain and provided the free Navigation of the said River above the said Degree of North Latitude shall be acknowledged and guaranteed by his Catholic Majesty to the Citizens of the United States in Common with his own Subjects. It is the Order of Congress at the same Time that you exert every possible Effort to obtain from his Catholic Majesty the Use of the River aforesaid with a free Port or Ports below the said 31st Degree of North Latitude, for the Citizens of the United States, under such Regulations and Restrictions only as may be a necessary safe Guard against illicit Commerce.

By order of Congress.

SAM. HUNTINGTON, PRESIDENT

LS. C, with notation "previous and main entry passed in the affirmative," in JP; Dft, in James Madison's hand, in DLC: Misc. PCC, endorsed by Thomson: "Motion Respecting the Mississipi by the delegates of Virginia, Feby. 1, 1781." *JCC,* XIX, 152–53; *RDC,* IV, 257; *SDC,* VII, 403–06; *MP,* II, 302–03. For the original instructions, see n. 2 of the 4 Oct. 1780 Congressional instructions, above.

The revised instructions were adopted on 15 February by a vote of seven states. Massachusetts, Connecticut, and North Carolina voted in the negative; New York was divided; New Jersey and Maryland could not vote because their delegations lacked a quorum. *JCC,* XIX, 153–54.

From William Livingston

Trenton, 20 March 1781

Dear Sir,

The French fleet sailed from Rhode Island for Chesapeak about a fortnight ago to intercept Arnold's escape, and the British fleet in these parts, two days after them, so that we hourly expect some important intelligence. It is said that the French are superior by one ship of the line and three or four Frigates, and as they will probably be in the bay first, that circumstance will greatly add to their superiority.[1]

I am happy to find that Congress have at last consented to what I know was agreeable to your Idea before you left us, and I hope that their coming into the measure at so late a period may not have occasioned some stops at a certain court that may be past recalling, by the time their resolutions on that Subject reach you.[2]

I have just now seen his Britannic Majesty's manifesto against the States General,[3] and I hope it will convince all Europe of the necessity of humbling a Prince, who, while at war with three powerful nations, thinks proper to commence hostilities against a fourth. I am, Sir, Your most humble servant

WIL. LIVINGSTON

Tr. See *JJ,* I, 123–24 for Livingston, JJ's father-in-law.

[1]The French expeditionary force under Admiral Charles-René-Dominique Sochet Destouches sailed for Virginia from Newport, R.I., on 8 March, with the British under Admiral Arbuthnot starting in pursuit thirty-six hours later. In a brief engagement on 16 March off Chesapeake Bay, Destouches' forces fared better than Arbuthnot's. Destouches, however, abandoned the expedition to link up with Lafayette at Annapolis, while Arbuthnot joined forces with Arnold. The latter, after a raid in Virginia, had moved up the Elizabeth River to Portsmouth, Va.

[2]Livingston alludes to Congress' altered instructions to JJ.

[3]A reference to the British declaration of war, 20 Dec. 1780, against the United Provinces. England's pretext for this action was the discovery, among Henry Laurens' papers when he was captured, of a draft of a proposed commercial treaty drawn up in September 1778 by William Lee and Engelbert François Van Berckel (1726–96), an agent of the burgomasters of Amsterdam. *Peacemakers,* p. 25.

To Floridablanca

Madrid, 2 April 1781

Sir,

Be pleased to accept my Thanks for having ordered the Ballance due on the Cloathing, purchased by Mr. Harrison, to be paid, and for having so arranged the Payment of the Money to which the Bills of this month amount, as to enable the Embassador of France effectually to interpose his kind offices to relieve me from the distressing necessity of protesting them.[1]

I lament the Embarrassments which your Excellency has experienced on this Occasion, and am persuaded that both his Majesty and your Excellency are sincerely disposed to realize the assurances of Friendship made through me to the United States. I flatter myself that this Friendship will continue to be manifested by such additional Aids, as it may be convenient to his Majesty to supply, and I am confident that they will meet with such Returns from my Country, as Gratitude may dictate, and the Situation of their affairs permit.

It will I hope soon be in my power to speake more explicitly on this Subject, and to give your Excellency higher Proofs, than Professions, of the Sincerity with which Congress desire, that a friendly Connection between the two Countries, may be formed and rendered convenient and agreable to both, by a constant Interchange of mutual good offices.

I have the Honor to be with perfect Respect and Consideration, Your Excellencys most obedient and most humble Servant

JOHN JAY

ALS in AHN Estado, leg. 3884, exp. 4, doc. 116, with the notation (trans. from the Spanish): "He gives thanks for Cabarrus' paying for the clothing. He mentions the necessity of new help and expresses the extensive cordiality of his Congress." ACS in CP E 604: 19.

[1]See above, Notes of a Conference with Floridablanca, 8 Nov. 1780.

To Samuel Huntington

Madrid, 21 April 1781

Dear Sir,

Accept my Thanks for your Favor of the 18 December which was delivered to me on the 13 of March last. I am happy to hear that your Health permits you still to continue in <Your import[ant]> the Chair and to sustain the Weight of Business which the Duties of that office impose upon you.

<We have within these five Days> The interesting news of General Morgans glorious victory[1] and the Success of the French in the Chesapeake reached us three Days ago <Never was Intelligence more welcome> and our Joy has been since increased by Intelligence which is credited tho not quite confirmed of the English Troops in the E. Indies have been defeated in a decisive Battle by a Prince of the Country in alliance with France.[2] This Campaign opens much to our advantage, and I hope the Blessing of Heaven on our arms will bring it to a conclusion equally prosperous.

<My public Letter[3] will give you an Idea of the State of Things since the Date of my very long Letter which Col. Livingston forwarded from France and which I doubt not has already come to your Hands, three Copies having been sent by different Vessels. There is really but little Corn at present in Egypt and those who would have it must purchase it and you know the price. This seems to be the present System. How long it may last no Mortal can tell. Friendships like the English Funds too generally rise and Fall according as Events are favourable or adverse.>

By the Letter from Doctor Franklin herewith enclosed <was sent me by the Return of the Express Courier I sent to him; and as his other Dispatches> and which he was so obliging as to leave open for my perusal I find he has requested Permission to retire on account of his age and Infirmities.[4] How far his <Constitution has been> Health may be impaired I know not, since the <many and long> Letters I have recieved from him bear no marks of age, and there is an acuteness and contentious Brevity in them <very seldom found in the Compositions of a declining Mind impaired> which do not indicate an understanding injured by Years. <Whatever> I have many Reasons to think our Country much indebted to him and I confess it would mortify my pride as an American, if <this worthy Citizen and public Servant should not recieve Marks of Honor and Approbation from his Constituents> his Constituents should be the only people to whom his Character is known that should deny his Merit and Services the Testimony given them by other Nations. Justice demands of me to assure you that his Reputation and Respectibility are acknowledged and have weight here and that I have recieved from him all that uniform attention and aid which was due to the Importance of the affairs committed to me. <God forbid that any future Historian should have occasion to remark the same Singularity in our Republic, what an

Ancient one with great Justice did in the Athenian "That tho Athens < <was actually blessed> > produced many Great Generals and able Statesmen yet there was scarce one whom she did not"[5] >

<I percieve> The affectionate mention he makes of his only descendant on whom the Support of his name and Family will devolve[6] is extremely <natural and> aimiable, and flows in <Terms of great Delicacy> a delicate manner from that virtuous Sensibility by which nature kindly extends the Benefits of Parental affection to a Period beyond the Limits of our Lives. This is an affecting Subject and minds susceptible of the finer <Feelings> Sensations are insensibly led <by it> at least to wish that <rather the name or worth of a Man whose Birth> the feelings <and merits> of an ancient Patriot <retiring with well earned Honor> going in the Evening of a long Life early devoted to the public to Enjoy Repose in the Bosom of a philosphic <Retreat> Retirement, may be gratified by seeing some little spark of the affection of his Country rest on the only support of his age and Hope of his Family. Such are the Effusions of my Heart on this occasion and I pour them into yours from a Persuasion that they will meet with a hospitable Reception from congenial emotions.

< < <With Respect to> > Of this Young Gentleman < <Character I wish I> > I have no personal knowledge except what < <I might be> > may be drawn from the real and accurate Manner in which as his Grandfathers actual Secretary he did such Business as respected me and of Course came under my Observation < <and which was neat and accurate> > and from a < <Letter he wrote me on the Subject of a particular Occasion> > very well written Letter I recieved from him on a particular Occasion. I have been told that his Genius < <bears his Grandfathers Mark and that> > tho not yet matured is strong and that he has derived from Education the Acquirements which figure in Courts. I have also been informed that tho not dissipated he < <does not possess> > is gay and fond of Dress and Diversions. This is all I know or have heard about him. These latter Circumstances do not always form the same Indication. The < <best fruit Trees blossom before they produce> > most valuable introduce their Fruit by previous Blossoms and < <when the latter> > as the one shook out the < <former fall> > other disappears. There are also Trees which only bear blossoms and < <are a gaudy scented Spectacle and for no other purpose> > < <that tho ornamental in the Spring are useless and from which> > make those who cultivate them < <are to expect> > no other return than perhaps very pretty and well scented Flowers < <while only> > in the Spring. A Tree is always known by its Fruit.

As the Character of this young Gentleman will on the Arrival of the Doctors Letter probably become a Subject of Inquiry and Discussion I wish I was enabled to give you clear and positive Information relative to it. The only Knowledge I have of it results from Circumstances and <<the opinion what I have at different Times heard of him from>> the Reports of others. <<He has for some Time past been the Doctors actual Secretary, and the manner in which that>> All I can say is that they inclined me to think well of him.

<<Opinions so formed>> From such materials you know it is not easy to form a decided <<opinion>> Judgment <<because>> circumstantial Evidence seldom rising <<any>> higher than Probabilities more or less convincing. <<In this case I have no>> The Doctor's <<opinion>> Recommendation of him indeed is clear and positive. His Situation and Discernment enables him to know this Gent[leman] perfectly, and <<I should think>> his Integrity and Prudence <<would not permit him>> afford good Security for his saying nothing more than what he thinks. How far Affection may have imperceptibly influenced the coloring the Character of the Painter will help us to ascertain. <<So that is well known>> <<I believe.>>>

I hope the Idea of putting your foreign Affairs on the Footing you mention will not be laid aside. A responsible, able Secretary for that Department would be more useful than all the Committees you could appoint.

Mrs. Jay presents her Compliments to you and Mrs. Huntington. We have had a fine Winter, far more <agreable> mild and temperate than our northern <Climates> States afford <There is a Prospect of a more plentiful Harvest than has been known here since the Year 1756> and were it not for the extreme Droughts and Heats of Summer from which I suffered greatly the last Year I should <like> be much pleased with this Climate <exceedingly>, not so much however as to wish to <remain longer> spend my Days in it. My Eyes and Affections are constantly turned towards America, and I think I shall return to it with as much real and cordial Satisfaction as ever an exiled Israelite felt on returning to his Land of Promise.

I am Dear Sir with very Sincere Regard and Esteem Your most obedient and humble Servant.

Dft in PPInd. Endorsed by JJ: "... In answr. to 18 Decr. last." E in JJ to Franklin, 20 Aug. 1781, Dft in JP; LbkC in DLC: Franklin VI, 27–29. E in DLC: Washington 7, and in *RDC,* V, 684. *HPJ,* II, 17–19, omits JJ's deletions, among them the third, sixth, seventh, and eighth paragraphs. Enclosure: Franklin to Samuel Huntington, 12 March 1781, *RDC,* IV, 281–84; *BFS,* VIII, 217–23.

[1]Brigadier General Daniel Morgan won the Battle of Cowpens, South Carolina, on 17 Jan. 1781. For Morgan, see *JJ,* I, 440.

[2]In 1780 Hyder Ali Khan, France's ally in India, overran the Carnatic, a region in southern India which had been virtually a client state of the British East India Company.

[3]JJ to Huntington, 25 April 1781, LS, body of letter in Carmichael's hand, in PCC 89, I, 148–53; LbkCs in JP, PCC 110, I, and in CSmH; E in JJ to Franklin, 20 Aug. 1781, in PCC 82, II, 231–32, and in French in CP E 16; *RDC,* IV, 384–89; E in V, 684; *HPJ,* II, 21–30; *SDC,* VII, 406–15.

[4]Franklin to JJ, on 12 April 1781, enclosed his of 12 March to Congress for JJ's perusal, forwarding, and comment. In his March letter to Congress Franklin stated his desire to retire, hoped that a replacement would be sent, and requested that Congress "take under their protection" his grandson, William Temple Franklin, giving reasons thereto. In his April letter to JJ, Franklin wrote he "desired a dismission from the service in consideration of my age, etc., and I wish you to succeed me here. No copy of the letter is yet gone from France, and possibly this which I send you may arrive first; nor have I mentioned my intention to anyone here. If therefore the change would be agreeable to you, you may write to your friends in Congress accordingly. I purpose recommending these Changes myself in another Letter." JJ, in addition to this 21st April private letter, included in his public dispatch of 25 April to Huntington a paragraph in support of Franklin as to his conduct and character. The following year, on 3 Sept. 1782 to Secretary for Foreign Affairs Robert R. Livingston, Franklin included extracts of JJ's 21 and 25 April letters to Huntington. Franklin to JJ, 12 April 1781, ALS in PPAmP: Feinstone; LbkCs in DLC: Franklin V, 49–52, VI, 75–77; *RDC,* IV, 357–59; *BFS,* VIII, 238–41.

[5]Sentence unfinished. JJ undoubtedly meant "ostracize" or "disgrace."

[6]Franklin's grandson William Temple Franklin, who served as his secretary in Paris. See also *JJ,* I, 769.

To Charles Thomson

Madrid, 23 April 1781

Dear Sir,

On the 30th January last I had the Pleasure of recieving your very acceptable Letter of the 12 October 1780.[1] The able Manner in which it treats the important Subject of american Finances induced me to give that part of it to the Minister,[2] and to send a Copy of the same Extract to Dr. Franklin[3] who in his answer says, "I thank you for communicating to me the Letter of the Secretary of Congress on our Finances. It gives Light which I had not before, and may be useful here."[4]

I wish in my Heart that you was not only Secretary of Congress but Secretary also for foreign Affairs. I should then have better Sources of Intelligence than Gazettes and Reports.

My public Letter[5] contains a State of our Affairs here, and I flatter myself that Congress will never again attempt to form an alliance on

Principles of Equality in *Forma Pauperis.*[6] <Their Bills have done more Harm than five times their value can do good. I am indeed as their servant only responsible for the Manner in which I execute their orders and not for the Wisdom of them. But as an American I feel an Interest in both and must take the Liberty of judging accordingly.>

Before their ingenious Letter on our Right to the Mississippi arrived, it was known in Europe; and the Substance of my last Instructions on that Head were no secret here,[7] before they reached this Side of the Ocean. I would tell you more, had I now Time to write in Cyphers, but the Gentleman who is to carry these Dispatches is waiting for them.

The Want of a regular and safe Communication between Congress and their foreign Ministers, gives occasion to various Inconveniences. Every Letter known or suspected to be for or from me that gets into the post offices is opened, often kept back for a while and to my certain Knowledge sometimes suppressed entirely. Hence it happens that Congress recieves from me fewer Letters than I could wish, or than their Affairs may demand. The Expence of private Couriers is intolerable, nor can many in that Character be found who merit Confidence, <but I have already written so much and so often to Congress on this Subject that Little remains to be added.>

The unseasonable arrival of Bills without being preceded by Funds, and the Train of Perplex Consequences resulting from that and other Causes not in my power to prevent have given me some anxious Hours, and often rendered my Situation uneasy. It is my Business however to reflect, that Pleasure was not the Object for which I came here, and that obstacles should rather excite, than repress Perseverance. <It is my Business however to press on in the political Course in which public Troubles have engaged me, and I therefore shall persevere steadily in it, not withstanding any obstacles that may lay or be laid in my way. I am confident that Liberty and Independence will sooner or later be firmly established and should I live to see that blessed Day, I think if I know my own Heart I shall return with inexpressible Pleasure to dwell securely and happily under the Shade of my Vine and Fig Tree.>

Be pleased to present Mrs. Jay's and my Compliments to Mrs. Thompson,[8] and believe me to be with sincere Regard and Esteem Your most obedient Servant.

Dft. Endorsed by JJ. ALS in DLC: Thomson. With deletions and errors in *RDC,* IV, 381–82; *HPJ,* II, 19–21.

[1]Thomson to JJ, 12 Oct. 1780, ALS in JP; LS in NHi: Jay; C in Carmichael's hand in AHN Estado, leg. 3884, exp. 8, doc. 25. *LMCC,* V, 418–20, omits first and last paragraphs. Thomson's account of the state of America's finances, submitted by way of explanation for Floridablanca, detailed the handling of the money or paper bills previously issued for carrying on the war, including an updating of revisions by Congress subsequent to the ceiling placed on emissions of bills on 3 Sept. 1779 (*JJ,* I, 512) and information about the retirement on 18 March 1780 of bills in circulation at one-fortieth of their face value.

[2]The last version of Thomson's letter in n. 1 was designated by JJ to Floridablanca.

[3]JJ to Franklin, 11 March 1781, Dft in JP; LbkC in DLC: Franklin VI; E in NN: Bancroft: American I, 264.

[4]Franklin to JJ, 12 April 1781, see n. 4 of preceding letter.

[5]JJ to Huntington, 25 April 1781, see n. 3 of preceding letter.

[6]"In the character of a pauper," who can sue without liability for costs.

[7]Huntington to JJ, 15 Feb. 1781, above.

[8]Hannah Harrison Thomson (c. 1728–1807), Thomson's second wife.

To Robert R. Livingston

Madrid, 25 April 1781

Dear Robert,

I scarcely ever address you in the familiar Stile, but I am insensibly led to reflect on what Clermont[1] and we were fifteen or sixteen Years ago. Nature seems to have given me a Propensity to Reverie, and I have long found pleasure in indulging it. Past Scenes recalled to view in this Species of perspective appear much softned, the lesser asperities are lost in the Distance, and the more pleasing parts of the object chiefly brought into view.

In your Letter of the 27 August, which I recieved the 30 January last, you refer to two or three sent by the way of France.[2] The only Letters I have recieved from you since I left america, are of the following Dates, vizt. 6 October 1779 and 22d December, 10 February, 6th July, 26th August, and 27th October 1780.[3] The two last came under one Cover. The Length as well as matter of the first of them, amply compensated for the great Difficulty I had to read it. I have never seen Ink so near the Color of the Paper. Had I been a little older, I should have suspected that my Eyes began to fail me.

I am glad to hear that the manner of conducting the Business committed to me has met with approbation.[4] Had not your Bills intervened, I believe Congress would have had more Reason to be satisfied. That measure placed me here in forma pauperis, and inspired a very mortifying Idea of the State of our affairs. It involved me in Perplexities too tedious to enumerate, and occasioned Doubts and Delays very unfriendly to our affairs. I am responsible, it is true, only for the

Execution of the Resolutions and Orders of Congress, and not for the wisdom of them, but I cannot help regretting these Circumstances. I have done my best, and shall persevere in doing my Duty with the same Patience and activity as heretofore. If my Endeavours meet with Success, so much the better. If not, I shall have nothing to reproach myself with.

Morgans Victory, the Successful Enterprize against Arnolds little Fleet, and the Enemys Disasters in the E. Indies make a deep Impression here, and I shall endeavour to proffit by it before Time or a Change of Fortune shall erase it.

Your Cypher[5] is intelligible, but as I suspect the Letter which enclosed it was opened before it came to my Hands, I think it would be prudent to alter it a little. If I understand your Explanation right, what you call the *Key Letters,* are the Letters which spell what you call the *Key word.* In this Instance you have in Fact no Key *Word,* tho the Letters over each Column answer the purpose just as well as if they spell any particular word. The Cypher I enclose is on the same plan with your's, and yet sufficiently different. I will now in your Cypher give you a Key word for it. I am persuaded that the Route in which this Letter will pass is very different from that in which I suspect yours was opened, and therefore that I may without much Risque use your Cypher on this occasion. 24 · 2 · 18 · 3 · 4. I must observe however that whoever gets a copy of the enclosed Cypher may use it without the Key word, for be the Key word what it may, the numbers 1 · 2 · 3 · 4 · 5 · or any numbers corresponding with the number of Columns and applied in like manner as a Key word, will answer the same purpose. Try it and you will find it so. I have on Experiment found 1 · 2 · 3 · perfect Substitutes for your x · z · a.

Mr. Toscan,[6] who is appointed Vice Consul at Boston, has been so obliging as to wait a few Days for my Dispatches. Favor him with your notice and attention. I have written several Letters to your Governor and General Schuyler, but have not recieved a Line from either of them.

Remember us to all your Family. Tell me whether the little Girl grows finely.

I am Dear Robert, your affectionate Friend.

JOHN JAY

ALS in NHi: Robert R. Livingston. Endorsed. Enclosure not located. DftS and ARC of key to YESCA cipher in JP. See *JJ* I, 661–62, 664–65, 809–13 for the XZA and YESCA ciphers.

[1]The ancestral estate of the Clermont branch of the Livingston family in Dutchess County where Robert R. Livingston lived.

America 27
army 28
Fleet 29
Congress 30
King 31
minister 32
General 33
Spain 34
France 35
England 36
Holland 37
Boston 38
N York 39
Frigates 40
Ship of ye Line 41
Chs Town 42
W. Indies 43
Governor 44
Russia 45
Emperor 46
Portugal 47
Secretary 48
the 49
by 50
and 51
to 52
from 53
all 54
Enemy 55
that 56
Washington 57
Virginia 59
Chesapeake 60
Rh. Island 61

Express numbers as you propose with a stroke under the figures —

write the key word over the five columns — a letter over each, beginning with the first —

The explanation of your cypher serves for this, as to the mode of writing & decyphering —

If the word you use contains fewer letters than the key word, dont begin the key word again, but continue on with the remaining letters of it, & then begin again —

tinder

	1	2	3	4	5
	y	e	s	c	a
a	1	26	11	6	10
b	2	25	10	5	11
c	3	24	9	4	12
d	4	23	8	3	13
e	5	22	7	2	14
f	6	21	6	1	15
g	7	20	5	7	16
h	8	19	4	8	17
j	9	18	3	9	18
i	10	17	2	10	19
k	11	16	1	11	20
l	12	15	12	26	21
m	13	14	13	25	22
n	14	13	14	24	23
o	15	12	15	23	24
p	16	11	16	22	25
q	17	10	17	21	26
r	18	9	18	20	1
s	19	8	19	19	2
t	20	7	20	18	3
u	21	6	21	17	4
v	22	5	22	16	5
w	23	4	23	15	6
x	24	3	24	14	7
y	25	2	25	13	8
z	26	1	26	12	9

Transatlantic Cryptology. Jay's Yesca Code. *(Papers of John Jay. Rare Book and Manuscript Library, Columbia University)*

[2]Not in 26 Aug. 1780, in *JJ* I, 809–13; no doubt mentioned in 27 Oct. 1780, not located.

[3]For 6 Oct. and 22 Dec. 1779 and 6 July 1780, see above, JJ to Livingston, 6 Oct. 1780 and nn. 1 and 2; 10 Feb. 1780 is in *JJ* I, 727–29.

[4]Probably mentioned in 27 Oct. 1780.

[5]The key to the XZA cipher, enclosed in Livingston's of 26 August.

[6]Jean Toscan, who served under l'Étombe, for whom see above, JJ to Huntington, [30 Nov. 1780], and n. 4.

To George Clinton

Madrid, 25 April 1781

Dear Sir,

Where you live, whether still at Poughkeepsie,[1] or at Kingston or elsewhere. Whether any of my Letters have reached you, whether you have been too sick, too busy, or too lazy to answer any of them.[2] How Mrs. Clinton and her little Family does?[3] And whether Vermont is to be or not to be[4] are Points of which I am as ignorant as if I resided among the Ten Tribes whose Habitations no Travellers have hitherto found. And yet these as well as many others are Points upon which I wish now and then to recieve a little Information from you. I am determined not to write you another long Letter till I recieve at least a short one from you.

Mrs. Jay presents her Compliments to Mrs. Clinton, to which be pleased to add mine, and desire her to remind you sometimes how much Pleasure a few Lines from you would give Your Friend and Servant

J. J.

P.S. Be pleased to forward the Letters herewith enclosed.[5]

DftS.

[1]The Clinton home during 1777–83 was in Poughkeepsie, in New York's Dutchess County. See E. Wilder Spaulding, *His Excellency George Clinton, Critic of the Constitution* (New York, 1938), pp. 99–100.

[2]See above, JJ to Robert R. Livingston, 6 Oct. 1780, and n. 17.

[3]The children of the Governor and Cornelia Tappen Clinton (1744–1800) were: Catharine (b. 1770), Cornelia (1774–1810), George Washington (b. 1779), and Elizabeth (b. 1780).

[4]Clinton's 6 April 1781 letter contained a brief reference to the Vermont dispute: "The Controversy with the Inhabitants of the Grants is yet undecided but my last advices from our Delegates give me Reason to hope for a speedy and just Decision. The Completion of the Confederation (on which I cordially congratulate you) will facillitate this Business." The Governor omitted all reference to his recent role in postponing a decision on the Vermont lands. On 21 Feb. 1781 the New York Senate agreed to appoint commissioners to make a settlement with Vermont commissioners,

which would virtually have conceded Vermont statehood. On 27 February Clinton sent a message to the Assembly reminding that body that, as the Senate resolution reversed earlier legislation, their concurrence would necessitate his proroguing the Assembly. See *JJ,* I, 102–05 *et seq.; PPGC,* VI, 430–37, 642–44, 741–45; Hiland Hall, *The History of Vermont* (New York, 1868), pp. 329–36; Spaulding, *Clinton,* pp. 142–48.

[5]Probably JJ to Peter Jay, 24 April 1781, under "Keeping in Touch," below. JJ to Philip Schuyler, [*c.* 25] April 1781, Dft in JP; *HPJ,* II, 13–14.

To John Laurens

Madrid, 2 May 1781

Dear Sir,

I have been favored with your very polite and obliging Letter by the Return of my Courier.[1] None of the Letters for me from America, which you mention to have committed on your arrival to the Care of Doctor Franklin have as yet reached me.

The nature of the Warrant under which your good Father is detained, is if I am rightly informed, such as that I fear his Enlargement on *Parole*[2] will not be easily obtained.[3] Indeed I much doubt its being effected in any other way than that of Retaliation. Whether we have among the Prisoners any of sufficient Importance, I am not informed. There were some Parliment men taken with Gen. Burgoyne who might be called though not perhaps imprisoned.[4] From my Ideas of the Coasts and Disposition of many Parts of Britain and Ireland, I should think it practicable to surprize and take off some ministerial men of Consequence in both Islands, but of this you are better able to judge than I am.

Your Remarks on our pecuniary Resources are exceedingly just, and the Conclusion you draw from them corresponds perfectly with my Sentiments on that Head.

When I did myself the Honor of writing to you last,[5] I had been led to suppose that your Residence in Europe would probably be for a considerable Time and therefore wished to provide immediately for the means of deriving advantage to our Country and Satisfaction to myself from a Confidential Correspondence with you. Your speedy Return to America will disappoint these views, but be assured that the same motives which induce me on this occasion to cultivate your Friendship will on all others render me desirous of evincing the Esteem and Regard with which I am, Dear Sir, Your most obedient and humble Servant.

JOHN JAY

Mr. Toscan who is appointed Vice Consul of France at Boston, and who set out from here for Bilboa last week, is the Bearer of your Letter to America. This opportunity is very seasonable, and the more so as few private ones offer from hence even to the Sea Coast. I have very little Reason to confide in the Post Office.[6]

Mrs. Jay is much obliged by your polite attention and assures you of her Regard and best Wishes.

ALS in John Jay Homestead. Dft in JP. *HPJ,* II, 31–32 omits postscripts.

On 21 Dec. 1780 Congress appointed John Laurens minister to France to solicit additional aid for the American cause. With Franklin's tactful cooperation, Laurens, who returned to America on 25 Aug. 1781, raised 2,500,224 livres and obtained three shiploads of military supplies. *JJ,* I, 652; *JCC,* XVIII, 1141, 1177–78, 1184–88 and 1197–98 contain his commission and instructions; David D. Wallace, *The Life of Henry Laurens* (New York, 1967), App. I, esp. pp. 478–84.

[1]Laurens to JJ, 11 [April] 1781, ALS in JP. La Guerre was the messenger of JJ and Carmichael. For the letters from America, see below, JJ to Franklin, 31 May 1781.

[2]While abroad, Laurens concerned himself with his father's plight, but, failing to secure his release, deposited £2,400 to his credit. Wallace, *Laurens,* p. 481.

[3]In the Dft, JJ had deleted: "any of the Parliament taken with Gen. Burgoyne . . . unless already exchanged would make very good Subjects to retaliate upon."

[4]Among the Members of Parliament who had surrendered at Saratoga in 1777 were Burgoyne himself, Major General William Phillips, and Major John Dyke Acland (d. 1778). For Burgoyne and Phillips, see *JJ,* I, 417, 538.

[5]JJ to Laurens, 26 March 1781, ALS in NjP: Misc. Mss.; DftS in JP.

[6]In the Dft, JJ deleted "The Post Office merits no Confiden[ce]."

From Gouverneur Morris

Philadelphia, 7–9 May 1781

Dear Jay,

I have received yours of the 5th November and a Duplicate of it.[1] I sincerely thank you for this only Favor I have received. Your Laconick Style has not forsaken you. Congress have by the same Opportunity which brought this Letter of the 5th November received some of a much later Date.[2]

I suppose it was Deane who wrote to you from France about the Loss of my Leg.[3] This Account is facetious. Let it pass. The Leg is gone and there is an End of the Matter. Thank you most heartily for your Condolance and I pray you to say every Thing to Mrs. Jay <and the Colonel> for me which I ought to say.

LEE is where HE OUGHT to be. I mean as to the PUBLIC ESTIMATION. CONNECTIONS have done and will do NOTHING for him. DEAN may complain of DUPLICITY and perhaps justly but he should recollect that it is his own CHARACTER to which may be added AVARICE. He and I had no DIFFERENCE. There are men in the World who think they can dupe the World. They themselves become the Dupes of this Idea and then they are enraged simply because they are undeceived. You and I have seen such men. The BARGAIN ABOUT MASTS which you mention is a thing which I would advise you to give yourself no Concern about.[4] Leave such Things to the Principles which give Birth to them.

THAT INTELLIGENCE of the EMBASSADOR by no means surprizes me.[5] How can it be otherwise? That YOU should want the same is equally natural for CONGRESS has not yet made PROVISION for it.[6]

I do not bury my Talents as you suppose. And yet let me tell you I know no Soil where I would so soon chuse to dig them a Grave. I understand clearly your Meaning. You would urge me to public Life. Take my decided Answer. I will neither seek for nor avoid it. Yet I beleive I am not an useless Citizen even at present.

I have written to you three Letters which I should be sorry you did not receive. One of the 2d January, one the 4th March and one the 31st March.[7] Among other Reasons why I wish they in particular may come to Hand is this, that they are not in Cypher, consequently no Duplicates.

Robert Morris is our Financier and will probably write to you on that Subject.[8] I lament very much the Loss of your little Infant chiefly on Mrs. Jay's Account. You have more Vigor of Mind than to sink under Misfortunes. Present to her my tenderest Condolances. Comfort her. (There is one thing indispensible, SIX MILLION DOLLARS AT LEAST MUST BE LANDED HERE BY THE SPANISH COURT. This I say is indispensible and I mean that the Word should be taken in its fullest Force.) Your Brother Sir James has been at Philadelphia last Summer as you heard. He has continued here untill the present Moment. His Silence does not surprize me.[9] Nil mirari,[10] is an useful Maxim even to a private Citizen. Our Friend Livingston writes me that he has received no Letters from you and that he is surprized at it, I am not.

We have no News worth Writing to you. Cornwallis a few Days after the Action of which I enclosed you an Account in my Letter of the 31st of March decamped in the Night and marched very rapidly for Wilmington by the Way of Cross Creek.[11] A few Hour's Stay would have exposed him to an Attack. He left his sick and wounded. Green pursued. He came up to a small River (I am not certain about the Name of it)[12] just as Cornwallis had crossed it. He would have still pursued and have compleated the Ruin of his Lordship, but the Time of the Virginia Militia was out and they quitted him.[13] Cornwallis went on to Wilmington. He will not carry 1500 men with him. Green has since that Period marched into South Carolina with about 1500 all continentals and crossed the Pedee River. I think he is between Cambden and Charlestown and will be there joined by General Marian and some excellent Militia, perhaps a thousand.[14] He will then act according to Circumstances. Should he be able to carry the Posts of Cambden[15] and ninety-six[16] he may be soon strong enough to detach to Augusta[17] and will confine the Enemy to Charlestown and Savanna for the Post at George Town[18] will I dare say be called in. It is not impossible that Green may attempt Charlestown. It is garrisoned by about 400 British and 800 Hessians besides sailors, Tories, etc., etc. 1000 are sufficient to stand the Assault of 10,000. Yet the Attempt would probably succeed for the British and Hessians have a bad Understanding together and the Tories have lately been disarmed on Suspicions. Cornwallis may either be reinforced or transported to Charlestown by Water. Neither will enable him to do much. The Climate alone will soon forbid very active Operations. The Enemy are scourging the Virginians at least those of lower Virginia. This is distressing but it will have some good Consequences. In the mean time the Delegates of Virginia make as many Lamentations as ever Jeremiah did and to as good Purpose perhaps.

I am very sorry that YOU CONTEND for NAVIGATION. In my Letter of the 2d January I was very full on that Subject.[19] To every Thing I have said or can say let me add, OUR WANT OF MONEY. This is an Article which YOU MUST INSIST ON HAVING. It must not be meerly ASKED AS a FAVOR BUT REQUIRED AS a RIGHT. One Thing I will also mention which I think will give you Pleasure. YOUR MASTERS ALL APPLAUD YOU. Adieu.

9 May

The above is duplicate. I am informed that the Account given me of Green's Situation was untrue. It has been reported for some Time and it gains Ground that the Enemy's Fort at ninety six is taken. It is also said that Lord Rawdon has abandoned the Post at Cambden. Be these Things as they may I beleive Green intends a Junction with Marian. I am sure it is a good Game and tho a bold is a secure one. This is every Thing where popular opinion is of any Consequence. Again Adieu. Yours,

GOUV. MORRIS

Duplicate ALS, partly in cipher, decoded by JJ. Endorsed: ". . . Recd. by Salem Packet via Bilboa, 2 July 1781." ALS in JP; DftS in NNC-RBML: Gouverneur Morris.

[1]JJ to Morris, 5 Nov. 1780, above.

[2]A reference to JJ's letters to the President of Congress: 6 Nov. 1780 was read in Congress on 24 April 1781; 30 Nov. 1780 was read the following day; 28 Jan. 1781, above, was read on 27 April. *JCC,* XX, 437, 451.

[3]See above, JJ to Morris, 5 Nov. 1780.

[4]*Ibid.,* and JJ to Deane, 2 Oct. 1780, above.

[5]See JJ to Morris, 5 Nov. 1780, above.

[6]Acting on JJ's dispatch of 6 Nov. 1780, James Duane moved on 7 May and Congress ordered "That Thursday next be assigned for electing a consul to reside in Spain." *JCC,* XX, 484. See also William Bingham to JJ, 13 July 1781, below, for the dispatching of David S. Franks.

[7]Morris to JJ, 2 Jan. 1781, DftS in NNC-RBML: Gouverneur Morris; 31 March 1781, DftS in *ibid.* and ALS in JP; 4 March 1781, not located.

[8]In organizing the civil executive departments, Congress, in addition to the Secretary for Foreign Affairs, resolved on 7 Feb. 1781 that posts of Superintendent of Finance, a Secretary at War, and a Secretary of Marine be established. On 20 February Robert Morris was unanimously elected Superintendent of Finance, but he assumed his duties on 27 June. Morris informed JJ of his new position on 5 June 1781, ALS and LS in JP; *HPJ,* II, 35–37; *RMP,* I, 4n., 5n., 9n., 112–14; *JCC,* XIX, 126, 180.

[9]Sir James was about to launch an explosive attack on Gouverneur Morris, among others, for which see below, Morris to JJ, 17 June 1781.

[10]*Nil [ad]mirari:* "Marvel at nothing." Horace, *Epistles* 1.6.1.

[11]Lord Cornwallis, commander of British forces in the South, retreated toward Cross Creek (present-day Fayetteville), N.C., en route to Wilmington three days after the battle of Guilford Courthouse, N.C. Although won on the field on 15 March over Greene, Commander of the Southern Department, at a cost of almost 100 killed and over 400 wounded, it was a strategic defeat for Cornwallis, necessitating retreat. Cornwallis reached Wilmington, N.C., on 7 April. For the Southern campaigns of Greene, see Christopher Ward, *The War of the Revolution* (2 vols., New York, 1952), II, 748–57, 762–88 *passim.*

[12]Nathanael Greene reached Deep River, N.C., on 28 March when the British were crossing the river.

[13]Greene dismissed the Virginia and North Carolina militias upon the completion of their six weeks' service.

[14]Greene's army was to number 1,500 Continentals, including: the 1st and 2d of both Maryland and Virginia; Lieutenant-Colonel Henry ("Light-Horse Harry") Lee (1756–1818) with his legion; Washington's dragoons; and partisan forces of Marion, Pickens, and Sumter. Brigadier-General Francis Marion (c. 1732–95), known as "the Swamp Fox," commanded South Carolina militia, at this time in the Peedee swamps harassing the British, while Thomas Sumter (1734–1832) was on Broad River, and Brigadier-General Andrew Pickens (1739–1817) in western South Carolina.

[15]Greene had fought Lord Rawdon, Francis Rawdon-Hastings (1754–1826), at Hobkirk's Hill, near Camden, S.C., on 25 April, a victory for the British. Rawdon had been left in command of South Carolina and Georgia after the battle of Guilford Courthouse. On 10 May, however, Rawdon abandoned Camden.

[16]The Patriot siege of Ninety-six, S.C., 22 May–19 June 1781, was unsuccessful.

[17]The Patriot siege and capture of Augusta, Ga., took place 22 May–5 June 1781.

[18]General Benjamin Lincoln had yielded Charleston, S.C., on 12 May, 1780. Savannah, Ga., was occupied by the British until 11 July 1782. The British abandoned Georgetown, S.C., on 23 May.

[19]Morris' lengthy letter included the following: "The faithful Guarantee of Our

Union would insure to Spain her American Dominions, and our Ambition or Avarice would tear them away <from> her, and ruin us by the Possession. We are poor and Spain can serve us now; we can serve her always; our mutual Interests are therefore united. They are indeed the same. . . . We must have specie from the Havanna up the Mississippi, in small Boats properly guarded to Fort Pitt and thence to Philadelphia. This is very practicable, and of infinite Consequence to the Defense of America."

The Issue of United States Citizenship

Notwithstanding an occasional challenge from the States, Congress asserted authority over the allegiance of the inhabitants of the Thirteen States in a variety of ways. It exacted loyalty oaths, defined and punished treason, required nationalization or naturalization, and admitted or excluded aliens. In all these areas the States exercised a coordinate authority.[1] Although Congress sought to avoid a definitive resolution of the issue of national as opposed to individual state citizenship, it did not hesitate to issue passports in the name of the President of the Congress of the United States of America.[2]

The exchange of letters between JJ and Benjamin Franklin regarding a request made by John Vaughan on his arrival in Spain that JJ administer to him an oath of allegiance to the United States raised the technical issue as to whether Congress had authorized ministers abroad to confer national citizenship. As a lawyer JJ felt that for him to do so would be to act beyond his powers,[3] a point which, in its narrow and technical sense, had not occurred to Franklin, who had in fact been taking oaths and issuing passports in the name of the United States as a matter of course.[4]

Whatever may have been the difference between Congress and Franklin or his consuls or agents—and it is not evident that Congress ever formally objected to the administration of oaths of national citizenship and national passports—the issue was to be settled by the Definitive Treaty of Peace of 1783, in whose writing JJ and Franklin were to play central roles. The treaty recognized both "the Citizens of the United States," in article VIII, and the citizens of the separate states, in article VII.[5] Neither the British nor the American peace commissioners appear to have contested this resolution of the issue, and there is no evidence of any challenge in Congress to the provisions of the treaty recognizing United States citizenship. In ratifying the treaty and directing the states to carry out its provisions, Congress asserted the authority of the Confederation to confer citizenship in the collectivity, as distinguished from the traditional rights of the separate colonies, assumed by the states, to grant state citizenship.[6]

[1]See Richard B. Morris, "The Forging of the Union Reconsidered," *Columbia Law Review,* LXXIV (1974), 1083–87. For Congressional directives to the states regarding

naturalization, see James H. Kettner, *The Development of American Citizenship, 1680–1870* (Chapel Hill, 1979), p. 219. For the effect of the "comity clause" in the Articles of Confederation and the emergence of a concept of common citizenship, see *ibid.*, pp. 220–24.

[2]See passport issued by JJ, President of Congress, to Capt. Joseph Deane, June 1779, *JJ*, I, 609–10.

[3]JJ saw no difficulty when in Spain in issuing passports to American citizens, although not to aliens. JJ to Del Campo, 26 Feb. 1782, Dft in JP; ALS in AHN Estado, leg. 3885, exp. 8, doc. 1.

[4]Numerous examples are found in the Franklin Papers, PPAmP. See also, *e.g.*, passport to the Messrs. Jones, "citizens of the United States," issued 8 Oct. 1780 by Franklin, "Minister Plenipotentiary of the United States of America," in [R. G. Adams, comp.], *The Passports Printed by Benjamin Franklin at His Passy Press* (Ann Arbor, Mich., 1925), p. 7.

[5]DNA: Treaty ser., no. 104; Miller, *Treaties*, II, 151–56.

[6]If any doubts did remain about the powers of the federal government to confer citizenship in the collectivity, they were removed by the adoption of the Constitution. The power to "establish an uniform rule of naturalization" was among the enumerated grants to Congress (Article I, §8 cl. 4). Congress promptly exercised this power by enacting a statute in 1790 which prescribed the rules for the acquisition of U.S. citizenship by persons of foreign birth. Act of 26 March 1790, 1 *Stat.* 103.

To Benjamin Franklin

Aranjuez, 31 May 1781

Dear Sir,

Your favor of the 20th Inst. reached me two Days ago.[1] The Intelligence <contained in> transmitted with it had reached us by the Way of Cadiz. I am nevertheless <consider myself> much obliged by this Mark of your friendly Attention. The Packet from America <sent me by the Courier> about which you inquire came safe to Hand. It contained only some old Letters of January last from Governor Livingston and his family. The Vessel which lately arrived at Cadiz from Philadelphia brought several Letters <from thence>. I have not however recieved a Line from Congress since January last, tho some of my Correspondants inform me that the President had written.[2] I am much perplexed for Want of regular Intelligence and expect to continue so till some other than the usual mode of conveyance is adopted. The enclosed extracts of Letters from Mr. Harrison <at Cadiz, will give you some Idea of these Embarrasments> to me shew that this Remark is not without Foundation. These Extracts are from Letters of 8, 11, and 0 [*sic*] Days of May 1781[3] about Letters brought by the Virginia and stopped. Bills upon me have lately arrived dated in March. How can this be reconciled to the obvious Dictates of Prudence and Policy?

I hear Mr. Laurens has left <us> you to return to America. He promised to give me previous Notice of it, but not a Line. I have lately recieved a Letter from Mr. Adams requesting but not containing Intelligence.[4] It is the first I have had from him these six Months. I wait only for a proper Opportunity to reply particularly to your Letter by my Courier.

Mr. Vaughan[5] who brought a recommendatory Letter from you to Mr. Carmichael is here. He desired me on his Arrival at Madrid to administer to him an Oath of Allegiance to the United States, in order to justify his calling himself an American and to facilitate his pursuing his object in this Country, and <then pass to that> his passing from hence to America. I have <not the least> no Doubt but that his Character and Intentions are fair. He seems to be a sensible Young Gentleman and I would <wish to be useful to him> with pleasure do him Service but as I knew he was not an American I could not represent him as such, nor could I comply with his Request as to administring the Oath, having no power for that purpose either expressed or implied in my Commission or Instructions. He told me you had advised him to take such an Oath at Bordeaux and had appointed a person there to administer it, but that prudential Considerations had induced him to postpone it till his arrival here. <He is much embarrased and I am sorry for it.> I advised him <at first> to wait on the Minister and communicate to him a true state of his Case, being of opinion that such a Step supported by your Letter to Mr. Carmichael would <placing him here in a fair point of view> have silenced Doubts and Enquiries and enabled him to obtain such Passports as might be necessary for his travelling in this Kingdom. He nevertheless thought it best to delay it for the present <in Hopes that your Answer to my Letter would remove Difficulties as to the oath being administered to him> and to go and stay at Toledo till I should recieve your Answer to a Letter I promised to write to you on the Subject of administring the Oath, and he accordingly went to Toledo, but not having a Passport the Governor would not permit his remaining there. This Circumstance brought him here. I shall endeavor to obtain a Passport for him to return there on the Ground of your Letter in his Favor.[6] I believe it to be the Inclination as well as the <policy> Interest of America to augment her Number of Citizens but still her Consent to <recieve him is as> admit a Foreigner must be as necessary as his <to become one> Consent to be admitted. Besides <properly> it appears to me that an oath of Allegiance to the United States can <not be> with propriety be only administered to <any

but> Servants of Congress, <the allegiance of mere Citizens as such being> for tho a Person may by Birth or admission become a Citizen of *one* of the States I cannot concieve how one can either be born or made a Citizen of them *all.* I wish these Difficulties did not oppose my complying with the Request of Mr. Vaughan who I am the more desirous of serving as he appears to possess your Regard <and shall therefore>.[7]

Be pleased to present my Compliments to your Grandson and be assured that I am with <real> Sincere Esteem and Attachment Dear Sir, Your obliged and obedient Servant.

Dft. Endorsed. LbkC in DLC: Franklin VI, 21–22; Tr in PPAmP: Vaughan; without deletions in *RDC,* IV, 462–63.

[1]Franklin to JJ, 20 May 1781, not located.

[2]Two letters have been located: William Livingston to SLJ, 14 Jan. 1781, below, and to JJ of the same date, ALS listed in Sweet Catalogue, #141, For the intercepted instructions from Congress, see editorial note, "Issues in Negotiation," above.

[3]Richard Harrison to JJ, 8, 11, and n.d. May 1781, all E versions in JP.

[4]John Adams to JJ, 28 March 1781, LS in JP; *JAW,* VII, 384–85, *RDC,* IV, 334–35.

[5]John Vaughan (1756–1841) was the third son of Samuel Vaughan, Sr., an erstwhile West Indian planter, and Sarah Hallowell Vaughan of Boston, where John was born. His family was staunchly pro-American during the war; his father and brother Benjamin were intimate friends of Franklin, who sponsored John's stay in France, beginning in 1778, to "acquire the language, learn business, and form connections" (Samuel Vaughan to Franklin, 5 March 1778, ALS in PPAmP: Franklin). With letters of introduction from Franklin, Vaughan set off for Madrid in the spring of 1781 on the first leg of a proposed journey to America.

[6]See Carmichael to del Campo, 2, 7 June 1781, both AL in AHN Estado, leg. 3884, exp. 19, docs. 1, 3; and JJ to del Campo, 3 Nov. 1781, ALS in *ibid.,* doc. 5; Dft in JP; *HPJ,* II, 144–45.

[7]JJ gave Vaughan a letter of introduction to Richard Harrison, informing him that the bearer planned to spend the winter at Cádiz and leave in the spring for America, "where he intends to settle and become a citizen of one of our States." JJ to Harrison, 6 Nov. 1781, ALS in PPAmP: Vaughan.

From Silas Talbot[1]

Mill Prison, Plymouth, 4 June 1781

Sir,

Your Excellency will find by the date hereof that it comes from a prisoner, and which is the cause of my present address. Theirfore on the Confidence of your favour, beg leave to inform you, that in October last being then in, and having the Command, of the Armed Ship of war called the General Washington, in which Vessel had the Misfortune to be Captured by his Brittannick Majesties Ship Culloden, and taken into N. York from whence in consiquence of orders from Admiral

Rodney, seventy men with my self mostly Capital officers of armed ships of the United States, were put on Board the Ship Yarmouth and Brought to this place, whare I am deprived of eviry friendly connection whereby I might receive some Relief in this my present unhappy condition of Captivity, have therefore in consequence of your Excellencys favors taken the Liberty of thus addressing you, in hopes that you may be pleased to contribute toward my relief. A Request which the nature of my Situation, I trust, will sufficiently apologize for this, and least your Excellency should not immediately Recollect my person and Rank, beg leave to acquaint you that am the same pirson who had the honor to receive from Congress several Considerable promotions of Rank and Honor, the last of which was a Captance in the Navy during your Excellency[s] Presidency in Congress. The difrent appointments in the Military Line (as well that of the navy) was in consequence of my singular and distinguished services, and as all manner of correspondance and Negotiation between this Country and the United States of America at present stopt, and for the want of an Honorable Credit here, I am deprived of those necessary Supplies which the peculiar nature of my present distressed State of Captivity doth Require, am thereby induced to Request your Excellency will favor me with a sum of about Fifty Pounds Sterling which may be charged to me in account of my Service either in the Millitary or Navle Departments, in both of which, the United States are considerably in Arrearages to me, other ways if pleased to advance me this som on my own privet account.[2]

In hopes of your Excellencys speedy, and effectual relief, I have the honor to be, with all due Respect, Your Excellencys obliged humble and Obedient servant,

SILAS TALBOT

ALS. Addressed: "His Excellency John Jay Esqr. Plenipotentiary, etc. for the United States of America at Madrid." Endorsed: ". . . Copy Recd. and ansd. 14 July 1781." ACS, misdated 11 June 1781, in JP.

[1]Silas Talbot (1751–1813), a New Englander, was a lieutenant-colonel in the Continental Army before being commissioned a naval captain in 1779. Captured in October 1780, Talbot was taken to England and confined at both Dartmoor and Mill prisons. Exchanged in 1781, he reached home in the spring of 1782. H. T. Tuckerman, *The Life of Silas Talbot* (New York, 1859), reprinted in *Magazine of History,* XXX (1946), no. 4, pp. 203–57.

[2]Too embarrassed financially to make an advance from public funds, JJ sent a copy of Talbot's letter to Franklin on 9 July, and informed Talbot of this on the 14th, stating therein that, if necessary, JJ would advance funds from his private account through Jonathan Williams, Jr. (1750–1815), Franklin's grandnephew, merchant at Nantes and sometime agent of the American ministers.

As early as 1777, without Congressional authorization, Franklin had provided funds for American prisoners and had established a cartel with Britain, the first prisoner exchange taking place on 1 April 1779. Franklin advanced both private and public funds to American prisoners regardless of rank, but had to act circumspectly because of the frequency of requests. Franklin was able to be of assistance to Talbot, and in November 1781 had his allowance increased and further aids supplied when Talbot reached Paris. JJ himself during his Spanish mission advanced funds for American prisoners abroad, for which see DNA: RG 39, Foreign Ledger of Public Agents in Europe, I, 192. Talbot to Franklin, 4 June, ALS in PPAmP. Talbot to Adams, 5 June ALS and 8 June CS in MHi: Adams, reel 355. JJ to Franklin, 9 July, DftS in JP; *WJ,* II, 83–84; *HPJ,* II, 51–53. JJ to Talbot, 14 July, DftS in JP; *WJ,* 284–85; *HPJ,* II, 53–54. Franklin to JJ, 20 August, LS in JP; LbkCs in DLC: Franklin V, 156–62, VI, 29–33; Tr in PPAmP: Benjamin Vaughan; *RDC,* IV, 643–47; *HPJ,* II, 60–65. Talbot to JJ, 24 Aug. 1781, ALS in JP. See also Catherine M. Prelinger, "Benjamin Franklin and the American Prisoners of War in England During the American Revolution," *WMQ,* XXXII, (1975), 261–94; Tuckerman, *Talbot,* p. 242.

To Silas Deane

Aranjues, 16 June 1781

Dear Sir,

Your Letter of the 8 April is particular on a Subject, on which I confess I wished to be minutely informed.[1] I approve of your having conveyed to the Minister what you concieved to be a true State of our Affairs. On such Occasions Policy, as well as Candor, forbids Deception. How far it was necessary or proper to mention the same Things in public Conversations, is less clear, and if that was the Case, I think it was not prudent.

AS TO CARMICHAEL, HE IS IGNORANT OF THE CONTENTS OF any LETTERS THAT HAVE PASSED BETWEEN US. I ONCE had MY GOOD OPINION OF HIM, AND MIGHT HAVE RETAINED IT, IF almost FROM THE TIME WE SAILED FROM AMERICA HE had NOT GIVEN ME SUFFICIENT CAUSE TO REPENT HIS being WITH ME. I CANNOT NOW GO INTO DETAILS. I WISH TO BE IN A SITUATION OF FORGETTING THEM AND HIM. This must be entre nous.[2]

I am told that PAINE is in France, but as far as I can learn, the Objects of his voyage remain a secret.[3] Mr. S. political Reflections do not surprize me.[4] I wish however they had been spared, as many may be led from the Extravagance of them to consider such assertions rather as Gasconades than well founded Facts.

It gives me Pleasure to hear that France has lately granted very considerable aids to our Country. They will be very seasonable, in more than one point of View. They will strengthen our Hands, and confirm our Confidence.

Spain [is] going to do something great, if we may judge by appearances. I allude to the armament preparing to sail from Cadiz. Gibralter is supposed to be the Object, and the Duke de Crillon is said to be the Commander in Chief.[5]

I am rejoiced to find that G. M. was not alluded to in your former Letter. He is still at Philadelphia, tho not in Congress. It is a Pity that his Time should be spent in private Life, when it might be employed with much advantage to the public.[6]

Mrs. Jay desires me to present her Compliments to you and I am, Dear Sir sincerely, Your Friend and Servant

JOHN JAY

ALS in CtHi: Deane. Endorsed. The cryptographic passages are in a code utilizing a list of words with numerical equivalents, supplemented by a monalphabetic cipher. The code book and grid cipher are in JP; inaccurate in *Deane Papers,* IV, 438–39.

[1]Deane to JJ, 8 April 1781, in which Deane spelled out his pessimistic views about the outcome of the war as relayed to Carmichael. LbkC in CtHi: Deane; *Deane Papers,* IV, 296–301.

[2]These remarks were provoked by previous correspondence. Carmichael had been critical of Deane for admitting publicly in France that the U.S. had serious military and economic problems. Informed of this by JJ, Deane had defended himself in his 8 April letter, arguing that candor about the nation's situation was more likely to induce European aid than a denial that any need existed.

[3]Paine was John Laurens' choice to be his private secretary on the latter's mission abroad, but Congress, to avoid contention, chose William Jackson (1759–1829) instead. Paine nonetheless accompanied Laurens to France, paying his own way. For Paine's previous contretemps with Congress and JJ, see *JJ,* I, 508. See also Philip S. Foner, ed., *The Complete Writings of Thomas Paine* (2 vols., New York, 1945), I, 1233–34.

[4]James Searle, an ardent Lee-Adams supporter, was then in France claiming, according to Deane, that the British forces were bottled up and perishing in Charleston, that Washington had over 20,000 men under his command, and that the U.S. was quite able to carry on the war alone. Although Searle was himself a merchant, Deane claimed that he characterized all Americans employed in trade as "Rogues and Speculators." Deane to JJ, 8 April 1781. For James Searle, see also *JJ,* I, 791.

[5]French General Louis de Berton des Balbes de Quiers, 2d duc de Crillon (1718–96), had served in the Spanish armed forces since the Seven Years' War. Instead of moving against Gibraltar, Crillon's force landed on Minorca, 23 Aug. 1781. Only after that island fell to the attackers in February 1782 did Crillon turn his attention to Gibraltar. Jonathan R. Dull, *The French Navy and American Independence* (Princeton, 1975), pp. 235–67.

[6]As early as June 1781, Gouverneur Morris was acting unofficially as Robert Morris' assistant in the Office of Finance at the latter's request, but was not sworn in until 7 August. *RMP,* I, 96n.

FROM GOUVERNEUR MORRIS

Philadelphia, 17 June 1781

Dear Jay,

Although I beleive myself thoroughly acquainted with you yet I cannot tell whether I ought to congratulate or condole with you ON YOUR LATE APPOINTMENT. Ere this reaches you you will have learnt that you are on the PART OF THIS COUNTRY ONE OF FIVE COMMISSIONERS TO NEGOCIATE for PEACE.[1] So far you are SOMETHING but when you come to find BY YOUR INSTRUCTIONS THAT YOU MUST ULTIMATELY OBEY THE DICTATES OF the FRENCH MINISTER, I am sure there is some thing in your Bosom which will REVOLT AT THE Servility of the SITUATION. To have relaxed on all Sides, to have given up all Things might easily have been expected from those Minds which softened by Wealth and debased by Fear are unable to gain and unworthy to enjoy the Blessings of Freedom.[2] But that the proud should prostitute the very little little DIGNITY THIS POOR COUNTRY was possessed of would be indeed astonishing if we did not know the near Alliance between Pride and Meanness. Men who have too little Spirit to demand of their CONSTITUENTS THAT THEY DO THEIR DUTY, who have sufficient Humility to beg a paltry Pittance at the Hands of ANY AND EVERY SOVEREIGN, such men will always be ready to pay the Price which Vanity shall demand from the Vain.

Do I not know you well enough to beleive that you will not ACT in THIS NEW CAPACITY? I think I do and therefore I will express my Concern that you must DECLINE THE HONOR, if that Name can indeed be applied to SUCH OFFICE. DECLINE, however with Decency tho with Dignity. I mean always if no Alteration takes Place which shall be done if I can effectuate it tho I almost despair.

Having declared what I think you will do let me advise what I wish you to do as the only Mode to BE OF CONSEQUENCE when the Affair is TREATED OF in EARNEST. Let Carmichael GO TO THE MEETING.[3] I must be most egregiously mistaken if SPANISH COURT IS DESIROUS OF PEACE. MEET THEM FULLY and in APPEARANCE WITH CONFIDENCE. TELL THEM WE are determined to persist untill the last Necessity. STATE OUR PRESENT TERMS, TO[4] COMPREHEND THE CESSION OF THE FLORIDAS AND EVEN OF Jamaica as an ULTIMATUM OF PEACE. THEIR MINISTER at the CONGRESS CAN DELAY, AND DELAY IS every Thing. No other CONGRESS WILL SURRENDER ALL AS THIS has to an ALLY. I am more moved on this Occasion than I have ever been and therefore it is possible I may be mistaken but I think so strong and deep an Impression cannot be false.

Your Brother has been pelting at me in the News Papers.[5] I am sorry for it because it renders your Brother ridiculous and indeed contemptible. Remember me properly and beleive me yours.

GOUV. MORRIS

ALS. Addressed: "Honle. Mr. Jay Minister plenipo. of the United State of North America at Madrid. Forwarded by Cuming & Macarty. L'Orient 2d Augt. 1781." Endorsed: ". . . Recd 18 Augt. 1781. ansd. 24 Do." Incomplete in *HPJ*, II, 38–39. Morris used a code based on Boyer's *Royal Dictionary;* see also JJ to Morris, 28 Sept. 1781, below.

[1]At Luzerne's urging, Congress, resolved to concur with France in accepting the proposed Russo-Austrian mediation, hammered out the instructions for the American peace commissioner, John Adams, between 6 and 11 June, and enlarged the peace commission. JJ, nominated by John Mathews of South Carolina on 11 June, was elected on 13 June; Franklin, Thomas Jefferson, and Henry Laurens were elected on 14 June. *JCC,* XX, 605–06, 608–10, 611–19, 625–28, 638, 648; Morris, *Peacemakers,* pp. 212–17. See also Huntington to JJ, 5 July 1781, below.

[2]This controversial clause in the instructions reads: "For this purpose you are to make the most candid and confidential communications upon all subjects to the ministers of our generous ally, the King of France; to undertake nothing in the negotiations for peace or truce without their knowledge and concurrence; and ultimately to govern yourselves by their advice and opinion, endeavoring in your whole conduct to make them sensible how much we rely upon his Majesty's influence for the effectual aid in everything that may be necessary to the peace, security, and future prosperity of the United States of America." *JCC,* XX, 651–52.

[3]Carmichael was one of the unsuccessful nominees for the enlarged peace commission. *JCC,* XX, 628.

[4]"(be the effect of their Backwardness. Hint a private Treaty to)" appears in the version listed in the Sweet Catalogue, #141.

[5]Sir James Jay's newspaper attacks on Gouverneur Morris and James Duane seem to have been prompted by their failure to support his money claims against Congress as well as his disappointment at not being put in charge of the newly created Department of Marine. Using the pseudonyms "Pro Bono Publico," "Lucius," "A Citizen," and "Plain Truth," Sir James denounced Duane as a Tory and British agent, and ridiculed Morris for wanting "to go to New-York to see his Mammy" (Sarah Gouverneur Morris [1714–86]), a Loyalist sympathizer, adding other irrational charges. For the Jay-Morris exchange, see *Freeman's Journal,* 16, 23, and 30 May; 6, 20, and 27 June; 4 and 25 July 1781; for the Jay-Duane exchange, *ibid.,* 23 May; 6 and 27 June; 8, 15, and 22 Aug. 1781; also Edward P. Alexander, *A Revolutionary Conservative: James Duane of New York* (New York, 1938), pp. 144–49. For Sir James' claims against Congress, see the editorial note below, "Sir James Kicks Over the Traces"; for his connection with the Marine Department, see Catharine W. Livingston to JJ, 29 March 1781, ALS in JP.

To Floridablanca

Madrid, 28 June 1781

Sir,

Agreable to your Excellencys Request I have now the Honor of again submitting to your Consideration a particular State of the Case of the unfortunate Americans who after Capturing the Dover Cutter and bringing her safe to Santa Cruz in the Island of Teneriff the 15th April 1780 have not as yet reaped the Fruits they expected from that successful though dangerous Enterprize.[1]

Your Excellency's answer to my Representation on this Subject in June 1780[2] Induced me to advise these People to abide Patiently the Result of the necessary Inquiries which were then proposed to be made, being well persuaded that if the Facts as stated by them should on enquiry prove true there would be no Difficulty in bringing the affair to a speedy and equitable decision. The Capture of some of the Packets passing between Spain and Teneriff gave occasion nevertheless to unavoidable Delays and protracted the business to the Month of December last.

In a Conversation I then had the Honor of having with your Excellency on the Subject, the Circumstance of the Cutters having been Captured by her own Mariners was mentioned as a Reason against their Claim, and such Captures not being warranted by the Law of Nations, and although they might be Americans yet that as they acted without Commission, they could not legally avail themselves of it. In order to remove these Objections I informed your Excellency, that the British Nation having thought Proper to encourage the Masters and Mariners of American Vessels to bring them by Force or Fraud into British ports and to reward their Treachery by adjudging such Vessels to be lawful Prizes, Congress found it necessary to retaliate by granting the like Indulgence and Encouragement to such Crews of British Vessels as should bring them within the Ports of the United States. I further informed your Excellency that Congress had on the Application of the Captors of the Dover Cutter passed a particular Resolution whereby I was instructed to endeavour to obtain for them the Benefit intended by the before mentioned Resolution, and that it was the Wish of Congress that the whole Profit of the Capture might be divided among the Captors.[3] Your Excellency was thereupon pleased to promise that the Prize should be appraized and the Value of it paid to the Captors, and authorized me at the same time to inform them of it. I was thence led to conclude that no important obstacles remained, and I had no Doubt but that orders would have issued for making the Appraizment in Question, and the affair soon drawn to a Conclusion.

Permit me to remind your Excellency that one of these Americans has been several Weeks and still in this City, and that he is ready to answer on oath to all such Question relative to the Capture of the Cutter etc. as may be put to him.[4]

As the Petition of Thomas Shuker (the Chief of these Captors) to Congress, of which I have before had the Honor of transmitting Copies at different Times to your Excellency, contains a precise Account of the Transaction, I again subjoin a Copy of it, together with an Inventory of the Prize, her stores etc. which I received from the American now here.

I have the Honor to be with perfect Consideration and respect, Your Excellencys Most obedient and most humble Servant,

JOHN JAY

LS, body in Carmichael's hand, with copy of Shuker's petition and inventory of supplies on *Dover* cutter at time of capture, in AHN Estado, leg. 3884 bis, exp. 12, doc. 6; Dft in JP.

[1]For the earlier correspondence and the petition of Shuker of 27 April 1780, see *JJ,* I, 784–86. Congress on 26 May 1780 had referred Shuker's petition to the Board of Admiralty. *JCC,* XVIII, 460.

[2]See *JJ,* I, 783.

[3]Congress so resolved 27 Sept. 1780. *JCC,* XVIII, 868–69.

[4]Possibly the Mr. Elford whom Carmichael refers to in his letter to JJ, 27 June 1781. ALS in JP.

To Montmorin

Madrid, 2 July 1781

Sir,

I have the Honor of transmitting to your Ex[cellenc]y herewith enclosed a copy of a Letter I have this Day written to his Ex[cellenc]y the Count De Florida Blanca. I have thereby informed him of my Being authorized to remove the objections hitherto made by the Court of Spain to a Treaty of Alliance with the United States, <I have communicated it to his Ex[cellenc]y and again requested that> and again requested that the measures necessary for <that> the Purpose may *now be taken.*

Permit me Sir to request that the favorable Interposition of <France> our kind and generous ally with his Catholic Majesty may be exerted to commence, the proposed Negociation, and bring it to a speedy and happy Conclusion. The Confidence justly reposed by america in the amity and assurances of his most Christian Majesty <will not permit> forbids me to <press> urge this Request by any arguments, <as being persuaded that the many valuable repeated and unequivocal proofs we have recieved of his Friendship convince us that> Persuasives being indelicate where <there ought to be no> not warrented by Doubts of Inclination, and I am happy in reflecting that his Instructions on this Subject are committed to the Execution of a Minister from whose attachments as well as from whose Talents and Address <may promise themselves much> the american Cause may expect to derive advantages. <Many Reasons induce me to view the present Moment as particularly favorable to the completion of this Business.>

I have the Honor to be with <perfect> real Esteem and Regard, Your Excellency's most obedient and most humble Servant.

Dft. C in French in CP E 605: 5. LbkCs in JP, CSmH, PCC 110, I; C in JJ to McKean, 3 Oct. 1781; without deletions in *HPJ,* II, 95 and *RDC,* IV, 747–48. Enclosure: JJ to Floridablanca, 2 July 1781, see editorial note, "Issues in Negotiation," above, n. 9.

From Samuel Huntington

Philadelphia, 5 July 1781

Sir,

You will receive herewith enclosed, a Commission constituting yourself and the three other Gentlemen therein named, in Addition to Mr. Adams, our Ministers for negotiating Peace.[1]

Also another Commission and Duplicate to the same Ministers, authorizing them to accept of the Mediation of the Emperor of Germany and Empress of Russia,[2] in one of which you will observe the Emperor is first named and in the other the Empress. These are to be made Use of as Circumstances shall render expedient.

I have also enclosed Instructions (in Cyphers) for your Government in Addition to those formerly given to Mr. Adams and now in his Possession, for negotiating Peace with Great Britain.[3]

Similar Dispatches are forwarded to Doctor Franklin and Mr. J. Adams with Direction to give you the earliest Advice on their Arrival, which you may probably receive before this comes to Hand.

I have the Honor to be, with the highest Regard, Sir, Your most obedient and most humble Servant,

SAM. HUNTINGTON PRESIDENT

LS in RAWC. Endorsed.

[1]Commission to the Ministers Plenipotentiary of the United States for Negotiating a Peace, 15 June 1781: DS, signed by Huntington, attested by Thomson, in JP; Dft in Thomson's hand in PCC 25, I; C (3) in FO 27/2, 95/511, and, countersigned by JJ on 1 Oct. 1782, in 97/157; C in PCC 24, I; E in MiU-C: Hartley, III; *JCC,* XX, 652–54; *RDC,* IV, 503–04.

[2]Commission to the Ministers Plenipotentiary to Accede to the Mediation of the Empress of Russia, and the Emperor of Germany, 15 June 1781: DS (2) in JP, signed

by Huntington, attested by Thomson. *JCC*, XX, 655; *RDC*, IV, 502. LbkC of Adams' instructions, 14 Aug. 1779, in JP.

[3]Instructions to the Ministers Plenipotentiary on Behalf of the United States of America to Negotiate a Treaty of Peace: Huntington to Adams, Franklin, Jay, Laurens, and Jefferson, 15 June 1781, LbkCs in DLC: Franklin VIII, 10–11 and VIIIa, 9–11; C in CP EU 17: 254–55. LS, n.d. [15 June 1781], partly in code, listed in Rendell cat. 92 (1973). *JCC*, XX, 651–52; *RDC*, IV, 504–05.

John Jay on the Pensacola Capitulation

When news reached Philadelphia at the end of May 1781 that the British fort of St. George at Pensacola had finally capitulated to Don Bernardo de Gálvez and his troops on 9 May, the Spanish victory was greeted with enthusiasm by the Americans. The military events were reported in the *Pennsylvania Packet* on 12 June, but no mention was made of the capitulation terms.[1]

By the closing days of June the Spanish success had begun to cause some apprehension among Americans as rumors of the capitulation agreement circulated. The Livingston family was concerned that JJ be alerted to this. Late in June Catharine Livingston wrote to her brother-in-law, and a fortnight later William Bingham sent JJ further details.[2] Huntington alerted Washington on 2 July that he had a report that the "prisoners lately taken at pensecola were to be sent to N. York." Appended to his letter was information that the captured British garrison was charged not to serve against Spain and its allies until exchanged.[3] Huntington was reluctant to accept the validity of the report, as was Washington, both men finding it difficult to believe that the pro-American Gálvez would agree to terms so inimical to the American cause.[4] The terms, however, were verified in the *Pennsylvania Packet* on 21 July. American leaders were quick to point out that since the United States was not yet allied with Spain, the released British troops were free to rejoin the conflict against America.

After much discussion and correspondence,[5] on 10 August Congress ordered the Committee for Foreign Affairs to transmit all the information on the capitulation to JJ in Spain, that he might remonstrate directly to the court.[6] Lovell complied with the order on 15 August.[7]

In his 3 October 1781 dispatch, JJ reported that he had brought up the Pensacola affair with Floridablanca at a conference on 8 September. JJ drew from Floridablanca a grudging admission that "it was ill done," . . . "very unexpected," and that it would be better had the prisoners been sent to Europe, along with a promise "that the like should not happen in the future." However, the Spaniard could not desist from entering a weak defense of the terms, arguing that "those troops were restrained by the capitulation from taking arms against the allies of Spain till exchanged, and could not operate against our troops without also operating against those of France, who were joined with them, and who, it was well known, were the allies of Spain."

[1]For the capitulation terms, see also N. Orwin Rush, *The Battle of Pensacola* (Tallahassee, 1966), pp. 84–92.

[2]On 30 June 1781 (ALS in JP) Catharine W. Livingston wrote to SLJ that: "The Spaniards have not used us well in permitting the Garrison at Pensacola to go to New York. They will most undoubtably be employed against us, & I fear it will defeat our Genl's design against New York." Therein she mentions having sent a letter to JJ "a few days ago," not located. Bingham to JJ, 13 July 1781, following.

[3]Huntington to Washington, 2 July 1781, LS in DLC: Washington; *LMCC,* VI, 132 and n. William Smith, *Memoirs,* II, 427, 433.

[4]See Huntington to Washington, 2 July 1781; Washington to Huntington, 10 July 1781, *GWF,* XXII, 356–57. See also John W. Caughey, *Bernardo de Gálvez in Louisiana, 1776–1783* (Berkeley, 1934), pp. 210–11.

[5]See *LMCC,* VI, 150, 151, 153, 154, 156, 187; *MP,* III, 196–98; *PPGC,* VII, 111.

[6]On 10 Aug. 1781, Congress ordered that the Committee for Foreign Affairs send JJ information on the Pensacola surrender and the British garrisons' arrival in New York "to the end that he may make such representation thereon as shall appear to him to be proper." Order in PCC 4; C in *ibid.* 6, III; *JCC,* XXI, 854. But, on 13 July 1781, JJ had already congratulated Floridablanca on the Pensacola capitulation and had enclosed two gazettes containing information about it. C in JJ to McKean, 3 Oct. 1781.

[7]LbkC in PCC 79, I, 293. Enclosures (not located) : (1) information which Lovell had "been able to obtain" for use by JJ according to his "discretion, and the Spirit of the enclosed resolution"; (2) the 10 August resolution, which did not pass, on the Mississippi River, which Lovell deemed "not amiss to enclose": "That the minister be empowered to make such further cession on the right of these United States to the navigation of the river Mississippi as he may think proper, and on such terms and conditions as he may think most for the honour and interest of these United States." *JCC,* XXI, 853; *LMCC,* VI, 187.

From William Bingham

Philadelphia, 13 July 1781

Dear Sir,

I did not know of Major Frank's[1] Intentions of embarking for Spain, untill this very Moment. I cannot suffer him to depart without addressing you a few Lines, should they only serve to congratulate you on the pleasing Prospect of our Affairs.

In every part of the United States, the Enemy are now acting on the defensive, and seem to have renounced the vain and hitherto transitory Idea of Conquest and Subjugation. A Revival of public Spirit has taken [the] place of that listless Apathy we were involved in, and our Friends to the Southward are making Exertions, that were thought far beyond their Competency. We seem to be convinced of the Necessity of a firm Reliance on ourselves, and have renounced the Illusions that a dependance on foreign Assistance occasioned. I believe the best Mode of procuring Services from others, is to show them, that we do not stand in Need of them.

Our Army under General Green in S. Carolina, have reduced every British Port, except Ninety Six and Charlestown, the former of which was closely besieged, and would inevitably have fallen, if it had not been for the unfortunate Arrival of a Reinforcement, which enabled Lord Rawdon to take the Field, and Report says that he has raised the Siege, altho no official Dispatches have as yet confirmed it.[2]

In Virginia a most respectable Corps of Troops is now opposed to Lord Cornwallis, which has forced him to retreat, and take Port at Portsmouth.[3]

The sanguine hopes of Conquest, which our Enemies flattered themselves with have been completely baffled in this Quarter.

New York is now invested by the federal Army,[4] and I should have hoped much from the Event of their operations, had it not been for a *faux pas* of our good Friends the Spaniards, who gave a Capitulation to the Garrison at Pensacola, which permitted them to reinforce the Enemy at New York or any other Port of the United States.

By a Late Gazette from New York it appears that upwards of eleven hundred of them have already arrived there, which is a most important Acquisition to the Enemy at this critical Moment, and has occasioned the greatest Murmurings and Discontents. Indeed I Know of no palliation that can be offered for such blind and erring Conduct.

Your late Appointment by Congress[5] will postpone your Return to this Country longer than you at first imagined, however it will enable you to return with greater Eclat, as I hope you will bring the Olive Branch along with you. No one partook of greater Satisfaction at your Nomination than I did.

Mr. Huntington has lately resigned the Chair, to which Mr. Johnson of N. Carolina was elected, but he has declined that honor, and Mr. McKean from the State of Delaware has been since chosen.[6]

My best Respects wait on Mrs. Jay, and my Compliments on the Colonel. Believe me to be with sincere Regard and Respect, Dear Sir, Your Friend and obedient humble Servant

WM. BINGHAM

ALS. Endorsed: ". . . by Maj. Franks, ansd. 8 Sept. 1781 by Do."

[1]David Salisbury Franks (c. 1740–93), son of the prominent Montreal merchant Abraham Franks, joined General Richard Montgomery's forces upon the capture of Franks' native city of Montreal in 1775. Following four years of service in the Northern army, Franks became a major and aide-de-camp to General Benedict

Arnold, but was exonerated (November 1780) of any complicity in Arnold's treason. Prior to Arnold's defection, Franks had written Brockholst Livingston about the possibility of his going to Spain. Franks sought to recoup the substantial losses he had suffered in exchanging the gold he had brought in from Canada for Continental money. Dispatched to Spain by Robert Morris in July 1781, Franks temporarily solved JJ's problem of intercepted letters. A. B. Hart, ed., *The Varick Court of Inquiry* (Boston, 1907), p. 169; Jacob R. Marcus, *Early American Jewry* (2 vols., Philadelphia, 1951), I, 251–55; *GWF,* XX, 442–43; Hersch L. Zitt, "David Salisbury Franks, Revolutionary Patriot," *Pennsylvania History,* LXI (April 1949), 77–95; Herbert Friedenwald, "Jews Mentioned in the Journal of the Continental Congress," American Jewish Hist. Soc., *Publications,* I (1893), 76–86.

[2]See above, Gouverneur Morris to JJ, 7–9 May 1781.

[3]By 13 July Cornwallis positioned his main base in Suffolk, while detaching 3,000 men to Portsmouth preparatory to sailing to Philadelphia or New York, a trip which never transpired as planned.

[4]The reference is to the Continental forces under Washington. At Wethersfield, Connecticut, on 22 May 1781 Washington met with Jean Baptiste Donatien de Vimeur, Comte de Rochambeau (1725–1807), commander of the French expeditionary force. They agreed to a plan to lay siege to New York, but held open the possibility, upon the arrival of De Grasse's fleet, of shifting operations southward to Virginia. *JCC,* XX, 557–59; John C. Fitzpatrick, ed., *The Diaries of George Washington, 1748–1799* (4 vols., Boston, 1925), II, 216–18; *GWF,* XXII, 105–07; Douglas S. Freeman, *George Washington* (7 vols., New York, 1948–57), V, 289; Henry P. Johnston, *The Yorktown Campaign and the Surrender of Cornwallis, 1781* (New York, 1881), p. 76.

[5]JJ's appointment as peace commissioner, for which see above, Gouverneur Morris to JJ, 17 June 1781.

[6]On 6 July Huntington informed Congress that because of his "ill state of health" he was resigning the Presidency of Congress. Samuel Johnston (1733–1816) of North Carolina was elected to the post on 9 July, but because of ill health declined the next day, when Thomas McKean (1734–1817) of Delaware was elected in his place. LbkC in PCC 15, p. 58; *JCC,* XX, 724, 732, 733; *LMCC,* VI, 139–40, 160n.

To Samuel Huntington

Madrid, 1 August 1781

Sir,

Your Ex[cellenc]ys Favor of the 28 May[1] and the Duplicate have come to my Hands thro those of the minister by whose Courier they were brought from Cadiz to this City.

Every Thing which that Letter rendered proper for me to do has been done. The Issue is as yet uncertain. The Court are gone to St. Ildefonso. I follow Tomorrow. For the Captors of the Dover Cutter I have as yet only been able to obtain Promises.[2] Mr. Gardoqui is still here.[3] It is said he will soon depart. The Duke of Crillons Fleet has passed by Gibralter, and Report says he is gone to Port Mahon.[4]

I cannot by this opportunity enter into Details nor indeed it is very important that I should.

Congress may rest assured of my utmost Endeavours to fulfill their Instructions, and that the approbation with which they have honored my past Proceedings will stimulate me to render my subsequent ones as worthy of their Commendation as unremitted Attention and unceasing Zeal in their Service can atchieve.

I have the Honor to be with great Respect and Esteem your Excellencys most obedient and humble Servant.

Dft.

[1]Huntington's 28 May letter, based on a Congressional committee (James Duane, Samuel Adams, James Madison) report of 2 May, informed JJ of Congress's decision to recede from insistence on the navigation of the lower Mississippi and empowered JJ to omit any "express reference" to the Franco-American treaty in any agreement he might make with Spain. Committee Dft of report in Madison's hand, 2 May 1781, in PCC 25, I, 411–16; Huntington to JJ, 28 May 1781, LS and Duplicate LS in NHi: Jay; C of Duplicate LS in JP; *JCC,* XX, 437, 472, 551–55; *RDC,* IV, 451–53; *HPJ,* II, 32–35; *SDC,* VII, 415–19. See also editorial note below, "The Second San Ildefonso Conference."

[2]See above, JJ to Floridablanca, 28 June 1781.

[3]Diego de Gardoqui, who, JJ expected, would be sent to America to succeed Miralles.

[4]The duc de Crillon took Port Mahon on Minorca by way of preliminary to his attack on Fort St. Philip, for which see above, Deane to JJ, 16 June 1781, n. 5.

To Robert Morris

St. Ildefonso, 1–8 September 1781

Dear Sir,

Major Franks arrived here last Evening.[1] I have not yet got thro the Dispatches he brought.[2] I have read sufficient however to percieve that I am soon to have the pleasure of writing long Letters to Congress and yourself.[3] I shall Dispatch the Major as soon as possible. I cannot say precisely when, because it will depend in some Measure on others.

THE BILLS <up> ON ME FAR EXCEED THE FUNDS FOR THEIR PAYMENT AND UNLESS OTHER THAN FUNDS IN THE AIR, ARE <supplied> afforded ME, PROTESTS WILL PROBABLY END THIS GAME OF HAZARD. DR. FRANKLIN HAS AS YET SAVED THAT necessity, BUT UNLESS BY EXPRESS ORDER OF CONGRESS HE CAN NOT ADVANCE MUCH MORE. SPAIN HAS LESS MONEY THAN URGENT <Demands> CALLS FOR IT, HER FINANCES, BEING ILL MANAGED, AND HER CREDIT LOW. I HAVE BUT little HOPES OF LOANS OR SUBSIDIES FROM HER. EVERY THING IN MY POWER SHALL BE DONE. CONGRESS SHOULD KNOW THAT THEIR SHIPS ON THE STOCKS ARE NEITHER SOLD NOR ENGAGED.[4]

THIS COURT SEEMS determined TO DO NOTHING UNTILL THE CAMPAIGN ENDS.

I am etc.

8 September 1781

P.S. BILLS AMOUNTING TO BETWEEN 68 AND 70 THOUSAND DOLLARS ARE NOW <in Jeopardy and absolutely> UTTERLY UNPROVIDED FOR.

Dft. ALS, encoded interlineally, in Charles Hamilton Catalog (1971). The letter utilizes the cipher sent to JJ by Robert Morris on 7 July 1781. On the same date, 1 September, JJ wrote a private letter to Morris, sending in his care goods for his father's family. Dft in JP.

[1]Franks had arrived in San Ildefonso on 29 August. See JJ to McKean, 20 Sept. 1781, below.

[2]See below, JJ to Floridablanca, 3 Sept. 1781, n. 2.

[3]See, *e.g.,* JJ to McKean, 20 Sept. 1781, below; to Gouverneur Morris, 28 Sept. 1781, below; to McKean, 3 Oct. 1781.

[4]The offer to sell to Spain at "prime cost" an unfinished "74 Gun Ship" had been made by JJ at the first San Ildefonso Conference of 23 Sept. 1780; see JJ to Samuel Huntington, 6 Nov. 1780, in *JJ,* I, 832. On 16 May 1781 Congress authorized JJ to dispose of the hull of such a gun-ship on the stocks at Portsmouth "on such terms as he may judge best for the honor and interest of the United States." *JCC,* XX, 508.

The Second San Ildefonso Conference

19 September 1781

When JJ had notified Floridablanca on 2 July that he had received altered instructions regarding the Mississippi, Spain's principal minister kept putting off a face-to-face meeting. Finally, to JJ's note of 3 September, printed below, Floridablanca suggested that JJ visit him on Saturday of that week (8 September), and invited him to bring along Major Franks. After questioning the pair about military affairs, to which Franks, on JJ's prompting, pointed to the inexpedient terms given the Pensacola garrison, Floridablanca ended the talks, pleading ill health. "Thus the conference ended as fruitless as the last," was JJ's laconic comment.[1]

Beside himself over Spanish procrastination, JJ again turned to Montmorin, and along with a note of 16 September sent him a proposed draft of a letter to Floridablanca, both below. Montmorin looked over this strongly worded letter, with its implied threat, and advised JJ that his draft was "just" but apt to give offense. JJ took his advice and never sent it. His original draft is more strongly worded than the revised form which he sent to Montmorin and included in his 3 October dispatch to Congress. To Floridablanca he substituted a brief, temperate note for his outspoken and less diplomatic first effort.[2] JJ merely informed Floridablanca of the imminent return of Major Franks to America and stressed the significance that would be attached "if the letter I may then write by him should not contain the desired intelligence." Congress might thereby be led "to apprehend that their expectations of forming an intimate union with Spain were not well founded."[3] The combination of Montmorin's backstage diplomacy and JJ's implied threat brought a quick response. On 19 September Floridablanca invited JJ to visit him that very same evening, "either alone or with Major Franks."[4]

When, at long last, the conference took place,[5] Floridablanca, contrary to his customary dilatoriness in treating American affairs, seemed eager on this occasion to forge ahead. He requested JJ to draw up the outlines of a proposed treaty within four days. JJ was to consider three major points: financial aid to the Americans, commercial relations between the two countries, and, finally, a treaty of alliance.

With a speed that must have astonished the leisurely moving occupants of the Escorial, JJ took only three days to draw up a set of propositions.[6] "Mr. Jay presumes," as he put it in his prefatory statement, "that it is not expected that he should offer a Plan of a Treaty drawn at Length, but only *General Propositions,* which may be so modified and enlarged, as on One Consideration and Discussion may appear expedient. With this view he begs Leave to present the following as the Basis of a Treaty of *Amity and Alliance.*" These propositions included: perpetual peace between the two nations; most favored nation commercial and navigation rights; a guarantee by Spain of United States' territories and by the United States of Spanish territories in North America; and, finally, a proposal to relinquish the navigation of the Mississippi from 31° N.L. —"that is, from the point where it leaves the United States—down to the ocean." JJ was careful to add: "The offer of this proposition . . . must necessarily be limited," and as a consequence, "if the acceptance of it should, together with the proposed alliance, be postponed to a general peace, the United States will cease to consider themselves bound by any propositions or offers which he may now make in their behalf." JJ justified his reservations to the President of a Congress which should have thought of them, but did not, by advancing this argument: "Your excellency will be pleased to observe that among my remarks on the sixth proposition I have limited the duration of the offer contained in it. I did this from a persuasion that such limitation was not only just and reasonable in itself, but absolutely necessary to prevent this court's continuing to delay a treaty to a general peace."[7] Thereby JJ gave an early demonstration of his readiness to use his discretion in carrying out instructions from his government whenever, in his judgment, the national interest justified an altered course. Congress was now on notice, and should not have been surprised by the independent course he would later pursue in Paris.

Floridablanca did not accept JJ's proffer. Unready to recognize American independence, Spain chose to remain a co-belligerent and leave the question of the Mississippi and the Florida boundary to future settlement. To JJ's credit, when, in the postwar years, the parties would resume negotiations, America's bargaining posture would be strengthened while Spain's would be deteriorating.

[1]JJ to McKean, 3 Oct. 1781.
[2]*Ibid.*

[3]JJ to Floridablanca, 17 Sept. 1781, LS in French in Carmichael's hand in AHN Estado, leg. 3884, exp. 15, doc. 3; LbkCs in JP, CSmH, and PCC 110, I; C in JJ to McKean, 3 Oct. 1781.

[4]Floridablanca to JJ, 19 Sept. 1781, LS in French in JP; Dft in French in AHN Estado, leg. 3884, exp. 15, doc. 4; LbkCs in French and English in JP, CSmH, PCC 110, I; C in JJ to McKean, 3 Oct. 1781.

[5]Notes of a conference held at San Ildefonso between Floridablanca and JJ, 19 Sept. 1781, LbkC in JP; C in JJ to McKean, 3 Oct. 1781.

[6]Draft treaty, San Ildefonso, 22 Sept. 1781: ADS and Spanish trans. in AHN Estado, leg. 3884, exp. 13, docs. 3, 4. C in French in CP E 605: 420–25. C in JJ to McKean, 3 Oct. 1781. LbkCs in CSmH, JP, PCC 110, I. JJ's covering letter, 22 Sept. 1781: LS in Brockholst Livingston's hand and Spanish trans. in AHN Estado, leg. 3884, exp. 13, docs. 2, 5. C in French in CP E 605: 420–25. C in JJ to McKean, 3 Oct. 1781. LbkCs in CSmH, JP, PCC 110, I.

[7]JJ to McKean, 3 Oct. 1781.

To Floridablanca

St. Ildefonso, 3 September 1781

Sir,

When I consider that the delicate state of your Excellency's health demands a greater degree of leisure and relaxation than the various business of your Office will permit, it is with great reluctance that I can prevail upon myself, to remind your Excellency that since our conference at Aranjuez, the Affairs of the United States at this Court, have made no progress.[1]

The short residence of his Majesty at Madrid, I am persuaded, made it necessary to postpone the discussion of these Affairs to this place, and since my arrival here on the 4th August last, I have daily flattered myself with being enabled to communicate to Congress his Majesty's pleasure on the important subjects, which, by their Order, I have had the honor of laying before your Excellency.

It has also for some time past been my duty to have requested your Excellency's attention to some other objects, which, though of less public importance, are nevertheless interesting to Individuals, as well as to the commercial Intercourse of the two Countries, but it did not appear to be consistent with the respect due to your Excellency to solicit your attention to new Objects while the former remained undispatched for want of time.

It would give me great pleasure to have it in my power to regulate all my applications by your Excellency's convenience, and though I am happy to see the connection between our two Countries daily encreasing, yet as that circumstance will naturally render necessary applications to Government more frequent, I fear the duties of my situation will often press me to be troublesome to your Excellency.

On Friday Evening last I received some important dispatches from Congress,[2] which I shall do myself the honor of communicating at any time which your Excellency may be pleased to name. The Gentleman who brought them,[3] will after passing on to Paris, return immediately to Philadelphia, and will, with pleasure, execute any Orders which your Excellency may honor him with, for either of those places. His stay here will be but short. As soon as I can ascertain the day of his departure, your Excellency shall have immediate notice of it. As Congress will naturally expect to receive by him particular information respecting their affairs here, I cannot forbear expressing how anxious I am to make him the Bearer of welcome tidings, and permit me to hope that your Excellency's sensibility will suggest an apology for the solicitude which appears in this letter.

I have the honor to be, with great Respect, Your Excellency's Most Obedient and Most Humble Servant,

JOHN JAY

LS, body of letter in Carmichael's hand, in AHN Estado, leg. 3884, exp. 15, doc. 1; C in JJ to McKean, 3 Oct. 1781; variances in *RDC,* IV, 752, and *HPJ,* II, 103–05.

[1]JJ had conferred with Floridablanca at Aranjuez on 19 and 23 May, reported in JJ to McKean, 3 Oct. 1781.

[2]JJ was alluding to dispatches including his commission as one of the peace negotiators, for which see Huntington to JJ, 5 July 1781, above. He had also learned that Robert Morris had become Superintendent of Finance and was authorized in that capacity to negotiate loans either in Spain or Portugal "in conjunction with Mr. Jay." Robert Morris to JJ, 4 July 1781, LS in JP; LbkC in PHi: Franklin I, 255 and DLC: Robert Morris, A, 27–35; C in French in AHN Estado, leg. 3884, exp. 20, doc. 2; D in Thomson's hand in JP; *RMP* I, 223–33; *RDC,* IV, 531–39. Resolution of Congress, 11 July 1781, C in CP; *JCC,* XX, 739. Morris composed the letter announcing his appointment and describing his plans in a form that could be shown to Floridablanca, as he explained in another note to JJ. Morris to JJ, 7 July 1781. LS in ViHi: LbkC in DLC: Robert Morris, A, 35–36; *RMP,* I. 250–51; *RDC,* IV, 552.

[3]David S. Franks.

To Montmorin

St. Ildefonso, 16 <Aug> September 1781

Sir,

The Paper herewith enclosed is the Draft of a Letter which I think of <addressing> writing to his Ex[cellenc]y the Count De Florida Blanca.[1]

The subject as well as the occasion < < <render> > call for much Circumspection necessary> demand that <cautious> dextrous and delicate management of which they only are capable who possess accurate Judgments and much Experience in affairs of this kind.

I am happy therefore that on such occasions I can avoid the Risque of committing Errors by recurring to your friendly advice.

Without Compliments but with Sincerity I am Sir your obliged <and obedient> Friend and Servant.

LbkCs in PCC 110, I and in CSmH; C in JJ to McKean, 3 Oct. 1781; Tr in Bancroft: American III, 162.

[1]Following letter.

To Floridablanca

Madrid, [n.d. 8–16 September 1781]

Sir,

Whatever may be the Issue of the American Revolution, whether that Country shall continue independent or be doomed to reunite her Power with that of Great Britain, the good will and affection of the People of North America <will never cease to> cannot in either Case be <of some Importance to> unimportant to their Neighbours; nor will the Impressions made upon their Minds <either> by the Benefits or the Injuries which they may recieve from other Nations in the Course of their <present Difficulties> present Struggles, ever cease <from having> to have a certain Degree of Influence on their future Conduct.

Various Circumstances led Congress, at <a very> an early period, to suppose that the Court of Spain <was> had wisely and generously determined to take a decided Part in their Favor. The Supplies granted to them by his Catholic Majesty soon after the british Armies became numerous in America, spoke this Language in strong Terms; and the assurances repeatedly given me by your Excellency, that his Majesty would firmly support their Cause, and never consent to their being reduced to the Subjection of Britain, left no Room to doubt of his friendly <Intentions and> Disposition and Intentions towards them.

Many obvious Considerations prompted Congress to desire that an intimate Connection might <be> speedily be established between the two Countries, by such Treaties <which by consulting the Interest of each <<would>> might forever be agreable and advantageous to both> as would take from the Enemy every Prospect of Success, and secure to Spain and the United States the <Bene[fit]> permanent Enjoyment of mutual advantages and reciprocal Attachment. With this

View Congress were pleased to send me to Spain, and the first Letter I had the Honor of recieving from your Excellency, gave me Reason to believe that the Object of my Mission was not displeasing to his Majesty. Unavoidable and long Delays were nevertheless created by <the Demands of Spain respecting a certain <<import[ant]>> Point, which America considered very interesting to obtain> Differences respecting a certain <article> <Claim in which both Parties> important Right which America wished to retain. So strong however was the Reliance of Congress on his Majesty's Assurances of Support, and such was their Disposition to render the proposed Treaties consistent with his Inclinations, that they have since agreed to remove the only Obstacle which seemed to prevent his Majesty from realizing those Assurances by substantial Aids, and an open Declaration of his Intentions.

But, unfortunately for America and perhaps for the general Cause, the Delays in Question have not ceased with the Causes to which they were ascribed <Your Excellency still forbears to inform me> and although the Confidence reposed by Congress in his Majesty's Assurances, will not permit them to doubt of his Determination to support their Independence; yet <it <<must>> would appear to them very singular, that> the silent Inattention with which their offers <made> to remove the former Obstacle<s> to a Treaty, <and their Requests that [we] be informed of his Majesty's Pleasure in the Subject, should <<so long remain unansw[ered]>> recieve no other Answer, <<but>> <<that what>> may be inferred from the profound Silence observed on this important Subject, and that,

Had I[t] <<been>> been in my Power to obtain the Honor of a Conference with your Excellency on that, or any other <<Bus[iness]>> American affair tho your Excellency had <<often>> from Time to Time promised me to name a Day for the Purpose> have long lain unanswered <be> <cannot be> must appear to them <as> as being very singular. Your Excellency has indeed <for more than nine weeks pro[mised]> repeatedly promised me to name a Time when I should have an opportunity of conferring with you on that and other Subjects <which press[ed]> submitted <forward[ed]> to your Consideration, <but it has as often happened that others> <but> <and> but it constantly happened that the Expectations excited by These Promises proved abortive.

<I most sincerely wish that all <<that>> my Letters <<I write>> to Congress may <<be>> <<contain such Facts only>> bear witness to the Wisdom, Candor and Amity of his Majesty and his

Ministers, and that nothing may ever drop from us.

It would mortify me exceedingly <<that>> if it should not be in my Power to communicate to Congress in my Letters by Major Franks any more welcome Intelligence than tedious> Knowing that Congress would expect me to recieve by the Return of Major Franks particular Information respecting their Affairs here, I was anxious <to avoid the Necessity of sending> to send <nothing> them some Intelligence more welcome than <I have Reason> I have Reason to think a Detail of <these> Delays and Procrastinations, <and that too> would be at a Season, when they <are> would be indulging the most flattering Expectations from the Measures they had taken to gratify his Majesty. For this Reason I <have hitherto> informed your Ex[cellenc]y that I <should> detained Major Franks for the present, and your Excellency promised me <last Saturday Evening> on the 8 Inst.[1] that you would <in the Course of this> appoint some Time in the ensuing Week <appoint when we should> for entering into a serious Conference about these Matters, and that Mr. Del Campo should give me Notice of it. That Week however <<is now>> <will> end<<ed>> to Night and has be> has passed away without having been Witness to <the> any such <Appointment> Notice or Conference.

I think your Excellency will do me the Justice to acknowledge that the utmost Respect, Delicacy and Patience have been observed in all my Transactions with your Excellency, and therefore I cannot forbear <thinking> hinting that my Constituents are at least entitled to that Species of Attention which <among civilized Nations is never withheld from those who make friendly Propositions in> the most dignified Sovereigns usually pay to the friendly Propositions of such States as sollicit either their aid or alliance in a decent Manner, <and<<particularly>> <especially> in Cases such Sollicitations had been previously encouraged by Royal> vizt. a candid Answer.

I am <well> sensible that Spain possesses a higher Degree on the Scale of national Importance than the United States, and I can readily admit that the Friendship of this Court is of more immediate Consequence to America, than that of America to the spanish Empire; but as his Catholic Majesty and his Ministers doubtless extend their Views beyond the present Moment, it would ill become me to remark how essential it is to the Happiness of neighbouring Nations that <they> their Conduct towards each other should be actuated <by only> by such Passions and Sentiments only, as naturally tend to establish and perpetuate Harmony and good Will between them. Most certain it is that <some consequences, good or evil, must necessarily

flow> in whatever Manner the Negociations between Spain and north America may terminate, <important> various <certain> good or evil Consequences <will necessarily flow> at <interesting to both> <must> will in future naturally and necessarily flow from it to both.

<America has long and assiduously cultivated the <<Friendship>> Alliance of his C[atholic] M[ajesty]. She is now ready to go great Lengths to obtain it, and the flattering Assurances she has recieved have excited sanguine Expectations, <<and>> If therefore these Negociations should end like a Dream, <<I fear>> there is Reason to apprehend that the Interpretations of it would <<not be a Prophetic of Evils>> <<[not be] a Prophecy of good>> not. <<Similar Causes will produce Similar>>

For my own Part I am <<most>> sincerely desirous to see the Seeds of future P[eace] and mutual good Will planted and cultivated in both Countries, and <<should be happy>> that the Annals of America may inform succeeding Generations <<how much they are>> that <<the Success of the present Revolution was owing to>> the Wisdom, Constancy and generous <<Policy>> Protection of his Catholic Majesty of Charles the 3d <<of Spain>> and of his Principal Minister of State the Count De Florida Blanca, are to be ranked among the Causes <<which>> that ensured Success to a Revolution which <<will always be>> <<will>> Posterity will <<certainly have Reason to>> concieve as one of the most important and interesting Events in modern History.>

There is good Reason to believe that the <indec[ision]> apparent Indecision of Spain relative to an open acknowledgment of the Independence of the United States has <had and continues to have <<great Influence>> an <<unforseen>> Unfavorable Influence on the Councils <<Conduct of>>> inspired other Nations <and <<there is>> it is> <very unfavorable to <<a>> the Am[erican] Cause> with Doubts and Conjectures unfavorable to the American Cause, and on the other Hand it is also more than probable that if his Catholic Majesty would <openly Honor us with his Protection and> be pleased to declare to the World that <he had honor> the United States were his Allies, and that he had given his royal Word to support their Independence, that <all Europe> Holland and many other Nations would follow his Example, <and thereby> <and a Period be thereby> <put the War on Terms> <On such an Event>

<Since therefore it is in the Power of Spain by a Measure worthy of <<the>> such a Sovereign, to, <<command the gratitude>> <<reign>> command in the Hearts and Affections of a rising Na-

tion, and < <thereby not only give new and warm Friends to his Crown and People, but> > and restore the Blessing of Peace to us.>

On such an Event also <I should suppose it> it might not be difficult to form a permanent Alliance between France, Spain, <Holland> the Dutch and the United States, and thereby not only prevent a seperate Peace between the <English and> Dutch and English, but effectually reduce the latter to <such> reasonable Terms of general Pacification.

The Limits of a Letter forbid my enlarging on these Topics. The Eyes of America and indeed of all Europe are turned towards Spain. It is in the Power of his Catholic Majesty to increase his Friends and humble his Enemies. I will only add my most sincere Wishes that the Annals of America may inform succeeding Generations, that the Wisdom, Constancy and generous Protection of his Catholic Majesty Charles the 3d and of his Minister the Count De Florida Blanca are to be ranked among the Causes <which> that ensured Success to a Revolution which Posterity will consider as one of the most important and interesting Events in Modern History.

Dft. Endorsed by Henry Brockholst Livingston: "San Ildefonso, Dr. Letter to the Ct. de F. Blanca; Ent. p. 9" (pp. 9–12 of JJ Lbk VI, in Brockholst Livingston's hand, in JP). Endorsed by JJ: "Not sent." C in JJ to McKean, 3 Oct. 1781; LbkCs in JP, CSmH, and PCC 110, I. *HPJ*, II, 109–13 and *RDC*, IV, 754–56, omit Dft deletions as well as paragraphs 5, 6, 8, 9, and 11.

[1]See JJ to McKean, 3 Oct. 1781.

To Thomas McKean

St. Ildefonso, 20 September 1781

Sir,

Your Excellency's Favor of the 5th July last, with the papers therewith enclosed, were delivered to me on the 29th ultimo by Major Franks, WHOM THE PROCRASTINATION OF the MINISTER STILL OBLIGES ME TO DETAIN.

The new Commissions with which Congress have honored me, argue a Degree of Confidence which demands my warmest acknowlegments, and which so far as it may be founded on an opinion of my zeal or integrity, they may be assured will not prove misplaced.

At the commencement of the present trouble, I determined to devote myself, during the continuance of them, to the Service of my Country in any station in which she might think proper to place me. THIS RESOLUTION, FOR the FIRST TIME, NOW EMBARRASSES ME. I KNOW IT TO be my duty, as a public servant, to be guided by my own Judgment only in matters referred to my discretion, and in other cases faithfully to execute my instructions without questioning the policy of them. But there is one among those which accompanies these commissions, which occasions sensations I never before experienced, and induced me to wish my name had been omitted.

So far as personal pride and reluctance to humiliation may render this appointment contra agreeable, I view it as a very unimportant circumstance and should Congress, on any occasion, think it for the public good, to place me in a station inferior and subordinate to the one I now hold, they will find me ready to descend from the one, and cheerfully undertake the duties of the other. My ambition will always be more gratified in being useful than conspicuous, for in my opinion the solid dignity of a man depends less on the height or extent of the sphere allotted to him than on the manner in which he may fulfil the duties of it.

But Sir, as an American, I feel an interest in the dignity of my country, which renders it difficult for me to reconcile myself to the idea of the Sovereign independent States of America, submitting in the persons of their ministers to be absolutely governed by the advice and opinions of the servants of another Sovereign, especially in a case of such national importance.

That gratitude and confidence are due to our allies, is not to be questioned, and that it will probably be in the power of France almost to dictate the terms of peace for us is but too true. That such extraordinary extent of confidence may stimulate to the highest efforts of generous friendship in our favor, is not to be denied, and that this instruction recieves some appearance of policy from this consideration must be admitted.

I must nevertheless take the liberty of observing that however our situation may in the opinion of Congress render it necessary to relax their demands on every side, and even to direct their commissioners ultimately to concur (if nothing better could be done) in any peace or truce not subversive of our independence, which France determined to accede to, yet that this instruction, besides breathing a degree of complacency not quite Republican, puts it out of the power of your ministers to improve those chances and opportunities, which in the course of human affairs, happen more or less frequently unto all men. Nor is it clear that America, thus casting herself into the arms of the King of France, will advance either her interest, or reputation, with that or other nations.

WHAT THE SENTIMENTS OF MY COLLeagues, ON THIS OCCASION, MAY BE, I DO NOT AS YET KNOW, NOR CAN I FORESee HOW FAR THE NEGOTIATION OF THE ENSUING WINTER MAY CALL FOR THE executION OF THIS COMMISSION. THUS CIRCUMSTANCED AT SUCH A distance from AMERICA IT WOULD NOT BE PROPER TO decline THIS APPointMENT. I WILL thereFORE DO MY BEST en-dEAVORS TO FULFIL THE expectATIONS OF CONGRESS ON THIS SUBJECT, BUT AS FOR MY OWN PART I THINK IT IMprobable that SERIOUS NEGOTIATIONS FOR PEACE WILL SOON TAKE PLACE. I MUST ENtreat CONGRESS TO TAKE AN EARLY opportunity of releiving ME FROM A STATION WHERE IN CHARACTER OF THEIR MINISTER, I MUST NECESSARILY receive (AND ALMOST UNDER THE NAME OF Opinions) THE DIRECTIONS OF those ON WHOM I REally THINK NO AMERI-CAN MINISTER OUGHT TO BE dependANT, AND TO WHOM, IN LOVE FOR OUR COUNTRY and ZEAL FOR HER Service, I AM SURE THAT MY COLLEAGUES, AND MYSELF, ARE AT LEAST EQUAL.

I have the Honor to be with great Respect, Your Excellency's most obedient and most humble Servant

JOHN JAY

P.S. I HAD AN INTERView LAST EVENING WITH THE MINISTER. NOTHING WAS PROMISED OR DENIED. A PERSON[1] is TO BE NAMED ON SUNDAY[2] TO CONFER *IN EARNEST*, AS IS SAID, WITH ME ABOUT THE TREATIES. I DO NOT DESPAIR, THOUGH HAVING SO MANY BILLS TO PAY, AND NO MONEY, PERPLEXES ME EXTREMELY. THE TREASURY OF SPAIN is VERY LOW, MUCH OF THE MONEY FOR THEIR EX-PENSES THIS WAR, COSTS THEM BETWEEN THIRTY AND FORTY PER HUNDRED, BY BAD MISmanagement, and WANT OF CREDIT. THIS OUGHT NOT TO BE PUBLIC. HIS EXCELLENCY STILL LOOKS AT YOUR SHIPS ON THE STOCKS BUT I SHALL, WITHOUT REFUSING, NOT CONSENT TO THEIR changing MASTERS.

LS, in Carmichael's hand, in PCC 89, I, 369–70, utilizing the Thomson code of 11 July 1781. LS (2) in PCC Misc. LbkCs in JP (2), CSmH, PCC 89, I, 371–75 and 110, I; minor verbal differences in *RDC,* IV, 716–18. For the reception of this letter in Congress, see below, Livingston to JJ, 13 Dec. 1781.

[1]Bernardo del Campo; see *JJ,* I, 775.

[2]23 September.

FROM ELBRIDGE GERRY

Marblehead, 20 September– 9 October 1781

Dear Sir,

Agreable to your Excellency's Request of the 18th of November last,[1] which I have lately received, I inclose the Constitution of this

State, together with a News Paper containing the latest political Intelligence.

Since the Arrival of the Fleet of our allies at Virginia, We have a favorable Prospect of a happy Issue to the present Campaign, and I flatter myself that You will soon have the Pleasure of hearing of the Capture of Lord Cornwallis and his Army, and of the Removal of the Enemy from every Part of the southern States.

The Failure of the old continental Currency has nearly prevented a Circulation of the new, and I wish not to see either revive, as Specie is every Day increasing amongst us by publick as well as private Importations, which being greatly promoted by the Scarcity of Medium, must soon produce a competent Supply. Our Adventures in privateering have suffered since last Spring, by repeated Losses, notwithstanding which, We are furnished by those that are successful, as well as by Means of our Commerce, with a plentiful Supply of every Article of foreign Produce, insomuch that the best Sugars are now sold at 40/ lawful Specie per hundred, Coffee 8d and Cotton 16 per pound, the best of madeira 50 Dollars per *pipe,* which is less than half it's Cost, Salt 6/ per bushell, and other Articles in the same Proportion.

We have had in this Quarter, and I believe throughout America, as plentiful an Harvest as ever was known, which has reduced the prices of provisions here lower than they were last War, and at the same Time increased our Resources so as to enable us to finish the Campaign without being sensible of the Expences thereof.

In addition to these Advantages, the Powers of Congress, in Consequence of the Ratification of the Confederacy,[2] and the vigorous Exertion of Government on the several States, have produced the most salutary Effects, and convinced the People that We have not only Resources for continuing the War, but also the Power of drawing them forth in Quantities equal to the most pressing Necessities. Difficulties will nevertheless occur in so arduous an Undertaking as We are engaged in, but those are of a short Duration and serve as a political School for Improvement.

From this State of Facts, it is hardly possible to conceive that our Enemies should buoy themselves up with Hopes of reaping advantages by prosecuting the War, but they seem to be devoted to Destruction and verily the Maxim "Quem Deus vult perdere, prius dementat."[3]

Pray give my best Respects to your Lady, Mr. Carmichael, and your Family, and be assured that I remain Sir with every sentiment of respect your Excellency's very humble Servant,

E. GERRY

9 October 1781

Dear Sir,

I have deferred the inclosing a Duplicate, in Expectation of authentic Advice, from the Southard, but none have yet arrived. We have nevertheless every Reason to expect, from the superior Force of our Allies at Sea, the Strength of the allied Army in Virginia, and the Advantage gained by the former agreable to Rivington's Account over Admiral Graves, that Cornwallis with his Army will be captured and that Charlestown will be immediately evacuated, or share a similar Fate.[4]

I remain as before your Excellency's very humble Servant,

E. G.

Duplicate ALS in MHi: Gerry-Knight. Endorsed: ". . . Recd. 26 Nov. 1781." Enclosure: noted in JJ Ledger as received. Tr in NN: Bancroft: American III, 126b.

[1]Above.

[2]The Articles of Confederation were ratified on 1 March 1781. *JCC,* XIX, 208.

[3]"Whom the Gods would destroy, they first make mad."

[4]De Grasse's fleet reached Chesapeake Bay on 26 August, inflicting substantial damage (5 September) on Admiral Thomas Graves' fleet en route from New York to protect Cornwallis. De Grasse's maneuvers with the enemy for several days off the coast of Virginia and North Carolina induced Graves to turn back toward New York on the night of 9–10 September, leaving the French in control of the entrance to Chesapeake Bay, where, by bottling up Cornwallis at Yorktown, they insured his eventual capitulation on 19 October.

To Gouverneur Morris

St. Ildefonso, 28 September 1781

Dear Morris,

My last to you was of the 24th Ult. Triplicates have been sent. I have recieved none from you later than 10 July by Major Franks. Yours of the 2d January and 4 March never reached me.[1] There is Reason to believe that <minister> THE PRIME MINISTER HERE HAS THEM. Tell me what you think of MY LETTER TO <the President> CONGRESS OF THE [———][2] <Inst.> OF THIS MONTH. Peace does not appear very nigh. THIS COURT AND THAT OF FRANCE DO NOT DRAW perfectly well. Except A JEW, I CAN HEAR OF nothing SO perfectly ODIOUS TO A Spaniard AS A FRENCHMAN. THIS GOVERNMENT HAS little MONEY, LESS WISDOM, NO CREDIT, NOR ANY

RIGHT TO IT. <they have Pride without Dignity, Cunning without Policy, Nobility without Honor> I speake with Certainty; WHAT NEW MEN <may> MIGHT DO IS UNCERTAIN. YOUR BILLS HAVE DONE MUCH MISCHIEF. THE KING MEANS WELL BUT KNOWS NOTHING. VATTEL'S LAW OF NATIONS[3] WHICH I FOUND QUOTED IN a Letter from CONGRESS IS PROHIBITED HERE. <I confide in your Prudence and Secrecy.>

Some of your letters have you say been drowned; do you suppose that none of mine have <shared that> miscarried. You would have given me some interesting Intelligence, if my Letters had been less laconic. Is this like You? This Sentiment, if <it deserves that Name> I may call it so has indeed flowed from your Pen, but I am sure your Heart <had no Concern in> did not dictate it. I CONFIDE IN YOUR Prudence AND SECRECY. YOU DESIRE ME TO SAVE YOU THE TROUBLE OF Repetitions, BY MAKING AND IN TURN recieving Communications. THIS PLAN WOULD ONCE HAVE DONE, BUT THAT TIME is passed—FOREVER. I <told> WROTE YOU SO <before the last> IN JUNE 1780, THE LETTER ARRIVED <safe> at PHILADELPHIA, <to my certain knowledge> BUT I NOW FIND YOU HAVE NEVER SEEN IT[4]; AS IT WAS IN CYPHERS THE INSPECTOR GAINED NO INFORMATION FROM IT. WHILE WE <continue to> HAVE FULL CONFIDENCE IN EACH OTHER <I am persuaded that> NEITHER WILL BE DECIEVED. TO GIVE YOU DETAILS WOULD BE TO WRITE A HISTORY, BUT I WILL TELL YOU PLAINLY THAT <that Your Secretary[5] is the most decietful, insidious Man I ever met with in all my Life, and I have met with many. This I think is being confidential as well as particular. The Time may come when I shall give you more Facts than you will be pleased with> THAT THIS SAME MAN IS IN MY JUDGMENT, THE MOST FAITHLESS AND DANGEROUS ONE, THAT I HAVE EVER MET WITH, IN ALL MY LIFE. THIS IS STRONG LANGUAGE, BUT TWENTY TWO MONTHS CONSTANT EXPERIENCE ASSURES ME IT IS JUST. IF I COULD HAVE TRUSTED MY CYPHERS WHEN AT MARTINICO I WOULD FROM THENCE HAVE <written to you of this Subject> GIVEN YOU A HINT OF HIS SHAMEFUL DUPLICITY AND UNKIND CONDUCT. TO DO HIM HARM IS NOT MY WISH, revenge NEVER HAS NOR EVER SHALL, ACTUATE ME, BUT HAPPY SHALL I BE TO SEE THE DAY WHEN I SHALL <cease to> <and to have any Thing to do with him> NO MORE BE PLAGUED WITH HIS TRICKS.[6]

THERE IS SOMETHING VERY DISAGREABLE IN THUS MENTIONING MATTERS OF THIS SORT, especially considering HOW YOU STAND WITH RESPECT TO BOTH.

I am very much inclined to think that THIS COURT MEANS IF possible TO DELAY FORMING ANY political Connections WITH US TILL A GENERAL PEACE, THEREBY AVOIDING <the Loans and Subsidies> ADVANCES OF MONEY WHICH <in Reality> THEY ARE NOT <in Capacity> VERY ABLE TO

MAKE, <and as well as> A PRECEDENT WHICH MAY ONE DAY BE TURNED AGAINST THEM BY THEIR OWN COLONIES. < < <they remaining free from Engage toward Engagements> > toward Engagements to avail themselves of Contingencies, and> THEY wish also, BY FREEDOM FROM ENGAGEMENTS, TO BE READY to take Advantage of CIRCUMSTANCES. AS TO PAROLE Promises OF THE MINISTERS, THEY PASS HERE AS continentAL DOES WITH YOU.[7]

I hear so Seldom from and so little of my Fathers Family, that you will oblige me greatly by mentioning from time to Time what you may know or hear about them.

The Cypher I use is No. 1, the only one I have as yet recieved. I hope, a Duplicate of it will not be sent unless by a very safe opp[ortunit]y. I am very much yours,

J. J.

Remember us to our Friends at Philadelphia. You know who they are.

DftS. JJ put the indicated portions of this letter into the nomenclator code sent to him by Morris early in July. The code numbers have been entered interlinearly without any obliteration of the text in the Dft.

[1]JJ to Morris, 24 August and Morris to JJ, 4 March, not located. For Morris to JJ, 2 Jan. 1781, see above.

[2]Left blank; it is 20 September, above.

[3]Emmerich de Vattel's *Le droit des gens, ou Principes de la loi naturelle, appliqués à la conduite et aux affaires des nations et des souverains* (1758) was cited by delegates in Congress, notably James Madison, to deny the right of a nation holding the mouth of a river to bar "innocent passage." *Peacemakers,* p. 239; also James Madison to JJ, 17 Oct. 1780, cited in n. 2 of Instructions to JJ, 4 Oct. 1780, above.

[4]JJ to Morris, June 1780, not located.

[5]William Carmichael.

[6]JJ rendered the code for the word "Tricks" incorrectly, which Morris quoted back to him in his 21 May 1782 reply, below.

[7]JJ here gives the word "parole" its meaning in law, *i.e.,* oral or not executed under seal. Thus, Spanish oral promises are as worthless to JJ as the rapidly deteriorating Continental currency was in America.

FROM EGBERT BENSON

Poughkeepsie, [30 September[1]] 1781

Dear Sir,

You will observe I have deferred my Letter til the last day of the Month, in hopes that I should have had it in my Power to communicate Intelligence as agreeable as it would have been important.

When I wrote last[2] Gen. Washington with the Allied Army was in the lower part of Westchester County, waiting, as it was generally supposed, the Arrival of the French Fleet from the West Indies in order to commence Operations against New York. I had scarcely dispatched my Letter, when We were informed that the whole Army was moving into Jersey,[3] and the Arrival of Count De Grasse in the Chesapeak a few days after unfolded the Design of this Movement, and it was then discovered that the Capture of Lord Cornwallis with his Army in Virginia was its Object. Our Army made a rapid March to that State and reached the Head of Elks, where they embarked the 8th Inst., and at this time they have compleatly surrounded his Lordship, who occupies Gloucester and York, the former on the north and the latter on the South side of York River, and his Strength is estimated at 6,000 regulars and 2,000 Negroes.[4] Indeed it is the only operating Army of the Enemy on the Continent, as they have not more than competent Garrisons at New York, Charlestown, and Savannah, the only Places they now hold within the Territory of the United States.

Whether this Change, from the supposed intended Plan of Operations for the Campaign, was the Effect of Choice or Necessity, I will not determine, but should the present Enterprise prove successful it must inevitably produce Consequences decisive in our Favor. This Movement of the Army reflects the highest Honor on our General, as neither the Country nor the Enemy at New York, knew his Design til he had crossed the Delaware. Cornwallis was certainly unapprised of his Intentions, or he would doubtless have seasonably retired to South Carolina. Gen. Washington's Force, French and Americans, is at least 15,000 regular troops,[5] and Count De Grasse has with him in the Chesapeak, including the Squadron heretofore at Rhode-Island, 35 Ships of the Line,[6] and the British have about 20 at New York, so that there is scarcely a possible Releif for Cornwallis.

On Monday next our new Legislature meet, and the Election of Delegates will be as interesting as any other Business of the Session. It is difficult to form even a remote Guess who will be elected, though I think it probable there will be a Change, not so much from a Dislike to the Persons who compose the present Delegation, as to meet the Wishes of the Inhabitants of that part of the State which is not within the Power of the Enemy, who have expressed their Uneasiness that the State should be represented wholly by *Refugees.*[7]

Possibly before this reaches You Mr. Robert R. Livingston may have informed You that he is appointed by Congress Minister for Foreign Affairs. Should Mr. Livingston accept this Appointment and resign the Chancellorship I imagine it will in the first instance be offered to Mr. Duane.[8]

Your Father and the rest of the Family here are in statu quo; a disagreeable Incident however has happened. Mrs. Jay is gone to the City of New York on a Visit to her Freinds.[9] She went by the way of New Jersey and it is suggested without the Permission of our Governor, and as the Commissioners for Conspiracies have always *dealt* with Persons, Citizens of this State, who have gone under such Circumstances, She will find it difficult to return with Impunity. Except a Regret at this Affair the Family are comfortable and happy. Master Jay, the Solace of his Grandpapa, is still here. My best respects to *Your* Mrs. Jay. I am sincerely Yours,

EGBT. BENSON

ALS. Endorsed: ". . . Recd. 7 Decr. ansd. 8 Do."

[1]Benson misdated this letter 30 October.

[2]No letters from Benson to JJ between 4 Sept. 1779 and 30 Sept. 1781 have been located.

[3]On 21 August Washington's army crossed the Hudson, then, feinting toward Staten Island, struck out southward across New Jersey.

[4]Similarly, the Patriots enlisted substantial numbers of blacks. A foreign officer, who visited the White Plains headquarters on 4 July 1781, noted that the blacks composed a quarter of the army there assembled. Evelyn M. Acomb, ed., *The Revolutionary Journal of Baron Ludwig von Closen, 1780–1783* (Chapel Hill, N.C., 1958), p. 89. Some blacks served with the infantry or artillery, but most were body servants or engaged in labor, wagon, commissary, or forage service. For their role on both the American and British sides, see also Benjamin Quarles, *The Negro in the American Revolution* (Chapel Hill, N.C. 1961).

[5]The combined Franco-American forces numbered approximately 14,845, of whom 8,845 were American. Ward, *The War of the Revolution* II, 886–87.

[6]De Grasse had 24 ships of the line and six frigates, combined with the Newport fleet of about eight ships of the line commanded by Comte Melchior Saint-Laurent de Barras. *Ibid.,* p. 885.

[7]On 26 Oct. 1781 the New York State legislature elected its new Congressional delegation of James Duane, William Floyd, John Morin Scott, Ezra L'Hommedieu, and Benson himself. This delegation was identical to that of 1780 with the exception of Benson, a Dutchess County lawyer, who replaced Alexander McDougall, a "refugee" from British-occupied New York City—a slender victory for the long-time upstate residents. Benson did not attend Congress in 1781 or 1782. *JCC,* XVII, 892; XXI, 1132; See *JJ,* I, 281, 655 for Floyd and L'Hommedieu.

[8]For Livingston's election as Secretary for Foreign Affairs, see his 20 Oct. 1781 letter to JJ, below. Livingston kept his position as Chancellor.

[9]Frederick Jay, a member of the New York State legislature, requested General Washington's and Governor Clinton's permission for his wife's visit to friends and relatives in Yonkers, behind British lines. Clinton deferred to Washington's judgment, but it is unclear whether the General granted permission. For Frederick Jay's letter to Clinton and the Governor's reply, see *PPGC,* VII, 116–17.

To Thomas McKean

St. Ildefonso, 2 October 1781

Sir,

The Esteem and Regard I entertain for your worthy Predecessor, lead me greatly to regret the Indisposition which rendered his Resignation indispensable, though I am persuaded, that the same laudable Principles which actuated his Successor, while on the Bench, will continue to do Honor to his Conduct, in the Chair.[1]

I congratulate You Sir! on this Appointment. It is a distinguished mark of the Confidence of your Country, and will afford you further Opportunities of manifesting that attachment to her Interest, which has, on so many occasions, recommended You to the Choice of your Fellow Citizens.

I have the Honor to be, with Sentiments of Respect and Esteem, Your Excellency's most obedient and most humble Servant,

JOHN JAY

ALS in PHi: McKean, II, 27. Addressed: "His Excellency Thomas McKean Esqr., President of Congress, Philadelphia." Endorsed.

[1]McKean was in 1777 commissioned Chief Justice of Pennsylvania, the post to which JJ is alluding. McKean held his judicial post while serving as President of Congress, 10 July–5 Nov. 1781.

From Robert R. Livingston

Philadelphia, 20 October 1781

Dear John,

You will receive with this an official Letter informing you of my appointment to the Secretaryship for foreign affairs.[1] If there is any thing peculiarly pleasing to me in this appointment to compensate for the difficulties with which it is attended it must be found in that new bond by which it unites our publick, as a much earlier and more agreeable one has our private characters. My publick Letters will keep you fully informed of our news and our politicks; my private correspondence shall be consecrated to such matters as are important to ourselves only and those effusions of the heart which I wish to indulge till care or age render me incapable of them.

Before I left the State I called to see your father. I found him chearful and serene as ever though labouring under all the infirmities of age. He took peculiar pleasure in bringing our children together, conversed with some vivacity with Mrs. Livingston about them, and in your promising boy seemed in some measure to console himself for your absence. Your Brother Peter[2] retains his health, and all his affection for you, most ardently wishing your return.

Having but this day qualified, I am not yet let in to the arena of politicks nor have I even seen your last letters, some members having taken them out of the hand of the committee.[3] I shall correspond with you in Mr. Thompsons cypher sent by Mr. Franks as we have heard of his arrival at Cadiz. I could wish you to be as particular as you think prudent in your publick Letters, and to venture even upon imprudence in your private ones, as I think you may rely upon your cypher. Let us know every thing that passes in Holland. Our Minister there is zealous and laborious BUT I WILL NOT ANSWER FOR HIS PRUDENCE. TRULY HIS DISPLAY OF HIS PUBLIC CHARACTER, WHEN EVERY THING WAS AGAINST IT CAN NOT be accounted for on principles that will do him honor. But I am sliding into politicks contrary to my determination. We have both too much of them. Let me remind you that you are in my debt for a Letter written two months since.[4] Offer my compliments to Mrs. Jay and the Gentlemen of your family and believe me to be most sincerely your Friend and Humble Servant,

ROB. R. LIVINGSTON

ALS. Addressed: "The Honble John Jay, Esqr., Madrid." Endorsed: ". . . Recd. under Covr from Marquis de la Fayette, 24 Feb. 1782, pr[ivate] not dec[ode]d." Enclosure (not located): "copy Entry of Mr. Livingstons appt. 10 Augt. 1781," as entered in JJ's Ledger, in JP. DftS in NHi: Robert R. Livingston; E in NN: Bancroft: Robert R. Livingston. Livingston's ciphered passage was intended to utilize the Thomson cipher sent to JJ on 11 July 1781 (in JP), but Thomson mistakenly gave a variation of it, which was lost at sea with Colonel Palfrey; see also below, 13 Dec. 1781, Livingston to JJ. As indicated by JJ's endorsement, he was unable to understand the cryptogram, which is deciphered here from Livingston's DftS.

[1]Livingston took the oath of office as Secretary for Foreign Affairs on 20 October, although he had been elected to the post on 10 August. LbkC of McKean to Livingston, 11 Aug. 1781, congratulating Livingston on his election, is in PCC 16, pp. 60–61. McKean had also enclosed the 10 August Congressional resolution on Livingston's appointment. See *JCC,* XXI, 851–52.

[2]JJ's blind brother; *JJ,* I, 32, 33.

[3]The matter concerns finances, especially as in JJ's letter of 28 Jan. 1781 to President Huntington, above, as well as his 6 and 30 Nov. 1780 dispatches (cited in "Issues in Negotiation," n. 2, and in JJ to Gerry, 18 Nov. 1780, above). After the Congressional committee (James Duane, Edmund Randolph, John Mathews, Elias Boudinot, Roger Sherman) which had conferred with Luzerne reported in Congress on 15 Oct. 1781, Congress ordered that Adams', JJ's, and John Laurens' letters concerning American finances be referred to Superintendent of Finance Morris. *JCC,* XXI, 1052–53.

[4]Livingston's letter prior to this date which has been located is 22 July 1781, DftS in NHi: Robert R. Livingston.

To George Clinton

Madrid, 16 November–11 December 1781
Duplicate

Dear Sir,

The last, and indeed only Letter I have had the pleasure of recieving from you is dated the 6 april last. I wrote to you on the 26 September by Major Franks.[1]

If my Friends in your State knew how much pleasure it gives me to hear of, and recieve Letters from them, and I flatter myself they would give me less Reason to complain of Inattention.

We have long been kept in Suspence about the real State of our affairs with you, having had no direct and certain Intelligence from america since July last. Various Reports of good and bad Fortune have in the mean Time spread through this Country. At present we are told that Gen. Greene has defeated the Enemy to the Southward and captured the 19th Regiment,[2] that Lord Cornwallis's Entrenchments have been carried by assault and himself killed,[3] that Digby's Squadron had fallen into the Hands of Monsieur Barras, and consequently that Greaves cannot make Head against De Grasse.[4] God grant that all this may be true, and that Victory may ever support the Standard of Justice and Liberty.

Fort St. Philip continues besieged by about 16,000 french and Spaniards. How long it may hold out is uncertain.[5]

The approaching Winter will give occasion to various Speculations and Conjectures respecting the Probability and Terms of a general Peace. For my own part, I expect at least one more Campaign, unless our Successes in America should be much more decisive than I can yet flatter myself they will be, considering the advanced Season in which Count De Grasse arrived. To all appearance, Britain can only be delivered from her strong Delusions respecting america by repeated Losses and Defeats.

It gives me much pleasure to hear that G. Morris would probably be in your Delegation this Fall.[6] Independent of my Regard for him, it appears to me of great Importance to the State, that every valuable man in it should be preserved, and that it is particularly our Interest to cultivate cherish and support all such of our Citizens, especially young and rising ones, as are or promise to be able and honest Servants of the public.

Mrs. Jay presents her Compliments to you and Mrs. Clinton. Be pleased to add mine, and believe me to be, Dear Sir, Your Friend and Servant,

JOHN JAY

P.S. Be so kind as to forward the enclosed,[7] and as I scarce ever hear from my Father's Family, you will oblige me by writing me now and then what you may know or hear of them.

Madrid, 11 December 1781

Dear Sir,

I congratulate You on the Surrender of Lord Cornwallis, a most joyful and important Event.[8] We are waiting with Impatience to hear what Effect it has on the british Court, and whether it will abate their Pride, or excite them to still more vigorous Efforts. I hope our Country will prepare for the latter. Adieu, I am yours etc.,

J. J.

Duplicate ALS in NN: Emmet 2620. Addressed: "(to be sunk in case of capture), His Excellency George Clinton Esqr., Governor of the State of New York. Poughkeepsie." Endorsed by JJ. DftS in JP; *HPJ,* II, 146–48, omits the 11 December note.

[1]Clinton to JJ, 6 April 1781. JJ's slip of the pen; his letter to Clinton was dated 28 Sept. 1781. Dft in JP.

[2]JJ's information was inaccurate. The battle of Eutaw Springs (8 September) was a technical victory for the British forces under the command of Lieutenant Colonel Alexander Stuart (c. 1741–c. 1794), ending with General Greene's withdrawal, but the Americans succeeded in driving the British back to the vicinity of Charleston, paving the way for the liberation of the South.

[3]This is a reference to the Franco-British assault at Yorktown on redoubts nos. 9 and 10, led by Colonels William Deux-Ponts and Alexander Hamilton on 14 October against Cornwallis.

[4]A reference to the Battle off the Chesapeake Capes, 5 Sept. 1781, when De Grasse inflicted severe damage on the British, while Barras, arriving with his convoy from Newport, slipped into the Chesapeake on 10 September. On 14 September Graves abandoned the Virginia coast and sailed back to New York. In August 1781 British Admiral Robert Digby (1732–1814) had succeeded Thomas Graves as naval commander in chief in America.

[5]Fort Saint Philip on Minorca fell in early February 1782. Montmorin to Vergennes, 7, 25 Feb. 1782. CP E 606: 186–88, 219–20.

[6]Gouverneur Morris did not return to Congress, but continued as assistant to Superintendent of Finance Robert Morris; see above, Silas Deane to JJ, 16 June 1781, n. 6.

[7]On 11 Dec. 1781, JJ forwarded to Richard Harrison at Cádiz the Clinton letter, enclosing therein JJ to Benson, 8 Dec. 1781, below. Entry on p. 15, JJ Ledger, in JP.

[8]Following the signed capitulation on 18 October, Cornwallis' army laid down their arms the next day.

FROM ROBERT R. LIVINGSTON

Philadelphia, 28 November 1781

Dear Sir,

I wrote so fully to you not long since[1] that I should not trouble you at this time if I had not determined to omit no opportunity of Letting you hear from this side of the water and enabling you at all times to meet any falsehoods the enemy may find it politic to publish.

Since the capture of Cornwallis nothing very material has happened. The ravaging parties on the northern frontiers have been defeated with great loss by the militia. The armies have taken their stations for the winter, the French in Virginia and Mary Land, our troops on the Hudson excepting some detatchments under General St. Clair destined to reinforce General Greene. They have orders to take Wilmington in their way where the enimy have about 600 men. It is probable they will not wait the attack.[2] General Greene will have men enough to shut up the enimy but not to force their strong holds. Want of money cramps all our exertions and prevents our making a glorious winter campaign. The enimy are all shut up on two or three points of Land which is all they possess of the immense country they hope to conquer, and even these they hold by a very precarious tenure. Disaffection which has languished for sometime past died when Cornwallis surrendered.

Congress are occupied in taking measures for an active campaign and they feel themselves satisfied with every thing both at home and abroad EXCEPT THE RECEPTION YOU MEET WITH. Plain and ingenuous THEMSELVES THEY ARE astonished AT THE FINESSES OF THE COURT, THE CANDID MANNER IN WHICH FRANCE HAS TREATED WITH THEM leading THEM TO EXPECT LIKE CANDOR ELSEWHERE. THEY FEEL THEIR PRIDE HURT AT the measures OF SPAIN AND IN SPITE OF ALL THEIR attatchment to the MONARCH AND PEOPLE OF THAT COUNTRY THEY begin to talk of ceasing to APPLY WHERE THEY ARE CONSIDERED NOT AS AN INDEPENDENT PEOPLE BUT AS HUMBLE SUPPLICANTS.

Tell me seriously what your opinion [is] about being directed to GO TO PARIS. IF NO LOANS CAN BE OBTAINED, IF NO TREATY CAN BE OPENED, WHY STAY WHERE YOU [ARE] AND experience NOTHING BUT MORTIFICATION? But this is only mentioned to know your opinion in case it should become a subject of discussion here.[3] Congress have dissolved Mr. Adams's powers to make a treaty of commerce with Great Britain[4] and as you know joined you and Mr. Franklin and Mr. Lawrance in his other commission if England should at length be wise enough to wish for peace.

The Marquis De Lafayette is the bearer of this. He has promissed to convey it with safety to you and to correspond with you in such manner as to enable you to avail yourself of all the knowledge which he has acquired that may be useful to you. The resolves of which I enclose a copy shew the sense of Congress on this subject and the confidence which they very justly repose in him.[5] His aid[6] waits for this. I NEED NOT EXPLAIN THIS LETTER. Adieu my Dear Sir. Believe me to be with the highest respect and esteem, Your Most Obedient Humble Servant,

ROB. R. LIVINGSTON

Make this addition TO YOUR CYPHER: 69. 226–600; 598. 226–601; 346. 226–602; 216. 226–603; 209. 226–604; 259. 226–605.[7]

ALS (# 2) in NHi: Jay. Endorsed: ". . . Recd. 24 Feb. 1782 from marqs. de la Fayette; not dec[ode]d." Dft in NHi: Robert R. Livingston. Duplicate and quadruplicate LS in JP. Triplicate LS in NHi: Jay, endorsed as received on 15 March. LbkCs in PCC 79, I, 232–34 and in 118. Cipher passages omitted in *HPJ,* II, 153–55, and *RDC,* V, 29–30. The letter contains passages written in the variation of Thomson's nomenclator used in Livingston's 20 Oct. 1781 letter to JJ, above. JJ was unable to decode either letter. The LS and Lbk versions, executed after Livingston realized his error, employ the code for which JJ did have the key.

[1]Livingston to JJ, 1 Nov. 1781 (# 1), LS, partly in code, in NHi: Jay. Dft and RC in NHi: Robert R. Livingston. Triplicate LS in JP. LbkCs (2) in PCC 118 and in 79, I, 302–08.

[2]Shortly after Yorktown, Major General Arthur St. Clair was dispatched south with 2,000 regulars to reinforce Nathanael Greene.

[3]In his answer of 6 February, JJ acknowledged receiving on the day before the first letters from Livingston as Secretary, dated 28 Nov. and 13 Dec. 1781, saying: "I have not written you a single official letter, not having been ascertained of your having entered on the execution of your office. I have indeed sent you by more than one opportunity my congratulations on your appointment. You may rely on my writing you many Letters, private as well as official. . . . A Duplicate of my Letter of the 3d October to Congress which goes with this renders it unnecessary for me to go into particulars at present, nothing having since happened but a repetition of delays, and of consequence additional dangers to the credit of our Bills." LbkCs in CSmH, PCC 110, II; *HPJ,* II, 175; *RDC,* V, 149–50; *SDC,* VIII, 8–9. See also below, JJ to Livingston, 13 Feb. 1782.

[4]On 12 July 1781 Congress had revoked Adams' 29 Sept. 1779 commission to negotiate the commercial treaty. See *JCC,* XX, 746 and n.; *RDC,* IV, 562.

[5]See below, editorial note, "Lafayette, Jay's Self-Appointed 'Political Aide-de-Camp,' Takes on the Spaniards" and Lafayette to JJ, 15 Feb. 1783.

[6]James McHenry (1753–1816), later Secretary at War in the Washington and John Adams administrations.

[7]This is an attempt to simplify the Thomson code which Livingston began using

in his letter to JJ of 20 Oct., above, and 13 Dec. 1781, below, adding six symbols for syllables ending in "r." Livingston's passage is undecipherable, as explained in *JJ,* I, 664.

From Robert R. Livingston

Philadelphia, 13 December 1781
Triplicate

Dear Sir,

My last letter of the 28th of November sent by the Marquis de la Fayette must for the most part have been unintelligible to you, owing to an unfortunate mistake of Mr. Thomson's who delivered me a Cypher sent by Mr. Palfrey which you never received, instead of that sent by Franks. The quadruplicate enclosed is in the last, so that you will no longer be at a loss for my meaning.

Since the date of that Letter, the Enemy have thought it prudent to abandon Wilmington in North Carolina. This Post was extremely important to them, not only as it checked the Trade of that State but as it directly communicated with the disaffected Counties. For it must be confessed that though in other parts of the Continent they had only well wishers, in North Carolina they had active Partizans. These they have left to the Mercy of their Country, and abandoned as disgracefully as the capitulation of York did those of Virginia. It is not improbable that when General St. Clair joins the Southern Army, the Enemy will evacuate Savannah, as they are at present extremely weak there, and unless they reinforce from New York, may be attacked with a prospect of Success.[1] Your Letter of the 20th of September has been received, and read in Congress. They have not been pleased to direct any particular Answer thereto, so that you are to consider it as their wish that you execute the Commission with which they have invested you. I was not in Congress at the time the INSTRUCTIONS OF WHICH YOU COMPLAIN WAS GIVEN,[2] BUT HAVE HEARD IT JUSTIFIED UPON MANY PRINCIPLES WHICH arise out of our local politicks. It was done before your appointment, so that it would NOT IMPLY THE SMALLEST DISTRUST OF YOUR ZEAL OR ABILITIES. THERE WERE AND ALWAYS WILL BE A VARIETY OF DIFFERENT INTERESTS AMONG THE RESPRESENTATIVES OF SO [extended] A COUNTRY. To bring them TO CONCUR IN ONE point IN WHICH EACH MUST SACRIFICE SOMETHING WAS extremely dificult and would have been attended with the most dangerous delays as THEY THEN SUPPOSED. THEY KNEW THAT THE PEACE WAS absolutely IN THE POWER OF FRANCE AND

THEY THOUGHT IT MORE PRUDENT TO INTEREST HER generosity THAN TO GIVE HER A PLEA TO DO AS SHE CHOSE FROM OUR insisting upon WHAT SHE MIGHT DEEM UNREASONABLE, OR NOT BEING WHAT WE INSISTED UPON. You will easily see, my dear Sir, that your Abilities and Address will not be less serviceable to your Country in the management of this Business than in any other of the great Affairs in which they have hitherto been employed.

The Minister has communicated to me a letter from the Count de Vergennes,[3] expressing his Master's satisfaction AT THE CONFIDENCE REPOSED IN HIM and assuring us that NOTHING BUT THE MOST ABSOLUTE NECESSITY SHALL induce him to make the smallest sacrifice OF THE INTEREST WE HAVE ENTRUSTED TO HIS CARE, that he has no reason to conclude from the operations of the present Campaign THAT SUCH NECESSITY WILL EXIST. HE expresses great pleasure at your appointment. I ought also to tell you that Doctor Franklin has accepted the Commission with marks of Satisfaction. From Mr. Adams, we have not heard since.[4] I congratulate you upon the determination of Spain at length to open a way to a treaty, THOUGH I MUST CONFESS I HAVE NO GREAT HOPE OF SUCCESS IN IT FROM THE CHARACTER OF THE NEGOCIATOR.[5]

We wait with the utmost impatience your next dispatches, we have heard THAT YOU HAVE OFFERED THE NAVIGATION OF THE MISSISSIPPI,[6] BUT WE ARE IGNORANT UPON WHAT CONDITIONS, and what is still worse we hear that the ANSWER to this important OFFER IS DELAYED THOUGH the ground on which we stand ENABLES US TO SPEAKE IN A FIRMER TONE THAN WE HAVE DONE. You are acquainted with facts. The rest may safely be left to your Judgement, on which we have the greatest reliance. My last letter may be of use to you, if you think that SPAIN REALLY WISHES EVEN [to] BE CONNECTED WITH US and only stands ALOOF TO TAKE ADVANTAGE OF OUR NECESSITY.

You see that I neglect no opportunity of writing. I flatter myself you will be equally attentive to let us hear from you. It is not without some degree of pain that we receive our earliest Intelligence frequently from the Minister of France. I know you may retort upon us with too much justice, but I hope to give you less reason to do so in future. I send a packet of News Papers with this. I sent an other some time ago. I hope they may reach you. In one of them you will find an Ordinance of Congress which comprizes all their Resolutions with respect to Captures, and forfeits all British Goods, which have not been taken as prizes.[7] Perhaps this may make some arrangements with the Court of Spain necessary, that is if any prize Goods are reshiped from there to America.

I am, my dear Sir, with the greatest Esteem and Regard your most Obedient and humble Servant

ROB. R. LIVINGSTON

A — over signifies E, a · under, FINAL S.[8]

Triplicate LS (# 3), utilizing 11 July 1781 Thomson cipher, deciphered by JJ and entered in JJ Ledger (in JP) as received 24 March 1782. Dft in NHi: Robert R. Livingston. LS in JP, endorsed by JJ as received 5 Feb. 1782. Duplicate LS in NHi: Jay, endorsed as received 15 March 1782. LbkCs in PCC 79, I, 234–36, and 118, pp. 51–55. Quadruplicate LS not located. All ciphered portions omitted in *HPJ*, II, 163–64, and *RDC*, V, 44–46.

[1]The British evacuated Wilmington, N.C., on 14 November. St. Clair reached Greene's camp in January 1782, with limited reinforcements, and the opposing armies remained stalemated through the winter. Savannah was not evacuated until July 1782.

[2]Livingston's last term in Congress had been extended to March 1781, but he had not attended since September 1780 and did not return to Philadelphia until the autumn of 1781, when he took the oath of office as Secretary for Foreign Affairs. *LMCC*, V, ix.

[3]Vergennes to Luzerne, 7 Sept. 1781. LbkC CP EU 18; 212–17. Luzerne informed Livingston of this letter in conversations which the latter reported to Congress on 23 November. For Livingston's "Heads of an oral communication made to the Secretary by Luzerne, Minister of France," see *RDC*, IV, 859–60.

[4]For Franklin's letter to the President of Congress, 13 Sept. 1781, accepting the commission, see *Ibid.*, pp. 709–10. Adams received his copy of the new commissions on 24 August. Illness interrupted his attention to public business, however, and it was not until 15 Oct. 1781 when he wrote the President of Congress acknowledging receipt of the commission and accepting it, with considerably less enthusiasm than had Franklin. *Ibid.*, pp. 661–63, 767–68, 779–80, 776–79.

[5]Livingston's skepticism probably resulted from JJ's and Carmichael's letters to Congress in which they indicated reservations about the appointment of Del Campo, regarded as pro-British. Although Del Campo was appointed to treat with JJ in September, the appointment was not announced to JJ until 10 Dec. 1781 and the JJ-Del Campo negotiations remained a polite diplomatic fiction until JJ left Spain in 1782. For the circumstance surrounding the Del Campo appointment, see JJ to McKean, 3 Oct. 1781; also JJ to Robert R. Livingston, 28 April 1782, both cited above in "Issues in Negotiation," nn. 3 and 26. William Carmichael to the Committee for Foreign Affairs, 28 Sept. 1781, *RDC*, IV, 731–33.

[6]A reference to JJ's 3 October letter, for which see below, Livingston to JJ, 27 April 1782.

[7]Ordinance of 27 March 1781, entitled "An Ordinance relative to the capture and condemnation of prizes." *JCC*, XIX, 314–16.

[8]The postscript, decoded by the editors, which was left in both the Dft and LS versions, describes a modification in the Thomson code.

To Matthew Ridley

Madrid, 8 January 1782

Sir,

Your Favor of the 10th Ult. with the four Letters and Picture mentioned in it arrived safe this morning.[1] Be pleased to accept my thanks for your Care and Attention in forwarding them.

The Paris Gazette gave us the first certain Intelligence of the Surrender of Lord Cornwallis—a most joyful and important Event.

I am happy to hear that Mr. Morris's two Sons are safe with you in France.[2] My Regard and Esteem for that Gentleman, interest me in every thing that concerns him. It is not very probable that I shall have an Opportunity of being useful to these young Gentleman. Be pleased nevertheless to assure them of my constant Readiness to render them every Service in my Power, and you will oblige me by giving me Directions for addressing Letters to them when at Geneva. I am in the Way of hearing often from Mr. Morris, and will with Pleasure transmit to them any interesting Intelligence which I may from Time to Time have of or from the Family.

I much fear that Miss Livingston's Sollicitude for her Brother is but too well founded.[3] There is Reason to apprehend that the Report of his having been carried to England was premature.

The Terms in which my Letters make mention of you, make me regret that I had so little opportunity at Philadelphia of cultivating the acquaintance of a Gentleman so much esteemed by my Friends there.

Mrs. Jay desires me to make her Compliments to you. I am Sir with great Respect, Your most obedient and humble Servant,

JOHN JAY

ALS in PHi: Dreer. Endorsed: "Recd. Jany 25 1782, Answd. Do. 1782." Dft and C in JP.

British-born Matthew Ridley (1749–89) emigrated to Maryland in 1770 as a representative of a London business firm. He went back to England in 1775, but in 1779 he returned to Maryland, becoming involved in business ventures with French and American merchants. Acting as Robert Morris' purchasing agent in Maryland and Delaware, Ridley, in March 1781, was appointed state agent for Maryland to negotiate loans and purchase supplies in France, Spain, and Holland. He arrived in France on 20 Nov. 1781. See Herbert E. Klingelhofer, ed., "Matthew Ridley's Diary during the Peace Negotiations of 1782," *WMQ,* XX (1963), 95–133.

[1]Ridley to JJ, 10 Dec. 1781, ALS in JP; Tr. in MHi: Ridley, *HPJ,* II, 162–63. The enclosed letters to JJ that have been located, and are in JP, are from: Robert Morris, 19 October, ALS and LS; *HPJ* II, 135–37; Catharine W. Livingston, 18 October, AL; *HPJ,* II, 134–35; and Susan Livingston to SLJ, 1 Oct. 1781, ALS. JJ's reference is to the Du Simitière portrait of Catharine W. Livingston; see below, JJ to Catharine W. Livingston, 21 Jan. 1782.

[2]Robert, Jr. (1769–c. 1804) and Thomas Morris (1771–1849), sons of the financier, were entrusted to Ridley's care for the completion of their education abroad. See also below, JJ to Morris, 13 Oct. 1782.

[3]Catharine W. Livingston had asked Ridley to check on the rumor that her brother John, feared lost at sea, had been imprisoned in England; see below, William Livingston to SLJ, 21 Aug. 1781, n. 2.

To Elbridge Gerry

Madrid, 9 January 1782

Dear Sir,

I should have much wondered what could have detained my Letter mentioned in yours of 20 September[1] last so long from you had not My Correspondence been strangely interrupted ever since my arrival.

Your Constitution[2] gives me much Satisfaction. It appears to me to be upon the whole wisely formed and well digested. I find that it <places> describes your State as being in *New England* as well as in America. Perhaps it would be better if these Distinctions were <entirely forgotten> permitted to die away.

Your Predictions respecting the Fate of Lord Cornwallis have thank God! been verified. It is a glorious, joyful and important Event. Britain feels the Force of that Stroke, and other nations begin to doubt less of the Continuance of our Independence. Further Successes must <pave> prepare the Way for peace, and I hope that Victory will <rather> stimulate instead of relax our Exertions.

Although myself and my Family have most severely suffered by the continental <Currency> money, I am resigned to its Fate. Provided we preserve our Liberty and Independance I shall be content, under their auspices, in a fruitful Country and by patient Industry, a Competence may always be acquired; and I shall <always think myself a gainer when I < <exchange> > find my civil Rights secured at the Expence of my Property> never cease to prefer a little with Freedom, to oppulence without it.

Your account of the Plenty which abounds in our Country is very flattering, and ought to excite our Gratitude to the Hand that gives it. While our Governments <can prevail upon themselves to> tax <justly> wisely, reward merit, and punish <Evil> offenders we shall have little to fear. The public have <too long> been too much a Prey to <private> Peculation. Economy and strict accounts ought to be and continue among the first objects of our attention.

I have not heard any thing for a long Time respecting our disputed Lines. In my opinion few Things demand more immediate Care than this Subject, and I differ from those who think that such Matter < of this kind > had better be postponed till after the War. At present a Sense of common Danger guaranties our Union. We have neither Time nor Inclination < to wrangle > dispute among ourselves. Peace will give us Leisure, < for both > and Leisure often finds improper occasions for Employment. I most sincerely wish that no Disputes may survive the War, and that on the Return of Peace we may congratulate each other in our Deliverance, and Prospects of uninterupted Liberty, without finding ourselves exposed to Differences and Litigations < among us > which never fail to make Impressions injurious to that Courage and Confidance which both < uses > our Interest and our Duty call upon us to cultivate and cherish.

Mrs. Jay charges me to present her Compliments to You. I am Dear Sir with great and sincere Esteem, Your most obedient and very humble Servant.

Dft. Endorsed by JJ: ". . . In ansr. to 20 Septr. 1781." ALS not located.
[1]See above, Gerry to JJ, 20 Sept. 1781.
[2]The Massachusetts Constitution of 1780. See *ibid.*

From Gouverneur Morris

Philadelphia, 20 January 1782

Dear Jay,

< It is so long since I have received a Letter from you that I will not pretend to account for the. > I have received but one Letter from you in a very long time and by an Inattention I can only describe and not date it.[1] It was chiefly in Cypher in answer to mine announcing a certain Appointment and Part of it was copied by your private Secretary. The Cypher I shall use in this if I have Occasion is our official No. 8 which Franks delivered to you.

Your friends are all well, your Child perfectly so. And if you do not receive Letters from < one of them > your Sister in Law now here[2] you may rely that it is not because she does not write. As to those on Hudson's River (and by the bye your Brother James is somewhere thereabout)[3] I incline to think that their Silence is the Cause why you do not hear from them. I pray you present me most tenderly to Mrs. Jay and assure her that although I do not love her in the common Sense of the Word I have all the Regard and Esteem which she would wish.[4] May many happy years attend you both and your Virtues meet some greater Reward than themselves which they certainly must do for they will be a Reward to each other. This my dear Friend is very much a conjugal Sentiment and such my Bosom is not incapable of altho the Chapter of Accidents has made them but improper Guests. May I felicitate you on an Increase of Family? I think I may for Carmichael announces Some thing of the Sort.[5]

WE HAVE REASONS TO BELEIVE THAT THE COURT ARE INCLINING TO TREAT WITH YOU. BY WE, I DO NOT MEAN THE PUBLIC. THE MINISTERS I FIND ARE DESIROUS OF KNOWING OUR SITUATION. DEPEND ON IT THEY SHALL HAVE GOOD INFORMATION, AND DEPEND ALSO THAT YOU SHALL KNOW WHAT IT IS. IF WHAT I HAVE JUST SAID WERE NOT OF VAST IMPORTANCE, I WOULD NOT (AS I DO) RECOMMEND SECRECY.[6]

THE OPERATIONS ON THIS COAST HAVE BEEN SUCCESSFUL. IF THE FRENCH ADMIRAL WOULD, OR COULD, HAVE ASSISTED IN PURSUING THE BLOW, THEY WOULD HAVE BEEN DEFINITIVE. WHAT MAY BE THE SUCCESS OF THOSE NOW CARRYING ON IN THE WEST INDIES, IT IS IMPOSSIBLE TO FORESEE. THIS IS CERTAIN THAT A FLEET AND ARMY, SUCH AS THE COMBINED FLEET AND ARMY THERE, ALL OF ONE NATION AND WELL COMMANDED OUGHT TO TAKE JAMAICA. I HAVE SOME HOPES THAT IT WILL BE ACCOMPLISHED.[7] YOU MUST BE I THINK THOROUGHLY CONVINCED, THAT IT IS THE SPANISH POLICY TO EXCLUDE ALL THE WORLD FROM THE GULF OF MEXICO. I THINK OUR DUTY AND INTEREST COMBINE ON THIS OCCASION TO DIRECT THAT WE SHOULD COOPERATE WITH THEM IN THIS OBJECT. THEY WILL I AM PERSUADED, FOR THEIR OWN SAKES, GIVE US A FREE PORT IN EAST FLORIDA AND IF THEY DO, OUR COMMERCE WILL DO EVERY THING FOR US WHICH IT OUGHT, AND SOMETHING MORE. FOR HEAVEN'S SAKE, CONVINCE THEM OF THE NECESSITY OF GIVING US MONEY. NOT IN EUROPE, FOR THEY WANT IT TOO MUCH THEMSELVES, BUT AT THE HAVANNA. WE CAN BRING IT AWAY, AND THE COURT WILL NOT CONSIDER SO DEEPLY A GRANT THERE, BECAUSE IT IS IN EFFECT ONLY AN ANTICIPATION OF THE NEXT YEARS REVENUE. WITH MONEY WE CAN DO EVERY THING. BUT IF IT IS OBTAINED, GIVE NO NOTICE TO CONGRESS, FOR WE MUST PLEAD POVERTY TO THE STATES IF WE WERE RICH AS CROESUS.

Dft in NNC: Gouverneur Morris, utilizing the Robert Morris code enclosed in his letter to JJ, 7 July 1781. The code equivalents were entered interlineally in the Dft without any deletions in the text. Dft deletes opening incomplete sentence: "It is so long since I have received a letter from you that I will not attempt to account for the . . ."

[1]JJ to Gouverneur Morris, 28 Sept. 1781, above.

[2]Catharine W. Livingston was in Philadelphia visiting the Robert Morrises.

[3]In November 1781, Sir James Jay returned to New York with his brother Frederick, ending an eighteen-month stay in Philadelphia.

[4]For Gouverneur Morris' earlier expressions of affection for SLJ, see *JJ,* I, 123–24.

[5]SLJ was pregnant with their third child. Carmichael to Gouverneur Morris, not located.

[6]Morris' "good information" was contained in his letter to JJ of 10 March 1782, enclosing "Copies of a Letter from Mr. Rendon the Spanish Agent to me & of my Answer. I need not tell you that he was led to make the Request," *i.e.,* for a detailed explanation of American finances. Morris to JJ, 10 March 1782, RC in NNC-RBML: Gouverneur Morris, enclosing: (1) C of Francisco Rendón to Gouverneur Morris, 4 March 1782, in JP; deciphered C in JJ's hand in JP. (2) Morris' reply to Rendón, 5 March 1782, C entirely in cipher in JP, utilizing the Morris-Jay cipher. For Rendón, Spain's unofficial representative in America, see *RMP,* I, 272.

[7]Morris' hopes were to be dashed, as De Grasse was defeated in the British West Indies at the Battle of the Saints on 12 Aug. 1782.

To Robert R. Livingston

Madrid, 13 February 1782

Dear Sir,

Major Franks has delivered my Dispatches to Captain Manly who I hope will deliver them together with this Letter to You.[1]

These Dispatches were directed to Congress because at that Time I was ignorant of your appointment.[2] They properly belong to your Department, and I not only authorize but desire you to treat them exactly as if they had been directed to you <and not to the President of Congress>.

I had the Pleasure of writing to you last week by Mr. Codman who is to embark at Cadiz.[3] With great Regard and Esteem I am Dear Sir, Your most obedient and humble Servant.

Dft. Entry in JJ's Ledger, in JP, that on 14 February: "Sent to Mr. Nesbit to deliver to Captn. Manly."

[1]On 7 February JJ sent with Stephen Codman of Boston his 6 February letter to Livingston, his duplicate letter of 3 Oct. 1781 to President of Congress McKean, and his 6 February letter to President of Congress John Hanson, LbkCs in JP, CSmH, and PCC 110, II; *RDC,* V, 150–51; *HPJ,* II, 176–78; *SDC,* VIII, 10–11. See JJ Ledger, in JP. See above, Livingston to JJ, 28 Nov. 1781, for JJ's 6 February letter.

[2]JJ is referring to his 3 Oct. 1781 dispatch to McKean; see also Livingston to JJ, 28 Nov. 1781.

[3]JJ to Livingston, 6 Feb. 1782.

From Benjamin Franklin

[Passy, after 14 February 1782]

Your Comparison of the Keystone of an Arch is very pretty, tending to make me be content<ed> with my Situation.[1] But I suspect you have heard our Story of the Harrow. If not, here it is.

A Farmer in our Country sent two of his Servants to borrow

<a Harrow> one of <his> a Neighbour, ordering Them to bring it between them on their Shoulders. When they came to look at <the Harrow> it, one of them, who had <plenty of> too much Wit, says <to the other>, What could our Master mean by sending only two Men to br[ing] this Harrow? <There is> No two Men upon Earth are strong enough to carry it. Ooh! says the other who was vain of his Strength, what do you t[hink] of two Men? One Man may carry it; help it up upon my Shoulders, and you shall see. As he proceeded with it, the Wag kept exclaiming, <Good God> Zounds, how strong you are! I could not have thought it! Why you are a mere Samson! There is not such another Man in America. What amazing Strength God has given you! But you will kill your self! Pray put it down and rest a little, or let me bear a Part of the Weight. No, no, says he, being more encouraged by the Compliments than oppressed by the Burthen, you shall see I can carry it quite home. And so he did. In this particular I am afraid my part of the Imitation <may> will fall short of the Original.

Dft in DLC: Franklin. JJ Ledger records the receipt of no letter from Franklin between the latter's 19 January (received 5 February) and 16 March (received 26 March). Hence this letter was either never sent or miscarried. Franklin wrote this Dft on the back of a letter of 14 Feb. 1782 from Jean Paul Marat (1743–93), inviting him to witness an electrical experiment.

[1]This is a reply to JJ's letter to Franklin of 30 Jan. 1782, below, in which JJ wrote: "Our Credit in Holland leans upon you on one Hand and, in Spain, on the other. Thus you continue, like the Key Stone of an Arch, pressed by both Sides and yet sustaining each."

To George Clinton

Madrid, 23 February 1782

Dear Sir,

My last to you was written on the 16 November[1] since which I have not had the pleasure of hearing from you.

Three Days ago Mrs. Jay was delivered of a Daughter and I take the Liberty of enclosing a Letter on that Subject for my Father, which be so kind as to send him.[2]

I congratulate you on the successful Issue of the last Campaign, to the Brillancy of which the late Surrender of Fort St. Philip at Mahon, has much contributed.

Your Hemisphere brightens fast, and there is Reason to hope another vigorous Campaign will be followed by Halcyon Days.

Be pleased to present our best Compliments to Mrs. Clinton. My old friend Cornelia, I suppose, is so grown that I should not readily know her again. Tell her however that we remember both her and her Sister.[3] When you see Mr. Benson and Capt. Platt[4] assure them of my Regard.

Mr. Benson writes me that your Judges are Industriously serving their Country, but that their Country had not as yet made an adequate Provision for them.[5] This is bad Policy, and Poverty cannot excuse it. The Bench is at present well filled, but it should be remembered that altho we are told that Justice <is represented> should be blind, yet there are no Proverbs which declare that she ought also to be hungry. Assure these Gentlemen of my Esteem and believe me to be dear Sir with sincere Attachment, your Friend and Servant.

Dft. Endorsed by JJ. *WJ,* II, 93–94, and *HPJ,* II, 180–81, omit paragraphs 1 and 5 and JJ's deletions.

[1]JJ to Clinton, 16 Nov. 1781, above.

[2]Maria Jay (1782–1856) was born on 20 February. Her godfather was Robert R. Livingston. JJ to Peter Jay, 21 February, DftS in JP; *HPJ,* II, 179–80. JJ to Robert R. Livingston, 14 June 1782, ALS in NHi: Robert R. Livingston; DftS in JP; *HPJ,* II, 309.

[3]JJ's references are to Clinton's daughters Catharine and Cornelia. See above, JJ to Clinton, 25 April 1781.

[4]Jonathan Platt, Clinton's neighbor; *JJ,* I, 791–92.

[5]In his 27 Oct. 1781 letter to JJ, ALS in JP, Egbert Benson commented: "I am at this place [Albany] attending the Supreme Court, for, thank God, the Streams of Justice, although interrupted in their Course by the Accidents of the War, still continue to flow, and, as We have upright Judges, with Purity. Messrs. Morris, Yates, and Hobart remain yet on the Bench, but what with the Poverty of the State and the Parsimony of the Legislature, the Salaries are as incompetent as ever." For John Sloss Hobart and Robert Yates, see *JJ,* I, 547.

From John Adams

Amsterdam, 28 February 1782

Sir,

I have the pleasure to inform you that Friesland has taken the Provincial resolution to acknowledge the Sovereignty of the United States of America, and to admit their minister to an Audience, and have instructed their Deputies in the Assembly of their high Mightinesses at the Hague to make the motion in eight days from this.[1]

The States of Holland have also taken my last Requisition and transmitted it to the several Cities, and tomorrow it is to be taken into Consideration in the Regency of Amsterdam. Dort has made a motion in the States of Holland to acknowledge American Independence and admit me to an Audience. Their high Mightinesses have encouraging News from Petersburg and from the East and West Indies, so that at present there are Appearances that our affairs will go well here, and come to a Speedy Treaty. If anything should delay it, it will be the Example of Spain; but I don't believe that will a great while. One thing is past a doubt, if Spain should now make a Treaty with you, this Republic would immediately follow the Example, which, if anything can, would accelerate the Negotiations for Peace.

By the 10th Article of the Treaty of Alliance between France and America, the Parties agree to invite in Concert other Powers to make Common Cause and accede.[2] Permit me to suggest an Idea. Suppose you write to the French Ambassador at Madrid, and cite the words of that 10th Article, and request him to join you in an Invitation to the King of Spain. Excuse this Freedom, you will judge whether it will do. I should be obliged exceedingly to you for the earliest Intelligence, whether there is any prospect with you or not.[3]

With great Esteem and Respect, I have the Honor to be, Sir, your most obedient and most humble Servant,

J. ADAMS

LS, body of letter in Thaxter's hand. Endorsed: ". . . Recd. 15 March 1782, ansd. 18 Do." Omission in *HPJ*, II, 181–82; *JAW*, VII, 531–32.

[1]The action taken by Friesland on 26 February was followed by the States of Holland 28 March, by the other five provinces shortly thereafter, and by the States General on 19 April. *AP*, III, 4n.; J. Osinga, "France and Friesland and American Independence, 1776–1783," unpublished Ph.D. dissertation, University of Amsterdam. See also Adams to Livingston, 19 April 1782, LbkC in MHi: Adams, reel 356; *RDC*, V, 315–19.

[2]"The Most Christian Kingdom and the United States agree to invite or admit other powers who may have received injuries from England, to make common cause with them, and to accede to the present alliance, under such conditions as shall be freely agreed to and settled between all the parties." Treaty of Alliance with France, 1778, art. X. William M. Malloy, comp., *Treaties, Conventions, International Acts, Protocols, and Agreements Between the United States of America and Other Powers, 1776–1909* (2 vols., Washington, 1910), I, 479–82.

[3]JJ wrote Adams a congratulatory reply on 18 March, regretting that he could not convey "intelligence equally agreable." Dft in JP; Tr in NN: Bancroft: American I, 262; *HPJ*, II, 186.

From Lafayette

Paris, 28 March 1782

My dear Sir,

I take this Opportunity of a Spanish Courier's Going to Madrid to let you know that St. Kitts Has Been taken by the French. The Intelligence has been Received Yesterday, and it is the More pleasing as British Accounts had Rendered us very Uneasy Upon the fate of the Expedition.[1]

Your letter of the 1st[2] having Come to Hand I made what Communications I thought to be Serviceable, but will be more particular upon this point. You know the Bills have been Immediately Accepted by Mr. Franklin.

It was said the British Ministers would Resign and a New set be introduced.[3] But the Matter is at least very doubtfull. You will certainly hear of the Dutch being about Aknowledging our Independance. As a Frenchman and of course a zealous lover of the House of Bourbon I earnestly hope the King of Spain will not leave to Holland the credit of first Entering into this Measure. Generosity and frankness are the Pillars of the Spanish Character, we shall certainly experience both in the Negotiation that is going on between that Court and the United States.

I beg, My dear Sir You will present my Respects to Mrs. Jay and Remember me to My friend Carmichael. I will write to you both by the Next Safe Opportunity. With the Highest Regard I have the Honor to be Your Affectionate Humble Servant,

LAFAYETTE

ALS. Endorsed: ". . . Red. 6 Ap. 1782." Tr in NN: Bancroft: American I, 281.

[1]Following his return to the Caribbean after Yorktown, De Grasse engaged Admiral Samuel Hood's (1724–1816) fleet off St. Kitts on 24 Jan. 1782, and the island capitulated to the French on 12 February.

[2]JJ to Lafayette, 1 March 1782, not located.

[3]Lord North resigned on 20 March 1782, to be succeeded by Charles Watson-Wentworth, Marquess of Rockingham (1739–82), who headed a ministry for the second time in his career.

When the United States Defaulted

21 November 1781–29 March 1782

The financial strains, at least for a moment, were further eased by another loan from Spain on 23 December 1781.[1] Most of the $51,083 obtained from this source was turned over immediately to the Marquis d'Yranda, a Spanish treasury official, to be credited against the April '81 advance, but JJ was able to use the unexpended balance of several thousand dollars to meet some bills during January and February 1782, but not for his back salary, whose want he began to feel "severely."[2]

Real trouble lay ahead, however. A thick sheaf of bills were scheduled to fall due in March, with Franklin apparently less and less able to supply timely assistance. Receiving no reply to his December letter, wherein he commented that "your aid daily becomes more necessary, and will soon be indispensable," JJ wrote Franklin again on 11 January, stressing Cabarrús' increasing anxiety and pointing out that securing further loans from him or anyone else depended on assurance that present obligations would be speedily repaid.[3] Made apprehensive by Franklin's continuing silence, JJ sought unsuccessfully on 26 January to interest Montmorin in having France advance him £30,000, reminding the French ambassador of the ill effects that a protest of United States bills would have on the reputation of both France and Spain as well as America. Should his country be unable to make payment, JJ threatened to publicize the fact that the default had come about because he "had placed too great confidence in the assurances of his Catholic majesty."[4]

The very next day JJ received a letter from Franklin enclosing a copy of one from Vergennes, from which he hastily concluded that his financial troubles were about to end. The French minister implied that the Dutch were on the verge of making a loan to the United States, and indicated that his own government was prepared to make a separate grant of one million livres to Franklin. Beyond that, Vergennes stated, his court could not go. In fact, Vergennes reproved Congress for its irresponsibility in drawing on its ministers abroad.[5] Nevertheless, to Jay, the "general tenor" of Vergennes' communication held out "a Prospect of terminating the Difficulties which the Bills drawn upon me have occasioned," and, accordingly, on 30 January, below, he wrote Franklin expressing his gratitude for France's generosity.

Soon JJ had to re-assess his situation. On 5 February he received Franklin's 19 January letter, below, in which Franklin, though immediately helpful, painted a gloomy pictures of his own financial resources, while sharply criticing the Spanish court. Two days earlier Del Campo had notified JJ[6] that he was not yet prepared to discuss matters of mutual interest, although he had been assigned this responsibility back on 10 December. He attributed his delay to the delicate state of Floridablanca's health, and to other unspecified difficulties.[7]

A crisis now confronted the American mission. JJ had no funds to settle either the debt to Cabarrús or the bills falling due in March.[8] Franklin could not help him; Spain evidently would not. For his part, Cabarrús had shown a willingness to supply any sum that Spain would authorize, and on the same terms by which he had procured funds for the Spanish government, but Floridablanca barred his making further such advances on the alleged ground that his own government needed all the funds the banker could conceivably command. Cabarrús then offered to cover the March bills if Montmorin would guarantee repayment, a commitment that the French ambassador did not feel authorized to make.[9] One by one the alternatives available to JJ were vanishing.

The month of February wore on with meetings at the Pardo and frantic consultations in JJ's and Montmorin's lodgings. When speaking to Montmorin Floridablanca held out the promise of aid to the Americans, but to Cabarrús he painted a gloomy picture of Spanish relations with the United States. By now quite concerned, the banker wrote to JJ on 10 February asking when he might expect repayment of some $40,000 then outstanding, and followed it up on 25 February with a letter which, in JJ's words, breathed "the fears and precautions of a creditor striving to make the most of a failing debtor." To JJ the communication was "inauspicious."[10] News that Spain was preparing to make a final $26,000 loan to be applied against the debt did allay some of Cabarrús' fears, and by the end of the month he appeared in a more cooperative frame of mind.[11]

When on 1 March JJ learned that a new Cabarrús loan was being processed, he sent off to Floridablanca a letter of thanks the following day (see below), urging him at the same time to furnish desperately needed help with the March bills. A week of silence ensued. On 9 March JJ paid a call on Floridablanca, who sounded cordial and supportive, but sought to delay any Spanish loan until he was certain that no French livres were forthcoming. With pressures mounting, JJ sent Cabarrús to the Pardo on the evening of 11 March. The mercurial Floridablanca, recently so amiable, now turned uncooperative. JJ, he said, must have misunderstood him; Cabarrús was to come only in "the last extremity."[12]

JJ now found the last door shut. When the creditors arrived on 14 March, he succeeded in gaining another twenty-four hours, which he used to dispatch an urgent note to Floridablanca soliciting such help as Spain could proffer. When Montmorin met with Floridablnca the next day, the latter denied any knowledge of JJ's communication. Montmorin set forth JJ's embarrassments, only to be told that the American "might accept the drafts to the amount of $50,000, provided M. Cabarrus remains in the same disposition he displayed hitherto, relative to the time he would wait for the reimbursement of the sums . . ."[13]

JJ's suspicions were aroused. "Why and by whose means," he wondered, had his letter been withheld from the Spanish minister. Why was Floridablanca so explicit in having these proposed arrangements hinge on Cabarrús' disposition?[14] Events now moved swiftly to their climax. Carmichael took to Cabarrús the note from Montmorin describing Floridablanca's promise to guarantee the $50,000 advance. The banker, whose earlier propositions had called for repayment over ten or twelve months, now demanded four equal payments over the next four months. JJ held off his creditors and returned to Floridablanca. The latter announced on 16 March that Spain would make no loans because the new conditions were unacceptable. Thwarted by the change in the banker's terms which he presumed had been dictated by the Spanish minister, JJ had no alternative but to deliver a protest of the bills that same day.[15]

JJ's protest was as explicit as he had warned Montmorin in January that it would be. The declaration asserted that the bills had been accepted in the first place because "he had good reason to expect to be supplied with funds necessary to pay them," and that only disappointment in such "expectations" now reduced him to the mortifying necessity of protesting the bills. The protest, too, included the specific amount of the bills: £25,000 sterling. Montmorin's aide, Bourgoing, sought to have this sum deleted on the ground that the smallness of the amount would reflect on the good faith and generosity of France as well as Spain. JJ was adamant, and the protest stood.[16]

On the very day that JJ protested the bills, Franklin wrote from Passy that a six-million livre French loan would enable JJ to meet all of his obligations.[17] The exhilarating news reached Madrid on 26 March,[18] and with an immense feeling of relief JJ undertook "to make it known among the bankers, that I had received supplies equal to all my occasions, and was ready to pay to every one his due." "Our credit," JJ reported with evident satisfaction, "was re-established." For the remaining weeks of his Spanish mission, JJ employed Yranda and Drouilhet and Co. as his bankers and did without the services of Cabarrús, whom he treated with "reserved and cold politeness" and about whom he wrote that "as a Christian I forgave him, but as a prudent man I could not again employ him."[19]

[1]See above, Spanish Loans Obtained by JJ, [1 Jan. 1781–21 March 1782]. See also Joseph Nourse, Register of the Treasury, to Alexander Hamilton, Secretary of the Treasury, 9 Oct. 1792, "Estimates and Statements, 1791 and 1792," Old Loan Office, Treasury Department, in Samuel Flagg Bemis, *Pinckney's Treaty: America's Advantage from Europe's Distress, 1783–1800* (rev. ed., New Haven, 1960), p. 328.

[2]The Spanish court still held out in the amount of $25,165 on the "old promise" of $150,000. JJ to Franklin, 11 Jan. 1782, Dft in JP; LbkCs in CSmH and in PCC 110, II; Tr in NN: Bancroft: American I, 55; C in JJ to Livingston, 28 April 1782, cited above, "Issues in Negotiation," n. 26.

[3]JJ to Franklin, 11 Jan. 1782, and 31 Dec. 1781: Dft in JP; LbkCs in CSmH and PCC 110, II. C in JJ to Livingston, 28 April 1782.

[4]JJ: Notes of a Conference with Montmorin, 26 Jan. 1782, ALbkC in JP; C in JJ to Livingston, 28 April 1782.

[5]Vergennes to Franklin, 31 Dec. 1781, C in French in Franklin's hand enclosed in Franklin to JJ, 15 Jan. 1782: ALS in JP; LbkCs in CSmH, PCC 110, III; DLC: Franklin VII, 7; C in JJ to Livingston, 28 April 1782; *BFS*, VIII, 362; *RDC*, V, 114. For JJ to Franklin, 30 Jan. 1782, see below.

[6]Del Campo to JJ, 3 Feb. 1782, LbkCs in CSmH and in PCC 110, II: C in JJ to Livingston, 28 April 1782.

[7]JJ to Livingston, 28 April 1782.

[8]Carmichael to Livingston, 18 Feb. 1782, *RDC*, V, 174.

[9]Bourgoing to JJ, n.d. [11 Feb. 1782], LbkC in French in JP, trans. in PCC 110, II; C in JJ to Livingston, 28 April 1782.

[10]JJ to Livingston, 28 April 1782.

[11]JJ to Franklin, 1 March 1782: Dft in JP; ALS in PPAmP: Franklin 85ba; LbkCs in CSmH and PCC 110, II; C in JJ to Livingston, 28 April 1782.

[12]JJ to Livingston, 28 April 1782.

[13]JJ to Floridablanca, 14 March 1782: ALS in AHN Estado, leg. 3884, exp. 4, doc.

149; LbkCs in CSmH and in PCC 110, II: C in JJ to Livingston, 28 April 1782. Montmorin to JJ, 15 March 1782: ALS in French in JP; LbkCs in French in CSmH and PCC 110, II; C in JJ to Livingston, 28 April 1782.

[14]JJ to Livingston, 28 April 1782.

[15]JJ to Franklin, 18 March, below.

[16]*Ibid.*, n. 1, and JJ to Livingston, 28 April 1782.

[17]Franklin to JJ, 16 March 1782, LbkCs in JP, CSmH, PCC 110, II, and DLC: Franklin VII, 80–81; C in JJ to Livingston, 28 April 1782; *BFS*, VIII, 398–99; *RDC*, V, 244.

[18]JJ to Franklin, 29 March 1782, below.

[19]JJ to Livingston, 28 April 1782. For Cabarrús' unsuccessful attempt to get back in JJ's good graces, see Cabarrús to JJ, 29 March 1782, LbkCs in CSmH and PCC 110, II. JJ to Cabarrús, 2 April 1782, Dft in JP; LbkCs in CSmH and PCC 110, II; C in JJ to Livingston, 28 April 1782. Bourgoing to JJ, 5 April 1782, ALS in JP. JJ to Bourgoing, DftS in JP, ALS in CP E 607: 405.

On several occasions, JJ took it upon himself to protest certain bills drawn on the American Treasurer of Loans, which seemed to have countenanced illicit trade with the enemy. JJ: Reasons for not accepting certain bills presented 4 Aug. 1781, Dft dated 17 Oct. 1781 in JP, endorsed by JJ: "18 Octr. 1781 sent Copy to Congress via Bordeaux." As JJ wrote to McKean on 18 Oct. 1782: "I now send Copies to Congress, to prevent their being alarmed at any general Report that may arrive in America of my having refused to accept their Bills drawn upon me." Dft in JP; ALS in PCC 89, I, 452–53; LbkCs in CSmH and PCC 110, I. See also protests of [26 Nov. 1781] and [February 1782], Dfts of both in JP.

To Benjamin Franklin

Madrid, 21 November 1781

Dear Sir,

It seems as if my chief Business here was to fatigue you and our good Allies with incessant Sollicitations on the Subject of the ill-timed and, I had almost said, cursed Bills drawn upon me by Congress. It is happy for me that you are a Philosopher, and for our Country that our allies are indeed our Friends. Amicus certus in re incerta cernitur.[1]

This Court continues to observe the most profound Silence respecting our Propositions. I cannot as yet obtain any answer <of any kind> to any of my applications for aids. Heretofore the minister was too sick and too busy. At present his Secretary is much indisposed. I have requested that he would lend us for the present only as much as would satisfy the Bills of December, viz. 31,809 Dollars. No answer. What is to be done. I must again try and borrow <again of my Banker> a little, and as usual recur to you. Thank God no new Bills arrive. If they did I should refuse to accept them. Only a few straggling old ones now and then appear. <Dont you think> Would not the Court of France on your representing this Matter to them enable you to put an End to <all our Dangers on this Head> this unhappy Business.

Thirty thousand pounds Stirling would do it. I am sure the Evils we should experience from the protest of these Bills would <cost our Country> cost even France a vast Deal more. You see my Situation. I am sure I need not press You<r speedy answer> to deliver me from it if in your power. I cannot yet believe that all the assurances of this Court will vanish into air. I still flatter myself that they will afford us some Supplies tho not in Season. I think we might very safely offer to repay the French Court the proposed Sum in America, for surely Congress would not hesitate to prefer that to the Loss of their Credit.

I enclose a news Paper which gives us <much> Reason to indulge the most pleasing Expectations. God grant they may be realized. I have a Letter from Mr. Gerry dated at Marblehead the 9 October.[2] He was then in daily Expectation of hearing that Lord Cornwallis and his Army were our Prisoners. He describes the last Harvest as very abundant and the general State of our affairs as very promising, much more so indeed than ever they have been.

I am dear Sir, with <perfect Gratitude and> sincere Regard and attachment, Your obliged Friend and Servant.

Dft. Endorsed by JJ. LbkCs in JP; CSmH; PCC 110, II; *RDC,* V, 346; *HPJ,* II, 234–36.
[1]"An undoubted friend proves himself in doubtful circumstances." (Ennius.)
[2]Above, 20 Sept.–9 Oct. 1781.

From Benjamin Franklin

Passy, 19 January 1782

Dear Sir,

In mine of the 15th[1] I mentioned my Intention of writing fully to you by this Days Post. But understanding since that a Courier will soon go from Versailles, I rather chuse that Conveyance.

I received duly your Letter of November 21, but it found me in a very perplexed Situation. I had great Payments to make for the extravagant and very inconvenient Purchase in Holland together with large Acceptances by Mr. Adams of Bills drawn on Mr. Laurens and himself; and I had no Certainty of Providing the Money. I had also a Quarrel upon my hands with Messrs. de Neufville and others, Owners of two Vessels hired by Gillon[2] to carry the Goods he had contracted to carry in his own Ship. I had wearyed this friendly and generous Court with often repeated after-clap Demands, occasioned by these un-advised (as well as ill-advised) and therefore unexpected Drafts, and was ashamed to show my Face to the Minister. In these Circumstances I knew not what Answer to make you. I could not encourage you to expect the relief desired, and having still some secret Hope, I was unwilling to discourage you, and thereby occasion a protest of Bills which possibly I might find some means of enabling you to pay. Thus I delayed writing, perhaps too long. But to this moment I have obtained no Assurance of having it in my Power to aid you, though no endeavours on my part have been wanting. We have been assisted with near 20 millions since the Beginning of last Year, besides a Fleet and Army, and yet I am obliged to worry with my Sollicitations for more, which makes us appear insatiable. This Letter will not go before Tuesday, perhaps by that time I may be able to say explicitly Yes or No. I am very sensible of your unhappy Situation, and I believe you feel as much for me.

You mention my Proposing to repay the Sum you want in America. I had tryed that last Year. I drew a Bill on Congress for a considerable Sum to be advanced me here and paid there in Provisions for the French Troops. My Bill was not honoured!

I was in hopes the Loan in Holland, if it succeeded, being for 10 Millions, would have made us all easy. It was long uncertain; it is lately compleated.[3] But unfortunately it has most of it been eaten up by advances here. You see by the Letter of which I sent you a Copy, upon what Terms I obtain another Million of it. That, if I get it, will enable me to pay till the End of February; and among the rest to pay the 30,000 Dollars you have borrowed, for we must not let your Friend suffer. What I am to do afterwards God knows.

I am much surprised at the dilatory and reserved Conduct of your Court. I know not to what Amount you have obtained Aids from it, but if they are not considerable, it were to be wished you had never been sent there, as the Slight they put upon our offered Friendship is very disreputable to us, and of course hurtful to our Affairs elsewhere. I think they are short sighted, and do not look very far into Futurity, or they would seize with Avidity so excellent an Opportunity of securing a Neighbour's Friendship, which may hereafter be of great Consequence to their American Affairs. If I were in Congress, I should advise your being instructed to thank them for past Favours and take your leave. As I am situated I do not presume to give you such Advice, nor could you take it if I should. But I conceive there would be nothing amiss in your mentioning in a short memoir, the Length of Time elapsed since the Date of the secret Article,[4] and since your Arrival to urge their Determination upon it, and pressing them to give you an explicit definitive immediate Answer, whether they would enter into a Treaty with us or not, that you might inform Congress, and in case of Refusal solicit your Recall, that you may not be continued from Year to Year at a great Expence in a constant State of Uncertainty with Regard to so important a matter. I do not see how they can decently refuse such an Answer. But their Silence after the Demand made should in my Opinion be understood as a Refusal, and we should act accordingly. I think I see a very good Use that might be made of it, which I will not venture to explain in this Letter.

Speaking of your Expence puts me in mind of something that has passed between Mr. Adams and me relating to certain Charges in our Accounts, which I think ought to be communicated to you, that if you should be of the same Opinion with us, you may charge as we propose to do, or if you are of a different Opinion, we may conform to it for the Reasons you will be kind enough to offer us. I therefore enclose Copies of the two Letters that contain the Points in question.[5] I wish not to be burthensome to our Country, and having myself no Expensive Habits, having besides no Wife or Family to bring up, and living out of Paris, perhaps I should be as little incommoded by a Reduction of some of those Charges as any of my Brethren. But as we are to establish Precedents, I would not have them such as may be oppressive to another or to a Successor differently circumstanced.

I advanced to Major Franks Fifty Louis as you desired, and took his Note payable to you. His stay has been so long, and he bought so many things, that it did not prove sufficient.

I cannot express sufficiently my Thankfulness to you for the kind and friendly Manner in which you wrote concerning me and my Grandson to the President of Congress.[6] Be assured I shall ever bear it in Remembrance.

I am of the same Opinion with you as to the Instructions you mention.

Mr. Deane has written a very indiscreet and mischievous Letter, which was intercepted and printed at New York, and since in the English Papers.[7] It must ruin him forever in America and here. I think we shall soon hear of his retiring to England, and joining his Friend Arnold.

I know not how the Account of your Salary stands, but I would have you draw on me for a Quarter at present which shall be paid, and it will be a great Pleasure to me if I shall be able to pay up all your arrears.

I forwarded to you General Washington's Dispatches,[8] by which you would learn the Reduction of York town and Gloucester. A great and important Event! The Infant Hercules has now strangled his second Serpent that attacked him in his Cradle, and I hope his future History will be conformable.

My Grandson joins with me in best Wishes and Happiness to you and Mrs. Jay.

Mr. Laurens being now at Liberty[9] perhaps may soon come hither, and be ready to join us if there should be any Negociation for Peace. In England they are made for a separate One with us, that they may more effectually take Revenge on France and Spain. I have had several Overtures hinted to me lately from different Quarters, but I am deaf. The Thing is impossible. We can never agree to desert our first and our faithful Friend on any Consideration whatever. We should become infamous by such abominable Baseness.

With great and sincere Esteem, I am ever, Dear Sir, Your affectionate and most obedient humble Servant,

B. FRANKLIN

I am writing to Mr. Carmichael, but it will be too late for this Opportunity.

The Letters between Mr. Adams and me are mislaid.

LS. Endorsed: "... Recd. 5 Feb. ansd 11 Do." LbkCs in PCC 110, II, CSmH, DLC: Franklin, VII, 19–23. C in JJ to Livingston, 28 April 1782, cited above in "Issues in Negotiation," n. 26. *BFS,* VIII, 364–67; *RDC,* V, 119–21.

[1]See above, editorial note, "When the United States Defaulted," n. 5.

[2]For Alexander Gillon, see *JJ,* I, 629–30.

[3]For the Dutch loan, see below, John Adams to JJ, 8 July 1782.

[4]See above, Adams to JJ, 28 Feb. 1782, n. 2.

[5]The issue of accounting for expenses was covered by Franklin to Adams, 11 June 1781, and Adams to Franklin, 4 Oct. 1781, *BFS,* VIII, 268–70, *RDC,* IV, 491–92, 767, *JAW,* VII, 456–66. C of both letters, endorsed by JJ, in JP.

[6]See above, JJ to Samuel Huntington, 21 April 1781.

[7]See above, editorial note, "Silas Deane: A Worrisome Correspondent."

[8]Washington to JJ, 22 Oct. 1781, ALS in RAWC; Duplicate ALS in JP; LbkC in DLC: Washington 3A; *HPJ,* II, 137–38. Enclosures (not located): (1) Yorktown capitulation terms, 18 October; (2) summary return of the prisoners and cannon captured at Yorktown and Gloucester, 22 October. In addition, Washington had written a letter on the 22d jointly to Adams, Franklin, and Jay; *GWF,* XXIII, 253–54.

[9]On 31 Dec. 1781 bail was posted for Henry Laurens by Richard Oswald and Oswald's nephew, John Aulem, and the prisoner was released. *Peacemakers,* p. 265.

To Benjamin Franklin

Madrid, 30 January 1782

My dear Sir,

I had Yesterday the Satisfaction of recieving your Favor of the 15th Instant. You will find by a Letter which I wrote you on the 11th Instant[1] that I imputed your Silence to its true Cause, being well persuaded that the same Attention which you have always paid to the public Affairs in general would not be withheld from those which call for it in this Kingdom.

I am happy to find that you have a Prospect of terminating the Difficulties which the Bills drawn upon me have occasioned, and tho I cannot but observe that Count De Vergennes Letter is peculiarly explicit and precise, yet I must confess I should not have been surprized if it had been <still less smooth> concieved in Terms still less soft.[2] Would it not be well to transmit a Copy of it to Congress?[3] <It certainly is high Time for us> France has done, and is still doing so much for us that Gratitude as well as policy demands from us the utmost moderation and Delicacy in our applications for aids. And considering the very singular <Manner> plan of drawing Bills <on the Bank of <<Hope>> Chance> at a Venture, I think we have no less Reason<s> to admire the Patience, than to be satisfied with the Liberality of our good and generous Allies.

Mr. De Neufville had given me a Hint of the Embarrassments occasioned by "the affair of our Goods in Holland."[4] It seems as if Trouble finds its Way to you from every Quarter <and between Holland and Spain> <supporting the public> Our Credit in Holland leans upon you on one <Side> Hand and, in Spain, on the other. Thus you <seem> continue like the Key Stone of an Arch, pressed by both Sides and yet sustaining each. How grateful ought we to be to France for enabling you to do it!

Mr. Joshua Johnson in a Letter dated the 18th Instant mentions the Arrival <there> at Nantz of the Brig Betsey from Philadelphia that she brought Letters for me, and that the Captain put them into the Post Office. <I> None of them have <not> as yet <recieved any of them> reached me.[5]

I have recieved too many unequivocal Proofs of your kind Attention, to render a punctilious Return of Line for Line necessary to convince me of it. Let such Ideas therefore be banished, and be assured that matters of Ceremony and Etiquette can never affect the Esteem and affectionate Regard with which I am very sincerely, Dear Sir, your much obliged and obedient Servant.

Be pleased to <remember me> present my Compliments to your Grandson. If the appointment of <the> a Secretary to the Commissioners for treating of Peace <be left> should become necessary and the Choice be left to them, <I think> he shall have more than mere verbal Evidence of <the> my Regard for you and yours.[6]

Dft. Endorsed by JJ: "... In ans. to 15th Inst." LbkCs (without postscript) in CSmH and in PCC 110, II; Tr in NN: Bancroft: American I; C in JJ to Robert R. Livingston, 28 April 1782, cited in "Issues in Negotiation," above, n. 26.

[1]Cited above, editorial note, "When the United States Defaulted," nn. 2, 5.

[2]*Ibid.,* n. 5.

[3]JJ included it in his letter to Livingston of 28 April 1782.

[4]The details are set forth in Franklin to John Adams, 26 Nov. 1781, *BFS,* VII, 331–34.

[5]Letters reached JJ a week later. The JJ Ledger contains no entry for the Johnson letter, but enters the receipt on 5 Feb. 1782 of a dispatch from Livingston of 1 Nov. 1781, with this notation in JJ's hand: "under Cover to Casa Major from Jon. Williams at Nants. It was forwarded from Boston by John R. Livingston and arrived here with marks of Inspection." Enclosed with this dispatch were "Copies of articles of Capitulation from York Town," other documents relating to the surrender, and "18 newspapers." On that date JJ also received the ciphered letter from Livingston of 13 Dec. 1781, above.

[6]See below, Appointment of William Temple Franklin, 2 Oct. 1782.

To Benjamin Franklin

Madrid, 11 February 1782

Dear Sir,

I have been so engaged these two Days as not to have had Time to <write> reply fully to yours of the 19th Ult. but though it is <now> late I must not let the Post depart without a few Lines for you.

Circumstanced as it seems we are, nothing more can be expected from us by our Country than our best Endeavours, and if they fail of Success, the Disappointment <is> will be imputable only to those whose immature Counsels have produced the Embarrassments under which we labor. The Evils which must follow are nevertheless to be lamented and the more so at this Season when they <will create> would form a black <cloud> and inauspicious Cloud in the present bright Aspect of our Affairs.

I flattered myself that the Loan in Holland would have afforded Funds for all our Bills and present Demands, and am sorry to hear that is not the Case. Could not that Loan be extended to a further Sum?

The Conduct of this Court bears few Marks of Wisdom. The Fact is they have little Money, less Credit, and very moderate Talents.

My Ideas correspond exactly with yours respecting the propriety of presenting such a memoir as you propose. The Embassador of France however is decided in his opinion against it, and it appears to me imprudent to disregard his opposition.[1]

I agree to the Rule for our Charges specified in your Letter to Mr. Adams of the 11 June last and his Answer of the 4th October following.[2]

There is half a Years Salary due to Mr. Carmichael and myself. I shall agreable to your Permission draw for a Quarter's, deducting the money advanced <to Maj. Franks> on my Account.[3]

I have recieved the Dispatches from Gen. Washington which you was so obliging as to forward. I am much mistaken if the Young Hercules <remains satisfied with the ne plus Ultra of the old.> does not one Day shake the pillars of the old. Mr. Laurens Enlargement will not in my opinion be unconsequential. I am told he behaved with Firmness and came into no Conditions repugnant to the Honor and Independence of the United States.[4]

Be so kind as to send me Copys of Mr. Deanes Letters.[5] I am surprized to hear that <their> the Contents are so exceptionable, and can not otherwise account for it than by supposing that the Mortifications he has experienced have <poisoned his Heart and turned his Brain> had an unhappy Influence on his Heart and Head. I confess I had a better opinion of them both. <Perhaps too the Honorable Silas Deane Esqr. one of the Commissioners of the United States of America etc., etc., etc., met with a very different Reception in France from that which Mr. Silas Deane of the State of Connecticut Gentleman, afterwards experienced.>

Britain <it seems is determined in her offers to keep one Step behind our Demands> though for some Years constantly advancing towards our Demands seems still to want the Wisdom and Decision to overtake them by one large and manly Step. I should be ashamed of the Country I now glory in, if she could for a Moment forget her Obligations to France, for while France treats us fair and friendly we should prefer Destruction in abiding by our <Engagements, rather than purchase> Treaty to ignominious Peace and Safety purchased by basely deserting our first and as yet faithful Ally.

I have not as yet received a single Letter from or by the Marquis De La Fayette. Mrs. Jay joins with me in assuring you and your Grandson of our best Wishes. I am, Dear Sir, your obliged and obedient Servant.

Dft. LbkCs in JP, CSmH, PCC 110, II, 74–75; Tr in NN: Bancroft: American I, 144–1/2; extracts in *HPJ,* II, 256–57 and *RDC,* V, 356.

[1]See the editorial note above, "When the United States Defaulted," and n. 4.

[2]See above, Franklin to JJ, 19 Jan. 1782, n. 5.

[3]See *ibid.*

[4]See *ibid.,* n. 9.

[5]Franklin enclosed a copy on 24 April 1782, below, but the letter has not been located. On Deane's intercepted letters, see the editorial note on Silas Deane, above.

To Floridablanca

Madrid, 2 March 1782

Sir,

Mr. Gardoqui informed me yesterday that he had received an order to pay to Mr. Cabarrus on my account 26,000 Dollars, being somewhat more than the Ballance due on the 150,000; and for which be pleased to accept my thanks and acknowledgments.

As the Residue of the Bills drawn upon me by Congress does not amount to a great sum, and as Mr. Cabarrus had generously offered to furnish it, provided Your Excellency would give him Assurances of its being repaid in ten or twelve months, I had flattered myself that his Majesty's Friendship for my Country would have induced Him, by this further proof of his goodness, to save me the Necessity I shall otherwise be under to protest them, and thereby ruin the Credit of Congress at so critical a Period.

It is with great pain that I hear his Majesty is displeased with the Silence of Congress respecting Returns on their part to the Friendship of Spain; and particularly in not having offered to comply with the propositions made by your Excellency relative to the Ships building in New England.

Permit me to observe to your Excellency that the long and constant expectation of Mr. Gardoqui's arrival in America,[1] with full powers on these Subjects, naturally induced Congress to postpone coming to any Resolutions on them, until they should have the pleasure of seeing him. They were well apprized of my Ignorance respecting such matters, and therefore could not with any propriety refer to my Direction, the entering into Engagements on Subjects with which I was wholly unacquainted.

I am authorized to assure Your Excellency of the readiness of Congress to make every return in their Power, to the kindness of his Majesty; and there is reason to hope that by the End of the next Campaign, their Abilities may be more proportionate to their wishes, than they have hitherto been.

Your Excellency will also be pleased to recollect, that the Propositions of Congress respecting the Mississippi, evince a strong desire to oblige his Majesty; and that Reason has been given me to hope, that their Compliance in that Instance, would be followed by new Proofs of his Majesty's good disposition towards us.

I must candidly confess to your Excellency that I now find myself entirely without resources. The Embassador of France can afford me no assistance, and my only remaining Hope arises from the Reliance on his Majesty's Friendship and Magnanimity which Your Excellency has so often encouraged me to entertain and confide in.

I have the honor to be with great Respect and Consideration Your Excellencys Most obedient and most Humble Servant,

JOHN JAY

LS, body of letter in Carmichael's hand in AHN Estado, leg. 3884, exp. 4, doc. 148; Dft in JP; LbkCs in JP, CSmH and in PCC 110, II; C in JJ to Livingston, 28 April 1782; variations in *RDC,* V, 360–61; *YU,* II, 352–53; incomplete in *HPJ,* II, 182–83.

[1]It was not until 1784 when Don Diego de Gardoqui was appointed chargé d'affaires to the United States, about which the King of Spain notified Congress on 25 Sept. 1784; *RDC,* VI, 820.

To Benjamin Franklin

Madrid, 18 March 1782

All our Trouble and anxiety about the Bills payable here this Month has been in vain. They are protested. The following are the Reasons which I have desired the Notary to recite exactly in the Protest viz. (here insert Reasons verbatim[1]). It is proper you should be informed that Mr. Garbarrus [sic] <many> some Months ago voluntary offered (through Mr. Carmichael) to furnish me even with <any Money we might want> 100,000 Dollars per Month provided the Minister would agree to <reimburse him within a Reasonable Time> put it on the same footing on which he had contracted to furnish certain Supplies to Government. <but since the Court was at St. Ildefonso all our Affairs have been at a Standstill> I need not observe that this did not take place. You know that Mr. Cabarrus had advanced about 30,000 Dollars towards our Bills. The Minister lately gave him an order for 26,000 Dollars being somewhat more than the Ballance due on the 150,000 Dollars of which my former Letters have often made mention so that my Debt to Mr. Cabarrus has been considerably diminished.[2] This Gentleman has also often <offered> authorized Mr. Carmichael to assure me of his Readiness to advance what might be necessary to pay the Residue of our Bills if the Minister or the Embassador of France would become responsible for the Reimbursement with Interest in a convenient Time. The twelve Day of this Month he renewed this offer to me in very express Terms telling me he would wait ten or twelve Months for the Money.

On the 15th Inst. the Minister <offered> consented that Mr. Cabarrus should <advance> supply me to the Amount of 40 or 50 thousand Current Dollars on these Terms.[3] But Mr. Cabarrus then insisted that the Rents of the post office <should be pledged to him and> should be charged with the Repayment of this Sum at the Rate of 200,000 Reals of Vallon[4] per Month. With this *new* Condition the Minister refused to comply,[5] and the protest of the Bills became inevitable.

This is a Subject on which I could make some interesting Remarks and add some singular Circumstance but they must be deferred to another Opportunity.

<If these Bills could be taken up and paid> Would it be possible to take up and pay these Bills at Paris? <France would in my Opinion not be a Loser by it, at least gain much Reputation by it>.

I am Dear Sir with <perfect> sincere Esteem and Regard your obliged and obedient Servant,

J. J.

DftS. Tr in NN: Bancroft: American, I, 265.

[1]The following protest, translated by Gardoqui and delivered to the Chevalier de Bourgoing, Montmorin's secretary, was entered in JJs Lbk I in JP and included in JJ to Livingston, 28 April 1782 (cited in editorial note, above, "Issues in Negotiation," n. 26):

> Mr. Jay says, that when he accepted the Bills hereunto annexed, he had good reason to expect to be supplied with the funds necessary to pay them. That he has been disappointed in the Expectations he was encouraged to entertain on this subject, and that his Endeavors to obtain Monies for the purpose both here and elsewhere, have been unsuccessful, although the Bills which remain to be paid by him, together with all his other Engagements, do not exceed twenty-five thousand pounds sterling. That these disappointments being unexpected, he cannot, for want of Time, have recourse to Congress, and, therefore, finds himself reduced to the mortifying necessity of Permitting them to be Protested.

[2]"I paid duly all former bills drawn in favor of M. Cabarrus," Franklin to JJ, 16 March 1782, see editorial note, above, "When the United States Defaulted," n. 17.

[3]Montmorin to JJ, 15 March 1782, ALS in French in JP; LbkCs in French in JP, CSmH, and PCC 110, II; C in JJ to Livingston, 28 April 1782.

[4]Or $10,000 (Mexican).

[5]As reported in JJ to Livingston, 28 April 1782.

To Benjamin Franklin

Madrid, 29 March 1782

Dear Sir,

On the 18th Instant I informed you of my having been reduced, by Mr. Cabarrus's want of good Faith to the mortifying Necessity of protesting a number of Bills which were then payable.

Your Favor of the 16th Instant[1] reached me three Days ago. It made me very happy, and enabled me to retrieve the Credit <which> we had lost here by those Protests <had injured>. I consider your Letter as giving me sufficient authority to take the necessary arrangements with the Marquis D Yranda for paying the Residue of my Debts here as well as such of the protested Bills as may be returned <here> for that Purpose. The account you request of all the Bills I have accepted is making out, and when finished shall be transmitted by the first good opportunity that may offer. You may rely on my best Endeavours to render my Drafts as little inconvenient to you as possible.

The british Parliament it seems begin to entertain less erroneous Ideas of us, and their Resolutions afford a useful Hint to the other Powers of Europe.[2] If the Dutch are wise they will proffit by it. As to this Court their system (if their Conduct deserves that appellation) with Respect to us, has been so opposite to the obvious Dictates of sound Policy that it is hard to devine whether any Thing but Experience <will make them wiser> can undeceive them. For my Part I really think that a Treaty with them <is not> daily becomes less important to us.

That Britain should be desirous of a separate Peace with us is very natural, but as such a Proposal implies an Impeachment of our Integrity I think it ought to be rejected in such a Manner as to shew that <our Feelings are hurt by such invidious Suspicions of our Honor> we are not ignorant of the Respect due to our Feeling on that Head.[3] As long as France continues Faithful to us I am clear that we ought to continue Hand in Hand <with them in> to prosecute the War until all their as well as all our reasonable Objects <are obtained> can be attained by a peace; for I would rather see America ruined than dishonored. As to Spain and Holland we have as yet no Engagements with them and therefore are <at present> not <further> obliged to consult either their Interest or their Inclinations further than may be convenient to ourselves, or than the Respect due to our good allies may render proper.

France in granting you six million has acted with Dignity as well as Generosity. Such gifts, so given, command both gratitude and Esteem, and I think our Country possesses sufficient Magnanimity to recieve and to remember such marks of Friendship with <all the> a proper Degree of Sensibility, <very different has been the Conduct of this Country, pompous in assurances, niggardly in their grants, daily making promises and daily breaking them. All

high and mighty in words, all mean and little in>.

I am pleased with your Idea of paying whatever we owe to Spain.[4] Their pride perhaps <would> might forbid them to recieve <our> the money; but <my> our Pride has been so hurt by the littleness of their Conduct that I would in that Case, be for leaving it at the gate of the Palace and quit the Country. At Present such <Conduct> a Step would not be expedient, though <I think> the Time <may and> will come when Prudence <will> instead of re[s]training will urge us to hold no other Language or conduct to this Court than that of a just, a free, and a brave People who have nothing to fear from nor to <hope or expect from> request of them.

With perfect Regard and Esteem I am, Dear Sir, your obliged and affectionate Servant.

Dft. Endorsed by JJ. Tr in NN: Bancroft: American I, 26. Misdated 19 March in *RDC,* V, 369–70, wherein Yranda's name is consistently misspelled as "Aranda."

[1]Franklin to JJ, 16 March 1782, cited above in "When the United States Defaulted," n. 17. That letter contained the news that Franklin had just obtained a grant of six million livres from the French court, whereby he was able to discharge all of JJ's debts to Cabarrús and satisfy all future bills. Franklin requested "a complete list of all the bills you have accepted, their numbers and dates, marking which are paid and what are still to pay."

[2]With the reopening of Parliament on 21 January, opposition leaders renewed their attacks on the North ministry. On 27 February they carried a resolve demanding an end to "the further prosecution of offensive warfare on the continent of North America, for the purpose of reducing the revolted colonies to obedience by force . . ." This resolve still fell short of recognition of independence. See Ian R. Christie, *The End of North's Ministry, 1780–1782* (London, 1958), pp. 299–325; *Peacemakers,* p. 253.

[3]Such sentiments matched those of Franklin, who had regularly rejected intimations by British agents that their government would welcome a separate peace, and had made clear to his British friend David Hartley his determination to abide by America's treaty obligations to France. See William Alexander to Franklin, 15 Dec. 1781, *BFS,* VIII, 346; Hartley to Franklin, 2 Jan. 1782; Franklin to Hartley, 15 Jan. 1782, *BFS,* VIII, 358–61; and all in *RDC,* V, 50–51, 80–84, 112–14.

[4]Here JJ is taking his cue from Franklin's query in his letter of the 16th: "And since Spain does not think our friendship worth cultivation, I wish you would inform me of the whole sum we owe her, that we may think of some means of paying it off speedily."

The End of the Spanish Mission

16 April–21 May 1782

With peace talks beginning in Paris in April 1782, Benjamin Franklin wrote JJ: "Spain has taken four years to consider whether she should treat with us or not.

Give her forty, and let us in the mean time mind our own business." He urged JJ to make the journey: "[H]ere you are greatly wanted, for messengers begin to come and go, and there is much talk of a treaty proposed, but I can neither make nor agree to propositions of peace without the assistance of my colleagues."[1] Only JJ might be available. Adams was still in the United Provinces; Laurens, still a paroled prisoner; Jefferson had not yet left the United States.

JJ, however, hesitated to leave Spain. He had received new promises of a negotiation to be opened later that spring,[2] with the possibility of official recognition or a treaty. Once again, he turned to the faithful Montmorin, asking the French ambassador to inquire of Floridablanca "if this Court really means to treat of an alliance," in which case his going to Paris might be postponed.[3] Floridablanca, on the contrary, was not averse to JJ's departure: he promised that instructions for the negotiation of a Spanish-American treaty would be sent to Aranda, the Spanish ambassador in Paris, to conduct talks with JJ there. Taking the hint, JJ decided that the time had come to move.[4]

It was perhaps typical of eighteenth-century diplomacy that what was to be JJ's last brush with the Spanish minister Floridablanca centered upon an invitation to dinner. On 30 March JJ received an unaddressed, undated, and unsigned note in Spanish: "The Conde de Floridablanca has been to take your Excellency's orders for Aranjuez, where he hopes to have the honor of your Excellency's company at his table every Saturday after next May 11th."[5] JJ subsequently learned that the other foreign ministers had received similar notes, none of them addressed to the envoys by name.[6]

Montmorin promised to make inquiries, and on 23 April reported to JJ that Floridablanca had "said that it must have happened by mistake, for that he intended only to ask my [JJ's] orders for Aranjuez, but he was, nevertheless, glad the mistake had happened, as it would give him an opportunity, by mentioning it to the king, to obtain his permission for the purpose. . . ." The result was that Montmorin was authorized to extend the invitation to JJ "as a private gentleman."[7] To this new invitation JJ responded to Montmorin on the 27th with a declination: "For my part I consider it, as a general rule, that although particular circumstances may sometimes render it expedient for a nation to make great sacrifices to the attainment of national objects, yet it can in no case be expedient for them to impair their honour, their dignity, or their independence. . . ."[8]

William Carmichael remained as acting *chargé d'affaires,* to be received by the Spanish court in August of the following year.[9] Carmichael was to keep JJ informed of developments, including the subleasing of JJ's still rented house, the disposition of his possessions which had been left behind, the settlement of his private accounts, and, more importantly, the settlement of JJ's public accounts on behalf of the American government.[10] By April 1782 the last of the promised Spanish loans had been received, making a total of $174,011. For their settlement and eventual reimbursement, see the editorial note, "Settling the Spanish Accounts," 28 January–15 May 1784, below.

While JJ was preparing to leave Spain, Congress was considering his last lengthy dispatch to its President. In a resolution adopted on 30 April 1782, Congress endorsed JJ's actions. Secretary Livingston, whose 27 and 28 April letters elaborating Congressional views and instructions regarding Spain are also published below, transmitted the resolution to JJ.

JJ left Madrid for Paris on 21 May 1782, accompanied by his wife, infant daughter, and nephew. In Paris a whole new world opened up, posing greater challenges and the chance to recoup his diplomatic setbacks by a stunning triumph.

[1]See n. 7 in Franklin to JJ, 24 April 1782, below. Richard Oswald was the newly appointed emissary dispatched by the Earl of Shelburne, Secretary of State for Home, Colonial and Irish Affairs, to negotiate with the Americans in Paris.

[2]Spanish officials had reviewed JJ's draft treaty proposals on 21 March 1782. Notes of the conference in Spanish are in AHN Estado, leg. 3884, exp. 13, doc. 1.

[3]JJ to Montmorin, 1 May 1782, ALS in CP E 608: 2; Dft in JP.

[4]JJ to Franklin, 8 May 1782, below. Montmorin, in reporting this step to Vergennes, concluded that JJ "doubtless has determined to leave this Court which so greatly annoys him, and which in fact cannot have been agreeable to him during the two years of residence here." See *HPJ,* II, 301n.

[5]L in Spanish, trans. by the editors, in JP; LbkC in Spanish with English trans. in CSmH and in PCC 110, II.

[6]JJ described the circumstances of the invitation and his reaction to it in his 28 April 1782 dispatch to Livingston, cited in editorial note, above, "Issues in Negotiation," n. 26.

[7]In *ibid.*

[8]JJ to Montmorin, 27 April 1782, ALS in CP E 607: 523; DftS in JP; LbkCs in CSmH, JP, and PCC 110, II; *HPJ,* II, 199–202.

[9]See Carmichael to JJ, 23 Aug. 1782, below, and 1 Sept. 1783, ALS in JP. For the form of Carmichael's letter of credence, approved by Congress on 9 Oct. 1779, see *JCC,* XV, 1159–60; *RDC,* III, 369–70; see also Carmichael to JJ, 28 May 1782, ALS in JP.

[10]Carmichael to JJ, 8 June; 3, 9, 23 July; 19, 21 Aug., and 18 Oct. 1782; 29 July, 28 Sept., and 12 Oct. 1783; 16 Feb., 12 March, 15 April, and 12 May 1784, all ALS in JP.

FROM ROBERT R. LIVINGSTON

Philadelphia, 16 April 1782

Dear Sir,

Returning from an excursion to the State of New York I found your letter of October 3 which on account of my absence had been committed to a committee of Congress. They have shown me their report. It will try their sentiments on a very interesting point if it goes through,[1] but as they may not suddenly come to a resolution, and I have just heard of a vessel which will sail in two hours for Cadiz, I avail myself of it to inform you that your conduct through the whole of your negotiation has been particularly acceptable to Congress.

The condition you have annexed to the proposed cession is extremely well calculated to hasten the Spanish Ministry and I think ought to be adhered to for unless some important advantage can be gained by it, the claim with the means we have of enforcing it is too valuable to be relinquished. Spain may flatter herself with the hopes of gaining that at a general peace by the favor of the mediators which she is unwilling to purchase of us by the smallest concession. In this, however, I conceive she will find when too late that a partial regard to triffling interests has led her to sacrifice those of a more extensive and important nature. Spain can have no claims to the Mississippi but what are derived from her late conquests. Our claims are valid, those of Britain are at least specious, both will be opposed to her's at a general peace. And as she has made the cession of Gibraltar a preliminary to a peace she can hardly expect that the mediators, if they gratify her in that, will add to it other countrys to which she has no claim, more particularly as the right of Britain is next to ours incontestably the best that can be set up, so that there is little doubt if the negotiation should open when the success of our affairs gives us importance in the eyes of the mediators that they will recognize our right. If, on the other hand, we should meet with any reverse of fortune, those of Britain will become more respectable thereby, and the weak claims which Spain may set up from the conquest of a few inconsiderable posts in a country of such immense extent, already in part conquered and possessed by us, can only serve as arguments of unbounded ambition without establishing a right.

Sound policy then certainly dictates as a sure means of attaining this great object such a vigorous prosecution of the war as will reduce Great Britain to the necessity of making the mortifying cessions which Spain requires, and give more validity to the rights with which we are willing on certain conditions to invest her. Pecuniary aids afforded to us will be the most effectual means of destroying the common enimy and reducing them to accept such terms as Spain may chuse to dictate, while the purchase of our rights will enable her to support them with dignity and to appear at the congress as a sovereign power who has supported a distressed ally without availing herself of that distress to deprive her of rights which she has paid no equivalent for.

America considers her independence as placed beyond all doubt. She begins now to look forward to other important objects. She knows the value of the country which is washed by the Mississippi. It is also well known to the nations of Europe. By the cession of her right to it she is satisfied that she can procure important advantages in commerce from any of the maritime powers in Europe. Some of the northern potentates, who have means of giving validity to our claims, would consider an establishment, under the restrictions with which we have offered it to Spain, as cheaply purchased by an alliance with us, and a much greater advance in money than we have yet thought of asking from Spain, if our present wants should make it expedient to pursue this Idea. Spain has not laid such obligations upon us, notwithstanding our respectful and patient attention to her, as to render us chargeable with the slightest degree of ingratitude in so doing.

You will therefore persist in the line in which you now are, declaring explicitly that the sessions you propose are only dictated by your desire to make early and vigorous efforts against the common enemy; that if they are not accepted so soon and upon such terms as to afford you a prospect of obtaining this desirable end, you will not consider your offers as binding upon you. I am persuaded that in this I speak the sentiments of Congress, and you may deliver them as such.

Your never having spoken of the answer of France, Spain and Great Britain to the proposals of the mediators makes me doubt whether you have seen them. That of Spain I have not seen. If I can get the others copied and cyphered before this vessel sails, I will send them to you. If not, I will enclose so much of the answer of France as relates to Spain. I see and you will see a use that may be made of it.[2]

No incident has turned up since my last worth communicating. The enimy are drawing lines across New York Island at Mr. Eliots[3] and making every preparation for defence. The Eastern and Northern States and some of the Southern States are using the most vigorous exertions to obtain a respectable force for the opening campaign. FRANCE HAS GRANTED AN ADDITIONAL AID of 6,000,000.[4] of Dollars from Spain is all that is necessary to enable us to make the most spirited exertions. Our Army is at present well clad and well fed and as well disciplined as any in the world. The force at West Point by the twentieth of May will amount to about 10,000 men and will gradually increase till September as the recruits can be collected; so that our operating force there, including the French troops, will amount by the beginning of June to about 15 or 16,000 men exclusive of militia, which may be called in if necessary. I mention this because I know great misrepresentations have gone abroad on this subject.

I have just received a letter from Mr. Carmichael which I shall answer if possible by this conveyance.[5] Be pleased to present my compliments to him and the rest of your family. I am, Dear Sir, With the greatest respect and esteem, Your Most obedient humble Servant,

ROBT. R. LIVINGSTON

DftS in NHi: Livingston Family: Robert R. Livingston. Endorsed: by Livingston: "Dr. of Letter to Mr. Jay. . . ." Duplicate LS (# 6) in JP, therewith appended JJ's "Explanation of the Cyphers in Mr. R. R. Livingstons Letter of 16 April 1782, No. 6, 2plicate, recd. 18 July 1782." JJ states: "N. B. there appears to be several Errors in the Cyphers, some Letters being mispelled, others omitted and some misplaced, the words however being pretty evident. I shall take no notice of these mistakes in this Copy." The LS and Lbk versions, utilizing the Thomson code, contain many errors by Livingston. LbkCs in PCC 79, I, 404–05, and 118, pp. 136–44; triplicate LS not located; *HPJ*, II, 187–90.

[1]See below, Livingston to JJ, 27 April 1782, n. 1.

[2]Great Britain declined the Austro-Russian offer to mediate the war in June 1781, and France did so in August. Luzerne had informed Livingston of France's response but had not made it clear that Vergennes' declination was endorsed by Spain. *Peacemakers*, pp. 185–86.

[3]Presumably Andrew Elliot, Royal Collector of Customs in New York before and during the Revolution and Superintendent General of Police and Lieutenant Governor during the war years. Thomas Jones, *History of New York During the Revolutionary War*, Edward Floyd DeLancey, ed. (2 vols., New York, 1879), II, 121–24; William Smith, *Historical Memoirs*, II, viii, *passim*.

[4]This is the only deciphered section of the Dft. In the duplicate LS, JJ deciphered the passage as "France has lent us six million of Livres for this year"; the dollar amount is left blank. This is the way it reads in *HPJ*.

[5]For Carmichael's letter to Livingston of 20 Dec. 1781 and Livingston's reply on 1 May, see *RDC*, V, 61–65, 383–84; see also *JCC*, XXII, 141.

From Robert R. Livingston

Philadelphia, 20 April 1782

Dear John,

It gives me extreme pain not to have received a single line in answer to my public or private Letters to you[1] though no vessel has sailed from this or any of the nieghbouring ports for <any part of Europe> France or Spain since October without being charged with one or the other <for you> not because I infer therefrom the least neglect on your part. I have too much confidence both in your punctuality and your friendship to entertain an idea so derogatory to both, but because I argue from it the difficulty of conveying any thing to you and the care with which the avenues to you are guarded. I foresee notwithstanding the expence with which it will be attended, we shall be under the necessity of using expresses of our own.

My official Letters[2] and the papers that accompany this will give you the little news and politicks going here. I must only add to it that we yesterday received advise from Baltimore by a vessel arrived there from the West Indies that the French Fleet had arrived with out loss at Martinico which is rendered probable from the time of their sailing. This once more restore[s] the superiority to the Count De Grasse and will enable him to prosecute the great objects of the present campaign.[3] Since my last of yesterday too we have received advises from Charles Town (though not officially) that the enemy are preparing to embark their troops and most probably to evacuate it altogether. Whether Jamaica, New York, or Rhode Iland is their object I can not say. The first is almost defenceless. The second can not be preserved with [out] a much greater body of troops than its present garrison and the third is absolutely necessary if they mean to have any fleet here this summer since in case of a defeat they could hardly fly to New York as an assilym where they must wait at the Door till high waters and even then disarm themselves perhaps in the presence of a victorious enemy before they can gain admittance.

I enclose a letter from your Brother which will give you some account of your Family which I had the pleasure of seeing ten days ago. They were all in health except your father who I am sorry to say you have little prospect of seeing again in this world.[4] He will shortly increase that circle of friends whom we shall both join in a better and talk over with contempt the cares which distracted us in this.

You can hardly experience more pleasure than I do in knowing the satisfaction which Congress express at your conduct. <your character stands extreamly high with them while> ADAMS AND DANA <are proportionably low though they have a party which still support them> <daily losing ground they> even SUPPOSE THE DIGNITY OF THE UNITED STATES TO CONSIST IN DIFFERING WITH THE MINISTER OF FRANCE, AND the <the whole of their measures may be induced by> whole of their measures may be explained by that principle. <EVERY STEP THAT THE FIRST HAS TAKEN HAS ONLY SERVED TO DISGRACE THE UNITED STATES> AND THE LAST HAS HAD THE WEAKNESS TO AVOW THE PRINCIPLE IN HIS <LAST> LETTERS <to Congress>.[5]

Adieu, my Dear Sir. Remember me affectionatly to your family. Tell Mrs. Jay her friends here are all well, though a little dispersed, her papa at Trenton, her Mama at Elizabeth, Caty on a Jaunt to Maryland, Susan at Clermount and Mrs. Watkins at Puramus. She has had the misfortune to loose her Son who was a very fine boy.[6]

This jumble of news, politicks and family affairs which would expose me to the censure of a critic will be received by you as marks of the confidence I place in your friendship and of the little restraint I impose upon my thoughts when I write to one from whom I am used to conceal nothing that passes in my mind though I am some time at a loss to express all that passes there and never more than when I would declare the attatchment I feel for you. <your friend> etc.

Dft in NHi: Robert R. Livingston. It uses the nomenclator code supplied to JJ by Charles Thomson on 11 July 1781, code passages entered interlineally by Livingston above words.

[1]For JJ's letters to Livingston after the latter took the oath of office as Secretary for Foreign Affairs, see: Livingston to JJ, 28 Nov. 1781, above, for 6 Feb. 1782. For 13 February, see above. LbkCs of 16 and 18 Feb. 1782 in CSmH, JP, and PCC 110, II; 16 Feb. in *HPJ*, II, 178–79, *SDC*, VIII, 12; both in *RDC*, V, 171. Dft of 14 March 1782 in JP. For 28 April 1782, JJ's last lengthy dispatch from Spain, see the citation above in "Issues in Negotiation," n. 26. In this dispatch JJ summarized his concluding activities in Spain since 3 Oct. 1781.

[2]Livingston to JJ, 16 April 1782, above.

[3]After the successful campaign against St. Kitts, de Grasse turned his fleet back to Martinique where he anchored 26 February.

[4]Frederick Jay's letter, possibly of 3 April 1782, not located. See Frederick Jay to JJ, 20 April 1782, below.

[5]Arrived at St. Petersburg 27 Aug. 1781, Dana quarreled with the Marquis de Vérac, France's envoy to Russia, over approaches to Catherine's court, both envoys being ignorant of the other's tongue and forced to turn for help to Vérac's son-in-law and the fifteen-year-old John Quincy Adams (1767–1848), who accompanied Dana as his secretary. See *RDC*, IV, 683–85, 695–99, 705–07, 710–14, 773–76.

[6]The son, born in 1781, of SLJ's sister, Judith. See Catharine W. Livingston to SLJ, 30 June 1781, ALS in JP.

From Benjamin Franklin

Passy, 24 April 1782

Dear Sir,

The Prince de Masseran,[1] being so good as to desire carrying a Letter to you, I sit down to write you a few Lines, though I hope soon to see you.

Enclosed I send a Copy of one of Mr. Deanes Letters.[2] I shall shew you more when you come.

In consequence of a Proposition I sent over, the Parliament of Britain have just passed an Act for exchanging American Prisoners.[3] They have near 1100 in the Goals of England and Ireland, all committed as charged with high Treason. The Act is to impower the King, notwithstanding such Commitments to consider them as Prisoners of War according to the Law of Nations, and exchange them as such. This seems to be giving up their Pretensions of considering us as rebellious Subjects, and is a kind of Acknowledgment of our Independence. Transports are now taking up to carry back to their Country the poor brave Fellows who have borne for Years their cruel Captivity, rather than serve our Enemies, and an equal Number of English are to be delivered in Return. I have upon Desire furnished Passports for the Vessels.

I believe you will find the Marquis D'Yranda the *surest* Friend upon Occasion, and his Connection with our Banker here, makes the Money Transactions more easy than with another. But I hope those perplexing Affairs are over. You will be right in taking the Arrangements with the Marquis which you mention in yours of March 29.[4]

Our Affairs in Holland are *en bon Train,* we have some Prospect of another Loan there,[5] and all goes well here.

The Proposal to us of a separate Peace with England, has been rejected in the manner you wish,[6] and I am pretty certain they will now enter into a General Treaty. I wrote you a few Lines by last Post, and on the same Day a few more by the Court Courier.[7] They were chiefly to press your coming hither to assist in the Affair.

With great and sincere Esteem, I am ever, Dear Sir, Your most obedient and most humble Servant,

B. FRANKLIN

I inclose what I suspect to be a pretended American Paper,[8] which, however, though it should be found fiction, as to the *Form,* is undoubtedly true as to the *Substance.* For the English cannot deny such a *Number of Murders* having been really committed by their Instigation.

LS in RAWC. Endorsed: ". . . Recd. 9 May 1782." *BFS,* VIII, 434–35, *HPJ,* II, 194–95, and *WJ,* II, 95, omit paragraph 4 and postscript.

[1]The Prince de Masserano, who served as an aide-de-camp on Crillon's staff. See *JJ,* I, 774–75.

[2]Not located. See above, JJ to Franklin, 11 Feb. 1782, and editorial note, "Silas Deane: A Worrisome Correspondent."

[3]Dr. William Hodgson (1745–1851), an English radical, had kept Franklin informed about a bill for a general exchange of prisoners that Edmund Burke had introduced in Parliament in early 1782. See Hodgson to Franklin, 1 and *c.* 22 March and 14 April 1782, all written from London, in PU: Franklin.

[4]JJ had written Franklin that he had put the payment of his debts exclusively in Yranda's hands; see above, JJ to Franklin, 29 March 1782.

[5]John Adams obtained a loan of 5 million florins at five percent interest from a consortium of Amsterdam bankers on 11 June 1782. F. van Wijk, *De Republiek en Amerika, 1770–82* (Leiden, 1921), p. 167; Pieter J. Van Winter, *American Finance and Dutch Investment,* James C. Riley, trans. (2 vols., New York, 1977), II, 1086.

[6]In his meeting with Richard Oswald on 12 April 1782, Franklin had rejected the idea of a separate peace. *Peacemakers,* p. 261.

[7]Franklin to JJ: 22 April 1782, LS in RAWC; *BFS,* VIII, 433–34; *HPJ,* II, 193; *RDC,* V, 320–21; *WJ,* II, 94. 23 April ALS in JP, *HPJ,* II, 193–94.

[8]While the enclosure is missing, it is undoubtedly Franklin's *Supplement to the*

Boston Independent Chronicle, No. 705, a fictitious account concocted by the Doctor and printed on his press at Passy, purporting to report a massacre of New England farmers by the Seneca Indians. Franklin also sent a copy of the *Supplement* to John Adams and Charles W. F. Dumas. *BFS*, VIII, 432–33, 437–47.

To Robert Morris

Madrid, 25 April 1782
Read this at Your *Leisure*

Dear Sir,

Some of my Letters to You have I find miscarried by the Capture of the Vessels that were carrying them, and there is Reason to suspect that two others were stopped here, as the Letters inclosing them did not reach the Persons at the Sea Ports, to whom they were directed.

I have heretofore mentioned the Reciept of the Picture you was so kind as to send me by Mr. Ridley, and the arrival of Your Sons. I dont know the Fate of that Letter, and that uncertainty induces me to repeat my Thanks for the one, and my Congratulations on the other.[1] The Estimation in which I hold your Friendship, and the marks I have recieved of it, interest me in every Thing which concerns You and Your's, and be assured that no opportunity of giving higher Proofs of it, shall be omitted.

Caty's late Letters have given us Reason to be anxious about her Health, and to be grateful for your and Mrs. Morris's attention to her. She is a valuable and affectionate Friend, and I am happy that in these unsettled Times, she has a pleasing Retreat in your friendly and hospitable Family.

Mrs. Jay's Time is much employed in nursing, and amusing herself with her little Girl. She is writing to Mrs. Morris.[2] We are chearful, and not unhappy, tho distant from our Friends and deprived of the Pleasures which result from that free and unreserved Conversation, which can only be indulged in the Company of safe Companions, or in a Country like ours.

We remove next Week to Aranjues, where I expect again to spend some agreable Weeks. It is a charming Place, containing a Tract of several miles in Circumference, and divided into Gardens, meadows, Parks, cultivated Grounds, and Wilds—full of fine Trees, fine Roads, and fine Walks, and watered by a slow winding River which if more clear, would be very beautiful. But still my Friend! it is not america. A Genius of a different Character from that which presides at your Hills and Gardens, reigns over these. Soldiers with fixed Bayonets present themselves at various Stations in these peaceful Retreats; and though none but inoffensive Citizens are near, yet Horsemen with drawn swords guarding one or other of the royal Family in their little Excursions to take the air, daily renew and impress Ideas of Subjection. Power unlimited and Distrust misplaced, thus exacting Homage and imposing awe, occasion uneasy Reflections, and alloy the pleasing Sensations which nature, smiling in such delightful Scenes, never fails to excite. Were I a Spaniard, these decorated Seats would appear to me like the temporary Enchantments of some despotic magician, who by re-extending his Wand, could at pleasure command them to vanish, and be succeeded by Presidios, Galleys and Prisons.

Nothing is more true than that all things figure by Comparison. This elegant Seat being surrounded with extensive Wastes, appears like a blessed and fortunate Island in a dreary Ocean. The contrast heightens it's Charms, and every Traveller arrives with a mind predisposed to admire and enjoy them, but as the first Impression wears away, and he begins to recollect the more happy though less magnificent abodes in his own Country, the attractions and allurements of this insensibly diminish. I have more than once experienced this, and though not difficult to please or be contented, yet I confess that I find little here which resembles, and nothing that can fully compensate for, the free air, the free Conversation, the equal Liberty, and the other numerous Blessings which God and Nature and Laws of our own making, have given and secured to our happier Country.

I would not be understood to insinuate that good Society and agreable Companions are wanting here. They may perhaps abound more in some other parts of the world, but they are also to be found here, tho an unsocial kind of Policy requires unceasing attention to the most austere Rules of Caution and Prudence. The little that I have seen and observed of this People, induces me to think that, except the Generality of those who compose the highest and lowest orders, they possess many Qualities which are praise worthy; and that two or three long and wise Reigns would make them a very powerful, and an amiable Nation. But as I have not yet had sufficient opportunities of mixing with and personally knowing many of them, Time and further Information may either confirm or alter this opinion. The evident Suspense and Indicision of the Court respecting us, has kept many at a Distance, with whom I should otherwise have been on a very familiar Footing, and some of them have been so candid as to tell me so. This is a kind of Prudence which naturally grows out of a jealous and absolute Government, under which the People[7] have, for many Generations been habituated to that Kind of Dependence, which constrains every Class to watch and respect the opinions and Inclinations of their Superiors in Power.

The prosperous Tide of our affairs however has for some Time past run so strong that I think many of our obstacles here must soon give way. Shyness will then cease, and I shall not afterwards find it difficult to be recieved into more of their Houses, and that in the only manner in which I ever wish to be recieved into any, I mean at the Front Door, by direct Invitation from the masters of them, and without the precursory good offices of upper Servants or unimportant Favorites, whom I never can submit to court.

Until this Period arrives, I shall continue to cultivate the few acquaintances I have, and without giving offence to any, endeavour to encrease their number whenever it may be done with Propriety and to advantage, but I shall as heretofore avoid embarrassing and intruding upon those who in the mean Time may think it necessary to be reserved. Self Respect joins with Prudence in pointing out this Line of Conduct, and as I have no Enemies of my own making, I am persuaded that instead of losing, I shall eventually be a Gainer by adhering to it, especially as those who may have been led to ascribe this Conduct to improper motives, will then immediately find themselves undecieved.

Be pleased to present our Compliments and best wishes to Mrs. Morris, Mr. and Mrs. Meredith[4] and our other Friends with you. I am Dear Sir with sincere Regard Your affectionate Friend and Servant,

JOHN JAY

ALS in CtY. Duplicate ALS in DLC: Robert Morris; Dft in RAWC. Endorsed by JJ: ". . . by Majr. Franks with Dup. to be left with others at Nantz." Paragraph 3 omitted in *WJ,* II, 96–99, *HPJ,* II, 195–99, and *RDC,* V, 328–30.

[1]JJ's letter to Morris not located. For Morris' sons and Ridley, see above, JJ to Ridley, 8 Jan. 1782. For the Du Simitière portrait of Catharine W. Livingston, see below, JJ to Catharine W. Livingston, 21 Jan. 1782, under "Keeping in Touch."

[2]No letters from SLJ to Mary White Morris in the spring of 1782 have been located.

[3]In the Dft JJ wrote "Minds of Men" before changing it to "People."

[4]Samuel and Margaret Cadwallader Meredith; see *JJ,* I, 756.

From Robert R. Livingston

Philadelphia, 27 April 1782

Dear Sir,

I informed you in my Letter of the 16th inst. that yours of the 3d of October had been received and submitted to Congress during my absence, and, as I had then reason to think, that it would be answered by them. This I wished, because I was persuaded it would express their approbation of your conduct and afford you that intimate knowledge of their sentiments which the delicacy of your situation renders peculiarly important. They have however judged it proper to refer the letter to me.[1] I shall endeavour to preserve the advantages I have mentioned to you, by reporting this answer, so that you will consider it as containing nothing which they <have not explicitly> disapproved.

Acquainted with the expectations of Congress and the grounds on which they formed them, you will easily believe, that they are equally surprized and concerned, at the little attention hitherto shewn by Spain to their respectful solicitations. They had learned from every quarter that his catholick Majesty among the princely virtues he possesses was particularly distinguished by his candour, and that open dignity of character which is the result of having no views that he found any reluctance in disclosing. And that the ministers in whom he confided, breathing the spirit of the prince, were above those artifices which form the politicks of inferiour powers. They knew the insults which Spain had received from Great Britain and they could conceive no reason why she should conceal or refuse to return them, with interest, by supporting openly the people Britain unjustly endeavoured to oppress. These principles confirmed by the frequent recommendation of those whom they believed to be acquainted with the sentiments of the court of Madrid induced them to send a minister to solicit the favourable attention of his catholic Majesty to a people who were strugling with oppression and whose success or miscarriage could not but be important to a sovereign who held extensive dominions in their vicinity. Give me leave to add Sir, that in the choice of the person, they were not inattentive to the dignity of the court or to the candor and integrity by which they supposed it to be influenced. <It> I would <give me pain to supp[ose]> not have you infer from what I have said that the favourable sentiments which the United States have hitherto entertained of the court of Madrid have undergone the least alteration. <I am> They are satisfied nothing would be more injurious to both nations than to permit the seeds of distrust or jealousy to be sown among them.

But <my dear Sir> though those who are well informed feel no abatement of respect or esteem for the virtue and magnanimity of his majesty, and do full justice to the integrity and abilities of his ministers accepting the appologies you mention, and attributing to their true causes the delays and neglects which you have unhappily experienced, yet they are in the utmost pain lest they should work some change in the sentiments of the people at large, in whom, with us, the sovereignty resides, and from thence defusing themselves in to the government be productive of measures ruinous to that friendly intercourse, that spirit of amity, which it is the earnest wish of those who are acquainted with the true interests of both countries to promote.

After the war was declared by Spain those among us who had formed the highest Ideas of her magnanimity < found consolation in the hour of their greatest distress by from a persuasion that Spain would then most readily declare in our favor; > persuaded themselves that she would act decidedly for us when she found us in distress. They grounded their beliefs upon the avowed spirit of the nation, and the policy of adopting measures to reanimate us, and damp the ardour of the enimy and to make such impressions upon our hearts, as to give them in future an considerable influence on our councils.

Our disappointment in this expectation, though perhaps to be accounted for upon very natural principles, has been greatly agravated by the sedulous endeavours of the enimies of both countries to create distrusts and jealousies. They artfully insinuate that Spain seeks only to draw advantages from our wants without so far interfering in our affairs as to involve herself if we should be unsuccessful. These insinuations are gaining ground, and it becomes daily more necessary for Congress to be furnished with reasons to justify to their constituents the concessions they have proposed to make or to withdraw those concessions, when they are found ineffectual. Yet they feel such reluctance in discovering the least want of confidence in the court of Madrid, that though their present situation might fully justify them in not parting with the important rights you are impowered to concede[2] without stipulating some very valuable equivalent yet they cannot be induced to make any alteration in your instructions on this subject, till you shall have reason to conclude that nothing can be done towards forming the alliance they have so much at heart, not only because of the influence it will immediately have in accellerating the peace, but because of the advantages which Spain and America may reciprocally promise each other in future from the lasting connection which will be erected thereon.

<It has you say been frequently hinted to you that the United States have hitherto only discovered their attachment to Spain by words. What then is expected of them? Had Spain explicitly declared her expectations they should honestly have told her how far it was in

their power to comply with them. But we have been left to guess at them. The cession we have offered to make because we presumed it would be agreeable to his Catholic Majesty, is certainly no insignificant proof of the value we put upon his friendship. You will easily conceive the mortification of Congress on learning the cold and indifferent manner in which this important offer has been received, more particularly when the only return they asked, was alliance < <of> > with his majesty.[3] Such < <concession> > priviledges as Spain might conceive could be < <obtained> > granted without injury to herself and a loan or subsidy to be employed in distressing more effectively the common enimy. While Spain continues the war the United States flatter themselves that they are of some use to her while they not only distract the enimies councils, but keep the greatest part of their force employed, thereby facilitating the designs of France and Spain upon their other possessions. The first of these powers has thought that this consideration alone entitled us to the aids which they have so liberally continued to afford without ever complaining that we had not purchased them by the sacrafice of our commerce or territory.>

Tho the delays you have met with afford room to suspect that Spain wishes to defer a particular treaty with us till a general peace yet I see so many political reasons against such a measure that I can hardly presume they will adopt it.

At the close of a successful war, a great and powerful nation, to whom a character for justice and moderation is of the last importance, can in no case demand more than a compensation for the injuries received. This compensation will indeed be measured in part by this success, but still it has bounds beyond which a nation can not go with dignity. Spain has insisted upon the cession of Gibralter as a preliminary to a peace. This is of itself a considerable compensation for any damage she may have sustained. Should she carry her demands further and, agreeable to the Ideas of [the] Spanish minister, expect to have an exclusive right to the gulph of Mexico and the river Mississippi,[4] she must not only demand East and West Florida of the British, but she must support the claims of Great Britain against those of America, the claims of an enimy against the rights of a friend, in order that she may make still further demands.

Will it consist with the dignity of his catholic majesty to ask for the short space in which he has been engaged in the war not only Gibralter, but the two Florida's, the Mississippi, and the exclusion of Great Britain from the trade to the bay of Hundorous, etc., while the other branch of the house of Bourbon who engaged early in the controversy confines her demands to the narrowest limits? Will she expose herself to the imputation of dispoiling an ally (for such we are in fact tho we want the name) at the instant that she is obtaining the greatest advantages from the distress which that ally has, at least in part, contributed to bring upon her enimy? And this too without the least necessity, when she may by accepting our cession and purchasing our right appear to have contended for the rights of the United States. As this will then make no part of the satisfaction to which she is intitled from Great Britain, she may justly extend her demands to other objects or exalt her character for moderation by limiting them to narrower bounds. This mode of reasoning will come with much more weight when we displayed our rights before impartial mediation, and shew that recent conquests have been added to our antient title, for it can not be doubted that we will at the close of the war make the most of those rights which we obtain no equivalent for while it continues. I persuade myself therefore that Spain will not risk the loss of so important an object as the exclusive navigation of the Mississippi by postponing the treaty to a general peace, more particularly as a treaty with us will secure our concurrence in their views at a general congress as well as save them the necessity of making demands inconsistent with that character for moderation which their great power renders important to them.

Congress flatter themselves that the surmises on this subject are groundless, and that before this reaches you the Treaty will be far advanced. Should they be mistaken you will take measures to know from Spain whether she accepts your concession as the price of an alliance, and upon what terms. If they are such as you can not close with, and the treaty must break off, be persuaded that any steps you have taken, or shall take, not inconsistent with the respect due to his catholic majesty to prevent the cessions you are empowered to make from militating against our rights, will be approved by Congress.

Congress presume you will find no difficulty in knowing the intentions of his Majesty on this subject since they wish you to treat his ministers with that unreserved confidence which becomes the representative of a nation which has no views that it does not avow and which asks no favor which it does not hope to return. And as in the present happy state of his majesties affairs they can conceive no reason for disguising his designs they are satisfied that your frankness will meet from his ministers with the confidence it merrits.

I make no observation on the hint the Count de Florida Blanca gave you with respect to the restitution of such sums as Spain might be pleased to advance to us.[5] Because whatever claims we might set up to a subsidy from the share we take in the burden of the war, and the utility of our exertions in the common cause, we are far from wishing to lay ourselves under any pecuniary obligations for a longer time than is absolutely necessary. A few years of peace will enable us to repay with interest any sums which our present necessities compel us to borrow.[6]

I can not close this Letter without expressing the grateful sense that Congress entertain of the Disinterested conduct of Spain in rejecting the proffers of Great Britain which must undoubtedly have been considerable if they bore that proportion to the importance of his catholic Majesty in the great system of politicks, which those that have been frequently thrown out to lead the United States to a violation of her engagements have done to their comparatively small weight in the general scale.[7] But, as America never found the least inclination to close with the insidious proposals of Great Britain, so she finds no difficulty in believing that the wisdom and magnanimity of his catholic majesty will effectualy guard him against every attempt of his natural enimy to detatch him from those who are daily shedding their blood, to avenge his injuries in common with their own.

Dft in NHi: Robert R. Livingston. LS (# 7) in JP; LbkCs in PCC 79, I, 409–16 and 118, pp. 150–62; duplicate and triplicate LS not located. *HPJ,* II, 202–09; *RDC,* V, 332–35; *SDC,* VIII, 14–20. An earlier Dft of this letter, dated 26 April, is in NHi: Robert R. Livingston; E in PCC 125.

[1]Due to Livingston's absence from Philadelphia, JJ's 20 Sept. and 3 Oct. 1781 letters, along with other "foreign despatches," were on 18 March 1782 referred to a committee, which on 20 March recommended referral to a "Special Committee" to determine the disposition of their contents. On 22 April that committee—John Morin Scott, Daniel Carroll, and James Madison—submitted its report on JJ's 3 October letter, approving his stance in negotiations, referring it to Secretary Livingston as a reply to JJ. Dft of report, in Madison's hand, is in PCC 19, III; *JCC,* XXII, 140–41 and n., 207–08; *MP,* IV, 168–69. This report is the basis of Livingston's 27 April letter.

[2]The cession of American rights to the Mississippi, treated more fully in Livingston to JJ, 16 April 1782, above.

[3]See editorial note, "The Second San Ildefonso Conference."

[4]In his dispatch of 3 Oct. 1781 to McKean, JJ summarized Floridablanca's response to every argument on behalf of American rights to the navigation of the Mississippi: ". . . the King of Spain must have the Gulf of Mexico to himself; that the maxims of policy adopted in the management of their colonies required it; and that he had hoped the friendly disposition shown by this court towards us would have induced a compliance on the part of Congress."

[5]In his 3 October dispatch JJ reported Floridablanca's reaction to the suggestion by Robert Morris that Spain might provide some of the $400,000 needed to launch the proposed Bank of North America. Floridablanca, remarking on the magnitude of the American proposal, stressed that "great punctuality was requisite in such

transactions . . . that on the part of America it must be ascertained what compensation they should make, as well as the time and manner of doing it." For the proposed bank, see Robert Morris to JJ, 13 July 1781, LS in JP; LbkC in DLC: Robert Morris, A, 41–44; *RDC,* IV, 562–68; *RMP,* I, 287–90.

[6]This paragraph follows the deleted paragraph beginning, "It has, you say, been frequently hinted . . ." Livingston indicated in the margin that it was to be transposed as hereinabove.

[7]In view of the opéra bouffe aspects of the Hussey-Cumberland mission, Livingston's reference to the "importance of the offers" of Britain is unintentionally ironic. The "mission" is referred to in *JJ,* I, 771–83, *passim.* For a full account, see Samuel Flagg Bemis, *The Hussey-Cumberland Mission and American Independence* (Princeton, 1933); also *Peacemakers,* pp. 56–66.

From Robert R. Livingston

Philadelphia, 28 April 1782

Dear Sir,

You will receive with this, a letter dated yesterday. Reasons which need not be explained induce me TO MAKE THIS A SEPARATE DISPATCH. I beleive with you, that the COURT OF MADRID DOES NOT WISH TO enter into engagements with [us] during the war, influenced as I presumed not only by the reasons you suggest, which our late success must have weakened, but by another, that ALARMS ME MORE. THEY APPEAR TO EXTEND THEIR views TO THE COUNTRY ON THIS SIDE OF THE Mississippi AND TO ENTERTAIN [hopes] OF HOLDING IT IN VIRTUE OF THEIR LATE CONQUEST. THEY PRESUME that the acceptance of OUR CESSION WOULD MILITATE AGAINST THEIR FURTHER CLAIM, AND BE CONSIDERED AS AN ACKNOWLEDGMENT OF OUR RIGHT TO ALL WE DO NOT CEDE.

It is not improbable that they are acquainted with the POWER WHICH THE COURT OF FRANCE WILL HAVE OVER THE negotiations FOR PEACE. They may build much upon THEIR FRIENDSHIP, AND EXPECT to obtain through it MORE THAN WE WILL YIELD. Should you believe these apprehentions to [be] well founded, you will doubtless endeavour to shew on every proper occasion THE RIGHT OF THESE STATES TO ALL THE COUNTRY IN QUESTION. You will urge the right, if Conquest can give any, which may be derived from WILLING'S.[1] You will judge how far it may be expedient to ground demands on the right we have to a compensation for our Share of the Burden and expence of the war, if the issue should be as favorable as we have reason to expect. Our Strength is so much underated in Europe that you will find it proper to represent it, as it really is. Our regular Army including the French Troops will consist of about TWENTY THOUSAND men. They are well disciplined, cloathed and fed and having for the most part seen a seven years hard service, I beleive they may be counted equal to any Troops in the world. Our Militia are in excellent order and chiefly disciplined by Officers, who have left the regular service. While the Army lies in the middle States it can in ten or fifteen days receive a reinforcement of EIGHT OR TEN THOUSAND men for any particular service. Facts that you can easily call to mind will evince that any deficiency in the regular Corps is amply made up by this supply. These are loose hints, by no means directory to you. Congress mean[s] as little as possible to clog you with instructions. They rely upon your judgement and address to reconcile whatever differnces may appear to be between the views of Spain, and the interest of these States.

I have the honor to enclose an important Resolution, which I fear to put in cypher both because you seem to be at a loss about your Cypher, and because it would be of little use, considering the accident which you say has happened to it.[2] I have the honor to be Dear Sir, with great respect and esteem, your most obedient humble servant,

ROB. R. LIVINGSTON

CONTINENTAL CONGRESS: RESOLUTION APPROVING JAY'S CONDUCT IN SPAIN

30 April 1782

Resolved, That the minister plenipotentiary of the United States at the Court of Madrid be informed, that Congress entirely approve of his conduct as detailed in his letter of the 3d of October last; that the limitation affixed by him to the proposed surrender of the navigation of the Mississippi in particular, corresponds with the views of Congress; that they observe, not without surprise and concern, that a proposition so liberal in itself, and which removed the only avowed obstacle to a connexion between the United States and his Catholick Majesty should not have produced greater effects on the counsels of the latter; that the surrender of the navigation of the Mississippi was meant as the price of the advantages promised by an early and intimate alliance with the Spanish monarchy; and that if this alliance is to be procrastinated till the conclusion of the war, the reason of the sacrifice will no longer exist; that as every day which the proposed treaty is delayed, detracts from the obligation and inducement of the United States to adhere to their overture, it is the instruction of Congress, that he urge to the ministers of his Catholick Majesty the obligation it imposes on Spain to make the treaty the more liberal on her part, and that in particular he use his endeavours to obtain, in consideration of such delay, either an enlargement of her pecuniary aids to the United States, a facilitating of the use of the Mississippi to the citizens thereof, or some peculiar indulgences in the commerce of the Spanish colonies in America.[3]

LS (# 8) in NHi: Jay, decoded by JJ. Endorsed: ". . . Recd. 18 July." Enclosure (not located): 30 April 1782 resolution of Congress. The code employed is the nomenclator sent by Thomson on 11 July 1781. Dfts (3) in NHi: Robert R. Livingston. Triplicate and quintuplicate LS in JP; quadruplicate LS not located. LbkC in PCC 118, pp. 163–66. Code passages omitted in *HPJ*, II, 210; *RDC*, V, 377; *SDC*, VIII, 20–21.

[1]"Willing's" was left undecoded by JJ. James Willing, youngest brother of Thomas Willing (1731–1821) of Philadelphia, and a merchant in British West Florida before the Revolution, was commissioned, in 1777, a captain in the American navy and dispatched to the lower Mississippi to win support for the Patriot cause in West Florida, either by persuasion or force. His successful raids in 1778 at least temporarily blocked British supply routes but won the enmity of West Floridians. See John Caughey, "Willing's Expedition Down the Mississippi, 1778," in *Louisiana Historical Quarterly*, XV (1932), 5–36.

[2]JJ had expressed doubts about the reliability of the Thomson code, fearing that a copy of the code had been inspected while in transit to him. He had also reported his inability to decode several of Livingston's letters.

[3]The resolution was entered in the Secret Journals only: original in PCC 4, C in PCC 6, III; *Secret Journals*, III, 98–99; *JCC*, XXII, 219–20. Dft in Madison's hand in PCC 36, IV, 7; *MP*, IV, 189–91.

From Lafayette

Paris, 28 April 1782

Dear Sir,

The Opportunity I now Embrace is offered By the Prince of Masserano who Sets of[f] this Minute for Spain, and Intends to Act a part in the daring Siege of Gibraltar.[1] I will Communicate a few intelligences Which it May Be Agreable for You to know and Which I Hope I may safely Intrust to this Conveyance.

Holland is now Quite determined, and Has Agreed to Acknowledge our Independence. They are About Making A treaty of Commerce and Have Received Mr. Adams in His Public Character.[2]

I will Also Give you an Account of what Has Lately past Respecting Negotiations.

A few days before the fall of the late Ministry France Had some Advances Made to Her Under Hand Wherein it Appeared the Great point was to Make Her Abandon American Independence. The Answer was Very proper, Very finely Expressed, and Such as Would please Every American Mind.[3]

Some time After that Mr. Adams Was Applied to at the Hague. He also said Independence was the prime Step, and Nothing Could be done But in Common with France.[4]

The New Ministry Have sent Emmissaries to the French Administration, to Mr. Adams, and to Mr. Franklin. The French Ministers Have Repeated their making terms [is] out of the Question Untill American plenipotentiaries Were Admitted Into the Negotiations. Mr. Adams, and Mr. Franklin once More Said that America was not less Averse to a seperate peace, and that Any Attempt was Nothing But a loss of time.[5]

Under those Circumstances, I think we must very soon know What the Intentions of the Ennemy Are, either to try the Course of this Campaign or to propose a General Negotiation.

Mr. Mithon who Commanded an Important Convoy Has Safly Arrived into Martinique Harbour. He Has Under His Care a Vast Quantity of Military Stores much wanting for the French Fleet, and His Safe Arrival Affords us Great Satisfaction.[6]

Some Vessels Going Under Convoy to the East Indies Have Met An English Squadron and were obliged to put Back. It is feared some may Be taken, but Nothing Material.[7]

I am in Hopes a Northern power not of the first Rate, will Before long Enter into a Treaty of Commerce.[8] But I Request from You the Utmost Secrecy. The telling of it to you Now Cannot be a Breach of Confidence.

I Beg the Whole of this Letter May be Considered as Confidential, and I do Not know whether Communications Have Been Made to your Friends. God Grant them a Good Success at Gibraltar. I wish the devilish Rock was out the way. Most affectionately and Respectfully yours,

LAFAYETTE

My Best Respects wait upon Mrs. Jay, and My Compliments [to] you My friend. Your fellow Sufferer.

ALS. Endorsed.

[1]In the late spring of 1782 the Duc de Crillon brought a large Franco-Spanish force to join in the siege of Gibraltar, which had been in progress since June 1779.

[2]The treaty was not signed until 8 Oct. 1782.

[3]Nathaniel Parker Forth, an agent of the North ministry, sought unsuccessfully on 14 March to interest Vergennes in a peace settlement that did not include U.S. independence. *Peacemakers,* p. 254.

[4]The exploratory visit to John Adams was made by Thomas Digges. *Ibid.*, pp. 255–56.

[5]For the missions of Thomas Grenville and Richard Oswald to Paris to explore peace negotiations, see below, editorial note, "The Status of the Peacemaking on Jay's Arrival in Paris." Henry Laurens, after release on parole, went to the United Provinces at Shelburne's request to probe Adams' attitude toward a separate peace. *Ibid.*, pp. 261, 264–67, 271.

[6]Mithon de Genouilly, a French naval officer, evaded Rodney's patrols and reached Martinique on 26 March with two ships of the line and the transports they were convoying. James, *The British Navy in Adversity*, pp. 330–31, 432, 442.

[7]Admiral Samuel Barrington sailed from Spithead early in April to intercept a French fleet bound for the East Indies. In engagements northeast of Ushant on 21 and 22 April, the British captured two French ships of the line and twelve transport vessels. *Ibid.*, pp. 366–67.

[8]The first informal conversations regarding a Swedish-American treaty took place in Paris in April 1782, reputedly arranged by Lafayette between Franklin and Count Gustav Philip Creutz, the Swedish ambassador to France. Not until December 1782, however, did Creutz and Franklin begin serious negotiations, and the treaty was not signed until April 1783. See Adolph B. Benson, *Sweden and the American Revolution* (New Haven, 1926), pp. 48–55, and Amandus Johnson, "Swedish Constributions to American Freedom, 1776–1783," *The Swedes in America, 1638–1938* (Philadelphia, 1953), part. VI, vol. I, 572–81.

To Benjamin Franklin

Madrid, 8 May 1782

Dear Sir,

I have recieved your Favors of the 22 and 23 Ult. They have determined me to set out for Paris. I shall leave this Place the latter End of next Week. Mrs. Jay and my Nephew go with me. Be pleased to take Lodgings for me, and to inform me of them, by a Line to Mr. Delap or Mr. Bondfield at Bordeaux.[1]

The Embassador of France does not dislike this Step, and the Count de Florida Blanca will refer the Instructions intended for Mr. Del Campo, to the Count de Aranda at Paris.

I am, Dear Sir, with great Regard and Esteem, Your obliged and obedient Servant,

JOHN JAY

ALS in PU. Addressed: "His Exy. Doctor Franklin." Dft in JP. *HPJ*, II, 301.

[1]As per instructions, William Temple Franklin notified JJ on 5 June that he had found an apartment for him in Paris. ALS in JP; *HPJ*, II, 308. John Bondfield was American commercial agent at Bordeaux; Samuel and J. H. Delap, a mercantile firm there.

Keeping in Touch

The Jays made a sustained effort while abroad to maintain contacts with relatives and close personal friends. At best, news crossed the Atlantic at an erratic and deliberate pace, letters sometimes taking more than six months to reach their destination. Exacerbating the problem were breaks in communication caused by lost ships and intercepted letters. Such correspondence as did reach the news-hungry Jays in Spain and France, however, brought them a lively sense of how their intimates at home were coping with the various wartime crises—from the British incursion of Elizabethtown, which placed the Livingstons' persons and property in danger, to the robbery suffered by JJ's family in Fishkill. In return, JJ and SLJ disclosed aspects of their personal lives which would not be detailed in the more formal official correspondence and which included innumerable comments on people, manners, fashions, and the rigors of travel in foreign climes. The Jays relied heavily on the news provided by SLJ's sister Catharine. "You are really a charming Correspondent as well as a charming every Thing else," JJ acknowledged. "We have more Letters from you than from all our other Friends in America put together."[1]

JJ's abiding concern for the well-being of his aged father, his afflicted brothers and sisters,[2] and his competitive elder brother Sir James, reveal the strain of the separation under which he labored. It was months before JJ learned of his father's death on 17 April 1782 or the details of Peter Jay's complicated will and codicils. Considering JJ's subsequent prominence in the movement to manumit slaves, it is of some relevance to learn the names and numbers of the black slaves bequeathed to the family members by his father.

During the course of the Spanish stay JJ's and SLJ's relations with Henry Brockholst Livingston deteriorated. At the start there seemed to be an atmosphere of congeniality. Late in 1780 JJ requested Congress to extend Brockholst's military leave in order for him to continue his duties as JJ's private secretary, and that body obliged.[3] In February, 1781 Brockholst wrote his sister that "Mr. Jay is daily loading me with kindness. He is heaping obligations on me which I am sure it will never be in my power to repay."[4] Nonetheless, within less than five months SLJ was moved to pour her heart out in a letter to her father, in which she described her brother's sulky attitude, his rude behavior, and the undiplomatic outbursts which were proving to be a continuing source of embarrassment to the American envoy and his wife.[5]

[1]JJ to Catharine W. Livingston, 13 Sept. 1780. Again, he wrote on 23 November: "You are without Exception the best Correspondent I have in America, and for that and twenty other good Reasons, every Letter I write to Congress shall enclose one for you." Dfts of both in JP. For the absence of letters from JJ's family in Fishkill, see SLJ to Catharine W. Livingston, 1 Dec. 1780, below.

[2]See JJ to Egbert Benson, [20] Nov. 1780. Dft in JP; *HPJ,* I, 447; *WJ,* II, 68.
[3]See above, JJ to Samuel Huntington, [30 Nov. 1780].
[4]Henry Brockholst Livingston to Catharine W. Livingston, 3 Feb. 1781, ALS in MHi: Ridley.
[5]See SLJ to William Livingston, 24 June 1781, below.

To Peter Jay

Madrid, 20 November 1780

Dear Sir,

I never send a Letter to Congress, but one for you accompanies it. Sir James and Fœdy must also have recieved several letters from me, and yet to this Day I have not been favored with a single Line from either.[1] They must either have been too inattentive or their Letter remarkably unfortunate.

Some of my former Letters informed you that I had sent you <some> cloathing etc. from Bordeaux and ten or fifteen of Salt from Cadiz.[2] If they arrived safe you have doubly recieved them, as they were consigned to Mr. Robert Morris who I am very sure would take care to acquaint you or one of my Brothers of it.

My little family are well. The enclosed is a Letter from Peter with whom I am well satisfied. He is much proven and in perfect Health.[3]

I am really very anxious to hear of the Health of the family and should be exceedingly obliged to one of my Brothers for a few Lines on that Subject. Be pleased to send the enclosed to <Doctor Van Wyck> Mr. Benson.[4] Remember me to Doctor Van Wyck[5] and your Neighbour.

<With> my love to all the family, I am, Dear Sir, your dutiful and affectionate Son,

J. J.

DftS. Endorsed by JJ. ALS not located.

[1]Only two other letters from JJ to Peter Jay, 23 May 1780, in *JJ,* I, 698–702, and 14 July 1780, DftS in JP, have been located. No letters from Peter Jay have been located, nor between JJ and Frederick Jay prior to Frederick's 28 Dec. 1780 letter, ALS in JP. Only an extract from one letter between JJ and Sir James has been located: that is from JJ's 4 Jan. 1776 from Philadelphia to Sir James at Bath, England. E in CO 5/40, p. 399, in the "intercepted letters from American colonists."

[2]The invoice for this trunk, dated 24 June 1780, consigned to Robert Morris, is in JP. The trunk, containing fabrics, clothing, snuff, hardware, and spices, was shipped by Bondfield Haywood and Company under the command of Captain Joseph Bradford.

[3]Enclosure not located.

[4]See letter immediately below.

[5]Dr. Theodorus Van Wyck. See *JJ,* I, 319.

Sarah Livingston Jay to Catharine W. Livingston

Madrid, 1 December 1780

How invaluable, my dear Kitty! is a real friend; had I been ignorant of its worth till now, the pleasure I've derived from your affectionate attention to our happiness, would have taught me to estimate the blessing in a proper manner. I am at this instant overjoyed with the receipt of three charming long letters from you, just handed to me, which added to those I had received before makes 11 that I return you my sincere thanks for. Sister Susan has wrote me one letter, and one I've been favored with from Mrs. Meredith;[1] not a single line has reached us from any of the family at Fishkill. Thus you see how extravagantly kind you have been, and how highly we must value your correspondance.

I willingly flatter myself that even those of my friends who have not time to throw away in writing to me, may yet have no objection to hear that I'm still in the land of the living, and therefore have taken the liberty of introducing myself to their recollection by scribbling to them; whether or not my letters have been lost I can't tell, though I almost believe they have since they have not provoked an answer. You alone seem sensible of the interest I take in the concerns of my friends, since but for your letters I should remain in ignorance of any alteration that takes place in my absence. Some of my friends indeed have experienced changes that I much lament; but others again have received an increase of happiness. Among the latter it's my joy to find the Chancellor and Mrs. Livingston. The pleasure I felt upon hearing of the birth of their little daughter induced me to trouble Polly with a letter to tell her that I shared her felicity. Notwithstanding Peter's caveat I had hopes to engage his affection for a lovely little sister, and yours for a sweet god-child, but alas! my dear Kitty, she is now beyond the regards of either.[2]

When I first took up my pen, I thought I should be unable to quit it, but really so many things crowded upon my mind that one displaces the other. Let me see, I'll begin with a reference to your last letters, and pray my Lady, why was the place you was at, omitted in the date? And why did not you inform me of your retrogade manuvre from Elizabeth Town? Whether the family still reserve the house at Persipiney or not? And whether my little heroe shared in the glory of the retreat? Was you not ashamed to abandon a post that Susan alone had once maintained with so much good conduct?[3] But jesting apart, I assure you I suffered exceedingly on your account till Mr. Jay received a letter from Mr. Morris, and another from Mr. Gerry,[4] in which the safety of the family were mentioned. The death of our amiable friend Mrs. Caldwell[5] affected me beyond description, and even now I can't think of it without feeling such uneasy emotions that I'm afraid to indulge the recollection. How chequered is life! And how unimportant do our pursuits appear when contrasted with the value and shortness of time!

But you'll think I'm relapsing in my usual moralizing strain, and therefore as I think we cannot better improve our time than by the cultivation of virtuous friendships, I shall change the subject by a gradual transition, when I tell you how much the mutual friendship subsisting between my dear Mrs. Morris and you contribute to my happiness. I have written two letters to her to express the satisfaction I've received from that circumstance; but to tell the truth I never yet wrote a letter that pleased me, I always wish to describe the sentiments of my heart to my friends, but the letters convey so faint an image of them that I can only trace a distant resemblance. I shall be happy if you tell me you resolve to accept her friendly invitation this fall,[6] and when you write to me continue to mention every thing relative to our friends though to you they may appear trivial circumstances.

I wish our dear Susan would visit our friends on the *banks* of Hudson, their society and the change of air would be agreeable and useful to her. I long to receive a letter from mamma were it to contain but three lines; methinks I could kiss the name written with her own hand. Pray give my love to papa. I fear he is less fond of his pen than gratitude to that little instrument of his fame will justify. I repent my not bringing with me some of his compositions. As to William, we are all downright angry with him for his invincible silence. When Judy[7] has leisure to recollect that she has more friends than one I shall be obliged to her if she'll reckon me of the number. Her silence 'till now I forgive, but if after my frequent admonitions she still continues in the fault of omission she'll find absolution not readily obtained.

The betts depending between you and the Chevalier[8] I hope are considerable since you are certainly intitled to the stake (I don't mean a wooden one, but such as I suppose a lady like yourself would naturally lay; as a Cap, Fan etc.) for I have not used any false colouring, nor have I amused myself with plays or any other diversions on Sundays. If this finds you at Philadelphia please to remember my Compliments to the Chevalier, Mr. Marbois and the Consul.[9]

I thank you my dear, for the plan inclosed in your letter which the ladies have adopted for the relief of our worthy soldiers.[10] You must know when I perceived the folded paper I immediately fancied it contained your picture, and should have been much disappointed if it had not been so agreeable and honorable a representation of my lovely country-women. I am quite charmed with them, and indeed with every thing truly American. One piece of advice I'll whisper in your ear; whatever false notions travellers may endeavor to palm upon you, don't you ever say that such a lady is handsome enough to please even at Court. Believe me it requires a greater degree of beauty to be only passable in America, than to out-shine all the grandees of—I won't say where.

I would not wish to damp the ardor of a youth who has entered the service of his country, but I must confess I don't think Jack[11] will be pleased with the region of Neptune. However, he has my best wishes. My fingers are tired of holding the pen, if I recollect any thing more before an opportunity offers, I'll resume my pen and begin another sheet, in the mean time believe me most affectionately yours,

SA. JAY

Please to present my most respectful Compliments to General and Mrs. Washington.

ALS. LbkC in JP.

[1]For Catharine W. Livingston's four extant letters to SLJ and JJ abroad, see *JJ*, I, 689–91, 698n., for [26 Dec. 1779] and 13 Feb. 1780; 23 May (marked "No. 10") and 10 July 1780 (marked "No. 12"), AL of both in JP. For Susan Livingston's letters, see hers to SLJ, 27 May 1781, below. Margaret Cadwalader Meredith's letter has not been located.

[2]A reference to the birth and death of the Jays' infant daughter Susan.

[3]A reference to Susan Livingston's bravery during a previous raid on Liberty Hall; see SLJ to JJ, 5 March 1779, and Robert R. Livingston to JJ, 6 July 1780, *JJ*, I, 572–73, 787–89. See Susan Livingston to SLJ, 27 May 1781, below, for the more recent episode.

[4]Robert Morris to JJ, 6 July 1780, ALS in JP; Elbridge Gerry to JJ, 10 July 1780, not located; mentioned in JJ to Gerry, 18 Nov. 1780, above.

[5]Hannah Caldwell, wife of the Reverend James Caldwell, was killed by the British during their June raid into New Jersey. The Caldwells were neighbors of the Livingstons. See *JJ*, I, 693. Theodore Thayer, *As We Were: The Story of Old Elizabethtown* (Elizabeth, N.J., 1964), pp. 136–37.

[6]In her 10 July 1780 letter, AL in JP, Catharine W. Livingston wrote that Robert and Mary White Morris had invited her to pay "them a visit in the fall or winter."

[7]SLJ's brother, William (see *JJ*, I, 451), and sister, Judith Livingston Watkins, for whom see below, Susan Livingston to SLJ, 27 May 1781.

[8]On 26 April 1780, Catharine wrote: "I suspect I shall win a wager of the Chevalier [La Luzerne], Mr. Carmichael must determine it, by informing the parties if you do or do not make use of paint in France; Another respecting your attending Public Places on Sunday Evenings. Had I been in doubt I should be encouraged

from Mr. Witherspoon to flatter myself I had not been mistaken in you." On 10 July Catharine added: "The Chevalier is not to be convinced that he has lost his bet to me, til Mr. Carmichael informs me that he was questioned by many at Martinique if you do not." On 1 September SLJ indignantly rejoined in a letter to Mary White Morris: "you will tell the Chevalier that Kitty is not mistaken in her sister; she has really won the bett." A friend of the Livingstons as well as SLJ and JJ, the Reverend John Witherspoon, President of the College of New Jersey from 1768 to 1794, served as a delegate to Congress from 1776 to 1782. Catharine W. Livingston had seen Witherspoon in Trenton where he was serving on the New Jersey Council. Catharine W. Livingston to SLJ, 26 April, and to JJ, 10 July, both AL in JP; SLJ to Mary White Morris, 1 Sept. 1780, ALS in CSmH and LbkC in JP. Varnum Lansing Collins, *President Witherspoon* (2 vols., New Jersey, 1925), II, 47; for Witherspoon, see also *JJ*, I, 371.

[9]The Chevalier de La Luzerne; probably Martin Oster, French vice consul in Philadelphia, see JJ to Huntington, [30 Nov. 1780], above.

[10]The Ladies Association of Philadelphia, founded in May 1780, subscribed a substantial sum in specie and paper money for the relief of Washington's army. J. Thomas Scharf and Thompson Westcott, *History of Philadelphia, 1609–1884* (3 vols., Philadelphia, 1884), II, 1690.

[11]On 10 July 1780 Catharine wrote: "Brother Jack received a summons to his duty on board the Saratoga as senior midshipman; the ship being shortly to sail on a cruize."

To Catharine W. Livingston

Madrid, 17 December 1780

Dear Kitty,

It is uncertain whether this Letter will ever come to your Hands. Two or three others are now on the Way to you. I fear your late Letters have been unfortunate, the last that reached us was dated in July,[1] since which we have not heard anything of the Family. We suspect that several Letters from our Friends were committed to Mr. Laurens Care. If so they may one of these Days have the Pleasure of seeing themselves in Print. It is said all his Papers fell into the Enemy's Hands. He, poor Man, is still in the Tower, where his Reputation as well as Person lies at the Mercy of the Ministry. They have insinuated that he has said many Things, which without better Evidence than their Words, I cannot believe he ever said.

All the World here are cursing Arnold and pitying his Wife. *Arnold's Plot* is the Subject of every Conversation. Do you know at what Price he sold his Conscience and Reputation? A Report prevails here that General Clinton agreed to give him 80,000 Stirling and a Major General's Commission, and Major Andrews[2] Life in the Bargain. I had a Letter a few Days ago from France which informs me that one Smith of Haverstraw was one of Arnolds Accomplices, and soon to be hanged. Should this be Thomas Smith? If so, I suppose he is in some Measure indebted to his Brothers Politics. His Brother James is in Holland and has written to me. His Letter bespeakes him a staunch Whig.[3]

Your Brother is gone to Bilboa,[4] from whence you will probably hear from him. How long he may stay is uncertain. Some say it has more Charms than any other part of Spain. If he should be of that opinion, I shall not expect to see him again very soon.

We are daily promising ourselves the pleasure of recieving some very long Letters from you. You have hitherto been very attentive. Dont fall off. Your Letters are always doubly welcome. The Hand that writes them has few equals, and they contain more interesting Information than most others we recieve.

Kiss our little Boy for us. I will repay you when we meet. In the mean time accept my best Wishes. I assure you they extend to every thing that can make you happy here and hereafter. Our Love to all the Family. I am Dear Kitty your affectionate Brother,

JOHN JAY

ALS in MHi: Ridley. Endorsed.

[1]Catharine W. Livingston to JJ, 10 July 1780.

[2]Error for André. JJ had an inflated notion of Clinton's offer. Arnold was promised £20,000 if he handed over West Point to the British, but was later awarded £6,315, as compensation for the losses he had suffered in joining their side.

[3]Joshua Hett Smith (1736–1818) was acquitted on 26 Oct. 1780 of the charge of complicity with Arnold. Thereafter held as a "suspected" Tory in a Goshen jail, he escaped in May 1781 and fled to Manhattan. Thomas Smith was his older brother. Both were brothers of William Smith, Jr., the prominent Loyalist, and James Smith, the "staunch Whig" who wrote JJ on 12 Sept. 1780; see *JJ,* I, 813–21. Van Doren, *Secret History,* pp. 289, 325, 391; William Smith, *Memoirs,* II, 334, 421.

[4]To insure secrecy and expedition, JJ often sent Henry Brockholst Livingston to Bilbao with dispatches to Congress as well as personal letters. See also above, JJ to Huntington, 28 Jan. 1781.

William Livingston to Sarah Livingston Jay

Trenton, 14 January 1781
Duplicate

My dear Child,

I cannot express the pleasure I felt on the News of the birth of your Daughter in a foreign Country, where, having so few connections, it must have given you still more joy, than mothers generally receive from so joyful an occurrence. I was proportionably afflicted by the account of her death, though I cannot pretend to form an adequate Idea of the distress into which you must have been thrown by so unfortunate an event. But the magnanimity and resignation with which you have borne that, as well as the other disasters with which it has pleased Providence to try your Patience and submission, do you great honour, and give me not a little comfort. I hope my dear Child that you will be restored to my arms as soon as circumstances will admit, and that the same kind Providence that protected you in your voyage to Spain will grant you a safe return to your native shore. I ardently long for the happy day.

Peter is a very fine boy, and I have within these few days received a Letter from him written with his own dear little fingers, though guided by his Aunt Sukey's[1] hand. The writing was his own, and he tells me that if I will buy for him a continental Primmer,[2] he will mind his book. I immediately procured and sent him one with the picture of his favourite, General Washington, in the frontispiece, and a Letter which I wrote in Characters in imitation of Printers types, which he was able to read and understand.

In your correspondence with the rest of the family, I am sorry that you have hitherto not included your affectionate Father,

WIL. LIVINGSTON

Duplicate ALS. Addressed: "Mrs. Sara Jay, Madrid." Endorsed.

[1]Susan Livingston.

[2]This primer, printed for Walters and Norman of Philadelphia, was published 23 June 1779, and contains what is generally believed to be the first engraved portrait of Washington executed in the U.S. Evans, 16480.

Henry Brockholst Livingston to Sarah Livingston Jay

Nantes, 1 March 1781

My dear Sister,

Your favor of the 4th Ult.[1] was delivered me Yesterday. It gave me very great pleasure to find you had heard from the family, which I have not been able to do at L'Orient; notwithstanding the most diligent Enquiries, and the many vessels which have lately arrived from our Country. You were right in reading Susan's Letters, and in not sending them forward. I had rather defer the pleasure of perusing them a month or two, than risque it altogether by putting them in a Post-Office. I employed a large part of my time at L'Orient in writing to our friends, and since my return here have met with another most excellent opportunity. Mr. Romain[2] an old acquaintance and fellow student of mine is on his return to New Jersey from his Studies at Edinburgh. He thinks his Father's family is at Morris-town and has promised to pay a visit to ours as soon as he arrives. If he lands at Boston he will call at Mr. Jay's on his way to New Jersey. I wish the Packet You are making up may arrive in time to go with him. He expects to sail in a fortnight, though I much doubt his getting away in less than a month.

Mrs. Johnson has been too unwell to execute your Commissions yet.[3] In a few days she will venture out. She has shewn me a riding suit for Mrs. Bingham.[4] It is very rich and elegant. The feathers alone in the hat cost several Guineas. Our Affairs must be in a promising train while the Ladies can afford such Extravagance. Several Gentlemen lately from America assure me, the female Headdresses in Philadelphia exceed by some feet those of their fair Allies on this side of the water.

I went last night to a Masquerade. It was the last of the Season, and the first I had ever seen. It was too crowded to be agreeable. There were not far short of fifteen hundred men and women the greater part of whom resembled Demons more than human beings. I wonder any Lady who has the least Pretensions to Modesty will be seen at a place where disorder, double-Entendres, and Indecency are so prevalent. Perhaps none there laboured under this Embarrassment. It was certainly fortunate for me not to be sufficiently acquainted with the language to understand the half of what was said. By this Ignorance the *delicate* organs of my hearing escaped, and spared me the Imputation of Modesty, which must often, in spite of every effort, have discovered itself by the blushes which would have overspread the cheeks of a much less bashful fellow than myself. It was not till sometime after sun-rise the Company broke up.

These diversions only prevail during Carnival which ended Yesterday. Lent of course commenced to day, though from what I have seen the People of this Country are not quite so Scrupulous in the observance of it, as their Neighbours of Spain. At the Hotel where I dined to day there was scarcely a dish of fish to be seen, unless they had assumed a masque which a great many dishes here wear even after Carnival, and often puzzle a Stranger to know what he has before him; nor is his taste always sufficient to determine the doubts of his Eyes.

I will not forget the Umbrella. Don't neglect to encrease your commissions through fear of giving me trouble. You will find by a former Letter of mine that I had advised you to do it. I wrote to Mr. Jay yesterday.[5] With my best wishes for you both, I am Dear Sister, Your Very Affectionate Brother,

HENRY BR. LIVINGSTON

P.S. If you meant to make any alterations in your directions respecting the feathers, you have not done it, for on comparing your Letter with the Memorandum, I find the same colours mentioned in both.

HBL

ALS.

[1]Letter not located.

[2]Nicholas Romayne (1756–1817), who matriculated at King's College in 1774, but completed his medical studies at Edinburgh in 1780, and was a leading, if controversial medical figure in post-Revolutionary New York City. David C. Humphrey, *From King's College to Columbia, 1746–1800* (New York, 1976), p. 261.

[3]Joshua Johnson's English-born wife, Catherine Nuth (c. 1757–1811), whom he married in that country c. 1772. For SLJ's order for the purchase of goods to be shipped to her sister, see JJ to Catharine W. Livingston, 21 Jan. 1782, below.

[4]Anne Willing (Mrs. William) Bingham (1764–1801), a daughter of Thomas Willing (1731–1821), Philadelphia merchant and former partner of Robert Morris.

[5]Livingston to JJ, 28 Feb. 1781, ALS in JP.

Sarah Livingston Jay to William Livingston

Madrid, 14 March 1781

My dear Papa,

The receipt of your letter last evening gave me inexpressible satisfaction but it was rendered less compleat than it otherwise would have been by a hint that you entertained some doubts of my remembrance of you. As I always preferred the virtues that flow from the heart before any accidental acquirements in any one, I cannot feel satisfied till every doubt of that nature is banished from your mind. I must therefore inform you that while on board the Confederacy I wrote to nobody but Mamma unless that letter was written jointly to you and her,[1] the weather being too tempestuous to admit of handling the pen with convenience.

When I arrived at Martinique my time [was] so much engaged by company that I could not take the rest that my indisposition required. As soon therefore as we re-embarked I began to write to you, and Mr. Jay's father[2] that in case when we arrived in port a vessel might be ready to sail for America my letters might be conveyed by it. My expectations were answered, for at Cadiz Mr. Dessesuer was waiting a fair wind, and after adding a postcript of equal length with what I had before written, it was delivered to the Captain and we never heard of the fate of them 'till a few months ago when we learnt that the vessel was captured and had been carried to Gibralter. As I kept a copy of what I wrote on the passage I shall enclose it in this. Several other letters I have sent but find they must have shared a similar fate.

You were too well acquainted with my Sensibility to be mistaken when you thought it had been greatly wounded by the death of my lovely babe, nor was my dear Sir mistaken when he concluded I had obtained resignation on the occasion, that gently soothed my grief and made me view the providence as if some guardian angel had offered to conduct her home without encountering the dangers of the sea when we were about returning to our native Country. And is she not gone home before me escaped from a more perilous ocean than that which parts me from my Country? Yes she is safe, but what trials may await her surviving friends is concealed in the bosom of futurity. I sincerely sympathize with Uncle and Aunt Livingston on the death of their sons[3]: those two worthy families have experienced many trials in a few years and they have followed so closely upon each others heels that the wounds could scarcely heal before they were made to bleed afresh. Wisdom is the companion of reflection and must be sought oftentimes in the habitation of Adversity found in sea[rch] of mirth and gaiety.

Some gay ladies there are who if they perused this letter would conclude it was written during the influence of spleen and vapours but they would be greatly mistaken. I am unacquainted with those disorders which I believe seldom visit any bosoms but those which are destitute of Thought. My situation is as agreeable as absence from my very dear friends will permit. I'm neither so hurried with company and trifling amusements as to exclude more rational entertainments, nor so much alone as to be tired of myself. My health is perfectly restored and I feel as happy and as chearful as if inspired by the season which is really enchanting. You would be pleased with this climate in the winter; already the leaves are opening and the trees blooming as with you in May.

The present King of Spain has greatly improved this City and the adjacent Country by beautiful walks, handsome fountains and excellent roads; the trees alone with which he has adorned the roads and walks would be to you sufficient proof of his taste. He has four sitios or Country seats[4] with palaces which he alternately visits and as he takes great delight in the Chase he prefers them to Madrid. Aranjuez is generally thought to be the most beautiful but as I only saw it en passant in my way here I cannot form any opinion of it, but intend in the month of May to make a short visit there, our finances not permitting me to <remain there all the while that Mr. Jay> spend all the time with Mr. Jay that he will necessarily be there. In the king's

Armoury is some very curious and very compleat armour. I had no idea that the antients were so well guarded from spears. As they are preserved with great care they really make a pretty appearance. There are three equestrian statues in it of the Emperor Charles the 5th[5] one of which represents him with the very clothes he wore and the saddle he rode on that occasion as Conquerer of Tunis. The other when crowned king of the Romans and a third as King of Spain. The horses are likewise in armour and upon their sides is a kind of styrup to support one end of an immense spear. Poor Motezuma's wooden spear and painted Armor make but an humble appearance among those of the Europeans. The large Mourning coach in which the foolish queen[6] (for that is the epithet given her) used to ride and always carry with her the corpse of her dead husband the Arc-duke father of Charles is likewise preserved in that place.

There are a great many things here very worthy of notice. The Palace is magnificent, and the Cabinet of natural curiosities well supplied, but of those things I suppose Brockholst has given you discriptions as his pen can do them more justice. Don't you already think me unconsciable to engross so much of your attention when so small a portion of your time is your own.

Heaven grant success to your unremitted attention to the benefit of our country. May peace and tranquility soon succeed to the toil and dangers of my Countrymen: the sun shines not on a more worthy people, even in their errors virtue is conspicuous, for does not the generosity that governed the actions of those soldiers who were lately discontented cast a veil over their precipitation.[7] <But my great attachment to that part of the world> As the season advances that must open the Campaign my solicitude increases though but certain I am that victory will one day give to the Americans that liberty they have had the virtue to defend. Adieu my dear Papa. Never again admit one idea to the disadvantage of the affection with which I am your very dutiful daughter,

S. J.

As you are often absent from the family I shall likewise write to Mamma but as we often divide the pacquets perhaps both letters may not arrive at the same time and if that should be the case please to remember me affectionately to her.

I felt the tenderness you express for my little boy with a great deal of gratitude and am very thankful for the continuance of his health. You have encouraged me to write to him by telling me that he begins to read. If we are absent more than a twelve-month I hope his Aunt Susan will teach him to write.

DftS. Enclosure: C of SLJ to William Livingston, 30 Dec. 1779, not located. LbkC in JP.

[1]SLJ to Susannah French Livingston, "on board the Confederacy," 12 Dec. 1779, LbkC in JP.

[2]SLJ to William Livingston, see source note; to Peter Jay, see *JJ*, I, 687–89.

[3]SLJ's uncle, Peter Van Brugh Livingston (1710–92), lost his son William Alexander (b. 1757) in a duel on 1 Aug. 1780; his youngest son was James Alexander (b. 1763). Reynolds, *Family Hist. of So. N.Y.*, III, 1325–26.

[4]See *ibid.*, p. 759.

[5]Charles V (1500–58), emperor (1519–58) and King of Spain (1516–56), was the son of Philip I and Juana of Castile.

[6]Juana "la Loca" (1479–1555), Queen of Castile and Aragon, daughter of Ferdinand and Isabella, and wife of Philip I (1478–1506). Philip's death had been the final blow to Juana's already unstable mind.

[7]Apparently a reference to the mutiny of the Pennsylvania Line, 1 Jan. 1781, followed on 20 January by a mutiny of the New Jersey Line.

To Frederick Jay

Madrid, 15 March 1781

My dear Brother,

I was just <writing> dispatching the enclosed Letter[1] to you when yours of the 28 December last[2] was delivered to me, as this is the first I have had the pleasure of receiving from you since my <my safe> arrival, I shall take this and several other opportunities to inform you of its having come safe to Hand. There is but little Prospect of my receiving yours of the 1 November last.[3] I regret it the more as you tell me it was particular.

The short Stay you purposed to make at Philadelphia pleases me; it evinces your Attention to our good old Father and his Family. The Proofs you have given of filial affection make me love and esteem you more than ever I did, and be assured I shall never neglect a single Opportunity of giving you higher Evidence of it than words.

I am exceedingly happy to hear you left the Family well. God grant that they may Continue so and <may soon cease to> that every obstacle to my seeing <my Family soon> them and contributing to their Welfare may soon cease. The account you give me of my dear little Boy is flattering. I fear he will soon begin to lose by my Absence, it is hard (though proper) to make such tender Sacrifices to public Good. I neither do or shall much regret his not going to Fish Kill. I have doubts on that Subject. I have received a ridiculous Letter from Mrs. M.,[4] but neither have or shall answer it. I wish to be excused from that correspondence <with her> <for the> at present.[5] Have no Hand therefore in conveying any of her Letters to me. As to our Knight of the Order of Sisiphus,[6] I am not much surprized to hear of his being still at Philadelphia, where I suppose <where> he is <sweating> labouring hard to roll some new Stone up Hill. I wish he may succeed for once. Had I flattered his foibles and been less sincere I should have been more agreable.

Tell Peggy I charge her to keep up her Spirits. Give the same <Advice> Injunctions to Peter and Nancy.[7] We shall all yet be happy together, and I shall be much mistaken if the Time does not come even in this world when we shall rejoice for the Days wherein we have seen adversity. In the next we certainly shall. Comfort each other, and be assured that I shall not delay joining you a moment longer than <my> Duty to our Country may detain me from you.

You may remember that I left a Chest of Law Books at Poughkeepsie. Take a Catalogue of them and let Mr. Hobart have them on his signing a Receipt at the foot of it.[8] Present my Compliments to him <and assure him of my>. I Esteem <and Regard> him much.

Dont neglect drawing upon me for the <money> 50 £ Sterling mentioned in the enclosed Letter,[9] and in three months after <you may again> draw again upon me for the like Sum out of which pay twenty pounds (that is fifty hard Dollars) to Mr. Bancker,[10] twenty to Peter, twenty to Nancy, and <twenty> you will be pleased to lay out twenty more in something clever and present to Peggy.[6] Sally and Peter are well and desire to be affectionately remembered to you all.

Write often to our Elizabeth Town Friends.[11] We have frequent Letters from them. As to Letters for me, send them often by the Way of Boston. You have several acquaintances there who would readily enclose them in some of their Correspondents in this Kingdom and many more Vessels come to Spain from New England than from all the Rest of the Continent. Remember that you have a Cypher, and that you will greatly oblige me by frequent, long, and particular Letters.

Remember me to my old Friends, the Doctor and Billy, Capt. Platt etc.[12] Assure the Doctor that I shall never forget his Kindness to the Family, and that if I live he shall not be a Loser by it. Tell all the Servants that I remember them, <and that> the Trunk I sent from Bordeaux contained something for each of them. It is lost and I am sorry for it.

Adieu my Dear Friend, continue to comfort and aid our good old Father and the Family and rely on the gratitude and Sincere attachment of Your affectionate Brother,

J. J.

P.S. Dont let Mrs. M. want but be guided by her real not ostensible Necessities. *I am sure you wont forget poor Guss.*[13]

DftS. Endorsed by JJ: "... In ansr. to <13 March> 28 Decr. 1780. Sent to Mr. Harrison. 22 Do. to Messrs. Gardoqui for Capt. Trask. See my Letter of 9 March which this covered. 25 Ap. sent Copy by Mr. Toscan."

[1]JJ to Peter Jay, 14 March 1781, DftS in JP.

[2]ALS in JP.

[3]Not located.

[4]JJ's sister, Eve Jay (Mrs. Harry) Munro, Peter Jay Munro's mother.

[5]No letters between JJ and Mrs. Munro have been located.

[6]Sir James Jay.

[7]JJ's blind brother and blind sister Anna Maricka.

[8]On 28 Dec. 1780, Frederick wrote that John Sloss Hobart wanted to borrow JJ's law books. See *JJ,* I, 208, 546, 547, for Hobart, a judge of the New York State Supreme Court of Judicature.

[9]JJ had heard that the ship which embarked from Bordeaux carrying the supplies that he had purchased for his father's family had been taken by the British. He therefore wrote his father: "I think it will be best to purchase what you may want in your own Country tho at a higher price, and for this purpose have desired Fœdy immediately to draw upon me for fifty pounds Sterling." See n. 1. See also JJ to Peter Jay, 20 Nov. 1780, above.

[10]For Gerard Bancker, see below, JJ to Egbert Benson, 8 Dec. 1781, n. 6.

[11]The family of Governor William Livingston.

[12]Dr. Theodorus Van Wyck; his son William (1769–1841); for Jonathan Platt, see above, JJ to George Clinton, 23 Feb. 1782.

[13]JJ's eldest brother Augustus. See *JJ,* I, 32, 33.

From Frederick Jay

Fish Kill, 10 April 1781

My Dear Sir,

Since your favours of the 17th and 18th September last I have not had the pleasure of hearing from you.

My last was of the 10th February via Philadelphia,[1] which I hope is come safe to your hands. Neither of the articles mentioned in your former letters have arrived, they would have been of service to the Family, but as we did not depend entirely upon them, the loss is not so great.

As my last letter gave you a full account of everything relative to the Family it will be needless at present to renew the Subject. I shall only say that our situation is not the most agreeable but at present there is no releif. We must be content and endeavour to do the best.

Sir James still continues at Philadelphia where he has resided since last June. When he intends to return is uncertain, he has not favoured the Family with a line since January last.

Farming goes on but badly, a large and helpless Family to be provided for. We have only old and young Platt with your Boy (who hitherto behaves well and is of use) and Kingston to do the work. Of consequence much hireing is necessary. The old Fellow has been laid up since October last with a locked jaw and is of very little use. Frank is sold for his good behaviour. Peter and myself have used our best endeavours to persuade the old Gentleman[2] to reduce the Number of Blacks, but without affect, the expence of supporting them at this present time is beyond conception. We are under the necessity of purchasing a great part of both their Cloathing and bread. A hint from you to Papa might perhaps be of service.

Our public affairs the last Year were in Such a Situation as prevented your little Boy paying us a visit. At present there appears to be no obstruction, and I shall by the 1st of May go for him. A few days ago I was honoured with a *letter* from him reminding me of the promise I made him last winter, that of fetching him in the spring. I have the pleasure to inform you that he and every branch of the Livingston Family at Elizabeth Town enjoy perfect health.

Our Old Parent is much the same in every respect as when you left him. Nancy is but in indifferent health, the rest of the Family as usual. Nancy, Peter and Peggy join me in our affection to you and Sally. Remember us to Peter Munro, the Colonel and Mr. Carmichael and believe me to be with great Esteem, Yours Affectionately,

FRED. JAY

P.S. Gussey remains at his old Quarters and behaves well. Mrs. Munro continues with us.

Your Negroe Clau's[3] is one of Sir H. Clinton's Family.

Part of the beans you sent we planted in October by way of Experiment. They grew finely and were not injured in the least by the frost 'till late in December. I imagine they will answer in this Climate. We shall plant the remainder the 1st of may.

FR. J.

ALS.

[1]None of these three letters has been located.

[2]JJ's father Peter. For the black slaves of Peter Jay, see editorial note below, "The Estate of Peter Jay."

[3]For Claas, see *JJ,* I, 166, 167.

To Peter Jay

Madrid, 24 April 1781

Dear Sir,

The Number of Letters I have lately written to you and Fœdy leaves me very little to say in this. I have as yet received no other Letter from him than the one he wrote at Philadelphia.[1]

I send you enclosed a Print of one of your Family,[2] and flatter myself that the time allotted for the absence of the original is already more than half spent. You will recieve by this Opportunity a long Letter from Sally[3] which I hope will compensate a little for the Brevity of this. Indeed as the Gentleman who carries this to America is waiting for my Dispatches, I cannot indulge myself in writing such long ones as I should otherwise do.

It seems one little parcel of Salt I sent you from Cadiz has arrived safe at Philadelphia so that you will not be greatly distressed for Want of that necessary article. I wish the Trunk from Bordeaux had been equally fortunate, you would have found in it a little of almost every thing for Family Use.[4]

Peter is busy in writing you a french Letter,[5] which I shall send in Statu quo that you may the better Judge of his Progress. He never looked better in his Life. He has Masters both for Head and Heels.

We have had a charming winter, clear mild sunshine almost every Day. The Spring is very favourable and there is a better prospect of a plentiful Crop than has been known here <than> since the Year 1756. It has already lowered the price of Grain, and Barley which is the common Food of Horses and mules and which was at the long price of fourteen Shillings for a measure a little larger than a Bushell is now sold for Eight Shillings (your money). The most disagreable Season here is Summer, the Heats of which exceed any thing you experience in America. The Droughts are also excessive, so much so that the Face of the whole Country looks as if Fire had passed over it, no <nothing green> verdure to be seen except a pale sickly green in the withering Leaves of the Trees of which there are very few. Wood for Fuel is sold here by weight. Chimnies are not common, a pot of live Coals being a cheaper though less pleasant Substitute.

Be pleased to make my Compliments to the Doctor and your Neighbours.

My Love to all the Family. I am Dear Sir, your very dutiful and affectionate Son,

J. J.

DftS. ALS not located.

[1]28 Dec. 1780, ALS in JP.

[2]JJ had just received from William Temple Franklin several sets of engravings of American Revolutionary figures, including himself, executed by Benoit Louis Prevost after Pierre Eugène Du Simitière. JJ sent one engraving of himself to his father and another to his sister-in-law, Catharine W. Livingston. In 1779, Du Simitière, one of the curators of the American Philosophical Society, had given his collection of portraits to Conrad Alexandre Gérard before the latter's departure from America to be "engraved in france by subscription." The original drawing of JJ by Du Simitière, done in Philadelphia in February 1779, has since disappeared. JJ to Catharine W. Livingston, 23 April 1781, DftS in JP, William J. Potts, "Du Simitière, Artist, Antiquary, and Naturalist, Projector of the First American Museum, with Some Extracts from his Notebook," *Pennsylvania Magazine of History and Biography,* XIII (1899–1890), 341–75, 482–83; *JJ,* I, 247, 248; John Jay Ide, *The Portraits of John Jay* (New York, 1938), pp. 2–3.

[3]Not located.

[4]The list of articles in the trunk shipped by JJ on 10 July 1780 is in *WJ,* I, 111.

[5]Not located.

Susan Livingston to Sarah Livingston Jay

Elizabeth Town, 27 May 1781

It has given me real concern to find that of all my letters to my Dear Sister one only has reached her. I cherished a hope that some written last Summer would undoubtedly have gone safe, but Kitty's letter of the 1st December[1] has decided the matter, for that mentions the arrival of no more than a single one. It is impossible to recollect the number I have written, nor can I account for the miscarriage of all of them,[2] without suspecting that some have never reached Phil[adelphi]a and others having never left it; the carelessness of People with respect to letters is really unpardonable, many have been lost betwixt Kitty and me since her residence in Philadelphia by Gentlemen that one would have imagined would have made a point of honour of their safety.

I penned a number of sheets last July at Baske, part of which contained a particular detail of the British maneuvres in this State the preceding month, the civilities we received from the officers on their March to C. Farms, and I must mention that one or two of them enquired for Mrs. Jay, who I am sure never saw you. While the enemy lay at the Point (for they returned from the Farms the same evening) we all made good our retreat,[3] except Mama and Mrs. Linn.[4] During the 3 weeks they were at the Point, our House was between two Fires, for the Enemys Piquet was a little below us. The day before they left Jersey they advanced to Springfield and after burning the Village they retreated again,[5] while they were on their march, Mama had a forced march 5 miles across the Country. She was so terrifyed that she was sure she could not survive the sight of them upon their retreat. Your little *Heroe*[6] was here when they first pushed into the Country, and was much amused with the sight of such an Army. He shook Hands with a British Gentleman who bid him not be afraid, and said he supposed the Child had been taught to think they would tear him to Pieces.

I hope we shall not be favored with another such a visit this summer; I have another enemy likewise to fear. Last summer I was greatly harrassed with the intermittent fever, and it's an established opinion that having had it, you are subject to a relapse. However I take a preparation that's to operate as an antidote.

You must do me the justice my dear Sister to believe that I have wrote very frequently to you since the last mentioned Letter. In the Fall I gave you an account of Arnold's Perfidy, and several other interesting matters in Letters that went with Colonel Palfrey who sailed from Phil[adelphi]a with some other Gentlemen in a new Merchantman, the best that has been built since the War; Mr. Morris was principal owner. There's great reason to think the Ship is lost, as she has never been heard of since; one that sailed in Company with her was captured and carried to England.[7] It was said that General Arnold was to be recompensed for his treachery by the value of the Stores at West Point which amounted to £30,000. He has carried on the War with great acrimony to the Southward. Does Spain furnish any examples of such finished Villains?

I wrote you the 10th of this month,[8] and Brother Henry a little while before; I write now in great haste, otherways I shall lose the opportunity of sending this to Phil[adelphi]a. Harry[9] recommends it to us to send our Letters from Newberry Port as the safest Channel of conveyance, but the risk they run of being lost, in such a long Journey is almost equal to the dangers of the voyage. Otherways presuming on Mr. Gerrys acquaintance with you,[10] I would throw a letter into his care, as we are allways fond of trusting our Ventures with the most fortunate.

The three unarmed Vessels Harry wrote by from LOrient are all safe in Port; he reasoned prudently when he declined sending any thing in those Ships, and prefered the Luzerne, but our wisest measures are often baffled by events; the Luzerne was captured 9 Days after she left France. I can only say we are truly unlucky. Mr. Morris is a great loser by that Capture, her Cargo was very valuable.

W[illia]m sent 2 long epistles about a fortnight ago, to Phil[adelphi]a for Harry; he has at last broke *bulk,* as a certain outlandish acquaintance of ours used to say. I expect to hear from Judy every moment by Colonel Burr, who I suppose will announce the arrival of a little Stranger in the Family.[11] It has not been Mr. W. fault that Judy has not written to you. He has urged her to it often. I leave her to excuse herself if she can. They have received yours and Harry's Letters.

Sister Linn is likely to be a Widow very soon.[12] Mr. Linn lies very ill at Dr. Darbys and little hopes of his recovery; I left him very low indeed a few days ago; he parted with me with great reluctance. Molly is allmost worn out with fatigue; Billy[13] went up a few days ago, and Mama went to day in pursuance of his request. Little Bess[14] is with us, she and Peter are both very hearty.

Adieu my dear Sister. God bless you, and all that are dear to you.

AL.

[1]Above.

[2]A reference to her 21 Oct. 1780 letter, ALS in JP.

[3]Susan Livingston to SLJ, n.d. [July 1780], recounting the Springfield, N.J., raid has not been located. Baske is Basking Ridge, just west of Elizabethtown; C. Farms is Connecticut Farms, now Union, N.J., a settlement just southeast of Springfield; the Point is Elizabethtown Point. The Springfield raid and Knyphausen's retreat are discussed in *JJ,* I, 787–89, 812–13.

[4]Mrs. Linn is SLJ's sister, Mary (b. 1753), who married James Linn (1749–1821) in 1771.

[5]General Knyphausen burned all but four of the nearly fifty homes during the Springfield raid.

[6]Peter Augustus Jay.

[7]The *Shelaly,* as Brockholst Livingston informed JJ from L'Orient on 15 Feb. 1781, "sailed with the Franklin, and was separated the first night, after leaving the capes, in a very heavy gale. Colonels Palfrey and Laurens were on board." ALS in JP. Lieutenant-Colonel William Palfrey, former paymaster general of the army, had been appointed U.S. consul to France on 4 Nov. 1780. *JCC,* XVIII, 978, 1041, 1056, 1134–36.

[8]Susan Livingston to SLJ, 10 May 1781, AL in JP.

[9]Henry Livingston Jr., for whom see JJ to Benson, 8 Dec. 1781, above.

[10]Nearby Marblehead was the home of Elbridge Gerry.

[11]Judith Livingston (Mrs. John W.) Watkins, was expecting her first child. Colonel Burr is Aaron Burr, who held the rank of lieutenant colonel prior to his resignation from the army in 1779. For the Watkinses, see *JJ,* I, 561.

[12]The prospective widowhood of sister Mary Linn did not materialize, since James Linn recovered (see SLJ to Catharine W. Livingston, 22 July 1781, below), and lived some forty years longer.

[13]The Van Wycks' twelve-year-old son William.

[14]The Linns' daughter Elizabeth.

Sarah Livingston Jay to William Livingston

Madrid, 24 June 1781
Duplicate

My dear Papa,

I had the pleasure of writing you a long letter by Mr. Toscan and likewise sending a duplicate of one which had been written a long while ago.[1] I hope you will soon receive them as they may serve to show you that those sentiments of gratitude and esteem to which you are intitled from me have not been obliterated by absence. The reluctance I feel to lessen the satisfaction of my dear Papa, already sufficiently involved in cares, has prevented me from disclosing a circumstance from which we have received not a little distress. I scarcely know where or in what manner to introduce a subject which I could wish buried in eternal silence. But since justice to ourselves as well as duty to you require it, I will undertake the painful task.

You know my dear sir in what manner the prospects both of your family and Mr. Jay's in respect of wealth have been destroyed by this war; that both you and Mr. Jay had disregarded all private considerations and intirely devoted yourselves to the service of the public. In the midst of the career you was elected Governor; Mr. Jay was appointed Minister; neither of those offices impeded your public services but rather prepared a prospect of more extensive usefulness. They were accordingly accepted. You resigned the repose which you had long ardently wished. Mr. Jay considered in what manner he might render his appointment beneficial to his friends as well as serviceable to his Country. Education so necessary to render men useful to Society being interrupted, he concluded to take his Nephew with him, that he might at the same time that he inspired him with patriotic sentiments ennable him to render future services to his Country. My brother had received his education it's true, but Mr. Jay still thought Brockholst might derive advantages from making the voyage with us, for which purpose the consent of Congress and yourself was obtained, and Mr. Jay hoped that the pleasure you relinquished by giving us his company would be compensated for by the advantages Brockholst would receive by residing some time in Europe. As I've often heard Mr. Jay say that here he might perfect himself in two useful languages, gain a knowledge of mankind, form useful connections, and at the same time make such a proficiency in the study of the Law as might ennable him with a little practice on our return to make himself master of it if Congress should not choose to place him in a political line.

But alas! instead of an affectionate and chearful Brother we too soon discovered a discontent and disgust which astonished us. My brother's temper I always knew to be irritable to an unhappy excess, but I flattered myself that that generosity of disposition which I had remarked with pleasure in our family would secure us from impoliteness except at times when his passions were not under the influence of his reason and which I would readily have pardoned. But I was mistaken. A constant captiousness and sulkiness has without ceasing marked his conduct, and I'm sure that if you had been a witness of the forbearance that Mr. Jay has imposed upon himself, even when most insolently treated by him, you would not have been less surprised at his moderation or less wounded by the want of delicacy in B——t than myself.

To confess the truth, my feelings have been too much hurt always to admit concealment which has induced me two or three times to bring on an explanation, hoping that when he perceived how much I was pained, he would endeavor to cultivate a more happy disposition. But Mr. Jay always disapproved those eclaircissements in the presence of B——t as well as when we were in private, telling me that his situation with respect to Brockholst was too delicate to admit of those remonstrances which friendship would justify, and that he hoped to conquer his disgusts by a repetition of good offices. But Mr. Jay was mistaken in his opinion of Brockholst. Instead of being gained by gentleness the idea of his own importance rose with our condescension and he has twice or thrice threatned to return to America, which Mr. Jay with uncommon meekness as often disuaded him from.

When he returned from France we resolved to continue the utmost caution, and even to avoid such subjects of conversation if possible as might excite his captiousness not omitting our endeavors to please him. Unfortunately the other day the Colonel and a young gentleman from France who had dined with us, conversing on the manners of different Countries, the Colonel took occasion to be very severe on the Americans on the score of sobriety, adding that it was more rational to drink wine like the French with their dinner than to oblige their Guests to get drunk after, as was the custom in England and America. The gentleman who had been educated in England asked permission to assure him that that barbarous custom was at present abolished there, and I took the liberty of rescuing my country-men from the same disgrace. However, the Colonel did not relinquish his assertion but was polite enough to believe that I thought as I spoke, since the ladies were excused from that ceremony. The gentleman smiled and inquired if Congress gave into that fashion. Congress, replied the Colonel, I have seen them all drunk at a time. Colonel, said I, it may have happened that upon the celebration of our Independance or some other public festival those gentlemen have drank more freely than usual, but surely you would not infer from that, that it was a practice they were often guilty of. Oh Congress are like other men, and the custom of getting drunk after dinner is general.

Soon after the two young gentlemen retired, and I observed to Mr. Jay that my brother's remarks upon Congress appeared to me imprudent considering the Country we were in, and that he himself was a servant of that Assembly, since such reflections might make deeper impressions than if dropt under other circumstances. He told me that his sentiments corresponded with mine upon that subject but that he feared to mention them lest he might provoke him, and that there was a probability the like conversation might not soon happen again.

The next day I was amusing myself with drawing when the same gentleman came in to thank Mr. Jay for the permission he had obtained through him to reside at Toledo some time, adding that he should have feared to trouble him had he thought so much time and difficulty would have been necessary to acquire a permission that might be granted in a few hours, but these monarchical governments, continued the gentleman, choose sometimes to shew their power. Mr. Jay made the usual reply to the gentleman's Comp[limen]ts, but the Colonel took up the reflection upon these kind of Governments and said that Congress exceeded them far, for that to his knowledge a person had been detained at Philadelphia three months to receive a pass-port from that Assembly after they had resolved to grant him one. Ay but, says that gentleman, they ought to be excused from the consideration of the multiplicity of business that demands their attention. Mr. Jay with his ordinary good humor said they should at least be spared the censure of Americans, and then as he had his hat in his hand when the gentleman came in, he recommended him to my attention and bid us good morning.

The Colonel was displeased with that observation, and after Mr. Jay withdrew, said that for his part he thought the Americans ought to speak their sentiments of Congress with the utmost freedom, that they were like other men, and he doubted not but that there were among them as great rascals as in other assemblies, and that indeed he knew some. I said that in America no ill could arise from scrutinizing their conduct, but that here, as the independance of America had not been publicly acknowledged, we should be careful not to lessen the respectability of the representatives of our Country.

Some conversation passed on that subject in the course of which I could not forbear requesting that even if he differed from me in opinion on that matter he would spare my feelings in future whether they arose from prejudice or esteem, promising likewise that I would observe silence on any one topic that would be disagreeable to him, upon which his warmth increased and he declared he was sorry to find me so deficient in good sense, then turning to the stranger, asked him to go with him to Mr. Carmichael's. He, says the Colonel, can abuse Congress, though formerly a member of it, and thank God there we can say what we please.

When Mr. Jay returned I mentioned to him what had passed. He told me he feared I had been angry, since he had sometimes observed that when my brother was unpolite I appeared too sensible of it. In the evening B——t returned from Mr. Carmichael's, and after supper he told Mr. Jay that he had reflected on the conversation that had passed between Mrs. Jay and him and that he preferred going to America to remaining like a slave here. Mr. Jay endeavored to reason with him but that was in vain, and indeed some indecencies in B——t's conversation made me quite as angry as himself, which Mr. Jay perceiving, told us we were both too warm to be reasonable and advised the Colonel to go to bed and me to compose myself.

I slept but little that night. The insinuation of slavery which the Colonel had dropt was an idea I could not account for, as it was impossible to act with greater delicacy than Mr. Jay had observed towards him. From the time that Mr. Jay's sallery commenced he allowed the Colonel two hundred and fifty spanish dollars a year to furnish him with Clothes and pocket-money, his washing and mending being done in the family, and even chose that the money should pass through my hands to him to avoid giving rise to any disagreeable feelings that B——t might be sensible of upon those occasions. As to any restrictions upon his pleasures, there have been none. Few persons in Madrid are less acquainted with the manner in which he spends his time than we are. He is studious, I believe, but we are both unacquainted with his studies. Mr. Jay's advice was never kindly taken by him. On the contrary, Brockholst has not been sparing of his sarcasms on his brother for advising him to pay considerable attention to some particular books as preludes to the study of the Law, offering at the same time to send by the way of Holland for such Law books as would have been necessary. But as B——t treated almost every thing recommended by

Mr. Jay as unessential and frequently as ridiculous, that plan was not executed. Thus my dear Papa have I day after day experienced mortification that can only be imagined by those who have the welfare of a brother as much at heart as myself, who, like me, admire the tenderness and delicacy of a husband, and, like me, lament his endeavours for a brother's happiness repaid with hatred.

But think not, sir, I ascribe the whole of my brother's conduct solely to the dictates of his own head or heart. No, there is another cause and one that has not given us less pain. Good God! papa, so dearly as we love America! that all our unquiet should proceed from those who received their birth in that favored Country. My emotions are very great when I reflect upon the insidious and cruel manner in which Mr. Carmichael has treated Mr. Jay. The friendly part he had assumed while we were at Philadelphia was thrown aside soon after the Confederacy was dismasted, and though the masque has at times been reassumed, the cloven foot was not concealed as formerly. With this gentleman the Colonel has formed the strictest intimacy, swallowing unwarily his artful baits. I soon percieved the seeds of jealousy grow in the breast of Mr. Carmichael. He knew the reputation which you sustained in America and feared a rival in your son. He saw the strong attachment of Mr. Jay to the Colonel and likewise was sensible of his application and speedy attainment of the spanish language. He observed with pain that Mr. Jay was anxious for the advancement of my brother and employed him in copying for Congress, which increased his jealousy so much lest Congress by that should be reminded of him, that he could not conceal it, but told Mr. Jay in my presence, that it had so odd an appearance that a Member of Congress had inquired of him in a letter the reason why the papers were not in his hand-writing. But for his part he said he supposed it arose from Mr. Jay's desire of making the Colonel acquainted with business and of promoting him.

A variety of circumstances too tedious to enumerate in a letter leave me not the smallest doubt that he has made B——t act a part so foreign to the welfare of himself and the interest of the family. I'll only mention one instance by which you may judge of B——t's devotion to him. Last summer Mr. Jay gave B——t a paper to copy, which not choosing Mr. C——l should be acquainted with, desired my brother, who had acted always as his private secretary, not to mention it to him. Yet in a few days after he did, and Mr. C——l spoke to Mr. Jay about it and said he had it from the Colonel. Shortly after I myself heard Mr.

Carmichael apologizing to the Colonel for mentioning it, upon which the Colonel replyed Oh, it's no matter, I'm glad of it, such caution is all d—n nonsense. In short, I'm well persuaded he has in the most artful manner endeavored all along to make Mr. Jay and the Colonel disatisfyed with each other,[2] which though Mr. Jay saw through I'm not sure the Colonel did not.

I remember last fall Mr. C——l happened to be present when the Colonel in one of his ill-humours threatned to return to America. After B——t had withdrawn Mr. C——l said he was very sorry for what had passed. Mr. Jay said he was the more hurt by such conduct as he had a great affection for B——t. Upon which Mr. C——l replyed that young folks would often abuse the affection their friends had for them, that he himself had done so when in Scotland with the Uncle that brought him up, but that when the Colonel grew older he would know better. Mr. Jay thought that an extraordinary manner of apologizing for the Colonel, who, you know sir, is no child, but seeing that those observations were rather calculated to irritate than reconcile matters, determined to frustrate his unfriendly designs by behaving to B——t as if nothing had happened.

Though I'm well convinced that Mr. C——l for a long time feared a future rival in Brockholst and took immense pains to infuse into his mind discontents against Mr. Jay in order to make the stay of both of them in this Country disagreeable to themselves, yet I begin to suspect that having accomplished his aim on the part of B——t and not only made him an enemy to his brother, but also persuaded <him> Brockholst to think that his own interest and his were united. He would rather the Colonel should stay here not only to trumpet him, as is the present system, but also to lessen and behave rudely to Mr. Jay which B——t very frequently does, even at our own table before company, and that in the most indecent and unprovoked manner, which Mr. C——l is not ignorant of, having been present more than once upon those occasions. Had I been in Mr. Jay's place I never could have observed such moderation and civility to that gentleman after being acquainted with his baseness as he has done, but if moderation and prudence are virtues, I'm sure [he] has enough of them.

The subjects I've been obliged to dwell so long upon are so interesting that I know not where to stop. I would avoid a single hard reflection on B——t that was not necessarily occasioned by the justice due to ourselves, but I value your good opinion too much to be willing to forfeit it when I know that I have not ceased to deserve it. If the

Almighty answers our wishes for the safe arrival of B——t in America, my breast will be composed, and I will continue to trust in his providence to be one day delivered from the snares with which we are beset by a designing man. Indeed were I not blessed with confidence in Heaven I never could have supported a chearful disposition at such a distance from friends whose value is enhanced by the dangers that surround them, separated from my son, deprived of a lovely daughter, distressed by a mistaken brother, and convinced too late of the insincerity of a person I believed our friend, when already in a foreign Country. Yet there is a sweet consolation in innocence which soothes the mind under every perplexity and prevents the most disagreeable circumstances from destroying our peace. Should my brother attempt to excuse his return with plausible reasons, I wish they may be accepted. You cannot but see the disadvantage it would be to him should his conduct be scrutinized or exposed.

I wish that when I write again to my dear papa a more agreeable subject may employ my pen. At present I'm sure we are both too much fatigued for you to read or me to write more than that I am, with the greatest sincerity, Your affectionate daughter,

SA. JAY

Duplicate ALS. Addressed: "His Excellency Governor Livingston." Endorsed by JJ: "N.B. The Letter of which this is a Copy, was enclosed to Miss C. Livingston with an Injunction not to Deliver it unless Brockholst's misrepresentations to his Father should be such as in her opinion to render it absolutely necessary. N.B. it never was delivered to him, his confidence in him remaining undiminished."

[1]No letter from SLJ to her father dated in late April or early May, when Jean Toscan left for America, has been located. For the letter written "a long time ago," see 14 March 1781, above.

[2]For Carmichael's impact on JJ's household, see SLJ to Catharine W. Livingston, 25 July 1781, below, and *JJ,* I, 769–71.

PETER AUGUSTUS JAY TO SARAH LIVINGSTON JAY

Elizabethtown, 18 July 1781

I thank my Dear Mama for her kind letter, and good advice, and my dear Papa for his remembrance.[1]

I hope when you return to our Country you will find your little son as you expect, and not be disappointed.

Aunt Susan teaches me to read; every hour the bell rings, and then I go in the office to say my lesson. Aunt Caty sends me books from Phil[adelphi]a. I learn in a very pretty book of Tales, one page has a picture and the opposite one a tale to explain it, all the book through. I have finished with the Continental Primmer and given that and the dull Ass[2] to cousin Betsey.[3]

As soon as I read well Aunt Susan will teach me to write, and then I can have the pleasure of writing to my absent friends. I have a pocket-book full of letters that Grand-Papa printed for me last winter. Every fortnight allmost I received a letter from him,[4] and last month Grand-Mama and I went to meet Grand-Papa and spend a few days with him at Cousin David Clarksons,[5] who lives three miles this side of Princeton. It was a long ride for such a little fellow as me.

Aunt Caty sent me a top, and Uncle Watkins made me a Kite for pastime. I am quite a country boy clad in a striped linen waistcoat and trowsers, and sometimes I hoe in the garden and gather the gooseberries and currants, and I helped to rake hay on the Lawn in the hay harvest.

We have plenty of fine fruit this summer, while we had cherries, the boys collected from all parts of the Country here, not less than fifty in a day, and soon stripped our trees.

Mama says I must write her what I wish her to bring me. I should like a hat, a pair of shoe and knee buckles, and a pair of sleeve buttons —if she pleases.

Hannah[6] says I must not forget to mention her, but she won't tell me what to say about her. She has not left me, and is very good to me, and gives her love to Mama. She has received the fine handkerchief and is much obliged to Papa for it.

Wealthy has been to see her mother 3 or 4 weeks, and is not the better for her visit. She does not learn her book as well as I do.

Please to give my love and duty to Papa and my love to Uncle Henry and Cousin Peter. I am dear Mama, Your very Affectionate Son,

PETER AUGUSTUS JAY

LS, body of the letter in the hand of Susan Livingston; the block letter signature is Peter's. Addressed: "Mrs. Sarah Jay, Madrid."

[1]Not located.

[2]*The Dull Ass* is probably one of Aesop's fables, which were published in a variety of translations. See below, William Livingston to JJ, 8 Jan. 1783, n. 3.

[3]SLJ's niece, Elizabeth Linn.

[4]William Livingston to Peter Augustus Jay, 8 Feb. 1781 and 16 Dec. 1783, ALS in JP; 6 and 12 Dec. 1783, below.

[5]David Clarkson, Jr. (1751–1825), SLJ's first cousin. For his parents, see *JJ*, I, 451.

[6]Hannah Benjamin, Peter Augustus Jay's nurse; see *JJ*, I, 414.

Sarah Livingston Jay to Catharine W. Livingston

Madrid, 25 July 1781

The happiness I receive from my dear Kitty's affectionate attention would be compleat did I not regret that by the miscarriage of a number of my letters she herself loses the satisfaction of knowing that hers are received with the sensibility they deserve. Your disappointment upon the arrival of vessels from Cadiz have as often arisen from our ignorance of their sailing as from the miscarriage of our letters, for I doubt not but that Mr. ———[1] has frequently received intelligence of vessels from Mr. Harrison who has naturally concluded that it would be mentioned to us. But he was less acquainted with [———][2] than unfortunately for us we are, for permit me to assure you my dear sister that in whatever style policy may induce him to mention me to those whom he thinks already my friends in America, neither Mr. Jay nor myself are in the least indebted to him for acts of friendship or even justice in this country. But in a letter from Aranjuez I've already explained to you my ideas of that gentleman,[3] and as his conduct towards Us has not ceased to give us more pain than pleasure we'll quit the subject.

The birth of my little nephew and sister's health are circumstances in which I participate their joy, and am obliged to Mr. Watkin for his three letters[4] all of which I shall answer by the Major.[5] My heart is quite dilated with the information of the amiable disposition of my dear little son and I'm confident that mamma and Susan will omit no opportunity to cultivate it. I shall desire Major Franks to purchase if possible a set of maps in France like those which Miss Loudon Robinson once had, for Peter, that he may learn Geography while he only thinks of amusement.

I confess that I regret with you the step that my father-in-law's family have taken in quitting Fishkill,[6] but really they have been so persecuted by misfortunes that I'm not surprised they should be embarresed in their measures. Poor Mr. Jay's feelings are so affected by their difficulties that he can't mention them to me but with emotion.

In the 2 years that we have been absent from America Mr. Jay has received but two letters from Fady, and not one from Sir James, though he has written to both, to Fady frequently. You may imagine our anxiety is not a little increased by their silence, but patience is a virtue, as Lord North told Col. Fanning,[7] and I think we are in a way of acquiring it. Three weeks ago I was distressed by my dear Mr. Jay's illness, but my fears have given place to the more delightful sensation of gratitude for his recovery. His situation is not in general the most desirable, for besides the perplexity oftentimes of his business, he receives little pleasure or satisfaction from some near him who ought to behave differently from what they do. One of them[8] is the most insidious and deceitful man I have ever known and is unfortunately too much the others tutor. Indeed, I never shall in future expect any virtue to spring from a soil that has not been softened and enriched with filial and fraternal affection. I acknowledge that the delicacy and forbearance that Mr. Jay has observed towards him, have heightened if it was possible my esteem and affection for him, while the unfeeling, sulky rudeness of the others conduct daily wears away my attachment, and sometimes puts me out of all patience.

As I'm not sure but what I shall commit this letter to the flames as I've done several before now in which I had mentioned this unfortunate circumstance I shall bid you adieu at present and resume my pen after dinner. Let me charge you however not to mention a syllable of this in or out of the family. Indeed I should not have ventured to say what I have at present, but as this letter will be carried by Maj. Franks I've no reason to be afraid that it will be opened by any body but yourself. Be cautious therefore of this secret, should it be exposed it might do harm and can do no good.

May you my dear Kitty never lament the insensibility of those you love, but may all who are favored with your friendship feel for you an affection not less ardent than Your ever affectionate sister,

S.J.

Major Franks has been so obliging as to answer with good nature the longest Catechism I believe he has ever heard, and I tell him he'll have a second part to go through on his return. Remember me to Mrs. Thompson the Secretary's Lady, Mama Lawrance and Miss Polly. Likewise to Mr. Randals family.[9]

ALS.

[1]Carmichael.

[2]Carmichael.

[3]See, above, SLJ to William Livingston, 24 June 1781.

[4]John Flint Watkins, born to John and Judith Livingston Watkins, 10 June 1781. Watkins' letters have not been located.

[5]David S. Franks.

[6]See below, Frederick Jay, to JJ, 18 Nov. 1781.

[7]For Edmund Fanning, see *JJ*, I, 379n.

[8]Carmichael.
[9]The Randalls were neighbors of the William Livingstons.

To Peter Jay

Madrid, 1 August 1781

Dear Sir,

<As I have written particularly to Fœdy by this opportunity, it will be unnecessary to repeat in this letter what is contained in the one to him.>[1]

<We have heard>

Several Letters I have recieved from Jersey and Philadelphia mention your having been robbed in April[2] last by a number of armed men. It is said they behaved with uncommon Respect to You, and Humanely towards Peter and Nancy. If this be true they deserve Credit for the Manner in which they executed their Purposes. The Loss sustained on that occasion must have been the more severely felt, <at the Time when> as the Situation of the Country and <your farms> the <other> Injuries you had suffered from the Enemy and the Depreciation of the Paper Money rendered it difficult for you to repair it. I thank God however that you lost nothing but Property—your Lives were spared.

I beseech you not to permit an improper Degree of Delicacy to prevent your deriving such Succours from me as may from Time to Time be convenient. I assure you the Reflection that my absence may be the Means of rendering the Situation of the Family less distressing, makes me more reconciled to it than I otherwise should be. You have denied yourself much for the sake of your Children and I am much mistaken if some of them have not inherited Dispositions somewhat similar to those of their Parents. Had you been less attentive to my Education, I should not have been as and where I am.

<Those who plant near Trees, have a right to expect fruit.> Economy will enable me to give you aid, <and I assure you will really oblige me> for tho I shall spare no Expence here which my <public good> <public character> situation may require, yet a Tax upon avoidable Pleasures, amusements, and Luxuries will produce a little Fund that may and shall be useful to you. In my Letter to Fœdy I have been more explicit on this Subject.

I am <very> much embarrassed by not hearing oftner from the Family, but two Letters from Fœdy have come to my hands and none from James. Fœdy and Peggy would do well to enclose many of

<all or this great part of> their Letters for us to Miss Caty Livingston who I believe is at Philadelphia from whom we have recieved at least twenty Letters, under cover at the same time to Mr. Robert Morris or some other member of Congress in whom Fœdy may have Confidence and who will immediately deliver his Letter to Miss Caty. The enclosed is a French Letter from Peter.[3]

My Love to all the family. I am, Dear Sir, Your dutiful and affectionate Son.

P.S. <The enclosed> I enclose a Copy of the Invoice of the Articles sent <shipped> last Summer from Bordeaux for you and which were unfortunately taken.[4]

Dft. Endorsed: "... carried by Ruthd. Cook to Cadiz to Mr. Harrison under covr. to Rob. Morris at Pha." Without JJ's deletions in *HPJ,* II, 59–60, and in *WJ,* II, 87–88. For Captain Cook, see the editorial note below, "Jay and Franklin Reminisce," n. 1.

[1]JJ to Frederick Jay, 31 July 1781, Dft in JP; *HPJ,* II, 56–58.

[2]The Jays learned about the robbery from Susan Livingston to SLJ, 10 May, AL in JP; Catharine W. Livingston to JJ, 12 May AL and 30 June 1781 ALS in JP; Robert Morris to JJ, 5 June 1781, ALS and LS in JP; *HPJ,* 35–37. For further details of the robbery, see below, Frederick Jay to JJ, 18 Nov. 1781 with Deposition of John Bennett, 11 Nov. 1785.

[3]Enclosure not located.

[4]See above, JJ to Peter Jay, 20 Nov. 1780, n. 2.

William Livingston to Sarah Livingston Jay

Trenton, 21 August 1781
(Duplicate)

My dear Child,

I have received your Letter of the 14th of March, and at the same time that of the 30th of December,[1] and read them with great pleasure.

Your description of Martinico is very lovely and picturesque, and I dare say, drawn to the life. Nor is your Account of the Armory at Aranjuez less entertaining, especially as the Curiosities there, were altogether new to me.

Our political affairs have this summer assumed a very favourable Aspect. Mr. Robert Morris at the head of our finances, will it is hoped extricate us out of all the difficulties we laboured under for want of Cash. Our Success in the Southern States has been astonishing, the Enemy having lost all their possessions in South Carolina except Charlestown. In Georgia, they are reduced to Savannah. In Maryland and Virginia the mighty parade of Cornwallis, is like to end like the fable of the mountain which produced a mouse. General Washington with the Troops of our Allies is beseiging New York, and we hourly expect a French fleet to co-operate with him in the reduction of that metropolis. If we succeed in this Enterprize, I think the British must abandon America, and Lord North, may if he pleases, go and hang himself. If the nation had any virtue remaining, they would spare him that trouble.

It is so long since we have heard of the Saraghtoga that there is the greatest reason to believe that she is lost, and that my poor John Lawrence is buried in the Ocean.[2] Alas how much misery is the Ambition of our Tyrant capable of introducing into the World!

Peter Jay came the other day with his Grand Mamma and met me at Maples Town, where we spent three or four days. In crossing Raritan River he was greatly delighted with the water, and observed to your mother that the more we went abroad, the more we saw of the World.

Remember me to Mr. Jay and Brockholst. I am your affectionate Father,

WIL. LIVINGSTON

P.S. I have received no Letter from Brockholst dated at L'Orient.

Duplicate ALS in RAWC. Addressed: "Mrs. Sarah Jay, At Madrid." Endorsed.

[1]SLJ to William Livingston, 14 March 1781, above, and source note.

[2]Midshipman John Lawrence Livingston, SLJ's younger brother, was lost at sea on 18 March 1781, when the ship on which he was serving, the sloop-of-war *Saratoga,* perished in a sudden storm off the Bermuda coast. In obtaining a midshipman's berth for his son, Livingston had declared that the "public interest requires our navy to be officered by the children of respectable families." At the same time, he instructed his son that officers should treat their men "with respect and dignity." Rumors of the *Saratoga's* capture and John's imprisonment prolonged the Livingston family's, and especially William Livingston's, anxiety over his fate for almost a decade. Theodore Sedgwick, Jr., *A Memoir of the Life of William Livingston* (New York, 1835), pp. 345–47.

From Frederick Jay

Poughkeepsiee, 18 November 1781
(Copy)

Dear Sir,

Above you have a Copy of my last to you.[1] I left with my Friend in Phi[ladelphi]a a Bill of Exchange drawn on you for £50 Sterling in favour of [———] at Sixty days Sight, and dated the 9th Instant. Bills being very low, and as I could not dispose of it to any Person while in Philadelphia is the reason of my leaving it with my Friend and the name to be inserted whenever he disposed of it.

From several letters received from you I find to my great Mortification that you had not received from me any Account of the Robbery we met with at Fish Kill; thought I wrote you a long letter on that Subject soon after it happened.[2] I will now relate to you the particulars of that cruel affair. On the 12th April a Party of thirty armed men surrounded the House, twelve of them entered with Fixed Bayonets and So silent that I did not discover them untill they had me in Custody. This done they seized all the Arms and then fell a plundering every thing they could lay hands on. All the Plate that we had (except a Tea pott which Mrs. Jay put into the Stove) together with every Farthing of hard and paper money they could find (of which they got the greater part) they took from us. They left me but one shirt, which I had on—my shoe buckeles, hatt, etc. did not escape them. In short they compleatly stripped me of almost every thing that I had. They took no Cloathing from any other Person, except a waistcoat from Peter and a few Shirts from Sir James. They continued with us from 8 oclock untill near one in the Morning and after putting me upon Parole (which I never answered) bid us good night, and happy was we to get rid of such Company.

A few days after a Party of ours fell in with them near Dobbs Ferry, killed one and retook the greater part of the Plate, a Sword and some small articles which we again got after paying nearly the Value. None of the Family received any personal insult from them. Mrs. Jay received a slight wound in her Arm by a Bayonet and I believe by Accident. We lost no papers.

Finding it necessary to remove Mrs. Jay and myself from so dangerous a Situation (especially as I did not answer my parole), we thought it most prudent to purchase a place in this town and to reduce the Family as small as possible. However I must confess this plan did not altogther please me, but Papa, Peter, and Nancy did not rest easy, I thought it best to comply with their wishes (though a loss to me), and we accordingly purchased the place of Mr. John Davies, about two or three Acres of Land, and where we are pretty comfortable and happy.

We have got rid of some of our servants. Gasieda is sold, old Plat and Zilpha Papa has given Free, tho she at present lives with us. Moll and Susan are put out in good comfortable places. Phoebe is dead and London with us. The Elder Mary being very unwell owing to a cold she got at her *laying in* is at Dr. Van Wycks. She will be an Invalid as long as she lives. The Younger Mary is out and will be sold. I have also put out Kingston during the pleasure of the Knight, so that we now have a Family of five Whites exclusive of my little Son[3] and Six servants and I am in expectation we shall make out pretty well, though our Situation is not so advantagious to me as I could wish, however as I have already sacraficed my all for the sake of the Family, I am determined to remain with them as long as Papa lives. I could say a great deal to you, but as it would rather give you pain than pleasure, shall omit troubling you with it untill I have the pleasure of seeing you.

Sir James is still with us and intends returning soon to Philadelphia to learn Politicks. Mrs. Munro is in good Lodgings which is much better than having her here. Gussey behaves well. I cannot conclude this letter without assuring you that your Son reads well for a Child of his age and much better than I would have expected as he could not read a line when I brought him here. He is fond of learning and has got a very great memory. Papa, Peter and Nancy enjoy their health as usual, Peggy never more hearty, and was my situation such as would admit of my doing business I should be happy.

Remember me to all your Family and believe me to be, Dear Brother, Yours Sincerely,

FR. JAY

CS, enclosed in Frederick Jay to JJ, 1 Dec. 1781, ALS in JP.

[1]CS of 8 Nov. 1781, in his of 1 Dec. 1781 to JJ; duplicate ALS in JP.

[2]See *ibid.*, referring to Frederick Jay's 22 April 1781 to JJ about the robbery at Fishkill. ALS not located.

[3]An affectionate reference to his nephew Peter Augustus Jay then resident at the Frederick Jay household.

Deposition of John Bennett

Ulster County ss. 11 November 1785

(Copy)

John Bennet of full age being duly Sworn, now a Prisoner in Ulster County Goal appeared before me Johannis Snyder one of the Justices of Said County, deposed and said while he the said Bennet being a Prisoner confined in the Ulster County Goal, in company with Jonas Carle, James Jones, Joel Westbrouk and William Case, the said Jonas Carle deserted from Dutchess County, and joined the british army, and being a Soldier in Delancey's Core,[1] the Said Jonas Carle, told this deponant that he with Several others while in the british Service he had committed Several murders, Roberies, and other misdemeanors upon the good People of the United States. (To wit) That he, with five others, Vizt. Elijah Chaane, Samuel Hols, the others unknown entered the House of Mr. Peter Jay and Frederick Jay, on a certain Night at Fishkill in Dutchess County and the Said Carle with three others entered the House of the said Jay, at the same Time several of the Inhabitants was aiding and assisting the said Carle as a Guard to prevent the Escape of any of the Family, where the said Carle, threatened the said Family on the Peril of their Lives not to Stir, while the said Carle was plundering and robbing the House of Several valuable Effects, Vizt. Money, Plate, and other Household Furniture, to a considerable Value, and brought out Wine, and carried out and put it out of Door. Also gave the Inhabitants Money for their Services, and the said Carle with the first five abovementioned carried off as much as they were able, and further this Deponent Said that the said Carle told him that he, with Several others, while in the british Service had taken Several of the Light Infantry of the United States Prisoners, and Hung them by the neck on Apple Trees at the white Plains, where this Deponent soon after passed by and saw them hanging, and the Said Carle confessed that he was in the Party committed the Fact, and further said that the said Carle with another Party killed one Mr. June going from his Field home, And further Said not.

(signed) JOHN BENNETT

Sworn before me this 11th Day of November 1785.

JOHANNIS SNYDER

C. Endorsed by JJ: "1785, abt. Robbery of P. Jays House at Fishkill."

[1]The "De Lancey corps," a Loyalist force raised by Oliver De Lancey, Sr., was known variously as De Lancey's New York "Volunteers" or "Refugees." For De Lancey, see *JJ,* I, 347.

To Egbert Benson

Madrid, 8 December 1781
Duplicate

Dear Benson,

I had yesterday the pleasure of receiving your favor of the 30th October last,[1] the only one that has come to my hands since I left Philadelphia. The letter, you mention to have written when General Washington was in West Chester County, has miscarried, and I the more regret it, as it probably contained some particulars about my Father's family, of whom I hear little except by reports transmitted by Persons at a distance from them. But two letters from Fœdy, and none from James, have come to my hands since we parted. You need not be informed how this circumstance operates upon my feelings, nor how much you will oblige me by supplying their Omissions. Remember however that your letters will probably be inspected before they reach me.

I thank you sincerely and cordially for this instance of attention, and the Intelligence you favor me with. Thank God! Lord Cornwallis and his Army are our Prisoners. A most joyful and important Event. The news must have arrived in England at the opening of Parliament. We are impatient to know what influence it will have upon the British Counsels. In my opinion, it will either lead the Enemy to think more seriously of Peace, or excite them to make the most strenuous efforts for prosecuting the War. I hope and pray that our Success may not relax our Exertions.

I have had no letters for many months past from R. Livingston though I have wrote him several. His appointment gives me pleasure. Our State will nevertheless lose an able Counsellor by his absence.

Peggy's visit to her friends gives me concern.[2] I wonder at the unreasonable compliance of her husband. Your Committee[3] cannot be Respectors of Persons, and clemency without Justice is no less reprehensible than Justice without Mercy.

I have been informed that my Father had been robbed, that he removed his family to Poughkeepsie, and that on the way he lost one of his Servants (but which I know not) by an unfortunate accident. I am to this moment ignorant of the Particulars, except so far as they have been conveyed by report. I wish to know where he lives, and how he does. Nobody writes me a syllable about Peter and Nancy. This distressed family are never out of my thoughts or heart. Harry Livingston Junior has been so kind as to write a letter to Mrs. Jay for which we are much obliged to him.[4] I wish however he had been as particular about my Father etc. as about my Son. You tell me he is the Solace of my Father. This circumstance makes me regret their parting. So few rays of comfort beam on that good and affectionate Parent of mine, that it is a pity he should be deprived of those which it seems he derives from the company and prattle of his little Grandson. It must not be. You my good friend must manage this matter for me.

Harry Livingston, I imagine, lives in the Neighbourhood. His wife is an excellent woman, and in my Opinion a *rara avis in Terra.*[5] I believe they both wish us well, and would not refuse to oblige me, by taking my Son to live with them, and treating him as they do their own. In that Family he would neither see nor be indulged in Immoralities, and he might every day or two spend some hours with his Grandfather, and go to School with Harry's children, or otherwise as you may think proper. At any rate, he must not live with his Grandfather, to whom, he would in that case be as much trouble as Satisfaction. This is a point, on which I am decided, and therefore write in very express and positive terms. Unless objections strike you, that I neither know or think of, be so kind as to speak to Mr. and Mrs. Livingston about it. I will chearfully pay them whatever you may think proper, and I would rather that you should agree to a generous allowance than a mere adequate compensation. Mr. Livingston will keep a separate account of his cloathing which shall be punctually repaid. In case Mr. and Mrs. Livingston should consent to this, be pleased *then* to mention it to my father and the family.

To fetch Peter from Jersey will be the next step. For this purpose, it will be proper either that Fœdy or Mr. Livingston should undertake it. I would advise that either the one or the other should, as soon as the Season will permit, go down alone in a carriage, and bring one of his Aunts or his former Nurse, Hannah Benjamin with him. Either of them would reconcile him to the Journey, and save him the painful Sensations which children of his age often experience on abruptly leaving those by whom they have been accustomed to be caressed. Whatever expence may, in any manner, be occasioned by this business, shall be on my account, and on the first advice I may have of its taking place, I will immediately furnish you with a Sum amply sufficient for the whole. I prefer committing this affair to you, rather than to my Brother, because I apprehend that my Father will be desirous of having the Boy with him, and it would not be proper that a question of that kind should be agitated between them, for I repeat it, that upon this point I am determined.

I entreat your attention to this Subject, and beg that you will extend your attention to this Subject, and beg that you will extend your Regard for the father of the Son and Family of Your Affectionate Friend,

JOHN JAY

Mrs. Jay desires me to assure you of her esteem and best wishes. Remember me to my Friends, and when you see Dr. Van Wyck, assure him that my Father's leaving his farm and neighbourhood does not in the least abate the attachment and gratitude I owe him for his kindness to the family, but that on the contrary, I shall rejoice in every opportunity I may have of being useful to him and his.

Peruse, and forward the enclosed to Mr. Bancker, and be pleased to remember the Reciept mentioned in it to be delivered to You.[6]

Duplicate LS, body of letter in Henry Brockholst Livingston's hand and the last sentence in JJ's hand. Endorsed by JJ. *HPJ,* II, 155–58, omits paragraph 3.

[1]Benson to JJ, 30 [Sept.] 1781, above.

[2]*Ibid.,* n. 8.

[3]JJ was unaware that Benson was no longer on the Commission for Detecting and Defeating Conspiracies, on which he had served since 1778, having declined reappointment in 1780.

[4]Henry Livingston, Jr. (1748–1808), SLJ's second cousin, served four months as a Major in the 3d New York Continental before retiring to his farm at Locust Grove, near Poughkeepsie, N.Y. Rev. George B. Kinkhead, "Gilbert Livingston and Some of His Descendants," *New York Geneal. and Biog. Record,* LXXXIV, 170–72. Livingston's letter has not been located.

[5]Sarah Welles Livingston (1752–83), the first wife of Henry, Jr., described here as "a rare bird upon the earth." *Ibid.*

[6]JJ to Gerard Bancker, New York State Treasurer, 9 Dec. 1781, LS (body of letter in Livingston's hand) and Dft in JP. Therein JJ asked Bancker to draw on him for the amount of the £150 bequest of JJ's Aunt Anne Van Cortlandt Chambers to Bancker's sister, Mary, which amount JJ had loaned out at interest for her before the war. He asked that the signed receipt be given to Benson. The transaction was completed on 19 Jan. 1785, ADS in JP. See *JJ,* I, 33, 144 for Bancker and Mrs. Chambers.

To Catharine W. Livingston

Madrid, 21 January 1782
Duplicate

Dear Kitty,

Sally will mention the Date of the last Letter we had the Pleasure of recieving from you.[1] Mr. Ridley was the Bearer of it, as well as of a Picture for which I esteem myself greatly indebted to our good Friend Mr. Morris.[2] I think it greatly resembles You, and that Circumstance gives it a value with us, which it is neither necessary nor easy to express. I have seen and admired many ancient paintings of celebrated masters, but their Effect on ones Feelings is cold and momentary, compared with the Impression made by a less finished portrait of a favorite absent Friend.

Simitiers really appears to have done his best, and I confess has somewhat softened by his Pencil, the Resentment excited by the Impropriety of his Conduct. I think he has given you a few Years too many, and if there be any other material Fault, it is in not having transfused into the Eyes, the exact and full Expression of the originals, but this I believe can seldom be done, except in Cases where nature has not been very liberal. I like the neat Simplicity of the Head Dress, but the Ringlet on the Shoulder might have flowed in Lines more easy. The air and mien of the whole Picture is graceful, the Dress well fancied, and though the Countenance is rather sedate, it is nevertheless free from Severity, serene, and pleasing.

I wrote to you on the Subject of this picture etc. in September last,[3] and as I have since sent two Copies of that Letter, I presume that one or other of them has reached You, especially as it contains nothing which could induce the post office to suppress it. I also wrote to you in October, November and December last.[4] Indeed I generally make it a Rule to write once a Month to almost all my Correspondents, and often more frequently to You.

A Letter dated the 27 August last from my old friend and Companion Mr. Benson, arrived here ten Days ago.[5] He gives me the most particular and satisfactory account of my Fathers Family which I have as yet recieved. I have not had a Line from Fœdy of later Date than April,[6] and I have been too plain and sincere with no. 11[7] to be admitted into the Number of his Correspondents. What is he doing?

In one of my former Letters I mentioned to you that my Family would probably be increased this Spring.[8] We expect this Event will take place in march. Sally's Health is in some Respects better than usual, though still delicate. The Rheumatism has left her, but her Strength is not in proportion to her Spirits.

I much fear that your apprehensions about the Saratoga are too well founded.[9] We can hear no Tidings of her. It is possible nevertheless that she may have been captured, but the Probability of it decreases daily. A Regard for your Feelings as well as my own, prevents my enlarging on this Subject. Our Inquiries shall be continued and you shall be informed of the Result of them.

Mr. Morris it seems has sent his two eldest Sons to Europe. They have had a fine passage, and I rejoice at it. I have desired Mr. Ridley to send me their Address, when settled at Geneva.[10] I have always found myself strongly attached even to the Children of my Father's Friends, and unless my Heart decieves me, the Children of my own Friends will always find a Place in it. My Ideas of an European Education were never very exalted, and I confess they are less so now than ever.

I had heard of Mr. R. Livingstons Appointment, and have been for some Time past expecting a Letter from him, but I suppose he has been so engaged in preparing for his Removal as not to have found Leisure. If this Letter should be more fortunate than mine to him, present him my Congratulations and best Wishes.

What has become of John Penn.[11] I have written him two or three Letters, but have never had a single Line from him, which I am surprized at as well as sorry for. I am much indebted to his Civilities, and should regret his thinking me unmindful of them.

Sally has sent Mr. Johnson at Nantz an order, of which the following is a Copy vizt.

"Be pleased to send for Miss Kitty W. Livingston, to the Care of the Honorable R. Morris, Esqr. at Philadelphia, by the first three good vessels bound there, the three following Parcels vizt.

No. 1 to contain 2 white embroidered patterns for Shoes, 4 pair Silk Stockings, a pattern for a negligee of light pink colored Silk, with a Set of Ribbons suitable to it, 6 pair of Kid Gloves, 6 Yards of Cat Gut, and Cap wire in proportion, 6 Yards of white silk Gauze.

No. 2 to contain The same as above, except that the Silk for the Negligee must not be *pink* colored, but of any other color that Mrs. Johnson may think fashionable and pretty. The shoes and Ribbons to be adapted to it.

No. 3 to contain The same as above, except that the Silk for the Negligee must be of a different Color from the other two, and the Shoes and Ribbons of a proper color to be worn with it."

We hope that one at least of these parcels will reach you, and be agreable to your Taste. You will be pleased to observe that they are not merely sent to your Care but for *your* wear.

Present my Compliments and best wishes to Mr. and Mrs. Morris, Mr. and Mrs. Meredith, Mr. and Mrs. Peters, Mr. and Mrs. Powel. I have written to G. Morris and Mr. Bingham but nevertheless remember me to them and to Mr. Matthews.[12]

Adieu. I am very sincerely Dear Kitty, your affectionate Friend and Brother,

JOHN JAY

Duplicate ALS in MHi: Ridley. Dft in JP. As recorded in JJ's Ledger, in JP, the ALS was sent to Richard Harrison, the duplicate to Joshua Johnson.

[1]Catharine W. Livingston to JJ, 18 Oct. 1781, AL in JP. *HPJ,* II, 134–35.

[2]Catharine W. Livingston had commissioned Du Simitière to paint her portrait for JJ. When she critized it as "fanciful," and her friends thought it more closely resembled SLJ, Du Simitière declined to turn over the portrait, to Catharine's astonishment. Robert Morris then stepped in, purchasing the portrait from Du Simitière as a gift for JJ, which Matthew Ridley took to Europe in October. Catharine W. Livingston to JJ and SLJ, 12 May, AL in JP; JJ to Catharine W. Livingston 28

September, DftS in JP; Robert Morris to JJ, 19 Oct. 1781, ALS and Duplicate LS in JP.

[3]JJ to Catharine W. Livingston, 28 Sept. 1781,

[4]JJ to Catharine W. Livingston, 23 Oct.–Nov. 1781, DftS in JP, is the only letter over the three-month period which has been located.

[5]Letter not located.

[6]Frederick Jay to JJ, 10 April 1781, above.

[7]Sir James Jay.

[8]See below, JJ to Peter Jay, April 1782.

[9]William Livingston to SLJ, 21 Aug. 1781, n. 2, above.

[10]JJ to Matthew Ridley, 8 Jan. 1782, above.

[11]John Penn (1760–1834), eldest son of Lady Juliana Penn, received his M.A. from Cambridge in 1779, and traveled on the continent until his return to Pennsylvania in 1783. For details of Penn's role in protecting his family's interest in Pennsylvania, see Lady Juliana Penn to JJ, 23 Nov. 1782, below. No letters between John Penn and JJ during this period have been located.

[12]Richard Peters (1744–1828), a Philadelphia attorney and member of the Board of War until December 1781, and his wife Sarah Robinson Peters (1753–1804); Samuel Powel (1739–93), last mayor of Philadelphia under the Provisional government and Speaker of the Pennsylvania Assembly in 1780, and his wife Elizabeth Willing Powel (1742–1830); John Mathews (1744–1802), a native of Charleston, S.C., and a delegate to Congress, 1778–82.

To Frederick Jay

Madrid, 13 February 1782

My dear Brother,

On the 8th Instant I recieved the third Letter which has reached me from you, since we parted at Philadelphia in the Year 1779—a very small Number! It is dated the 8 November last. The six which you mention to have written to me since last May have all miscarried. There seems to be a Spell upon your Letters. The Way to breake it will be to enclose them in future to Mr. R.R. Livingston or Mr. R. Morris at Philadelphia. Their Letters have been more fortunate, and I have no doubt but that yours would be less unlucky if inclosed with theirs. You do not inform me what Letters you have recieved from me, which I wish you had not omitted. I am glad that the one of 15 August reached you and that it contributed to your Convenience.[1]

I have written to Mr. Benson about Peter. He must not return to Eliz[abeth] Town, as I am informed that his Grandfather chuses to keep him. I am content that he should remain in the Family or at a convenient Distance from it, or let him live at Mr. Henry Livingston's Junior to whom I have desired Mr. Benson to speake on the Subject.[2]

I have sent you Blankets and Linnen, but I hear that one parcel of them was taken in the Virginia near the Capes of Delaware. However as I ordered six parcels to be sent in different vessels, I hope that some will arrive safe. Miss Kitty Livingston informs us that some Silk which Sally sent for Peggy had arrived at Philadelphia. A subsequent Vessel carried some for Nancy.

Mr. Benson informs me that the Family are now at Poghkeepsie[3] and that my Father has resigned the Management of it to you.[4] I am pleased with this Circumstance especially as it will now be in your Power to make the Remainder of his Days free from Care and consequently as easy and agreable as Age and Infirmities will permit. It gives me pleasure to reflect that it is also in your Inclination as well as power to be a Father to this distressed Family, and that Mrs. Jay has now an opportunity of acquiring the Reputation of a domestic Matron, as well as that of an agreable Woman.

I flatter myself that your future Letters will be as particular as Prudence may allow. I think it probable that some Family Matters which I must not particularize may give you Embarrassments, and on such occasions I advise you to be firm as well as discreet. You will find excellent Counsellors in Peter and Nancy, and to them I may add Mr. Benson who I am sure has a most sincere Regard for us all. Much depends upon and is expected from you, and consequently much Circumspection becomes indispensable.

Remember poor Guss. Make his Life comfortable. If necessary I will furnish the Means. The Profession of the others will enable him to stand upon his own Legs. <The Parsons Wife> Mrs. <M> must not be neglected. It is best however if practicable, that you should not be too near Neighbours. Without great Care and œconomy you will find your Expences constantly exceeding your Calculations. One of the best ways to avoid this is to keep a very regular account of Expenditures and never to purchase on Credit. As I offer these Hints from the best of motives, I hope they will be taken in good part. I hear Mr. Livingston has purchased <your> the Carriage.[5] So much the better the less you have to do with pleasurable Carriages of any kind the better. This War has put us all far back, but Prudence and Attention and all the Fruits of them are within our Reach, and peace and liberty will more than compensate our Losses. Many of my Correspendents mention a late <visit> unadvised Excursion to New York, and the Fact seems so well authenticated that I am obliged to believe and to regret it.[6]

Peter is very well and much grown. Sally expects to give you another nephew or niece in a few Weeks. Remember us most affectionately to my Father, and to our Brothers and Sisters. Rely on my constant Attachment and believe me to be, Dear Fœdy, your very affectionate Brother.

Dft.

[1]Not located.

[2]JJ to Egbert Benson, 8 Dec. 1781, above.

[3]Egbert Benson to JJ, 30 [Sept.] 1781, above.

[4]Not located.

[5]Susan Livingston to SLJ, 1 Oct. 1781, ALS in JP: "The Chancellor has bought your Papa's Chariot for £50. It is not worth while to pay taxes for what is not used."

[6]For Margaret Jay's visit to her relatives behind British lines, see Egbert Benson to JJ, 30 [Sept.] 1781, above.

The Estate of Peter Jay

27 May 1782

JJ's father Peter Jay made his last will and testament on 28 May 1778, and followed it with three codicils dated 22 June 1780, 11 September 1781, and 18 December 1781. The will and codicils were probated 3 June 1782 in the Probate Court at Poughkeepsie before Judge Thomas Tredwell.[1] Therein Peter Jay made the following disposition of his estate.

To Augustus he bequeathed a trust fund for life in the amount of £ 500 lawful money of New York, and to Eve Munro a similar trust fund in the amount of £ 1800 for her maintenance and the maintenance and education of her son Peter Jay Munro, the full sum going to the latter on Eve's death. To Anna Maricka he bequeathed £1,800. Peter Jay bequeathed the residue of his estate to his four remaining sons—James, Peter, John, and Frederick—and their heirs forever as tenants in common. However, the will made provision for a method of appraisal and division into four equal parts to be held in severalty. In JJ's absence overseas, a codicil designated George Clinton, Melancton Smith, and Egbert Benson as trustees whose consent would be required to the residuary estate's division. Included in the division, however, were specific provisions giving Peter the farm at Rye, JJ a choice of his father's farms or tracts in the township of Bedford in Westchester County, and Frederick the lot and water lot on which he had built a storehouse situated at the Dock Ward Wharf in New York City. As regards Sir James' share, the will provided that the sum owed by James to his father should be charged against his share of the estate.

The will and codicils disposed of Peter's slaves as follows: Zilpha and the elder Mary were, "in consideration of their long and faithful services," to be allowed to choose their future masters, but if they preferred any of Peter's four sons, excluding Augustus, the legatees so named could take them at a charge not exceeding £30 each. JJ was given Plato, who, in the meantime, should serve such member of the family as the slave might choose. Again, the younger Mary was given her choice of family members with whom to live, with "reasonable compensation" from Peter's personal estate to be made to the new owner should she become a burden "by reason of her infirmities." In the event that none of Peter's children was prepared to accept the responsibility for Mary, the executors were authorized to draw upon the estate for such sum as the annual income thereon would suffice for her maintenance. Administration was granted to Frederick Jay and Egbert Benson.

[1]C in New York State, Surrogate's Court, Record of Wills, Liber 33, pp. 489–95. See also Rivingston's [New York] *Royal Gazette,* 3 Aug. 1782.

FROM FREDERICK JAY

Poughkeepsiee, 20 April 1782

My last to you was of the 3rd Ult. covering a Duplicate of mine of the 1st December, a Copy of which I had not time to make. It was short, and contained very little more than giving you an account of Papa's illness and that he was past recovery.[1]

It gives me pain to inform you that it pleased God to take him from us on the morning of the 17 Inst. and was yesterday interred in the Vault of Gysbert Schenck Esqr. at Fish Kill. It is very remarkable that he expired on the same day and month and the very hour that our poor Mother did.[2] To give you an Account of his illness would only add to your Grief. His greatest complaint was frequent and violent pains in his breast and the last attack proved fatal.

Poor Nancy and Peter are much distressd, Nancy especially, but nothing to make them easy and comfortable shall be wanting on my part. I will not forsake them. In a Word, ever Since and long before our Robbery I have had the burthen of the Family upon me, and the weight has been almost too heavy for me to bear. However I am determined to do all I can and shall be happy if what I have done and will still do will be satisfactory.

Your not hearing as often from me as you had reason to expect or I would wish, must in a great measure be attributed to the great charge I had upon me, and being under the necessity of attending Papa every other night during his Illness which commenced early in December, realy effected both my Body and mind to such a Degree as rendered me almost incapable of doing any thing.

Sir James left us in the beginning of February and went to Elizabeth Town to sollicit some of his Friends in New York to lend him money, and was to have returned in three weeks. He remained in Jersey untill the 15th Inst. when a Party of the Enemy took him out of his Bed at Arent Schuylers and carried him to New York where he is now confined in Provost. Such another Man surely was never born.[3]

I have it not in my power to send you by this Conveyance a Copy of the Will and Codicil, they being at Kent. There is no material alteration made by the Codicil. Mr. Benson is an Executor, to which I make no doubt you'l have no Objection.[4]

I shall continue here with Peter and Nancy this Summer, in order to settle matters as well as the times will permit, when and where I shall move to is uncertain, but it will be highly necessary for me to get in business and endeavour to make up for lost time.

Your Son is still with me, but will in a few days return to Jersey with his Aunt Susan.[5] It gives me pleasure to inform you, that he has greatly improved, and if he could speak plain would read as well as any Boy of his Age ever did. I am sorry you have not given some Person directions about his Education; this I hinted to you in my former Letters. It will not be to his advantage to remain long at Elizabeth Town.

The only Articles we have received from you are, thirty bushells salt, one bale coarse cloth with linnings, a bale of blankets and some Oznabrigs,[6] in all of which you have been greatly imposed upon. The Cloth not much superiour to brown paper, the oznabrigs rotten, and the Blankets only fit for Cradles. I shall write you again shortly.

Peter, Nancy and Mrs. Jay join me in assuring you and Sally of our affection and that I am, yours,

FRED. JAY

P.S. I am just informed that another Bale of blankets is arrived at Philadelphia.

Inform P.M. that his Mother is very well. Mr. Benson has informed me that you have given him directions about Peter. I am glad of it and will assist him all in my power. Mr. Benson is now in Albany.

F. JAY

ALS. Endorsed. Omissions in *HPJ,* II, 191–92.

[1]For 1 Dec. 1781, see above, Frederick Jay to JJ, 18 Nov. 1781; 3 March 1782 not located.

[2]On 18 July JJ first learned of his father's death from letters of Robert R. Livingston (see below, JJ to Livingston, 13 Aug. 1782) and Margaret Beekman Livingston, 21 April 1782, below. No letters from JJ to his brother concerning his father's death prior to 3 Oct. 1782, below, have been located. JJ's mother, Mary Van Cortlandt Jay, died 17 April 1777. Members of the Jay family had traditionally been buried in the graveyard of St. Mark's Church in the Bowery in New York City. British occupation of Manhattan made interment in the family plot impossible. Peter Jay and many of his descendants are buried in the family cemetery in Rye. Laura Jay Welles, *The Jay Family of La Rochelle and New York* (New York, 1938), pp. 15–16.

[3]See editorial note below, "Sir James Kicks Over the Traces." Arent Schuyler was the second cousin of General Philip Schuyler.

[4]See below, Frederick Jay to JJ, 15 Aug. 1782. The will and codicil were probably at the home of the Reverend Joel Bordwell of Kent, Conn., with whom JJ and SLJ had temporarily stayed at the outset of the Revolution.

[5]Susan Livingston had completed a winter of visiting in Dutchess County and was about to take Peter Augustus Jay to Elizabethtown.

[6]Or osnaburg, a heavy, coarse cotton fabric, originally manufactured in the German city of Osnabrück.

From Margaret Beekman Livingston

Claremont, 21 April 1782

My Dear Sir,

I hope you'l not think me capable of neglecting to acknowlege the honor and pleasure your Letter gave me in mine wrote sixteen months agoe and sent to the committee at Philad[elphia] to transmit to you.[1]

Sorry I am to have occasion to condole with you upon the Death of your Honoured Parent.[2] Your long Separation from him, his advanced Age together with his infeebled State for Some time past, must have Lessened the Shock, which you doubtless felt upon the melancholy occasion. This at least we hope for your peace. This must be your consolation that he is safe in the Haven of Bliss. We have still to contend with the tempests of trials and trobles and often ill furnished for the combat. But Infinite wisdom has declared, as thy day is, so shall thy strength be. The truth of this I hope my Friend finds under his great remove from his dearest connections, and the important duties of his elivated Station. Doubtless you have often your head and Heart so full that such Supports are necessary. Will you permit a friend who loves and honours you to beg of you not to Let your Immortal Soul to Starve under the weight of cares and business. Altho that must necessarily take up much of your time and thoughts, but not your whole time I hope. Your God has blest you with many talents. Those I trust you improve for his Glory and the good of your country. Wisdom is the gift of God, and he has promised additions of it, to those that ask it. For he giveth Liberally and like himself you are ingaged in a Just and Virtuous cause. You know an Holy God befriends it, so that you may come boldly with affiance to the throne of Grace for every requisite, to enable you for the dutys of your exalted Station. I am perswaided that you believe these truths nor will the repetition be irksom, altho known and practised by you.

I have the happyness to inform you that my Robert has paid me a Visit a few weeks Since and that he is in perfect health. His Little Bess[3] you would be delighted with was you to See her, you cant think what a Little Cherub she is, her temper the finest you can immagine. But I think I hear his Excellency tell his Sweet Lady Sitting next him, Set an old woman a writing or talking about a favorite Grandchild and She will so profuse etc. My Edward has always been honored with your particuler attention. I must say something of him. He has past through his College Education Last Fall,[4] and Except a little Jaunt to Boston with me last winter, he has applied to Learning the french Language under Mr. Tetard,[5] who with a German refugee minister, I took in the house to teach him German. He is Master of the french and reads and understands the other. You may form an oppinion of him from this annecdote. He was 3 days at Albany on a Visit to his sister Lewis.[6] He refused going to a dance with the young patron Saying he did not know the Company. He is now going to Study Law under Benson.

I long much to hear how my cousin your Lady does. I shall be made happy to hear of an addition to your family, which cousin Susan Informs me is expected. She left us this morning on her way to your parents. Last week a noted partizan was taken near Albany with Letters wrote in Cypher from Canada to New York. I hear three more are taken. I Sigh for the evacuation of Our Capital. When shall we meet? You can have no Idea of the sufferings of many who from affluence are rendered to the most abject poverty, and others who Die in Obscurity. But I forgit that it is unpolite to make too long a Visit to a statesman. But as I have had no opportunity of a little conversation with you, since I had the pleasure of receiving your Letter, you will forgive my Rusticity. Please to present my Love to my cousin and compliments to my friend Brockhurst, and believe me to be My Dear Sir, with the most perfect Esteem yours Sincerely,

MARGARET LIVINGSTON

P.S. I must thank you for the melon seed you sent.[7] The Seeds were distributed but nobody had the luck to raise any melons but my self by the meer dint of watching every morning to kill the buggs. I shall be much obliged by a new supply next year. Will you indulge me with some flower Seed in a Letter or shrubb Seed. I forgot to tell you that your Son grows a very fine Boy.

ALS in JP. Endorsed: ". . . Recd. 18 July 1782." *HPJ,* II, 298–300.

[1]Not located.

[2]See below, JJ to Robert R. Livingston, 13 Aug. 1782.

[3]See above, JJ to Robert R. Livingston, 6 Oct. 1780, n. 7.
[4]See *ibid.*, n. 15.
[5]For the Reverend John Peter Tetard, see *JJ*, I, 584, 585.
[6]Her daughter, Gertrude Lewis. See JJ to Livingston, 6 Oct. 1780, n. 8.
[7]See *ibid.*

Susannah French Livingston to Sarah Livingston Jay

Elisabeth Town, 21 April 1782

My Dear Sally,

I hope you dont harbour a thought that my not writing to you proceeds from any abatement of my affection for you, but rather impute it to the true reason, which is the attention of your Sisters, by which means you have every information concerning our family, and Likewise every thing intresting out of it. My dear Child of my heart, I love you most tenderly and have often attempted to write to you but was two much affected to finnish a letter. I have felt more for you than I chose to discover. I long and pray for the happy period that shall bring you to my embraces. It is my daily prayer that you may be preserved in health and Safty to your native Country. Your absence is one of the afflictions of my life. I feel distrest at the thoughts of Brockhols leaveing you,[1] least it make it more lonesom for you, other wise I shall be very happy to see him, if a kind Providence permit that blessing.

Your dear little son is a great Comfort to me he is amiable and has the love and esteem of all that know him. He is not yet returned from his Viset to his grand pappa Jay, where he went last August, acompanyd by his aunt Susan. Mr. F. Jay came here to try to get Mrs. Jay into New York. He Succeeded. This made a way for our little master, to pay the Viset we all wished for. I heard from him a few days ago by Docter Latham who lives some whare up the river. He says that the old gentleman Mr. Jay is declineing fast; he dont get out of his bed. The rest of the family embrace health, and that Petter and Susan would have returned with him if they had known it sooner.

Mr. Jay has been called on by the Committy of the State of New York, to give Security for Mrs. Jays future good behaviour. Mrs. Jay wont consent to it. How the matter is Settled I have not heard. Sir James Jay has been one of my family since the first of February. I often told him that he was in a very unsafe place, and that my house was in dangerd by him, to be plunderd. I was told so, and that they were only waiting an oppertunity. Last monday morning he left us with an intent to be back again in two days, but unfortunately, he was taken off from Mr. Scylars and carried into the king's lines ware he is at present.[2] His Clothing are here, at my house.

Your pappa keeps a Constant Correspondence with his little grandson. He prints all his letters so that my Dear little Petter can read them, for himself. This is such a Scroll that I am asshamd to Send it. Susan is my pen maker, when at home. I expect Kitty to Spend the Summer with us at home.

Give my love to Mr. Jay and B. if with you.

AL. Endorsed: ". . . From Mama." Omissions in *HPJ,* II, 298–300.
[1]See editorial note below, "Sir James Kicks Over the Traces."
[2]*Ibid.*

To Peter Jay

Madrid, [29] April 1782

My Dear Sir,

Sally, Peter, and myself have written you many Letters.[1] Some of them we know miscarried by the Capture of the Vessels which were carrying them and others we hear arrived safe in America.

I lately informed You of the Birth of a Daughter whom we call Mary,[2] and that I had Peters Picture taken, which <I waited only for a> should be sent You by the first good opportunity. I now commit it to the Care of Major Franks.[3] If he arrives safe I make no Doubt but that it will be immediately and safely transmitted to You. It should have been properly set, but as I <thought> knew you would not value it on that account, the Risque of its falling into the Enemies Hands determined me to avoid that Expence.

We are all well <thank God [in] good health and not a little> and anxious to revisit our Friends and Country. I hope my Letters directing that my Son should remain with you have arrived safe.[4] No Consolation in my power shall ever be withheld from You. My absence is in nothing so painful <to me> as in depriving me of the Satisfaction of making you thoro Returns of affectionate Attention, which a grateful Sense of the innumerable obligations I owe to your kindness, will never cease to prompt. God grant that we may embrace each other in this world as well as in the next.

Remember me to my Brothers and Sisters, and believe me to be Dear Sir, your very affectionate Son,

J. J.

DftS.

[1]Letters to Peter Jay in JP that have been located are: SLJ to Peter Jay, 9 Jan. 1780, *JJ,* I, 687–89; 29 April 1782, ALS. JJ to Peter Jay, 23 May 1780, *JJ,* I, 698–702; 14 July, DftS; 20 Nov. 1780, above; 14 March, ALS; 24 April, above; 23 May, Dft; 29 May, ALS; 1 August, above; 20 September, DftS; 16 Nov. 1781, ALS; 21 Feb. 1782, DftS; and 29 Jan. 1781, ALS in NNMus: Jay. No letter from Peter Jay Munro to Peter Jay has been located.

[2]The Jays' third child, Maria, was born on 20 Feb. 1782.

[3]David Franks arrived in Salem, Mass., on the ship *Thomas* on 18 July 1782. *Pennsylvania Gazette,* 31 July 1782.

[4]JJ to Egbert Benson, 8 Dec. 1781, and JJ to Frederick Jay, 13 Feb. 1782, both above.

Lewis Littlepage: An Insubordinate Protégé

Eighteen-year-old Lewis Littlepage[1] arrived at Madrid in late October 1780[2] to study "law and politics" under JJ's tutelage, a responsibility JJ assumed as a favor to Littlepage's uncle, Benjamin Lewis, a Virginia planter. In fact, it was delegate Thomas Adams of New Kent County, Virginia, who brought Littlepage to JJ's attention, in response to Lewis' request.[3] Recommended as a person "whose talents and disposition merited better opportunities of improvement,"[4] Littlepage had been tutored by the Reverend Thomas Hall (1750–1825) from 1774 to 1777, was a Nottoway Scholar at the College of William and Mary from 1778 to 1779, and a volunteer in the Virginia Artillery in the Matthew-Collier Raid of 1779.[5] JJ took at face value Littlepage's professions to engage in serious study, and prior to the latter's departure for Spain in 1779 offered to provide him room and board at Madrid. Nonetheless, the newly-appointed minister cautioned Colonel Edward Fleming[6] of his limited ability to finance his new charge.[7]

Littlepage expected an exciting world of diplomats, but instead found a sober minister who was unrecognized and snubbed by the Spanish Court. Bored with his studies, Littlepage broached JJ about joining the duc de Crillon as a volunteer in the Minorcan campaign.[8] JJ emphatically disapproved. He had "recieved" Littlepage under his "direction" as well as his "protection" and possessed neither the authority nor the funds to sanction Littlepage's military career.[9] Ignoring JJ's objections, Littlepage elicited from Crillon personally the promise of a post as aide-de-camp subject to Floridablanca's approval.[10] While he thought it unlikely that Littlepage would receive Floridablanca's permission to join the Duke, JJ, having failed to dissuade Littlepage, wrote to the Spanish minister on 17 June stating therein that, although he withheld his consent from Littlepage's venture, he would not restrain him.[11]

Much to JJ's surprise, on 23 June Littlepage received Floridablanca's permission to join Crillon.[12] Provided with no funds from the Spanish army, as JJ had forewarned, Littlepage lacked the resources to join Crillon, who had already left for Cádiz, en route to Minorca. To spare Littlepage embarrassment and "disgrace," JJ reluctantly offered to fund his venture in part, allowing him to draw enough money through Richard Harrison for his expenses until he joined the Duke, and instructing him to draw upon him further only if he was taken prisoner.[13]

Following Littlepage's departure, JJ informed Benjamin Lewis of the youth's decision to join Crillon, and enclosed an account of Littlepage's expenses.[14] Wishing to keep Lewis appraised of his actions in this affair, JJ also enclosed copies of his 15 June letter to Littlepage stating his opposition to the youth's plans, his 17 June letter to Floridablanca, and his 24 June letter to Montmorin absolving himself from any further responsibility.[15] Only JJ's prior promises to Littlepage's friends and his own good conscience kept him from relinquishing all responsibility for Littlepage.

On 3 July 1781 Littlepage requested that his credit be doubled, for although he was honored with the position of aide-de-camp, volunteers in the Spanish army were unpaid.[16] Despite Harrison's assurances that Littlepage's expenses were justified, JJ questioned both the necessity of Littlepage's employing a servant and his overly expensive journey from Cordova to Cádiz,[17] and refused to honor a bill from Harrison for Littlepage in excess of the established credit.[18] Littlepage continued, however, to importune JJ for further funds.[19]

At the conclusion of the Minorcan campaign, Littlepage solicited JJ's advice on his future plans. In reply, JJ authorized Littlepage to draw on him for twenty guineas, and to return to Madrid by the least expensive means.[20] By the time Littlepage had arrived in Madrid on 9 April, JJ had formed a permanent impression of him as a shallow, impetuous spendthrift, and there was no real chance for a reconciliation. Nevertheless, lacking any communication from Benjamin Lewis or Littlepage's friends in America, JJ felt unable to relinquish his responsibilities to his young ward.[21] Before departing for Paris, he agreed to give Littlepage a room and a small allowance until March 1783, but Littlepage left Madrid in June, 1782—again in spite of JJ's objections—to rejoin Crillon's forces at the massive siege of Gibraltar.[22]

The JJ-Littlepage correspondence reveals the growing rift between the pair. Letters from Littlepage included below are typical of the inflated demands of the ward, while JJ's lengthy reply of 26 October documents a rising irritation, not entirely bereft of understanding. JJ did not escape Littlepage's importunities even when he went to Paris, and, later on, in America the two would have a notorious confrontation.

[1]See *JJ*, I, 769–70. See also *Letters, Being the Whole of the Correspondence Between the Honorable John Jay, Esq. and Mr. Lewis Littlepage; A Young Man Whom Mr. Jay, when in Spain, Patronized and took into his Family.* A New and Correct Edition. To which is added an Appendix, not before Published. Printed by Eleazer Oswald. (New York, 1786).

[2]Littlepage arrived at Nantes on 11 Feb. 1780, and remained in France until September 1780 to study French. Curtis Carroll Davis, *The King's Chevalier* (Indianapolis, Ind., 1961), pp. 31–32.

[3]Benjamin Lewis of New Kent County (b. 1744) to JJ, 20 Nov. 1780, ALS in JP.

Thomas Adams (1730–1788), delegate to Congress, 1778–80, wrote JJ on Littlepage's behalf, describing him as "the Youth you was so kind as to promise to take into your Notice and Care." Thomas Adams to JJ, 30 May 1779, ALS in JP.

[4]See below, JJ to Littlepage, 26 Oct. 1781.

[5]Nottoway scholars were students who could not afford to pay for their education. By 11 May 1779, British forces under the command of Sir John Collier (1739–95) and Major General Edward Matthew (1729–1805) had taken Fort Nelson, Va., captured and/or burned 137 vessels and caused £ 2,000,000 worth of damage. Davis, *The King's Chevalier,* pp. 19–20, 26–27.

[6]*JJ,* I, 252.

[7]See below, JJ to Littlepage, 26 Oct. 1781.

[8]Crillon's forces on Minorca were reinforced in September 1781 by 4,000 French troops under the command of Baron de Falkenheim (b. 1724). The British surrendered to Crillon on 5 Feb. 1782. Jack Russell, *Gibraltar Besieged* (London, 1965), pp. 157–60.

[9]Through 12 April 1782, JJ paid a total of 594.9 hard dollars to and for Littlepage. Account with Lewis Littlepage, 26 Sept. 1780–12 April 1782, AD in JP; see also JJ to Littlepage, 26 Oct. 1781, below.

[10]Davis, *The King's Chevalier,* p. 41.

[11]JJ to Floridablanca, 17 June 1781, C in JJ to Benjamin Lewis, 25 June, Dft and C in JP.

[12]Davis, *The King's Chevalier,* p. 41. Floridablanca dispatched Minister of War de Muzquiz to inform Littlepage of his decision. No letters survive.

[13]JJ allowed Littlepage 150 hard dollars to be drawn through Richard Harrison, 127 pieces of eight in hand, and paid his remaining debts of 50 hard dollars. See below, JJ to Littlepage, 26 Oct. 1781.

[14]By 25 June 1781, JJ had paid sums to and for Littlepage of 2108 Livres Tournois and 446.16 hard dollars. JJ to Benjamin Lewis, 25 June 1781.

[15]Dft and C of the three letters in JJ to Benjamin Lewis, 25 June 1781.

[16]Littlepage to JJ, 3 July, ALS in JP and C in 26 Oct. 1781, below, and 8 Oct. 1781, ALS in JP and C in 25 Nov. 1781, below.

[17]Littlepage to JJ, 3 July; Richard Harrison to JJ, 20 July, ALS in JP; Littlepage to JJ, 8 Oct. 1781, below.

[18]Richard Harrison to JJ, 20 July 1781.

[19]Prior to his 26 Oct. 1781 reply to Littlepage, JJ received at least four letters from Littlepage concerning finances: Littlepage to JJ, 6 and 20 July; 20 July 1781, all versions ALS in JP, and 8 Oct. 1781, below.

[20]Littlepage to JJ, 4 Feb. 1781, ALS in JP; JJ to Littlepage, 26 Feb. 1781, DftS in JP, and 6 March 1782, Dft in JP.

[21]On 28 Sept. 1781 JJ wrote Lewis of his nephew's activities with Crillon, and enclosed a duplicate of his 25 June letter; Dft in JP.

[22]Davis, *The King's Chevalier,* pp. 56–57, 74.

From Lewis Littlepage

St. Laurent, 15 July 1780

Dear Sir,

Your favor of the 16th of June,[1] agreeably interrupted my application to the barren rudiments of the French language. All the polite assiduities of the worthy family in which I reside, have been able to render my situation little better than a pleasing hermitage. Unaquainted with the principles of their tongue, without society or even one companion, you may suppose I feel rather sensibly the change from dissipation and the amusements of a populous city.

The memoirs of *Noailles*[2] are not to be procured in this place, but as your advice was in general terms, I presume any productions of the same kind are to be understood as equally instructive. My present study is the history of France, though I have lately perused some of *Voltaires* works, and a few moral and political performances of *Marmantelle.*[3] I find the French language extremely difficult both from irregularity and redundancy. To acquire, in a few months, a sufficient collection of elegant words in a foreign language, is an evident impossibility, and was never my expectation. I flatter myself that my present knowledge of its fundamental principles will enable me hereafter to read with some degree of satisfaction, its most useful Authors. If you have no objection, I would proceed immediately to Madrid. Be pleased to write to me and let me know your sentiments.

I am with the greatest respect, Sir, your humble servant,

LEWIS LITTLEPAGE

P.S. If you think it more advantageous for me to remain in this Kingdom till, I acquire the language in any tolerable degree of propriety, my residence here must be at least the remainder of this year.[4]

ALS. Endorsed: ". . . Recd. 28 Do."

[1]JJ to Littlepage, 16 June 1780, Dft in JP.

[2]Adrien Maurice, duc de Noailles (1678–1766), Marshall of France and great-grandfather of Adrienne Noailles de Lafayette; *Mémoires politiques et militaires pour servie à l'histoire de Louis XIV et de Louis XV,* compiled by the Abbé C. F. X. Millot (Paris, 1777), previously (16 June 1780) recommended by JJ as basic reading for Littlepage.

[3]Jean François Marmontel (1725–99), a French philosophe.

[4]On 19 Aug. 1780 (Dft in JP) JJ wrote Littlepage urging him to remain in France in order to acquire a proficiency in French, but the latter, following a midsummer bout with malaria, quit that country, arriving in Spain at the end of October.

From Lewis Littlepage

Aranjuez, 15 June 1781

Dear Sir,

Notwithstanding your friendly endeavors to dissuade me from my intention of accompanying the Duke of *Crillon,* in the ensuing campaign, I find my inclination, honor, and let me add, my interest too nearly concerned to admit the most distant idea of desisting. Perfectly convinced, however, of the *generous and candid motives* which influence your conduct, I think it indispensably incumbent upon me to explain to you, in the most serious manner, my reasons for persevering.

In this unhappy era of war and commotion, Politicians and Soldiers are equally necessary. At a distance from my Native Country, and consequently incapable of serving it immediately in a military line, I think it still my duty to embrace every opportunity of acquiring a degree of experience which may one day prove beneficial. Your partiality to my abilities induces you to suppose politics my proper sphere. Friendship seems more prevalent than judgement in that conjecture. My present object is the attainment of the Spanish language. The alternative is to retire to some village, or spend a few months in the army. The latter is infinitely more agreeable, less expensive and more consistent with my future plans of life. Here, Sir, permit me to call your attention to some minute particulars relative only to myself.

Neither your friendship nor my own caution can, I find, protect me from the *machinations of a powerful and insidious Enemy.* To his malicious insinuations I can alone impute that universal coldness with which every person in the least influenced by *him* continually avoids me. Suspicions to the prejudice of my character are infused into the minds of all who appear disposed to treat me with civility. Attempts have been, and are daily and hourly made, to irritate, and render me discontented with you, and at the same time to seduce me into pursuits which would tend to lessen your good opinion of my honor and morals. The most infamous falsehoods have been reported even to yourself by the same persidious and cruel Author. Your Secretary Mr. William Carmichael is the person to whom I allude.

Justly incensed and disgusted at this unprovoked and inhuman treatment; actuated by the most honorable and ardent desire of exculpating myself from aspersions equally odious and ill founded; and of obtaining some degree of respect amongst my present deluded acquaintances, I have formed the design of entering, if possible, into the family of His Grace of *Crillon,* and serving as a Volunteer in the intended Embarkation from *Cadiz.* The connexions which I may there form, the reputation which only a decent line of conduct will inevitably procure, may, perhaps, convince the world that malice, not candor, could injure me. Mr. Carmichael at first warmly opposed my intention, but at present, for obvious reasons, stimulates me to it, with the artful appearance of disinterested friendship.

Whether I shall succeed or not is as yet uncertain; but whatever may be the event, these considerations maturely weighed, will I hope induce you to think more favorably of the design of Your Excellencys Most Obedient Humble Servant,

LEWIS LITTLEPAGE

ALS. Endorsed: ". . . ansd. same Day."[1]

[1]JJ's 15 June 1781 reply, Dft in JP, is a shorter and more temperate version of his 26 October letter, immediately below, which includes an extract from his 15 June letter.

To Lewis Littlepage

Madrid, 26 October 1781

Sir,

I have received your letter of the 8th Instant.[1] I have paid Mr. *Harrison* the money he advanced to You, as far as my letter of credit to him in your favor extended. Your Bill upon me, *drawn without my consent,* for a Sum, beyond the limits of that credit, I did not accept.[2]

It is true Sir! that I was so far the cause of your leaving your friends, as my offering to receive you into *my Family, Care, and Protection, in case they should think proper to send you to Europe,* might have been Inducement. This offer was disinterested, and in my opinion as generous as my circumstances, and my duty to those who stand in the nearest of all relations to me, would permit.

I then understood that your principal Funds consisted in the generosity of a worthy Uncle, and one or two other friends, and I had some reason to suppose, that the supplies with which they might be willing to furnish you would, though equal to your necessary Expences, be nevertheless such, as *to require* a constant attention to Eoconomy; for I remember that on speaking with Colonel Fleming,[3] shortly before I left Philadelphia about the probability of your following me, he told me that *the difficulty of providing Funds* for the purpose, would be the *principal Obstacle;* but, this being a matter without my Province, I could only desire him to assure your friends, *that in case they should conclude to send you, they might depend* [*up*]*on my taking care of you.* Hence I have constantly thought myself particularly bound, ever since your arrival, to take care that *these Funds,* so far as the disposition of them might depend upon me, should be confined to their *proper objects,* and not diverted to *such foreign Ones* as might, from time to time, spring up in a warm and youthful fancy. I neither considered myself, nor did I suppose that you would consider me, merely in the light of *your Bancker.* I expected to recieve you under my *Direction,* as well as *Protection;* and that the Expences, which your friends might be willing to be at on your Account, should be regulated, in a certain degree, by *my Judgement* as well as *your's.*

A moment's reflection ought to convince you, that *no selfish* Considerations influenced me to undertake this Task. You was represented to me as a young gentleman whose talents and disposition merited better opportunities of improvement than those you had, and my regard for a rising genius, opposed by difficulties, prompted me to patronise you, *though a perfect Stranger to me,* and no way connected with any of my Family.

With this view it was, that my house and patronage were at first offered to you, and hence it was that I have, from time to time, taken the liberty of advising you with respect to the books and Studies most proper for you, in my opinion, to read and to pursue. You may remember also, that in a conversation about your Expences, brought on by Mr. De Francy's[4] letter, I shewed You your Uncle's letter to me,[5] remarking it's too great Want of particularity on that head, and expressing my wishes that it had been more explicit; for, that as I was ignorant of the extent of your Funds, it was impossible to determine the proper Extent of your expences, which I thought the more necessary, because, in my Judgement, the plan of your education should be more or less extensive, in proportion as you might be more or less able to support the expence of it. I mention these circumstances to remind you, that I early considered myself in another light than that of your *Bancker.*

When you first mentioned to me your plan of going a Voluntier with the Duke de Crillon, and requested me to speak to him upon the Subject, I well remember that *the Expence of it* became one of the topics of the conversation which then ensued; and I am *surprised* you should forget that you urged the *cheapness* of the plan as an argument to reconcile me to it.[6] You observed particularly, that if you should be admitted into the Duke's Family, you would be at scarce any *other expence* than that of *Regimentals,* and that it would not only be a more expeditious and agreable, but also a less *expensive* way of learning Spanish, than that of going to a Country Village, as Mr. Vaughan[7] had done, and as you would otherwise be also inclined to do.

In the course of that, and all other Conversations which I have ever had with You or others on the subject of this Project, *I pointedly disapproved of it;* and though many reasons for my disapprobation were submitted to your Consideration, it seems that all except two have escaped your memory vizt; *"as being contrary to the designs of your Friends, and from personal danger."* For the *first,* you say, you looked upon yourself to be responsible, and I will add, that so far as I might be concerned in it, I considered myself as responsible both to your friends and to my own judgement. As to the circumstance of *personal danger* you desire me to judge whether you ought to have been influenced by it? I forbear remarks on the Repitition of this question. It wants explanation, and you will find that, as well as an answer to it, in the following Paragraph of a letter I wrote You on this subject the 15th June last,[8] vizt. "I know that you ought, and I advise you steadily, to follow wherever your duty may lead you, *without being deterred by dangers, or Evils of any kind whatever;* and were it your duty to go on the proposed Expedition, I should cease to esteem you, if you suffered *any personal consideration* to restrain you. You seem to admit that your duty does not require you to take this step, and I think you would do well to consider how far it will *authorize* it. This is a delicate subject; and yet the Relations you stand in to your Country, your Family, and your Friends, ought to be well weighed, before you embark in a measure that may affect each of them. But you know my Sentiments on all these Points, having before dwelt minutely on them. All I can do, is to give you my advice—this I have done fully and candidly."

The objections you mention are only *two* of the reasons which I urged against your Project. They were accompanied with those others which, naturally arising from the Subject, must present themselves to all who consider it with attention. It would be as unnecessary to enumerate them now, as it proved useless to urge them at first. Besides, the manner in which you refer to my objections, seems to be more with a view of shewing what they *were not,* than what they *were,* for if I understand you right, you mean to infer from these *two* being the *sole* reasons for my Dissent, that the *expence* of the plan could not have been one of them, and therefore that I ought either to have afterwards furnished you with *as much* money as you might find Occasion for in the execution of it, or have told you that I would not supply you with *any.* There is a difference, Sir! between advancing *no money* at all, and advancing *as much* as a young Gentleman may please *to ask for,* beyond the probable extent of his Funds. There are also some matters of fact, which I wish to recall to your memory; and that this may be done with less risque of mistake and confusion, it may not be amiss to consider the whole time in which the business of this Project was in agitation as coming within three Periods:

1. The time which passed between your *first* mentioning it to me, and your acquainting me with your determination *to persist* in pursuing it, notwithstanding my disapprobation.

2. The time which passed between this determination, and the grant of your request by the Court.

3. The time subsequent to the grant of your request, including your departure for, and arrival at Cadiz.

During the *first* of these periods I flattered myself with being able to convince you, that your project, being ill adapted to *your Situation,* and little calculated to promote your *proper* views, ought to be relinquished. It was then sufficient only so far to touch upon the matter of *Expence,* as it gave occasion to *general* Remarks. At *that* time it had not become seasonable, nor necessary to tell you, *I would not advance you any money in case you persisted,* for I could not presume that *you would persist against my advice and consent.* Such a *threat* would have been too harsh and indelicate, to have had a good effect; and would have been very distant from the manner in which I always had treated, and always wished to treat you.

On the Commencement of the *second* Period, the State of the whole affair was changed. The moment you ceased to respect my Opinion and Consent, it became *your* business, and ceased to be *mine,* to provide for the means of executing a scheme, you had *resolved to adopt against my approbation.* So that if I had afterwards observed the most profound Silence respecting the Expence, and all other Articles connected with this project, you would have had no sort of right to complain.

But, Sir! Although my advice had hitherto been neglected, I again took an occasion of troubling you with it; for, on hearing that the Duke had, on your application, consented to take you into his family, provided you could obtain the leave of the Court to go, I thought it a good opportunity of calling your attention to a matter, about which your expectations appeared to be rather too sanguine, I mean *the Expence.* I advised you, in so many words, immediately to take such explicit arrangements with the Duke, as that *no matter of expence* might be left unascertained, in case you should obtain the permission in question. I expected that the propriety of this advice would certainly strike you; and, not doubting but that you would mention to me the Result of your Conversation with him on this Subject, I suspected it would afford me *new arguments* to prevail upon you to desist.

But this advice, however proper, met with *no attention.* You applied to the Court for leave to accompany the Duke, and permitted him to set out for Cadiz, without having said a word to him about the expence you might expect to incur.

Here arose the following question of prudence, vizt. Whether it would be best for me to tell you plainly, that I would not supply you with any money, in case you should obtain leave to go, and thereby oblige you to abandon, from *necessity,* a Scheme which you could not be persuaded to relinquish from *Reason.* On considering this Question, I saw that the necessity, and consequently the propriety of this Step, must depend entirely on the *probability* of your obtaining the leave of the Court. A little time and consideration convinced me, that Probability was decidedly against your obtaining it, for:

1. You was a Protestant, and it was said that no Officers of that Profession were to be found in the Spanish Service.

2. You was a Citizen of North America, whose Independence had not yet been acknowledged by this Court.

3. I had made no Secret of my disapprobation, and in a letter of the 17th June, informed the Minister of State, that I could take no part in your application, the Trust reposed in me by your friends, as well as my *private judgment,* opposing it.

4. The Duke himself had told you, he did not believe that your request would be granted.

The Conclusions deducible from these circumstances, need not be specified. The language of them made the same Impression upon you, that it did upon me; and it was not long before we both became persuaded that your application would prove fruitless, and in all probability die away without further notice.

There not being therefore the least appearance of *necessity* for the step in question, it would have been very improper to take it, especially as it would have unavoidably excited in your Breast, Sensations and Feelings very destructive to that confidence in my friendly attention, without which I could expect to be of very little use to You. We had differed in Sentiment without anger; and though the warmth and enthusiasm, inspired by a desire of sharing in the Eclat of a brilliant Coup de Main, had hurried you too far; yet neither my opposition on the one hand, nor your pertinacity on the other, had produced disgust on your part, or Crimination on mine. Besides as *interested motives* had never found a place among those which activated my Conduct towards You, it would have been imprudent, by a measure, capable of such a Construction, to have given you reason to impute to *those* considerations, an opposition which proceeded from the *purest principles of friendship and candour.*

We were nevertheless mistaken in our conjectures as to the Improbability of your obtaining the Permission you sollicited. Without entering into the reasons which, it seems prevailed with the Court, I shall only observe, that, very unexpectedly to us both, it was granted.

Here the last Period began. The Duke had gone to Cadiz, and you was to follow him immediately. You reflected that money would be necessary, and *you proposed to draw Bills upon me, as your Occasions should require;* assuring me that you would only draw for as much as might be absolutely necessary.[9] This Proposition did not appear to me in the *most proper light,* though I did not tell you so. You had no money in my hands, nor any pecuniary demands upon me; and this was at least an *unusual* way of applying for Favors. As this Project was adopted without my approbation, and pursued against my advice, I might, with great justice, have refused to furnish any money for its Execution. But, Sir! I saw and I felt the unhappy dilemma to which you had imprudently brought yourself. Without money, you could not proceed, and without proceeding you would suffer disgrace. I also considered what was due to your Friends, whom you had thus subjected to the disagreeable alternative of either seeing you resign with an ill grace, or submit to the Expence of preventing it. The latter was more consistent with my own judgment and feelings, and therefore I presumed that *they* would also prefer it.

How much you should be allowed then, became a necessary question, as well as a difficult one; because, in determining it, Respect was to be had to the *Abilities and Inclination* of your friends, which I could only *conjecture;* to *your Ideas of necessity,* which were very *vague,* and to your *proper and unavoidable Expences,* which we neither knew, nor had then time to enquire about; and which would greatly depend on your *being admitted,* or *not,* into the Duke's Family. As to your proposition of *unlimited Credit,* I declined it; not from doubts of the sincerity of your Assurances, but because it would in itself have been improper.

I could easily suppose, that either in the capacity of a Voluntier-

Gentleman-Soldier, or as a Voluntier Aid de Camp to the Duke, you might spend a great deal of money, and yet spend much less than some others in the same Situation. But I could also suppose that a Sum which, measured by their fortunes, would be very moderate, would, if compared with *your Funds,* be very extravagant: *Their* Expences, therefore, could furnish no Rule for *your's.* Admitting also, for the sake of Argument, that this Project was capable of affording you, not only much pleasure, but also much advantage, yet, if the Expence of it exceeded your means to supply, your attention should return, as soon as possible, to objects more within the limits of your Powers and Circumstances. Had you followed my advice and previously ascertained the Expences incident to the place promised you by the Duke, your way would have been plain and obvious.

I had several months before written to your Uncle *to fix the sum* beyond which he would not choose that your Expences should extend, and I purposed immediately to repeat that request.[10] As his answer would releive me from the risque of all differences with you on so delicate a Subject in future, I thought it most prudent to make you such an allowance *in the mean time,* as I had reason to think fully adequate to *your real wants,* though perhaps not to *your desires.* For this, however, some *rule* was necessary, and I could find none better than the allowances on which *the Spanish Officers appeared to live decently.* I thought that if you was enabled to live in the Stile of a *Spanish Captain of Foot,* until the Instructions of your Uncle should arrive, you would have reason to be satisfied. I therefore agreed to allow you *the same pay,* and to advance you the amount of it *for six months.* Over and above this, I agreed not only to pay off your little debts here, which I afterwards found to amount to fifty odd hard Dollars, but also to furnish you with money for your Expences between this and Cadiz, and for Regimentals etc. In short, I gave you at setting out 127 Peices of Eight *on hand,* and a credit on Mr. *Harrison* for 150 more, which you accordingly received on your arrival. I also authorized you, *in case you should be taken Prisoner, and not otherwise,* to draw upon me for sufficient to releive you from the distresses in which such an Event might involve you. I acknowledge that you expostulated with me warmly, though not indecently, on the subject of this Provision, and that you was discontented with it, though in my opinion, without reason. I thought it was doing as much as, all things considered, could prudently be done for you. I did not know how far your Uncle might either find it convenient, or be disposed to defray even these Expences, expecially considering the Amount of those which he had already incurred on your Account; and I thought it my duty to pay some regard to his convenience, as well as to your's.

A few days after your arrival at Cadiz, you wrote me the following Letter:[11]

"Cadiz, 3rd July 1781

"Dear Sir,

I arrived here on Saturday last, after a very fatiguing and disagreeable journey. *The extreme heat of the weather* obliged us to *hire a Coach.* The General received me with the greatest cordiality, and has even honored me with the Office of Aid de Camp. Our Destination is yet uncertain, though I begin to suspect it is not for Gibraltar. The expences of my journey, and those which I must still unavoidably incur, so greatly *exceed my Expectations,* that I must absolutely request you to double my Credit on Mr. *Harrison,* or my situation will be infinitely distressing. I entreat you to write immediately, or it will be too late.

I am your Excellency most obedient humble Servant.

LEWIS LITTLEPAGE."

This Request was afterwards repeated almost in the same words, in your Letter of the 6th July,[12] in which you also mention some articles of news, and inform me that though your Quartan[13] had returned the last Postday, you was then recovered.

You now complain that these letters were never answered. It is true, that though I have since written to you, vizt. on the 10th day of September last,[14] yet *I never did take any notice of these Letters.*

I have known many Gentlemen, with ten times your allowance, in daily distress for want of money; and yet it would not have been proper to indulge them with more.

You informed me that unless your allowance *was doubled,* you might be infinitely distressed. This I knew to be very *possible,* but still the insufficiency of your allowance for your *necessary* Expences could not *thence* be argued. From what could I argue it? You mentioned no Facts. You sent me no Estimate. You did not assign a single reason for your apprehensions. You informed me, indeed, that the Expences of your Journey, and others unavoidably to be incurred, greatly exceeded your Expectations; but how was I to divine either the one or the other? Or with what propriety could you expect that I would be guided by your Opinion, or apprehensions, further than they might *appear* to be well founded? I would have encreased your allowance, *if evidently incompetent,* but that Incompetency was first to be manifested. The obvious impropriety of such summary, unexplained applications for money, *in such cases,* affords a sufficient answer to them; and I should indeed have ill answered the Expectations of your Friends, if I could have given them no better reason for advancing you money on their account, than that *you had asked for it.*

Your request to *double your allowance* being accompanied with no Facts or Reasons to shew its Propriety, I could continue to judge of it only from the general appearance of things. I considered that you had set out with an ample supply of Cloaths, and with money to purchase Regimentals, etc., that you had also been furnished with money for your journey, and thereby enabled to enter the Duke's Family with *six months pay of a Captain untouched in your Pocket.*

I considered that your admission into his Family and to his table, had actually realized those Expectations, from which you had before argued the *Cheapness* of your Plan; and that, though you might associate with Gentlemen of *Fortune* and *Expence,* yet that, not being equal to them in the *One,* you ought not to follow them in the *other.* I could perceive without any difficulty, that if you meant to keep pace in Expence with many of your Companions, your allowance would prove very inadequate, and I had my fears that this, in a certain degree, might be the case; for though you had been at the Expence[15] of an Order for Post-horses, to carry you from hence to Cadiz, yet it seems the *"extreme heat of the weather obliged* you and a Fellow-traveller to *hire a Coach* on the way". This, no doubt, was a more *agreeable* way of going, and yet (unless made necessary by sickness, which I have not heard was the case) it was travelling rather like a Gentleman who needed not to regard Expence, than like one whose funds did not admit of such Indulgences. You may say, perhaps, that it made no great difference in the Expence; if so, it was a slender reason for encreasing your allowance; and if, on the contrary, it was considerable, it ought to have been avoided.

Now, indeed, at this *late* day, you inform me that you are obliged to find not only your own Horse, but even Forage for him. This is undoubtedly a good argument in favor of encreasing your allowance, but surely, Sir! You could not expect that I should be influenced by this circumstance, before it had come to my knowledge.

Thus, Sir! I have, by a full and temperate answer, treated your letter with a degree of Respect, which it would not probably have received from many others. I forbear making any Remarks on its Improprieties, being persuaded that they are to be considered rather as the incautious violences of a generous mind, revolting against narrow, though necessary restraints, than as the virulent Efforts of a bad disposition, to give unmerited pain. I flatter myself that some future moment of dispassionate self-Examination, and a more impartial review of my uniform Conduct towards you, will yet make room for Reflections and Sensations of *another kind.* My Doors, my Heart, and my Purse are still as open to you as ever. I rejoice to hear that you have been left above *Dependence,* and I advise you to take care that *that Consideration,* does not reduce you to it.

In whatever Situation you may think proper to place yourself, my best wishes will still attend you; and I shall be pleased with Opportunities of indulging the Inclination I yet have to give you further proofs of the disinterested regard with which I am, Sir, Your most obedient and very humble Servant,

JOHN JAY

P.S. Messrs. French of Bordeaux have, as they say, by your Orders, sent to Col. Livingston for you, a pair of Shoe and Knee buckles; but as the price amounts to between thirty nine and forty hard Dollars, I must decline interfering further than to give you this Information.

Your Orders, respecting your Cabinet, shall be executed as soon as I shall be informed by You, or otherwise, that you remained of the same mind, after the Fit of the Fever in which they were written.

Duplicate LS. The body of the letter is in the hand of Henry Brockholst Livingston containing JJ's corrections. Endorsed by JJ.

[1]Littlepage to JJ, 8 Oct. 1781.

[2]On 26 July 1781 (Dft in JP), JJ had requested Harrison to advance 150 hard dollars to Littlepage. On 6 November, JJ returned Littlepage's bill to Harrison, accepting only the amount of credit he had authorized. ALS in PPAmP: Vaughan; enclosure not located.

[3]Colonel Edward Fleming; see *JJ,* I, 249, 252.

[4]Theveneau de Francy was an agent for Beaumarchais in America. Letter not located.

[5]Benjamin Lewis to JJ, 20 Nov. 1779.

[6]See above, 15 June 1781.

[7]See the editorial note above, "The Issue of United States Citizenship."

[8]JJ to Littlepage, 15 June 1781.

[9]This was a verbal assurance Littlepage made to JJ in a conversation prior to departing for Cádiz.

[10]JJ to Benjamin Lewis, 25 June and 28 Sept. 1781, both Dft in JP.

[11]Littlepage to JJ, 3 July 1781, ALS in JP.

[12]Littlepage to JJ, 6 July 1781, ALS in JP.
[13]A fever characterized by a violent recurrence every fourth day.
[14]JJ to Littlepage, 10 Sept. 1781, Dft in JP.
[15]Note in JJ's hand: "This included the whole expense for Horses to Cadiz."

From Lewis Littlepage

Camp before Gibraltar, 29 December 1782

Sir,

Your letter of the 18th of November was transmitted to me a few days past by Mr. *Harrison.*[1]

I cannot but regret that my unhappy circumstances will not permit me to discharge immediately the debt which I have incurred from your generosity in the prosecution of designs, which once flattered me with the prospect of a more pleasing issue. I regard your letter as an ultimate refusal on your part to afford me further assistance, and delicacy in my present situation, as *well as gratitude for what you have already done,* prevent me from incommoding you with *reiterated,* and too probably, *vain* sollicitations.[2]

Since I have nothing to expect from your partiality as a *friend,* I appeal to *your candour as a man of honor,* for my justification! I have forfeited your *confidence* and *protection,* but *I am mistaken in your character, or I shall ever possess your esteem.*

The Marquis de La *Fayette* is arrived at Cadiz, and informed me the other day by the Count de *Crillon,* that he is desirous for me to accompany him to America. I shall in consequence repair immediately to Cadiz to take explicit arrangements with him for that purpose.[3]

I have recieved an official letter from the Count de *Florida Blanca,* in the King's name, containing the most flattering acknowledgements from his Majesty, for my conduct in his service, with permission to retire from my post of Aid de Camp.[4] *I have only to request you to inclose immediately* to Mr. Harrison, *a state of the account between us, which be assured shall be remitted to you as soon as possible.*[5]

With the sincerest gratitude for the many instances of friendship and generosity, which I have received from you, I have the honor to be your Excellency's most Obedient and respectful humble Servant,

L. LITTLEPAGE

ALS. Addressed: "His Excellency John Jay. Paris," In an unidentified hand: "Hotel d'Orleans, rue des Petits Augustins." Endorsed: ". . . Recd. Jany 1783."

[1]JJ to Littlepage, 18 Nov. 1782, AL in JP.

[2]In his 18 November letter, JJ told Littlepage that his disapproval of the latter's joining the Gibraltar campaign was "sincere advice," and declined giving Littlepage any more money or discussing the matter further.

[3]On Lafayette, see the editorial note below, "Lafayette, Jay's Self-Appointed 'Political Aide-de-Camp,' Takes on the Spaniards."

[4]The Floridablanca letter has not been located.

[5]There is no evidence that JJ replied to this letter or fulfilled this request.

II

PARIS AND THE CHALLENGE OF PEACEMAKING

The Status of the Peacemaking on Jay's Arrival in Paris

Long before JJ reached Paris to take up his post as peace commissioner, peace feelers had been put out by the belligerents as well as certain neutral powers. Back in 1778 the British had dispatched the Carlisle Commission to America to effect reconciliation by offering home rule,[1] a proposal that contained too little and came too late. That same year Spain proposed a long-term truce with America's ultimate fate left unresolved.[2] In 1779–80 Jacques Necker, France's Director General of Finance, acting in secret and behind the back of his country's foreign minister, suggested a partition scheme, but nothing came of it.[3] Meantime, as the war dragged on, plunging France and Spain into serious financial difficulties without compensating military successes, Vergennes found merit in proposals of the self-appointed comediators, Catherine II of Russia and Joseph II of Austria, for a peace conference on the basis of a long-term truce and settlement on the ground then held. Since under this plan the American Congress would be by-passed and the Thirteen States be represented by delegates of their own choosing, such a proposal, considering the military realities, would have meant the eventual partition of the United States.[4] It was John Adams, however, then still serving as the sole American commissioner to negotiate the peace, who scotched any idea of a further pursuit of this proposal by reminding Vergennes that under the Articles of Confederation only Congress, not the separate Thirteen States, had authority to enter into diplomatic negotiations.[5]

Adams had already succeeded in ruffling French feelings, and Vergennes saw to it that Congress redefine Adams' authority and limit his initiative. Acting in response to proddings from France's minister in Philadelphia, the Chevalier de la Luzerne, Congress in the spring of 1781, as previously mentioned, instructed Adams to keep France fully informed, indicated a willingness to accept comediation accompanied by independence and a truce, provided England evacuated the ground she held, and clipped Adams' powers further by enlarging the peace commission to include JJ, along with Franklin, Thomas Jefferson, and Henry Laurens. Luzerne scored a further success when Congress chose the pro-French Robert R. Livingston to serve as Secretary for Foreign Affairs.[6]

Yorktown not only administered the coup de grâce to the idea of mediation but cut the ground from under the North ministry, which resigned on 20 March 1782. The new ministry was headed by Charles Watson-Wentworth, Marquess of Rockingham (1730–82), as First Lord of the Treasury, with Charles James Fox, known as a friend of American independence, named Secretary of State for Foreign Affairs, and his rival, William Petty Fitzmaurice, Earl of Shelburne (1737–1805) as Secretary of State for Home, Colonies, and Irish Affairs.[7]

An immediate rift developed in that uneasy coalition. Fox, considering the United States to be a de facto independent nation, insisted that negotiations with America came under his jurisdiction, whereas Shelburne, who hoped to retain the Thirteen States within the Empire on some basis, countered that, since American independence had not yet been formally conceded, the negotiations belonged to his office. Shelburne acted first, dispatching Richard Oswald (1705–84) to Passy to start talks with Franklin. Oswald was an elderly Scottish merchant, boasting a long record of close friendship with prominent Americans, including Franklin and Henry Laurens.

Shelburne did not put all his chips on Oswald, however. Still determined to avoid if possible a commitment to independence, the Earl dispatched his private secretary, Maurice Morgann (1726–1802) to New York with instructions to the top-ranking military and naval officers there to make a final attempt at conciliation. Sir Guy Carleton and Admiral Robert Digby, who were named joint peace commissioners on 25 March 1782, spread the word to Washington and Congress that the new ministry would welcome reunion, only to be quickly repulsed. Carleton's role was not to be a peacemaker but rather one who would be charged in a most essential way in promoting peace by evacuating British troops in America. With an inflated notion of his importance, he defied a Parliamentary order to evacuate all troops from New York, and had troops from other points diverted to New York instead of Halifax in order to be able to negotiate with Washington from a position of strength. The long-drawn-out process of evacuation, for which Carleton was responsible, contributed to JJ's suspicions of British intentions of recognizing American independence.[8]

The idea of a separate peace was pressed in France as well as in America. Soundings were taken by Oswald when he met with Franklin at Passy on 12 April 1782. Playing an ambivalent role, Franklin took Oswald to Versailles, where Vergennes reminded them that France's treaty with the United States barred such a separate agreement. However, at a leave-taking breakfast two days later, Franklin turned over to Oswald a confidential paper advising the cession of Canada, while not pressing the proposal as an ultimatum. Oswald reacted favorably. Franklin had gone so far as to hint at a reparation to Tories for their forfeited estates, such compensation to come out of Canada's vacant lands, which might also provide funds to indemnify Americans for homes burnt by the British troops and their Indian allies. This last point Franklin, on second thought, was careful not to disclose to John Adams, then in the United Provinces.[9] In any event, Oswald had found in Shelburne neither a readiness to concede independence nor a disposition to yield Canada, while the Earl appeared adamant on the score of compensating the Loyalists and honoring all debts owed British subjects.[10] Some time later and several weeks after JJ's arrival in Paris, Franklin, reading from notes, outlined to Oswald the conditions he considered might form the basis of a treaty under the categories of *necessary* and *advisable* articles. The "necessary" articles were independence, a settlement of boundaries, including a confinement of the boundaries of Canada to what they were prior to the Quebec Act of 1774, and freedom of fishing on the banks of Newfoundland and elsewhere, although the Doctor did not specify leave to dry fish on shore. The "advisable" were an indemnity to Americans who had suffered by the war, perhaps in an amount of £500,000 to £600,000, a public acknowledgment of England's error, equality of commercial privileges, and the cession of Canada.[11]

In the weeks and months following Franklin's initial discussions with Oswald, the commissioners set out on the road to Paris. One of them arrived almost at the final moment of the negotiations. That was Henry Laurens, who, following his capture at sea, was imprisoned in the Tower of London until paroled on 31 December 1781 through the good offices of his long-time friend and business associate Richard Oswald. The terms of that parole clouded over Laurens' role as a commissioner, and he did not join the negotiations until 29 November 1782, the day before the signing of the Preliminaries. From JJ's arrival in Paris on 23 June[12] until 26 October, when Adams reached Paris in response to JJ's urgent summons and after successfully negotiating a commercial treaty with the Dutch, Franklin and JJ constituted the American negotiating team.

By the time JJ was able to join in the discussions Richard Oswald had virtually assumed full command of the British side of the negotiations with the Americans. The feud between Fox and Shelburne was rapidly reaching a climax. Fox's emissary to Paris was Thomas Grenville (1755–1846), a son of George Grenville, the author of the ill-starred Stamp Act. Young Grenville had come prepared to concede independence and complete the evacuation as well as to undertake separate negotiations with the United States in the event a general peace were to prove impractical.[13] The adamant stands of France and Spain convinced both Grenville and Oswald of the need to settle privately with America, a notion implicitly encouraged by Franklin himself.[14] Once Franklin understood that Grenville's powers did not encompass treating with the United States, he lost interest in him and became convinced that he could secure better terms from Oswald, to whom he indicated that separate negotiations would provide the smoothest road to achieving a general peace.[15] This approach suited Oswald, while it had in fact been originally suggested by Vergennes.

On 17 June Parliament had passed the Enabling Act authorizing peace with America, and the Cabinet was obliged to take sides between Fox and Shelburne. To force a showdown, Fox demanded the immediate recognition of American independence and the blocking of the appointment of Oswald as sole negotiator with the United States.[16] The victory went to Shelburne on both issues, making Fox's position untenable. At this moment of crisis the titular head of the Cabinet, Rockingham, died of influenza on 1 July 1782, and the King promptly named Shelburne to head the government. Thereupon Fox resigned, stripping Grenville of his sponsorship, and leaving American peace issues for some months to be negotiated in Paris between Oswald for the British and Franklin and JJ for the United States.[17]

In Britain the break-up of the coalition ministry propelled two new men into posts critical to the peace negotiations. Hereafter Franklin, Jay, & Co. would have to take into account the views not only of Shelburne but of Thomas Townshend (1733–1800, later 1st Viscount Sydney) who assumed Shelburne's post as Colonial (Home) Secretary, and Baron Grantham (Thomas Robinson, 1738–86, 2d Baron Grantham), who replaced Fox as Foreign Secretary. Shelburne lost no time in notifying Grenville in Paris of the changes in the government and instructing him to assure the French and Americans that Fox's departure would not alter the direction of negotiations nor dampen the King's "ardent desire for peace."[18] The dispatch, which arrived 8 July, prompted Grenville's trip to Versailles the following day, when he acquainted Vergennes, Aranda, and Franklin with its contents.[19] Grenville then resigned,[20] to be replaced by Alleyne Fitzherbert (1753–1839), a young career diplomat who had been serving as minister at Brussels.[21] Meantime Oswald was concerned about reassuring Franklin that the change in ministries did not signify any "reserve intended in the grant of independence."[22] Now that JJ had joined the negotiations, Oswald was anxious to "lose no point of the ground gained to date." In turn, Shelburne insisted "that there never have been two opinions since you were sent to Paris, upon the most unequivocal Acknowledgment of American Independancy" and that he himself had long since given up "decidedly and reluctantly" the idea of maintaining territorial ties.[23]

With the negotiations for peace entering a new and critical phase, the Jays arrived in Paris on Sunday June 23rd, taking up quarters arranged for them by William Temple Franklin at the Hôtel de la Chine at the Palais-Royal.[24] JJ plunged into his diplomatic rounds at once. That same day he went to see Franklin at Passy, then the next day the pair journeyed to Versailles to pay a call on the Comte de Vergennes, who briefed them on the state of the negotiations with Great Britain. On the Spanish side, he now took up negotiations directly with Spain's ambassador at Paris, Pedro Pablo Abarca de Bolea, conde de Aranda (1718–98), with whom he opened negotiations on 25 June (see below).[25]

[1]Weldon A. Brown, *Empire or Independence: A Study in the Failure of Reconciliation, 1774–1783* (Baton Rouge, 1941), is the definitive study of the Carlisle Commission. See also *JJ,* I, 474–78.

[2]*Peacemakers,* pp. 150–51.

[3]*Ibid.,* pp. 98–111, 149.

[4]Vergennes always insisted publicly that France would settle for nothing less than American independence. Count Lusi (Prussian envoy to London), to King Frederick II of Prussia, 11 June 1782, E in MiU-C: Shelburne RGA.

[5]*Peacemakers,* pp. 204–09.

[6]For the commission, instructions, and the revision of the instructions, see above,

Gouverneur Marris to JJ, 17 June 1781, and Huntington to JJ, 5 July 1781.

[7]*Peacemakers,* pp. 251–53, 257–60.

[8]Shelburne to Carleton and Digby, 5 June 1782, LbkC in CO 5/178. Robert R. Livingston to JJ, 9 May 1782, LS in JP; Dft in NHi: Robert R. Livingston; LbkCs in PCC 79, I, 417–23 and 118, pp. 166–76; *HPJ,* II, 302–06; *RDC,* V, 404–07; *SDC,* VIII, 105–10. D'Annemours to Castries, 13 June 1782, LS in MAE: CC Baltimore, I, 18–19. For a critical estimate of Carleton's role, see Paul H. Smith, "Sir Guy Carleton, Peace Negotiations, and the Evacuation of New York," *Canadian Historical Review,* L (1969), 245–64.

[9]*Peacemakers,* pp. 261–64.

[10]*Ibid.,* pp. 269–70. Vergennes had received a report that England did not contemplate an explicit recognition of independence. Francès (first secretary of the French legation in London), to Vergennes, C in CP A 537: 218–19.

[11]Franklin, reading from a memorandum, reported these "Hints" to Oswald on 10 July, and the latter that very same day communicated the points to Shelburne. ALS in FO 27/2, C in 95/511, LbkC in 97/157 and in MiU-C: Shelburne 70. Hale, *Franklin in France,* II, 68, erroneously attributes the Franklin-Oswald meeting to 9 July.

[12]See "Jay's Diary of the Peacemaking," below.

[13]For Fox's powers and his readiness to concede independence unconditionally, see Grenville to Fox, 4 June 1782, ALS in FO 95/511 and C in 27/2; Fox to Grenville, 10 June 1782, Dft in FO 27/2, C in 95/511. Conferences between Vergennes and Grenville, Paris, 5, 15 June 1782, Dft in the hand of Rayneval in CP A 53: 171–72; Doniol, *Histoire,* V, 116–17.

[14]*Peacemakers,* pp. 271–74.

[15]Franklin voiced his wish that arrangements could be made permitting him to treat with Oswald rather than Grenville. Franklin to Oswald, 27 June 1782, ALS in FO 97/157; *BFS,* VIII, 554–55; *RDC,* V, 584.

[16]The Enabling Act received the royal assent on 19 June 1782. *Journals of the House of Commons,* XXXVIII, 1028; *Journals of the House of Lords,* XXXV, 529, 535. JJ quickly found out that Fox and Shelburne were feuding. JJ to Robert R. Livingston, 25 June 1782, LbkCs in JP, CSmH, and in PCC 110, II; *HPJ,* II, 312–14; *RDC,* V, 516–17; SDC, VIII, 113–15; *WJ,* I, 142.

[17]*Peacemakers,* pp. 278–81.

[18]Shelburne to Grenville, 5 July, C in FO 27; Dft in MiU-C: Shelburne 71.

[19]French Notes on Conference Relating to the Preliminary Peace Negotiations: 7th Conference, 9 July 1782, CP A 537: 324.

[20]Grenville to Shelburne, 9 July 1782, ALS in FO 27/2. That Fox's resignation was prompted in no small part by his commitment to unconditional American independence, a view which the new ministry did not share, is the argument of Loren Reid, *Charles James Fox: A Man for the People* (London, 1969), pp. 146–47. For Vergennes' misgivings about the readiness of the new ministry to make sacrifices, see Vergennes to Montmorin, 13 July 1782, LS in CP E 606: 48–49. See also Francès to [Vergennes], 2 July 1782, ALS in CP A 537: 245–46; *Peacemakers,* pp. 283–86; Hansard, *Parliamentary History,* XXIII, 152–200.

[21]Fitzherbert received powers to negotiate with France, Spain, and the Netherlands, arriving in Paris at the beginning of August. Grantham to Fitzherbert, 23, 27 July 1782, C of both in FO 27/3; Fitzherbert to Vergennes, 2 Aug. 1782, ALS in CP A 538: 9.

[22]Oswald to Shelburne, 12 July 1782, (private), ALS in FO 27/2; C in MiU-C: Shelburne 70, and in FO 95/511 and 97/157.

[23]Shelburne to Oswald, 27 July 1782, C in MiU-C: Shelburne 71.

[24]William Temple Franklin to JJ, 5 June 1782, ALS in JP; *HPJ,* II, 308.

[25]See JJ to Robert R. Livingston, 25 June 1782.

To Robert R. Livingston

Bordeaux, 14 June 1782

Dear Robert,

My Letter of the 11 May[1] mentioned my being called to Paris by a Letter from Dr. Franklin. Our Journey thus far afforded much Variety, and excepting some bad Roads, Fleas, and Bugs, was not unpleasant. Both Spanish and French Biscay contain a number of romantic pretty Scenes, and I assure you we found ourselves perfectly disposed to enjoy the Beauties of this charming Season. Our Health has been greatly improved, or I may say, restored by the Journey. The Rheumatism has left me, and the only disagreable Circumstance which at present attends us is the Indisposition of our little Girl, who has the hooping Cough, and is cutting her Teeth. We have taken the Liberty of naming you for her God Father. I hope Mrs. Livingston will one of these Days give you an opportunity of laying the same obligation upon me.

We have recieved many Attentions and Civilities both here and at Bayonne. Mr. Bondfield has been particularly obliging.

The Inhabitants of this City are preparing to present their King with a Ship of the Line. Commerce flourishes here, some say more than before the War. Bayonne, I hear, is soon to be declared a free port.

Remember us to Mr. and Mrs. Morris, Mr. and Mrs. Meredith,[3] Gouv. Morris, and such of your Family as may be with You. Adieu.

I am Dear Robert Your Friend

JOHN JAY

ALS in NHi: Robert R. Livingston. Addressed: "The Honb. Robt. R. Livingston, Esqr., Philadelphia." Endorsed. AC in *ibid.;* DftS in JP; *HPJ,* II, 309, with omissions.

[1]JJ's letter to Livingston was actually dated 14 May, although the DftS in JP bears date of 11 May. The 14 May version is in: LbkC in PCC 110, II and in CSmH; Tr in PPAmP: Force; *HPJ,* II, 307; *RDC,* V, 417.

[2]The Robert Morrises and the Samuel Merediths.

To Aranda

Paris, Hotel de la Chine, 25 June 1782

Sir,

On leaving Madrid his Excellency the Count De Florida [Blanca] <assured> informed me that the Papers relating to the objects of my mission there had been transmitted to your Ex[cellenc]y with <such

instructions> authority and Instructions to treat with me on the Subjects of them.[1]

I arrived here the Day before Yesterday <afternoon> and have the Honor to <assure> acquaint your Ex[cellenc]y of my being Ready to commence the necessary Conferences at such Time and Place as your Ex[cellenc]y may think proper to name.

Your Ex[cellenc]ys Character gives me Reason to hope <that the proposed> that the Negociation<s> in question will be conducted and terminated in a manner agreable <and useful> to both our Countries, and permit me to assure you that nothing on my Part shall be wanting to manifest the Respect and Consideration with which I have the Honor to be, Your Excellencys most obedient and most humble Servant.[2]

Dft. C, misdated 29 June, in AHN Estado, leg. 3885, exp. 1, doc. 13; LbkCs in CSmH, JP, PCC 110, II, and in CP E 608: 398; C in JJ to Robert R. Livingston, 17 Nov. 1782, see n. 2.

[1]Floridablanca to Aranda, 17 May 1782, LS in Spanish in AHN Estado, leg. 3885, exp. 3, doc. 1.

[2]Aranda courteously replied on 27 June, LS in French in JP; LbkCs in French in CSmH and in PCC 110, II; C in JJ to Robert R. Livingston, 17 Nov. 1782. Two days later, JJ and Franklin paid a visit to Aranda (JJ to Aranda, 29 June 1782, Dft in JP, ALS in AHN Estado, leg. 3885, exp. 1, doc. 13), which Aranda reciprocated the following day. But because of sudden illness, JJ was unable to accept Aranda's dinner invitation, and they did not meet again for a month. See JJ to Robert R. Livingston, 17 Nov. 1782, LbkCs in JP (2); CSmH, and PCC 110, II; E in MH: Sparks; *HPJ,* II, 366–452; *RDC,* VI, 11–51; *WJ,* II, 456–95.

From Lafayette

St. Germain, Tuesday, [25 June 1782]

Dear Sir,

Your Arrival in Paris which I just Now Happened to Hear Affords me an Heartly felt Satisfaction. I shall Leave this place to Morrow in order to Wait Upon You at Paris, and also to Present My Respects to Mrs. Jay whom I Have the Honor to Congreatulate Upon Her Arrival.

Dr. Franklin will No Doubt make you some Communications in Consequence of Which He Has desired I should delay My departure.[1] Notwithstanding the Inclination I felt to Join My Colours, I Have thought Every Sacrifice ought to Be Made to the Expectation of Rendering Myself Useful to the public, and as we were of the Opinion, which I fancy You will also Be Sensible of, that My presence Here was By far more Serviceable to America, than My presence upon the Continent Could possibly Be at this period, I Have Resolved Not to go this fortnight or three weeks, provided You and Dr. Franklin are pleased to write to Congress, that in this delaying I have followed their Advice.[2]

With the Highest Regard and Most Affectionate Sentiment I Have the Honor to Be Dear Sir, Yours,

LAFAYETTE

ALS. Endorsed: ". . . Recd and ansd 25 June 1782."

[1]Benjamin Franklin urged Lafayette to remain in Paris "a few weeks longer" rather than to return to the field in America, as he "is of great use in our affairs here, and as the campaign is not likely to be very active in North America." Franklin to Robert R. Livingston, 25 June 1782, *BFS,* VII, 548–53 at 550; *RDC,* V, 510–13.

[2]JJ, writing for himself and Franklin, recommended that Lafayette "postpone his return for the present." JJ to R. R. Livingston, 28 June 1782, LbkCs in JP, CSmH, PCC 110, II; *HPJ,* II, 317–19; *RDC,* V, 527–28.

To Lafayette

[Paris], Tuesday, 25 June 1782

Dear Sir,

Accept my Thanks for your friendly Letter, and kind Congratulations on our arrival here.

It gives me Pleasure to find that I shall have an opportunity of seeing you before your Departure, and am <much> greatly obliged by your Intention of doing me that Honor To Morrow.

I have had some Conversation with Dr. Franklin on the Subject to which I believe you allude, and <expect to see him> shall take the first opportunity by conversing further with him about it to enable myself to give the advice you do me the Honor to ask.

Mrs. Jay presents you her best Respects, and permit me to assure you of the great Regard and Esteem with which I have the Honor to be, Dear Sir, Your most obedient and humble servant.

Dft. Endorsed: ". . . in Inst. to his of same Date."

To Montmorin

Paris, 26 June [–19 July], 1782

Dear Sir

I devote this <moment of> first Leisure moment which has occurred since my arrival <on Sund[ay]> <on Tuesday last> to the Pleasure of writing a few Lines to You.

Our Journey was pursued without any avoidable Intermission to Bayonne where it became adviseable to rest a few Days, and where we recieved many kind Attentions from <the imperial Embassador> Monsieur Formalaguer to whom it seems you and the Chevalier[1] <or both>, had been so obliging as to make friendly mention of us. That City is turning its Attention to the american Trade, and its Situation in certain Respects is favorable to that <Purpose> Design.

Your Friend Monsieur Risleau at Bordeaux pleased me much. There is a Frankness in his Manner and a Warmth about his Heart that <pleased me much> is very engaging. <His attachment to you is strong> I made some agreable acquaintances in that City and wish <that Circumstances had been such as to admit of my staying> I could have stayed longer with them. Commerce appears to flourish there, and if their Trade with America could be properly protected, there is Reason to believe that it would soon become an object of great Importance.

On leaving Bordeaux Mrs. Jay catched an intermitting Fever which with the great Demand for post Horses made by the Prince du Nord <prev[ented]> delayed <my arriving here so soon as I expected> us greatly.

I went with Dr. Franklin to Versailles the Day after my arrival. The minister[2] spoke of you in Terms very friendly and very just, and my next Visit would have been to the Countess de Montmorin[3] but as we learned that a mail was to be dismissed <to> for Philadelphia to Day, we returned immediately to prepare our Dispatches, so that I have been obliged to deny myself the Honor of paying my Respects to a Lady whose Character and Connection with you render me particularly desirous of seeing. Tomorrow we are promised <the Honor> a visit from the Marquis <and Marchioness> de la Fayette and his Lady, after which I shall take the first opportunity "<de> me poner a los pies de la Condesa de Montmorin."[4] I <do not know whether> am not sure that this is good Spanish. If not, I wish the Inspectors of the post office <w[ill]> may be so obliging as to correct it.

<Politics must for obvious Reasons be reserved for some future Letter.>

[19 July][5]

I had written thus far when a variety of Interruptions prevented my <continuing> proceeding for several Days, and then I became violently attacked with the Influenza from which I am now just beginning to recover. It has been very severe on all my Family, none except my nephew having escaped. Mrs. Jay has been obliged to struggle with that and the intermitting Fever together, and this is the first Day that she has been out of the House since our Arrival.

I am much mortified at not having yet seen the Countess de Montmorin. The Day before I was taken sick I did myself the Honor of calling at her House, but she was from Home. As soon as the Doctor sets me at Liberty, the first use I shall make of it will be to renew my visit.

What I have seen of France pleases me exceedingly. Doctor Franklin has recieved some late Noble proofs of the King[s] Liberality in the Liquidation of his Accounts and the Terms and Manner of paying the Balance due on them.[6] No People understand doing civil Things so well as the French. The aids <we hav[e]> they have afforded us recieved additional Value from the generous and gracious Manner in which they were supplied, and <we sensibly find our Hearts uniting with our Interest> that circumstance will have a proportionable Degree of Influence in cementing the connection formed between the two Countries.

I think the late Resolution<s> and Conduct of America respecting Mr. Carltons proposed <Negociation> correspondence with Congress must have given you Pleasure.[7] As Monsieur de Clonard[8] passed through Spain he doubtless brought you Copies. Some Letters and Instructions <brought me> I have recieved by the same Vessel, contain strong Evidence of the Determination of Congress to <be faithful Allies to France in al[l]> consult the Interest and wishes of France upon all occasions.[9]

I have seen and dined with the Count D'Aranda.[10] His Conversation <and Professions> leads me to <hope> suspect that his Court is at last in earnest. This however is a Question which Facts and not words <can> must determine. <has lost somewhat of its Importance, and which> It is hard to judge of Men especially of old politicians. At present I like the Count, for he appears frank and candid as well as sagacious. They say he is a little obstinate, but for my part I <like a> prefer <a> plain Dealing obstinate <man> men <infinitely better than <<one>> those> to those unstable ones who like the Moon change once a Fortnight and <feebly shine by> <only with a feeble> are mere Dispensors of borrowed Light.

I cannot forbear mentioning that I am particularly indebted to the polite Attention of your Friend Count D'Estaing. He is at Passy enjoying otium cum Dignitate.[11] There is a singular Taste <on the orname[nts]> displayed in the ornaments of his <Rooms> House. The very walls (like Portius in Addisons Cato) are *ambitiously sententious,* <but you> <as you have doubtless been there, this> and shew that they do not belong to <a common> an ordinary Man.

I am Dear Sir with great Esteem and Attachment, your most obedient and very humble Servant.

P.S. I intended to have written also to the Chevalier, but I must defer it <till Tomorrow.>

Dft. Endorsed by JJ. ALS in CP E 608: 405–06; without deletions in *RDC,* V, 522–24. This letter was written over a period of three weeks and not completed until 19 July. Montmorin acknowledged JJ's letter on 22 Aug. 1782, ALS in JP; Tr in NN: Bancroft: American IV, 64.

[1]Chevalier Bourgoing.

[2]Vergennes.

[3]Montmorin married his cousin Françoise-Gabrielle de Tane in 1767. She has been described as "la grosse Madame de Montmorin," "moins jeune et moins riche que son cousin, mais autrement intelligente, fine, délice et ambitieuse." Frédéric Masson, *Le Départment des affaires étrangères pendant la revolution, 1787–1804* (Paris, 1877), pp. 57, 57n.

[4]To pay my respects to the Countess of Montmorin."

[5]This date appears on the addressee's copy.

[6]On 16 July 1782 Franklin and Vergennes concluded an agreement which provided for repayment of loans from February 1778 to July 1782. The principal, amounting to 18 million livres, was to be repaid in twelve equal yearly installments of 1,500,000 livres, payment to begin "the third year after a peace." As "a new proof of his affection and friendship," the King provided that the 5% annual interest on these sums would not be computed from the dates on which the loans were made, but from "that day of the date of the treaty of peace." Provision was also made for American assumption of the Dutch loan of 1781. The contract is reprinted in French and English in *JCC,* XXIV, 51–63.

[7]In a brusque reply to Carleton's peace feeler, Congress resolved: "That the Commander in Chief be, and hereby is, directed to refuse the request of Sir Guy Carleton, of a passport for Mr. Morgan to bring despatches to Philadelphia." *JCC,* XXII, 263.

[8]Ambrose Sutton, Chevalier de Clonard, a French naval officer and privateersman during the Revolution who remained with a small squadron left behind by de Grasse after Yorktown. In May 1782, Luzerne picked Clonard to run the British coastal blockade to deliver dispatches to Europe. Clonard was in Spain in early July. See William Carmichael to JJ, 3 July 1782, ALS in JP; see also G. Rutherford, "Ambrose Sutton, Chevalier de Clonard, The Irish Sword," Military History Society of Ireland, *Journal,* I (1952–53), 253–61.

[9]A reference to a resolution of Congress reaffirming its determination to uphold the Alliance of 1778 and make no separate peace with Great Britain. Proposed by Livingston to quiet the French Court's anxiety concerning the recent British attempts to open separate peace talks in America, drafted by Madison and finally accepted in altered form on 31 May 1782. *JCC,* XXII, 302–05; 311–13; *RDC,* V, 464–65; *MP,* IV, 192–93; 302–04. See also Robert R. Livingston to JJ, 9 May 1782, cited above in "The Status of the Peacemaking," n. 8.

[10]JJ and Franklin met with Aranda on 29 June 1782. The invitation to dinner was extended to them within the next week. Both matters were reported by JJ

to Secretary Livingston on 17 November; see above, JJ to Aranda, 25 June 1782, n. 2.

[11]"Leisure with dignity."

NOAILLES DE LAFAYETTE TO SARAH LIVINGSTON JAY

Paris, this Tuesday the 29 June 1782

Mme. de Lafayette has only just learned that Madame Jay has come to Paris. She is most anxious to have the honor of making her acquaintance, and would have liked very much to have gone as early as this evening, to learn from her about her trip, but her health does not permit her to go out today. She begs Madame Jay to find some way for her to make it up by allowing her to come tomorrow, and of asking her at what hour she will be at home, without imposing upon her.

Mme. de Lafayette dares to hope that the kindness and friendship of M. Jay for M. de Lafayette, about whom he has so often spoken, will serve to persuade Madame Jay to overlook an eagerness, perhaps a little indiscreet, and to hope that her initial respects will be well received. M. de Lafayette is at Versailles, from which he will return tomorrow, to have the honor of seeing Monsieur and Madame Jay.

Tr in French, trans. by the editors.

FROM JOHN ADAMS

The Hague, 8 July 1782

Sir,

The Duke de la Vauguion has this Moment, kindly given me Notice, that he is to Send off a Courier this Evening at Eleven, and that the Dutch Fleet has Sailed from the Texel this Morning.

I Shall take Advantage of the Courier Simply to congratulate you on your Arrival at Paris, and to wish you and Mrs. Jay, much Pleasure, in your Residence there. Health, the Blessing which is Sought in vain, among these Meadows and Canals, you can Scarcely fail of enjoying in France.

Shall I beg the Favour of you, to write me, from Time to Time the Progress of the Negotiation for Peace? The States of Holland, go upon my Project of a Treaty, the 10th and I dont foresee any Obstacle to the Compleation of it, Slowly however.[1] After which I fancy I shall make a further Proposal, with great Modesty and Humility as becomes me, but which the English, if not the Russians and the Danes, will think very forward and assuming.[2] How the Loan here is likely to Suceed I cannot as yet inform you. I am flattered with Hopes of getting a Million and an half, but I dare not depend upon one Quarter Part of that Sum, nor insist upon any Part, untill the Money is received.[3] Appearances in this Country are not less uncertain now than they were in the Times of D'Avaux and D'Estrades.[4]

I hope, in God that your Spanish Negotiation has not wrecked your Constitution as my Dutch one, has mine. I would not undergo again, what I have Suffered here, in Body and mind, for the Fee Simple of all their Spice Islands.[5] I love them however, because with all their Faults and under all their Disadvantages, they have at Bottom a Strong Spirit of Liberty, a Sincere Affection for America, and a Kind of religious Veneration for her Cause.

There are Intrigues, going on here, which originate in Petersbourg and Copenhagen, which Surprise me.[6] They Succeed very ill, but they are curious. Have you discerned any coming from the Same Sources at Madrid or Versailles? Whether the Object of them is to Stir up a Party in favour of England to take a Part in the War, or only to favour her in Obtaining moderate Terms of Peace or whether it is Simply, to Share Some of her Guineas by an amusement of this kind, like a game at Cards is a Problem.

As to Peace, no Party in England Seems to have Influence enough to dare to make, one real Advance towards it. The present Ministry are really to be pitied. They have not Power to do any Thing. I am surprised they dont all resign. If they dissolve Parliament, I dont believe they would get a Better. Is Mr. Carmichael at Paris with you, or does he continue at Madrid? With great Esteem I have the Honor to be Sir your most Obedient Servant,

J. ADAMS

ALS. Endorsed: ". . . ansd 2 Augt." *HPJ,* II, 322–23, omits most of 3d paragraph.

[1]Adams was officially received by the Dutch on 19 April, and on the 23d he formally proposed the formation of a committee to treat with him in drawing up a Dutch-American treaty of amity and commerce. The protracted negotiations culminated in the signing of the treaty at The Hague on 8 Oct. 1782. *AP,* III, 3–4, 16–17; *RDC,* V, 325, 803–05.

[2]The "further Proposal" was doubtless Adams' scheme to gain America's admission into the League of Armed Neutrality, thereby obtaining *de facto* recognition of the U.S. See below, Adams to JJ, 10 Aug. 1782.

[3]On 11 June Adams signed a contract with three Dutch banking firms for a loan of 5 million guilders ($2 million). Although Adams was unduly skeptical about receiving most of it in the near future, virtually the full amount was subscribed by the end of 1782. Rafael R. Bayley, *The National Loans of the United States from*

July 4, 1776 to June 30, 1880 (Washington, D.C., 1882), p. 17; Adams to Robert R. Livingston, 5 July 1782, *JAW*, VII, 599–600, *RDC*, V, 594–95.

[4]Jean Antoine de Mesmes, Comte d'Avaux (1640–1709), and Godefroi Louis, Comte d'Estrades (1607–86), French authorities on diplomatic negotiations with the Dutch, whose tracts Adams had read. See *AP*, IV, 146n., for citations of their works.

[5]Adams had been seriously ill the previous summer and remained in weakened condition as late as the spring of 1782. Page Smith, *John Adams* (2 vols., Garden City, N.Y., 1962), I, 502, 511, 516.

[6]These "intrigues" concerned renewed proposals for Russian mediation of the Anglo-Dutch War, for which see Friedrich Edler, *The Dutch Republic and the American Revolution* (Baltimore, 1911), pp. 193–201, and Isabel de Madariaga, *Britain, Russia, and the Armed Neutrality,* (New Haven, 1962), chs. 12, 13, 16; and editorial note above, "The Status of the Peacemaking on Jay's Arrival in Paris."

From Lafayette

Paris, 9 July 1782

Dear Sir,

Mr. Grenville's Courier is Arrived, and Mr. Grenville Himself is Gone to Versailles. Any thing further I Hear, I will make a point to Communicate, and Beg You will do the same, as I think this Business is pretty Interesting. I am just Going to St. Germain, But will Return to Morrow. My Best respects wait upon Mrs. Jay. Most Respectfully and Affectionately Yours,

LAFAYETTE

ALS. Endorsed.

Sir James Kicks Over the Traces

Throughout the war the vain and strident Sir James seemed to relish taking public positions discomforting to his younger and more distinguished brother and associating with persons and causes which proved embarrassing to the Jay family. Craving the kind of recognition his brother had earned, he became increasingly competitive. When JJ aligned himself with Franklin and Silas Deane in the controversy over Arthur Lee, Sir James espoused the latter's cause.[1] As a member of the New York Senate (October 1778–April 1782) he joined forces with JJ's oldtime foe, John Morin Scott, to push through the legislature the punitive Act of Attainder (22 October 1779), confiscating the property of conspicuous New York Loyalists, an action which JJ deplored. Writing to Governor George Clinton from Aranjuez on 6 May 1780, JJ observed that if the legislation as reported in an English newspaper was "truly printed," New York was "disgraced by injustice too palpable to admit of palliation."[2]

Using the wartime family home at Fishkill as a base of operations, Sir James continued to serve in the legislature and hobnob with celebrities. Around 8–9 September 1780 we find him stopping off at Haverstraw at the home of Joshua Hett Smith, an intermediary between Major André and Benedict Arnold. He then traveled on to West Point with the General, who was frantically awaiting his wife's arrival from Philadelphia before making his fateful move.[3] On returning to Fishkill, Sir James dutifully communicated some unspecified request of Benedict Arnold's to Governor Clinton, probably soliciting permits for some friends of Smith's to pass within the enemy's lines.[4] Two days after Sir James' letter was received, Arnold defected.

Sir James was not shy about pressing his claims upon Congress for reimbursement. On 14 December 1780 Congress awarded him $400 in bills of credit "in full compensation for the damage he sustained by Depreciation and otherwise, on the Money advanced to Otis Andrews, Clothiers, in Boston on the 16th July, 1778." Insisting that he had been prompted to advance the money, "not by a desire of promoting the public service," as was reputed, but "by the view of transferring my property from Boston to Philadelphia with ease and safety," Sir James pressed Governor Clinton for recovery of sums allegedly due him as a result of the depreciation of the bills of credit, for a balance remaining of some £7,000.[5]

Whether or not the alleged ingratitude on the part of Congress could be held accountable for the elder sibling's increasingly bizarre conduct, it might have been predicted that more embarrassments could be in store for the staunchly patriotic Jay family. In April 1782, by prearrangement, Sir James was captured in New Jersey and brought within the King's lines. There he was reported to have expressed his fear and revulsion of the French and to have first launched his project for reuniting the colonies with Great Britain.[6] Sir James then arranged with Sir Guy Carleton to be allowed to go to England. Soon thereafter JJ's and SLJ's families broke the news to JJ of his brother's alleged capture,[7] and some months later Gouverneur Morris implied that Sir James had defected.[8] The unsettling news prompted JJ to indite a stern letter of repudiation of his erratic and suspect brother.[9]

JJ's instincts were sound. Despite his later professions of steadfast loyalty to the American cause,[10] Sir James proved a wilful meddler, losing little time once in England. In June we find him officiously tendering Shelburne a draft of a bill relinquishing or modifying Parliament's jurisdiction over America and authorizing the King to make a peace or truce with America and form a union by incorporating the colonies "into one grand body politic on the solid basis of affection and common interest."[10] Most pernicious was his proposal for treating with the assemblies of the separate States and bypassing Congress, a plan long since repudiated and one that would have cut the ground from under Congress' Peace Commissioners in Paris, including JJ.[11]

In addition to being a turncoat, Sir James proved himself as much of a nuisance in England as he had in America. Shelburne complained to Thomas

Townshend (before the July cabinet shift, Secretary at War and thereafter Home Secretary and chief government spokesman in the Commons) that JJ's brother had refused to disclose any information concerning America unless he would listen to an "idle story about a naval invention." Perhaps the best way out would be to send him back to Carleton in New York, the Earl added, and if he refused, to cut off his stipend.[12] Failing to clear up the suspicions about himself which Shelburne had conveyed to Townshend, Sir James soon abandoned his ill-timed efforts in England and slipped away to the Continent, where he busied himself arranging an exchange with a captured British officer in order to free himself from his parole.[13]

Before departing Sir James thrust himself into two controversies, both involving appeals to General Washington on behalf of British military prisoners, the first on 12 July when he urged the exchange of Captain Eld of the British guards, a prisoner at Yorktown.[14] Then, on 19 July he entered his plea on behalf of Charles Asgill.[15]

The Asgill affair, which escalated to an international incident, arose when Sir Henry Clinton released an artillery captain hailing from Monmouth County, New Jersey, by the name of Joshua Huddy. The Patriot officer was placed in the custody of Richard Lippincott,[16] a so-called "refugee" from the same county. On 12 April 1782 Lippincott hanged Huddy at Middleton Point in reprisal for the death of Philip White, a Tory kinsman of Lippincott's. Moved by a memorial from the inhabitants of Monmouth County, Washington wrote Clinton demanding that Lippincott or an officer of equivalent rank be handed over for condign punishment. His action was endorsed by a resolution of Congress of 29 April. When Clinton declined to comply, Washington directed Brigadier General Moses Hazen to designate by lot "a British Captain who is an unconditional prisoner." As a result of carelessness or misunderstanding, Hazen failed to exclude all protected officers from the drawing. The lot fell on Captain Charles Asgill (1762/3–1823), member of a prominent aristocratic British family and an officer covered beyond dispute by Cornwallis' terms of capitulation. When Washington proved adamant, the young man's mother appealed to the Comte de Vergennes. The British took up the Asgill case with JJ and Franklin in Paris, but both Commissioners refused to intervene on the ground, as Richard Oswald reported their views, that "the Execution of Huddy was undoubtedly a cruel murder; and for which Lippincott who commanded the Party ought to suffer."[17] In the light of JJ's long and steadfast support of Washington, his reaction might have been forecast. In the end, as a result of the intercession of Louis XVI, Congress voted on 7 November that Asgill be released, and Washington complied.[18]

By curious coincidence both Sir James and Henry Brockholst Livingston managed to get involved in the Asgill affair. Brockholst, whose break with the Jays had been forecast by SLJ a half year earlier,[19] left Madrid on 7 February 1782 and sailed from Cádiz on 11 March, carrying dispatches to Congress. His ship was captured by the British frigate *Quebec* on 25 April, not before Brockholst had destroyed the dispatches.[20] Brought to New York, he was confined to the Provost jail on order of the British Military governor of New York, Lieutenant General James Robertson, on the alleged ground that he was the bearer of dispatches to Congress. During the course of his detention he was also regarded as a potential hostage against the life of Captain Asgill. Livingston's cell-mate was none other than Sir James Jay. The latter pumped JJ's brother-in-law for all he could get, and then revealed the gist of his conversations to the Loyalist William Smith, retailing with some relish an account of the discontents which had riddled the Spanish mission.[21]

Failing to persuade Livingston to help establish diplomatic contact with Congress, Sir Guy Carleton released him on parole.[22] Thereafter Brockholst began the study of law under Peter Yates at Albany, was admitted to the bar in 1783,[23] and time on end would prove to be a thorn in the side of JJ.

[1]*JJ,* I, 571, 572.

[2]JJ to George Clinton, 6 May 1780, Dft in JP; *HPJ,* I, 314–15 and *PPGC,* V, 684–86. See also Jones, *History of New York,* II, 524–40.

[3]William Smith, *Historical Memoirs,* II, 488, 495, 505, 506. *New York Royal Gazette,* 17 April 1782.

[4]See James Jay to Benedict Arnold, 14 Sept. 1780, below. See also A. B. Hart, ed., *The Varick Court of Inquiry* (Boston, 1907), pp. 89–91, 96–99.

[5]Computed at a year's interest on $6,366. *JCC,* XVIII, 1152, 1153; *PPGC,* VI, 492, 500.

[6]William Smith (*Historical Memoirs,* II, 488, 503–506) reports conversations at first and second hand with Sir James, making it clear that the latter arranged his own capture to promote his notions of a reunion with the Mother Country, and that "by veiling his Intentions," he sought to deceive Washington about the purpose of his planned secret trip abroad. Aside from belittling the role of his brother in Spain, Sir James was reported to have spread information damaging to the Patriot cause.

[7]Frederick Jay to JJ, 20 April 1782, and Susannah French Livingston to SLJ, 21 April 1782, above.

[8]Gouverneur Morris to JJ, 6 Aug. 1782, below. Robert R. Livingston, who also reported to JJ on Sir James' departure, took a more charitable view of the matter, saying "many people here attribute it to design. I for my part acquit him of every thing but imprudence." See below, Livingston to JJ, 17 Sept. 1782.

[9]JJ to Peter Van Schaack, 17 Sept. 1782, below.

[10]Sir James to John Adams, 21 Nov. 1782, below, which hardly conforms with the evidence (Shelburne to Townshend, n.d. [June–July 1782], below) that Sir James was receiving a stipend from the British, behavior which placed him in the category of either a refugee or an intelligence agent.

[11]Sir James to Shelburne, 15 June 1782, below.

[12]Shelburne to Townshend, n.d. [June–July 1782], below.

[13]See below, Sir James to Franklin, 27 Oct. 1782.

[14]Sir James to Washington, 12 July 1782, C in DLC: Washington 4.

[15]Sir James to Washington, 19 July 1782, below.

[16]See Larry Bowman, "The Court-Martial of Captain Richard Lippincott," *New Jersey History,* LXXXIX (1971), 23–27.

[17]Oswald to Strachey, 31 July 1782, C in FO 95/511.

[18]See *JCC,* XXII, 217–18; XXIII, 652–53, 663 and n., 689–91, 695n., 715, 718–20; *GWF,*

XXIV, 135–39, 144–45, 146–47; XXV, 40–41, 112, 243, 295, 336–37, 349 *passim; RDC,* V, 462–64, 617–18, 634–36 *passim;* VI, 64–65. Townshend to Oswald, 28 Aug. 1782, C in FO 95/511. See also Henry Steele Commager and Richard B. Morris, eds., *The Spirit of 'Seventy-Six* (New York, 1958), pp. 884–91.

[19]See above, SLJ to William Livingston, 24 June 1781. JJ secured a passport from the Spanish government for his brother-in-law. JJ to Bernardo del Campo, 1 Feb. 1782, AL in AHN Estado, leg. 3885, exp. 12, doc. 1; LbkCs in PCC 110, II, in JP, and in CSmH.

[20]Brockholst confessed to being "prudent enough to destroy" the papers. Henry Brockholst Livingston to General James Robertson, The Provost in New York, 8 May 1782, C in DLC: Washington 4. JJ's instructions had been that the dispatches be sunk in "Case of Danger." See JJ to John Vaughan, 5 Feb. 1782, ALS in PPAmP: Madeira-Vaughan. Sent by Codman on 7 February, the packet contained the following letters to Congress: a duplicate of JJ's 3 Oct. 1781 to McKean; his 6 Feb. 1782 to Secretary Livingston (cited above in Livingston's 28 Nov. 1781, n. 3); his 6 Feb. 1782 to President of Congress John Hanson, LbkCs in JP, CSmH, PCC 110, II; *HPJ,* II, 176–78; *RDC,* V, 150–51; *SDC,* VIII, 10–11.

[21]William Smith, *Historical Memoirs,* II, 504.

[22]See below, Henry Brockholst Livingston to William Livingston, 3 May 1782, and to Washington, 16 June 1782, ALS in DLC: Washington 4.

[23]Gerald T. Dunne, "Brockholst Livingston," in Leon Friedman and Fred L. Israel, eds., *The Justices of the United States Supreme Court, 1789–1969* (4 vols., New York, 1969), I, 387–98.

Sir James Jay to Benedict Arnold

Fishkill, 14 September 1780

Dear General,

I communicated what you desired to the Governor. He assured me he would write to you on the Subject, and was disposed to give the matter all the assistance in his power.

I am but this moment returned from Poughkeepsie. The day before yesterday, the Legislature elected Delegates to Congress for the ensuing year. General Schuyler declined, and General McDougal was chosen in his room. All the other Delegates were reelected.[1] This is all the news I have to tell you. I hope by this time you have the happiness of Mrs. Arnold's company. If so, I beg my best regards to her; and wishing you both all the happiness which it is possible to enjoy in such a Country, and in such a neighbourhood.

I remain, with great regard, Dear General, Your Most Obedient and humble Servant,

JAMES JAY

ALS in DLC: Washington 4.

[1]The New York delegation to Congress in the fall of 1780 comprised: James Duane, William Floyd, John Morin Scott, Ezra L'Hommedieu, and Alexander McDougall. *JCC,* XVIII, 891–92.

Henry Brockholst Livingston to William Livingston

[New York], 3 May 1782

My dear Sir,

If You have received my letter by the Commerce you already know of my leaving Cadiz on the 11th of March last. The 25th of the month following I was taken by the Quebec frigate, and yesterday by General Robertson's order committed to the Provost of this City.[1] I have taken the liberty to remonstrate with that Gentleman on this measure. Enclosed You have a Copy of my letter to him.[2] I hope you will think it conceived in spirited and at the same time in decent terms. Whether it will work out my release I cannot tell.

It has been hinted to me by the Provost Marshal,[3] and perhaps you will hear it, that I shall not be set at liberty, until Lippincott's affair be settled, and that if General Washington puts his threat into Execution, I may be thought a proper subject for retaliation. I laugh at this Insinuation, and am so fully persuaded of the justice of our General's Conduct on this occasion, that did I beleive any thing of the kind would be <hinted> mentioned to him, I would Entreat him myself to pay no attention to it. On this I am determined, that let what will happen, I will never stoop so low as to ask the smallest favor at their hands, and could I beleive that my letter to General Robertson could be considered in that light, I would rather have burnt than sent it. Pray give yourself no uneasiness on my account. I must do Capt. Cunningham the Justice to say that he does every Thing in his power to render my situation comfortable.

Mr. and Mrs. Jay are well. Sally had another daughter in february.

I am my dear Sir Your dutiful Son,

HENRY B. LIVINGSTON

ACS in DLC: Washington 4.

[1]The Provost Gaol, used in the British military occupation of the city, was the New Gaol or Debtors' Prison erected c. 1757 on a corner of the Common near the site of New York's present City Hall.

[2]See source note of H. B. Livingston to Washington, 16 June 1782, below.

[3]The notorious William Cunningham (c. 1717–91).

From Gouverneur Morris

Philadelphia, 21 May 1782

Dear Jay,

I write these Lines to acknowledge yours from San Ildefonso of the twenty eighth of September[1] to enclose you a short Resolution of Congress to tell you that Colonel Livingston and your Brother James met in the Provost at New York.[2] Livingston is with us. James is at large in New York. Your Family except one are alive and well. I am sorry to add that your Father is no more. I know how much you will feel on this Occasion and I know you too well to offer a Consolation. This must always come too soon or too late. Some Arrangements now before Congress will I think be agreable to you. You tell me BUT HAPPY SHALL I BE TO SEE THE DAY WHEN I SHALL NO MORE BE PLAGUED WITH HIS TRICKS. This Day will I think speedily arrive in a Manner agreable to all Parties.[3]

I will write you fully by the next Opportunity.

Adieu. Yours,

GOUV. MORRIS

DftS in NNC: RBML: Gouverneur Morris. Endorsed by Morris: ". . . Dr letter to Mr. Jay 21 May 1782, wrote per same offering a Billet to Carmichael." The code employed is the nomenclator that Robert Morris used on 7 July 1781.

[1]Above.

[2]See James Jay to President of Congress, 16 Aug., 29 Sept. 1781, ALS in PCC 78, XIII, 253–54, 273, pressing his claim for monies due him; denied by Congress 29 Sept., *JCC,* XXI, 1026.

[3]Morris is quoting from JJ's letter to him of 28 Sept. 1781, above, referring to Carmichael. A week after Morris wrote JJ, Carmichael, at Livingston's nomination on 9 May, was picked by Congress to serve as Franklin's secretary in Paris, an appointment revoked on 10 July. *RDC,* V, 402; *JCC,* XXII, 258, 307, 380.

Sir James Jay to Shelburne

Saturday, from the same place as before,
[London], 15 June 1782

My Lord,

With an aching head, and a parched Tongue, I set down to the subject I undertook. I beg you will keep this in mind when you read what I am going to write; and that you will also remember that when a Person is giving his sentiments on a political subject without knowing the whole of what has been done, or is proposed to be done, it is scarcely possible to avoid proposing something that is not inconsistant with the General Plan laid down.

As I am too much oppressed with sickness to enter into the Subject at large, I shall just make an observation or two in the Bill,[1] and inclose a rough Sketch of One with such Additions as appear necessary to remedy the *seeming* Defects of the other.

Your Lordship will observe that the Bill before the House goes no further than to Enable His Majesty to make a *Peace* or *Truce* with the Colonies; and for that End to *repeal* or *suspend* any Act or Acts etc. which relate to the Colonies.

The Complaints and Claims of the Americans go much further. They contend against the principle of some of those Acts. They deny the Right of Parliament to Tax Them, and to interfere in their internal Police.

The Bill therefore does not come up to their Ideas. This was observed, with much uneasiness, by some friends of Government in New York. Where the contending Parties differ widely about principles, is it likely that a Bill which does not go to those principles, will remove Difficulties and reconcile Differences, with a jealous, irritated people, under the influence of men whose Interest will lead them to prevent any Accommodation short of total Independency? If Government mean to give up the Right of Taxation, I imagine it should be done in plain clear Terms; because that will put it out of the power of bad men in America to mislead the people of that Country. If Government, on the other hand, mean to leave that Point doubtful, the Objection I have made falls of Course.

A great deal may be said on this Bill. Considering the State of Britain, of America, and of other Countries; the risk and consequence of disappointment, t'is a very important One, and the Time very Critical. But the condition I am in will not allow me to add more, than that I am, My Lord, with great respect, Your Lordships Most Obedient and humble Servant.

N.B. Lest the Bearer might lose this Letter, I decline putting my name to it.

Sketch of a Bill etc.

N.B. The principal additions in the following Sketch are underlined.

Whereas *certain points respecting the Jurisdiction of the British Legislature over the Colonies or Plantations of New Hampshire etc. etc., have never been ascertained and settled; in consequence of which the present unhappy war with the people of those Colonies hath arisen.* And whereas it is essential to the Interests, Welfare, and Prosperity of Great Britain and the said Colonies, that Peace should be restored between them, and *proper Measures taken to incorporate them into one Grand Body Politic on the Solid Basis of Affection and common interest.*

Wherefore, and for a full manifestation of the earnest wish and desire of His Majesty and His Parliament, to put a speedy end to the Calamities of war, *to satisfy the people in America in what is just and reasonable, and to remove all cause of future distrust,* Be it Enacted by the Kings most Excellent Majesty, by and with the advice and consent of the Lords Spiritual and Temporel, and Commons, in this present Parliament assembled, and by the authority of the same, that it shall and may be lawful for His Majesty to treat, consult of, agree, and conclude, with any Body Corporate or Politic, or any Assembly or Assemblies, or Description of men, or any Person or Persons whatsoever, a Peace, or Truce, with the said Colonies or Plantations, or any of them, or any Part or Parts thereof; any Law, Act or Acts of Parliament, Matter, or Thing, to the contrary in anywise notwithstanding.

And *for the more effectually answering the aforesaid Ends,* and to obviate any Impediment, Obstacle, or Delay, to the carrying the intentions of His Majesty and His Parliament into full Effect, which might arise from any Act or Acts of Parliament affecting or relating to the said Colonies or Plantations; *or from any Right or Claim of Jurisdiction of the British Legislature over them.* Be it further Enacted by the authority aforesaid, that for the concluding and establishing of a Peace, or Truce, *and forming such Union as aforesaid* with the said Colonies or Plantations, or any of them His Majesty shall have full Power and Authority, by virtue of this Act, by His Letters Patent under the Great Seal of Great Britain, to repeal, anul, and make void, or to suspend for any Time or Times, the operation and effect of any Act or Acts of Parliament which relate to the said Colonies or Plantations, or any of them, so far as the same do relate to them, or any of these, or any Part or Parts thereof, or any Clause, Provision or Matter therein contained, so far as such Clauses, Provisions, or Matters, relate to the said Colonies or Plantations, or any of them, or any Part or Parts thereof: *And also to maintain or relinquish and finally adjust and settle any Right or Claim of Jurisdiction of the British Legislature over the said Colonies and Plantations in such manner as He shall think reasonable, and most conducive to the Honour and Happiness of both Countries.*

And Be it further Enacted, that this Act, as to the exercise of the Powers and Authorities hereby given to His Majesty, shall continue to be in full force until the———.[2]

AL in MiU-C: Lansdowne 71: 287-90. Endorsed: "Sir James Jay. his observations on the Act to enable His Majesty to make Peace with America etc. etc."

[1]Sir James enclosed a printed copy of Stat. 21 Geo. III, c. xlvi (1781), "An Act to enable His Majesty to conclude a Peace or Truce with certain Colonies in North America therein mentioned." Printed by Charles Eyre and William Strahan (London, 1782).

[2]Blank in manuscript.

Henry Brockholst Livingston to George Washington

Elizabeth Town, 16 June 1782

Sir,

Considering the various and important objects of your Excellency's constant attention, it is with the greatest reluctance I prevail upon myself to engage it a single moment by any thing not of some immediate public consequence; yet such is my present Situation that I flatter myself your Exc[ellenc]y will pardon my freedom in requesting your Attention to it.

On the 11th of March last I sailed from Cadiz, and was taken by an English frigate the 25th of the month following. At New-York I was committed to the Provost, and continued in it until the arrival of Sir Guy Carleton who liberated me on parole. Having been absent from America on furlough, without exceeding the term thereof, and having a Lieut. Colonels Commission in pocket, I did not think there could be any impropriety in signing a parole as such, and in being exchanged accordingly. But on perusing the Journals of Congress, I find by Resolutions passed the 31st of December 81, and 21st January 82,[1] that I am among those Officers who are considered as retiring from Service on half pay, the first day of the present year. Those Resolves your Exc[ellenc]y will readily beleive I must have been a perfect Stranger to at the time of my capture, neither of them having had time to reach Madrid when I came away, which was on the seventh of february last. This circumstance will, I trust, exculpate me from any censure, and will induce your Excellency to permit me to be considered as a Lieut. Colonel in any future Exchange agreeable to the tenor of my parole.[2]

I cannot conclude without taking notice of that part of Sir Guy Carleton's first letter to your Excellency,[3] in which he appears to make a merit of my enlargement, and to think himself entitled therefor to some return on the part of your Excellency. Lest this circumstance may induce a suspicion, that some part of my conduct, while in confinement, may have given the Enemy reason to beleive that I considered my liberation in the light of a favor, or took improper steps to obtain it, I think it incumbent on me to lay before your Exc[ellenc]y a narrative of what passed on that occasion.

Immediately on landing at New-York, Mr. Sproat informed me, on the part of General Robertson, that I was to be confined in the Provost, and Mr. Chief Justice Smith was sent thither to apologize for my being treated in that manner. I told Mr. Smith that throwing a Person into a common Jail merely on suspicion of his being the Bearer of important dispatches, appeared to me an unprecedented and a very extraordinary measure, but that as it could answer no purpose to enter into an altercation with him, I should write to General Robertson himself on the Subject; and on pen, ink and paper, being brought me I wrote him a letter, of which the enclosed is a copy.

In answer thereto, the General sent me a polite message by Major Wymms, the purport of which was that "reasons of state rendered my confinement necessary, but that I might rest assured it would be of very short duration." The Major concluded by apologizing for my not receiving a written answer, the General's time being wholley engrossed by very pressing business. Major Wymms had scarcely retired when Captain Cunningham, the Provost-Marshal, mentioned to me for the first time, Lippincott's situation, and what had passed between your Exc[ellenc]y and Sir Henry Clinton on that subject. He did not seem to speak from authority, but gave me to understand, as politely as he could, that it might be well for me to interest myself on the occasion, as it was impossible to say, to what lengths retaliation might be carried in case your Exc[ellenc]y should execute the threat you had thrown out. I was not then apprized of all the circumstances relative to the murder of Captain Huddy, but had I been a total stranger to your Excellency's character, Cunningham's own state of the matter might have convinced me of the perfect propriety of your requisition. I told him so and (after laughing at the Idea of any Interest of mine or of my friends being sufficient to induce your Excellency to recede from so just a demand) promised to comply with his request, provided he would first engage to transmit to your Excellency whatever I might think proper to write on the matter. He replied General Robertson must first see it. This convinced me, it would be useless to write from a certainty that my letter would not correspond with his wishes, and of course not be forwarded. I set down however and wrote what is enclosed to my Father.

I had now determined to make no further application to General Robertson, nor did I hear any thing more from Head-Quarters until the arrival of Sir Guy Carleton, who sent for me without my applying to him either verbally or by letter. On being introduced to his Excellency, he informed me, in the presence of Mr. Smith, of his being much surprized at hearing of my confinement, and very happy to have it in his power so soon to put a period to it. Without leaving time to reply, he acquainted me with his Intention to send his Secretary with a *complimentary* letter to Congress, and begged of me in order to facilitate Mr. Morgan's[3] Journey to accept of a seat in his carriage. After thanking him for his Attention, I asked whether Mr. Morgan had permission from Congress or your Exc[ellenc]y to proceed to Philad[elphi]a and on being answered in the negative, told him that I recollected Mr. Ferguson's having been stopped on a like errand for want of such passport, and that Mr. Morgan would probably be obliged to return should he undertake the Journey without one. He said the Idea was perfectly new to him; he did not conceive any necessity of a flag's being furnished with a passport, and if so in Mr. Ferguson's case, my going with his secretary must supersede that necessity in the present one. I observed to him that his Exc[ellenc]y must allow there was a wide difference between sending a military flag to an out-post of our army, and sending a person in Mr. Morgan's character through so great a part of the Country to Philadelphia, and that without such a pass I must beg leave to decline the pleasure I should otherwise derive from travelling in that Gentleman's company. Sir Guy then proposed that his Secretary and myself should go together, and in case of the former's being stopped, I was to proceed with his dispatches to Congress. This also I refused, telling him, that as it was probable his letters contained some overtures, I could not consent to charge myself with them, unless his Excellency would assure me they contained an acknowledgment of our Independence, or a promise to withdraw their fleets and armies, that these were the only terms on which Congress had agreed to open a treaty in 78, and that it was not probable they would listen to any thing short thereof now. He seemed somewhat surprized, and after a little hesitation assured me upon his honor that he was vested with no such Powers, that his intended letter to Congress was a matter of mere compliment, but if there was any danger of Mr. Morgan's meeting with difficulties, he would postpone his Journey until he could hear from your Exc[ellenc]y on the subject. This closed our conversation for that day. The next morning agreeable to his desire, I waited on him again. He received me very politely, talked much of the King's pacific dispositions, of his own earnest desire of an honorable peace, of his wishes to carry on the war, while it did prevail, more consonant to the dictates of humanity than heretofore. He was persuaded of meeting with corresponding sentiments in your Exc[ellenc]y, that both Countries were interested in supporting the british character, that if England and America must separate, it would be their mutual Interest to part like men of honor, and in good humour with each other. After a great deal more of the same purpose he informed me a barge was ready to take me to Elizabeth Town. He then put into my hands a letter for my father,[4] some English prints, with a few is[sues] of the Bill and the votes of the house of Commons which he said should be transmitted to your Excellency by another flag. After signing a parole I took my leave.

I hope your Excellency will forgive my having been so very prolix on this occasion, as nothing but an idea of it's being my duty has led me to be circumstantial in every thing that passed between the Commander in chief and myself during my captivity in New York.

I have the honor to be, With the highest Respect, Your Excellency's most Obedient and very Humble Servant,

HENRY BROCKHOLST LIVINGSTON

ALS in DLC: Washington 4. Endorsed: ". . . answd. July 3d, 1782." Enclosures: Henry Brockholst Livingston to William Livingston, 3 May 1782, above, and Henry Brockholst Livingston to Lieut. Gen. James A. Robertson, 2 May 1782, ACS.

[1]*JCC,* XXI, 1186–87; XXII, 40–42.

[2]Washington accepted Livingston's explanation. Washington to H. B. Livingston, 3 July 1782, *GWF,* XXIV, 394–95.

[3]Maurice Morgann (1726–1802), Shelburne's private secretary, dispatched to New York to aid the mission of Sir Guy Carleton and Admiral Robert Digby to approach Congress with a view to reconciliation. *Peacemakers,* p. 269.

In his 7 May 1782 letter to Washington, Carleton stated that the paroling of Livingston was "the first Act" of his command. Therein he requested a passport for Morgann, on which Congress resolved negatively on 14 May (*JCC,* XXII, 263). Carleton's 7 May ALS is in DLC: Washington 4, enclosing Parliamentary debates on concluding a peace or truce with America, which commenced on 4 March 1782 (*Parliamentary History,* XXII, 1102 *et seq.*). See also *GWF,* XXIV, 241–44, including Washington to President of Congress Hanson, 10 May 1782.

[4]Carleton to William Livingston, 12 June 1782, LS in NHi: Misc. Mss. William Livingston; Cs in MHi and NN: Livingston; also in DLC: Washington 4.

SHELBURNE TO TOWNSHEND

Saturday, [London], [June–July 1782]

Dear Sir,

Sir James Jay has been with me. Nepean[1] can tell you everything about him. He has been with me with an Idle Story about a naval Invention, and says he finds he can be of more use of those things than about America. I wish you would get us rid of him, for he has been an expence, and will prove an Intolerable one, if you don't speak very plain to him. He told me he could not call on you about America, till I determined about his naval business. However he is now gone to you, and I would submit to you whether after talking to Nepean it would not be better to order him back to Carleton by the Pacquet, or to let him know that he'll have no more money, if he does not go.

Ever yours,

SHELBURNE

Tr in BM, Add. Sydney Papers 3: 17.
[1]Sir Evan Nepean (1751–1822), Undersecretary of State.

SIR JAMES JAY TO THOMAS TOWNSHEND

[London], Tuesday Evening, 9 July [1782]

My Lord,

Agreeable to the message delivered me this morning from Your Lordship, I called at the Office. I had some conversation there with Mr. Napean, in consequence of which I am apprehensive that you labour under a mistake in regard to me, which I feel myself urged to undeceive You in. At the same time, I am not insensible that in the great Circle of business in which You move, Appearances may arise in a particular Case which have no foundation in reality. Satisfied that on a little reflection your Lordships sensibility will lead you into my ideas on the occasion, I think it unnecessary to enter into particulars; or to shew the propriety of my knowing your determination as soon as possible.

I am now to request of Your Lordship an audience of a few minutes. Sensible of the load and hurry of business in which you are involved, I wish not to press on your time. But allow me, my Lord, to add, that I shall esteem your indulging me with it soon a real obligation.

I have the honour, My Lord, to be, with the greatest respect, Your Lordship's Most Obedient and Very humble Servant,

JAMES JAY

ALS in MiU-C: Sydney. Endorsed.

Sir James Jay to George Washington

London, 19 July 1782
Copy

Dear Sir,

I writ to Your Excellency the 12th instant.[1] I hope that Letter will be forwarded by the same conveyance with this. I am now called upon to address you by one of those very affecting instances of private distress which deeply wound the heart; and excite all our tenderness in favour of the unhappy Sufferers. This melancholy Case is occasioned by the confinement of Captain Asgill as an Object of retaliation; the news of which arrived here about six days ago.

T'is a truly melancholy situation to be in, when the misfortunes of others affect our feeling, and prompt us to wish for their relief, at the same time that our reason tells us there may be insuperable obstacles to the exercise of this humaine disposition. Unable as I am, in the present instance, to form a competent opinion on that point, I readily yield to the solicitations of friends, and the suggestions of my own feelings for the distressed family, to lay their condition before you: confident that your humanity and judgment will make a proper use of the information; and that your candour will put a proper interpretation on my conduct. My acquaintance with the family, and frequent visits to it in this hour of affliction, enable me to give you the melancholy detail from my own knowlege.

Sir Charles Asgill,[2] the father of the unfortunate youth, is very much indisposed, and in so critical a situation, having been of late severely threatened with an Apoplectic fit, that the News of his Son's confinement etc. is kept from him. His Lady, oppressed with grief, dare not see him, lest her behaviour might betray the secret, which would probably put an end to his existence. His Daughter, a lovely young Lady of great delicacy of mind and person, has ever since been delirious, raving almost perpetually about her brother, his execution and death. In this complicated Scene of woe, on account of her husband, Son, and daughter, Lady Asgill herself is sinking into a condition that is easier to be imagined than described.

Melancholy as these circumstances are, worse are still to be apprehended. Should the rigid hand of retaliation cut the Thread of life of the unfortunate youth, the stroke would reach beyond himself. When I view the present distressing Scene, and think on what may happen, I feel, from the very bottom of my soul, for this amiable family. There is reason to fear that inadvertence or accident may carry the news of the Son's situation to the father, which would certainly precipitate him into great danger, if not immediately prove fatal: that agitation of mind may distroy the daughter: that complicated distress may sink the wretched mother. Yet nature may overcome the violence of the present shock: Hope may protract their wretchedness and their lives till they hear the Event: but should that prove contrary to their prayers and their hopes, the consequences will probably exhibit a Scene which humanity shudders to view even in imagination.

This, Sir, is the Case that looks up to you for relief. T'is the Case too of a friend; for Sir Charles has always been the decided and steady friend of our Country. I have the honour to be, with great regard and respect, Dear Sir, Your Excellency's Most Obedient and very humble Servant.

JAMES JAY

ACS in DLC: Washington 4.
[1]ACS in DLC: Washington 4, on behalf of Captain Eld.
[2]Sir Charles Asgill, baronet, died in 1788.

Sir James Jay to Benjamin Franklin

Hague, 27 October 1782

Sir,

The restriction I was subjected to by my parole, not to go to France, determined me not even to write to any person in that kingdom, till I should be exchanged. The officiousness however of some persons in London, in converting me into a messenger of peace from Congress, inclined me, for very obvious reasons, to break through the restraint I had imposed upon myself, and to give you an account of my captivity. But on a little reflection I could not but think that such a step would be a work of supererogation.

Agreeably to the determination I have just mentioned, I thought of transacting the business of my exchange with Mr. Adams. As that

Gentleman is now also in France, and I of course stand in the same situation with regard to you both, I take the liberty to write to you on the subject, flattering myself that both of you will do every thing in your power to expedite my exchange. Mr. Townshend, the Secretary of State, consents to accept of a Lieutenant Colonel for me, and that either Colonel Tarlton or Colonel Dundas,[1] both of whom were taken at York Town, may be the man. I beg Your Excellency will take the matter into your consideration, and favour me with your determination upon it as soon as possible.

I remain, with great respect, Your Excellencys Most Obedient and humble Servant,

JAMES JAY

P.S. Please to direct for me to the care of Monsieur Dumas.[2]

ALS in PHi: Society. Endorsed by W. T. Franklin.

[1]Banastre Tarleton (1754–1833), to be appointed lieutenant colonel in December 1782, was on parole in England; Thomas Dundas (1750–94), was to be brevetted colonel in Nov. 1782.

[2]For Dumas, see below, Adams to JJ, 10 Aug. 1782, n. 6.

Sir James Jay to John Adams

Hague, 21 November 1782

Dear Sir,

The Letter I received under your Cover from my brother,[1] informs me that injurious suspicions were entertained of me by some people in America. I suppose you have heard the same. Had I had the happiness of meeting you here, I should easily have shown you the futility of those suspicions, pointed out their source, and convinced you of my attachment to the Liberties of our Country, and to the common Cause of America and her Allies. Deprived of that opportunity, I must refer you to his Excellency the Duke de Vauguion who will satisfy you on those points. I flatter myself therefore that I shall soon have the pleasure of seeing you in Paris: and in the mean while I beg that you will believe me to be with great regard and esteem, Sir, Your most obedient humble Servant,

JAMES JAY

ALS in MHi: Adams, reel 359.

[1]Not located.

To John Adams

Paris, 2 August 1782

Sir,

Your friendly Letter of the 8th Ult.[1] should not have remained so long unanswered had I not been obliged by sickness which lasted several weeks to postpone writing to any of my <Friends> correspondents.

Mrs. Jay <and indeed all my Family have> has also been indisposed; indeed neither of us have been blessed with much Health since we left America.

Your Negociations in Holland have been honorable to yourself as well as useful to your Country. I rejoice in both, and regret that your Health has been so severely taxed by the Business of your Employment. I have also had my share of perplexities, and some that I ought not to have met with.

I congratulate you on the Prospect of your Loan succeeding, and hope that your Expectations on that Subject <will> may be realized. I commend your prudence however in not relying on appearances. They <often> deceive us sometimes in all Countries.

My Negociations have not been discontinued by my leaving Madrid. The Count d'Aranda is authorized to treat with me, and the Disposition of that Court to an alliance with us seems daily to grow warmer. I wish we could have a few Hours Conversation on this Subject, and others connected with it. As we have no Cypher I must be reserved. I had flattered myself with the Expectation of seeing you here, and still hope that when your Business at the Hague will admit of a few Weeks' absence you <will> may prevail upon yourself to pay us a visit. I really think that a free Conference between us might be useful as well as agreable, especially as we should thereby have an opportunity of making many Communications to each other that must not be committed to paper.

As to Negociations for peace, they have been retarded by the late Changes in the British Ministry. <I have very little confidence in that Court and shall always expect more from this.>

Mr. Oswald is here <and it is said>, and I hear that Mr. Fitzherbert is to succeed Mr. Grenville. <The Brit[ish]> Lord Shelburne continues to profess <his> a Desire of peace, but his Professions unless supported by Facts <ought to> can have little Credit with us. He says that our Independence shall be acknowledged, but it is not done and therefore his Sincerity remains questionable.[2]

War must make peace for us, and we shall always find well appointed armies to be our ablest Negociators.

The Intrigues you <mention> allude to I think may be also traced <every where> <here and> at Madrid, <and> but I believe have very little Influence <any where except perhaps at London. Russi[a]> <at either> anywhere except perhaps at London. <Russia> Petersburgh and Copenhagen in my opinion wish well to England but are less <with a Desire to take part> Desirous to share in the War than in the proffits of it. Perhaps indeed further accessions to the power of the House of Bourbon may excite Jealousy, especially as America as well as Holland is supposed to be <almost entirely> very much under the Direction of <her Ally> France.

Did you receive my Letters of 18 March and 15 April?[3] <I left Mr. Carmichael at Madrid.>

Think a little of coming this way. I am Dear Sir with great Esteem and Regard Your most Obedient and very Humble Servant.

<P.S. I left Mr. Carmichael at Madrid.>

Dft. Endorsed: "... in ansr. to 8 July." AL in MHi: Adams, reel 357. Omissions in *HPJ*, II, 324–25; *JAW*, VII, 602–04; *RDC*, V, 638–39.

[1]Above.

[2]Fearful that Fox's resignation would adversely effect the ministry's willingness to concede independence, Franklin suspended his talks with Oswald, who appealed to Shelburne to reassure the Doctor on this point. Shelburne's attempts to mollify Franklin seem only to have strengthened the American's conviction that the Earl was trying to split the French and Americans. Oswald to Shelburne, 12 July 1782, cited above in "The Status of the Peacemaking," n. 22; Franklin to Vergennes, 24 July 1782, ALS and French trans. in CP EU 21: 460–61; *BFS*, VIII, 570. See also Grantham's reassuring letter of introduction for Fitzherbert. Grantham to Franklin, 27 July 1782, FO 27/3. For Fitzherbert, see above, "The Status of the Peacemaking," and n. 21.

[3]For JJ to John Adams, 18 March 1782, see above. In his 15 April letter JJ dealt with the prospect of Dutch recognition of the United States, among other matters. Dft in JP; ALS in MHi: Adams, reel 356; E in NN: Bancroft: American II, 187.

Jay Opens Negotiations with Aranda

3 August 1782

Laid low with influenza in July, JJ was unable to commence his negotiations with the Conde de Aranda until 3 August. As described in Aranda's "Journal" below, the initial talks concerned the boundaries claimed by the United States.

It quickly appeared that the differences between the negotiators were vast. JJ insisted on the Mississippi as the western boundary, and on the southern boundary's extension to 31° N.L. Aranda then drew a red line on his own map which he turned over to JJ.[1] The Aranda line ran vertically from the westernmost shore of Lake Erie southward, bisecting Georgia. In the ensuing deadlock the Conde appealed to Vergennes. At a meeting on 23 August below, Aranda indicated that he was not prepared to "quibble over some leagues more or less in such a vast extent of territory." Vergennes suggested that his undersecretary, the English-speaking Gérard de Rayneval, might serve as an intermediary in the negotiations between Aranda and JJ, a proposal acceptable to the Spaniard. On 25 August Vergennes proposed a compromise, moving the Aranda line westward to the lower junction of the Wabash and the Ohio. In turn, Aranda countered with an alternate line, roughly splitting the distance between the Wabash and his original longitudinal line. This one would bisect the present state of Ohio. Some discussion also took place regarding the southwest boundaries of the United States. The following day Aranda found JJ to be obdurate on the Mississippi as his country's western limits.

The French now took a more active role. On 30 August Rayneval sketched out for Aranda a counter-proposal, which, incorporating some of Aranda's modifications, he presented to JJ about a week later.[2] This was a zigzag line running from the intersection of the Wabash and the Ohio, along the course of the Cumberland, and southwards to the Flint River, still far short of American claims.

On receipt of this memoir JJ sat down and drafted a reply, in which he made the following points: (1) he was transmitting a copy of the memoir to Congress; (2) he was not authorized to treat with Aranda either in the latter's private capacity or as ambassador, since Aranda was "not authorized ex officio to treat" with JJ; (3) while he had shown Aranda his commission from Congress to treat, the latter had shown him no "power whatever." (4) Accordingly, he had deferred further negotiations since his commission barred him from treating except "with persons vested with equal authority." (5) Finally, he had informed Aranda that he had no power "to cede any territory of the United States to Spain," but only to frame treaties of alliance and commerce.[3] On second thought JJ withheld the letter.

[1]A marginal note, in JJ to Robert R. Livingston, 17 Nov. 1782, in JJ's letterbook version, reads as follows: "This map was sent to the Secretary's Office the 17 Augt. 1786 for the Inspection & Information of the members of Congress where it still remains." For the 17 Nov. 1782 letter, cited above in JJ to Aranda, 25 June 1782, n. 2; see also *JCC,* XXXI, 540; (22 Aug. 1786).

[2]See Rayneval, "Suggestions concerning Boundaries between Spain and the United States," 6 Sept. 1782, below.

[3]JJ to Rayneval, 7 Sept. 1782. Tr in JP. Endorsed by JJ: "Proposed draft letter to Mr. Rayneval but never sent."

BOUNDARY DISCUSSIONS BETWEEN JAY AND ARANDA, 3–30 AUGUST 1782

1st session, Paris, 3 August 1782

On Saturday the 3rd of August, Sir John Jay came at ten o'clock in the morning, and on his entering my study, I shewed him a big Map of North America, whose title read:

"Amérique septentrionale avec les routes, distances en milles, villages et établissements—les 8 feuilles françois et anglois—parle Dr. Mitchel traduit de l'anglois par Le Rouge Ingenieur Geographe du Roi rue des grands Augustins 1753."

"North America so Doctor Mitchel zu London in 1775 den jahr ansgegeben jetzaber in des französische übersetzet."[1]

He informed me that there were other partial and provincial maps. I replied that I would show them to him later, because we should first consider the matter in the large and in its totality in order to draw a line of demarcation between the territories that would be kept by Spain and those by the 13 United States; such line, in my opinion, should run from the principal and ineffaceable points without arguing over a hundred leagues more or less; that in any case that dividing line would have to run, in greater part, through the lands of the Indians, whom each of us would have to pacify in order to have peaceful boundaries between both Empires.

This observation having been accepted in general, I asked Jay where he would draw his dividing line. He replied that a separation was already marked out, notably the Mississippi River, and pointed with his finger to its source, tracing it down almost to New Orleans. I asked him then, if his idea was to deprive us of all of Western Florida which, besides having been ours in former times, we had recently reconquered from England.

He replied that inasmuch as the Colonies had claimed for themselves the rights of England, including these acknowledged boundaries, one could not deny them boundaries running from the source of the Mississippi to where the true boundary of Western Florida began. I immediately used his own argument to refute his proposition, pointing out that Spain, having reconquered Florida, which had been the basis for fixing the whole of the Mississippi as the boundary in the treaty of Paris, Spain had claimed for herself, through the reconquest of that province, all rights under that treaty.

He rejoined, arguing that when the Colonies had been settled under the authority of the British Crown, they claimed, according to

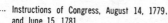

THE PEACE NEGOTIATIONS, 1779-1783: THE BOUNDARIES OF THE UNITED STATES

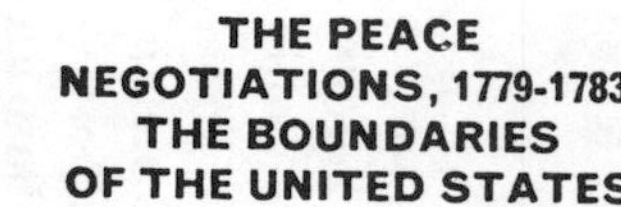

Instructions of Congress, August 14, 1779, and June 15, 1781

La Luzerne's proposal to Congress, January 1780 (Proclamation Line of 1763)

Shelburne's instructions to Oswald, April 28, 1782

Western line proposed by Aranda, August 3, 1782

Compromise line proposed by Vergennes, August 25, 1782

Aranda counterproposal, August 25 1782

Rayneval's proposed line, September 6, 1782

Jay's provisional treaty draft, October 5, 1782, Including Franklin's proposal to defer N.E. boundary for settlement after the war

Strachey's alternative proposals, October 20, 1782

Great Lakes and alternative 45th parallel lines agreed upon by British and American Commissioners, Nov. 30, 1782 (embodied in Jay's revised draft)

Preliminary and definitive treaty lines of November 30, 1782, and September 3, 1783

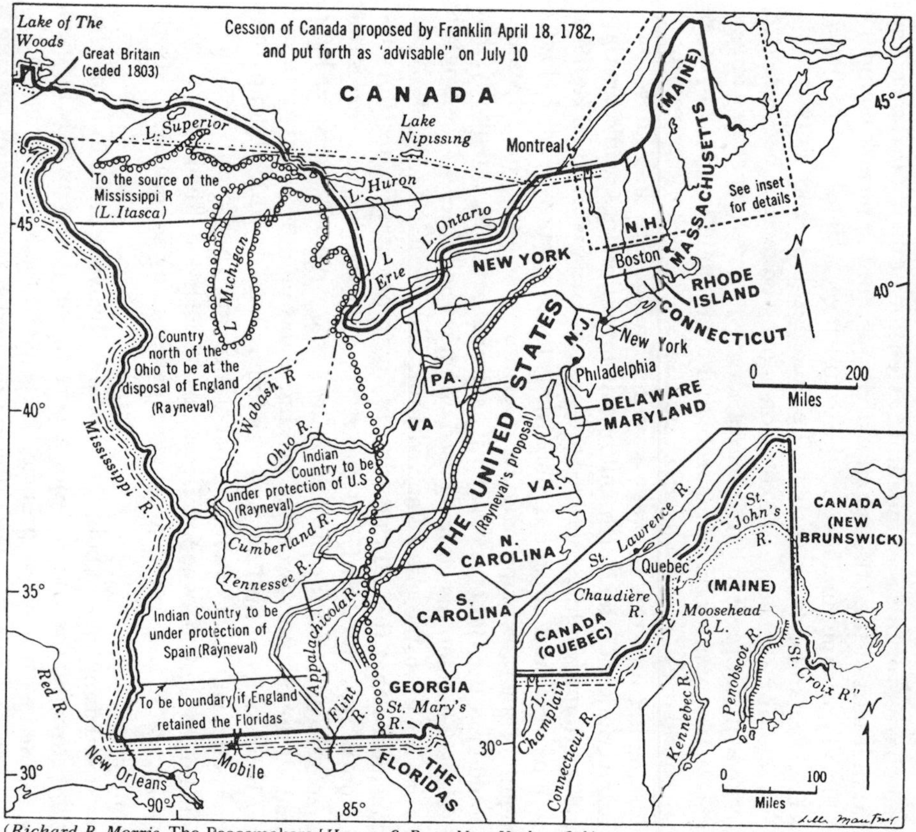

(*Richard B. Morris,* The Peacemakers [*Harper & Row, New York, 1965*])

their charters or titles, an indefinite extension at their backlands, and that that part of the Mississippi which was not the former boundary of Florida, was not included in the Spanish reconquest, but belonged to England and consequently to the Colonies, her representatives.

I told him that such an extension conceived to have been granted by the British Crown to her Colonies, gave equal rights in these imaginary spaces to any other monarch; and even Spain was able to draw her boundaries from Louisiana and the coast of Florida, from both sides, going upwards between parallel lines, to the less known and frozen country of the North, but in this form the lines would overlap, and the maps would be reduced to lineal squares, with equal rights to each party: that it appeared more likely that he who already held the mouth of the Mississippi, and its interior course over a long distance, would have the right to consider it as his perpetually; and finally, that he must abandon his claims based on undefined lines on the English maps, for even the one I showed him, had them, and I had always considered that they did not signify anything; that the territory the Colonies had inhabited and possessed, appeared on the very same map, as well as on the provincial ones that we would consider later; that all the territory, we were looking at, beyond the principal line of the boundaries of the Colonies, was Indian land, to which both parties had equal rights, or equally unjust claims, and that for this reason we should divide it between us by means of clearly defined points, after which each one would dress that naked body according to its resources.

I aired my views about the division, always bearing in mind that the course of the rivers, from a certain point downwards at least, remained with only one proprietor. He asked me to mark it out on the map clearly, and I agreed, offering to send him one map bearing a clear demarcation which he might peruse, reserving for a later occasion his doubts, concerning which in turn I would seek to give satisfaction.

Let me now state my reasons:

As regards that part of the line in controversy, I explicitly picked the end of the Lakes, starting in at *Superior,* following their borders until the end of the Erie or Oswego, in such position that there would be nothing disputable to its rear, and with the idea in mind that Spain would erect forts at certain points, which were in sight of her neighbor, and would be able to permit, or otherwise, trade within her possessions. Then I went down to the junction of the Great Kanawha with the Ohio, tracing it to the largest entry into North Carolina, with the idea of continuing to run the demarcation line through some line of sight, such as a lake, in the land of the Apalachees, or George River, but without reaching it and only marking the end of the line as an indication, and without continuing it when it approached the boundary between Georgia and Florida, until finding out which would be the definitive one.

Mr. Jay asked me why I stopped there, without continuing the line to the lake; I answered him that, since East Florida was still an English possession, we should not draw interior lines therein, to which he agreed.

The point that I had in mind in fixing the principal boundary in that way, was to force the Americans to adopt a more moderate position, and to counteract Mr. Jay's pretension to the whole Mississippi as a boundary line.

Don Gilberto Maxent showed me a map with a dividing line that he had drawn and which he had sent to Señor Don José de Gálvez, and of which I took a copy. In this he had drawn a straight line, starting above the Lakes, passing through [Lake] Michigan, and continuing directly to the same point in East Florida, next to the Guillmard River,[2] and to what is called the tip of Florida.

My first explanation embraces whatever modification, from the Lakes downwards, that is from North to South, which is the territory known to us, and therefore more important to us, than that from the Lakes upwards. To leave the use and navigation of the Lakes, which are interconnected, such as the so-called Superior, Michigan, Huron, Erie or Oswego, and Ontario, to the Americans, shall please them, while to us they are useless because they do not connect with our rivers. To divide them would cause disturbances in that distant wilderness.

This first proposal, which had been formulated early in the day, was meant to demonstrate that we were entering into negotiations, and that we have opened the door to the Americans to set forth all their own views, by which we shall be governed subsequently.

The dividing line that I have drawn, therefore, is marked with red, and the others that were to come would each be indicated by a different color.

Paris, 19–30 August 1782

On Monday the 19th of August when I was leaving the house of M. de Vergennes, Franklin and Jay were getting out of their coach. We greeted each other, and I asked Jay whether he had amused himself with the atlas of the colonies I had given him, and whether he had found it useful. He answered, "Yes. It was very good," adding that he did not know which were better maps, mine or the English ones. I added that whenever he wanted we would talk, and he volunteered that he would arrange for it as soon as possible.

On Wednesday the 21st I returned to Versailles, and M. de Vergennes showed me the big map of Mitchell, which I had loaned to Jay last Monday, with the demarcation of boundaries I proposed.

On seeing this, I expressed my gratification to M. de Vergennes that Jay had taken His Excellency into his confidence, and I told him that we had put off discussions for another day as he seemed busy then.

On Friday the 23d I returned to Versailles with the sole purpose of acquainting myself with M. de Vergennes' ideas, and to instruct him properly about what was advisable. He took the map and I demonstrated to His Excellency how Jay first proposed to draw the boundaries along the entire length of the Mississippi River, which, of course, he [Vergennes] considered unacceptable; I recapitulated several reasons that I had advanced to Jay, which he deemed appropriate, and I explained to him that the reason I had drawn the red line in that form was to seek out known and clearly legible spots as principal points of those boundaries, while at the same time, to persuade Jay to modify his original pretension, by proposing a counter-line of a different color to serve as a basis for further discussion.

M. de Vergennes informed me that Jay had pointed out to him that the colonies already had some outposts far beyond their back-country, and consequently beyond the red line. I replied that I wanted Jay to identify that very spot on the map, that I was ready to acknowledge as many posts as they had already established, but that, until he would point these out, we ought to govern ourselves by the boundaries on the maps; and that, for the express purpose of giving Jay the opportunity to make his nominal claims, I had started drawing such a line. Indeed so far as I could see, considering his poverty of words, compounded by his difficulties in understanding French and Spanish, it was not possible to carry on a long discourse with him. That according to my instructions I could not accept the Mississippi as the boundary line, which for many obvious reasons was not suitable. Apart from this, I would not quibble over some leagues more or less in such a vast extent of territory; and that if His Excellency wanted to take the trouble to mediate, I would appreciate it; but he should begin by requiring Jay to explain himself clearly and concretely.

M. de Vergennes showed himself disposed to do that, and asked me if I had any objection to dealing also with his first deputy, M. de Rayneval, a person well informed on the issue in question, and the only one who was capable of arguing with Jay, because he had had more frequent dealings with him and spoke English. I replied by accepting, and he sent for him.

M. de Rayneval came down just when the Duke de Civrac, who had to talk with the said Minister, arrived, and then Rayneval and I repaired to another chamber with the map. I began by explaining the background of my conversations with Jay, and by observing that Jay's claims were rendered all the more extreme when one considers those English possessions as consisting of two parts: The first might be designated the Colonies, with definite limits; the other, the possessions of the Crown conquered from other empires, for instance Canada and both Floridas, whose internal extension was no concern of the Colonies, but also that the same English monarch, who had allowed the Colonies to draw indefinite boundaries from East to West, in distant times and arbitrarily, proved no longer disposed to consenting to these boundaries, but sought to cut the Colonies off by others running from North to South, from Canada to Florida, which two possessions he considered to be a conquered patrimony of the Crown. Moreover, situated in the center were several nations not even as yet brought under control by any one. Yet, despite all these considerations, Jay proposed to extend his line all the way to the Mississippi.

M. de Rayneval told me that my observation was correct while Jay's was excessively optimistic; in support thereof he informed me that, while Louisiana and Canada had belonged to France, she had always considered all the intermediate territory as hers, even the lakes, without stopping to fix a middle line, according to the principle that Canada, or Louisiana, all belonged to the same proprietor. But what could be advanced against Jay even further was the fact that once France had lost Canada, it was then that the issue arose regarding her boundary with respect to Louisiana, which remained French. The English argued that the limits of Canada extended along the entire course of the Ohio and the Mississippi, for so M. de Vaudreuil, the French Governor of Canada, had described them in a provisional protocol that had been entered into between the commanding officers of both nations when the English conquered Canada. In support of this argument, when the treaty of peace was signed, the English continued to bound Canada by the Mississippi, running the length of this river to the sea, on the ground that Florida had been conquered from Spain, as well as the French part of Mobile. On this ground, the Americans could not claim that their territory extended beyond the right bank of the Ohio, for not having taken possession of Canada, it belonged to England. On like grounds, they could not acquire the left bank, because the same British Crown could claim an extent of territory from both Floridas up to the Ohio, behind Georgia, the Carolinas, and Virginia.

M. de Rayneval sought to find the fort called Toulouse[3] which we located on the Alabama River; and he told me that when France had possession of part of Mobile, on the other side of the Mississippi, between this point and Spanish Florida, she built up that fort as a point of support as well as a limit for the English and the Spaniards, and that the territory from the mouth of the said river upwards had always been called under the generic name of Louisiana, which, as such, was joined at its upper limits with Canada.

Considering M. de Rayneval's ideas as so far removed from Jay's, with due respect to his fund of information about those places, I told him that he could return that map to Jay in order to dissuade him from pursuing his ends and to moderate his pretensions. For a start he could disabuse him of the notion that the settlements were in an advanced state. Having an abundant supply of similar maps, I would transmit one to the Comte de Vergennes for his personal use. Then we could mark the maps with the controversial lines, and once the final boundaries had been fixed, they would be entered separately in other maps similar to that. He appeared satisfied, and even assured me he would prepare a relevant report, for which I expressed my gratitude.

M. de Vergennes came in. We informed him about our discussion. He seemed agreeable, and we concluded our conversation.

On Saturday the 24th I sent the promised map.

Sunday the 25th was Ambassadors' Day, moved up from last Tuesday on the occasion of the celebration of the great festival of St. Louis, which everybody was obliged to attend at Versailles, according to custom. I met M. de Rayneval as he was coming out of the Minister's study, with the map under his arm, and since I recognized it as mine, I started to talk about it. He replied, repeating that he would make all the necessary annotations; and I encouraged him to do so, not only as a service to the Catholic King, but also for the kindly treatment he had accorded me.

In turn, I went in to confer with M. de Vergennes. He asked me if I insisted on the red line. I responded "No," provided that we would keep the colonists a considerable distance away from the Mississippi, and that we could settle upon some clear points. He appeared satisfied with my answer. He told me that if Jay could not understand this argument, there would still be room for an agreement, one which would leave the Indian nations in the intermediate areas neutral and free to trade with both Spaniards and colonists. "No doubt," I replied, but I pointed out the consideration that such an arrangement would in time have to be altered because the colonists were a new and growing nation, which, concerned with restricting or punishing the barbarians, would be pressing to take possession of those much better and more temperate lands than the ones along the coast. It would be always good policy, even in the case of the neutrality of those nations, to set some kind of meridian or clear line across which no one on either side could pass.

His Excellency picked up Jay's map, which he still had. We reexamined it, and he told me that in order to satisfy the Americans it was necessary to concede them more territory at their rear. To accomplish this I could move the line that crossed the junction of the Great Kanawha with the Ohio, to the lower junction of the Wabash with the Ohio, pointing out that even with this change considerable distance remains to the Mississippi. I proposed to His Excellency that it would suffice to draw it as running between the two lakes that are located midstream of the aforesaid two rivers, in whose gap is inscribed Etang Castor. He replied that he himself would not oppose it, but because it was the intent of the Americans to trade along the interior rivers, they would resist the loss of the Wabash which, once preserved by his more westerly divisional line, would remain entirely in their hands as far as the Ohio, and thus open up for their use a considerable distance beyond the Colonies, as well as the Great Kanawha, claims which they would have to curb or moderate.

I remarked to M. de Vergennes that France once claimed Canada as extending northwards from the Ohio, and belonging now to the English. It was necessary to remember that while we were treating the boundaries between the Americans and us, the territory could be said still to belong to the English, and that neither one nor the other of us had exercised such control over it as to justify a claim to possession. Bearing this consideration in mind, the agreement should, while substantially the same, provide that if there would be any case in which either nation were to extend beyond its actual boundaries—whether because the territories were uninhabited or because of war with the Indians located in between—and having reached any one of the points designated as the frontier line, assuming it to be fixed now, then neither party would be allowed to go beyond that point, whether by reason of its being vacant or of the presence of the uncivilized Indians. Accordingly, should Jay refused to be reasonable and to renounce claims to the Mississippi, he would have to yield to the objection that Spain would not treat on that subject with the Americans, but instead with the English; and that in any case the divisional line already acknowledged, or preparatory for the future, had always been accepted as being far distant from the Mississippi.

M. de Vergennes said that to draw the line from the fort of Toulouse on the Alabama River could not be opposed by the Americans, because when that part called Mobile belonged to France, that was her boundary. To this I added that, if Fort Toulouse and the Alabama River were the limits of the French possessions when they adjoined Spanish Florida, now it had been retroceded to Spain not only on the grounds of original ownership but because it was essential to leave the Alabama River as an interior line, and to draw another line which would include Pensacola and adjacent areas already reconquered by Spain.

M. de Rayneval returned. He offered to work to clarify all the details; and in the presence of M. de Vergennes himself I asked him to do what was proper, according to his understanding. With that our conversation was then terminated.

On Monday the 26th Jay came to see me between one and two o'clock in the afternoon. I asked him if he was satisfied with my maps. He answered me that, as regards the atlas, he was very much so, but less so with the big map, because it seemed to him to be inaccurate. I told him that there was a general map in the atlas, too, and that to me it made no difference which was used, but obviously none better was available. Then, in a candid manner, I remarked that no map would be satisfactory to him unless he abandoned his first proposition of the Mississippi as the boundary, because to draw the boundary in that way one needed no maps, but merely a pen to write it down.

He replied that on his departure from the Colonies, he had been so instructed without discretion, and that, therefore, he was not able to alter it.

I had carefully noted that the copy of his powers, which he had given to me and whose transcription I sent to the Court on the 10th of August with the number 2266, did not touch on the issue of adjusting boundaries, but only those of commerce and amicable relations; yet I did not wish to tell him this explicitly for I would have given him a pretext to affirm that he was not so authorized and then to justify his insistence on the Mississippi.[4]

Bearing this in mind, I took the contrary position, and reminded him that instructions were one thing, powers another; that in dealing with the issue of boundaries one always proposed what would be agreeable; yet, considering the fact that there could be no negotiation or practical discussion, unless the ground rules were already agreed upon: first, it would have to be confirmed—*prius est esse, quam operari.*[5] That the Congress was sufficiently intelligent to appreciate the fact that it would be accorded like intent; that it could not have failed to bear in mind that there would be conflicting claims; that to treat with a totally new establishment, a thousand leagues away, concerning a large and indeterminate interior navigation, when it had not sent an attorney with power to make concessions to another's arguments, and to set the matter in such a form that it would satisfy everyone; that a man of the stature of Mr. Jay, who had been its President, who was loved and respected by his countrymen, and whom all of us considered a plenipotentiary, and that if he himself claimed to have done the bidding of Congress without any power to agree to alterations —then all the conferences, geographical maps, and persuasive arguments were absolutely fruitless.

He repeated that in the matter of the Mississippi Congress had neither told him anything, nor did he have any powers. I asked him immediately how he had made out in Madrid when he had had to deal with boundaries. He replied that only once, when he had entered into a general explanation of them, had he made a reference to the Mississippi River, to which he was plainly told *that it was unacceptable,* without giving him a further explanation; and having left the matter in that status, he had decided not to budge under any circumstances.

I explained that the reply of my Court had been natural and proper considering his extraordinary claim, and since he learned that it was inadmissible at the outset, it was his duty to inquire what Spain was prepared to offer, and then rebut her notions by advancing the views of Congress. Although he had lacked sufficient powers to enter into an agreement, at least he would have made clear the converse pretensions, and with enough time he would have informed his superiors about the aspect and state of this issue; in view of which they would have dispatched to him their final instructions to complete the partial ones; and, as a result, he would have them to explain to me and to serve as a basis for discussion. He answered me that since no one in Madrid had raised the issue any further, he had left the matter as it then stood.

Disagreeing with him, I said that, according to what he had told me, we would have to remain as we were; because I had denied not only the Mississippi, but I had drawn a line with more fundamental *right* to support it than he had had on his part to back up his claim of extension to the Mississippi. He replied that by virtue of my line I was compelling him to enter into an argument because he now had seen several grounds that neither the Congress nor he himself had been able to foresee, and that, now having been enlightened quite differently from his understanding when he had left his own country, he would be able to explain to the United States the difficulties he had encountered.

I asked him if under his commission Dr. Franklin was equally authorized to act. He answered "No," that only he had powers with regard to Spain.

Holding firm to my position that I had considered him in the character of plenipotentiary, I repeated to him that he ought to peruse his papers closely, that he should distinguish between instructions and the credentials of a plenipotentiary. I pointed out that it was not possible, since the fate of the Colonies was to be dealt with in Europe, that its commissioners were supposed to ask advice from Philadelphia, as if the business were to be transacted between Paris and Madrid, for which latter case an answer by safe passage could come in a fortnight while in this case it was a matter of a half year's navigation jeopardized by enemies and storms.

Observing that my argument threw him off guard and unable to respond, I asked him if he would have confidence in placing his case in the hands of the ministry at Versailles and in listening to what it would have to say about this matter. He answered, "Yes," and I persuaded him to do so; but, pointing out by way of concluding, that if he would find upon reviewing his documents that he was not authorized to discuss the boundaries, nor to arrange them, he would let me know in writing; because, having once started to set them down formally, I now found that I would not be able to continue with it; to which he replied that he would inform me after duly reflecting on his position.

In the course of the conversation I considered it appropriate to remind him how much Spain had helped the Colonies with the secret aids as well as with the declaration of war, which had diverted the forces of the enemy. Jay responded very coldly that it was true in regard to some financial assistance, but so far as the war was concerned, he said that Madrid had promised him that they would help the Colonies with the Spanish army, and at most the army had been deployed in the conquest of Florida for itself, and this had not helped them at all in New York or Charleston. In reply, I stated that I did not anticipate, with due respect to his intelligence, such a curious assumption that attacking the enemy in its possessions was not distracting it, that according to basic rules of warfare, any binding ally ought to move on his own course. Therefore, with Spain in possession of Louisiana, and thereby able to draw towards Florida that part of the English army which could have been situated on other fronts, Spain had done what reason dictated.

He replied that he wished we would not have taken Pensacola, because then the British troops were removed to New York, and their strength provided a considerable reinforcement for the English. I answered him that he was offending us by assuming that we had acquiesced in the removal of the English troops from Pensacola to New York; that it had been an interpretation on the part of the English and in bad faith; and the only thing that I was able to say was that the terms of capitulation could have been more specific, pointing out that they must not take up arms again against any one of the belligerents, instead of the allies, or to have demanded explicitly their return to Europe, and although there might have been a certain carelessness in this matter, it should be put down to the official who signed the articles, not to the Court.

He left, stating in his customary few words, that he was looking at the matter in a very different manner from when he had come, and that he wished that his commission could be satisfactorily carried out.

On Friday the 30th I went to Versailles, and at a meeting with M. the Comte de Vergennes and M. de Rayneval, informed them of the visit of Sir John Jay last Monday the 26th, and since they both expressed doubts about the observation I had made to them to the effect that Jay's powers only embraced commerce and amity, without touching the issue of boundaries, I showed them a copy of them, which surprised them both.

They told me that according to the correspondence of the Chevalier de la Luzerne, the Court of Spain had initiated the discussion about boundaries, in the Colonies themselves, through Don Juan de Miralles; to which I replied that that explained why this matter had not been advanced in Madrid.

Having to go to a meeting at the house of the comptroller,[6] M. de

Vergennes left M. de Rayneval and me to continue the discussion of boundaries.

We reexamined the map, and drew a line from the mark that indicated the beginning of Eastern Florida in the direction of Fort Toulouse, to include Western Florida and attach her to Louisiana.

From the said Fort Toulouse, to reach the Ohio, M. de Rayneval had drawn a line going upwards throughout the Toulouse River, following the Cherokee or Hogohegee River, which flows into the Ohio, but a very short distance from the Mississippi; and after I had made the observation that this would place the Americans too close to the course of the Mississippi, we changed the line to pass across the Cherokee through the confluence of the Pelisipi, going upwards until its source, then to take the Cumberland River, and following it to the Ohio, to move downwards to its junction with the Mississippi. In this form the Americans would be positioned far from the latter. Granted that the English would always be the owners of the territory between the Mississippi and the Ohio northwards, still it was impossible to deny it to them as a part of Canada yielded by France.

M. de Rayneval read to me the report on which he was working, giving information about all those lands, and whether England had considered them to be hers, or to belong to other independent and neutral nations, and after having asked him for a copy of it, he promised me one.

From the discussion that we had in the meantime, I inferred that Jay had indicated how little pleased he had been with the Court of Madrid; yet, he had also begun to realize that his claim to the Mississippi River would be neither as legally based nor as sufficiently supported as he originally had conceived.

M. de Rayneval told me about an English map of North America of the year 1753, which had been published with a printed appendix of explanations, of which only one copy was known to be extant, but that he had never been able to acquire the map because, while highly regarded in its time, all copies had disappeared.[7] I told him I believed I had a copy, and that I would send it to him. This I did the next day, for which he was greatly appreciative.

D in Spanish in AHN Estado, leg. 3885, exp. 1, doc. 6, trans. by the editors; partly in *YU,* II, 355–364.

[1]This version of the Mitchell map—engraved by Thomas Jefferys (d. 1771), geographer to the King—with both French and German titles, was published by Georges Louis de Rouge, *Atlas amériquain septentrional* (Paris, 1778). For the famous Mitchell map, see below, editorial note, "Maps Used in the Peace Negotiations."

[2]The Chattahoochee, the eastern boundary of West Florida.

[3]The old French fort at Tuskegee, at the junction of the Talapoosee and Coosa Rivers.

[4]Aranda to Floridablanca, 10 Aug. 1782, ALS in AHN Estado, leg. 3885. JJ had been instructed originally to insist upon the free navigation of the Mississippi and to obtain a free port on the lower portion of that river, for which see *JJ,* I, 650.

[5]"It must exist before it can be operative." Prior possession prevails.

[6]Jean-François Joly de Fleury (1718–1802) succeeded Necker as minister of finance, serving from 24 May 1781 until 30 March 1783.

[7]While the Mitchell map (1st ed., London, 1755) was the principal map used in the peace negotiations, Rayneval may have been referring to Thomas Jefferys, *A Chart of North and South America, including the Atlantic and Pacific Oceans* (London, T. Jefferys, 1753). This map was reprinted, along with a text entitled, "Reasons in support of the new chart of North and South America," in six sheets, by J. Green (London, 1768).

From Gouverneur Morris

Philadelphia, 6 August 1782

Dear Jay,

I received your Letter of the twenty eighth of April by Major Franks.[1] It came too late for I had already applied the Copy of a certain Correspondence in the Manner you intended when you sent it.[2] I decyphered and read your Letter to the Minister of foreign affairs. If I were with you or had Time to use my Cypher,[3] I would say somewhat on it. I think that Congress will not be silent. Should you have done Nothing I advise you to the Maxim festina lente.[4] You will know the Reasons when this reaches you or soon after, Wind and Weather permitting, for both must, you know, be consulted before Instructions can be ascertained to an ultramarine Agent.

I am surprized that you have not had [any] of my Letters since last Autumn but that Circumstance proves the Position I have just advanced. A Question. Are you acquainted with the organization of the Office for foreign Affairs? Letters from the Minister are submitted to Congress *in Toto.* I learn you are going to Versailles if the Account be true, and it came from yourself, this will find you there. I do not however expect any Thing like Peace at present, because I do not expect Peace. This may not be so intelligible to every Body else as it is to you. Sed festina lente I repeat again.

Your Friends here are well. Your Brother James has, I am told, gone to England. If so, his political Race like a New Market Course has run round in a Circle and brought him back to where he started. I am sorry for him, or rather I reciprocate your Feelings on the Occasion. It is somewhat extraordinary, Doctor Franklin's Son,[5] your Brother, and Mr. Lawrence's Self are in England. Mr. Adams I suppose has no Connection there, tho by the bye situated as he is, he should be cautious not to connect himself with those who have.

You will see by our News Papers that the States resolve away at an enormous Rate not to make Peace nor Truce, nor any Thing else with Britain: nimium ne crede Colori.[6]

Look at the other Side of the Question and you will find that, to use a vulgar Expression, they pay Taxes like nothing at all. I use this Expression almost literally for the only Difference is that they pay Nothing, instead of paying like nothing. With this Hint however you must combine our Consideration which is that nobody will be thankful for any Peace, but a very good one. This *they* should have thought on who made War with a Republic. I am among the number who would be extremely ungrateful for the Grant of a bad Peace. My public and private Situation will both concur to render the Sentiment as coming from me unsuspected. Judge then of others. Judge of the many headed fool whose Sense can feel no more than his own wringing. I am not extravagant in my Demands nor impressed with the Quixotism of destroying either a Giant or an Enchanter because I fear not the Force of one nor Charms of the other, but I wish that while the War lasts it may be real War, and that when Peace comes it may be real Peace.

Adieu. Yours,

GOUV. MORRIS

LS. Endorsed: ". . . Recd. Sep."

[1]Letter not located.

[2]A reference to letters between JJ and Lewis Littlepage. JJ had dispatched the packet to Morris, explaining that if Littlepage "should endeavour to gratify his ill-founded Resentment by misrepresentation, on your Side of the Water, they will put it in your Power to defeat his Design, in such a Manner as your Prudence and Friendship for me may dictate." JJ to Gouverneur Morris, 10 Nov. 1781, DftS in JP. See editorial note above, "Lewis Littlepage: An Insubordinate Protégé."

[3]The "Morris" cipher used by the Finance Office.

[4]"Make haste slowly," a favorite saying of Augustus. Quoted by Suetonius, *Augustus* 25, and by Aulus Gellius, *Attic Nights* 10.11.

[5]William Franklin (1731–1813), Benjamin Franklin's illegitimate son, former royal governor of New Jersey, who had been arrested at the start of the war, exchanged in 1778, and served for a time as president of the Board of Associated Loyalists at New York before leaving for England.

[6]Vergil's advice to a conceited youth: "Trust not too much in your good looks."

Independence as a Precondition to Peace Negotiations

7–29 August 1782

Long simmering suspicions of Shelburne, touched off, first, by news of the Carleton mission,[1] and, second, by Shelburne's elevation to the post of prime minister, now erupted when the wording of Oswald's commission[2] came to light. On 7 August Oswald visited both American negotiators to acquaint them with the instructions he had received the previous day from Thomas Townshend, and to show them a draft version of the commission that was to be forwarded to him once the seals were affixed. The nub of the issue was the wording of that document in which the United States was treated under the description of "colonies." JJ, who had only partially recovered from a severe bout with influenza, had by now assumed a key role on the American side of the negotiations. As Oswald's account below reveals, JJ found the commission unsatisfactory, insisting both on independence as a precondition to starting negotiations and on the total evacuation of British forces in America. The conversation (below) between JJ and Oswald was reported by Alleyne Fitzherbert to have been a "violent altercation," in the course of which JJ "let fall some very indecent expressions of animosity against Great Britain," views which the new British emissary to Versailles felt Franklin must have shared, since the two seemed to act "in the closest intimacy."[3]

The very next day Franklin dispatched his copy of Oswald's proposed commission to Vergennes, but, deferring to the latter's preference that negotiations be postponed until the British negotiator had in hand a signed and sealed commission, he used the intervening period to quiet Oswald's fears (as reported in Oswald's account to Townshend of 11 and 13 August below), without, however, dissociating himself from JJ's insistence on a prior, separate acknowledgment of independence, nor entirely allaying Oswald's apprehension about the prospective role of Congress, as JJ had intimated, in acting as guarantor of the peace.

Meantime, on 10 August JJ and Franklin conferred with Vergennes on the proposed Oswald commission. Vergennes urged the Americans to drop their objections on the ground that their formal exchange of powers with Oswald would carry an implied commitment on the British commissioner's part to make independence an article of the treaty itself, which, the French foreign minister insisted, would be the only appropriate way to secure such acknowledgment. In sum, Vergennes argued that, accepting the plenipotentiary powers of Franklin and JJ would *indirectly* concede American independence.[4] As Oswald reported in his 11, 13 August accounts, Franklin may have been persuaded, but JJ was obdurate.

When Oswald next conversed with JJ on 15 August, he queried the American as to the form of recognition he required. JJ then drafted a patent which he worked over with Franklin. Oswald forwarded it to London, not, however, before assuring JJ that such a patent would be unnecessary if the British would write into the treaty an unconditional acknowledgment of American independence. JJ was thus persuaded to move ahead in separate negotiations with England while suspending treaty talks with Spain. Oswald's accounts below of 15, 17 August relayed this advice to his superior, advice quickly supplemented by his report of 18 August disclosing that the Americans would not budge until a preliminary article on independence was forthcoming. By 29 August Thomas Townshend had prepared a compromise proposal, meeting JJ more than half way on the point of independence.

[1]See editorial note, above, "The Status of the Peacemaking on Jay's Arrival in Paris," and n. 8.

[2]Oswald's original commission and instructions were sent by Townshend on 3 August (without the seals) and on the 10th with the seals. The commission empowered him to treat for peace or truce "with any Commissioner or Commissioners named or to be named by the said Colonies or Plantations." Townshend to Oswald, 3 Aug. 1782, Cs in FO 27/2, 95/511, 97/157; 10 Aug., Dft in FO 95/511, Cs in FO 27/2 and 97/157, and in MiU-C: Shelburne 70.

[3]Fitzherbert to Townshend, 8 Aug. 1782, Royal Commission on Historical Manuscripts, *Reports,* LXXXVII, 185.

[4]Vergennes to Luzerne, 12 Aug. 1782, LS in CP EU 22: 46–51.

Richard Oswald: Conversations with Franklin and Jay

Paris, Wednesday, 7–[Friday], 9 August 1782

Yesterday Evening, at 7 o'clock, the Courier Roworth arrived; and brought my Commission for treating with the Commissioners of the Colonies and the King's instructions etc.

This forenoon I went out to Passy, and carried a copy of the Commission to Dr. Franklin. After perusal he said he was glad it was come. That he had been at Versailles yesterday, and Mons. de Vergennes had asked about it; and upon the Doctor telling him it was not come, he said he could do nothing with Mr. Fitzherbert till it arrived; as both Treaties must go on together hand in hand.

I shewed him Mr. Townshend's Letter accounting for a copy being only sent, as the Chancellor and Attorney General were at a distance in the Country. The Doctor seemed to be satisfied, and said, as on a former occasion, He hoped we should agree; and not be long about it. There were no particulars touched upon, and after sitting about a quarter of an hour, I proposed calling on Mr. Jay, the only other Commissioner at Paris. The Doctor said it was right, and returned me the

Copy of the Commission to be left with Mr. Jay, which he would bring back to the Doctor, as he was to dine at Passy.

I accordingly returned to Paris, and called on Mr. Jay. He is a man of good sense; of frank, easy, and polite manners. He read over the copy of the Commission and Mr. Townshend's Letter accounting for it's not being under seal, and then said, By the quotation from the Act of Parliament in the Commission, He supposed it was meant, that Independence was to be treated upon, and was to be granted perhaps as the price of Peace. That it ought to be no part of a Treaty. It ought to have been expressly granted by Act of Parliament, and an order for all Troops to be withdrawn previous to any proposal for Treaty. As that was not done, the King, he said, ought to do it now by Proclamation, and order all garrisons to be evacuated, and then close the American War by a treaty. He said many things of a retrospective kind; such as the happy effects a Declaration of that nature at earlier periods would have produced; if Great Britain had handsomely, and nobly, made this Grant, before such deep wounds had been given to that Bias and attachment, which till then subsisted all over that Country in favour of G. B. even in spite of their Petitions being repeatedly rejected. That in such case, they would undoubtedly have concerted such Plan of Treaty, as would have not only restored Peace; but would have laid a solid Bottom of amity and Conciliation, and such as would have obliterated from their memory, in a short time all remembrance of preceding Acts of Distress and Violence.

But by the continued Enforcement of the same cruel Measures, the Minds of the People in general all over that Continent were almost totally alienated from G. B. so that they detested the very name of an Englishman.

That it was true a number of older People had not forgot their former Connections, and their Inclinations might still lean towards England. But when they were gone, and the younger Generation came to take their place, who had never felt any of those Impressions, those Inclinations would be succeeded by grudge and resentment of every kind, upon reflecting on what they had seen, and their Parents had suffered; that few of them but could recollect the loss of Blood of some relation or other; Devastation of their Estates, and other Misfortunes.

On which occasion he run into a Detail of particulars, as unnecessary as unpleasant here to be repeated and which I would not have touched upon, if I did not think that a full Exposure of the Features of this Conversation may help to form a Judgement of what may be expected in the Issue, from the Determination of this Commissioner, and consequently what concessions on this very critical occasion it may be safe and proper to propose and insist upon.

As information, respecting the real sentiments of those Gentlemen, was the object I principally aimed at, in the Commencement of this Business, I allowed Mr. Jay to go on without Interruption; remarking only upon the whole, that supposing there had been capital Mistakes in the Direction as well as in the Execution of our Measures, it would be hard to bring the Charge home to the Nation in general; and there was a good deal to be said even Excuse of the Ministers, who presided over the Conduct of those Measures considering that they were not personally acquainted with the circumstances of that Country, and therefore could not but naturally listen to the information they received from those who were so acquainted; who came over from America as Refugees, and who had upon all occasions insisted, that We had so great a proportion of Friends in all the Colonies, as to require only a temporary support from Government to bring every thing back to the original state of Peace and Subordination. That it was the search after those friends of Government which, in consequence of personal Interference and correspondence in writing, has kept up and encouraged a continuance of the Measures of Coercion complained of, until they brought on at last the present unfortunate Crisis.

Mr. Jay admitted that some Blame was justly to be imputed to the Misrepresentation of the refugees, and other Correspondents abovementioned, who, he said, at least many of them, were in a particular manner concerned on account of their private interest, to have things brought back by any means to their original state.

As to the Military Men, I said it was natural for them to give credit to those Representations; and they were in general so inattentive to circumstances out of the line of their profession, that I had heard them insist that with a few Battallions, they could go from one End of the Continent to the other; and that I had upon such occasions told them that under the orders of a French or Spanish Court, they might surprize a defenceless country, and by Massacre and Devastation might terrify the People and compleat the Conquest. But having so done, it would be only for the present time, in such a Country as North America. But as Troops would receive no such orders from Great Britain, even a temporary Conquest of any Extent could never be made, by any Armies We could support in that Country. Mr. Jay admitted this to be true, without taking notice of what might have been the Conduct of the abovementioned Foreign Nations in the Reduction of revolted countries.

He returned to the subject of Independence as not being satisfied with its being left as a Matter of Treaty. I wished much to get him off it, and for that purpose said, that the Method proposed was much the same as what he meant, and perhaps such as the Nature of the British Constitution made necessary.

Independence on Great Britain in the most compleat sense would be granted without any reserve; always supposing that their states should be equally independent of other Nations. And so the Treaty might proceed in the Course which was thus marked out for it, untill it ended in Peace. He said Peace was very desirable, and the sooner the better. But the great point was, to make such a peace as should be lasting.

This brought back my attention to the same Expression in Monsieur de Vergennes's Discourse in April, when I first had the Honor of waiting on him. And the more so, that almost in every Conversation I have had with Dr. Franklin, he has made use of the same Words, and delivered as in the way of aphorism; and as an indispensable principle in the foundation of a final settlement between them and France.

I never at these times chose to ask for an Explanation, having no right to do so; I thought it was then too early to venture on such delicate ground; and so I remained at a loss as to the intended meaning of the Words; although I strongly suspected the Expression pointed at some unpleasant or unfavorable Limitations on the Conduct of Great Britain.

But now, being in a somewhat different situation, and having so fair an opportunity, which I wished not to miss of, in order to guess at the meaning of this phrase, I replied that such long Intermission of War was certainly very desirable. But what security could there be given for a continuance of Peace, but such as generally put an End to all Wars, being that of Treaty? But which was often found to be a very inadequate security; as was the Case of the last Treaty concluded at this Place, only twenty years ago.

To this Mr. Jay replied, he would not give a farthing for any Parchment security whatever. They had never signified any thing since the World began, when any Prince or State, of either Side, found it convenient to break through them. But the peace he meant was such, or so to be settled, that it should not be the *Interest* of either Party to violate it. This he said was the only Security that could be proposed to prevent those frequent Returns of war, by which the world was kept in perpetual Disturbance.

I could guess what he meant by the present Parties being bound by motives of Interest to be quiet; and asked for no explanation.

As I happened to mention the last Treaty of Paris, Mr. Jay said, We had taken great advantage of the French in that Treaty. I did not ask him as to the articles he objected to. But further to try his Sentiments on these Subjects, I said I wondered that he, being of America should complain of that Treaty, as if the French had not been tenderly enough dealt with in it; Since that long and expensive War, to which it put a Period, was entered into entirely on account of America; and to save them from the Consequences of that constant Course of Hostility which the French were avowedly carrying on against them on their Western Frontiers, in the times of profound Peace in every other Quarter of the World, and to which they were solemnly bound by the Treaty of Aix la Chapelle.

Notwithstanding which, he very well knew, that in that Interval, there was no intermission in their Endeavours to disturb the quiet of the Colonies by their constant intrigues among the Savages of all the Tribes from Canada down to the Chicasaws on the Gulph of Mexico.

That these Savages, prompted, paid and supported by the French continually lay upon the Borders of our colonies to take advantage of the defenceless state of the back settlers, to surprise and cut their throats as opportunities offered. That to repress the unceasing practice of those cruelties by the Savages, as well as from the French Settlements of Canada, that War was entered into and continued at great Expence, until the Colonies were put out of the reach of all farther Danger by the Conquest of Canada and the total Expulsion of the French from that quarter of the World. I therefore said I thought it odd that the Treaty should be complained of, which put a legal Period to that War; by which the future safety and quiet of the Inhabitants of every part of North America was thus firmly established, and which could not have been effectually done by any other means. Whether We ought to have been so tender of their safety, as to run into that extensive scheme of Exertion, was a Question I also ventured to touch upon, but needless to be repeated here.

To all this Mr. Jay made answer, that at that time North America being considered as a part of the British Empire, as much as England or Ireland, had an equal Title to the protection of Government as any other part of the Dominions, and therefore We could plead no merit by way of Distinction, so as to have any particular claim on america.

I admitted that america on that occasion had the same right to protection, in proportion to Circumstances, as the County of Kent had; and only thought it hard that, in america, there should be such Feelings for the Conditions to which the French were bound by a Treaty which concluded a War so necessary for its present and future Safety.

On this occasion I could not help thinking that Mr. Jay fell below the idea I wished to entertain of his Candour and impartiality, regarding objects not strictly american; and so we passed to other subjects.

At one or other of the periods of this conversation he said, you seem to think that France ought to consider the Independence of our States, as a sufficient Indemnification for all her expenses in the war. (This however I had never said to him, although I had often said so to Dr. Franklin.) But, continued Mr. Jay, that ought not to be admitted, as it in the first place, put us under a greater obligation to France than We incline to, as if to her alone we are indebted for our Independence. And in the next place (I have forgot the precise terms, but it was to this purpose) that in the course of the war France had made Conquests, and they the americans had a Treaty with them, by which they were bound not to give us Peace but in concurrence with our settlement with them. What the conditions might be he could not say: He believed we should agree. But that France had in the course of the war made Conquests and We could not expect to get back all we had lost. They of america must fulfill their Treaty. They were a young Republic just come into the World, and if they were to forfeit their Character at the first outset, they would never be trusted again, and should become a proverb amongst Mankind.

All this is true, I replied, but your Treaty does not oblige you to support their Demands after your Independence is acknowledged. He seemed to say they would think themselves obliged to support them in their Settlement with us, in general: only at last he said, unless unreasonable; then indeed—and paused—but afterwards went on and said, France had been very kind to them, and had lent them money very liberally etc.

After enlarging on these obligations, and the gratitude they owed to France, He proceeded to Spain and Holland, and talked also, though in a more general way, of their alliances with them, and their great obligations to them for advance of Money; and as if by the conditions of Treaty, they could not conclude or have Peace with Great Britain separately from those other two Powers.

I did not think it right to be over inquisitive as to their intentions regarding them; but it appeared to me as if he considered those two

Courts as much under their protection as that of France; and as if they, the Commissioners of the Colonies, would agree or refuse to close with us according as they should consider the Terms which these two Powers shall insist on, to be reasonable or unreasonable.

I don't recollect any thing more of material consequence that passed in the Course of the Conversation.

As beforementioned I think it best to give these Minutes, in the loose way in which they run; as in that dress I can keep more easily and closely to the precise strain of Conversation, than if formed into a proper state of official Correspondence, and therefore I hope to be excused for this Time.

Upon the contents of the beforementioned representation, I beg leave to make the following observations, Vizt.

1st. On the forenoon of the 7th being the next day after the Receipt of my Commission, I went out to Dr. Franklin with a Copy of it, as already mentioned; when he said very kindly, He hoped We should do very well, and not be long about it: as he had said to me upon a former occasion.

2nd. In an hour afterwards, I called on Mr. Jay at his House in Paris: a sensible Man, of plain yet civil Manners, apparently humane, and of a calm obliging Temper.

After reading the Commission, He said he hoped some good would be done. I replied, if I did not think so I should not be here. He said he was so informed by Dr. Franklin; and then began upon the article of Independence, and continued the Conversation in the manner as has been mentioned, in the coolest unreserved method, and determined stile of Language, that any common subject could be treated; and with a freedom of Expression, and disapprobation of our Conduct at home and abroad, respecting America, as shews We have little to expect from him in the way of Indulgence. And I may venture to say that although he has lived till now as an English Subject, though he never has been in England, he may be supposed (by anything I could perceive) as much alienated from any particular Regard for England, as if he had never heard of it in his Life. I sincerely wish I may be mistaken, but think it proper to Remark, as Mr. Jay is Dr. Franklin's only colleague, and being a much younger man and bred to the Law, will of Course have a great share of this Business assigned to his Care.

3d. I thought it remarkable that so soon after I left Dr. Franklin, I should have found this Gentleman's plan of settlement with Great Britain, so much less liberal, or at least so much more incumbered with relative Connections, Concerns and Interests, than had been insinuated in any Conversation I ever had with Dr. Franklin; or rather, on the contrary, seemingly very materially different; Excepting only in that making such a Peace as should be lasting, which the Doctor always said he aimed at.

4th. The Doctor and Mr. Jay having been today (the 8th) to see Mr. Fitzherbert, they called upon me, when the Doctor told me he had sent a Copy of my Commission to Monsieur de Vergennes at Versailles. They said no more, nor was there any notice taken of any Conversation having passed between Mr. Jay and me, the day before, nor anything else of business.

5th. From what has been said, and from anything I could ever learn while I have been here, there is good reason to apprehend that the Colony Commissioners think much less of their own Concerns than of those of Foreign Nations: or rather that they consider their business as good as settled, and that though the Dignity of their Congress may require a formal Acknowledgement of Release from their Dependence on Great Britain, yet they are not so much concerned about it, as to propose to give peace to Great Britain but on Condition of our settling with these other Nations. At first France was only named, but now Spain and Holland are included. Sometime ago, I believe France declared that they must be included in their Treaty, no doubt in Expectation of being supported in that claim by the Commissioners of the Colonies, and by Mr. Jay's Conversation with me, it would appear they seriously intend it. And although he had not said so, it might have been understood, since he has concluded a similar Treaty with the Ambassador of Spain now here, to that settled with France in America in 1778, for which I had the authority of Doctor Franklin some days ago. And I make not the least doubt they have connected themselves in the same manner with Holland.

The Business therefore of those Commissioners at this place seems to point at a superintendency over the general Peace, and not only to bring it to a Conclusion, but upon such terms and conditions, as to themselves seem just and reasonable, two words, which I remember Mr. Jay made use of when we happened to touch upon that subject.

In so far the Congress (in the Persons of their Commissioners) have assumed the right of arbitration between Great Britain and those Foreign States, and I wish I may be mistaken in thinking that they have taken those States also under such Protection, as that they shall not likewise, before the Close of the Business, be found to act the part of Dictators to Great Britain, believing that they can safely do so, without any new Act or Determination of their Congress; and only by going on as they do now in a Course of hostilities by Sea and Land, in consequence of their Treaties with those Foreign Powers; to which they profess such sacred Respect, and also without any Regard to the Conduct of Great Britain, although We should cease Hostilities by Sea as we have done by land; a state of Dilemma I am inclined to think not a little embarrassing to Great Britain. By Land, though We are inactive We may defend ourselves, and so can hardly suffer. But by sea, we must continue to act, since by a Cessation We could gain nothing upon the good Will of the Congress or others in America; they being bound to go on with the War, by virtue of their Treaties with our other Enemies.

When We set out upon this Business of Peace, We justly thought that a Relinquishment of the Sovereignty of America which France so strongly pleaded for, would have had some Weight in the scheme of Pacification with them, and that such grant of Independence would have also fully satisfied the Colonies; and then, that by a few Exchanges or Concessions of little Consequence, in the Course of the Negotiation with France the whole might have been quickly ended. But the affair seems to have taken a different Turn. France very wisely, I don't say consistently, disowns the Grant of Independence, as being no concern of theirs, and Mr. Jay will not allow them to share in the merit of it, lest the Colonies should be brought under a greater Obligation to France, than they should chuse, or more than they can easily discharge, by a Repayment of the Money borrowed of them, which his Colleague some time ago told me could be easily done, as their Taxes were coming in fast.

Thus France comes into Conference, with all her acquisitions in hand, clear of any Charge against her on account of North America; and out of the Reference of any Concessions expected from us, but that of the little Island of St. Lucia, and a few settlements on the continent of India: and therefore before she will listen to our Desire of Peace, is under no difficulty in telling us that We must agree to submit to great alterations respecting different quarters of the World, (besides others) as settled by the Treaty of Paris. And Mr. Jay, on the part of the Americans in support of that demand, feelingly complains of France having been hardly dealt with in that Treaty, as beforementioned.

To gain the Americans, we have nothing in hand but what they say they are possessed of, or if any formality is wanting, they insist it is so much their Right, that it ought not to stand as part of a Treaty. If in their Interposition in favour of Foreign States, We pretend to remonstrate, They plead Treaties, Conscience, and Character, under such Constructions of Determination as appears good to them, without any apprehension of Control, whilst they are gaining and We losing by a continuance of the War.

So much I have presumed to say as to my Ideas of the State of the present depending Treaty at this place, which I am unwillingly led to, with a view of paving the way to some modification in the Articles of His Majesty's Instructions, in case this negotiation should proceed in its intended Course.

But before I quit this Article, I beg leave in justice to myself, as to former Advices relative to my Conversations with Dr. Franklin, particularly in my Letter of the 10th July[1] as well as for the farther information of His Majesty's ministers to remark that there is a great Difference between those said advices, and the strain of Mr. Jay's conversation of yesterday's date. I never chose to teize Dr. Franklin with many questions, yet at different times he has freely declared, that having got the Grant of Independence, their Treaty with France was at an end; and on the 10th of July[2] explicitly specified the conditions which he thought must necessarily be granted, to obtain a Peace of any kind with the Colonies; but if granted would have that effect, adding at the same time others, as discretionary or adviseable, which if complied with, would not fail to diffuse a temper of Reconciliation all over the Country. These were the Doctor's Sentiments and Conditions of Settlement on the said 10th of July, and which he read to me from a Minute in writing, and only declined putting it into my hands from a motive of Delicacy regarding his Colleague then but just arrived. And so consistent the Doctor still appears to be, that upon the production of my Commission on the 7th Instant he repeated the Words which he used on a former occasion: "That he hoped, we should do well enough, and not be long about it," as already mentioned. That could not but be very agreeable to me, if my expectations had not been so soon after dampt by the said unpleasant Reception from Mr. Jay.

Having given my opinion as to what appears immediately to concern the present Treaty, I must take the Liberty to touch upon another Subject, principally regarding future Times, which I think is deserving of notice, and ought to be mentioned on this occasion, as the Object of it is perhaps intended by the American Commissioners, as well as the French Minister, to be connected with, and were inserted in the Body of the foreign Treaties now depending, whenever they are concluded. I mean a supposed Intention of some particular Scheme, of settling those Treaties in such a manner, as in their opinion shall make the Peace uncommonly solid and lasting.

Dr. Franklin, as I have said, had often touched upon this Subject in a general way: "That Peace could not be too dearly bought; and always ending with a wish that it could be made lasting; and at same time observing that England, in a State of Peace for a hundred years, would become a perfect Garden." I did not clearly perceive the meaning of the proposal, yet I own I did not much like any of these prescriptions of Quietism, as believing they would not be entirely suitable to the English taste, or Interest; nor did I foresee any Benefit intended for England, by what Monsieur de Vergennes, in Dr. Franklin's hearing, humanely proposed in April, of settling the Peace *solidement,* and for a long standing,[3] which I then suspected as an Intimation of an intended Scheme of some sort for putting the Naval power of England under some unusual and particular Limitation.

On those occasions with Dr. Franklin, I never chose to say much, or to ask for an Explanation as to his Idea of the effectual means of preventing the return of War.

But upon Mr. Jay's mentioning the same proposal the other day of their Design of settling the depending Treaty on such a solid foundation, as that the Peace should be lasting, I asked him, how a sufficient Security could be found, to make it so. He answered as beforementioned, the best Security in the World Vizt.: that it shall not be the *Interest* of either party to break it.

There was no Explanation necessary here, as I knew he could not mean Treaty, since he had just before declared, that he made no account of any Treaty whatever, when any Prince or State found it convenient to break it, and therefore I concluded he must mean a *Guarantee* of some intermediate Power who he thought would not chuse to be Principals in any War, and yet (in that State of Neutrality respecting their own Concerns) might be capable of controuling other States, by adopting the cause of those in whose safety they might be particularly interested, or to whom protection was due, under the Stipulations of a general Guarantee.

This Power or State I now conceive could be meant to be no other than their American Congress, who taking upon them the Guarantee of the general Peace intended to be settled at this Place, the Commissioners of the Colonies possibly suppose that they can make it stand for almost any length of Time they please; as believing that the united Power of their Confederacy will be of such weight, as to make it in the Interest of either of the present belligerent Powers to desist from War whenever they chuse to interpose, and consequently that the same being once understood, the said Powers would perceive, that it would not be for their Interest to break the Peace.

On this Occasion, to speak one's Sentiments freely, it is a fair Question, whether such States as are interested in Commerce, Navigation, and foreign Plantations (as is the Case of England, France, Spain and Holland,) would not, if at War among themselves, be obliged to give away, and put an End to the Quarrel, in case of a Declaration of the American Congress, against any one or more of them.

One may even go further than supposition, and I think may venture to say, that in Case of either of those parties persisting, and the Americans were called upon by their Guarantee, under the authority of the Congress to take a Side, the Objects of Prize and Depradation would bring forth from all parts of that Continent, such Swarms of armed adventurers, as would distress the Commerce and Settlements of the resisting party or Parties to such Degree, as to determine them without Delay to put an End to the War; and consequently knowing that this must ultimately be their fate, they would find, as Mr. Jay says, that it would not be their *Interest* to break the Peace.

This Capacity in the American Colonies, is admitted to exist at this time, must continue to increase, and become more decisive, from year to year, in proportion to the quick Increase of population in that Country, which abound in every necessary material for the equipment of Shipping, and every Conveniency of safe Roads and Harbours for their Reception. And where also they run no risk of suffering within Land, or on their Coasts, any Such Danger, in the way of Reprizal or Retaliation, from any Power in Europe, as shall prevent their enforcing and supporting the Effect of any Guarantee they may think fit to enter into as has been mentioned.

That I humbly own is my opinion, and I have always thought so since I came to have any knowledge of the particular circumstances of these Colonies, and have, I may say, trembled at, ever since I came to despair of our recovering them.

In these Sentiments I cannot but be sincerely sorry, that any such System of naval power should, in a State of Combination, have rose in competition with that of England. And more particularly that the application of the proposed Check thereof, (if really intended as suspected) should be thought of at this time. Which being undoubtedly and visibly so much courted by France, and our other Enemies, it is to be feared will unreasonably give the Colony Commissioners a predominancy in settling the Conditions of Peace with those foreign Nations, that may not be convenient for England, besides the Effect it must have in determining the Frame of their own Treaty almost at their Pleasure,

For if the Commissioners of the Colonies are determined to carry through this scheme of conditional Inteference, into real Execution, and to have it administered on this occasion, either by inserting their Guarantees as Parties in those foreign Treaties, or by Stipulation of Guarantee in separate Treaties of offensive and defensive alliance, I can not possibly see how they can be prevented.

As yet, their Intention has come out only in the unexplained manner which I have mentioned; But as something, (as has been said) was hinted by Monsieur de Vergennes, so early as in April, and has been from time to time since then, repeated by Dr. Franklin in the same way, and at last in a manner openly declared by Mr. Jay, upon the first perusal of my Commission, I think it my Duty to Say the same, (as far as I can yet judge of it) before His Majesty's Ministers, so as such Resolutions may be taken, and the necessary Instructions given in consequence thereof, as to their Wisdom may seem fit.

RICHARD OSWALD

Paris, Sunday, 11–[Tuesday], 13 August 1782

I went out this forenoon to Doctor Franklin, to know whether he was inclined to enter upon Business. He told me he had carried the Copy of the Commission I gave him to Versailles, the Day before, and had some conversation on the subject with Monsieur de Vergennes, who was of opinion with him, that it would be better to wait untill a real Commission arrived; this being neither signed nor Sealed, and could be supposed as only a draft or order, in which there might be alterations, as in the Preamble it said only "To the Effect following etc." To this objection I had nothing to say, as I did not incline to shew them the Instructions, though signed and Sealed.

Finding no alteration in the Doctor's manner, from the usual good natured and friendly way in which he had formerly behaved to me (as I had reason to apprehend from what had lately passed with his Colleague) and having a quiet and convenient opportunity, I was anxious to learn whether the Doctor entertained those Ideas, which, in the preceding Papers, I suspected Mr. Jay had in view, regarding the *means* of preventing future Wars, by settling the Peace in such a manner as it should not be the Interest of the Parties to break it.

With that Intent, I told the Doctor I had had a long conversation with Mr. Jay, of which no doubt he had been informed; and in which he had not spared Us in his Reflections on what had passed in the American war; and that I could not but be sorry he had just reason for the Severity of some of them; at same time I was pleased he was equally well disposed to Peace, and to bring it quickly to a Conclusion as We were, and also that it should be a lasting One, as he, the Doctor, had always proposed. And that I was only at a loss, as to how that could be ascertained otherwise than by Treaty, which Mr. Jay declared he paid no regard to; and said it could be only depended upon as lasting by its being settled so as it should not be the Interest of any of the Parties to break it. I told the Doctor this was certainly the best Security, if one could tell how to accommodate the terms so justly to the mutual Interest of the Parties, as to obviate every temptation to Encroachment or Trespass.

The Doctor replied, that the method was very plain and easy, which was to settle the Terms in the first projection on an equal, just and reasonable footing; and so as neither Party should have cause to complain, being the Plan which the Monsieur de Vergennes had in view, and had always recommended in his conversations with him on the Subject of Peace. And the Doctor said it was a good Plan, and the only one that could make the Peace lasting. And which also put him in mind of a story in the Roman History, in the early time of the Republic. When being at war with the state of Tarentum, and the Tarentines having the worst of it they sent to the Senate to ask for Peace. The Ambassador being called in, the Senate told him they agreed to give them Peace, and then asked him how long he thought it would last; to which he answered, that would be according to the Conditions. If they were reasonable the peace would be lasting. If not it would be short. The Senate seemed to resent this freedom of Expression. But a Member got up and applauded it, as fair and Manly, and as justly challenging a due regard to moderation on their part.

It is not easy to say how happy I felt myself at the conclusion of this Quotation. The Terms and Conditions it's true remained undecided; and comprehend, no doubt, a very serious Question, although not material to what I aimed at. Nor did I conceive them to lye so much in my way as in that of another Department, by the concern which the French Minister took in settling the Principle. Nor did I trouble myself about the possible inefficacy of it, as still depending in some degree on the obligations of Treaty, however cautiously adjusted. And therefore I did not think it proper to touch upon that point, nor to say anything on the Subject of Terms and Conditions.

I thought myself sufficiently satisfied in getting clear of my apprehensions of those ill founded Suspicions of a supposed American *Guarantee* being intended, as mentioned in the papers of the 9th Instant, and at the same time asking pardon of those to whom that design was unjustly imputed. And which upon my return from this visit, I should have certainly struck out of those Papers, if I did not, with all Submission, incline to think that by remaining under the Eye of Government, they might help to shew that the Question of the possibility of such Guarantee taking place on some future occasion, may still not be undeserving of attention. As to the consequences of such Measure whenever it happens (as pointed out in the said Papers of the 9th) there can be no doubt: nor do I think it requires much Ingenuity in the Americans quickly to discover the expediency and benefit of resorting to it on a variety of occasions; particularly, in case of our insisting on Terms in the present Treaty, or acting a part in our future correspondence with them which We cannot support in such a manner as to make it appear to them to be to their Interest (and consistent with their Engagements and the Character they have adopted) quietly and contentedly to submit to.

I am the more ready to hazard the freedom of these observations, and the danger of exciting into action the least experiment of this kind of combined Interposition of the American Provinces, upon reflecting on Doctor Franklin's hint or caution, as reported in one of my letters of last month. "Not to force them into the hands of other People." Which I hope will never happen; But on the contrary, after laying the foundation of Peace, in the best manner that can be done, on the bottom on which Congress wish it to stand, by an amicable and final agreement with their Commissioners here, every possible Measure may thereafter be taken to promote a temper of Reconciliation and Amity over the whole of that country. As yet there has been nothing done in a Separate way, however unjustly suspected, to interfere with the plan of such Preliminary and regular Settlement. And I hope the same will be followed out in such manner as to shew to the Americans, that all such concessions as are required and can be reasonably granted, do actually flow from a desire of His Majesty and His Ministers, of laying this foundation on the most just and equitable Principles, and in a mutual relation to the Benefit of one Party as well as the other.

After that is done, and consequently every pretence and occasion of Jealousy is obviated, and constitutionally out of the Question, I must take the liberty to say, That it will concern the Interest of Great Britain in the most sensible degree, as well in the hopes of returning benefit, as in that of avoiding contingencies of critical danger, to concert, from this time, every possible method of facilitating and perpetuating a friendly correspondence with those Countries.

The second thing the Doctor touched upon was Independence. He said by the Quotations of Acts of Parliament, he saw it was included in the Commission. But that Mr. Grenville had *orders to grant it in the first instance.* I replied it was true; And that though supposed to be granted under this Commission, and in the course of the Treaty, I hoped it would make no difference with Gentlemen, who were so well disposed to put an end to this unhappy Business as I knew him to be.

He then asked if I had instructions. I said I had, and that they were under his Majesty's hand and Seal; and that by them it appeared Independence, unconditional in every sense, would be granted, and that I saw no reason why it should not make the first Article of the Settlement or treaty. That I was sorry Mr. Jay should have hesitated so much on that head, as if it ought to have been done Separately, and by act of Parliament. And now Parliament being up, that the Grant should be made by Proclamation. That I did not pretend to judge whether the Right and Authority of a Grant of that kind, so conveyed, would be proper and effectual. There seemed however to be one Inconveniency in it, that a Proclamation became an address to the Congress, and to every part of their provinces jointly and Separately, and might in so far interfere with the progress of the present Commission, under which We hoped, that all pretensions would be properly and expeditiously settled. That in this matter he was a better Judge than I could pretend to be. I was only sure of one thing, that the affair might be as effectually done, as in the way proposed by Mr. Jay. The Doctor replied that Mr. Jay was a Lawyer, and might think of things that did not occur to those who were not Lawyers. And he at last spoke, as if he did not see much or any difference. But still used such a mode of expression as I could not positively say would preclude him from insisting on Mr. Jay's Proposition, or some previous or separate acknowledgement. I was glad to get clear of the Subject without pushing for further explanation or discussion or yielding further, as I have mentioned, than to a preliminary acknowledgement in the course of the Treaty.

I then said after that was done, I hoped there would not be many things to settle; and that the Articles called necessary, which he specified on the 10th of July, would pretty nearly end the business. And that those called Adviseable, which, as a Friend to Britain and to Reconciliation he had then recommended, would be dropt, or modified in a proper manner. That I had fairly stated the case at home, and could not but confess that I had this Answer from one of his Friends. To this I cannot say I had any reply.

I then told the Doctor there was a particular circumstance, which, of myself, I wished to submit to his consideration, as a friend to returning Peace. England has ceased all Hostilities against America by Land. At Sea it was otherways, and however disposed We might be to stop these proceedings there also, I could not see how it could be done until the People of America adopted the same plan. At the same time I was sensible, that by the strict Letter of their Treaty with France, the Americans could not well alter their conduct before we came to a final Settlement with that Nation. That this was an unfortunate Dilemma for both of Us. That We should be taking each other's ships, when perhaps We might, in other respects, be at perfect Peace, and that notwithstanding thereof We must continue in this course, waiting for a conclusion with France and other Nations, perhaps at a distant period. That although I had no orders on this head, yet as a Continuance in this Species of Hostility seemed to be so repugnant to the Motives and Principles which had determined a Cessation on the part of England by Land, and was certainly a bar to that cordial Reconciliation which he so much wished for, I could not avoid Submitting the Case to his Consideration, to see whether he could find some remedy for it. The Doctor replied he could not see how it could be done; it would be a difficult thing. However at last he said he would think of it.

I next touched upon the Subject of the *Loyalists,* but could not flatter myself with the hopes of its answering any good purpose; the Doctor having from the beginning assured me they could take no part in that Business, as it was exclusively retained under the Jurisdiction of the respective States upon whom the several claimants had any demands: and there having been no Power delegated to the Congress on that head, they as Commissioners, could do nothing in it. I only said that I was sorry that no Method could be suggested for a reasonable accommodation in a Matter, which I could not but suppose he would admit has a natural claim to the consideration of Government. I thought it to no purpose to go any further on the present occasion. If afterwards things of more immediate concern and importance should get into a smooth train of proceeding, and be established, and I could venture freely to appeal to their unprejudiced humanity and good sense I would try it; although without hopes of their taking any other part than in suggesting of Means and Expedients and perhaps favouring the proposals in the way of private recommendation to their Countrymen. As to the ungranted, or unappropriated Lands, although they were undoubtedly the reserved Property of His Majesty in all the States, I am afraid when I come to state that claim as a Fund towards Indemnification the Commissioners will pretend these Lands fell with the States, as much as the King's Court Houses etc.

Upon the whole of this Matter the Doctor said nothing, but that he was advised that the Board of Loyalists in New York was dissolved by General Carleton which he was glad of.

The Doctor at last touched upon Canada, as he generally does upon the like occasions, and said there could be no dependence on Peace and good Neighborhood, while that country continued under a different Government, as it touched their States in so great a stretch of Frontier. I told him I was sensible of that Inconveniency. But having no orders, the consideration of that Matter might possible be taken up at some future time. At my coming away, the Doctor said, that although the proper Commission was not come over, yet he said, Mr. Jay would call on me with a Copy of their Credentials. This being Sunday, he said the copy would be made out on Monday. On Tuesday he must go to Versailles, being the Levée day; but on Wednesday they would call with their papers. So that to-morrow I shall probably have the honour of seeing those Gentlemen, and of course may have something still to add to these tedious Writings.

RICHARD OSWALD

Paris, 15, 17 August 1782

In the Conclusion of the Papers of the 13th Inst. I said that Dr. Franklin and Mr. Jay were to call on me as [of] Yesterday to exchange Credentials, but they did not call. I went out therefore this Morning to the Doctor to inform him that the Commission had come to hand, of which I told him I would have informed him sooner, if I had not expected him Yesterday. He excused himself on account of Company coming in which made it too late for coming into Paris that forenoon, but that Tomorrow he and Mr. Jay would certainly call. He said he was glad the Sealed Commission was come. There was nothing material said on the subject of Business.

I returned to Paris and called on Mr. Jay to inform him in like manner of the Commission being arrived. At Meeting with this Gentleman I own I was under some Concern on account of Our former Conversation. But, I was agreeably disappointed having found him in the best humour, and disposed to enter into a friendly discussion on the Business I came about.

He did not seem desirous of going back upon past Transactions as on the former occasion and chiefly pointed at the object of a present Settlement. He said We had it now in our power to put a final period to the Misfortunes We complained of by carrying into execution what had been solemnly intimated to them, of which Sir Guy Carleton had Orders to communicate to the Congress in America, a Copy of whose Instructions they were in possession of. One Article of which says, that His Majesty was to grant unconditional Independence to the Thirteen States of North America, but that the way proposed of making the same rest upon the Events and Termination of a Treaty did not come up to that description and was a mode of Performance which would not give Satisfaction to the Congress or People of America, and could not be considered by them as absolute and unconditional, if only standing as an Article of a depending Treaty, and upon the whole that they could not treat at all until their Independence was so acknowledged as that they should be on an equal footing with Us, and might take Rank as Parties to an Agreement. That in this they had a fair precedent in the Settlement of the Dutch with the Spaniards who refused to enter into any Treaty until they were declared Free States. That if We wished for Peace that was the only way to obtain it, and if done with a becoming Confidence and magnanimity, We should not only get Peace in the result, but by the concurrence of better management hereafter, he also hoped that a happy Conciliation and Friendship would be restored and perpetuated between both Countries, notwithstanding all that had happened, which he said would give him great Pleasure. But, that if We neglected this Opportunity, and continued in Our Hesitation on that head as We had done, We should then convince them of the Justice of their Suspicions of Designs, which he would not name, and should force them into Measures which he supposed I had discernment enough to guess at, without coming to further Explanation, that he should be extremely sorry to see things run into that strain, and therefore, as the Method proposed was indispensable, he could not but seriously advise and recommend it.

A good deal more this Gent[leman] said to the same purpose without any Appearance of Resentment or Disgust. On the Contrary he delivered his Sentiments in a manner the most expressive of a sincere and friendly intention towards Great Britain. I should not do him Justice if I said less, and I am the more inclined to be particular in this part of the report that I was so free in my Remarks on his former Conversation, especially in my suspicions of an actual, or premeditated Connection with Foreign States, on account of his particular Idea of guarding against the Violation of Treaties, as mentioned in the preceding Papers, but which, although I could perceive was present to his mind on this occasion also, yet I am now convinced had gone no farther than Speculation, and, as he said himself and which I really believe he would be heartily sorry they should be forced to have recourse to.

At proper times I said what occurred to me as necessary to bring this Question to some sort of desireable period and in particular wished to have Mr. Jay's Idea of such way of declaring this unconnected ascertainment of Independence as would satisfy them.

His former proposal of doing it by Proclamation he gave up, as liable to sundry Objections needless to be here repeated. He then proposed it should be done by a particular and separate Deed, or Patent under the Great Seal, in which my Commission for a Treaty might also be narrated, and that such Patent should be put into the possession of the Commissioners to be by them sent over to the Congress and accordingly Mr. Jay brought me a Draft of the Patent. As I could see no other way of satisfying those Gentlemen, and it appearing highly necessary that some beginning should be made with them, since until that was done the Foreign Treaty could not proceed in its course, I agreed to send the Draft over to His Majesty's Secretary of State, by a Courier Express for that purpose with my own Opinion rather in favor of the proposal than otherways; and so it was settled with the Commissioners.

However afterwards on casting my eye upon the preamble of the Draft, where it is stated *as if Sir Guy Carleton had Orders to propose Treaties of Peace etc. to the Congress,* and believing this to be a mistaken Quotation of memory from the Copy of Sir Guy's Instructions in the possession of the Commissioners, and as such inferring an unjust Imputation on the Consistency of the Conduct of Administration and apprehending also that the Commissioners entertaining a Doubt of this nature, might have been the reason why they wished to be guarded with all this Caution in requiring this special Acknowledgement under the Great Seal, besides keeping their minds in suspense in all future proceedings where Confidence in good faith ought to smooth the Path on many Occasions to a happy Termination. I say in reflecting on these things I thought it my Duty, and I confess I was on my own particular Account, a little anxious to have an Explanation of this matter, and therefore after it had been agreed in the presence of Dr. Franklin and Mr. Jay that I should send off the Draft, I took the liberty to point out to them the said preamble, telling them that there might be a possibility of mistake or misquotation in the last part of the

Paragraph. Mr. Jay said he had not the Copy of Sir Guy's Instructions, and acknowledged he had inserted those Words from a general Impression that remained on his Memory and could not positively say but there might be some mistake. Dr. Franklin said he had the Copy of the Instructions and would send a Duplicate to Mr. Jay in a few Hours. He did so and I waited on Mr. Jay to see the Papers. Upon the Perusal, he owned he had been mistaken and that Sir Guy's Instructions went no further than an Order of Communication, to inform the Congress and General Washington that His Majesty intended (or had given Directions) to grant free and unconditional Independence to the Thirteen States etc.[4]

Finding this Prejudice entirely removed and that Mr. Jay was perfectly satisfied that the whole Course of proceeding in this matter was fair and consistent, I asked him what occasion there was then for this Extraordinary Caution of insisting on the Solemnity of such separate Deed under the Great Seal etc., since a preliminary Clause or Article in the Treaty, as always intended might do the whole Business by making it absolute and not depending in the view of ascertainment on the event of other or subsequent Articles, and which might be so expressed as to remove every Doubt as to the Independence being as free and unconditional as they desired it to be. In Confirmation of the greater expediency and dispatch of this method and that it was the sincere Intention of His Majesty to make this Grant in the precise way they desired, I thought myself warranted in telling him that I had a full power in my Instructions to give them entire Satisfaction on this head and make no scruple in shewing it him, as it stood in the 4th Article thereof. Upon the Perusal Mr. Jay said that was enough and he was fully satisfied, and there was no occasion for any other Writing on the Subject. That resting upon this would save time and he was happy also that the discovery of this mistake prevented their asking of His Majesty any farther proof of his good Intentions towards them than what were actually meant and conveyed in those my Instructions. Upon this I promised immediately to send off this Representation and also to desire leave and permission to make an absolute Acknowledgement of the Independence of the States to stand invariably as the first Article of the proposed Treaty with those Gentlemen. Mean time I think it proper to send inclosed the intended Draft (though now of no use here) to shew by the Words scored in the preamble the ground of those Gentlemens hesitation and what gave occasion to their insisting on a Separate Deed under the Great Seal.

I have now to add in relation to my last Conversation with Mr. Jay, that after having quitted the Subject of their particular Affairs, and thinking myself at liberty to enter into a greater freedom of Conversation I wished to take the Opportunity of saying something relative to Foreign Concerns to a man of good sense and temper, who in his present and future Situation may have it in his power here and elsewhere to exemplify by his good Offices, those favorable Inclinations respecting Great Britain which he so freely and warmly expressed on the present Occasion.

Accordingly at proper periods I made no scruple in throwing out the following Observations. That after settling with them which I hoped would end to the Satisfaction of both Parties our next Concern regarding a Settlement with France and other Foreign Nations. That as yet I understood We could make no guess as to what France aimed at. They kept themselves on the reserve perhaps, partly with a view of being in some measure governed in their proposals by the manner in which our Settlement of American Affairs may proceed.

That in the course of the American War they had taken the Opportunity of making separate Conquests for themselves and encouraged by this late Alteration in Our System, it may be supposed they were projecting some hard terms of Settlement for Us, by their delay in coming to particulars. Excepting only their Declaration of having no interest or concern in the Article of American Independence, and consequently that in every view of Equivalent, it is to have no place in abatement of their Claims of retention or further Requisition.

That having taken the Spanish and Dutch Concerns also under their Cover, and so as not to treat but jointly, or in concurrence with them, the prospect of a speedy and favorable Settlement for Great Britain became still the more unpromising, unless they, the Comm[issione]rs of the Colonies should interfere to check the Exorbitancy of the Terms which thus might be expected to be insisted on by such formidable Combination of Foreign States.

And this prospect, I said, was still the worse that I understood he himself (Mr. Jay) had concluded, or was about to conclude a Treaty with Spain on the same footing with that which the Congress had settled with France. That the restraining Clause in those Treaties regarding Truce or final Peace between England and America, until there was also a final Settlement with those Foreign States was a most unlucky Circumstance, and therefore the more of those Treaties the Comm[issione]rs entered into, so much the worse for England.

A great deal more I said, but being of a speculative kind, regarding future times and the different Situation We should be in from what We had formerly been, and the need We should feel of a friendly Attention on the part of the Colonies, with other things of so general a nature not necessary to be repeated here.

In answer, Mr. Jay replied to the following purpose. That We had only to cut this knot of Independence to get rid of many of those Apprehensions, that if We looked better to our Conduct for the future We might be sure of recovering and preserving a solid and beneficial friendship with the Americans, that for the last twenty Years he could not say much for Us, yet he said more particularly regarding the fairness and sincerity of Our professions, than I chuse to repeat.

He continued by saying that England under a wise Administration was capable of great things. Such a Country, such a People and blessed with such a Constitution had nothing to fear, and in Thirty Years would forget all her present Difficulties, etc., etc.

That as to the Spanish Treaty he had not proceeded far in it, and unless We forced them into those Engagements, he did not see that the People of America had any Business to fetter themselves with them and in the mean time he assured me he would stop as to this of Spain, which I was very glad to hear of.

He said he supposed the Terms of France would be moderate, and in that Case he would give his Advice, that when they came to light that the Court of England would consider them with temper; and after making a deliberate Estimate of the Price they can afford to give for Peace, to strike at once without haggling about it.

That if their Independence was once settled, he hoped that next Winter would put an End to the War in general. That it was true there was a look here towards another Campaign, and what might be the possible Consequences of the Operations in the interim, and touched upon the East Indies, as if great Expectations from thence were entertained at this Court etc.

Amongst other things I omitted when We were talking of Independence that I mentioned by the bye, as if it was understood that when America was Independent of England, they would be so also of all other Nations. Mr. Jay smiled and said that they would take Care of that, and seemed in his Countenance to express such disapprobation of any question being put on that head, as would make one cautious as to the manner in which any Stipulations on that Subject should be proposed to those Gentlemen.

RICHARD OSWALD

C in FO 95/511. Endorsed. C in MiU-C: Shelburne 70.

[1]Oswald to Shelburne, 10 July 1782, ALS in FO 27/2; C in 95/511; LbkC in 97/157 and in MiU-C: Shelburne 70.

[2]See above, "The Status of the Peacemaking," and n. 11.

[3]The 17 April interview was also reported in Franklin to Shelburne, 18 April 1782, LS in FO 95/511; C in CP EU 21: 57 (enclosed in Franklin to Vergennes, 4 May 1782, ALS in *ibid.*, 21: 136); see also Franklin's "Journal of the Negotiation for Peace with Great Britain," *BFS*, VIII, 465–68.

[4]Both JJ and Franklin had insisted on the clarification of Carleton's mission in New York, and it was Carleton's apparently competing role as peacemaker in America that impelled JJ to demand that Oswald's powers be clearly delineated. Oswald to Shelburne, 21 Aug. 1782, ALS in FO 27/2 and LbkC in 97/157.

John Jay: Draft of Patent

[15 August 1782]

George the Third etc. to Richard Oswald Esq. etc. Greeting. Whereas by a certain act etc. (here insert enabling act), and whereas in pursuance of the true Intent and Meaning of the said act, and to remove all Doubts and Jealousies which might otherwise retard the Execution of the same we did on the Day of last, instruct Sir Guy Carlton, etc., our General, etc., To make known to the People of the said Colonies in Congress assembled, our royal Disposition and intention to recognize the said Colonies as Independent states, *and as such to enter with them into such Treaties of peace amity and Commerce*[1] *as might be honorable and convenient to both Countries.*

And Whereas further in pursuance of the said act we did on the Day of authorize and commission You the said Richard Oswald (here insert commission).

Now Therefore To the End that a period may be put to the Calamities of War, and peace Commerce and mutual Intercourse may be the more speedily restored We do hereby, agreable to our royal word, for ourselves and our successors, recognize the said Thirteen Colonies as free and independent States. And it is our will and pleasure that You do forthwith proceed to treat with the Commissioner or Commissioners already appointed or to be appointed for that purpose by the Congress of the said States (and with him or them only) of and concerning the Objects of your said Commission, which we do hereby confirm; and that this Declaration be considered by You as a preliminary Article to the proposed Treaty and be in substance or in the whole inserted therein, or incorporated therewith. And it is our further will and pleasure that on recieving <this Declaration> these Letters[2] which we have caused to be made patent, and our great seal to be hereunto affixed, You do deliver the same to the said Commissioner or Commissioners to be by him or them transmitted to the Congress of the United States of America as an Earnest of the Friendship and Good Will which we are disposed to extend to them. Witness etc.

AD in FO 27/2. Endorsed by Oswald: "Draft proposed by Mr. Jay, 16 August 1782, But now dispensed with as not necessary," with the clerk's entry: "Inclosed with the Observations of 15 and 17 of August 1782." C in FO 95/511; LbkC, misdated 10 August, in MiU-C: Shelburne 70; C in JJ to Livingston, 17 Nov. 1782, cited above in JJ to Aranda, 25 June 1782, n. 2. For a variant version, see *RDC,* VI, 16–17.

[1]In *RDC:* "such a treaty of peace."

[2]In *RDC:* "these presents."

From Benjamin Franklin

Passy, 16 August 1782

Inclosed is a true Copy of the Extracts from Gen. Carleton's Instructions given to me by Mr. Vaughan from Lord Shelbourn.[1] You will see that the Instruction I mentioned as given to Mr. Grenville is acknowledged and recited. Is it not probable therefore that Mr. Oswald may have the same? And if he has, and will execute it by making ministerially in writing the Declaration intended, perhaps the Paper proposed to be sent to England may in this Case not be necessary.[2]

With great Esteem I have the honour to be, Sir, Your most obedient and most humble Servant,

B. FRANKLIN

ALS in PPAmP: Franklin 85, 177. Endorsed: "... Enclosing Ex. of Carltons Instructions of 5 June 1782," E in William Temple Franklin's hand. Tr in NN: Bancroft: American III, 299.

[1]Shelburne to Carleton and Digby, 5 June 1782, marked "Secret & Confidential," C in CO 5/178; E, under date 25 June, included in JJ to Livingston, 17 Nov. 1782 (cited above in JJ to Aranda, 25 June 1782, n. 2). Therein it is stated that George III had commanded his "ministers to direct Mr. Grenville that the independence of America should be proposed by him in the first instance instead of making it a condition of a general treaty." W. T. Franklin copied the end of the sentence as "the condition of a general peace."

[2]JJ's proposed Dft of 15 August, above.

Richard Oswald to Shelburne

Paris, Sunday, 18 August 1782

My Lord,

I am just now jointly with Mr. Fitzherbert, Sending off a Courier on the Subject of this American business, with So great a volume of writing, that I would be ashamed to touch upon it Seperately, and think it unnecessary, as I make no doubt your Lordship will desire to See Some part of it, which I very much wish for on different accounts. And amongst others that I may know your Lordship's Sentiments, and have your directions, and also corrections where you think necessary. In these Papers your Lordship will see that the American Commissioners will not move a *Step untill the Independance* is acknowledged. And all I have been able to gain upon them, is to take it into the body of a Treaty, but there as a preliminary Article to be Signed and Sealed as a ratified Deed, come of the subsequent Articles what may. I hope however in that way we may get on provided Orders are sent me to make the Acknowledgement in the final form as abovementioned. If that is granted the sooner the Order comes the better. Untill the Americans are *contented Mr. Fitzherbert cannot proceed.* I cannot pretend to advise any-thing, and therefor must leave the issue to Such Conclusions as can be inferred from the facts in the papers I now send over which I answer for.

There is one thing I beg leave to mention to your Lordship that may be material untill this business is further advanced that nothing of this correspondence gets over to this place, by the papers lying about or getting into other hands than those who have a right to See them. I could not use the freedom to hint this to Mr. Townshend, as if I doubted of these things being cautiously attended to in his Office, and yet if your Lordship would be so good to mention it to him, I should be the easier and write perhaps with greater freedom.

I have great pleasure in all occasions which occur in my communications with Mr. Fitzherbert, in whose appointment, as I mentioned before, I have reason to think your Lordship has made a happy choice.

I have the honour to be with Sincere regard and esteem, My Lord, Your Lordship's most obedient humble Servant,

RICHARD OSWALD

C in MiU-C: Shelburne 71. Erroneously in Hale, *Franklin in France*, II , 123–24.

Thomas Townshend: Propositions in Regard to Mr. Jay's Project

29 August 1782

That we are ready as Mr. Jay desires to Grant the Independence of the 13 Provinces in the Preliminary or First Article of a Treaty either of Peace or Truce.

The said Article to be <irrevocable> Invariable, unconditional and Independent of any other Articles of the Treaty.

That we are ready according to their repeated desire to Withdraw all our Troops and entirely Evacuate the 13 Provinces.

That we will settle the Boundaries of the Provinces and Control the Limits of Canada as desired by Dr. Franklin.

And that we will admit them to a part in the New foundland And Labrador Fisheries.

<And will en> These to be looked upon as Preliminary Articles.

And that we will enter freely into the Adjustment of the other Articles mentioned by Dr. Franklin as Adviseable.

And all the above we are ready to make parts of a General Treaty or of a Truce or Particular Treaty, whenever the Americans are disposed to enter into it.

Following as Dr. Franklin and Mr. Jay point out the Steps taken and the Acknowledgements made by the Plenipotentiaries of the Arch Duke Albert and the Crown of Spain to the United Provinces in 1607 and 1609, and Treating with the 13 Provinces of N. America in all things as with a Free and Independent State Over whom the Crown of England Pretend's to hold no Authority.

Dft in hand of Evan Nepean in MiU-C: Sydney I.

FROM ROBERT R. LIVINGSTON

[Philadelphia, 8 August 1782]
Quadruplicate

Dear Sir,

Your Letter of the 28th April was received by Major Franks, WHEN THE CONTENTS WERE COMMUNICATED TO CONGRESS. THE REPEATED SLIGHTS AND NEGLECTS YOU HAVE EXPERIENCED EXCITED THEIR WARMEST RESENTMENT. SEVERAL MEMBERS feeling that our Obligations to SPAIN WERE EXTREAMLY SMALL; THAT OUR AFFAIRS HERE AND IN EUROPE GAVE US A RIGHT TO THINK AS AN independent People WERE FOR ENTERING INTO RESOLUTIONS which might perhaps have presented a more lively Picture of their own SENSATIONS THAN GOOD POLICY COULD JUSTIFY.[2] After much Deliberation they came to the inclosed Resolution in which they have in some Measure entered into your Sentiments. THEY EXPECTED SOME EQUIVALENT FOR THE CESSIONS THEY HAVE OFFERED. If in this Expectation they are deceived, they see no Reason why they should STAND OPEN AGAINST

THEM. THE COMMERCE BETWEEN THIS COUNTRY AND SPAIN IS A VERY important object to AMERICA. THE TRADE THAT AN Industrious PEOPLE CARRY ON WITH THOSE WHO DO NOT manufacture FOR THEMSELVES IS ALWAYS valuable, and perhaps TREATIES OF COMMERCE WITH ANY OTHER NATIONS MAY BE CONSIDERED AS DISADVANTAGEOUS.[3] I could therefore have wished to see his CATHOLIC MAJESTY'S MINISTERS SENTIMENTS ON THAT POINT.[4] From the Conversation you relate in your Letter of the 3d October to have passed between you and the Count de Florida Blanca on that Subject, I am led to think he expected WE WOULD ASK PECULIAR PRIVILEDGES. How far it might be possible to OBTAIN A COMMERCIAL CONNECTION WITH THEIR COLONIES IT IS difficult TO SAY, BUT ANY INTERCOURSE WOULD BY THE INGENUITY OF OUR MERCHANTS BE TURNED TO ADVANTAGE.

What the Sentiments of Congress on the Subject OF THE PROPOSED GUARANTEE OF EACH OTHER'S TERRITORIES IN AMERICA, I know not, but I most heartily wish that we could avoid ENTERING INTO IT WITH SPAIN. IT MAY ONE DAY COMPEL US TO WHAT NEITHER OUR INTEREST OR consciences will justify, nor can it in any SENSE BE CONSIDERED AS EQUAL, SINCE THE GUARANTEE OF SPAIN WILL BE OF LITTLE Moment to us AFTER THE WAR. I need not remind you of the caution that will be necessary on your part to prevent this GUARANTEE FROM EXTENDING TO THEIR CONQUESTS ON THE MISSISSIPPI.

We have Reason to conclude from a variety of Circumstances, that you will see in the inclosed Papers, that Savannah is evacuated, though Congress have yet no official Account of that Event.[5] Our Army are still on Hudsons River. They amount to about TWELVE THOUSAND MEN. They are well appointed and better disciplined. The French Army, consisting of something less than FIVE THOUSAND, are on their march to the same post. A few days ago the Marquis de Vaudreuil[6] with thirteen Sail of the Line, having on board FOURTEEN HUNDRED, has arrived at the Capes, WHERE THEY WILL REMAIN SOME DAYS TO COVER THE SAILING OF THE TRADE AND PROCEED TO BOSTON TO REFIT. The Southern Armies retain their old Stations. Greene in South Carolina; and Wayne in Georgia.

I shall conclude this Letter that I may attend to an important Debate in Congress on the Subject of THE INSTRUCTIONS FOR MAKING PEACE. Should any ALTERATIONS TAKE PLACE I shall write to you again by this Conveyance.[7]

I sent to Dr. Franklin a set of Bills to enable him to pay you and other Ministers one Quarters Salary. I shall send a second set by this conveyance, together with Bills for the amount of your second Quarter, terminating the first of July 1782.[8]

I wish you to send me as soon as is convenient an exact State of your Account. The Bills are purchased at 6/3d. for 5 Livres.

This Letter is written in Dr. Franklin's cypher, which will do as well as any other I presume, when, agreeable to your Request conveyed in your Favour of the 12th of May,[9] I direct for France.

I have the honour to be with the greatest Respect and Esteem Your Excellency's most obedient and humble Servant

ROBT. R. LIVINGSTON

N.B. The Letter and Resolutions are written in No. 4 of Dr. Franklins Cypher transmitted by Mr. Morris.

By the United States in Congress Assembled, 7 August 1782

RESOLVED That the Minister Plenipotentiary of the United States at the Court of SPAIN BE INSTRUCTED TO FORBEAR MAKING ANY OVERTURES TO THAT COURT, OR ENTERING INTO ANY STIPULATIONS IN CONSEQUENCE OF OVERTURES WHICH HE HAS MADE, AND IN CASE ANY PROPOSITIONS BE MADE TO HIM BY THE SAID COURT FOR A TREATY WITH THE United States, TO DECLINE ACCEDING TO THEM UNTIL HE SHALL HAVE TRANSMITTED THEM TO CONGRESS FOR THEIR APPROBATION, UNLESS THE TREATY PROPOSED BE OF SUCH A TENOR AS TO RENDER HIS ACCESSION THERETO NECESSARY TO THE FULFILLMENT OF THE STIPULATION, ON THE PART OF THE UNITED STATES, CONTAINED IN THE SEPARATE AND SECRET ARTICLE OF THEIR TREATY WITH HIS MOST CHRISTIAN MAJESTY.[10]

Resolved that MR. JAY BE AT LIBERTY TO LEAVE SPAIN AND GO INTO ANY OTHER PART OF EUROPE WHENEVER THE STATE OF HIS HEALTH MAY REQUIRE IT.[11]

ROBT. R. LIVINGSTON

(Quadruplicate) LS (#12), and enclosure signed by Livingston, utilizing the Franklin-Morris code (C in DLC: Franklin) deciphered by the editors. Endorsed: ". . . Recd. 5 Nov. 1782, No. 12 quad." Dft (misdated 9 August) undeciphered and ARC in NHi: Robert R. Livingston; duplicate LS undeciphered and C of triplicate in hand of W. T. Franklin in *ibid.*, Jay; LbkC, partly deciphered, in PCC 118, 242–46, with the notation: "1st Copy by the Ship Washington, 2plicate by the Ship Queen of France, 3plicate by the Ship St. James, 4plicate by Washington Packet." *HPJ, II, 336–41; RDC,* V, 720–24.

[1]JJ's lengthy dispatch of 28 April 1782 recounted his many frustrations in Spain since the preceding October. Cited above in "Issues in Negotiation," n. 26.

[2]The receipt of JJ's 28 April letter ignited a fiery debate in Congress, followed by the passage of the amended instructions included herewith. See Charles Thomson, "Debates in the Congress of the Confederation, from July 22d to September 20th, 1782," in New-York Hist. Soc., *Collections,* XI (1878), 63–169; also *LMCC,* VI, 390–91, 410–11, 428–30, 431–38. See Madison to Edmund Randolph, 5 Aug. 1782, *MP,* IV, 220–21. The resolution on the instructions, submitted on 6 August by a committee comprising

John Rutledge, James Duane, James Madison, Samuel Osgood, and Joseph Montgomery, was debated and amended on 6 and 7 August and entered only in the secret journals, III, 146–49. See *JCC,* XXII, 449–51, 455–56; see also *LMCC,* VI, 424–27, 431–32.

[3]Livingston expanded his views on commercial treaties in the letter dated 12 Sept. 1782, Dft in NHi: Robert R. Livingston; LS in JP; LbkC in PCC 79, I; *HPJ,* II, 336–41; *RDC,* V, 720–24.

[4]See editorial note, above, "The Second San Ildefonso Conference," for the points raised by Floridablanca with JJ on 19 Sept. 1781.

[5]Savannah was evacuated by the British on 11 July.

[6]Vice Admiral Louis Philippe de Rigaud, Marquis de Vaudreuil (1724–1802), French naval commander.

[7]The antigallic ferment vented itself in the bitter debates of 8 August. Arthur Lee moved that the 1781 peace instructions "be reconsidered," singling out for special attack the provision that the American Commissioners be bound by the wishes of France. He contended that France would be "governed by her own interest and from her long and close connection with Spain," a position not unlike JJ's (in JJ to Livingston, 28 April 1782). Madison led the champions of the instructions, insisting that the sacrifice of "national dignity" was "a sacrifice of dignity to policy." He moved that a committee be appointed to consider and "report to Congress the most advisable means of securing to the United States the several objects claimed by them and not included" in the ultimatum for peace of June 1781. After further debate and the passage of additional resolutions, his motion prevailed. See *JCC,* XXII, 458–60; *MP,* V, 35–38; *LMCC,* VI, 432–38.

[8]The new arrangements by which the Superintendent of Finance would remit to Livingston as agent quarterly payments for U.S. ministers abroad were described by Livingston to JJ, 9 May 1782, cited above in "The Status of the Peacemaking," n. 8.

[9]The date of JJ's letter is 14 May 1782, wherein he informed Livingston of his impending departure for France. Dft in JP; LbkCs in JP, CSmH, and PCC 110, II; *HPJ,* II, 307; *RDC,* V, 417.

[10]The "separate and secret article" signed at Paris 6 Feb. 1778 reserved to the King of Spain "the Power of acceding to the said Treatys, and to participate in their stipulations at such time as he shall judge proper." Miller, *Treaties,* II, 45–46.

[11]Evidently worded to sanction covertly JJ's trip to Paris to join Franklin in the peace negotiations, as the latter had informed Livingston on 14 May; see n. 9.

From John Adams

Hague, 10 August 1782

It was with very great pleasure that I received this morning your kind favor of the 2d inst.[1] I am surprised to learn that your and Mrs. Jay's health have been disordered in France where the air is so fine.

That your anxieties have been very great I doubt not, that most of them were such as you ought not to have met with, I can easily conceive. I can sincerely say, that all mine, but my Fever, were such as I ought not to have had. Thank God, they are past, and never shall return, for nothing that can happen shall ever make me so anxious again. I have assumed the felicis animi immota tranquillitas.[2]

Nothing would give me more satisfaction than a free conversation between you and me, upon the subjects you mention, and all others, directly or indirectly connected with it or with any of our affairs, but I don't see a possibility of taking such a journey. The march of this People is so slow that it will be sometime before the Treaty of Commerce can be finished and after that I have other orders to execute, and must be here in person to attend every step.[3] But besides this, I think I ought not to go to Paris while there is any messenger there from England, unless he has full powers to treat with the Ministers of the United States of America. If the three American Ministers should appear at Paris, at the same time with a real or pretended Minister from London, all the world would instantly conclude a Peace certain, and would fill at once another years Loan for the English. In Lord Shelburne's sincerity I have not the least confidence and I think that we ought to take up Fox's idea, and insist upon full powers to treat with us in character before we have a word more to say upon the subject. They are only amusing us. I would rather invite you to come here. This Country is worth seeing and you would lay me under great obligations by taking your residence, during your stay, in the *Hotell des Etats Unis.*[4] Many People would be glad to see you.

I should be very glad however to be informed, from step to step, how things proceed, which may be done with safety by Expresses to me; or by those from the Court of Versailles to the Duke de la Vauguion, in whom I have great confidence, or it may be done even by Post, under cover to Messrs. Wilhem & Jean Willink, at Amsterdam;[5] or Mr. Dumas, at the Hague;[6] or to Mr. Charles Storer, chez Madame la Veuve Loder at the Hague.[7]

As you justly observe, further accessions of power to the House of Bourbon may excite jealousies in some Powers of Europe, but who is to blame but themselves? Why are they so short sighted, or so indolent, as to neglect to acknowledge the United States and make Treaties with them! Why do they leave the House of Bourbon to contend so long and spend so much? Why do they leave America and Holland under so many obligations. France has and deserves and ought to have a great weight with America and Holland, but other powers might have proportionable weight, if they would have proportional merit.

If the Powers of the Neutral Maritime Confederation, would admit the United States to acceed to that Treaty, and declare America Independent, they would contribute to prevent America at least, from being too much under the direction of France. But if any Powers should take the part of England, they will compell America and Holland too, to unite themselves ten times more firmly than ever to the House of Bourbon.

I don't know, however, that America, or Holland are too much under the direction of France, and I don't believe they will be, but they must be dead to every generous feeling as Men, and to every wise view as Statesmen, if they were not much attached to France in the circumstances of the Times.

I have received two letters from you in the Spring. One I answered, but have not the dates at present; the other kindly informed me of the arrival of my Son in America, for which I thank you.[8]

With great regard and esteem, I am, dear Sir, Your Most obedient humble Servant,

JOHN ADAMS

LS in Storer's hand. Endorsed. LbkC, in Adams' hand, in MHi: Adams, reel 107, pp. 69–70; with variations and omissions in *JAW*, VII, 606–07.

[1]See above.

[2]"The unbroken calm of the happy soul." Seneca, On Anger 2.12.6.

[3]Adams did not sign the Treaty of Amity and Commerce with the United Provinces until 8 October. *AP*, IV, 264.

[4]In February 1782 Adams arranged for the purchase of a house at The Hague for his official residence, the first which the United States acquired as a foreign legation. *AP*, III, 4–5.

[5]One of the three Houses Adams contracted with for a loan for America on 11 June. See above, Adams to JJ, 5 July 1782. Van Winter, *American Finance and Dutch Investment*, I, 86–96 *passim*.

[6]Charles William Frederic Dumas, Adams' counselor, translator, secretary, and intermediary with Dutch officials and journalists. German-born of French parents, Dumas settled at The Hague in 1756. A long-time admirer of America, he had served Congress and its commissioners in various capacities in the United Provinces since the start of the war. *AP*, III, 9–10n. For Dumas' earlier labors for the American cause, see Renaut, *Les Provinces-Unies et la Guerre d'Amérique*, V (Paris, 1925).

[7]Charles Storer (1761–1829), a relative of Abigail Adams', had recently joined the Adams' household at The Hague, serving without pay as Adams' private secretary. *AP*, III, 13n.

[8]JJ to John Adams, 18 March, above; for 15 April 1782, above, "Issues in Negotiation," n. 3.

To Robert R. Livingston

Paris, 13 August 1782

Dear Robert,

Almost ever since my arrival here I have had and still have a sick Family. The epidemic Disorder which has spread throughout the northern parts of Europe, has been severe upon us. I am free from it at present, but it has taken from me some Flesh and much Strength.

Mrs. Jay has frequent attacks of an intermitting Fever, and our little Girl is not yet wholly out of Danger.[1]

Your Letter of the 22d May,[2] and the one enclosed with it from your good Mother contain the first advices I recieved of my Father's Death. My last Letter from Frederick was of an earlier Date.[3] That Intelligence was not unexpected. I wish I had been with him, but it is a temporary Separation and I am resigned; it has added to the number of my Inducements to walk in his Steps, and thereby arrive at the same Home.

Sir James is in England, and at large, but whether on parole I can not say, having had no Letter from him, nor any particular Information respecting him.[4] I feel very sensibly for Peter and Nancy; they are ever in my Thoughts. I thank you sincerely for becoming my Agent. Doctor Franklin had paid me nine months Salary a few Days before your Letter arrived; and too great a part of it was preengaged to admit of my repaying it and waiting for Bills. I do not understand whether, or how far, we are to take the Chances of Exchange. Be pleased to explain this. However the case may be, I shall be content. I am paid up to the 18 July last, so that Mr. Morris will be pleased to consider my account as commencing on that Day; for although there are Reasons for computing my Salary from the Date of my Commission, yet I have conformed to the Letter of the Resolution of Congress on that Head.

I must request the Favor of you to pay twenty pounds York Money to Miss Kitty Livingston on account of my little Boy, and one hundred and fifty pounds like Money to Frederick, Peter and Nancy, to *each* fifty pounds; manage this through Benson. I hear my Father has given some of his Servants free, and that some others of the older ones have been put out. Old Servants are sometimes neglected. Desire Mr. Benson to keep an Eye over them, and not to let any of them want; and for that purpose place fifty pounds in his Hands which he will apply according to his Discretion, as Necessity may from Time to Time require. He must also reimburse himself for any Expences he may be at on their account.[6] I should write to him also on this Subject but have neither Health nor Time, having at present a violent headache and a little Fever, and my Letter must be sent to the Marquis de la Fayette this Evening.

I have begun to confer with the Count de Aranda. He proposes a Line between us which would leave near as much Country between it and the Mississippi, as there is between it and the Atlantic Ocean.[7]

Col. Livingston had no Letters from me.[8]
Adieu my Friend. Yours etc.

JOHN JAY

ALS in NHi: Robert R. Livingston; Dft in JP; E in NN: Bancroft: American III, 298; incomplete in *WJ*, II, 100.

[1]JJ does not seem to have been fully recovered from influenza until mid-October, when he reported that "both evils" ("want of health" and "want of Leisure") were beginning to abate, and that he could at long last enjoy the pleasures "of this Charming Country." Both Sally and their daughter had also recovered as of this date. JJ to Abbé O'Ryan, 16 Oct. 1782, Dft JP.

[2]Robert R. Livingston to JJ, 22 May 1782, ALS in JP; Dft in NHi: Robert R. Livingston; Lbk Cs in PCC 79, I, 417–21, and PCC 118, pp. 166–76; *HPJ*, II, 307–08. This letter enclosed Margaret Beekman Livingston to JJ, 21 April 1782, above.

[3]JJ's last letter from Frederick was dated 1 Dec. 1781, ALS in JP.

[4]Livingston had written JJ on the 22nd: "Sir James, as I informed you in my last, having been carried to New York and confined to the provost till the arrival of General Carlton, was enlarged but not permitted to leave the City. It is since said that he is gone to England but whether as a prisoner or of his own accord I cannot say, though I presumed, if the account is true, that it must be as a state prisoner."

[5]In his 22 May letter Livingston informed JJ that he had found it "impossible to get the amount posted to procure the bills on this short notice."

[6]Further directions for financial assistance to his family were included in JJ's 26 August letter to Egbert Benson, below.

[7]See above, editorial note, "Jay Opens Negotiations with Aranda."

[8]For the dispatches Brockholst Livingston carried from Europe, see above, editorial note, "Sir James Kicks Over the Traces."

From William Bingham

Philadelphia, 14–15 August 1782
(Duplicate)

Major Franks, on his Arrival here, the 1st Instant, delivered me your Letter of the 8th September,[1] in which I find You do not acknowledge the Receipt of several that I had wrote You, which renders your Precaution very necessary.

It is the prevailing Opinion in America that Negociations are on the Tapis for a general peace and your DEPARTURE from Madrid, to hold a CONFERENCE (as is said) with the OTHER COMMISSIONERS tends to strengthen the Conjecture.

I believe the new Ministry are wholly intent upon this favorite Object, as the untoward Events of War may occasion such Clamours in the Nation as may be fatal to their Views of keeping their places, which I imagine they must be very desirous of retaining after being so long engaged in the pursuit of them.

The United States have many Reasons to urge them to wish for Peace, but at the same Time, they are not disposed to make any Sacrifice of their Interests, or their Honor to obtain it. Many wish for a continuation of the War, until the PUBLIC DEBTS are properly SECURED to the PUBLIC CREDITORS, and some until our PREJUDICES against the ENGLISH are more DEEPLY RIVETED, for they have still a POWERFUL PARTY AMONG US.

It is perhaps fortunate that this Campaign is INACTIVE, and consequently not very EXPENSIVE; for its EXPENDITURES are to be drawn from TAXES alone, which must prove a very INTENSIVE REQUISITION for the purpose, especially since the DIMINISHING of our TRADE has removed the MAJOR SPRING, which set[s] the whole Machinery of Industry and Alienation in Motion, on the BASIS of which TAXES can alone be founded.[2]

It is really time to fund our National Debt, to appropriate Revenues for the punctual Payment of the Interest that we have already borrowed, and for any new Loans that we may make. We may perhaps then procure Credit from the Monied People of Europe, for the Interest of 6 per cent is a very tempting Bait.

The Administration of the Finances of this Country must have afforded, to hackneyed politicians in Europe, a very strange and uncommon Appearance. To support a War of seven Years, without encumbering the Nation with more than a Debt of about fifteen Millions of Dollars, is what neither of the powers of Europe, with the best protected Trade, and all the Resources that productive population and active Industry can procure, could effect. However, we have got to the LENGTH of our TETHER, and must begin to adopt their MODE of SUPPORT by BONDING and FUNDING.

The Campaign has hitherto passed over, without any Appearance of active Hostility. The Enemy have kept within their Lines, and we have wanted Force, and the co-operation of a Navy, to enter, and drive them out. The French Troops are now on their March from the Southward, to form a Junction with the American Army. The Marquis de Vadreuil, with thirteen Ships of the Line, is now on the Coast, cruising off the Capes of Delaware. He arrived from Hispaniola, I suppose, with an Intention of avoiding the Hurricane Months, as I can observe no Movements that imply the Execution of any projected plan of Operation.

Savannah is evacuated by the British, and the Garrison of Charlestown is preparing to do the same, having embarked all their heavy Artillery, and Stores. If their Destination is for New York, it is very probable the French Fleet may intercept them, in their Route. The

Enemy seem most effectually to have renounced all Idea of Conquest, and I believe will only endeavor to retain New York until a general pacification takes place.

The waste and uncultivated Lands of America begin to engage the Attention of Congress, and the Claims of the respective States to that part of them that falls within the BOUNDARY of their CHARTERS, will occasion some DISSENSION and CLAMOR. If the Maxims of Justice were to decide, the Matter would soon and easily be adjusted; but the INTERFERENCE of private INTEREST will delay the Determination, and will occasion considerable FERMENT and DISTRUST.[3]

DR. FRANKLIN begins to recover his FULL INFLUENCE IN CONGRESS. The punctilios of the LEE JUNTO have ceased to be attended to. Both ARTHUR LEE[4] and IZARD are in CONGRESS, the former from VIRGINIA, and the latter from SOUTH CAROLINA. An Interest is making by some of the Friends of CARMICHAEL to procure for him the place of SECRETARY to the EMBASSADOR at the COURT of VERSAILLES.[5]

You would oblige me by giving me your Opinion of the Credit that our LOAN OFFICE CERTIFICATE[s], which bear an INTEREST of 6 per centum, payable AT PARIS have obtained, and whether they could be NEGOTIATED for nearly their FULL VALUE in SPAIN.

In compliance with the Requisition of Congress, all the States, except Rhode Island, have passed the Law for laying a Duty of 5 per centum, ad valorem, on all imported Goods, for the Extinction of the Capital, and the regular payment of the Interest on the Debts due to the public Creditors.[6]

GENERAL CARLETON has proposed an Exchange of SAILORS for SOLDIERS with GENERAL WASHINGTON, and in order to invalidate the Objections that might arise from the LATTER being capable of being brought into SERVICE, whilst the others could add nothing to the CONTESTING FORCE, has engaged his Honor that they should not take THE FIELD for a twelve Month, and adds that, at the Expiration of the Time, he is confident there would be no FURTHER USE for them.[7]

The acknowledgement of our Independence, by the States General of the United Provinces, has diffused the greatest Joy amongst the Inhabitants of these States, as it adds a strong Link to the Chain that supports us.

August 13.[8] Since writing the above, Sir Guy Carleton has informed General Washington of the pacific Disposition of Great Britain, and that the King has directed Mr. Grenville, (who is invested with full powers to treat with all the parties at War,) to propose the Independence of America, in the first Instance, without making it a Condition of a general Treaty. This pleasing Intelligence inclines us to believe that we shall have a speedy peace, on honorable Terms.[9]

Mrs. Bingham requests her best Compliments may be made to Mrs. Jay, to which please to add my sincere Respects; and believe me to be, with great Regard, and Attachment Dear Sir, Your obedient humble Servant,

WM. BINGHAM

Duplicate ALS. E in NN: Bancroft: American IV, 47.

[1]JJ to Bingham, 8 Sept. 1781, not located.

[2]See Robert Morris' report to Congress on the public debt and the problems of financing the war. *JCC,* XXII, 429–46.

[3]With the cession by Virginia on 2 Jan. 1781 of her claims north of the Ohio River, a central issue of the "backlands" was resolved, but other disputes remained to be settled, including Connecticut's charter claims to the Western Reserve in Ohio and a reservation of bounty lands for Virginia. Still to come was Congressional legislation for the sale of the Western lands. See Francis S. Philbrick, *The Rise of the West, 1754–1830* (New York, 1965), chaps. 4 and 5.

[4]Lee's attacks on Franklin and JJ were one phase of the larger struggle to revise the peace instructions and change the peace commissioners. For Lee's resolution of 24 July 1782 to the latter end, see *JCC,* XXII, 415; for Madison's countervailing efforts, see Madison to Edmund Randolph, 26 July 1782, *MP,* IV, 434–35; V, 14–15, 33, 36.

[5]Carmichael's friends in Congress had sought without success to have him appointed secretary to the delegation at Paris. See *JCC,* XXII, 258, 260, 307, 380.

[6]For the issue of imposts and Rhode Island's objections to this revenue-raising proposal, see E. James Ferguson, *The Power of the Purse; A History of American Public Finance, 1776–1790* (Chapel Hill, 1961), pp. 152–53; David Howell to Governor William Greene, 30 July 1782, *LMCC,* VI, 399–404 *et seq.*

[7]For the Congressional resolution on the proposed exchange of prisoners, see *JCC,* XXII, 421–22 (29 July); XXIII, 462–63 (12 Aug.); and Charles Thomson's Notes on Debates, *LMCC,* VI, 440–41.

[8]Slip of the pen for "15."

[9]On 27 September Bingham sent JJ further domestic news and urged a treaty giving the Americans access to the British West Indian and Cuban trade. ALS in JP.

From Montmorin

St. Ildefonso, 22 August 1782

Dear Sir,

I received, sir, only a few days ago the letter that you were so kind as to write me, begun the 19th of June and completed on the 26th of July.[1] I trust that your health, and that of Madame Jay, are now restored. I would be very sorry if you had reason to complain of the Paris climate. Moreover, I trust that it will be the only subject of complaint that you have in France. You have seen for yourself how America is viewed there, and how the system of government reflects the point of view of the nation.

I believe you will have every reason to be satisfied with M. le Comte d'Aranda as regards attentions and honesty; as regards details, the instructions of his court determine the basis of his behavior. I hope moreover that you advance further than you did here.

We are very much occupied with Gibraltar. We stand at the threshold of great events. Pray God that they will be auspicious. I believe that they could bring very much closer the epoch of peace which we all wish for, a peace both good and solid. We must exploit the moment when this can be obtained; and not insist on making a bad peace which will not last, one which has no other object than to allow the enemy to get his wind back and give him the means to attack us anew when we will be less on our guard and less united than we are at the moment.[2]

M. le Comte d'Artois[3] arrived on the 15th of this month and was at the camp of St. Roch that very same evening. He comes from an operation which could cost us heavily but has not cost us a single man up to the present. Things go well. I do not believe that the English fleet will arrive before the siege will be ended. The operations are proving very troublesome to them. I do not speak of affairs generally. You are on the very spot where all affairs of peace or war are determined.

I very much hope that Madame de Montmorin might be of some assistance to Madame Jay, and that all which I have can provide proof of my esteem for you and of my sincere and inviolable attachment. I have the honor of being, Sir, your very humble and obedient servant.

LE CT DE MONTMORIN

Please give Madame Jay assurance of my respect and attachment, in which the Chevalier de Bourgoing joins.

ALS in French, trans. by the editors. E in NN: Bancroft: American IV, 64.

[1]Above, dated 26 June–19 July 1782.

[2]The final Franco-Spanish assault on the fortress of Gibraltar was not mounted until 13 September.

[3]Louis XVI had given permission to his brother, the Comte d'Artois (1757–1836), to participate in the siege of Gibraltar. The future King Charles X of France, the Comte was also a nephew of the King of Spain.

BENJAMIN VAUGHAN TO SHELBURNE

Paris, 24 August 1782

My Lord,

I have no knowledge of any right which I have to add to the number of letters (Already perhaps of a style that may seem improper) which I have at different times written to your lordship, but a fact or two has occurred to my knowledge which I beg to communicate in extreme confidence.

On monday last, the 19th, the American ministers went to communicate their late conferences with Mr. Oswald, and the news of his having proposed independence to his court, as a measure to be by them adopted. They went as if to say a thing that was to prove acceptable. M. Vergennes however, professed not to understand the good sense of their measures, and thought that independence should be a subject of general treaty. Much conversation passed, but he did not *choose to understand* their reason for the *measure* they had taken. In the course of what had passed M. Vergennes told them that he should send to or see Mr. Fitzherbert (I cannot find which were the exact words) on the Tuesday, which was the 20th. I understand Mr. Fitzherbert did see Oswald, by whom I did not write, having no notice of it. The quarter however whence I have this intelligence adds that M. Vergennes seemed to wear the appearance of being not a little embarrassed by the supposed approach of the acknowledgement of independence.

I have also to mention to your lordship, that Mr. Jay said to me one day, when alone in his carriage, "why will not your court cut the cord that ties us to France, and why can they suppose we can be quiet (while the very end of the treaty is independence) till independence is guaranteed." He also suffered me to understand that while on the one hand little was to be got by *bargaining* with America, that much would be done by conceding this one point to her, and that the best way England's making a good bargain with *France* was by making a good agreement with America (evidently because France could make better terms having America in *her* own interests than when America became in England's interests). He said if this thing was not guaranteed that was written for, there was end to all confidence, and he would rather the war should go on to his grandsons than independence be given up.

Much conversation of this sort passed in which he was wholly without reserve. Fearing however the most, I endeavored to state and prepare reasons, that I said *might* induce the English ministry to postpone their declaration, notwithstanding the best intentions and grounds of confidence still subsisting in their favor. But I cannot say that these arguments had entire weight. Such, my Lord, is the specimen of the many things I hear in this place. I am more of a doubting politician than your lordship suspects, but nevertheless I cannot but give weight to evidence, supported by the knowledge both of the *interests* and *temper* of the particular parties, when I find them combined in favor of the same general point.

They *talk* of five sail of the line with sixty more merchantmen being arrived at Bellisle from the French W. Indies, but the rest of the merchantmen are to come by another opportunity.

This is the third arrival of ships and trade lately from the W. Indies, if the present news is accurate. There are those who still talk of the attack on Gibraltar having begun on the 15th and Mr. Walpole and others have hinted to me that C. D Estaing is *possibly* to command the combined fleet at Cadiz. I saw him (Count D Estaing) a day or two ago, however, at the Italian Comedy, and have not heard of his leaving his house at Passy.

Dr. Franklin is very much indisposed this week with gravelly complaints, but to-day is somewhat better. In the warm bath he for some days has voided small stones. I have told him that I should at all events wait the return of Mr. Oswald's courier, to give him an opportunity of sending his last intimations, which he has promised to your lordship.

I have the honor to be My Lord, Your Lordship's faithful and respectful servant,

BENJAN. VAUGHAN

P.S. I am on the best terms with Mr. Oswald, and Mr. Jay tells me he has no jealousy, which Dr. Franklin indeed took pains to prevent. This letter goes by Mr. Walterstorff,[1] the Danish gentleman I introduced to your lordship by your lordship's obliging permission. If your lordship sees him, he has some important particulars to communicate, relative to a canal through Holstein, which I cannot but suppose it fitting for your lordship to know. May I beg to mention to your lordship that I have not received a letter, which Mrs. Vaughan informs me she wrote July 19th,[2] and forwarded to your lordship. This makes me uneasy as young people write *very* foolish things to each other and the letter may be mislaid.

Tr in PPAmP: Vaughan. Benjamin Vaughan (1751–1835), a protégé and confidant of Shelburne, was chosen by the latter as a private agent to make contact with the American Commissioners in Paris. A familiar of English radical leaders, he had brought out in 1779, with Franklin's authorization, an edition of the Doctor's writings. See also above, JJ to Franklin, 31 May 1781, n. 5.

[1] Baron de Walterstorff, Danish minister in Paris.

[2] Vaughan had wed Sarah Manning (1753–1834) on 30 June of the previous year. Her letter has not been located.

To Egbert Benson

Paris, 26 August 1782

My good old Friend,

The Day before Yesterday I received a Letter from Colonel Isaac Sears dated the 25th March last,[1] covering one from you dated the 27th November 1782.[2] You evidently mistook the year, and if the month be right, you have either been lazy or your Letters very unlucky. <I suppose the latter to have been the case.> The only Letters I have received from you since I left America are 30 October 1781 which arrived the 7 December following, 27 August 1781 which arrived 8 January 1782,[3] and the one above mentioned which arrived 24 August Instant.

From your account of the Vermont Business, it appears, to use a vulgar Expression, to have been *bitched* in its last as well as first Stages. Obsta Principiis[4] though an old and wise maxim was neglected, but as Putnam used to say, "It is not worth while to cry about spilt milk." The calfs have kicked over the pail <may yet be sorry for it> and there is an End of the matter. You have other Lines still to settle, and the sooner it is done the better.[5]

Every good American will zealously endeavor to remove all ground of future Dissention between the States. Our Power Respectability and Happiness will forever depend on our Union. Many foreign Nations would rejoice to see us split to pieces because we should then cease to be formidable and such an Event would afford a fine Field for their Intrigues. Let us keep peace among ourselves for whenever the members quarrel the whole Body must Suffer.

My last Letter from Frederick is dated the 1 December 1781.[6] It arrived here the 18th Ultimate and makes the fourth letter I have received from him since we parted. Tell me something of Peter and Nancy. Assure them of my fixed Resolution to return and spend the Remainder of my Days with them. They are never out of my Mind and Heart. I hope they keep up their Spirits and are careful of their Health which I am very anxious about, on my own account as well as theirs; for some happy tranquil Years with them forms one of the most pleasing of the prospects I have left. I have desired R. Livingston to pay (through you) to them and to Fœdy one hundred and fifty pounds York money, viz. fifty pounds to *each.* He is also to place fifty pounds in your Hands for the occasional Relief of such of our old Servants as may from Time to Time want it. It may not perhaps prove necessary; if not, say nothing of the matter.

Inform me of the Time and Manner of my Father's Death. I feel too much to enlarge on this Subject.

Sir James is in England, but I know not in what Capacity. I have not had a Line from him since I left Philadelphia.

Present my best Compliments to your Mother and Brothers.[7] Tell Doctor Van Wycke I remember him with Gratitude. Your Governor owes me some Letters. He has my Esteem and Regard. I have written two or three Letters to Charles DeWitt, but none from him ever reached me.[8]

We have all (except my Nephew) been very sick, but are now thank God better. God bless and preserve You.

J. J.

Dft. E in NN: Bancroft: American IV, 80.

[1]Sears' letter has not been located.

[2]Benson's 27 Nov. 1781 (misdated 1782), ALS in JP; *HPJ,* II, 149–53.

[3]The 30 Sept. 1781 (misdated October) is above. No letter of 27 Aug. 1781 has been located. However, JJ received one dated 27 Oct. 1781, endorsed as having arrived on 5 Feb. 1782, ALS in JP.

[4]"Resist the beginnings."

[5]In his 27 November letter Benson recounted developments in the continuing Vermont lands' dispute subsequent to JJ's departure for Spain. Congress had still failed to act decisively, while the New York State Senate made an offer of cession which the Assembly failed to support.

[6]ALS in JP.

[7]Catherine Van Borsum (Mrs. Robert) Benson (1718–92), and Anthony (1752–94) and Henry (1741–1823); for Robert, see *JJ,* I, 393.

[8]Letters between DeWitt and JJ in this period have not been located. For DeWitt, see *JJ,* I, 331, 389.

To Robert R. Livingston

Paris, 4 September 1782

Dear Robert,

I wrote to You on the 13 Ultimo, a copy of that Letter enclosing one for your good mother, and one for Mr. Benson, was given last week to

Mr. Wright,[1] who had appointed last Thursday for setting out to Nantes in order to embark there for America. He is still here, but leaves Paris Tomorrow. This gives me an Opportunity of writing you a few Lines more, for though I daily gain strength, yet the Dizziness to which I have been subject on the least application, since my Illness, will not permit me either to write or read more than an Hour at a Time without a Cloud before my Eyes.

Be pleased to forward Bills for my Salary as it becomes due, deducting the sums which I have, or may in future Desire you to pay in America. Whenever you write tell me what you may know respecting the Health of my Family, for I almost despair of a regular Correspondence with F———,[2] whose last Letter was dated in November. Sir James is at large in England, but I am still ignorant in what Light he is considered, not having yet had a Line from him.

Count de Montmorin writes me that the Spaniards continue making immense preparations for the attack of Gibralter.[3] This object requires enormous Expences. They have issued more Bills and the Depreciation has increased. I am preparing a map to shew you the Line which Count D'Aranda proposes for our western Boundary.[4] It will not be finished in Time for this Conveyance. I am persuaded it is best for us to take Time. My further Reasons shall be explained at large in a future Letter which I shall begin as soon as my Health will permit.

Assure my Friends of my Remembrance and Regard. Mrs. Morris and Mrs. Meredith are in Mrs. Jay's Debt on the Score of Letters. Tell them so. How does Duer[5] do. I have written to him, but never received a Line from him. I hope Mrs. Livingston and *our* little Girl[6] are well. My best Wishes always attend them.

I am Dear Robert Your Friend

JOHN JAY

ALS in NHi: Robert R. Livingston. Dft in JP.

[1]Joseph Wright (1756–93), portrait painter, modeler in clay and wax, and medallist, was the son of Patience Lovell Wright, and the first to sculpture General Washington from life. George C. Groce and David H. Wallace, *The New-York Historical Society's Dictionary of Artists in America, 1564–1860* (New Haven, 1957). For his portrait of JJ, see Illustration section. For his life mask of the General, see Gustavus A. Eisen, *Portraits of Washington* (3 vols., New York, 1932); Frances D. Whittemore, *George Washington in Sculpture* (Boston, 1933). For his mother, see below, Patience Lovell Wright to John Adams and JJ, 8 March 1783, n. 1.

[2]"Fœdy," Frederick Jay.

[3]See above, Montmorin to JJ, 22 Aug. 1782.

[4]See map, p. 271.

[5]During this time, Duer was involved in private commericial and financial

enterprises as well as furnishing supplies for the army. See also *JJ*, I, 331.
[6]Livingston's daughter Elizabeth.

FROM RAYNEVAL

Versailles, 4 September 1782

I would very much like, Sir, to have a conversation with you concerning your problems about boundaries with Spain, but it is utterly impossible for me to go to Paris.

You would therefore greatly oblige me if you would be good enough to come to Versailles tomorrow morning. I would be very happy to invite you to dinner. While awaiting the honor of seeing you, I have that of being, Sir, in perfect attachment, your very humble and obedient servant,

DE RAYNEVAL

ALS in French, trans. by the editors. Endorsed. LbkCs in French in JP, PCC 110, II, and in CSmH; Tr in French in NN: Bancroft: American IV, 84; C in JJ to Robert R. Livingston, 17 Nov. 1782, cited above in JJ to Aranda, 25 June 1782, n. 2.

FROM RAYNEVAL

Versailles, 6 September 1782

I am honored Sir, to send you as you wished, my personal ideas concerning the manner of ending your boundary dispute with Spain. I trust that they seem to you worthy of being taken into consideration.

I have reflected, Sir, on what you told me yesterday concerning the lack of powers of the Spanish ambassador. I do not believe that you should use this ground to forgo dealing with this ambassador without offending him and impeding the preliminary steps that you have taken with him. This thought leads me to advise you, Sir, to meet with M. le Comte d'Aranda again, and to make him a proposal on the aforementioned subject; the one which is covered in my memorandum seems the best one to effect a reasonable conciliation, but it is for you to judge if I am mistaken, because you alone have knowledge of the titles on which the United States lays claim to their territories at the expense of the nations whose independence England herself recognized.

Moreover, Sir, whatever use that you may wish to make of my

memorandum, please look upon it as a small proof of my zeal and my wish to be useful to the cause of your nation.

I have the honor to be, with perfect regard, Sir, your very humble and very obedient servant

DE RAYNEVAL

Since I will be absent for several days, please send your answer to M. Henin, Secretary of the Council of State, at Versailles.

Rayneval: Suggestion Concerning the Manner of Determining and Discussing Boundaries Between Spain and the United States from the Banks of the Ohio Towards the Mississippi

[Versailles, 6 September 1782]

There is a discussion between Spain and the United States of North America concerning the setting of respective boundaries towards the Ohio and the Mississippi. The Americans argue that their territory extends to the Mississippi, and Spain maintains the contrary.

Obviously the Americans can only borrow from England the right the latter claims to extend as far as the Mississippi. Therefore to determine this right, it is necessary to examine what the court in London has thought and done on this subject.

We know that prior to the Treaty of Paris, France owned Louisiana and Canada and that she considered the Indians living East of the Mississippi as either independent or as under her protection.

This claim has caused no dispute. England has only sought to raise the issue as regards the lands situated towards the source of the Ohio River, in the part where England named the river the Allegheny.

There ensued at this time a discussion about boundaries between the Courts of Versailles and London. But it would be useless to pursue these details; we can merely note that in 1755 England proposed the following boundary:

It started from the point where the River de Boeuf flows into the Ohio at the place called Venango. It extended up that river towards Lake Erie for a distance of twenty leagues, and starting again at Venango. England drew a straight line to the last mountains of Virginia which slope towards the ocean.

As for the Indians living between the aforesaid line and the Mississippi, the English Minister considered them independent.

As a result of these propositions of the London court, almost the whole course of the Ohio belonged to France, and the countries to the west of the mountains were considered as having nothing in common with the colonies.

When peace was negotiated in 1761, France ceded Canada to England. The setting of the boundaries of this colony and those of Louisiana was in question. France claimed that almost the entire Ohio River was part of Louisiana, and the Court of London, to prove that this river belonged to Canada, produced several authentic documents, among others the map that M. de Vaudreuil turned over to the English commander in surrendering Canada. The English Ministry maintained at the same time that part of the Indians living West of the Mississippi were independent, another part under its protection, and that England had purchased a part from the five Iroquois nations. France's troubles cut short the discussion. The Treaty of Paris fixed the Mississippi as a boundary between the possessions of France and those of Great Britain.

Let us look at the dispositions which the Court of London made as a result of the Treaty of Paris:

If she had considered the vast territories east of the Mississippi as part of her original colonies, she would have so stipulated and would have made the dispositions accordingly. Far from doing that, the King of England, in a proclamation of October 1763, made known in a precise and positive manner that these same territories are situated between the Mississippi *and the original English colonies.* Thus it is clearly evident that the English court itself when it was still sovereign over the Thirteen Colonies, did not consider the abovementioned lands as being part of these colonies. Hence, it clearly follows that at the present day they have no right to these lands. To maintain the contrary, it would be necessary to subvert every principle of the laws of nature and nations.

The principles now established are as applicable to Spain as to the United States. This nation cannot extend its territories beyond the bounds of its conquests. She cannot pass beyond the fort of Natchez situated near the 31st degree of latitude. Therefore her rights are limited to this degree of latitude; that which is beyond is either independent or belongs to England. Neither Spain nor the Americans have any claim to it; only the future peace treaty can settle the respective claims.

The consequence of all that has been said is that neither Spain nor the United States has any rights of sovereignty over the Indians in question, and that any such negotiations over this territory would serve no purpose.

But the future could well bring forth new circumstances, and this reflection persuades me that it would be useful for the Courts in Madrid and the United States to reach an eventual agreement.

This agreement could be drawn from the eastern angle of the Gulf of Mexico which separates the two Floridas to Fort Toulouse situated in the country of the Alabamas; thence that it would ascend the river Locushatchee from the mouth of which a right angle should be drawn to the fort or factory Quanessee; from this last place, we would follow the course of the River Euphasee until it joins the Cherokee. We would follow the course of this last river until it meets the Pelisipi, and then follow this to its source, from whence a straight line is to be drawn to the Cumberland River whose course is to be followed until it falls into the Ohio.

The Indians west of the line described should be free, under the protection of Spain; those to the eastward should be free, and under the protection of the United States, or rather, the Americans may make such arrangements with them as they find most convenient. Trade should be free to both parties.

Glancing at the map, we can see that Spain would lose almost the whole course of the Ohio River and that the American establishments on this river would remain untouched, and that even a very extensive space remains to form new towns.

As to the course and navigation of the Mississippi, they would follow with the property, and would belong, therefore, to the nation to which both banks belonged. If, then, by the future peace treaty, Spain keeps western Florida, she alone will be the sole owner of the course of the Mississippi from the 31st degree of latitude to the mouth of this river. Whatever the fate of that part which is north of this point, the United States cannot claim it, not being master of either bank of this river.

As regards the lands situated northward of the Ohio, there is reason to presume that Spain will lay no claims thereto. Their fate must be decided by the Court of London.[1]

ALS in French, trans. by the editors, in NHi: Jay. Endorsed. Enclosure: "Mr. Rayneval's Plan of a conciliatory Line between Spain and the United States towards the Mississippi. Recd. 7 Sep. 1782," D in French, trans. by the editors. C of letter and enclosure in both French and English in JJ to Livingston, 17 Nov. 1782 (cited above in JJ to Aranda, 25 June 1782, n. 2). RC of letter in French in CP EU 22: 197–98, with notation: "M. Jay, hotel d'Orleans, rue des Augustins, fauxbourge St. Germaine; sent copy to M. de la Luzerne on

21 July 1783" (translated). Dft of plan in French in *ibid.*, pp. 200–04, with notation (translated): "Sent copy to M. Jay on 6 September 1782; sent copy to M. le Chev. de la Luzerne on 21 July 1783." A variant and inaccurate translation is in *RDC*, VI, 25–27 and in *HPJ*, II, 393–98.

[1]Superimposing the antiquated and obsolete geographical references on a modern map, the Rayneval proposal constituted a line which zigzagged from the mouth of the Cumberland in a general southerly direction to the "eastern angle" of the Gulf of Mexico, at Apalachicola Bay. While it would have offered the Americans somewhat more territory to the westward than Aranda's proposal of a few days earlier, it would have left the Mississippi south of the Ohio under exclusive Spanish control and kept the United States far away from its entire length. See map, p. 271.

JJ drafted a reply to Rayneval's "conciliatory" line, in which he insisted that Aranda did not have formal powers to treat with him, and that JJ himself "had no power to cede any territories of the United States to Spain," his authority extending "only to the forming treaties of alliance and commerce." Dft in The Rendells, Inc., *Autograph Letters, Manuscripts, Documents* (1971), Catalogue 54, pp. 36–37. Endorsed by JJ: "Proposed draft letter to Mr. Rayneval but never sent."

The Rayneval and Vaughan Missions to England

September 1782

On 10 August the Comte de Grasse, who as a paroled prisoner had paid a courtesy call upon Shelburne,[1] returned to France with word that the British minister was prepared to make concessions to secure peace. Anxious to test Shelburne's sincerity and, if possible, to get peace negotiations moving, Vergennes directed his *premier commis* Joseph-Matthias Gérard de Rayneval, to journey incognito to England to conduct explanatory talks with the Prime Minister.[2] Rayneval left on 7 September, reached London three days later, and on the 13th entered upon a week's discussions with Shelburne either at the latter's country estate, Bowood Park in Wiltshire, or in London.

The primary purpose of the Rayneval mission was to bring about a quick settlement of the outstanding issues between France and Spain on the one side and Great Britain on the other. In fact, the formal written instruction which Vergennes handed to Rayneval scrupulously omitted the United States from the agenda. That did not, however, stop Rayneval from adverting to the claims of the United States, and, since he reported his conversations to Vergennes at once, it is clear that he had been relying on an oral understanding with his superior about the scope of his authority.

At the start of the initial conference on 13 September, Rayneval referred to "the propositions set down by M. de Grasse," which he reviewed with Shelburne, and of which the first was "Independence." His comment: "This article is settled; it will be without any restrictions."[3] A third proposition, "fishing in Newfoundland," was treated by Rayneval in such a way as to assume that "each nation would fish exclusively in its assigned territory," a stand which was clearly meant to exclude the United States. That point was made clear in the course of that afternoon's discussions and in talks later that week. During the first afternoon Shelburne remarked, according to Rayneval's account, that "most probably the Americans would formulate some designs concerning fishing rights," while expressing the hope that "the King would not support them," a view which he had already voiced to Fitzherbert.[4] Ingenuously denying knowledge of Congress's views on the fisheries, Rayneval assured Shelburne, "I can count on the fact that the King will never support unfair demands."

As regards the mediation by Russia and Austria, broached the same day, a subject which Rayneval conceded was agreeable to France, the Frenchman told Shelburne, "We ended it because of the Americans, and Spain, because of Gibraltar." Summing up the first day's talks, Shelburne informed the King, "the point of independence once settled," Rayneval "appears rather Jealous than partial to America upon other points, as well as that of the Fishery."[5]

Toward the conclusion of his next to the last session with Shelburne, held on 18 September, Rayneval discussed America at some length, and this is his own account:

". . . Following these opening remarks we came to the propositions set down by M. De Grasse. Milord told me that he had made no formal overtures to this officer, that they had merely spoken together about the war and peace and in the course of the conversation, Milord said that he had always been opposed to independence, that it was the hardest pill to digest, but that he felt it was necessary to swallow it and that this objective could be settled unconditionally. There was a discussion of St. Lucia and of Santo Domingo; India was mentioned briefly. He said nothing about either Africa or Dunkirk, even less about Gibraltar and the interests of the neutrals.

"After this explanation, Milord reiterated his desire for a speedy and lasting peace, and observed that he felt that independence alone would not satisfy us, as M. Fox had assumed; that we had other objectives to settle; that the King of England was willing to do us justice and that Milord-himself was very anxious that I make it possible for him to tell the King about our intentions in order to arrange a satisfactory resolution of the issue with me.

"Yielding to the entreaties of Milord, I took back the paper with the propositions set down by M. de Grasse and I reviewed and discussed them in order.

"1. Independence. This article is settled; it will be without any restriction."

At the close of the next day's session the issue of secrecy came up in the event that a preliminary agreement was reached. Shelburne confessed his fear of a leak to speculators in the public funds. Rayneval sought to reassure him. "I said that we could advise them of ways to keep everything a secret in order to foil the curious, but Milord is worried about the Americans and the Dutch. I repeated that there would be a way to lead them astray, principally by keeping them in ignorance of the state of the negotiations between France and Spain [on the one side] and England [on the other]."[6] Considering the French criticism of JJ for the secrecy in which he and his colleagues conducted negotiations from this time forward until the Preliminaries were concluded, the record of the clandestine talks of Rayneval and Shelburne reveal that America's ally pursued like tactics when national interests, and those of her Spanish ally, so dictated.

Apart from his written report of his conversations, Rayneval presumably, in an oral briefing, revealed other details concerning the bearing of his talks with Shelburne on the interests of the United States. As Vergennes was to inform Montmorin when the subject of equivalents for Gibraltar was raised, Shelburne proposed the restoration of West Florida in exchange for the Rock. Vergennes commented: "Considering the point of view with which the Spanish court had up to now adopted toward the American Revolution and the alarm with which she now regards it, it would seem to me, Monsieur, that, should Lord Shelburne's overture take on the firmness of a formal proposal, nothing would better serve the cause of the honor that Spain attached to recovery of Gibraltar than what she hopes to gain by not having as a neighbor a people she regards as rash and aggressive as the North Americans."[7]

Finally, as regards American boundary claims, Shelburne was to inform his Secretary of State: "Now Monsr. Rayneval gave me to understand that, Independence once granted, they were disposed to assist us as to the Boundarys no matter what motives they may have. It may be material in the first private Letter you write to Oswald and Strachey to give them suitable Instructions without precisely naming Monsr. Rayneval, and to advice them to consult with Fitzherbert on the French disposition."[8]

The day before his departure from Paris Rayneval had remarked to JJ in a letter, above, that he would be away for a brief spell. In view of JJ's unsatisfactory conversation with Vergennes, Rayneval, and Aranda, the American suspected that some covert move disadvantageous to the United States might be under way. Although Vergennes did not inform the American Commissioners of Rayneval's mission, JJ learned of it on 9 September from Matthew Ridley. His suspicions were heightened the next day when the British placed in his hands an intercepted cipher dispatch from Barbé-Marbois to Vergennes, which criticized the American position on the fisheries, while describing the Congressional instructions to its Peace Commissioners as making "the King master of the treaty of peace, excepting independence or treaties of alliance."[9]

Now, acting swiftly on his own, JJ dispatched Benjamin Vaughan to England to neutralize whatever Rayneval might be seeking to achieve there. During the summer Vaughan, who had been visiting Paris, had held long talks with both Franklin and JJ in an effort to reconcile the differences between the Americans and the mother country. He had diligently reported these conversations to Shelburne, along with a significant talk with JJ held around the middle of August, and included above, stressing the advantage to England of a prompt recognition of American independence by way of preliminary to treaty negotiations.[10]

Aside from his concern about the purpose of Rayneval's mission, JJ, having now drafted an alteration of the commission which Oswald, with his permission, had forwarded to his government, felt an urgency in the timing of Vaughan's trip. In his report to Secretary Livingston of 17 November 1782 JJ listed the substance of his instructions to Vaughan. The first of these was the necessity of England's treating with the United States on an equal footing. Once the acknowledgment of independence was avowed, "we should be at liberty to make peace the moment that Great Britain should be ready to accede to the terms of France and America, without our being restrained by the demands of Spain, with whose views we had no concern." JJ went on to caution against any division of the fishery with France to the exclusion of the United States or against France's obstruction on the issue of boundaries and the navigation of the Mississippi.[11] With these oral instructions from JJ, Vaughan set off for London on the evening of 11 September, only a few hours after Oswald's courier had departed with the British Commissioner's letter of 10 and 11 September to Townshend and Shelburne. Vaughan's two advance communications to Shelburne are printed below, along with his retrospective account of the mission, which he sent to James Monroe in 1795. The latter was penned in Basel, at a time when Vaughan was a political refugee from counter-revolutionary England.

How instrumental Vaughan proved in moving the ministry off dead center is a matter of speculation. Nevertheless, coincident with his mission, the British Cabinet on 19 September recommended to the King that a new commission be issued to Oswald to "treat with the Commissioners appointed by the Colonys, under the title of Thirteen United States, inasmuch as the Commissioners have offered under that condition to accept the Independence of America as the First Article of the Treaty."[12] Not until the 21st did the commission receive the seals, and on the 24th Townshend dispatched it to Oswald with the "hope that the frankness with which we deal, will meet with a suitable return."[13] In the weeks ahead, following his return to Paris on 27 September, Vaughan, who found JJ "a truly amiable and sensible man, with ideas of a gentleman, and a frankness and decision that do him considerable honor," possessed "of a fertile head in business, great shrewdness, great extent in his combinations, and much caution and experience," continued to press Shelburne for favorable action on reciprocal trade with America, one of the unsettled issued of the peacemaking, and to endorse the boundaries upon which JJ had been so insistent in his original instructions, along with America's position on the fisheries.

Summing up the concession made on recognition of the United States, Shelburne confided to Oswald: "We have put the greatest confidence, I believe, was ever placed on men, in the American commissioners. It is now to be seen, how far they or America are to be depended upon," adding, "I hope the public will be the gainer, else our heads must answer for it deservedly."[16]

[1]See De Grasse to Shelburne, 10 Aug. 1782, ALS in MiU-C: Shelburne 71, with enclosure, preliminary project between Shelburne and de Grasse, 17 Aug. 1782, D in *ibid.,* indicating the tentative terms to be accorded the belligerents, including entire and absolute indepen-

dence of the U.S. For a variant version with some deletions indicated, see D in CP A 538: 54–55. Still another set includes Spanish and French reactions to the British offer. D in CP A 538: 100–10. De Grasse reported to Vergennes the results of his meeting. De Grasse to Vergennes, 17, 18 Aug. 1782, ALS in *ibid.*, pp. 56, 58, and then notified Shelburne of the necessity of securing a Spanish agreement. De Grasse to Shelburne, 18 Aug. 1782, ALS in MiU-C: Shelburne 71. For Vergennes' reaction, see Vergennes to Montmorin, 18 Aug. 1782, LbkC in CP E 608: 210–11; also *Peacemakers,* pp. 319–20.

[2]Vergennes to Rayneval, 6 Sept. 1782, ALS in CP A 538: 117–18, with letter of introduction to Shelburne and Grantham, 8 Sept., Dft in *ibid.,* p. 124.

[3]In the confidential instructions Rayneval carried with him, the first article reads: "Since the independence of America is agreed to, no comment need be made on that subject." "Confidential remarks of the means of achieving the Preliminaries of the Peace," September 1782, MiU-C: Shelburne 71. From Rayneval's remarks, the editor Jared Sparks argued that the *premier commis* had insisted that acknowledgment of independence was "a preliminary step to further discussion." *RDC,* VI, 50n. The Rayneval-Shelburne conferences as reported by the former to Vergennes are in CP A 538: 146–206 *passim.* Except for the conferences on 15 and 16 September, they were published by Doniol, "Conference de M. Rayneval avec les Ministres Anglais," in *Revue d'Histoire Diplomatique,* VI, No. 1 (Paris, 1892), pp. 62–89.

[4]Shelburne had surely been apprised before this of Rayneval's hostility to America's fishery claims. On 29 August Fitzherbert reported to Grantham: "He [Rayneval] signified to me in pretty plain terms that nothing could be farther from the wishes of this court than that the said claim be admitted." Fitzherbert to Grantham, 29 Aug. 1782, ALS in FO 27/3.

[5]Fortescue, ed., *Corr. of George III,* VI, 125.

[6]Conference between Rayneval and Shelburne, 18 Sept. 1782, C in French in CP A 538: 172–92.

[7]Vergennes to Montmorin, 13 Oct. 1782, C in French in CP E 609:83–84. A note in the margin: "This still proves the suitability of the proposal for Spain. A reason which should prevent us from proposing it to the Spanish minister."

[8]Shelburne to Townshend, [28 Oct. 1782], ALS in FO 95/511.

[9]*Peacemakers,* pp. 323–35. The Barbé-Marbois letter, 13 March 1782, is printed with minor variations in *RDC,* V, 238–41, and in *WJ,* II, 490–94. An original is in MAE, despite French disclaimers at the time. JJ's suspicions about Rayneval's trip, as well as the impact upon him of the Barbé-Marbois letter, along with the New Yorker's exposition of the American position prior to Benjamin Vaughan's trip to England, are set forth in JJ to Livingston, 17 Nov. 1782, cited above in JJ to Aranda, 25 June 1782, n. 2. See also 9 September entry in Matthew Ridley's diary, at MHi: Ridley.

[10]Vaughan to Shelburne, Paris, 24 Aug. 1782, above. See also Vaughan to Shelburne, 6, 18 Aug. 1782, Tr of both in PPAmP: Vaughan. For Vaughan's contacts with Franklin and his consistent support of the Americans' peace terms, see Vaughan to Shelburne, 31 July 1782, wherein he describes JJ as "a very pleasant man, who has no unreasonable notions or passions."

[11]JJ to Livingston, 17 Nov. 1782. For Vaughan's contacts with Franklin and his consistent support of the Americans' peace terms, see Vaughan to Shelburne, 31 July 1782, *loc. cit.,* wherein he describes JJ as "a very pleasant man, who has no unreasonable notions or passions."

[12]Minutes of Cabinet Meeting, 19 Sept. 1782, in Townshend's hand forwarded by Shelburne to the King. Fortescue, ed., *Corr. of George III,* VI, 131.

[13]Townshend to Oswald, 24 Sept. 1782, Cs in FO 95/511; 97/157; 27/2; LbkC in Mi U-C: Shelburne 70.

[14]Vaughan to Shelburne, 3 Oct., 1 Nov. 1782, Massachusetts Hist. Soc., *Proceedings,* 2d ser., XVII (1903), 409, LbkC in PPAmP: Vaughan; Tr in MiU-C: RGA-Vaughan.

For an earlier comment about JJ, see Vaughan to Shelburne, 31 July 1782, Tr in PPAmP: Vaughan.

[15]Vaughan to Shelburne, 11, 29 Oct. 1782, LbkCs in PPAmP: Vaughan.

[16]Shelburne to Oswald, 23 Sept. 1782, RC in MiU-C: Shelburne 71.

BENJAMIN VAUGHAN TO SHELBURNE

[Paris], 9 September 1782

My Lord,

I am made abundantly happy by your lordship's kind letter.[1]

An affair has occurred which gives much alarm here. M. de Rayneval, Count de Vergennes' principal secretary, will probably soon be with your lordship, as we suspect on deep business. Will your lordship be kind enough to take no sort of measures till one of us comes over, or a courier arrives. The Marquis de Bouille[2] has left this place some days.

I have the honor to be, as ever, My Lord, Your Lordship's faithful and respectful servant,

BENJAN. VAUGHAN

In the Utmost haste.

Tr in PPAmP: Vaughan.

[1]Not located.

[2]Commander at Martinique (*JJ*, I, 741). As a result of the reported movement of 4,000 British troops from New York to the West Indies, Bouillé was ordered to return to Martinique to counter the British threat. Dull, *The French Navy and American Independence*, p. 308.

BENJAMIN VAUGHAN TO SHELBURNE

Paris, 11 September 1782

My Lord,

I mean to follow a few hours after the present courier (being called by private affairs), and hope to have the honor of being admitted to confer with your lordship.

In the meantime I think it necessary to inform your lordship, that the French court have given out that Mr. Rayneval's journey has for its object the bringing your lordship to some immediate decision; that they are dissatisfied with late transactions at particular coasts, and are determined not to be made *dupes to settle negotiations themselves.* Other objects for this journey are suspected. Some think an underhand bargain is intended to be proposed in favor of Spain, in which Britain is to be made to assist, by ceding some of her rights to Spain: but I cannot think England will hazard a measure which will be followed by the most unhappy circumstances. Others think that a fund of intelligence is meant to be established in London; and particularly that *the disposition of the North American troops* is meant to be an object of enquiry of the first consequence; which I myself think not improbable, as they have not been able to learn the fact here with any precision.

Be these things as they may, I have to suggest to your lordship on the footing of ancient indulgence and present danger, that this is a crisis of the first consequence, and that to procure delay is of the utmost moment in treating with M. Rayneval. If France could have favorable hopes for a moment she would be contented to wait perhaps your lordship's pleasure *in referring your answer to the medium of Mr. Fitzherbert;* but I dread her thinking she has nothing to hope but from war; for in this case M. de Vergennes (it is probable) would state conditions impossible to be received in order to break up all negotiations instantly, *before* America can adjust her pretentions. Perhaps your lordship is not yet informed of a private article, which forbids America to *treat* without the consent of France. We all know the public article about the *conclusion* of a treaty, but this relates to the very act of treating.

At the same time, my lord, that I speak of smoothness and delay to France, I must beg permission to suggest the most *instantaneous* despatch for the parties in America. My Lord, does your lordship consider the critical situation of the commissioners here after the precedents (of which Mr. Jay sends a catalogue by this courier) and the orders, of congress?[1] History, private honor, and even *life,* are perhaps all in question for the consideration of these commissioners upon this occasion. Under this commission I see *they will not act.* But I believe, if your lordship instantly endeavored to procure an *equivocal* commission, which made no specific recital of the act of parliament and called the colonies the "territories" of New Hampshire and so on, and the people here "commissioners on the part of the representatives of the people and inhabitants of the said territories"; and if at the same time the commission was equivocal, the instructions were definite and explicit for acknowledging these commissioners for acting on the part of the "United States of America"; I say, my lord, I think I have solid grounds for knowing that if this etiquette were thus settled, the formal deed of independence might with pleasure be reserved for the court of England to satisfy its own mind with, in the *course* of the treaty. But America *must have a character,* to use the words of Mr. Adams; and in America the British officers have allowed it.

My lord, I beg pardon for this freedom, but without it I cannot ease my conscience. If this moment is rudely managed, or slightly passed over, I conceive peace in *consequence* takes flight, and that America will be hurried back into war, at a moment when they have so ripened things that "three hours" would make you friends again.

The Marquis de la Fayette has given me the following short sketch of the war on the part of France. In the East Indies, a superior navy, some troops, and friendly country powers, *nothing* to lose and every thing to gain; in the West Indies, a great naval action lost, but no island conquered from them, and yet islands won by France when navies are only equal; at Gibraltar, a seige soon to finish in one shape or other (no matter which) and forces then *set free* to conquer elsewhere; allies, superior in money, troops, and navy; and England, in its best state, with revenue only just sufficient after a peace to pay the interest of its debts (which he intimated in private life could never be called *wealth.*) I answered him as well as I could, and pretty well for the moment.

I put these things on paper for your lordship to weigh. In my opinion the crisis was never more thoroughly ripe for the use of good sense on one side, or for ruin on the other.

I have settled a train for Lady Shelburne's business, whom I am proud and eager to be favored in attempting to serve.

I have the honor to be, as ever, My Lord, Your Lordship's faithful and respectful servant,

BENJN. VAUGHAN

P.S. I beg to mention to your lordship that some caution must be used in talking to M. Rayneval about what is doing here; as I am disposed to think this court has by some means contrived to obtain a knowledge of the instructions and part of the correspondence that has taken place.

Tr in PPAmP: Vaughan.

[1]Proceedings of Congress included in Oswald to Townshend, 10 Sept. 1782, below.

Benjamin Vaughan to James Monroe[1]

Basle, 18 September 1795

My dear sir,

Mr. De Witt, the Dutch minister here, gave me your favor of the 8th inst.[1] late last night, and you perceive that I lose no time in answering it.

You desire me to send you "a free exposition of the views of the Marquess of Lansdown, with his propositions, during the negotiation for the *American* peace; and of the grounds and motives of the American negotiators for suspecting the liberality of the French court, with regard to your boundaries, fisheries, etc.; and you seem to think the suspicions of the latter excited by the address of the English negotiators, rather than by well founded causes given by the French court". I shall reply explicitly <and directly>.

First, the views of Lord Lansdown were to render the two countries one and the same, as to commerce and intercourse, if not as to alliance; to remove all direct cause of war to arise from the ill-will of America, and all indirect cause to arise from the intrigues of France, and thus to diminish the causes of war even with France; and by these several means to pave the way for a more liberal system of politics in Europe, and consequently for the improvement of humanity. His steps for accomplishing this were, to remove, by the treaty of *peace,* all objects of jealousy from the mind of America, and to leave no prospect of gaining anything by war; that is, to leave no ground either for *fears* or *hopes,* which could disturb the tranquillity of the two countries; and then to follow the treaty of peace by a generous treaty of commerce. Next, to appoint a person to negotiate with America, who had corresponding views. The first facts are manifest on the face of the preliminary treaty of peace; and <from> in the bill respecting the American commercial intercourse, brought into the house of commons. The second fact appeared in the nomination of Mr. Oswald, as negotiator, who answered the description required; and for whom, had his character been different, I alone am answerable; since he was appointed upon my recommendation, as capable of fulfilling the wishes which I was told were to preside in the negotiation. Lastly, still farther to do justice to Lord Lansdown, though perhaps to pay little compliment to any thing besides the strength of his personal attachments, I must add, that my appearance was judged eligible at Paris; in order that the long and close acquaintance with which he had honored me, might enable me to assure Dr. Franklin and Mr. Laurens, with whom I was connected, and thence the other gentlemen, that <the views of> his views were liberal and sincere. So much for the first point.

What remains of your queries may all be comprised under a second head; since I can shew, that the American negotiators were *well authorized* to suppose, that France, on the subjects in question, took part with England. The evidence arose from the manner in which Count Vergennes recommended moderation to the American negotiators, respecting their demands on the head of boundaries, fisheries, and refugees. Perhaps the secret desire of M. Vergennes at this time, that Gibraltar should remain with the English, to perpetuate the attachment of Spain to France, seemed a case in point to the American negotiators. But be this as it may, they were intitled to suspect that their cause was intended to be sacrificed; not only because a jealousy of England in America, seemed held synonimous to a connection with France; but because the fewer concessions were bestowed by England upon *America,* the more might be spared to <England> *France.*

Mr. Jay, observing all this, desired me to go to London to endeavour to seek a remedy. When I arrived, I thought I saw reason to compliment Mr. Jay's sagacity. Lord Lansdown however rendered all suspicion superfluous, by declaring that he thought no policy rational, but that of a permanent and affectionate peace, instead of a truce. I therefore returned joyfully to Paris. During this treaty, no one in the British cabinet, unless Mr. Pitt, comprehended, and perhaps even did not fully embrace, this policy in all its extent; so that new security was taken against the liberality of Mr. Oswald, as it was necessary to conclude the treaty before the meeting of parliament, which was prepared to expect it. Mr. Fitzherbert (now Lord St. Helens) who was at Paris negotiating with France, and Mr. Strachey, from London, were made his coadjutors; but his good sense was allowed to take the lead, and the preliminaries with America were signed.

Such is the beginning and conclusion of this history. No intrigues on the part of England were known to Mr. Oswald or myself, and therefore I presume that none were practiced. The system of Lord Lansdown did not require them; and not only his temper disdained them; but considering the confidence which prevailed between [him] and Count Vergennes through Mr. de Rayneval, he would have esteemed such dishonorable; and if he had even betrayed a confidence which had been reposed in him, it would imply that the project of Count Vergennes had previously *existed.*

Independent of the above evidence, I may refer you to that of Mr. Genet;[2] who, after perusing the papers of the preceding French government, drew up for himself (as I have been <well> assured) the instructions which he carried to America as minister; and in those instructions, as published in the Moniteur, you will find many traces of the above particulars; which these instructions very severely reprobate. If I mistake not, the papers of Dr. Franklin contain full confirmation of the fact, though from delicacy to the old government of France, it may never perhaps be made public.

Had Lord Lansdown possessed sufficient power, the preliminary articles would have been materially enlarged, especially in one most essential particular; and the commercial treaty would not have been left for the present day. The systems of this statesman go to the abolition of wars, the promotion of agriculture, the unlimited freedom of trade, and the just freedom of man. He is in short against governing too much, and for reconciling the happiness of nations with that of their rulers. He is the first person in England who has ventured to espouse these principles in office and in parliament, and the experiment cost him his place, without his repining; and I am confident that he will accept of no public situation where he cannot more or less pursue them. If his character has been mistaken, you see the source of the mistake in the subsequent conduct of a part of the Rockinghams; for as they never could enter into his principles in domestic or foreign politics, it was natural that they should draw all their partizans to adopt their prejudices against him. His principles were too grand for them to comprehend, and therefore it was natural for them not to give him credit for sincerity in maintaining them. But, as time had proved *their* politics, it has also proved *his;* and if he has not rendered his own still more manifest, it is owing to the conduct and persuasion of timid friends; for his <own> courage and disinterestedness make him, as to his own person, careless of the issue.

It is hence that I have regretted, that his proceedings have been so ill understood and requited in America; and that the Americans have enjoyed advantages which they have not referred to their proper author. The truth is, that Lord Lansdown so compleatly removed by the peace all cause of quarrel; that it is forgotten that there was once a danger of such quarrel without it. His system, it was, which instantly calmed a struggle of near twenty years; and produced such a favorable impulse, that notwithstanding it may be queried, according to Mr. Jefferson, whether in the ten years which next followed, the British ministry had at any one time given way to America; yet every thing remained appeased, till disputes were reproduced by the present war.

True it is, that when Lord Lansdown was suddenly questioned in the house of Lords, he declared that the American preliminaries would have been null and of no effect, had the peace not followed with France. But (to avoid other explanations and to speak frankly) what does this prove, but that he thought the Americans still bound by their engagements with France, had the treaty failed? It is no argument that he designed to take advantage of America, had America been <insulted> deserted by France in consequence; for as his persuasion is, that nature must always be consulted, force being an abominable instrument of government, in such case he would probably have increased his confidence towards America, because the generosity would have been doubly valued. Any other interpretation than this, would reflect upon the feelings or judgment of him who adopted it.

When we see the tranquillity and satisfaction with which Lord Lansdown becomes a private life, after having twice been minister; when we find that he has never varied either in place, or out of place, respecting the necessity of a liberal conduct towards America; when he has had the good faith to declare in public debate, "that the people have rights, but that kings and princes have none"; it is needless to ask for private evidence of his sincerity towards America. Near twenty years, however, of confidential acquaintance, with which I have been honored by him, authorize me to say, that he has never deviated from his first opinions in favor of America; yet, without violating his duties to the country which he inhabits, because he conceives that both ought to stand upon a common basis, This assertion, instead of being weakened, will be fortified, when I add, that he does not confine his system to America; since he desires to see all nations viewing each other as brothers; and, in the necessity of separate governments perceives <sees> no reason why those separate governments should become enemies. On the contrary, he thinks, that as men are happy under their domestic governments, in proportion to their *union;* it is the principle of union, and not of separation, which ought to form the policy <of> between different nations. Thus, my dear sir, you perceive that Lord Lansdown in his conduct with America has pursued not only the true policy of an Englishman, but the liberality of modern philosophers.

In like manner, when he was at one time opposed to the grant of independence to America, it was not because he sought the subjugation of America; or even altogether because he wished to reserve the cession of independence, to count for something in a treaty of peace; but because he would not throw away the chance of an affectionate reunion with America, by a wise negotiation. In proof of this I must add, that when the American negotiators resolved not to treat in form with England, without a previous declaration of independence; and when Mr. Jay had, in consequence, prevailed upon me to make a preceding journey to London, to endeavor to remove this preliminary difficulty; I found nothing more necessary in addition to my <previous> former correspondence, than to state in person, that without it, the negotiation was at an end; when the affair soon became arranged, I returned again to Paris in a few days, with the courier in my chaise, carrying the act of independence under the great seal of England; no delay occurring <but> beyond what was necessary to procure the concurrence of the Lord Chancellor Thurlow, then at a distance in the country, and who, to his honor, acceeded without hesitation.

I may make slight mistakes in these narratives, being without a single paper or friend to aid my memory in my present situation; but the essence of everything asserted, is correct; and it is certainly impartial, as my political connections with Lord Lansdown have wholly ceased <in consequence of my family> and Mrs. Vaughan and myself have adopted the plan of settling in America which is rendered so natural to us by inclination, and numerous family, property, and my descent from an American mother, who is herself descended from some of the first settlers in America.

Before I conclude, permit me to say a word of Mr. Oswald. He was born, as I have understood in the Orkney islands; and came to the south in company with Sir Robert Strange, the celebrated engraver, in order to seek his fortune. He succeeded in acquiring one which was immense, though with a clear character; and his wealth, his qualities, and his country, had acquired him many friends. He knew America from having traded with and visited it; and he knew the operations of an army, from having been actively attached to that of Prince Ferdinand; and he therefore saw how impossible it was to render any connection with America beneficial, which was founded in force. He not only thought for himself; but was accustomed to transactions upon a large scale and of a novel nature, which both call for original ideas, and lend the experience which in time is to correct them. If he wanted the finish of a philosopher, he possessed, however, the strength and simplicity of conception, the candor, and the habits of meditation, which attach to that character; and as he was fond of retirement, even in the midst of a great city, he was a great reader. Happily, some of his friends in Scotland had written wisely upon general politics; and though he was prior to them perhaps in many of his first notions upon these subjects, yet he must naturally have felt courage from finding himself suported in them by literary men of note.

The modesty of Mr. Oswald and his real ignorance of some of the small things of the world, made him sometimes appear ignorant of some of the greater things; and especially in cases where he thought that silence was wisdom: But these qualities sometimes made others dupes to him without making him the dupe to others. He had also, not only calm manners, which enabled him to listen to everybody; but although by no means deficient in sensibility, he had great patience. The last was an important qualification in the negotiation; since every new conference produced a new claim; which was rendered the more critical, as it was commonly founded upon general principles, and supported by bold language and angry documents. It was therefore not only necessary for him to hear many things without replying to them; but that in his official correspondence he should suppress much, which would have offended either his king or some of the ministry. Happily, if he was cool, he was also generous; and though his fortune was partly procured by economy and firmness, his temper, where it was proper, was liberal and yielding. Happily also, he was by no means insensible to the ambition of concluding a treaty, which was big with results of the first magnitude, of which few were concealed from him. At the same time, he was so little given to jealousy, that although I never communicated any of my correspondence to him, and kept him wholly ignorant of the share which I happened to have in his appointment, he never discovered any umbrage towards me, notwithstanding his age was considerably more than the double of mine; but on the contrary, he always shewed me great personal confidence and affection.

Such is a part of the character of Mr. Oswald. It was necessary to have a negotiator acquainted with mercantile and military affairs; yet few of the English merchants had seen at once America and an army; and most of them have their business, and consequently their knowledge, confined to one particular object. It was requisite to have a person versed in the world; and yet devoid of the pride of aristocracy, without being suspected of democracy. It was proper to have a man old in experience, yet with a versatility of mind and temper, capable of entering into new affairs. It was indispensable to excite confidence; and Mr. Oswald was the most intimate and respected friend which Mr. Laurens had in the world. Judge then, my dear sir, how often I have felicitated myself, in having been the accidental means of so fortunate a choice in so great a concern, which has led to so many subsequent events; and that Lord Lansdown had enough personal acquaintance with Mr. Oswald to render him sensible of the truth of what I urged in his behalf.

I have the honor to be, with great regard and respect Dear sir, Your faithful and sincere humble servant.

BENJN. VAUGHAN

Tr in DLC: Monroe. Endorsed: ". . . To James Monroe, etc., etc."

[1]Not located in the Vaughan papers at PPAmP nor in the Monroe papers at DLC.

[2]James Monroe (1758–1831), at that time minister to France, failed to defend the Jay Treaty of 1794, and was recalled in 1796. See his *A View of the Conduct of the Executive, in the Foreign Affairs of the United States as connected with the Mission of the French Republic, During the Years 1794, 5, and 6* (Philadelphia, 1797).

[3]For Edmond Genêt, see editorial note below, "Jay's Diary of the Peacemaking."

Jay Proposes Altering Oswald's Commission

9 September 1782

Sympathetic with JJ's insistence on a prior acknowledgment of independence by the British,[1] Oswald met resistance from his superiors across the Channel, who still insisted that the Americans agree to accept independence as the first article of the treaty,[2] but not prior to the treaty or separately.[3] Townshend pointed out that acknowledging independence by a separate article, separately ratified, amounted to "a Treaty for the purpose of Independence alone," transcending the explicit power the Enabling Act conferred on Oswald.[4]

Duly impressed by Oswald's report of American intransigence on the point of independence, the British Cabinet reached what it hoped would be an acceptable compromise. Oswald was instructed to cede independence as the first article of a treaty and to offer to conclude a treaty immediately on the basis of this article and the four "necessary" articles that Franklin had proposed to Oswald on 10 July. While unwilling to yield on the point of prior acknowledgment, the British now evidenced a willingness to accept Franklin's four "necessary" points as the basis for peace.[5]

On 3 September Oswald received his instructions from Townshend, and during the week that followed sought to persuade the American Commissioners to accept the new counter-proposals. First, he informed Franklin that he had been authorized to declare American independence in the first article of the treaty. The old Doctor, incapacitated by gout and kidney stones since the last week of August, could only "hope Mr. Jay will agree to do this,"[6] as he confided to Rayneval. Then Oswald tackled an unpersuaded JJ, who reiterated his insistence on prior acknowledgment. Once again Oswald rendered a full account of his conversations with the American negotiators in his communication of 10 September, below.

JJ's growing suspicions of French designs made Oswald's task easier. Convinced that Vergennes was undermining his efforts to win prior recognition of American independence, JJ took it upon himself to set forth to Oswald what he believed "to be the natural policy of this court [France] on the subject, and to show him that it was the interest of Britain to render us as independent on

France as we were resolved to be on her." Oswald duly reported what JJ considered to be the best solution, Franklin consenting, and that would be "in place of an express and previous acknowledgment of Independence, to accept of a constructive Denomination of Character, to be introduced in the preamble of the Treaty, by only describing their Constituents as the Thirteen United States of America."

Picking up JJ's hint, Oswald requested him to draft the proposed alteration in the commission. The draft appears below under the date of 9 September, followed the next day by a draft of a proposed letter to Oswald, who persuaded JJ to turn it over to him. Oswald reported to his superiors Franklin's reservations as to procedure, and JJ later admitted to Livingston that the Doctor had reminded him of their obligations to consult the French court.[7] Perhaps, as Oswald's account indicates, JJ might have held back in deference to Franklin, but Oswald seemed too insistent to be denied.

On reflection JJ decided to give Oswald the draft letter with the understanding that he would make "only such use of it, as it should not appear in any publick way, and so as it should not be heard of either here or elsewhere, not even by some of his own Friends." So Oswald reported in his letters to Shelburne of 10 and 11 September below, enclosing JJ's draft of the altered commission along with his draft letter, and urging his superiors to revise his commission in accordance with JJ's proposal. Oswald's dispatches of the 10th and 11th were received on 14 September, and on the 20th Townshend informed the commissioner: "A meeting of the King's Confidential Servants was held as soon as possible to consider the contents of them, and it was at once agreed to make the Alteration in the Commission proposed to you by Mr. Jay. I trust that the readiness, with which this Proposal was accepted, will be considered as an ample testimony of the openness and sincerity with which the Government of this Country is Inspired to treat with the Americans."[8] It need also be pointed out that, once the negotiations with the British were stepped up, JJ discontinued his talks with Aranda, turning down Vergennes' proposal that he treat with the Spaniard without exchanging powers. *AP*, III, (3 Nov. 1782).

[1]See above, JJ: Draft of a Patent, [15 Aug. 1782]. JJ and John Adams were in agreement on this point of prior acknowledgment. Adams to JJ, 13 Aug. 1782, ALS in RAWC; *RDC*, V, 660–61, JJ to Adams, 1 Sept. 1782, ALS in MHi: Adams, IV, 358; Dft in JP; *HPJ*, II, 335; *Peacemakers*, p. 303.

[2]Oswald to Townshend, 17, 18 Aug. 1782, ALS in FO 27/2; LbkCs in FO 97/157 and in MiU-C: Shelburne 70; C in FO 95/511. See also *Peacemakers*, pp. 317–18.

[3]Oswald to Shelburne, 18 Aug. 1782, ALS in MiU-C: Shelburne 71.

[4]Townshend to Oswald, 1 Sept. 1782, Dft and partial Dft in FO 95/511; LbkCs in MiU-C: Shelburne 70; FO 27/2, and 97/157; E in CSmH; LbkC in PCC 110, II and in NHi: Jay. Enclosure: proceedings of Congress extracted from journals in possession of the American Commissioners relating to negotiations with Great Britain, 17 July 1776–18 July 1778, in FO 97/157.

[5]Minute of Cabinet, 29 Aug. 1782 (in Nepean's hand), MiU-C: Sydney I; Fortescue, ed., *Corr. of George III*, VI, 118 (in Townshend's hand); Townshend to Oswald, 1 Sept. 1782.

[6]See Franklin to Rayneval, 4 Sept. 1782, ALS in CP E 22: 186, *BFS,* VIII, 590–91; also Franklin to Oswald, 8 Sept. 1782, regarding clarification of art. 4 of the latter's instructions relating to the concession of independence. LbkC in FO 97/157; *BFS,* VIII, 591.

[7]JJ wrote Livingston a few days later that he believed France was trying to delay independence, but that Franklin disagreed. JJ to Livingston, 18 Sept. 1782, LbkCs in CSmH and in PCC 110, II; *RDC,* V, 740; *HPJ,* II, 345–47.

[8]Townshend to Oswald, 20 Sept. 1782, Dft in FO 95/511; Cs in *ibid.* 27/2 and 97/157, and in MiU-C: Shelburne 70. Oswald to Townshend, 11 Sept. 1782, is mentioned in the editorial note below, "First Draft Treaty," n. 4.

Jay: Draft of a Proposed Alteration in Oswald's Commission

[9 September 1782]

A commission (in the usual Form) to Richard Oswald Esquire to treat of Peace or Truce with Commissioners or[1] Persons vested with equal Powers by and on the Part of the thirteen United States of America, would remove the Objections to which his present Commission is liable, and thereby render it <justifiable> proper[2] for the American Commissioners to proceed to treat with him on the Subject of Preliminaries.

Dft in FO 27/2, LbkC in FO 97/57 (enclosed in Oswald's dispatch to Townshend of 10 Sept. 1782, below). Endorsed by Oswald: "... proposed by Mr. Jay, to be made in His Majestys Commission, for treating with the Commissioners of the Colonies, received about 8 days ago, 10th September 1782." The "8 days" refer to the receipt of the sealed commission, not to the date of the receipt of JJ's Dft. LbkC as dispatched by Oswald in FO 95/511 and in MiU-C: Shelburne 70; a slightly variant version, as enclosed by JJ to Livingston, 17 Nov. 1782, cited in JJ to Aranda, 25 June 1782, above. It is from this last version that Wharton reprinted the "alteration" in *RDC,* VI, 19.

[1]"Commissioners or" was added by Oswald. At the bottom of the page on which JJ drafted this "alteration" Oswald added the following note: "11th Augt. [error for Sept.]: In case the proposed Alteration in the Commission should be agreed on, I humbly Submit whether it will not be proper in the description of the American parties to be treated with, to leave out a great part or all that variety of Denominations of Colonies, Bodies Corporate, Persons etc. as they now Stand in the Commission, and to confine the Description to just what is necessary as in the Sketch abovementioned, or with Such farther addition only as may not give offence to the Commissioners.

"I have not Said any thing to Mr. Jay respecting the words of the above Memorandum, having forgot to do so, But I think the words—or *Commissioners*—would stand properly after or before the word *Persons* in the above Minute." Presumably Oswald informed JJ of his proposed alteration, since, in the version of the "sketch" which JJ sent to Secretary Livingston on 17 November (cited above in JJ to Aranda, 25 June 1782, n. 2), the phrase reads: "with commissioners, vested with," etc.

[2]The substitution of "proper" for "justifiable" was made by JJ.

To Richard Oswald

[10 September 1782]

Sir,

It is with Regret that we find ourselves obliged by our Duty to our Country to object to entering with you into negociations for Peace on the plan proposed. One Nation can treat with another Nation only on Terms of Equality, and it cannot be expected that we should be the first and only Servants of Congress who would admit Doubts of their Independence.

The Tenor of your Commission affords Matter for a Variety of Objections which your good Sense will save us the necessity[1] of inumerating. The Journals of Congress[2] present to you unequivocal and uniform Evidence of the Sentiments and Resolutions of Congress on the Subject, and their positive Instructions to us speake the same Language.

The Manner of removing these obstacles is obvious, and in our opinion no less consistent with the Dignity than the Interest of Great Britain. If the Parliament meant to enable the King to conclude a Peace with us on Terms of Independence, they necessarily meant to enable him to do it in a Manner compatible with his Dignity, and consequently that he should previously regard us in a point of View that would render it proper for him to negociate with us. What the point of view is, you need not be informed.

We also take the Liberty of submitting to your Consideration how far his Majesty's now declining to take this step, would comport with the assurances lately given on that Subject; and whether Hesitation and Delay would not tend to lessen the Confidence which those assurances were calculated to inspire.

As to referring an acknowledgment of our Independence to the first article of a Treaty, permit us to remark, that this implies that we are not to be considered in that Light until after the Conclusion of <it> the Treaty, and our <agreeing to it> acquiescing, would be to admit the Propriety of our being considered in another Light During that Interval. Had this Circumstance been attended to, we presume that the Court of Great Britain would not have pressed a Measure which certainly is not Delicate, and which cannot be reconciled with the recognized Ideas of national Honor.

You may rest assured Sir of our Disposition to peace on reasonable Terms, and of our Readiness to enter Seriously into Negociations for it, as soon as we shall have an opportunity of doing it in the only Manner in which it is possible for one Nation to treat with another, viz. on an equal footing. Had your Commission been in *the usual form,*[2] we might have proceeded, and as we can percieve no legal or other objection to this, or some other such like Expedient, it is to be wished that his Majesty will not permit an Obstacle so very unimportant to Great Britain, but so essential and insuperable with Respect to us, to delay the Reestablishment of peace, especially as in Case the Business could be but once begun, the Confidence we <repose> have in your Candor and Integrity would probably render the settling all our articles, only the work of a few Hours.

Dft in MiU-C: Shelburne 71. Enclosure in Oswald to Shelburne, 11 Sept. 1782, below. Endorsed in Oswald's hand: ". . . Scroll of a Letter proposed to be wrote by Mr. Jay to Mr. Oswald, Which with some difficulty I got out of his hands, after it had been settled with his Friend, that it was not proper to go before any public Board, etc. 10 Sept. 1782." Added endorsement by a clerk: ". . . In Mr. Oswald's of 11th Septr. 1782." LbkCs CSmH and PCC 110, II, 168–70; C in JJ to Livingston, 17 Nov. 1782, cited in JJ to Aranda, 25 June 1782, above; *HPJ,* II, 383–84; *RDC,* VI, 19–20. Variations between the original Dft and the version sent to Livingston are indicated in notes below.

[1]"Pain" in *RDC* and LbkC versions.

[2]Cited in source note of following letter.

[3]In the LbkCs and printed versions this phrase reads: "Had you been commissioned in the usual manner."

Richard Oswald to Thomas Townshend

Paris, 10 September 1782

Sir,

By the Courier Ranspach, who arrived here on the 3rd, I had the honour of your Letter of the 1st instant.[1] Upon receipt of it, I went out to Doctor Franklin. He asked me whether I had any directions relative to the points upon which the last Courier had been dispatched to England regarding a previous Declaration of their Independence before a commencement of Treaty. I told him I had got Instructions on that head, which although they empowered me only to make such Declaration as in the first article of the Treaty, yet I hoped upon a due Consideration of the matter, they would appear to be fully satisfying. He said, if there was no particular objection, he would wish to have a copy of that Instruction. I told him it should be sent to him. He was ill at the time; and as he could not come to Town, he gave me a Letter to Mr. Jay, desiring him to come out to him in the Evening.

I called on that Gentleman, When, informing him of the manner in which I was authorized to treat, he said they could not proceed unless their Independence was previously so acknowledged, as to be entirely different and unconnected with Treaty. In the course of this Conversation, and the day thereafter, a good deal was said of the Same nature with what had passed on former occasions relative to this Subject, as advised in my Letters of last month.

Two days ago, Doctor Franklin sent to me, desiring a Copy of the Instruction which I had promised, as abovementioned. I copied out the first part of your Letter of the 1st Instant, leaving out some immaterial words, and sent it inclosed in a Letter from myself. Of both of which papers there is a Duplicate under this cover.

Since then, I have seen Mr. Jay frequently, and have used every Argument in my power to get him over his Objections to Treating, without a separate and absolute acknowledgement of Independence. And for that purpose, I found it necessary (although unwillingly), yet as of my own private opinion, to tell him, that there might be a doubt whether the Powers in the Act of Parliament went so far, as to allow of making that Grant, otherways than as in the course of a Treaty for Peace; which, as you are pleased to observe, was the Sole object of the Act.

I said moreover, That if they persisted in this Demand, there would be nothing done untill the meeting of Parliament, and perhaps for some considerable time thereafter, That certain Articles had been already agreed upon; and if we went on and Settled the Treaty on that footing, with Independence Standing as the First Article of it, we might give opportunity to the foreign Treaties to be going on at the Same time; So as, for a Conclusion of general Peace there might be nothing wanting, at the meeting of Parliament but a Confirmation of the Said first Article, in case it should be then thought necessary; which I imagine would be the case.

In answer to this, Mr. Jay said, there could be no judgement formed as to when the foreign Treaties would end, and that untill that with France was concluded, they of the Colonies would not give us either Peace or Truce. Nor would they presume, so much as to give an Opinion of the Demands of France, whatever they might be; Since untill their Independence was acknowledged, absolutely and unconnected with Treaty, they were as no body and as no People. And France could tell them so, if it were to pretend to interfere; having failed in acquiring that Character, for which they had jointly contended and therefore they must go on with France, untill England gave them satisfaction on the point in question. That to this they were bound by

Treaty; which their Constituents were determined honestly and faithfully to fulfill.

That being the case, it could not be expected that they, as Servants, could take upon them to dispense with the said acknowledgement.

That by looking over the Sundry Resolves of the Congress, I might see that that Assembly did not mean to seek for their Character in an Article of any Treaty. And for that purpose, Mr. Jay recommended to me the perusal of Sundry parts of their proceedings, as they stood in the Journals of the Congress, which he would mark out for me; And if I would extract, and send them to England they would serve, at least as an Excuse, for them as Commissioners, in thinking themselves bound to abide by their demand. Mr. Jay accordingly gave me Four Volumes of their Journals, with Sundry Passages marked out as above. Mr. Whiteford has been so good to copy them out and they are inclosed.

Mr. Jay was kind enough also to read to me an Article of their Instructions to the same purpose and likeways contain paragraphs to two late Letters from his Colleague, Mr. John Adams in Holland, expressly declaring, that they ought not to proceed in a Treaty with England, untill their Independence is acknowledged.

In the course of these Conversations it may be Supposed this Gentleman took frequent Opportunities to refer to the Offer by Mr. Grenville, to acknowledge their Independence in the first instance. Which they always considered to be absolute, and unconnected in every shape with the process of a Treaty: and would not conceive the reason why that which we were willing to give them in May, should be refused in August. If it proceeded from there being less Confidence on our Side, on this occassion, the Change ought to make them still more cautious than usual on their part. Mr. Jay also insisted on that Offer of Mr. Grenville, as a proof, that the same thing being denied now, could not proceed from any Supposition of restraint in the Enabling Act.

To avoid being tedious, I forbear repeating a great many more things to the same purpose which passed in those Conversations with Mr. Jay.

Mr. Franklin being so much out of order, I would not think of disturbing him by frequent Visits to Passy and therefore continued taking proper Opportunities of talking to Mr. Jay; and the more readily that by any Judgement that I would form on his real Intentions, I would not possibly doubt of their pointing at a Speedy conclusion of the War; and also leaning as favourably to the side of England, as might be consistent with the duties of the Trust he has undertaken.

To convince me that nothing less than this stood in the way of agreeing to my requests of accomodating this Difficulty in some shape or other, he told me at last that if Doctor Franklin would consent he was willing, in place of an express previous acknowledgement of Independence, to accept of a constructive Denomination of Character, to be introduced in the preamble of the Treaty, by only describing their Constituents as the Thirteen United States of America. Upon my appearing to listen to this, and to Consent to the Substitution, He said, "but you have no authority in your Commission to Treat with us under that denomination. For the Sundry Descriptions of the Parties to be treated with, as they stand in that Commission, will not bear such application to the Character we are directed to claim and abide by, as to Support and authenticate any Act of your Subscription to that purpose, and particularly to the Subscription now proposed. There are such a variety of Denominations in that Commission, that it may be applied to the People you see walking the Streets, as well as to us."

When, in reply, I imputed that variety to the official stile of such like Papers, Mr. Jay said it may be so, but they must not Vest a Question of that Importance upon any such explanation. And since they were willing to accept this, in place of an Express Declaration of Independence, the least they could expect was, that it should appear to be warranted by an Express Authority in the Commission.

I then askt if, instead of States, it would not do to say Provinces; Or States or Provinces. Mr. Jay said neither of these would answer.

I then begged the favour of him to give me in writing, some Sketch of the Alteration he would have to be made in the Commission. He readily did so, in a Minute which is inclosed; to be more largely explained, if necessary when the Commission comes to be made out. He also said that this New Commission must be under the Great Seal, as the other was.

Before I quitted this subject, I tried one other expedient for saving time, and avoiding the necessity of a New Commission; by reading to Mr. Jay the Second Article of my Instructions, which empowers me to treat with them, as commissioned by Constituents of any denomination whatever. And told him that although this Power meant only to apply to Character as assumed by them, and not to <any> an admission by me without exception; yet in the present described Character of States. I would not only admit their assuming that Appellation, in the preamble of the Treaty, but I would venture to repeat it, so as it should appear to be an acknowledgement on my part. In doing so I could not suppose any hazard of objection at home, considering what had passed on a former occasion as abovementioned; together with the said power in my Instructions. But Mr. Jay said they would admit of no Authority but what was explicitly conveyed to me by a Commission in the usual form. And therefor, to put an end to this difficulty, there was an absolute necessity of a new Commission.

He at the same time told me, That to satisfy His Majestys Ministers of the propriety of their conduct, as Persons under Trust, he had Sketched out a Letter to me, which I might send home if I pleased. He read the Scroll of it to me, and promised to write it out fair, and give it me before the departure of a Courier.

So the affair rested yesterday the 9th, when I received a Letter from Doctor Franklin desiring a Copy of the 4th article of my Instructions which I had shewn to Mr. Jay, as formerly advised. Inclosed there is a copy of the Doctor's Letter.[2]

Doubting as to the propriety of giving such things in writing, I thought it best to go out to the Doctor, carrying the Instructions along with me, to see whether a Reading of that article would satisfy him. But after reading it, as he still expressed a desire of having a Copy, I told him that although I had no orders for that purpose, yet at any hazard whatsoever, since he desired it, I would not Scruple to trust it in his hands. And then sat down, and wrote out a copy, and signed it, which after comparing it with the original he laid by, saying very kindly, that the only use he proposed to make of it, was, that, in case they took any liberties, for the sake of removing difficulties, not expressly specified in their Instructions, he might have this paper in his hands to shew, in justification of their Confidence or some words to that purpose; for I cant exactly quote them.

The Doctor then desired, I would tell Mr. Jay that he wished to see him in the Evening. He did go out that night and again this morning, no doubt with a view of agreeing upon an expedient for removing those obstacles to their proceeding, as hinted at in the Doctors Letter to me. At Noon, and since writing the above, Mr. Jay called, and told me that upon further consultation and consideration of the matter it was thought adviseable not to press upon His Majesty's Ministers those arguments which he proposed to make use of in the Letter he intended to write me (of which it was understood I might send home) as considering it somewhat more than indelicate for them to pretend to see more clearly than The King's Ministers might do, the expediency, if not the necessity, at this critical time, to decide with precision and dispatch, upon every measure, that can be reasonably taken, for extricating Great Britian from out of the present embarrassing Situation, in which her Affairs must continue to be involved, while there remains any hesitation in coming to an Agreement with the States of America.

I liked the Scroll of the Letter so much when it was read to me Yesterday, that I was Sorry it was withheld. I even pressed to be entrusted with it, in gratification of my own private wish that the Writer of it might receive from good Men, that share of Applause that is due to those who wish well to the peace of Mankind in general, and who seem not to be desirous of expunging altogether from their Breasts the Impressions which had been fixed there by those habits and natural feelings by which Individuals are tied in attachment to particular combinations of Society and Country. But I could not prevail, and was obliged to be contented with a Recommendation to Say what I thought proper in my own way.

Finding it so, There remained for me, only to ask a Single and final Question of Mr. Jay. Whether in this his last Conference with Dr. Franklin, this morning (for he was just then come in from him) it was Settled between them, that upon my receiving from His Majesty a new Commission, under the Great Seal, such as the last, with an alteration only as before mentioned, of my being empowered to Treat with them as Commissioners of the Thirteen United States of America, naming the said States by their several provincial distinctions, as usual, I said Whether in that case, they would be satisfied to go on with the Treaty, and without any other Declaration of Independence, than as standing as an Article of that Treaty.

Mr. Jay's Answer was, that with this they would be satisfied, and that immediately upon such Commission coming over, they would proceed in the Treaty. And more than that, Said, they would not be long about it; and perhaps would not be over hard upon Us in the Conditions.

Having stated those Conversations and other Circumstances as they actually passed to the best of my remembrance, it would not become me to go further by giving any Opinion as to the measures proper to be taken in consequence therof. Yet, Sir, I hope You will excuse me, and I think it my duty to say this much, that, by what I have been able to learn of the Sentiments of the American Commissioners, in case the Compromise now proposed (which with great difficulty they have been persuaded to agree to) is refused, there will be an end to all further Confidence and Communication with them, the Consequences of which I will not presume to touch upon, either as regarding American or Foreign Affairs. On the other hand, if the expedient of a

New Commission is adopted, I beg leave to Say that no time ought to be lost in dispatching it.

There being now four Couriers here, and as they may be wanted at home, it is thought proper that one of them, as extra, may go along with the Courier Lauzun who goes from Mr. Fitzherbert's Office.

I have the honour to be Sir, Your most obedient and most humble Servant,

RICHARD OSWALD

ALS in FO 27/2. Enclosures: JJ's Dft of the commission, above; boundaries agreed on 29 Aug. 1782; proceedings of Congress (17 July and 5 Sept. 1776; 22 Nov. 1777; 22 April, 6 and 17 June, and 18 July 1778); and Cs of Oswald to Franklin, 5 Sept. 1782 (LbkCs in DLC: Franklin, FO 97/157, and in MiU-C: Shelburne 70; *RDC*, V, 699), and Franklin to Oswald, 8 Sept. 1782, with extracts of Townshend to Oswald, 1 Sept. 1782. Hale, *Franklin in France*, II, 131–39.

[1]Townshend to Oswald, 1 Sept. 1782, Dft in FO 27/2, C in 97/157, Dft (2) in 95/511. LbkCs in MiU-C: Shelburne 70 and in DLC: Franklin. E in NHi: Jay, CSmH, and PCC 110, II. *RDC*, V, 681.

[2]Franklin to Oswald, 8 Sept. 1782, LbkCs in DLC: Franklin and in FO 97/157; *BFS*, VIII, 591; *RDC*, V, 712.

RICHARD OSWALD TO SHELBURNE

Paris, 11 September 1782

My Lord,

I had the honour of your Lordships two Letters of the 3d Instant[1] in Consequence of which I took an Opportunity of talking to Dr. Franklin on the Subject of one of them in a general way, and by what he said, I believe he is very much attatched to his old Friends, and wishes it may be thought So, and does not encourage misrepresentations to their prejudice. He put into my hands a Letter from one of his Correspondents, which it would appear he don't like, otherways he would not have given it to me. There is a Copy of it enclosed.

I have wrote Mr. Townshend by this Courier, that I have now Settled with the American Commissioners, that they will not insist on a previous and absolute Acknowledgement of their Independence, provided the Commission for Treating with them shall give them the Denomination of the Thirteen United States of America. And then they will be contented with their Independence Standing only as an Article of Treaty. With great difficulty they have yielded to this mode of Compromise. I hope His Majesty will grant it. If it is refused Mr.

Fitzherbert as well as me, may go home. And in my opinion it will not be an easy matter for any others to take up the same Clue for extricating the Nation out of its difficulties which I think is within our reach. Both the Commissioners, I really think, are well disposed, much better than I expected some time ago. Mr. Jay seems to be particularly anxious, that as they have agreed to go even beyond the limits of their Instructions. His Majesty's Ministers may not balk their good Intentions either by refusal or delay. To prevent this he Scrolled out a Letter to be directed to me, Shewing the necessity of our attention and compliance, with a view to my Sending it home. But upon consulting farther about it, he was advised by his Friend to drop it and would not give me the Letter. I have mentioned this in my Letter to day to Mr. Townshend. However I afterwards with much Intreaty I got him to give me the Scroll upon condition of my making only <a particular> Such use of it, as it should not appear in any publick way, and So as it Should not be heard of either here or elsewhere, not even by Some of his own Friends. I take the liberty to Send that Paper inclosed. When Mr. Townshend Sees it, to which I can have no objection, I dare say he will excuse my not Sending it to him, Since I was not certain but that in Such Case it must be laid for Inspection with other papers in the Course of the Negotiation. It is a clear proof of this Commissioner being particularly desirous of Smoothing the path of this awkward business. If the proposal abovementioned be agreed to by His Majesty, Which is only treating with them as States instead of Colonies, I should think your Lordship may have the pleasure of meeting Parliament with a Peace in hand. At least there would be a kind of certainty, as far as appearances to be relied on, To have So far Satisfied America, as that she will not only Control but Spur on the other parties. This would calm the Disturbances at home, by disappointing those who may wish to inflame them. I was once afraid that if Mr. Grenvilles proposition would not be regranted or repealed, that all the Treaties must wait to have the full Parliament to that grant for laying the first foundation of the Negotiations. Now all that is required is to say States instead of Colonies, and the whole Machine is put into Motion and will go its course. I will not allow myself to doubt there being any hesitation on the Subject. The only Inconvenience is that there must necessarily be a New Commission. If that is agreed on, I hope there will not be an hour left in despatching it.

By what I can understand, the French Court, of all things, wish the Colonies may not be Satisfied, but rather that they should go on Treating without any acknowledgement of Independence, and have actually told them they were Seeking for the effect without the cause, Since it would only with propriety arise out of the Treaty. And so wishing that they should continue unfixed and unsatisfied untill their affairs and those of their allies were satisfied, and there might be then no fear of Checks but rather help from the American Quarter. The Marquis de la Fayette is always going about the Commissioners, anxious to know how they are like to proceed, over which head one of those Gentleman has had Sundry applications, and he makes no Scruple to give me these hints.[2]

Mons. de Vergennes who keeps these Agents in motion, it is said is to send his Secretary Mons. Gerard etc. over to London upon some particular Negotiation it's thought in favour of Spain. That Court wishes to have the whole of the Country from W. Florida, of a certain width, quite up to Canada so as to have both Banks of the Missisippi clear. And would wish to have such Cession from England before a cession to the Colonies takes place. If that Gentleman goes over, there can be no difficulty in amusing him. The Spaniards have the French Title and would gladly compleat one to the whole of that District by patches from the English pretensions Which they could not hope for once we have agreed with the Colonies.

I am very happy that your Lordship has so good an aspect of increasing Strength to the present System. A quick successive Settlement with the Americans will give it fresh vigour.

I therefore hope your Lordship will bestow some attention to have that matter speedily carried forward. If it Succeeds, it is thought France will be moderate. The Commissioners say they will be so in all events. In any thing I have to do with those Gentlemen I could not wish to be on better terms. I beg your Lordships pardon for Scratching away in this loose manner, but the truth is I have just done with my Official Dispatch and the Courier's hour of appointment being at hand, I cannot detain him.

I have the honour to be with Sincere regard and esteem My Lord, Your Lordships most obedient humble Servant.

RICHARD OSWALD

ALS in MiU-C: Shelburne 71, enclosing JJ's Dft letter above. Hale, *Franklin in France,* II, 140–44.

[1]Shelburne to Oswald, 3 Sept. 1782, C in MiU-C: Shelburne 70.

[2]For Lafayette's liaison role in the peace negotiations, see editorial note below, "Lafayette, Jay's Self-Appointed 'Political Aide-de-Camp,' Takes on the Spaniards."

Commission of Richard Oswald

[London], 21 September 1782

George the third, by the Grace of God, of Great Britain, France and Ireland and so forth, Defender of the Faith, King To Our trusty and well beloved Richard Oswald of our City of London Esquire. Greeting, Whereas by Virtue of an Act passed in the last Session of Parliament, intituled, An Act to enable His Majesty to conclude a Peace or Truce with certain Colonies in North America therein mentioned it is recited, that it is essential to the Interest, Welfare and prosperity of Great Britain and the Colonies or Plantations of New Hampshire, Massachusets Bay, Rhode Island, Connecticut, New York, New Jersey, Pensylvania, the three lower Counties on Delaware, Maryland, Virginia, North Carolina, South Carolina and Georgia in North America, that Peace, Intercourse, Trade and Commerce should be restored between them.

Therefore, and for a full Manifestation of Our earnest wish and desire, and of that of Our Parliament, to put an End to the Calamities of War, it is enacted, that it should and might be lawful for Us to treat, consult of, agree and conclude with any Commissioner or Commissioners named, or to be named by the said Colonies or Plantations, or any of them respectively, or with any Body or Bodies, Corporate or Politick, or any Assembly or Assemblies, or Description of Men, or any Person or Persons whatsoever, a Peace or a Truce with the said Colonies or Plantations, or any of them, or any part or parts therof, any Law, Act or Acts of Parliament, Matter or Thing to the contrary in any wise notwithstanding.

Now know Ye, that We, reposing Special Trust in your Wisdom, Loyalty, diligence and Circumspection in the Management of the affairs to be hereby committed to Your Charge, have nominated and appointed, constituted and assigned, and by these Presents do nominate and appoint, constitute and assign You, the said Richard Oswald, to be Our Commissioner in that behalf, to Use and Exercise all and every the powers and Authorities hereby entrusted and Committed to You, the said Richard Oswald, and to do, perform and Execute all other Matters and Things hereby enjoined and committed to Your Care during Our Will and Pleasure, and no longer, according to the Tenor of these Our Letters Patent.

And it is Our Royal Will and Pleasure, and We, do hereby authorize, empower and require You, the said Richard Oswald, to treat, consult of, and conclude with any Commissioners or Persons vested with equal powers, by and on the part of the Thirteen United States of America, Vizt. New Hampshire, Massachusets Bay, Rhode Island, Connecticut, New York, New Jersey, Pensylvania, the three lower Counties on Delaware, Maryland, Virginia, North Carolina, South Carolina and Georgia in North America, a Peace or a Truce with the said thirteen United States, any law, Act or Acts of Parliament, Matter or Thing, to the contrary in any Wise notwithstanding.

And it is Our further Will and Pleasure, that every Regulation, provision, matter or Thing, which shall have been agreed upon between You, the said Richard Oswald, and such Commissioners or Persons as aforesaid with whom You shall have judged meet and sufficient to enter into such Agreement, shall be fully and distinctly set forth in Writing, and Authenticated by Your Hand and Seal, on one side, and by the Hands and Seals of such Commissioners or Persons on the other, and such Instrument so authenticated, shall be by You transmitted to Us through One of Our Principal Secretaries of State.

And it is Our Further Will and Pleasure, that You, the said Richard Oswald, shall promise and engage for Us, and in Our Royal Name and Word, that every Regulation, Provision, Matter or Thing, which may be agreed to and concluded by You, Our said Commissioner, shall be ratified and confirmed by Us, in the fullest Manner and Extent, and that We will not suffer them to be violated or counteracted, either in whole or in part by any Person whatsoever.

And We do hereby require and Command all Our Officers, Civil and Military and all other Our loving Subjects whatsoever, to be aiding and assisting unto You the said Richard Oswald in the Execution of this Our Commission, and of the powers and Authorities herein contained, Provided always and We do hereby declare and Ordain that the several Offices, powers and Authorities hereby granted, shall cease, determine and become utterly Null and Void on the First day of July, which shall be in the Year of Our Lord, One thousand seven hundred and eighty three, although We shall not otherwise, in the mean time have revoked and determined the same.

And Whereas in and by our Commission and Letters Patent, under Our Great Seal of Great Britain, bearing date the seventh day of August last, We nominated and appointed, constituted and assigned you, the said Richard Oswald, to be Our Commissioner to treat, consult of, agree and conclude with any Commissioner or Commissioners named or to be named by certain Colonies or Plantations in America therein specified a Peace or a Truce with the said Colonies or Plantations.

Now know ye, that we have revoked and determined, and by these presents do revoke and determine Our said Commission and Letters Patent, and all and every Power Article and Thing therein contained. In witness whereof We have caused these our Letters to be made patent.

Witness our Self at Westminster, the twenty first day September, in the twenty second Year of our Reign.

By the King himself

YORKE

Paris 1st October 1782. I certify that the adjoining is a true Copy of the Commission of which it purports to be a Copy and which has been shewn to Mr. Franklin and Mr. Jay.

(signed) RICHARD OSWALD
the Commissioner therein named

C in CP EU 22: 248–52 (enclosed in Franklin to Rayneval, 13 Oct. 1782, ALS in *ibid.*, p. 367). French trans. in *ibid.*; Cs in PCC 106 and in MiU-C: Hartley III. Townshend's authorization of this commission addressed to the Attorney/or Solicitor General is dated 19 Sept. 1782, Cs in FO 27/2, 95/511 and 97/157. On its receipt from Townshend, Oswald enclosed a copy of this commission to Franklin on 24 Sept. 1782. *RDC,* V, 748–50, 762; *SDC,* IV, 21.

To Aranda

Paris, 10 September 1782

Sir,

Agreable to your Excellency's *Request*[1] I have now the Honor of repeating in writing, that I am not authorized by Congress to make any Cessions of any Countries belonging to the United States, and that I can do nothing more respecting the Line <and Propositions proposed> mentioned by your Excellency than to <request> wait for, and to follow such Instructions as Congress on recieving that Information may think <expedient> proper to give me on the subject.

Permit me nevertheless to remind your Excellency that I have full Power "to confer, treat, agree, and conclude with the Embassador or plenipotentiary of his Catholic Majesty, vested with equal powers; of and concerning a Treaty of Amity and Commerce and of Alliance,"[2] on principles of Equality Reciprocity and mutual Advantage.

I can only regret <the Reasons> that my <Propositions> overtures to his Excellency the Count de Florida Blanca, who was ex officio authorized to confer with me on such Subjects, <were never answered> have been fruitless. It would give me Pleasure to see this

Business begun, and I cannot omit This opportunity of assuring your Excellency of my wish and Desire to <commence the necessary Conference> enter upon it as soon as your Excellency shall be pleased to inform me that you are authorized and find it convenient to proceed.

I have the Honor to be with great Respect and Esteem Your Excellency's most obedient and most Humble Servant.

Dft. C and Spanish trans. in AHN Estado, leg. 3885, exp. 1, doc. 15; LbkCs in JP and in PCC 110, II; C in JJ to Livingston, 17 Nov. 1782, cited above, JJ to Aranda, 25 June 1782, n. 2.

[1]At their 26 August conference Aranda had asked JJ to state his instructions in writing, so that they could be conveyed "with greater accuracy" to the Spanish court. See JJ to Livingston, 17 Nov. 1782.

[2]Close quotes supplied by editors. This is a quotation from JJ's commission as minister plenipotentiary to Spain, 28 Sept. 1779. LbkC, in H.B. Livingston's hand, in JJ Lbk IV, 1–2; *JCC,* XV, 1121; *RDC,* III, 711–12.

From Aranda

Paris, 11 September 1782
Response to Mr. Ambassador

Sir,

I have the honor to reply to your letter of yesterday, and to state that I have the necessary instructions from my Court and am authorized to confer and treat with you on all the points on which you may be instructed and authorized to treat by your principals. As soon as you wish to send me your suggestions, we will review them and afterwards I will let you have my comments, which may serve to bring both sides closer together.

I have etc.

Dft in French in AHN Estado, leg. 3885, exp. 1, doc. 15, trans. by the editors. LbkC in French in JP, PCC 110, II; C in JJ to Livingston, 17 Nov. 1782, cited above, JJ to Aranda, 25 June 1782, n. 2. Variant translation in *RDC,* VI, 28, and *HPJ,* II, 401.

From Robert R. Livingston

Philadelphia, 17 September 1782

I have at length been favored with a private Letter from you[1] which gives me great pleasure, not only because it assures me of your health and that of Mrs. Jay but because it is expressive of that friendship which I should be sorry to see lost in the ocean of politics in which we have both launched our barks.

I am sorry for the ill health of my little god daughter[2] but as the disorders she complains of are such as must necessarily be visited upon all the children of our Epicurian Grandmother, I hope she bore them with becoming fortitude and that she is happily freed from them before this. I thank you for the interest you have given me in her and am not without prospects of being able ee'r long to return you the compliment.[3]

I have not heard for some time from your family. Sir James I suppose you know is in Europe. I mentioned his misfortune in having been taken and carryed into New York. What adds to that misfortune is that many people here attribute it to design. I for my part acquit him of every thing but imprudence. His going to England has given more credit to the aspertions of his enimies. The State of New York has made it the ground of a resolution for vacating his seat and electing Mr. Duane to it.[4]

Benson has refused to take a seat in Congress, has lost his election in Dutches, and is attentive to improve his fortune in the line of his profession. Hamilton has be[en] elected in his place and leaves for it the Law which he was just beginning to practice and a snug sinecure place under Congress.[5] I will not venture to discede or digne [sic] the palm of wisdom to either in preference to the other.[6]

I am just about to pay a visit to the banks of the Hudson but have a thousand things to do first. The length of my journey must therefore shorten my letter though it will lengthen my next by enabling me to speak of your friends. Adieu my dear Sir. Remember me affectionately to Mrs. Jay and believe me to be what I sincerely am, Yours with undiminished friendship,

ROBT. R. LIVINGSTON

ALS. Dft in NHi: Robert R. Livingston; omissions and variances in *HPJ,* II, 342.

[1]See above, JJ to Livingston, 13 Aug. 1782.

[2]Maria Jay.

[3]The Chancellor's second daughter, Margaret Maria, was born the following April.

[4]Seat declared vacant from Sir James' inability to attend, "being a prisoner." On 22 July the Assembly appointed James Duane to replace him. *N.Y. Civil List,* p. 371.

[5]Dft version: "I will not pronounce between them or say who best deserves the palm of wisdom."

[6]Hamilton accepted the post of Receiver of Taxes for New York on 17 June 1782. Elected a delegate to Congress on 22 July 1782, Hamilton commenced his term in November. He was admitted to practice as an attorney before the Supreme Court in July, and as counsel in October. *HP,* III, 93–94, 108, 122, 189; *N.Y. Senate Journal, 1782,* p. 91.

To BOURGOING

Paris, 26 September 1782

Dear Sir,

Accept my Thanks for your Favor of the 4th Inst. which together with the papers mentioned in it, came to Hand last week.[1]

There are few Things in this world that are not rated at more than their real <Value> worth, and that will always continue to be the Case while Wisdom and Integrity continue to be unequally <shared> divided among Men.

As to the Contents of these News papers <in Question>, they are much like common Conversations which serve to amuse a Leisure hour but are generally more abundant in Words <are not very replete with> than interesting matter. I am glad you sent them by a Courier, for otherwise their real postage from Madrid here, would have added considerably to their fictitious Transportation from Peru to Cadiz.

The more I see of this Country the better I like it, and whenever I leave it, I shall carry with me many favorable Impressions of it. Such a Kingdom, so governed, has little to fear from War, and in my opinion should make peace with as much Deliberation, as it is capable of prosecuting a war with Vigor.

The spanish Embassador shews me no powers to treat, and yet desires me to proceed. His Court does not appear to be apprized that tho his Catholic Majesty has not acknowledged our Independence, yet that the United States as well as France and Holland, have.

There is a Tide in human affairs which waits for nobody and political mariners ought to watch <and profit> it and avail themselves of its Advantages. Sat Verbum.[2]

Present my best Respects to the Embassador, and be assured that tho want of Time or Health may sometimes make me an unpunctual Correspondent, yet that you was led into a mistake when you <supposed> imagined that I might not be *disposed* to write to You. The Appearance of Objects <differs according to the> depends not a little on the Glass thro which we view them, and some are so fashioned as not to represent either men or things as they are.

Mrs. Jay presents you her Compliments. She is as much pleased with France as I am.

Adieu. I am dear Sir with great Regard your most obedient and humble Servant.

Dft. Endorsed by JJ: ". . . in ansr. to 4 Inst." E in NN: Bancroft: American IV, 171.
[1]ALS in JP, enclosing "a paquet of newspapers."
[2]Abridged for *Verbum sat sapienti,* "a word to the wise is sufficient."

From William Bingham

Philadelphia, 27 September 1782

Under Date of August 4th[1] I had the honor of addressing you, Since which we have the fullest Prospect of an approaching Peace, as it appears that the Negotiations in Europe will most certainly terminate in that desirable Event.

There is a Point of the greatest Consequence for the Interests of the MERCHANT STATES which is not consulted in the TREATY of COMMERCE with *France,* and which if unattended to in that with GREAT BRITAIN will involve us in considerable DISTRESS. I mean the liberty of TRADING to the WEST INDIA ISLANDS. The ACT of NAVIGATION of GREAT BRITAIN and the ORDER of FRANCE at present effectually exclude us, and I am afraid this jealous POLICY will Still be continued.

If so, the TRADE of EXPORT of MERCHANT STATES will be for several years after the War very much circumscribed, as from the expensive Equipment of Ships, freights will be very high, and will not admit of our BREAD PRODUCTS being carried to EUROPE on Such Terms as to enter into Competition with that raised on the spot. It is certain that the real Interests of both FRANCE and ENGLAND would dictate a very different Line of Conduct but the COMMERCIAL Legislation of the ISLAND has been always founded on a very NARROW POLICY. I have the honor to ENCLOSE you a Short ADDRESS to the GOVERNOR and INTENDANT of MARTINIQUE on the Subject, Some time after my ARRIVAL there.[2]

As for SPAIN it is not to be expected that she will throw off the confined System, she has long pursued in relation to the TRADE of the COLONIES. The PORT of HAVANNAH and of the HAVANNAS are now open for our EXPORTS and our VESSELS are permitted to NAVIGATE freely to and FROM these PORTS and carry off their PRODUCTS. It will be of very material Service to my COMMERCIAL Views to be informed whether this LIBERTY will probably be CONTRACT[ED] to us after the WAR, and for what length of Time, as by engaging too deeply in this TRADE, great hopes may ensue by too Sudden a PROLIFERATION of it.

I think it is very probable that the COURT of MADRID would find its

Interests in having the HAVANNAH furnished with FLOUR etc. by CONTRACT after the WAR. If Such Proposals would be accepted I should be very happy in having a COMMERCIAL HOUSE that I HAVE ESTABLISH[ED] in this Place, joined in the CONTRACT with Some of my FRIEND[S].

I must trust to your Friendship to excuse the Trouble I give you.

L'Aigle and La Gloire (two French Frigates) were pursued within these few Days by a Superior force of the Enemy, that had been laying in Wait for them. The first was under the Necessity of running ashore, but fortunately saved the whole of the Money that She had on board, and had the good fortune to land her Passengers in Safety. The Captain and Crew were made Prisoners.[3] La Gloire escaped.

I have not time to address you So fully by this opportunity as I would wish, as it is just on the Departure.

Please to make my respectfull Compliments to Mrs. Jay, with those of Mrs. Bingham, and believe me to be with Sincere Regard and Esteem, Dear Sir Your obedient and humble Servant,

WM. BINGHAM

ALS.

[1]Probably a slip of the pen for 14 August, above.

[2]For the address, not located, see Bingham to JJ, 25 Feb. 1780, in *JJ*, I, 738–41.

[3]*L'Aigle* was captured 14 Sept. 1782. Dull, *French Navy and American Independence*, p. 358.

To John Adams

Paris, 28 September 1782

Dear Sir,

Mr. Oswald received Yesterday[1] a Commission to treat of peace *with the Commissioners of the United States of America.* I have Reasons for wishing that you would say Nothing of this till you see me, which I hope and pray may be soon, very soon. This is a short Letter, but notwithstanding its Brevity be assured that I am with great Esteem and Regard Dear Sir your most obedient Servant.

Dft. ALS in MHi: Adams, reel 358.

[1]Oswald received the commission on 24 September, as he informed Franklin. See the Commission, above, 21 September, source note.

Jay Draws Up the Preliminary Articles: First Draft Treaty

1–8 October 1782

With the arrival of Richard Oswald's commission[1] Anglo-American negotiations began in earnest. As Franklin was "still in an indifferent state of health," the labor fell to JJ.[2] Oswald's talks with the Americans prior to 2 October had led him to believe that "in a few days . . . we shall agree with the principle Articles of which the Treaty is to consist."[3] It was his hope that he could limit the articles to those matters stressed by JJ in these conversations: independence, boundary lines, the cession of the "additional lands of Canada," and fishing rights. In JJ he discovered an enthusiastic convert to his project to regain West Florida for Great Britain.[4] Indeed, JJ's support for a British military campaign against the territory that Spain had reconquered during the war is a recurrent theme in Oswald's reports over the next month or so, although JJ was understandably reluctant to have his advocacy of so sensitive a subject publicized.[5]

JJ's sudden passion for the British re-acquisition of West Florida may in part at least have been a delayed reaction to the diplomatic snubs he had suffered at the Spanish court, coupled with indignation at the terms of the Pensacola capitulation.[6] This resentment may well have masked a careful calculation. Possession of West Florida by Great Britain would have divided control of the entire east bank of the Mississippi between the United States and England, and thereby provide a basis for a joint U.S.-British claim to the free navigation of that waterway, a pretension that is supported in both the Preliminary and Definitive Treaties but would have been difficult to press under prevailing international law against a power that controlled both banks of a river at its mouth, as Rayneval had already reminded JJ.[7] Finally, JJ may well have felt that a diversion of British troops from Patriot port towns would speed the evacuation of the Redcoats from posts still retained, notably New York, Charleston, and Penobscot. Had JJ succeeded in his efforts to relocate the British on the east bank of the Mississippi, he inadvertently might have blocked the later acquisition by the United States of the vast territories west of the river. As for Oswald, he regarded the West Florida re-deployment as a means of safeguarding British troops and stores when evacuating American ports, as he disclosed in his dispatch of 2 October below. Within a very few weeks, however, West Florida was being seriously considered by both Britain and the Franco-Spanish negotiators as an equivalent for Gibraltar,[8] and the British government shied away from a military solution of the Florida problem.

On 5 October JJ handed to Oswald "the Plan or Articles of a final Treaty . . . in his own handwriting," which Franklin had approved.[9] Oswald found the Articles acceptable, with the exception of the Nova Scotia boundary. The problems raised by that boundary, he felt, could be referred to later adjustment.[10]

The comments of the Commissioners upon the respective Articles in this draft are detailed in the notes to the version printed below.

Oswald's letters to Townshend reveal how readily he was persuaded to forgo pressing for additional points not included in JJ's draft. First, he abandoned his notion of an armistice on the high seas.[11] Then he accepted JJ's explanation why nothing could be done to establish a fund from ungranted lands in the States to be used for Loyalist reparations and that the Commissioners lacked powers to do anything further as regards debts due British creditors.[12]

Oswald prepared a copy of JJ's draft of the treaty to be forwarded to England, with JJ's minor corrections. On 8 October Oswald dispatched the treaty to England with a request for a "discretionary permission" to sign the articles as they stood if they should be "found to be right in the main." Oswald took satisfaction in what he considered a diplomatic coup, and particularly in having elicited from JJ comments indicating the latter's satisfaction at the separate negotiating course that he and his fellow Americans were pursuing.[13]

The Scotsman's optimism about a quick settlement would prove groundless,[14] but for the moment the Commissioners could congratulate themselves, relax, and enjoy Paris.[15] Coincident with JJ's negotiations, Adams was completing his Treaty of Amity and Commerce and the Convention concerning Recaptures, both of which were signed with the Dutch on 8 October. A slow traveler, and not in the most robust health, Adams informed JJ that it would take some time before he could get to Paris, but should anything in the meantime "be in exitation, concerning Peace, in which there should be any difference of opinion between you and your Colleague, you have a right to insist upon informing me, by Express, or waiting till I come."[16] Adams' arrival was just what Vaughan particularly dreaded. Let us get on with it, he urged Shelburne, lest the French or "Mr. Adams" interfere. "I will not answer for the mischief he may do."[17]

[1]Above, 19 Sept. 1782.

[2]JJ's time was also taken up with matters that properly fell to Franklin when in better health. See, *e.g.,* application for a waiver of the French import duty on a cargo of sugar. Nathaniel Barrett to JJ, 30 Sept. 1782, ALS in PHi: Franklin III, 52; C in French in PPAmP: Franklin XLVIII, 2.

[3]See Oswald to Townshend, 2 Oct. 1782, below. Vaughan shared this belief. Vaughan to Shelburne, 3 Oct. 1782, LbkC in PPAmP: Vaughan.

[4]Oswald had been prodding JJ about Florida for almost a month. On 11 September he had reported to Townshend: "I have mentioned to Mr. Jay a wish that the Limits of West Florida could be Stretched further to the Northward even though it should be at the Expence of Georgia. He did not Say it would be impossible. He thinks that Some time after last peace there was Some Change of Boundaries in those Colonies, by proclamation. If so, I should be glad to be informed of the particulars." Oswald to Townshend, 11 Sept. 1782, LbkCs in MiU-C: Shelburne 70; FO 27/2; 95/511; 97/157.

[5]Oswald to Townshend, 5, 7 Oct. 1782, below; also Townshend to Strachey, 23, 26 Oct. 1782, Tr of both in MiU-C; RGA. Vaughan joined in advocating the West Florida reconquest. Vaughan to Shelburne, 1 Nov. 1782, Tr in PPAmP: Vaughan.

[6]See editorial note above, "John Jay on the Pensacola Capitulation"; Townshend to Oswald, 26 Oct. 1782, below.

[7]See above, Rayneval's "Suggestion," 6 Sept. 1782.

[8]Vergennes to Montmorin, 13 Oct. 1782, C in CP E 609: 83–84; Montmorin to Vergennes, 12, 24 Oct. 1782, LS in *ibid.*, pp. 103–06, 135–36; Townshend to Strachey, 21 October, Tr in NN: Strachey.

[9]"The articles are drawn up very fully by Mr. Jay." Franklin to Livingston, 14 Oct. 1782, *RDC,* V, 811–12; *BFS,* VIII, 614–17.

[10]Oswald to Townshend, 7 Oct. 1782, below.

[11]Oswald to Townshend, 5 Oct. 1782, below.

[12]Oswald to Townshend, 7 Oct. 1782, below.

[13]Oswald to Townshend, 8 Oct. 1782, below.

[14]See editorial note below, "Preliminary Articles: Second Draft."

[15]JJ revealed his mood of confidence in a letter to Livingston of 13 Oct. 1782. "Mr. Oswald," he said, "is well disposed. You shall never see my name to a bad peace, nor to one that does not secure the Fishery." LbkCs in CSmH and in PCC 110, II; *RDC,* V, 809; *HPJ,* II, 348–49.

[16]Adams to JJ, The Hague, 7–8 Oct. 1782, ALS in JP; Tr in NN: Bancroft: American IV, 188; *RDC,* V, 803; *JAW,* VII, 645–46.

[17]Vaughan to Shelburne, 3 Oct. 1782, Tr in PPAmP: Vaughan.

Appointment of William Temple Franklin

[Paris], 1 October 1782

To all to whom these Presents Shall come, Benjamin Franklin and John Jay send Greeting.

Whereas the United States of America in Congress assembled did on the 15th June in the year of our Lord 1781 appoint and constitute the said Benjamin Franklin and John Jay and John Adams, Henry Laurens and Thomas Jefferson Esquires, and the Majority of them, and of such of them as should assemble for the Purpose, their Commissioners and Plenipotentiaries to treat of and conclude Peace in their Behalf.[1] And whereas the said United States in Congress assembled, did on the 26th June in the year of our Lord 1781 appoint Mr. Francis Dana, untill he could proceed to the Court of Petersburgh, either in a Public or Private Capacity to Secretary to the said Plenipotentiaries for negotiating a Peace with Great Britain, And in case Mr. Dana should have proceeded or there after proceed to Petersburgh or to any Part of the Dominions of the Empress of Russia the Ministers appointed by the Said Act of Congress of the 15th June 1781 or a Majority of such of them as should assemble, should be and thereby were authorized to appoint a Secretary to their Commission, and that he be entitled to receive in Proportion to his Time of Service, the Salary of one thousand Pounds Sterling per Annum allowed to Mr. Dana.[2] And whereas His Britannic Majesty hath issued a Commission dated the 21 Sept. 1782 to Richard

Oswald Esquire to treat of and conclude Peace with any Commissioners or Persons vested with equal Power By and on the Part of the thirteen United States of America. And whereas the said Richard Oswald is at Paris, ready to excute his said Commission, and hath exchanged with the said Benjamin Franklin and John Jay, Copies of their respective Commissions, and entered on the Business of the Same, Whereby the Appointment of a Secretary to the American Commissioners hath become necessary. And the said Mr. Dana now being at Petersburgh, the right of appointing such a Secretary hath in persuance of the afore recited Act of Congress, devolved on the Said Commissioners and on the Majority of them and of Such of them as have assembled for the Purpose of executing their said Commission. And whereas Mr. Jefferson one of the said Commissioners hath not come to Europe, and Mr. Laurans, another of these, hath declined to accept the said Office, and Mr. Adams another of them is at the Hague, So that the said Benjamin Franklin and John Jay are the only Commissioners now assembled to execute the said Commission.

Now Know Ye that they reposing special Trust and Confidence in the Ability and Integrity of William T. Franklin Esquire to perform and fulfil the duties of Secretary to their Said Commission have appointed and constituted And by these Presents do appoint and constitute the said William T. Franklin, Secretary to the said Commission. In Witness whereof the said Benjamin Franklin and John Jay have hereunto set their Hands and Seals this first day of October in the year of our Lord one thousand seven hundred and Eighty two and in the seventh Year of the Independence of the said United States.

(signed) B. FRANKLIN
(signed) JOHN JAY

Approved on my part, Mr. Franklin having acted with propriety as Secretary to the Commission from the time of my arrival here. Paris, 10th January 1783.

(signed) HENRY LAURENS

Approved on my part, Mr. Franklin having acted with Propriety as Secretary to the Commission from the time of my arrival here. Paris, 8 September 1783.

(signed) JOHN ADAMS

LbkC in PPAmP: Franklin LV, 9. *RDC*, V, 789–90; *SDC*, X, 83–85.

[1]*JCC*, XX, 652–55.

[2]*Ibid.*, p. 699.

RICHARD OSWALD TO THOMAS TOWNSHEND

Paris, 2 October 1782

Sir,

I had the honour of your Letters of the 20th and 24th September, the last accompanying his Majesty's new Commission, altered as desired. Upon receipt, I produced it to the American Commissioners, and they were entirely satisfied therewith. I have also to advise that yesterday I delivered to them a Copy of said Commission after its being compared with the original, and certified by me, and in exchange received from them a Copy of their Commission, which being in like manner compared with the original, was certified by Mr. John Jay one of the Commissioners. A Duplicate of said Copy, you have inclosed.

Dr. Franklin being still in but an indifferent State of health, he could not come to Town, and left this first part of the Business to Mr. Jay. From any thing that passed on the occasion, I have no reason to think worse of the farther progress of it, than as mentioned in my last Advices. In a few days I hope We shall agree upon the principal Articles, of which the Treaty is to consist. When that is done, I shall transmit the same so as to have your Instructions thereon. We have as yet only talked of them in a loose way, viz.:

First. Independence.

2d. Settling the Lines of separation or Boundaries between those of the thirteen States, and the British Colonies.

3d. Giving up the additional Lands of Canada.

4th. Freedom of fishing to the 13 States, for Fish and whales.

These, I say, are all that have as yet been mentioned between Mr. Jay and me. Whether any others will be proposed or insisted on by them, I cannot say, but I hope there will not.

Meanwhile, as there will probably be time for a Return of a Courier, before We proceed much farther, I would beg to hear an Explanation as to some of the particulars in my Letter of the 11th Ult., respecting the Article of Boundaries of Canada, Nova Scotia and Georgia, East Florida, and particularly West Florida. How its Boundaries are to be determined with regard to Georgia, that must depend upon the Charter of Georgia, by Grant or Proclamation. I have nothing here to go by but Maps, and they are no authority even though they agreed, which these do not.

By the former Courier I wrote Sundry things about this Colony of West Florida, rather in some haste, as the Messenger was just then upon setting off. I have given Mr. Jay an account of it, and he greatly approved of the Proposal. He is indeed anxious that Great Britain should regain possession of the Colony, on the same footing it stood before the War, since he said their States would not by any means like that the Key of that part of the Gulph should be in the hands of the Spaniards, as the whole, on the greatest part of the Trade and produce of that great back Country, would most naturally and beneficially issue there, and which he says would soon be very considerable and would ultimately fall into the hands of the English on the Mobile and Mississippi; both in the supply of English Merchandise, and Importation of American Commodities in return. Rather than leave it in the hands of the Spaniards, he said it would be worth while to embark some of the Troops from New York and Charles Town, and retake it. I mention this only to shew how desirous they are that that Colony should not remain with the Spaniards, and in confirmation of the Opinion I took the liberty to give on that subject in my former Letters.

In order to make it a Kings Government of some consequence, I again tried Mr. Jay, whether without regard to what might be the Chartered limits of Georgia, We might not settle it so in the Treaty, that West Florida should be extended to about the Latitude of 34. To which he answered that although he could wish to give every Encouragement to that Settlement, yet it would not be in their Power as Commissioners, to dismember any of the States, but that it was a matter of little consequence whether that upper part, which I aimed at, was under British Government or theirs. The People would agree very well, having one common Interest in the Settlement and Prosperity of that great and fertile Country, and in which their People would in a manner be dependent on Great Britain, as having the Command of the Navigation into the Gulph of Mexico, through which the bulk of that Trade must pass, He added that their Traders from the Northern Colonies have lately crossed the Mississippi into the Spanish Territories, and will continue to do so to a still greater extent after the War is over, and they begin to Stretch further back in their Settlements, which will occasion an additional Demand for British Merchandize, as those which are laid down near the spot, by Importation from the Gulph through the English Settlements, will have the preference on account of the saving of the Land Carriage from the Atlantic side. Consequently he thinks, as I do, that the Port of West Florida may be of great advantage to England, as this would become the Mart or Center of a great part of the Trade of America to the Southward, as would Quebec be to the Northern parts. By which means, upon the whole, England, having those two Keys in its hand, may still enjoy an exclusive Monopoly of a larger share of North American Commerce, and consequently may not happen to be, in point of Trade, so great a loser by the change, as is generally imagined.

In the course of this last Conversation with Mr. Jay, he repeated his Wish that the Spaniards might be dislodged from West Florida and said, "what are you doing with 20,000 Men (he called them so many) lying idle, spending of Money in New York and Charles Town, and keeping up a Jealousy and animosity between you and Us at a time when We are here endeavoring to bring about a Restoration of friendship and good Will? Why not employ some of those Troops to recover that Colony?"

Upon another occasion, he said, your Ministry ought to take the first opportunity to write to Sir Guy Carleton an account of Our being likely to come soon to an amicable and final agreement here, on the footing of an unconditional Independence; and to desire that he would immediately publish that Intelligence and at same time give orders to discountenance all those Murderous attempts by scouting Parties of what you call Loyalists, or Indians in the Remote parts of the Country etc. From this and other parts of that Gentleman's conversation, and the good Disposition which I suppose both the Commissioners entertain with respect to England, the following things have occurred to me, and which (trusting to the Indulgence which has been hitherto shewn to the freedom of my correspondence) I venture to mention on this occasion vizt.

1st. When the principal Articles of the Treaty are agreed upon, and reduced to Writing, it will surely be proper to resolve upon evacuating our Ports in the Thirteen States without delay.

2. The manner of doing it to advantage, and without discredit to the Troops, will be a matter of delicacy, if not of some difficulty, so as to save everything there that is valuable.

3. When such Evacuation is resolved upon an approbation from the Commissioners here accompanying the Transports, will greatly facilitate the Operation, as well as keep up the countenance of Our People at their departure.

4. An understanding between the Commissioners and me being privately Settled, that these Troops are to be employed in the Recovery of the Colony of West Florida, I should hope would be the means of procuring from them even a Recommendation to Congress and to General Washington to give every countenance and facility to such Evacuation, so as the Troops might quit those Ports with that Repu-

tation and honor that is due to their Character.

5. If the Article of my Instructions, relative to a general pardon for all supposed Trespasses and crimes charged upon the Loyalists, can obtain the consent of the Commissioners here, the personal safety of the Loyalists remaining at those Posts will be secured, so as they may dispose of themselves in the Country, as they think proper. Or such as do not chuse to trust themselves even under that Provision, may depart along with the Troops.

6. In the view or expectation of the said Loyalists recovering their property, or getting an Indemnification for their Losses, it cannot be supposed that these Garrisons will be kept there, in a State of inactivity, in the time of War, whilst any of our public Losses, such as the Colony of West Florida, can be recovered by their means. Therefore the consideration of what regards the said Sufferers cannot properly operate to the delay of the Evacuation of those Places, for any time after an amicable acquiescence thereto is obtained of the Commissioners here.

7. The Employment of those Troops having been particularly suggested by the Commissioners themselves, and so as to act against an intrenched Garrison, they must perceive that Artillery must be necessary, and of course can have no objection to our dismantling all our Works, and carrying off our Cannon and Military Stores from New York, Charles Town, Penobscot etc. I mention this because I have always had a doubt, whether there might not arise some Difficulty on this head, and that We might not by compromise or otherwise, and for the sake of getting quietly out of that Country, be glad to have a part of our valuable Artillery and Stores behind Us.

8. An avowal or private acknowledgement of the intended Employment of those Troops against Spain, I suppose would not, in the eye of the Commissioners appear as any Infringement of their Treaty with France, I have the authority as I have said, of the express Words of Mr. Jay, in a manner to the contrary: when upon my saying how hard it was, that France should pretend to saddle us with all their private Engagements with Spain, and perhaps try to bring them under cover of the Treaty with the Colonies. He replied, No, We will allow no such thing. For We shall say to France, the agreement We made with you We shall faithfully perform. But if you have entered into any Separate Measures with other People, not included in that Agreement, and will load the Negotiation with their Demands, We shall give ourselves no concern about them.

9. Supposing I am right in the Principles of the preceeding Arti-

cles, vizt. that any longer continuance of our Troops at their present Posts is unnecessary, except for keeping pace with a final Settlement with the Americans; there can be no objection to moving them on account of the Expence, not even that of Transports in carrying them to West Florida, for that cannot be said to be an extraordinary Expence, since the Transports must be removed and carried somewhere, either to Britain, or to our remaining Islands in the West Indies. To bring them home in the Winter would be distressing to them and very expensive. To send them to our own Islands perhaps is not necessary, as the French, I suppose, think they have got enough of them already, so that I hope what remains will be safe, and that those Islands We have lost, or most of them, will be recovered in an easier way, than by means of those American Detachments.

Besides such attempts against French possessions, even for the recovery of our own Settlements, would give that Nation a just pretence to call for an Intervention of the Americans, Which might not be convenient in this early State of Negotiation, and before a return of the sensible Feelings of a mutual conciliation takes place between Us and them.

10. To obviate these inconveniencies I would therefore propose that the object of this withdrawing the Troops from America, should be declared or hinted to the Commissioners to be the Recovery of West Florida, and upon that voyage they might proceed accordingly. When arrived they would enjoy the benefit of a fine Climate, and it might be contrived to supply them with the best Provisions at a much cheaper rate than they are now supplied at Charles Town, New York, and Penobscott; And also that the same would be done by the Americans themselves, greatly to their Content, and with much benefit and Satisfaction to the Troops. For the People of Georgia and North Carolina would drive their Cattle down there in Thousands, and deliver them to the Commissaries of the Troops, at 40 Shillings a head. As a proof of this I can shew that they drove Cattle to St. Augustine, and delivered them at 30 Shillings Sterling per head. There would then be no want of Meat, and the People of New York and Philadelphia I suppose would send them Biscuit and Flour, at less than one half the Cost they are now supplied at in those Countries. But it is to be considered, that times would then be changed, and instead of Enemies, the Americans would look upon those Troops as Friends and useful Customers.

If there is any thing improper in this Representation, I must plead the excuse of the Proposal having been suggested by one of the Commissioners, which I could not but think would be accepted, since, whether it is approved or not, it shews their wish that an amicable, and mutually beneficial correspondence between England and them, may not only be renewed as quickly as possible, but that in the particular case above mentioned, there may be a foundation laid for its extension and permanency. In which light as I considered the object of the Proposal, I could not avoid stating it.

I send under this cover Doctor Franklin's Discharge of Captain Fage's Parole. There being four Passengers now here, one of them, Long, returns Extra, along with North, by whom this goes.

I have the honor to be, Sir. etc.

RICHARD OSWALD

P.S. Since writing the above, I have had some farther conversation with Mr. Jay, about the conditions of the Treaty. I hope to get clear of the advisable Articles. But as to some of those in my Instructions I doubt I shall not succeed. For the present I only touched upon the following vizt.

Ungranted lands within the United States. He said all must go with the States.

Pardon to the Loyalists. The Congress cannot meddle in it. The States being Sovereigns, and the Parties in fault answerable to them, and them only. Besides he said, it is his opinion, that many of them could not be protected by their Governments, and therefore ought to depart with the Troops.

Drying fish in Newfoundland, I find is to be claimed as a privilege in common, We being allowed the same on their shores. I did not think it proper to say much on this Subject at present, and wish that granting this freedom may be found to be no material loss to England, being afraid if refused it may be a great loss in other things. Mr. Jay came again upon the Subject of West Florida, and expects and insists for the Common good, Our own as well as theirs, that it may not be left in the hands of the Spaniards. And thinks we ought to prepare immediately for the Expedition, to execute it this Winter. At the same time he earnestly begs it may not be known that he advised it, and wishes I had mentioned it myself. As I approved of the thing, I thought the Proposal should be strengthened by his opinion, and to speak the truth I could not suppress the Credit due to him for attending to it.

I am to Dine with Doctor Franklin to-morrow, when it is likely We shall talk farther of the Conditions of the treaty, and I am in hopes that the next Courier may carry a Sketch of them. When agreed on they must remain without Effect or Operation until We have closed with

France, so they positively say. I *really believe the Commissioners are sorry they are so tied up.* But they say there is no remedy.

C in FO 27/2, with enclosure of copy of the American Commissioners' commission, 15 June 1781, certified by JJ and Oswald; Cs in MiU-C: Shelburne 70, FO 95/511 and 97/157. See also Hale, *Franklin in France,* II, 168–70, for brief excerpts.

The letters mentioned herein are cited above: 24 Sept. 1782 in "The Rayneval and Vaughan Missions," n. 13; 11 and 20 Sept. in "Jay Proposes Altering Oswald's Commission," n. 8.

Richard Oswald to Thomas Townshend

Paris, 5 October 1782

Sir,

In my Letters of the 3d Instant to the Secretary of State,[1] I took the Liberty to propose our embarking the Garrisons of New York, Charles Town and Penobscott, and employing them in retaking Pensacola, and other places in West Florida, so as to recover possession of that Colony, by driving the Spaniards entirely out of the Country, on that side of the Missisippi. The motives to this undertaking were said to be as follows. Vizt:

1. The Benifit of Colony possession and profit as far as the Limits of West Florida will go.

2. Having the Command of the Mouth of the Missisippi, and the Navigation thereof to and from the Gulf of Mexico.

3. And consequently making our Settlement there an Entrepôt of the Trade of the great back Country of all the Provinces of the 13 States, that would naturally go to the Southward, and in the same manner as the other part to the northward would center the issue from Quebec.

4. And putting both together would satisfy the Nation, that in a mercantile view, We should still enjoy a beneficial Connection with those States. And considering that the Atlantic Side of said States lies open to the same Correspondence with us as formerly, there would be reason to hope that in a mercantile view, We should not lose much by the Change that has happened.

One of the Commissioners tells me that We should lose nothing, and should be saved the Expence and trouble of governing them. These are his words. And as an Encouragement to the Undertaking has agreed to give us in the Treaty a full freedom of Navigation on the Missisippi, all along their back Country as settled in the Treaty of Paris, without Duties of any kind, the same as for their own People, and I suppose will allow of the like privilege from Canada.

5. Another just motive to the Undertaking is that of indulging a Request of the Americans. I may say conferring an Obligation on them, as they detest the Thought of having the Key of that Trade in the hands of the Spaniards.

6. In my own mind I think it is not unworthy of notice, that were the Spaniards to be left in West Florida, and should find their situation uneasy there, on account of the incurable Inveteracy of the Indian tribes in the neighbourhood, Chactaws, Chicasaws, Creeks, etc. they might find it inconvenient to compromise some Agreement with the French, and give up the post of Trade into their hands, and so by letting in that active Rival upon us and thereby fixing a new Commercial Connection with the great stretch of that frontier Country to the westward, they might gain such an Ascendancy of Interest among those States in general, as to hurt Great Britain more ways than in that of Commerce.

7. Another Motive to the Undertaking is that of the Americans being thus interested in the Success of it, We might expect to get away our Garrisons, Effects, Artillery and Stores in a decent way, without danger or affront to the Troops, or any Loss of the abovementioned Articles. A Consideration which I must confess has lain upon my mind as of some Consequence, ever since I saw that We must evacuate those places, which is a long time ago. For the Americans being tied up so as not to make peace, there was no certainty but they might act hostily against us, upon this occasion of a Retreat Especially as there lyes in the neighbourhood of New York, as I am told a Body of French Troops, about 4000 men, under the Count de Rochambeau. These, though not to be feared in case of a trial in the Field, yet hanging upon the skirts of a retreating Army, and perhaps wishing to occupy our Outlines as We quit them, might, without exposing themselves, occasion some confusion and hurry in the Embarkation that would not be credible, and in some degree not safe, even supposing the Americans should continue in a neutral position which We could not be sure of; And might be certain that numbers of their Individuals would, on such an Occasion, take part with the French in incommoding our Troops, and putting every affront upon them in their Power. Those brave Troops have behaved so nobly and patiently during the whole of this distressing War, that one cannot help partaking of their feelings upon foreseeing the possibility of any Stain being thrown upon their Reputation, on so critical an Occasion as this might happen to be, considering the Delicacy of their Situation, in being tied up to a plan strictly defensive, and the possibility of its being necessary to take a different part to get

away in safety, and afterward to prove the expediency and necessity of doing so; without which We might come again to have the Circumstances of a new quarrel to explain and settle with those States, with whom we are now endeavouring to settle a Peace.

These Inconveniences, as hinted at in my late Letter, I am hopeful might be prevented by obtaining from the Commissioners here, such Recommendations to Congress and General Washington with respect to the Evacuation of those Garrisons, as should allow of the Troops quitting their posts and withdrawing their Artillery Stores and other Effects, in an easy safe and convenient manner. And in consequence of such Orders all Interference or Interruption from the Enemy might either be forbidden, or so discountenanced, that We should have nothing to fear from them.

In the Harbour and upon the Coast no doubt We must be so guarded against Squadrons or Cruizers, French or Americans, as to be under no Apprehension after We are embarkt. Considering the vicinity of Rhode Island, that must be effectualy taken care of.

That the American Commissioners will do what is necessary and consistent with their French Treaty I make no doubt, in securing a safe and decent Retreat to those Garrisons. I shall take the Liberty to give one Reason for thinking them well disposed to any such like Accommodation, where they are not strictly tied up by their Treaty with France.

About six or seven weeks ago, seeing the absurdity of War being carried on between them and us at Sea, whilst We had declared Peace at Hand, and considering that the Americans were so tied up by their Treaty with France, that they could agree to no kind of formal Cessation untill We had finaly closed with that Nation, I wished to try to make a sort of artificial Truce between the Americans and us, and stating the awkwardness of the Situation to Dr. Franklin, He admitted it, but said a Remedy would be difficult. However, he promised to think of it, as I had the honour to report in my Letters to Lord Shelburne.

However there was nothing further said of the Matter until lately, when seeing that we were likely to give the Americans Satisfaction in the main Question, I thought it proper to try Mr. Jay on the same Subject of a Truce at Sea, so as, independent of the proceedings of the French in their Treaty at this place, we might be getting on in our Amnesty and Friendship with the Americans. And so might not only move quickly toward a Conclusion with France, but also on better Terms than perhaps it might be otherwise possible to do. And in any Event were this to succeed, We should be more indifferent as to a longer Continuance of the War with France.

In these sentiments I stated to Mr. Jay the Impropriety of our situation in the above respect, of being at Peace on shore, whilst We were capturing each others ships at Sea etc. And said that I thought our Government ought to make an offer to them, to cease Captures at Sea, of every Ship that was not armed for War, and had not Cannon on board, and a Crew of men above 20 or 30 in number, so that all American ships of that description might go free to France, England or other Country, In which I intended to propose to except naval Stores, althought I did not mention it. That this should be declared to last a certain time, six months or so, and if the Americans should in like manner desist from their Depredations, the forbearance on our part should be renewed and continued. And so the War at Sea might be carried on on both sides, against Ships of War only. By which means their people would get the just Value of the produce of their Estates, and be plentifuly supplied in foreign merchandize, at a much cheaper rate than at present. And so our commercial Correspondence might open afresh, and quickly, without regard to the Operation of the French, Dutch or Spaniards.

I told Mr. Jay at same time that I observed in their Demands on us, they made great use of the Word Magnanimity, and that their Congress would probably be soon in such situation as to have a right to adopt the same term with propriety: And if this scheme could be rendered practicable, and my advice could be of any Weight with our Gouvernment, it should be to trust their Congress, that upon our making such an offer, they would act up to the pitch of that Character. His answer was (for I will give his own words,) that it was a noble proposal, and that although they were so tied up, that such Compromise could not have the Sanction of a public Act of their States, yet We might very well trust to the Consequences, and that after such an Order on our parts, no man of Character would fit out a Privateer, nor any Body else would be well lookt upon, that would be concerned in them. Upon the whole, this Gentleman so strongly approved of the Scheme, that I proposed, with his leave, to go to Passy, and open it again to F[ranklin]. He agreed, and I went hither. Whilst repeating what is abovementioned regarding the proposal, I was greatly pleased to find that he equaly approved of it, and at last said He thought they might write to Congress about it; but first wished to see Mr. Jay. I returned to Paris, and informed Mr. Jay. He accordingly went out to Passy. When they came to consider the matter together, I suppose, they found that such an Understanding between them and us, however adjusted, would not be consistent with their restraining article in the Treaty with France, for Mr. Jay upon his return, told me they found, it would not do: and so there it rests.

Although the plan has not succeeded, yet I have thought proper to mention it, to shew that where those Gentlemen can consistently with their particular Engagements open a way to a Speedy Restoration of Peace, (and perhaps partly prompted thereto by a friendly Disposition still remaining towards England), they will readily lend their helping hand. And on that foundation I may be justified in supposing as I have done, that in giving their Countenance to our withdrawing our Garrisons in a desirable manner, and proceeding to the recovery of West Florida (as being in such case under no positive Restraints), they will not be backward in any thing depending on them. Although for the sake of the Connection of Spain with their Ally, they might still wish to keep their part as much out of sight as possible.

As to what has yet passt it has been only between them and me; and which I know, they wish may remain so, and I should be very sorry they should have any Reason to repent of their Confidence, Being sensible that in the present situation of things, it ought to be considered with respect to me as a matter of delicate Trust. And yet in the Channel through which it passed it can do them no harm; but as it may possibly be some sort of Guide in our future proceedings in American Business, I think it my Duty to give this Intelligence the Chance of being taken into Consideration.

I shall only beg leave to add one thing, that if an attempt on the Spaniards should be agreed to, it was recommended that the utmost Secrecy should be observed, as to the particular Object.

The above was wrote two days ago to lye <ready>) for a courier as it could not be got ready to go by North <up>. I have the honour to be, sir, your most obedient humble servant,

RICHARD OSWALD

ALS in FO 27/2; Cs in FO 95/511 and 97/157; LbkC in MiU-C: Shelburne 70.
[1]The letter of 2 Oct. 1782 to Townshend, above.

Maps Used in the Peace Negotiations

The principal map used in the peace negotiations, and the basic reference source in subsequent boundary disputes, was Dr. John Mitchell's famous map of North America, first published in London in 1755.[1] Copies the negotiators actually worked with are still extant, and include: (1) the so-called "King George's Map" (the 4th English edition of 1775), annotated by George III and Richard Oswald, and now in the British Museum. On this map the boundaries in negotiation are superimposed, and a red line runs between Nova Scotia and Massachusetts (Maine since 1820) and continues down the Atlantic coast. The red line bears the annotation: "Boundary as described by Mr. Oswald." Other lines on this map designate—incorrectly—the lines of the Treaty of Utrecht according to British and French construction.

(2) The copy JJ used during the Preliminary negotiations is the 3d English edition, now owned by the New-York Historical Society (of which two sections are reproduced herein), and bearing the legend, "Mr. Oswald's Line" in JJ's handwriting fourteen times to designate the tentative line of 8 October 1782, provisionally agreed upon with Richard Oswald.[2] Other copies extant are (3) the Steuben-Webster Mitchell; (4) the "Sheet which contains the Bay of Passamaquoddy," sent by Franklin to Thomas Jefferson when the latter was Secretary of State (both maps in the Department of State); and (5) Aranda's transcription of the Franklin red-line map in Archivo Histórico Nacional, Madrid.[3]

Such maps, bearing markings made during the Preliminaries, have no legal standing. The final, formal, signed copies of both the Preliminary and Definitive Treaties bearing the attested signatures of the British and American Commissioners and submitted both to Congress and the British government for ratification contained no maps, nor were any maps attached thereto. What was approved and what was ratified was a handwritten text of the treaties unaccompanied by maps, drawings, or illustrations in any form. At most, they must be considered as working-papers providing clues to the intentions of the negotiators.[4] The Mitchell map does, however, explain certain geographical distortions and misconceptions, such as the location of the source of the Mississippi River and the existence of the "St. Croix River," both which figured in the treaty terms.[5]

[1] *Map of the British and French Dominions in North America, with the Roads, Distances, Limits, and Extent of the Settlements.* In this map, compiled before the Seven Years' War, Mitchell (d. 1768) claimed for Great Britain the vast territory between the Alleghenies and the Mississippi River, including areas "usurped" by the French. The first edition, published early in 1755, was withdrawn, and the second, with "numerous important changes," was issued with the same date. See John Jay II, "The Peace Negotiations of 1782–1783," in Winsor, ed., *Narrative and Critical History,* VII, 181.

[2] JJ implied that other maps were consulted, while John Adams asserted that upon the Mitchell map, "and that only," were the boundaries delineated. As previously suggested, another of Jeffreys' maps was also consulted in the JJ-Aranda negotiations. See also Franklin, Adams, JJ, and Laurens to Livingston, 13 Dec. 1782, below; testimony of John Adams, 15 Aug. 1797, in the St. Croix River arbitration, in John Bassett Moore, ed., *International Adjudications, Ancient and Modern* (8 vols., New York, 1929–36), *Modern Series,* I, 63; and deposition of JJ, 21 May 1798, *ibid.,* p. 65; C in NHi: Jay. Adams to James Sullivan, 2 Aug. 1796, LS in MHi: Adams, reel 382; *JAW,* VIII, 519–20.

[3]See also Richard W. Stephens, comp., "Table for Identifying Variant Editions and Impressions of John Mitchell's Map of the British and French Dominions in North America," and Walter W. Ristow, "John Mitchell's Map," in Ristow, ed., *A la Carte: Selected Papers on Maps and Atlases* (Washington, D.C., 1972), pp. 107–08. For John Mitchell, see Edmund and Dorothy Smith Berkeley, *Dr. John Mitchell: The Man Who Made the Map of North America* (Chapel Hill, N.C., 1974).

[4]See Miller, ed., *Treaties,* III, 332–33.

[5]Lester J. Cappon, *Atlas of Early American History: The Revolutionary Era 1760–1790* (Princeton, 1976), p. 125, discusses the distortions of the Mitchell map.

Richard Oswald to Thomas Townshend

Paris, 7 October 1782

Sir,

Referring to my Letters of the 2d and 3d,[1] by the Courier North, and to one of the 5th, which goes under this Cover, I have the honour to send you inclosed the plan or Articles of a final Treaty proposed between Great Britain and the Thirteen States of America, Which being Settled, was delivered to me by Mr. Jay on the 5th in his own hand writing, after it had been approved of by Doctor Franklin, as he at same time informed me.

And which, by any Conversation I previously had with those Gentlemen, or Since I received it, may be Considered as including the whole of their Demands, Necessary or Advisable and, if agreed to on our part, as a Compleat and finished Treaty, with an Exception only of the usual formalities of reference to Commissions etc. Also that, as to the point of Ratification, so as to establish Peace, it must wait for our Conclusion with France, as you will please to observe is declared in the preamble.

After considering the Terms, as they Stand in the Treaty, I thought there was no Reason to object to the Boundary Lines of the Thirteen States, excepting that there is a part of Nova Scotia cutt off on the Bay of Fundy. I called on Mr. Jay this Morning, and found him willing to Sett that matter to rights, so as the Massachusetts Government shall have no more of that Coast, than they had before the War. He took his directions from Maps, and they are not distinct, nor do they agree in this matter. This is in the mean time referred, to be afterwards properly adjusted.

I next talkt to him about the Claim of Drying Fish on the Island of Newfoundland, as not having been mentioned, or included in Dr. Franklins Necessary Articles. Mr. Jay said he put them into the Treaty to avoid an Appearance of unneighborly distinctions, and considering

<them> it as not material to us, there being room enough for both of us, as well as for the French. But if we thought otherways, he would not Say but they might give it up, rather than we should be dissatisfied about it, believing their People would not much value the Priviledge, and would in general chuse to bring their Fish to their own Coasts, as they used to do. On this Subject, if I might Speak my Opinion, it is a question whether we ought to insist on their Exclusion, while the French enjoy that Conveniency, and on that account, although the Americans had not desired a Similar priviledge, <if> whether there would have been any harm in offering it to them, Since their Exclusion would be always attended with a grudge.

In my last Letter I advised that the Value of the Ungranted Lands in the Several Colonies could not be Saved as a Fund at His Majestys disposal, as the Commissioners insist that every property belonging to the Crown must go with other Rights within the Thirteen States. In case, Sir, you should think it proper that I should press this matter farther, you will be pleased to let me know. At same time I must confess that considering the little chance of Success, and that I look upon the Treaty as now closed, I doubt whether it would be proper to open it on this account. In any other Case, one would not Say so. But where there is no Controul on one Side and Circumstances press for decisions, perhaps it may be proper, if other things are Right, not to insist on a provision of this kind Standing part of the Treaty. At Same time as a great Sum may be raised out of this Property, as well as out of what is Cutt off from Canada, it would not be taken amiss by the Commissioners if it was submitted to their Consideration and equity in a Seperate way.

A Seperate Letter on that Subject, laying Claim to their Justice and good Sense, in distinguishing <between> a Resignation of property no way connected with those of Legislation and Government, and intended for the relief of unfortunate Sufferers, may have some weight with the Several provinces in Softening their resentment against Some of those People, and extending their Indulgence to them accordingly in the way of Restitution or Indemnification. But as I have said, If the Treaty is otherways approved of, I offer it as my humble opinion, that an Expectation of this kind had best be Suggested independently, and sent me in a Seperate Letter, to be laid before the Commissioners.

I touched also upon the Debts due to British Subjects, and my apprehensions of Loss by Confiscations. Mr. Jay replied that he had heard of no Such Confiscations but in the province of Maryland, which he seemed not to approve of. However, as I had before been Satisfied that they, as Commissioners, could do nothing in the matter, I did not insist farther upon it.

Before we parted, this Gentleman came again upon the Subject of West Florida, and pled in favour of the future Commerce of England, as if he had been of her Council, and wishing to make Some reparation for her Loss. Amongst other things, he repeated, that there is Water Carriage by Rivers or Lakes all the way within Land, from Canada to the mouth of the Missisippi, excepting a few Short Stoppages of Portage, So that, for Outward Merchandize, we might engross the whole of their Supplies, for a Stretch of Country between two and three thousand Miles. And in like manner (chiefly by means of the Missisippi) receive their Country Commodities in return and particularly Should embrace the whole of the Fur Trade. In all which I am Satisfied he is well founded.

At last he Said he wished much to be informed whether our Government will adopt this measure of recovering that Colony, So as he might know how to Shape his conduct with respect to Spain, and desired to be at a Certainty before he had any farther Conference with their ambassador. To which he is much Sollicited with a view to entering into a Treaty with them, in which he understands they want, amongst other things, that we shall be entirely Shutt out of any part of the Gulph of Mexico from Cape Florida to Cape Catoche.[2]

In answer I told Mr. Jay that I should write immediately, and should inform him of any Commands I had on the Subject. But told him, there would be a difficulty, as I had mentioned before, regarding the Evacuation of those Garrisons, without the necessary Letters from them to make it Safe and easy.

To which he replied. The best way will be this: "Do you now Send over this Treaty to your Ministry. If they approve of it, You and We will Sign a Copy of it when it is sent back, and the same being returned to England, it may be Sent over to Sir Guy Carleton, with Orders to publish it as a finished business. And <also> he may at Same time upon the foundation of it, Settle a Convention with General Washington for the evacuation of the Garrisons, and We Shall also write him what is necessary, which may be sent from England along with the Treaty, adding at Same time that Count Rochambau is under General Washingtons Orders, and can do nothing Seperately.

"If this Should be approved of he said Your Court may keep a Frigate ready to go at a moments warning with these papers, and any orders that may be necessary for Convoys, Transports, etc."

He at the Same time Called for the inclosed Copy I had made of the Treaty, and Scored the Words which you See Struck out, being *That "they neither Should."* He also interlined the two words in the preamble, *"or accepted,"* and Sett out for Dr. Franklins Quarters to have his opinion as to their writing Letters to General Washington on the Subject of the Evacuation of the Garrisons, and also respecting the Boundaries of Nova Scotia. When he returns I shall make a Report of his Answer in a Seperate Letter.

In the mean time I have called on Mr. Fitzherbert and have Shewen him this Sketch of the Treaty, and have informed him of any thing which I think may be of use in his Business, And he has informed me of the Count de Vergennes Propositions, and has Shewen me the Memorial of the Count d'Aranda.[3] If the West Florida Scheme were to take place, I think it would Settle Some of the points in that Memorial, as well in the recovery of that Colony, as of all the Bahama Islands we have lost.

Untill Mr. Jays return, I have not farther to add, but that I am, Sir, Your most obedient, humble Servant,

RICHARD OSWALD

ALS in FO 27/2; Cs in MiU-C: Shelburne 70 and in FO 95/511.

[1]ALS in FO 27/2; Cs in 95/511; 97/157; and in MiU-C: Shelburne 70.

[2]Cape Florida is a point at the southern end of Biscayne Bay; Cape Catoche is the northeast extremity of the Yucatán peninsula.

[3]At this time, Vergennes was pressing Aranda to accept as equivalents for Gibraltar the two Floridas, New Orleans, and its environs. Contrariwise, Aranda demanded of the British all territories in the Gulf of Mexico ceded to Spain during the war, as well as a share in the Newfoundland fisheries. Propositions of Spain to England, sent by Aranda to Fitzherbert, 6 Oct. 1782, C in CP A 538: 260–69, and *Peacemakers*, pp. 390–92. See also editorial note below, "America and the General Peace."

Richard Oswald to Thomas Townshend

Paris, 8 October 1782

Sir,

Mr. Jay, upon his return last night from Passy, told me that Doctor Franklin could not determine as to the Boundary Line between Nova Scotia and Massachusetts Bay, and thought it was best to leave it to be Settled by an express Commission for that purpose, after the War, and accordingly added a Minute of that Clause to the enclosed Treaty, to Stand as a part of it when Signed.

He also told me that with respect to their writing Letters to General Washington on the Subject of the Evacuation of the Garrisons, the Doctor thought it would not be proper for them to appear in it, in that way, on account of particular Connections, And that it was unnecessary, Since upon Sight of the Treaty, Signed by them, General Washington would readily Settle a Convention with Sir Guy Carleton, that would make every thing easy in the evacuation of the Garrisons. They wish much to have an Answer from you as Soon as possible So as the Treaty may be finally closed.

After that is done, I will, agreeable to my Instructions, bespeak their attention to the Sundry Articles not included therein, but recommended to the justice and humanity of the Commissioners, And shall not forget that one in particular, respecting a closer Union hereafter. I have no great hopes of Such a thing, yet what Doctor Franklin once Said, That they might possibly at last enter into a Confederacy with us, will give me a fair pretence to touch upon the Subject. Mr. Jay also Said Something like it, the other day, But I did not Seem to attend to it, And think it best to defer touching upon things of that kind untill their Treaty is signed, and they are entirely free, as they have always appeared So jealous of its being thought that the merits of their Claim of Independence were to rest on Assurances of any other Conditions than what ought to constitute an Agreement between States treating on an equal footing.

With a view to a Smooth and quick Conclusion with those Gentlemen I would beg leave to Suggest that if the Inclosed Draft is found to be right in the main, and exceptionable only in immaterial Articles, that I may have Orders to Sign the Treaty, with the necessary Amendments respecting those Articles if they Can be Carried, but Leaving it to my best endeavour to obtain a Consent to those Amendments, if they are not So indispensible as not to be left under that Uncertainty.

Under Such discretionary permission I shall do the best I can; and if I find I cannot Succeed, I shall avail my Self of Such general power, and Sign the Treaty, and So put an end to all Differences with America in the way Mr. Jay Said to me last night. "Once we have Signed this Treaty, We Shall have no more to do but to look on and See what the People here are about. They will not like to find that we are So far advanced; and have for Some time appeared anxious and inquisitive as to our plan of Settlement; upon which Subject I was lately tried by a certain Marquis, but I gave him no Satisfaction, and wish that for Some time as little may be Said about it as possible." Upon the whole respecting the foreign Treaties, I am apt to think, if the Demands are unreasonable, even on the part of France, they will not be Countenanced by those Commissioners. Mr. Jay having Scored out the words, relative to *peace or Truce,* I thought was done under an Impression of that nature, And with respect to Spain, I believe they think themselves very little Concerned.

Mr. Fitzherbert being anxious to dispatch this Messenger immediately, I am obliged to write these Letters in Some hurry, and hope you'l be so good to excuse the Inacuracies which I have not time to alter or correct.

We have only one Courier remaining here, but hope Soon another will be Sent over. In case Georgia had no Chartered right to go back to the Missisippi, I can Still get W. Florida carried higher up than the Latitude of 38. At least I hope so And I beg leave to add that if the Line between Nova Scotia and Massachusets could be determined with certainty, by Charter or otherways, it would be very desireable, Since I own I do not like opening a Commission with the New England Men after all our other Differences we Settled by Treaty. I tried to avoid it, but could not. If a Line of Seperation is quoted, I Should wish that the time or period of Assertainment, and proofs or Signs of acquiessence on the part of Masachusets, was also mentioned. My Friend Mr. Richard Jackson[1] I believe could get those two points Settled.

I have the honour to be, Sir, Your most obedient humble Servant,

RICHARD OSWALD

ALS in FO 27/2. Addressed: "To Mr. Secretary Townshend, 8th Octr. 1782." Endorsed: ". . . Rd 11th. By Ogg the messenger." Cs in FO 95/511, 97/157, and MiU-C: Shelburne 70.

[1]Richard Jackson (c. 1721–87), M.P., former agent for Massachusetts, had been appointed by Shelburne lord of the treasury in July 1782.

Preliminary Articles: First Draft Treaty

Paris, [5–8] October 1782

Articles agreed upon by and between Richard Oswald Esqr., the Commissioner of His Britannic Majesty for treating of Peace with the Commissioners of the United States of America on the behalf of His said Majesty on the one part. And Benjamin Franklin, John Jay[1] of the Commissioners of the said States for treating of Peace with the Commissioner of His said Majesty on their behalf, on the other part. To be inserted in, and to Constitute the Treaty of Peace proposed to be Concluded between the Crown of Great Britain, and the said United States. But which Treaty is not to be Concluded untill His Britannic Majesty shall have agreed to the Terms of a Peace between France and Britain, proposed or Accepted by His Most Christian Majesty; and shall be ready to conclude with him Such Treaty accordingly. It being the Duty and Intention of the United States not to desert their Ally, <nor to conduct any Separate Peace or Truce,>[2] but faithfully, and in all things, to abide by and fulfill their Engagements with His most Christian Majesty.

Whereas reciprocal advantages and mutual Convenience are found by Experience to form the only permanent foundation of Peace and Friendship between States, It is agreed to frame the Articles of the proposed Treaty on Such principles of liberal Equality and Reciprocity, as that partial advantages (those Seeds of discord) being excluded, Such a beneficial and Satisfactory Intercourse between the two Countries may be established, as to promise and Secure to both, the blessings of perpetual Peace and Harmony.

1 His Britannic Majesty acknowledges the Said United States, Viz. New Hampshire, Massachusetts Bay, Rhode Island and Providence Plantations, Connecticut, New York, New Jersey, Pennsylvania, Delaware, Maryland, Virginia, North Carolina, South Carolina and Georgia, to be free, Sovereign, and Independent States; That he treats with them as Such; and for himself, his Heirs and Successors, relinquishes all Claims to the Government, Propriety, and territorial Rights of the same and every part thereof. And that all disputes which might arise in future on the Subject of the Boundaries of the Said United States may be prevented, It is hereby agreed and declared, that the following are, and Shall Remain to be, their Boundaries Viz.

The Said States are bounded North by a Line to be drawn from the North west angle of Nova Scotia along the High Lands which divide those Rivers which empty themselves into the River St. Lawrence from those which fall into the Atlantic Ocean, to the Northermost [sic] head of Connecticut River; thence down along the midle of that River to the forty fifth degree of North Latitude, and thence due West in the Latitude forty five degrees North from the Equator, to the Northwestermost Side of the River St. Laurence or Cadaraquii, thence Streight to the South end of the Lake *Nipissing* and then Streight to the Source of the River Missisippi; *West,* by a Line <by a str[aight]> to be drawn along the midle of the River Missisippi from its Source to where the Said Line Shall intersect the Thirty first degree of North Latitude. South by a Line to be drawn due East from the termination of the Line last mentioned in the Latitude of thirty one degrees North of the Equator to the midle of the River Appalachicola or Catahouchi, thence along the midle thereof to its junction with the Flint River, thence

Strait to the head of St. Marys River; and thence down along the <head> midle of St. Marys River to the Atlantic Ocean. And *East* (alteration as Undernoted) by a Line to be drawn along the midle of St. Johns River, from its Source to its Mouth in the Bay of Fundy Comprehending all Islands within Seventy Leagues of any part of the Shores of the United States, and lying between Lines to be drawn due East from the points where the aforesaid Boundaries between Nova Scotia on the one part, and East Florida on the other, shall respectively touch the Bay of Fundy and the Atlantic Ocean.

2 From and immediately after the Conclusion of the proposed Treaty, there Shall be a firm and perpetual Peace between His Britannic Majesty and the Said States, and between the Subjects of the one and the Citizens of the other. Wherefor all hostilities, both by Sea and Land, shall then immediately Cease, All Prisoners on both Sides Shall be Sett at liberty; And His Britannic Majesty Shall forthwith, and without causing any destruction, withdraw all his Armies, Garrisons and Fleets, from the Said United States, and from every Port, Place and Harbour within the Same; leaving in all Fortifications the American Artillery that may be therein, And Shall also order and [cause all Archives, Records, Deeds and Papers belonging to either of] the said States or their Citizens, which in the Course of the War may have fallen into the hands of his Officers, to be forthwith restored and delivered to the proper States and persons to whom they belong.

3 That the Subjects of His Britannic Majesty and People of the Said United States Shall continue to enjoy unmolested the Right to take Fish of every kind on the Banks of Newfoundland and other places where the Inhabitants of both Countries used formerly, Viz. before the last War between France and Britain, to fish; And also to dry and Cure the Same at the acustomed Places, whether belonging to His Said Majesty or to the United States. And His Britannic Majesty and the Said United States will extend equal Priviledges and Hospitality to each others Fishermen as to their own.

4 That the Navigation of the River Missisippi from its Source to the Ocean Shall for ever remain free and open, And that both there and in all Rivers, Harbors, Lakes, Ports and Places, belonging to His Britannic Majesty or to the United States in any part of the World, the Merchants and Merchant Ships of the one and the other Shall be received, treated and protected like the Merchants and Merchant Ships of the Sovereign of the Country. That is to say the British Merchants and Merchant Ships on the one hand Shall enjoy in the united States, and in all places belonging to them, the Same Protection and

Commercial priviledges, and be liable only to the Same Charges and Duties as their own Merchants and Merchant Ships. And on the other hand, the Merchants and Merchant Ships of the United States Shall enjoy in all places belonging to His Britannic Majesty the Same protection and Commercial priviledges, and be liable only to the Same Charges and Duties as British Merchants and Merchant Ships Saving always to the Chartered Trading Companys of Great Britain, Such exclusive Use and Trade, and their respective Posts and Establishments, as neither the other Subjects of Great Britain, nor any the most favoured Nation participate in.[3]

A true Copy of what has been agreed on between the American Commissioners and me, to be Submitted to His Majestys Consideration.

RICHARD OSWALD

Alteration to be made in the enclosed Treaty, respecting the Boundaries of Nova Scotia, Viz. at the Word East, the true Line shall be Settled by Commissioners as Soon as conveniently may be after the War.

ADS in FO 27/2. Endorsed by Oswald: "Articles of the Treaty proposed to be Concluded between His Majesty and the United States of America, 5th October 1782." Endorsed in an unidentified hand: "In Mr. Oswalds 7 Octor. 1782." The articles were dispatched by Oswald on the 8th. LbkC in MiU-C: Shelburne 34; *RDC,* V, 805–08.

[1]Apparently the space was left blank to include John Adams on his arrival.

[2]Significantly, deleted by JJ.

[3]The section involving reciprocal trade and shipping proved a casualty of subsequent negotiations despites its valiant and reiterated defense by Vaughan. See, *e.g.,* Vaughan to Shelburne, *c.* 8 Oct. 1782. Tr in PPAmP: Vaughan, where the former states that he had raised questions with JJ as to the extent to which Americans were to enjoy freedom of trade both within the British Empire and from the Empire to foreign parts. Vaughan repeatedly urged the advantages England might derive from serving as America's chief entrepôt to the European continent and proposed a free port scheme for America. Vaughan to Shelburne, 23, 29 Oct. 1782, Tr in PPAmP: Vaughan. See also editorial note below, "Negotiating a Trade Treaty," June 1783.

From Benjamin Franklin

[Passy, 9 October 1782]

Doctor Franklin regrets exceedingly that his Health does not permit him the honour and Pleasure of Waiting upon Mr. and Mrs. Jay, according to their obliging Invitation.[1] He hopes Mr. and Mrs. Jay will condescend to indemnify him for the Loss he sustains, by honouring him with their Company at Dinner on Saturday next. The Doctor would be happy to see Mr. Mo[n]rowe[2] at the same time.

L in hand of William Temple Franklin.
[1]Invitation not located.
[2]Peter Jay Munro.

To Gouverneur Morris

Paris, 13 October 1782

Dear Morris,

I have recieved your festina lente Letter, but wish it had been, at least partly, in Cypher. You need not be informed of my Reasons for this wish, as by this Time you must know that Seals are, on this Side of the Water, rather matters of Decoration, than of use. It gave me nevertheless great Pleasure to recieve that Letter, it being the first from You that had reached me the Lord knows when, except indeed a few Lines covering your Correspondence with a Don.

I find you are industrious, and of Consequence useful; so much the better for yourself, for the public, and for our Friend Morris, whom I consider as the Pillar of american Credit.

The King of Great Britain by Letters patent under the Great Seal, has authorized Mr. Oswald to treat with the Commissioners of the United States of America. His first Commission litterally pursued the enabling act, and the authority it gave him was expressed in the very Terms of that act vizt., to treat with the Colonies, and with any or either of them, and any part of them, and with any Description of Men in them, and with any Person whatsoever, of and concerning Peace, etc.

HAD I NOT VIOLATED THE INSTRUCTIONS OF CONGRESS THEIR DIGNITY WOULD HAVE BEEN IN THE DUST FOR THE FRENCH MINISTER EVEN TOOK PAINS NOT ONLY TO PERSWADE US TO TREAT UNDER THAT COMMISSION BUT TO PREVENT THE SECOND BY TELLING FITZHERBERT THAT THE FIRST WAS SUFFICIENT. I TOLD THE MINISTER THAT WE NEITHER COULD NOR WOULD TREAT WITH ANY NATION IN THE WORLD ON ANY OTHER THAN AN EQUAL FOOTING.[1]

We may, and we may not have a peace this Winter. Act as if the War would certainly continue; keep proper Garrisons in your strong posts, and preserve your army sufficiently numerous, and well appointed until every Idea of Hostility and Surprize shall have compleatly vanished.

I could write you a volume, but my Health admits only of short Intervals of application.

Present my best Wishes to Mr. and Mrs. Morris, Mr. and Mrs. Meridith, and such other of our Friends as may ask how we do.

I am dear Morris, very much, Yours,

JOHN JAY

ALS in NNC: Gouverneur Morris. Addressed: "The Honble Gouvr. Morris Esqr., Philadelphia." Endorsed. The decoding was done by Morris interlineally in the cipher paragraph. Dft in JP. Omissions in *RDC*, V, 810. This is in reply to Morris' 6 Aug. 1782 letter, above.

[1]See editorial note, "The Rayneval and Vaughan Missions to England," above.

Thomas Townshend to Richard Oswald

Whitehall, 26 October 1782

Sir,

When I wrote to you last by Mr. Strachey, wishing to avoid all delay, which was not absolutely inevitable, I was as concise as possible. I thought it better to refer you to him for my Opinion upon the subject of your Dispatches, than to enter at that time into a Detail.

There was one part of Your Letter which referred to a proposal of Mr. Jay's which seems to have been frequently and eagerly urged by him. I mean that of an Expedition against West Florida. I do not think that he went so far as to guaranty a quiet Evacuation of New York. This is a matter of great delicacy, and though in some points of view the proposal appears to be one, with which we might be tempted to close, Yet we might put ourselves too much in the power of Friends very newly Reconciled to us, as well as of those who might remain our Enemies, by carrying a large Force to the Southward of all Our West India possessions. To be sure we are not disinclined to prefer an Attack upon the Spaniards to one upon the French, provided we could by that means bring off our Army, Artillery and Stores without difficulty or Insult, and that we should not run a chance of meeting the whole Force of France and Spain in defence of the Possessions of the latter, when the former were apprized of our being tied up from attacking them or of having that of France employed in the mean time against our Islands. The Colony of West Florida is certainly an object of Our attention, and we should be extremely glad to adopt such measures as might ensure to Us the re-possession of it.

If you have an opportunity of Sounding the Commissioners on this head, or if Mr. Jay should return to the Charge, it seems adviseable to see how far he thinks himself enabled to engage for the Evacuation, and then we shall be better able to judge in what manner the rest of the Scheme might be put into Execution.[1]

I am etc.

T. TOWNSHEND

P.S. I have this moment received the inclosed Letters from Lord Shelburne relative to the Estate of the Penn Family, and particularly recommend their contents to your consideration.

Cs in FO 27/2; FO 97/157; FO 95/511, and in MiU-C: Shelburne 70. Enclosure: Shelburne to Townshend, 26 Oct. 1782, with documents for Oswald, "with the King's Commands, to interest himself in behalf of the Penn Family, and to communicate it to the Commissioners, if he thinks it will serve their cause." C in FO 95/511; LbkCs in *ibid.*, 97/157, and in MiU-C: Shelburne 70.

[1]In letters of 23, 26 October to Strachey, Townshend indicated some reservations about JJ's proposal to Oswald for a British expedition against Florida, expressed concern about "the quiet and creditable evacuation" of New York, and voiced the hope that West Florida might be recovered "by other means as well as by direct attack." Cs of both in DLC: RGA: Lamson-Strachey.

Preliminary Articles: Second Draft

4 November 1782

If JJ and Oswald had assumed for a moment that the former's first draft treaty would be acceptable to the British ministry, both were to be quickly disabused. On 17 October the British Cabinet directed Townshend to issue new instructions to Oswald, instructions which disclosed how badly the British Commissioner had misjudged the importance his government attached to several issues on which he had given way to the Americans. These new instructions covered five points: (1) Oswald was to extend the Nova Scotia boundary. (2) He was to "state" Britain's right to the back country "and urge it as a means of providing for the Refugees," while indicating Britain's willingness to yield this territory should America make some other provision for the Loyalists. (3) He should resist American claims to drying rights on Newfoundland. (4) He could agree to the freedom of navigation provided in the fourth article of the treaty draft, but the rest of the article was to be omitted and referred to a treaty of commerce "for which it is a proper Subject." (5) "The Discharge of Debts due before the War [was] to be again urged as strongly as possible."[1]

Significantly, the Cabinet resolves reflected a growing lack of confidence in Oswald, to whom instructions regarding the boundaries were to be dispatched "either in writing or by some proper Person."[2] Townshend chose the latter course, and his delegate was the unbending Henry Strachey,[3] an Undersecretary of State in the Home Office. Ostensibly, Strachey's mission was "to explain the Boundaries and authentic Documents, which were only to be found" in London.[4] In fact, his real role was much broader. At a conference with Shelburne on 20 October, Strachey had received both verbal and written instructions which dealt with matters far beyond the boundaries problem. He was to strive for "as much as possible" of Canada under the Quebec Act, i.e., the Old Northwest Territory, as a basis for Loyalist compensation. Enlarged Nova Scotia boundaries were also an important object. However, if the American Commissioners refused to alter their position, Strachey might accept the boundaries proposed in the 8 October draft treaty rather than refer the question to Commissioners. The only articles in the 8 October draft which were "totally inadmissible" were the provisions for drying rights on Newfoundland and the free trade section of the fourth article. Strachey could agree to the treaty minus these two points, but he was "to fight the matter as well as [he could] with Messrs. Franklin and Jay."[5] While it "must appear authentically" that he had done his best for the Loyalists and British creditors, nevertheless an enlarged Nova Scotia boundary and a promise of United States' aid in the recovery of West Florida would reconcile Shelburne to finding other resources for the Loyalists. "But the Debts require the most serious Attention," read Strachey's written instructions. "That *honest* Debts may be *honestly* paid in *honest* Money" was to be his object as well as "Some Security as to the American Courts of Justice."[6]

Although Townshend's letter of introduction for Strachey preserved the polite fiction that he was sent only to aid Oswald in determining "with precision" the historic boundaries of the former colonies,[7] the British Commissioner in Paris did not have to look far for Strachey's real mission. In stating that he could not accept "the Principle which you seem to have adopted of going before the Commissioners in every Point of Favour or confidence," Shelburne delivered a sharp rebuke to Oswald for his easy acquiescence to American demands and arguments. He made it clear that stronger attempts must be made to obtain the backlands for the Loyalists and reminded Oswald that the debts to British creditors "cannot be lightly passed over."[8] The Prime Minister's hint that Strachey's aid might be "a material point" in obtaining compensation for Loyalists and creditors, as well as in defining boundaries, could not be ignored.[9]

On 24 October Oswald informed JJ of Strachey's mission.[10] In the next several days the group of American and British negotiators was enlarged when John Adams arrived in Paris on Saturday the 26th,[11] and Strachey joined Oswald the following Monday.[12] As Franklin's health had improved markedly, Strachey had to deal with three forceful American Commissioners.

Negotiations were conducted continually from Wednesday, 30 October through Monday evening, 4 November. The boundaries were settled first, requiring some concessions on the part of the Americans but not the substantial ones for which the British Cabinet had hoped. Remaining to be settled were the disputes over the fisheries, Loyalist compensation, and debts. On the evening of 3 November, the Commissioners and Strachey agreed to an article, drafted by JJ, which provided for legal protection for British creditors and a Congressional recommendation to the States for nullifying the confiscation of the property of "real British Subjects." Between 11:00 A.M. and 3:00 P.M. and in the evening until eleven o'clock on 4 November, Adams, JJ, Oswald, and Strachey agreed to a new fisheries article which Adams had drawn up. The two Americans returned to Oswald's that evening and completed their work on the second draft treaty.[13] It was apparently at this time that JJ scrutinized and corrected the copy of the articles, reprinted below.

The British negotiators were uneasy on the score of the Loyalists. Oswald felt that though, on the whole, "some material points are gained" in the new draft, it fell "far short of what was wanted."[14] Therefore, after agreeing to JJ's article on the debts and confiscation, the British negotiators resorted to a last appeal which, Strachey admitted, was intended as much for propaganda in England as persuasion in Paris.[15] Oswald's letter of 4 November below to the Commissioners was, according to Strachey, made "in the view of having an authentic Proof that every Effort had been used, agreeably to my Instructions from Lord Shelburne; upon a Point wherein the National Honor is so deeply concerned."[16] Strachey drafted this letter as well as the one sent a day later over his own signature. Strachey left Paris on the afternoon of 5 November, taking with him the corrected text of the draft treaty agreed to the previous day, together with sundry of his and Oswald's "observations" on these articles.

Although the American Commissioners had not presented their reply to the Strachey and Oswald letters on the Loyalists before Strachey's departure, Oswald had already seen and described to Strachey an "intended Answer" to his letter of 4 November, in which the Americans were prepared to compensate the Loyalists provided Great Britain in turn "would compensate for all the Towns, Houses, Barns, etc. destroyed during the War!"[17]

On 6 November Oswald called on JJ for the expected reply to the letters of himself and Strachey of 4 and 5 November, below. JJ and Oswald reargued the Loyalist issue, with the former distinguishing between unforgivable Tories and "less obnoxious" ones, and threatening that, with the favorable turn of the war, Congress might be expected to revise its 1779 peace instructions and formulate tougher ones. All this Oswald dutifully reported in his account of 6–7 November, below.

At noon on 7 November JJ delivered the Commissioners' separate replies to Oswald. In the former the Commissioners recapitulated the legal obstacles which prevented them from making any general engagements concerning the recovery of confiscated property. In their letter to Strachey dated 6 November they rested their case on their reply to Oswald, a copy of which they enclosed, pointing out that these were "our unanimous sentiments."[18]

JJ also asked Oswald on the seventh for a copy of the treaty draft sent to

England. On re-examining the text, he listed certain variances which had apparently escaped his previous notice. This list of JJ's suggested changes was forwarded to Strachey by Oswald in a communication of 8 November, below.

In sum, the second draft treaty substituted the "St. Croix River's" source for the middle of the St. John River, proposed the "line-of-the lakes" boundary as an alternative to the line of 45° N.L. proposed as the northern boundary in the first draft, provided for drying fish at specific places not including Newfoundland, dropped the reciprocal trade provision, and contained various minor changes in phraseology. On the back country and the debts the Americans had proved adamant.

The matter did not end here, however. The British Cabinet, meeting on 11, 14, and 15 November, scrutinized the second draft treaty and was still dissatisfied with the provisions regarding the fisheries, the refugees, and the prewar debts. It drew up a counter-draft, transmitted to Strachey by Townshend on 19 November,[19] and submitted to Adams, Franklin, and Jay on 25 November at the Hôtel de Moscovie, where the British Commissioner lodged. Its variant proposals and modifications are included in the annotations to the second treaty draft below.

[1]Resolution of the Cabinet, 17 Oct. 1782, Tr in NN: Bancroft: Strachey and in MiU-C.

[2]*Ibid.*

[3]For Townshend's letter introducing Strachey to Franklin, 23 Oct. 1782, see Dft in FO 95/511; Cs in FO 27/2, 97/157, and in MiU-C: Shelburne 70. For a comment on Strachey's unlikable personality, see Vaughan to Shelburne, 4 Dec. 1782. Massachusetts Hist. Soc., *Proceedings,* XVII (1903), 421.

[4]Shelburne to Oswald, 23 Oct. 1782, LbkC in FO 97/157 and in MiU-C: Shelburne 70; C in FO 27/2 and in 95/511.

[5]Minutes of Shelburne's conversation with Strachey, 20 Oct. 1782, Tr in MiU-C; Royal Commission on Historical Manuscripts, *Reports,* LXXXVII, 209.

[6]Shelburne to Strachey, 20 Oct. 1782. Tr in MiU-C; Royal Commission on Historical Manuscripts, *Reports,* LXXXVII, 194.

[7]Townshend to Oswald, 23 Oct. 1782, LbkC in FO 97/157 and 95/511; C in MiU-C: Shelburne 70.

[8]Shelburne to Oswald, 21 Oct. 1782, LbkC in MiU-C: Shelburne 71. Townshend let it be known that he, too, felt that Oswald "has been in my opinion a great deal too easy upon these subjects, so as to appear here to have been quite in the hands of Mr. Franklin and Mr. Jay." Townshend to Strachey, 21 Oct. 1782, Tr in NN: Bancroft: Strachey and in MiU-C.

[9]Shelburne to Oswald, 23 Oct. 1782.

[10]JJ, Diary, 24 October, below. Promptly briefed by JJ, Adams observed, "Mr. Jay likes Frenchmen as little as Mr. Lee and Mr. Izard did. He says they are not a Moral People. They know not what it is." *AP,* III, 46 (5 November).

[11]*Ibid.,* p. 37 (26 October).

[12]JJ, Diary, 29 October, below.

[13]The commissioners—Adams, Franklin, and Jay, and Oswald and Strachey—met five times: 30 and 31 October, 2, 3, and 4 November, with Franklin absent on the last two occasions. Twice the commissioners dined at JJ's. *Ibid.; AP,* III, 39–46.

[14]Oswald to Shelburne, 5 Nov. 1782, ALS in MiU-C: Shelburne 71.

[15]See below, Strachey to the Commissioners, 5 Nov. 1782.

[16]Strachey to Townshend, 8 Nov. 1782 (public), below.

[17]Strachey to Townshend, *ibid.* Again, at the closing stage of the negotiations, Franklin proposed compensation to the "merchants and shopkeepers" of Boston, to the "Inhabitants" of Philadelphia, and to the planters of the Southern states for property, including slaves, seized by the British, as well as "Compensation for all the Towns, Villages and Farms, burnt and destroyed by his Troops or Adherents in the said United States." Franklin, Memorandum "read to the Commissioners," 29 Nov. 1782, in PPAmP: Franklin, with endorsement by Benjamin Vaughan.

[18]American Commissioners to Strachey, 6 Nov. 1782. LS in hand of John Thaxter, Jr., in FO 97/157. Cs in FO 95/511 and PRO: Chatham 30–8–343. LbkCs in PCC Misc. (2); FO 27/2; MiU-C: Shelburne 70. Tr in NN: Bancroft: Strachey. C in American Commissioners to Livingston, 14 Dec. 1782, for which see below, 13 Dec. 1782. *RDC,* V, 857; *SDC,* X, 101.

[19]Rough Cabinet Minutes, 11 Nov. 1782, in Townshend's hand, Fortescue, *Corr. of George III,* V, 155 (incomplete report); "Sense of the Cabinet," 15 Nov. 1782, Dft in MiU-C: Shelburne 72. Endorsed: ". . . Approved by Mr. Townsend and Mr. Pitt." For other memoranda on the Cabinet draft, see *Peacemakers,* pp. 367–68, n. 105; also Townshend to Strachey, 19 Nov. 1782, AL and Dft in FO 95/511; LbkCs in FO 97/157 and 5/8–3. Townshend also wrote to Oswald, 19 November, notifying him that Strachey was returning to Paris with a proposed treaty that satisfied Great Britain and should be acceptable to the Americans (Dft consisting of notes for letter in FO 95/511, LbkC in 95/157). He wrote again three days later to let Oswald know that Parliament had been prorogued until 5 December "to give time to receive a final answer from the Powers with whom we are in Negotiation." 22 Nov. 1782, C in FO 97/157 and 27/2.

Richard Oswald to the American Commissioners: Strachey's Draft

[Paris, 4 November 1782]

Gentlemen,

You may remember that from the very beginning of our Negociation, I insisted that You should positively stipulate for a Restoration of the Property of all those Persons, under the denomination of Loyalists or Refugees, who have taken part with Great Britain in the present War, or, that if the said Property (as you then asserted) had been resold and passed into such variety of hands as to render the Restoration impracticable, (which you asserted to be the case) You should positively stipulate for a Compensation or Indemnification to those Persons adequate to their Losses.

To those Propositions, You have refused Your Assent. Mr. Strachey, since his Arrival at Paris, has most strenuously joined me in insisting upon the said Restitution, Compensation, or Indemnification, and in laying before You every Argument in favor of these Demands, founded upon National Honor, and upon the true Principles of Justice. These Demands, You must have understood to extend, not only to all Persons of the abovementioned Description who have fled to Europe, but to all those who may be now in any parts of North America, dwelling under the Protection of His Majesty's Arms, or otherwise. But you have still refused your Assent.

We have also insisted upon a mutual Stipulation for a general Amnesty on both sides, comprehending thereby an Enlargement of all Persons, who, on Account of offences committed, or supposed to have been committed since the Commencement of Hostilities, may be now in Confinement, and for an immediate repossession of their Properties, and peaceable Enjoyment thereof under the Government of the united States. To this You have not hitherto given a direct Answer.

It is however incumbent upon me as Commissioner of the King of Great Britain to repeat all these several Demands, and (without going over all those Arguments upon Paper, which we have so often urged in Conversation) to insist, as I do hereby in the most peremptory manner, that You do enter into an express and unequivocal stipulation, for the said Restitution, Compensation, or Indemnification and general Amnesty before we proceed farther in the negociation for Peace.

Tr in NN: Bancroft: Strachey. A memorandum by the copyist at the beginning of this letter reads: "Mem. This Copy is made from the draft of a letter which has neither date nor signature." At the end of the transcript, in the hand of the copyist, is this notation: "(The Original is in the handwriting of Henry Strachey. HfB)." This copy, with its peremptory closing sentence, apparently was of Strachey's original draft. Letterbook and other copies, adhering to the variant text in *RDC,* V, 848, are found in FO 95/511, which ends with "signed H. Strachey," and carries the endorsement: "Copy of the Draft of Mr. Strachey's Letter to the American Commissioners dated 5 Nov. 1782 (No. 6)"; in FO 27/2, in CO 5/6–3 (in Oswald's hand, the copy enclosed in his letter to Townshend of 6–7 Nov. 1782, below); and in PCC 85, 106, and Misc.; Royal Commission on Historical Manuscripts, *Reports,* I, 239.

Preliminary Articles: Second Draft

[4–7 November 1782]

Articles agreed upon by and between Richard Oswald Esquire the Commissioner of his Britannic Majesty for treating of Peace with the Commissioners of the United States of America, on behalf of his said Majesty on the one part; and Benjamin Franklin, John Jay and John Adams, three of the Commissioners of the said States, for treating of Peace with the Commissioner of his said Majesty, on their behalf on the other part. To be inserted in, and to constitute the Treaty of Peace proposed to be concluded between the Crown of Great Britain, and the said United States. But which Treaty is not to be concluded untill his Britannic Majesty shall have agreed to the Terms of a Peace between France and Britain, proposed or accepted of by his most Christian

Majesty; and shall be ready to conclude with him, such Treaty accordingly; it being the Duty and Intention of the United States not to desert their Ally, but faithfully and in all things, to abide by and fullfill their Engagements with his most Christian Majesty.[1]

Whereas reciprocal advantages, and mutual Convenience are found by Experience to form the only permanent Foundation of Peace and Friendship between States, It is agreed to form the Articles of the proposed Treaty, on such Principles of liberal Equality, and Reciprocity as that partiall Advantages (those seeds of Discord) being excluded, such a beneficial and satisfactory intercourse between the two Countries may be established as to promise and secure to both perpetual Peace and Harmony.

His Britannic Majesty acknowledges the said United States Viz. New Hampshire, Massachusetts Bay, Rhode Island & Providence Plantations, Connecticut, New York, New Jersey, Pennsylvania, Delaware, Maryland, Virginia, North Carolina, South Carolina and Georgia, to be free Sovereign and independent States. That he treats with them as such, and for himself, his Heirs and Successors relinquishes all Claims to the Government Propriety and territorial Rights of the same, and every part thereof; and that all Disputes which might arise in future on the subject of the Boundaries of the said United States may be prevented, It is hereby agreed and declared that the following are, and shall be[2] their Boundaries Viz:

From the north west Angle of Nova Scotia, being that Angle which is formed by a Line drawn due north, from the source of St. Croix River to the Highlands which divide the Rivers that empty themselves into the River St. Laurence, from those which fall into the Atlantic Ocean, and along the said High Lands, to the northwestern head of Connecticut River, thence down along the middle of that River to the forty fifth Degree of north Latitude, following the said Latitude, untill it strikes the River Missisippi. Thence by a Line to be drawn along the middle of said River Missisippi, untill it shall intersect the northernmost part of the Thirty first Degree of Latitude, north of the Equator.[3] South, by a Line to be drawn due East from the determination of the Line last mentioned in the Latitude of Thirty one Degrees to the middle of the River, Apalatchicola or Catahouche; thence along the middle thereof, to its junction with the Flint River; thence straight to the head of St. Mary's River; and thence down along the middle of St. Mary's River to the Atlantic Ocean. East by a Line from the mouth of said St. Mary's River to the mouth of the River St. Croix in the Bay of Fundy and by a Line drawn through the middle of said River to its Source; and from its Source directly north, to the aforesaid High Lands which divide the Rivers that fall into the Atlantic Ocean, from those which empty themselves into the River St. Laurence, comprehending all Islands within twenty Leagues of any part of the Shores of the United States,[4] and laying between Lines to be drawn due East from the points where the aforesaid Boundaries of St. Croix River, and St. Mary's River shall respectively touch the Bay of Fundy, and the Atlantic Ocean; excepting allways such Islands as now are, or heretofore have belonged to the Colony of Nova Scotia, or have been within the Limits thereof.[5]

Upon a farther Consideration of the just Limits and Boundaries of the Province of West Florida it is agreed that its northern Boundary shall extend from the said thirty first Degree of Latitude to a Line to be drawn due East from the place where the River Yassous falls into the River Missisippi, and along the said Line due East to the River Apalachicola.[6]

It is agreed that all such Loyalists[7] or Refugees, as well as all such British Merchants or other Subjects, as may be resident in any of the United States at the Time of the Evacuation thereof by the Arms and Garrisons of his Britannic Majesty, shall be allowed six months thereafter to remove to any part of the World; and also at their Election to dispose of, within the said Term, or to carry with them their Goods and Effects. And it is understood that the said States shall extend such farther Favour to the said Merchants; and such Amnesty and Clemency to the said Refugees, as their respective Circumstances, and the Dictates of Justice and Humanity may render <fit> just[8] and reasonable and particularly that Amnesty and Indemnity be granted to all such of the said Refugees as may be unaffected by Acts, Judgments, or Prosecutions actually passed or commenced a month previous to such Evacuation.[9]

That the Subjects of his Britannic Majesty, and the People of the said United States shall continue to enjoy unmolested the Right to take Fish of every kind, on all the Banks of Newfoundland; also in the Gulph of St. Laurence, and all other places where the Inhabitants of both Countries used at any time heretofore to fish; and also to dry and cure their Fish on the Shores of the Isle of Sables, Cape Sables, and the Shores of any of the unsettled Bays, Harbours or Creeks of Nova Scotia, and of the Magdalene Islands. And his Britannic Majesty, and the said United States will extend equal Priviledges and Hospitality to each others Fishermen as to <his>[10] their own.

Whereas certain of the United States excited thereto by the unnecessary Destruction of private Property, have confiscated all Debts

John Jay. By Gilbert Stuart. London, 1783. *(Collection of John Jay Iselin, Courtesy of The New-York Historical Society)*

Sarah Livingston Jay. By David Huntington after a contemporary French miniature.

TWO AMERICAN CORRESPONDENTS OF JAY

George Clinton. By T. B. de Valdenuit
(Oneida Historical Society)

Egbert Benson. By Gilbert Stuart
(Long Island Historical Society)

THE AMERICAN PEACE COMMISSIONERS IN PARIS

Benjamin Franklin. By J. S. Duplessis. *(The New York Public Library, Astor, Lenox, and Tilden Foundations)*

THE AMERICAN PEACE COMMISSIONERS IN PARIS

John Adams. By Charles Willson Peale *(Independence National Historical Park Collection)*

THE AMERICAN PEACE COMMISSIONERS IN PARIS

John Jay. By Joseph Wright. New York, 1786. *(Courtesy of The New-York Historical Society)*

Henry Laurens. British school, eighteenth century. *(The United States Senate Collection)*

THE FRENCH AND SPANISH PEACE NEGOTIATORS

Vergennes. Steel engraving, French school, eighteenth century.

Aranda. Miniature by Michel Honoré Bonnieu *(Biblioteca Nacional, Madrid)*

Nekoubayistes
Abitibis
Gr. Discharge
French House or New Settlement
L. Beauharnois
L. Miskouaskane
Chomonchouanistes
L. Ouichigoubich
St. John's Lake
Chekoutimi
L. Oumamiouetz
Lake Begon
L. Naouagamiou
L. des Neiges
Achoupekahigan
Lake Kaouinagamich
L. Tamiscaming
Lakes St. Thomas
L. St. Croix
L. St. Charles
Lorette
Quebec
Antient Algonquins
Extirpated by the Iroquois
R. Masquinonge
Long fall
Bounds
Mataouan
Portage les Galets
Six Nations
R. Creux
Allumettes
L. du Borgne
Riv. of the Outaouais or Utawas
Les Calumets
R. Rouge
Montreal
La Prairie
Lake Nipissin
By the several Conquests here mentioned, the Territories of the Six Nations extend to the Limits here laid down; which they have been in Possession of about 100 Years.
Antient Outaouacs
Expelled by the Iroquois
R. de la Tortue
R. Ridoau
Petite R.
De L'Isle Du Fer and other Geographers
L. St. Francis
Limits of Canada and the Iroquois according to
Long Fall
Rapids
Moulinet
Falls St. Johns
Norridgewock
Iroquois
Northern Iroquois
L. Quento
La Galette
Ganeydoes
R. Chalytera
Tannaoute
L. St. Leon
Kente
Ganaraske
River of the Iroquois or Cataraqui
Irocoisia
The Original Country of the Iroquois and formerly so called
Lake Ontario or Catarakui
Middle Pt.
Bay of Nioure
Tegaogen
Toronto
Traverse Pt.
Assumption R.
Sable R.
Crown Point
White Mountains
New Hampshire
Bottom of Lake
Niagara Ft.
60 m.
Oswego Bay
Oswego
Oneyda Lake
Burnetsfield
Palatine T.
Mohawks R.
Fort Dummer
York
Onondago
Messesagues removed hereabouts
Schenectady
Albany
Green Bush
Massachussets Bay
Northampton
Hatfield
Springfield
Suffield
Enfield
Sunderland
Boston
Plymouth
Connecticut
Rhode Island
Buzards B.
Elizabeth I.
Block I.
Martha's Vineyard I.
Long Island Sound
Long I.
New York
Kingstown
Sheshequin
Shenango
Ohio
Pensilvania
Shawanoes

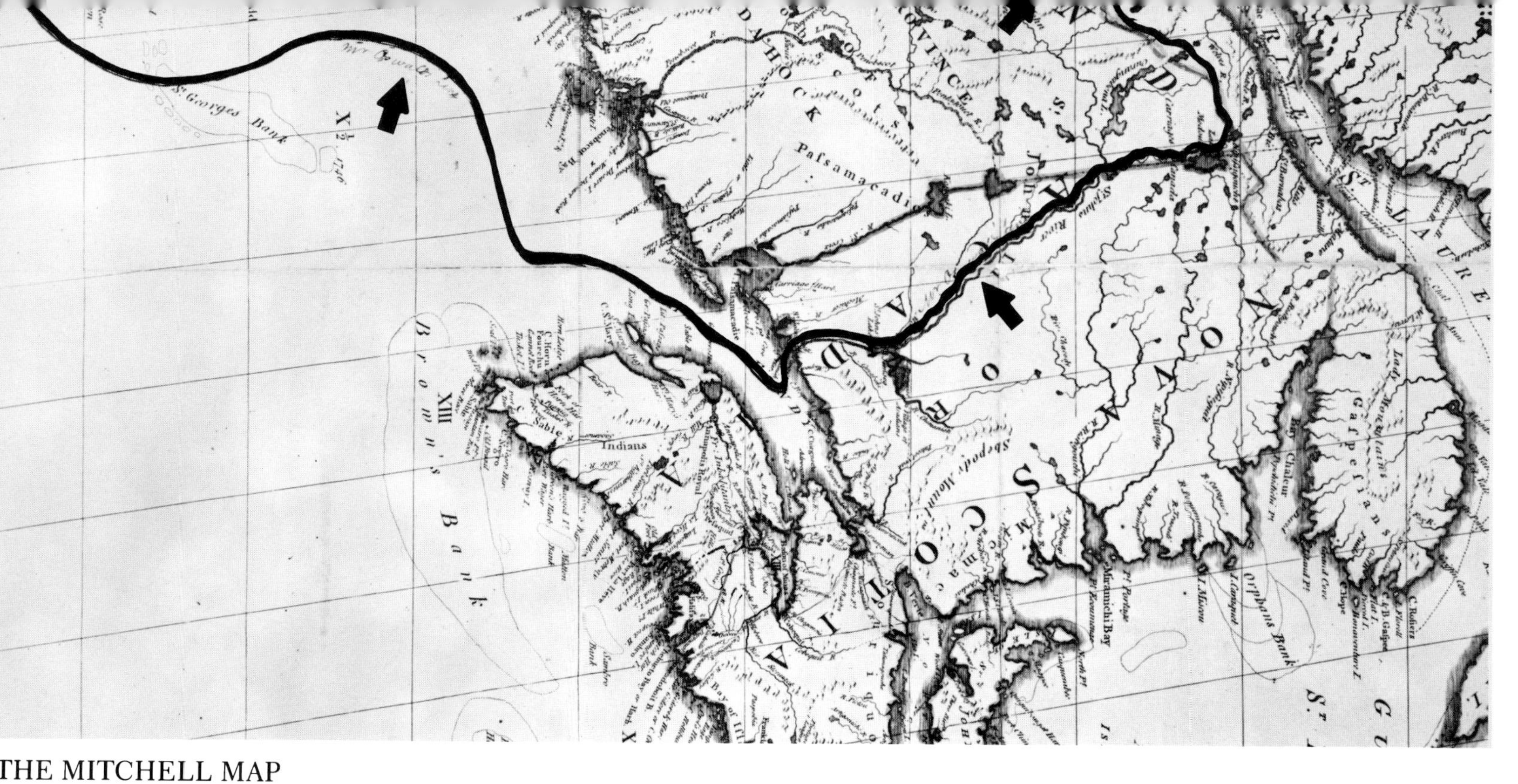

THE MITCHELL MAP

Northeastern Section, including the Fisheries.
A map of the British and French Dominions in North America by John Mitchell. Printed by Jefferys & Faden. "Published by the author, February 13th, 1755, according to Act of Parliament."

The heavy line and arrows indicate the line drawn and labeled as "Mr. Oswald's Line" by John Jay on the original map. *(Courtesy of The New-York Historical Society)*

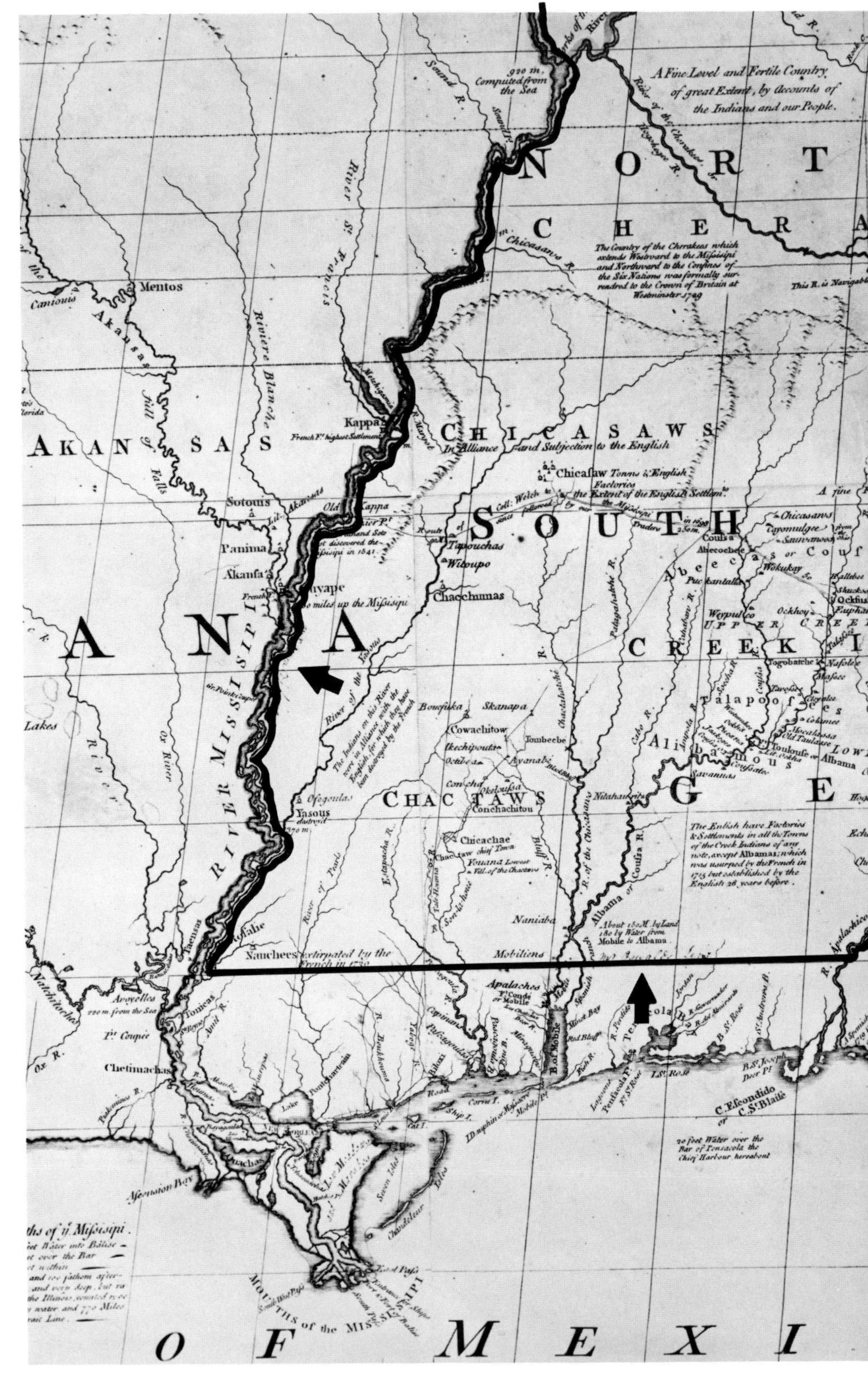
A Fine Level and Fertile Country of great Extent, by Accounts of the Indians and our People.
920 m. Computed from the Sea
NORT
CHERA
The Country of the Cherakees which extends Westward to the Misisipi and Northward to the Confines of the Six Nations was formally surrendred to the Crown of Britain at Westminster 1729
Chicasaws R.
Mentos
Canioüis
River St Francis
Riviere Blanche
Kappa
French Ft highest Settlement
AKANSAS
CHICASAWS
In Alliance and Subjection to the English
Chicasaw Towns & English Factories
the Extent of the English Settlem.t
Sotouis
Old Kappa
Panima
Akansa's
SOUTH
Tapouchas
Witoupo
Chacchumas
Coussa
Abecoche
Abeecas or Coussas
Puckantalla
Wokukay
Chicasaws
Chomulgee
Sauwanoos
Weypulco
UPPER CREEK
ANA
CREEK
River of the Yasous
Togobatche
Nafolee
Masace
Talapoosees
Toulouse or Albama
Alibamous
Savannas
LOWE
G
E
RIVER MISSISIPI
The Indians on this River were in Alliance with the English, for which they have been destroyed by the French
Boucfuka
Skanapa
Cowachitow
Ikechipouta
Tombecbe
Octibea
Ayanabi
Concha
Okoloussa
Conchachitou
CHACTAWS
Ofogoulas
Yasous destroyed
Chicachae
Chactaw chief Town
Youana Lowest Vill. of the Chactaws
The Enlish have Factories & Settlements in all the Towns of the Creek Indians of any note, except Albamas; which was usurped by the French in 1715 but established by the English 28 years before.
Lakes
Ox River
Naniaba
About 150 M. by Land 180 by Water from Mobile to Albama
Nauchees extirpated by the French in 1730
Mobiliens
Apalachicola
Arovelles
220 m. from the Sea
Tonicas
Pt. Coupee
Chetimachas
Apalaches
Ft. Condé or Mobile
Mobile Bay
B. of Mobile
Pensacola
I. St. Rose
B. St. Rose
St. Andrews B.
B. St. Joseph
Lake
Pontchartrain
Biloxi
Pascagoula
Ship I.
Dauphin or Massacre I.
Mobile Pt.
Corne I.
C. Escondido or C. St. Blaise
20 feet Water over the Bar of Pensacola the Chief Harbour hereabout
Ascension Bay
Chandeleur Isles
Seven Isles
East Pass
MOUTHS of the MISSISIPI
OF MEXI

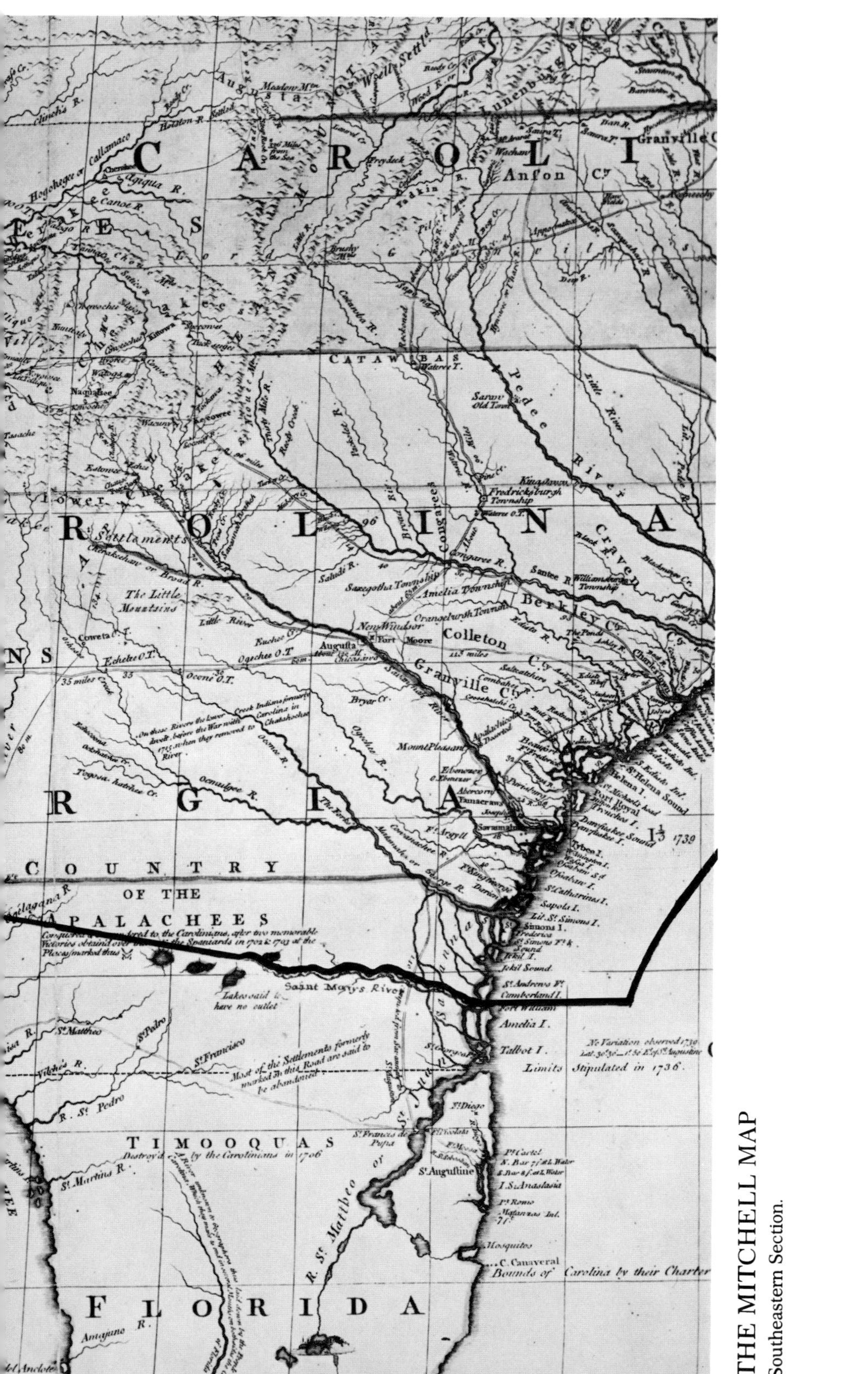

THE MITCHELL MAP
Southeastern Section.

BRITAIN'S NEGOTIATORS

Earl of Shelburne. From a mezzotint by Sir Joshua Reynolds, 1787.

Richard Oswald as a Young Man. By William De Nune, 1747. The only known portrait.

Thomas Townshend (Later First Viscount Sydney). By Gilbert Stuart, London, c. 1785. *(State Library of New South Wales, Sydney)*

David Hartley. Engraving by James Walker after the portrait by George Romney, 1783.

JAY'S VACATIONS IN FRANCE AND ENGLAND

Tour d'horloge, Rouen. Watercolor and pencil by David Cox the Elder *(Tate Gallery, London)*

The Pump Room, Bath. (Richard Warner, *The History of Bath* [Bath, 1801])

SALLY JAY'S FRIENDS IN PARIS AND AMERICA

Adrienne Noailles de Lafayette. Etching by Albert Rosenthal after French school, eighteenth century.

Mary White Morris. By Charles Willson Peale *(Independence National Historical Park Collection)*

Alice De Lancey Izard. By Thomas Gainsborough, 1775 *(Metropolitan Museum of Art, New York)*

Lady Juliana Fermor Penn. Pastel by Francis Cotes *(Newhouse Galleries, New York)*

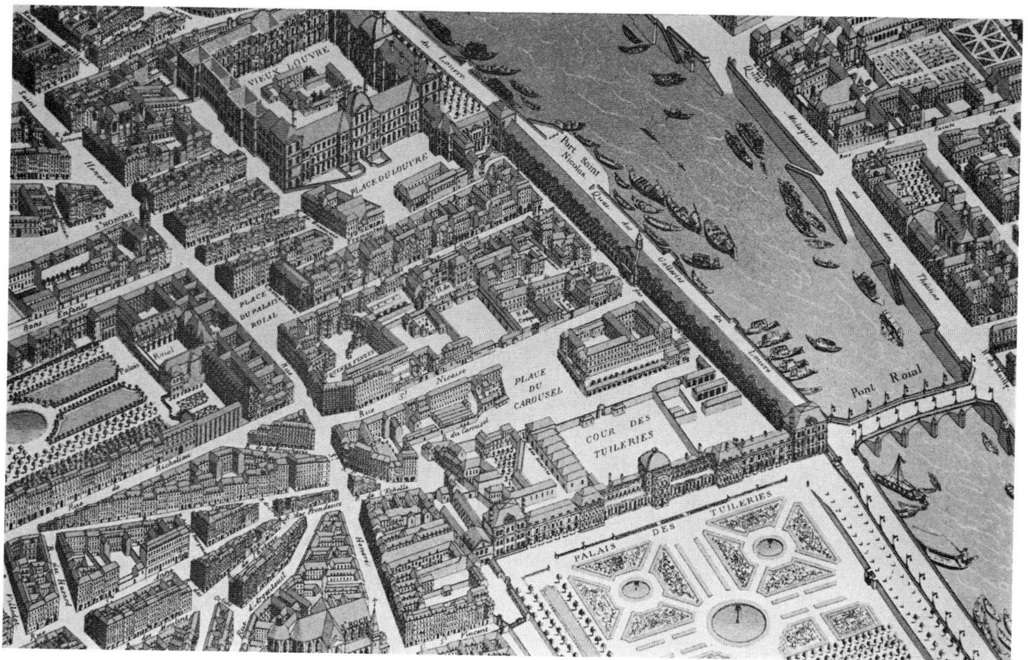

Paris at the Time of the Jays

The Peacemakers. Benjamin West's unfinished painting commemorating the signing of the Preliminary Peace, 30 November 1782. Left to right: John Jay, John Adams, Benjamin Franklin, Henry Laurens, and William Temple Franklin. The blank space on the canvas was presumably reserved for Richard Oswald and Caleb Whitefoord whom West was unable to persuade to sit for him. *(The Henry Francis du Pont Winterthur Museum)*

Montgolfier Balloon Ascension. Versailles, 19 September 1783, in the presence of the royal family. By Charles De Lorimier.

due from their Citizens to British Subjects; and also in certain Instances Lands belonging to the latter;

And whereas it is just that private Contracts made between Individuals of the two Countries before the War, should be faithfully executed; and as the Confiscation of the said Lands may have a Latitude not justifiable by the Law of Nations, It is agreed that British Creditors shall notwithstanding meet with no lawful Impediment to recovering the full Value or Sterling Amount of such Bona fide Debts as were contracted before the year 1775. And also that Congress will recommend to the said States so to correct (if necessary) their said Acts, respecting the Confiscation of Lands in America belonging to real British Subjects, as to render the said Acts consistent with perfect Justice and Equity.[11]

As to the Cession made of certain Lands in Georgia by a number of Indians there, on the first June 1773, for the purpose of paying the Debts due from them to a number of Traders. The American Commissioners say that the State of Georgia is alone competent to consider and decide on the same; for that it being a matter of internal police, with which neither Congress nor their Commissioners are authorized to interfere, it must of necessity be referred to the Discretion and Justice of that State, who without Doubt will be disposed to do, what may be just and reasonable on the Subject.

Similar Reasons and considerations constrain the Commissioners to give the like answer to the Case of Mr. Penn's Family.[12]

From and immediately after the Conclusion of the proposed Treaty there shall be a firm and perpetual Peace between his Majesty and the said States; and between the Subjects of the one, and the Citizens of the other: Wherefore all Hostilities, both by Sea and Land, shall then immediately cease: All Prisoners on both sides shall be set at Liberty and his Britannic Majesty shall forthwith, and without causing any Destruction, withdraw all his Armies Garrisons and Fleets from the said United States, and from every Port Place and Harbour within the same; leaving in all Fortifications the American Artillery that may be therein. And shall also order and cause all Archives, Records, Deeds and Papers belonging to <either> any of the said States, or their Citizens, which in the Course of the War may have fallen into the hands of his Officers, to be forthwith restored and delivered to the proper States and Persons to whom they belong.

That the navigation of the River Missisippi from its Source to the Ocean shall forever remain free and open.

Separate Article

It is hereby understood and agreed, that in case Great Britain, at the Conclusion of the present War, shall recover, or be put in possession of, West Florida, the Line of north Boundary between the said Province and the United States, shall be a Line drawn from the mouth of the River Yassous where it unites with the Mississippi, due East to the River Appalachicola.[14]

C in CO 5/8–3. This is the corrected copy enclosed in Strachey to Townshend, 8 Nov. 1782, below. Additions and corrections made by JJ on 7 November, as well as the Articles proposed by the British Cabinet in mid-November, are indicated in the notes below. On a copy of the draft treaty in FO 95/511 is this marginal comment, presumably by Townshend: "This Paper appears to me, though drawn in the form of a Treaty, to be in effect an Ultimatum from the American Comm[issione]rs to serve as the Foundation of a Provisional Treaty."

[1]The British Cabinet version of the treaty draft is identical except for the omission of the concluding clause: "It being the Duty and Intention . . . his most Christian Majesty." The Cabinet draft contained this instruction to Strachey: "N.B. If the American Commissioners wish to have the remainder of the Title proposed by them, which follows the words *Treaty accordingly,* they may be admitted."

[2]"Shall remain to be" in *RDC.*

[3]Alternative boundaries proposed by the American Commissioners: west on 45° to the Iroquois River, thence along the middle thereof into Lake Ontario, and through the middle of Lakes Ontario, Erie, Huron, and Superior, on to Long Lake and the Lake of the Woods, and thence to the northernmost part thereof (the later basis for the U.S. western boundary of 49° N.L.). See below, Oswald to Strachey, 8 Nov. 1782, with enclosures, for which see source note. In turn, the British Cabinet in their third draft version accepted this "line-of-the-Lakes" alternative. Early in the negotiations Strachey proposed a longitudinal line in the Northwest, which reminded JJ uncomfortably of the boundary proposed variously by Rayneval and Aranda. See *Peacemakers,* p. 358.

[4]On the seaward boundary of the U.S. and the claims of the U.S. versus various North Atlantic States to the continental shelf on the basis, among others, of this clause, see R. B. Morris, "The Treaty of Paris of 1783," in Library of Congress, *Fundamental Testaments of the American Revolution* (Washington, 1973), pp. 93–96; Report of Albert B. Maris, Special Master, in U.S. v. Maine *et al.,* No. 35, Original, October Term 1973, 420 U.S. 515 (1975).

[5]On 7 November JJ struck out of the treaty the exception as to the Nova Scotia islands. Oswald to Strachey, 8 November, below. The Cabinet accepted the new northeastern boundary line, which used the "St. Croix River," a cartographic fancy. The Cabinet draft excepts "such islands as now are, or heretofore have been, within the limits of the said province of Nova Scotia."

[6]This paragraph omitted in *RDC,* V, 852, and in Cabinet draft.

[7]"Royalists" in *RDC.*

[8]Interlinear correction from "fit" to "just." *RDC* has "just."

[9]Section beginning "and particularly," a marginal insert. The Cabinet sought to extend the protection of American courts to the victims of confiscation, both to the "real British Subjects" of JJ's first draft Article, as well as to the refugees, enclosing not only recommended texts but four modifications. See also Strachey to American Commissioners, 25 Nov. 1782, n. 4, below.

[10]"His" inserted; "their" remains in *RDC.* This article, drafted by Adams, was more explicit in listing areas where drying and curing might be performed. The

British Cabinet's instructions to Strachey of 19 November change "right" to take fish and dry and cure to "liberty," and in the Cabinet version the blanket "right" to fish "in all other Places, etc." was omitted. Under these latter instructions the fisheries provisions were no longer reciprocal and coastal fishing was forbidden.

[11]The original draft version of the Articles on British debts and Loyalists is in JJ's hand in MHi: Adams, reel 359. See also *AP,* III, 43–46 (3 and 4 Nov. 1782). As regards forfeiture, the Cabinet proposed a stronger version, providing for refunding to the person then in possession the bona fide price paid for the land.

[12]The Articles relating to the Georgia grants and the Penn family are omitted in the Cabinet draft.

[13]The Cabinet draft omitted the opening phrase and changed the provision regarding evacuation from "forthwith" to "with all convenient speed."

[14]*RDC* spells the river "Yazoo," the modern spelling, and following "Apalachicola," the text reads: "and thence along the middle of that river to its junction with the Flint River, etc." On 7 November JJ crossed out "recover" and substituted "be"; see Oswald to Strachey, 8 Nov. 1782, below. The *RDC* version uses JJ's wording and does not include the reference to the alternate version in the body of the treaty draft. The Cabinet agreed to the separate Article, but retained the phrase "shall recover, or be put in possession of."

Henry Strachey to The American Commissioners

Paris, 5 November 1782

Gentlemen,

Knowing the Expectation of the King's Ministers, that a full Indemnity shall be provided for the whole Body of Refugees, either by a Restitution of their Property, or by some stipulated Compensation for their Losses, and being confident, as I have repeatedly assured You, that your Refusal upon this Point will be the great Obstacle to a Conclusion and Ratification of that Peace which is meant as a solid, perfect, Permanent, Reconciliation and ReUnion between Great Britain and America, I am unwilling to leave Paris, without once more submitting the Matter to Your Consideration. It affects equally, in my Opinion, the Honor and the Humanity of Your Country, and of ours. How far You will be justified in risking a favorite Object of America, by contending against those Principles, is for You to determine. Independence, and a more than[1] reasonable Possession of Territory, seem to be within Your Reach. Will You suffer them to be outweighed by the Gratification of Resentment against <Men who adhered to their lawful King?> Individuals? I venture to assert that such a Conduct has no Parallel in the History of civilized Nations.

I am under the necessity of setting out by Two o'Clock today. If the time is too short for your Reconsideration, and for Determination, of this important Point, I shall hope that You will enable Mr. Oswald to dispatch a Messenger after me, who may be with me before Morning at Chantilly, where I propose sleeping tonight, or who may overtake me before I <reach> arrive in London, with <such an> a satisfactory answer <as> to this Letter. I have the honor to be, Gentlemen, Your most obedient and most humble Servant,

H. STRACHEY

Dft in FO 27/2. This is the draft enclosed by Strachey in his letter to Townshend of 8 Nov. 1782 (public), below. The RC is printed in *RDC*, V, 850, without, of course, the deletions which appear in the Dft and with a minor, but significant, inversion in wording in the first paragraph. LbkCs in FO 95/511, 27/2, in PRO: Chatham 30–8–343 and in MiU-C: Shelburne 70. Tr in NN: Bancroft: Strachey. In reply, the American Commissioners, 6 November, refer Strachey to their letter to Oswald of 7 November below. LS in hand of W. T. Franklin in FO 97/157; Dft in hand of Adams in PCC 85, p. 282; LbkCs in PCC 106, FO 27/2, and in MiU-C: Shelburne 70; Cs in PRO: Chatham 30–8–343 and in FO 95/511. Tr in NN: Bancroft: Strachey.

[1]"More than a" in *RDC*.

Richard Oswald to Thomas Townshend

Paris, 6 and 7 November 1782

Sir,

Referring to the Letter I had the honour of writing by Mr. Strachey, who left this Place yesterday afternoon, I beg leave to inform you, that I called on Mr. Jay this morning for an answer to a Letter from me to the American Commissioners delivered to him some days past, in relation to the Refugees and Loyalists, and also to one sent to him from Mr. Strachey yesterday on the same Subject. To this, Mr. Jay told me that he intended this day to call on Mr. Franklin and Mr. Adams on that Business, and to take their Sentiments thereon, and that whatever should be agreed between them, should be stated in a Letter to me, to serve as an answer to both Mr. Strachey's Letter and mine, which he hoped would be in my hands to-morrow, to be sent to England, if I thought proper.

This Interview gave Occasion to the subject of the Refugees being again taken up in the way of Conversation. When Mr. Jay went over much the same arguments against a Restitution of their Estates, as he and Dr. Franklin had done on many former Occasions, and particularly in their Conversation with Mr. Strachey, with an addition of sundry other Observations, relative to the American business Vizt.

That there are Certain of those Refugees they never would forgive, for various reasons that would be recited in their Letter to me. That they would not suffer them to live in their neighborhood, even although we had lands to set them down upon, nor would those Persons be sure of their Lives there. That however they were not of any great Number, and as to the others less obnoxious, the Clause of Amnesty in the Plan of the New Treaty, would make all such of them as were not under Judgement, or Prosecution, perfectly easy in their several Stations; and he made no doubt but, after a Peace the several States would treat them with as much lenity as their Case would admit of. And the bulk of these being besides of low rank, they would successively fall into the Sundry Occupations of the Country, and so Government would be saved the Expence of transporting and subsisting them.

That with respect to those abovementioned, under Exception, since, failing of a restoration of their Estates, We pressed to have a Fund for compensation allotted to us, they had given us Land; at a proper distance, which they might occupy, and if not occupied, it might be sold. That Money might be raised upon that Land. If not enough, the difference might be supplied without assistance. That such Difference would be a small Matter in comparison of the Expence of going on with the War another year, which he said would be the Certain Consequence of refusing to close with them on the present Occasion; And that according, as we Should determine they would be guided in their Reports and Advices to the Congress, and their Attention, more or less to this Court.

That they have just now received fresh advice from the Congress, dated in the end of September,[1] By which he found the People of that country were universally suspicious of the Intention of Great Britain towards them. That their printed Publications were brimfull of these Insinuations, and they were preparing themselves accordingly for the Consequences.

That they, the Commissioners, were, however perfectly Satisfied that England was Sincere, and meant to give them their Independence, and to put an end to the War. And as they equally, and most ardently longed to see their Country settled in Peace, Mr. Jay said he hoped we would not let this Opportunity slip, but resolve speedily to wind up this long Dispute, so as we might be again as one People.

That they had hitherto asked in this Negotiation under Instructions of the Year 1779 when their Affairs were not in quite so good a Situation as at present, and had gone to the full Stretch of them, and farther.

But if we broke up now, We might be assured of their receiving new Instructions, and of a very different kind from the present. In which, among other things, he made no doubt they would be directed to state all the Depredation, Plunder and unnecessary Destruction of Property over all their Country, in Charge against the British Demands of bona fide Creditors, for which in the body of the Treaty, they have now established an Independent Security.

That by the last Advices in September they understood the State of Pennsylvania had begun upon these Estimates; and there was a Committee actually sitting at Philadelphia for making up an account of all those Damages, not occasioned by the direct and necessary Operations of War; Which, when collected from the Reports of the several States, and brought to a head, would leave no room for any Claims in behalf of the said British Creditors. That now was the time for Great Britain to take the benefit of the Security offered to those Creditors; and wisely to avoid the Consequences of former Mistakes. For Mr. Jay was pleased to say, and which I think myself bound to repeat, That in every Stage of the War Our Offers and Acceptances had always come too late, and we had consequently worse Terms in the next propositions.

That with respect to those British Debts, he had at all times jointly with his Colleagues declared, that all that were contracted before the War must be duly paid; yet if their States by Our refusal of accommodation should be continued under their present expensive Establishment, he would not answer for the same favourable determination hereafter. The Time he said was precious, as they would soon be under a necessity of writing to their Congress in answer to their late Letters. Mr. Jay, after repeating his wishes that Great Britain might determine in a manner suitable to the present situation of Things, said, that in case we meant to close with them on this occasion, he would take the liberty to request, that His Majesty would order his ambassadors at the Neutral Courts to give so much Countenance to the peace with America, as formally to Intimate its being in the Train of Negotiation, and when signed, that the same should also be notified. The advice of this he said would soon reach America, and would produce the happiest effects there, as well to our benefit as theirs; even although the final Conclusions must wait a Settlement with France. That even that Conclusion would also feel the benefit of those Negotiations.

Soon after Mr. Adams, the other Commissioner, called upon me, and expressed himself equally anxious that there might be an end to all our Differences.

In the mean time he delivered me the inclosed Packet from their Congress to Mr. Laurens, with a Request that I would send it by the first Courier, and to Recommend it so as it might get safe to his hands.

Which I promised to do, and hope it will be taken care of. Mr. Adams also signified in like manner as Mr. Jay had done a Wish that the abovementioned Intimation might be made of the Neutral Courts. He seemed so earnest about it, that I could not avoid asking him as to the object of such Intimation. He answered, that among other Things, it would make them more Independent, or Indifferent about this Court, Which they wished exceedingly might be brought about. That neither he nor Mr. Jay had any particular Instructions relative to this Court, nor had any Correspondence with it, farther than as they were bound by the Letter of their Treaty with them. Farther than that, he said as much, as if they gave themselves no Concern about them. That in a Case of a particular Commission, long Residence and habits of Correspondence, it was natural to suppose a correspondent Complaisance would be created, even under the guidance of the most upright Intentions and Conduct upon the whole; but as to Them Two [sic], this Gentleman said, they were not even under those kind of biasses.

Under this Cover I send six Philadelphia Gazettes,[2] down to the 5th October. In the Paper of that date, there is an advertisement of the Committee sitting at Philadelphia for liquidating the Damages, which Mr. Jay mentioned, and which he apprehends will make part of the next Treaty, in case the present Plan is not adopted. It stands in the second column of the third Page of that Paper, scored with Red Ink. In the said 3d Page there is an Advertisement of the Resolutions of their Congress worth Notice. Also the Pennsylvania Bill in the 3d Page of the Pennsylvania Packet dated 21st September.[3]

Thursday 7th Mr. Jay called upon me about Noon, and delivered me the two inclosed Letters, one to Mr. Strachey, the other to me, in answer to our two Letters, addressed to the Commissioners as abovementioned. He repeated his request for a speedy decision, and his wishes for a favourable one. He said, he had seen a Letter from Mr. Morris, the Financier General of their Congress, wherein he says, that to his great Surprise, he finds the American Merchants, the most averse to Peace of any People of that Country. I told Mr. Jay that was easily accounted for, since the Circumstances of the times threw the Trade of Importation, as well as Exportation, into the hands of a few Merchants of a Superior Address, and who had Capital of their own, and an extensive Connection and Correspondence with Merchants in France, Holland etc. and by means thereof held a Monopoly of the Trade against all other Traders and the Country too; which they must perceive would fall to the ground, as soon as the present dangers and difficulties ceased, and their Ports were open to all Adventurers whatever. Mr. Morris, besides that, said that Supplies of all kinds came in so plentifully, that he had countermanded on this occasion sundry Orders he had before given for Cloathing for their Troops, and other Necessaries for the Publick Service, as they could be had at hand, without the risk of disappointment, and at a moderate price. Mr. Jay said it was natural to think so, and that there was a difficulty in getting Freight at Nantes, and other Ports in France, for the great Quantities of Goods the Merchants wanted to ship off for that Country.

There are now two Couriers here, besides the one this goes by. I shall have a Passport ready for another in case any thing new should require immediate dispatch.

I have the honour to be, Sir, Your most obedient humble Servant,

RICHARD OSWALD

ALS in FO 27/2. Endorsed: "... Rd. 12th by Staley, the Messenger; Four Enclosures." Cs in FO 95/511, 97/157, and MiU-C: Shelburne 70. The enclosed newspapers are missing. For the enclosure of the American Commissioners to Strachey and Oswald respectively, see immediately below and source note. Oswald sent his letter of 5 November to Townshend by Strachey. ALS in FO 27/2; C in *ibid.*, 95/511; LbkC in *ibid.*, 97/157, and in MiU-C: Shelburne 70.

[1]Joshua Barney arrived on 5 November with numerous dispatches. See Robert Morris' circular to Jay, 25 Sept. 1782, enclosing Congressional resolutions of 27 Nov. and 3 Dec. 1781, and 14 and 23 Sept. 1782 (LS and triplicate LS in NHi: Jay; quadruplicate LS in PPInd; LbkC in DLC: Morris; *RDC*, V, 763); 7 Oct. 1782 LbkC in DLC: Morris, which enclosed Philadelphia newspapers. See also Morris to Adams, 23, 25, 27 Sept. and 7 Oct. 1782 (*JAW*, VII, 641; *RDC*, V, 770–71, 858–59). See also Morris to Franklin, 27 (2), 30 Sept. and 1, 7 Oct. 1782 (*RDC*, V, 771–75, 791, 802).

[2]Marginal note: "11 Newspapers."

[3]The reference is to the Congressional resolution of 10 Sept. 1782 by James Madison directing the Secretary for Foreign Affairs to secure returns of "the slaves and other property carried off or destroyed" in the course of the war and of the Pennsylvania General Assembly's bill of 18 Sept. 1782 "for procuring an estimate sustained by the inhabitants of Pennsylvania . . ." *JCC*, XXIII, 562; *RDC*, VI, 78–80.

American Commissioners to Richard Oswald

Paris, 7 November 1782

In answer to the letter you did us the honor to write on the 4th instant we beg leave to repeat what we often said in Conversation, viz. that the Restoration of such of the Estates of Refugees,[1] as have been confiscated, is impracticable; because they were confiscated by Laws of particular States, and, in many instances, have passed by legal titles through several hands. Besides, Sir, as this is a matter evidently appertaining to the internal Polity of the separate States, the Congress, by the nature of our Constitution, have no authority to interfere with it.

As to your demand of Compensation to these Persons, we forbear enumerating our Reasons for thinking it ill founded. In the moment of conciliatory Overtures, it would not be proper to call certain Scenes into view, over which, a variety of Considerations should induce both Parties, at present to draw a veil. Permit us therefore only to repeat, that we cannot stipulate for such Compensation, unless, on your part, it be agreed to make retribution to our Citizens for the heavy Losses they have sustained by the *unnecessary* Destruction of their private Property.

We have already agreed to an Amnesty, more extensive than Justice required, and full as extensive as Humanity could demand. We can therefore only repeat, that it cannot be extended further.

We should be sorry if the absolute Impossibility of our complying further with your Propositions on this head, should induce Great Britain to continue the War for the sake of those who caused and prolonged it; but, if that should be the Case, we hope that the utmost Latitude will not be again given to its rigours.

Whatever may be the Issue of this Negotiation, be assured Sir, that we shall always acknowledge the liberal, manly, and candid manner, in which you have conducted it; and that We shall remain, with the warmest Sentiments of Esteem and Regard, Your Most Obedient humble Servants,

JOHN ADAMS
B. FRANKLIN
JOHN JAY

LS, body of letter in Charles Storer's hand, in CO 5/8–3. This is the LS enclosed by Oswald in his letter to Townshend of 6–7 Nov. 1782. From the internal evidence of the letter of the American Commissioners to Strachey of 6 November, it is apparent that this letter was also drafted on the 6th but formally delivered the following day. LbkCs in FO 27/2, 95/511, and PRO: Chatham 30–8–343. LbkC and Tr in MiU-C. These copies all correspond to that printed below. However, the version in *RDC,* V, 849–50, misdated 5 November, omits the phrase "on this head" from the fourth paragraph, an omission repeated in the undated copies of the letter forwarded by the Commissioners to Livingston, 14 Dec. 1782, for which see below, 13 Dec. 1782, and the two copies in John Adams' hand in PCC Misc.

[1] "Refugees" inserted by Adams.

Henry Strachey to Thomas Townshend

Calais, 8 November 1782
Private

Sir,

Considering the Anxiety of my mind and the Fatigues I have gone through, having travelled 16 and 18 hours a day, in very bad Roads, and with miserable Horses, you will not expect that I should have been perfectly clear in the Dispatch accompanying this. But I thought it necessary to send You some Account of the Business, and the Messenger will certainly reach You several hours before I can. On my arrival here this Morning, I found that the Wind had been adverse for seven days past, and that there were at least Sixty English in one House waiting for a Passage.

The Treaty must be written in London in a regular Form, which we had not time to do at Paris; and several of the expressions being too loose, should be tightened; for these Americans are the greatest Quibblers I ever knew. The paragraph about the Indian lands in Georgia (a Subject which I thought it right to take up, though I had no particular Instruction concerning it) seems to be too indecisive to be inserted at all in the Treaty. It was put in amongst the Articles that You might have everything before You.

From an accurate Attention to Words which fell from Jay and Adams in the course of our conversations, I venture to tell You, that I am inclined to think, if You make the Restitution or Indemnification to the Refugees, a sine quâ non, the American Commissioners will accede, rather than Break off the Treaty upon such a point; more especially if a Mode not too odious, could be devised of admitting exceptions of some few People, against whom they are particularly irritated. Mr. Oswald is not however of my opinion. The matter is too serious, either way, to be hastily determined. You are in some degree relieved from the inundation of Refugees that might have been expected from America; but still those at home will be a heavy load.

I am sorry that I have been able to do no more than I have done, but as my Journey has not been quite fruitless, I hope not to meet with your Disapprobation. I must add that not a moment of Time has been lost. We have been in Conference from Eleven o'clock every Morning, though Franklin lives at Passey, and dined all together Four times in order to pursue Our Business in the Evening.[1] They are apparently jealous of the French, and I believe wish to conclude with England.

The sudden Arrival of Dispatches from America prevented their answering Mr. Oswald's Letter, and mine. I heard nothing of their News but that General Lee was dead, and that Laurens's Son (a Colonel) had been killed in opposing a foraging Party from Charles Town.[2]

I am most truly Sir Your faithful and obedient Servant,

H. STRACHEY

ALS in CO 5/8–3. Endorsed. Cs in 95/511 and 97/157.

[1]See editorial note above, "Preliminary Articles: Second Draft," and n. 13.

[2]Retired to his Virginia estate, Major General Charles Lee was dismissed from the Continental army in 1780, and died on 2 Oct. 1782. John Laurens, who had wounded Lee in a duel fought in December 1778, was killed in action in South Carolina on 27 Aug. 1782.

HENRY STRACHEY TO THOMAS TOWNSHEND

Calais, 8 November 1782

Sir,

The Moment I arrive at Dover, I shall dispatch a Messenger with the enclosed new Terms of Treaty,[1] as a Paper which You will be most anxious to see. It is accompanied with a Map,[2] upon which are drawn the Boundary Line originally sent to You by Mr. Oswald, and Two other Lines proposed by the American Commissioners after my Arrival at Paris. Either of these, You are to chuse. They are both better than the original Line, as well in respect to Canada as to Nova Scotia, though neither of them equal to Your hopes. The Boundaries, according to the first-proposed of these Two new Lines, are described in an enclosed Paper, No. 2.[3] Those according to the second-proposed, are described in the Treaty, merely because they are contained in a lesser Compass of Writing.

It is unnecessary at present to trouble You with the Arguments urged by us, to enlarge the Circle of Canada and to extend Nova Scotia to Kennebeck, or even to Penobscot. The Limitation of this Province to the River St. Croix (which is the Boundary by the King's Commission to the Governor) being inadmissable under the Instructions Lord Shelburne gave me, could not be acquiesced in, and the American Commissioners would not recede from their Extention of the Massachusetts to that River. Nor would they agree to the Appointment of Commissaries, unless it were to settle where the River St. Croix really is, for it is not laid down in the same place in all the Maps.

No. 3 is what I contended for, as the proper Article concerning the Fishery, which I take to be precisely consonant with your Intention.[4] After a little Dispute, they gave up the Point of drying Fish on Newfoundland, but they insisted upon a Right to fish in the Gulph of St. Lawrence, and in all other Places where they and we used formerly to Fish; and also to dry on the Shores of the Isle of Sables, Cape Sables, the Magdalene Islands (which are said to be uninhabited) and on the Shores of any unsettled Bay in Nova Scotia. Mr. Oswald is satisfied with the Article, so expressed, and I enclose (No. 4) his Observations upon the Subject.[5]

The Recovery of the Property of the Refugees, and of the Debts due to British Subjects before and since the War, are Points which have been obstinately fought for. You will see by the Treaty all that could be obtained. The Debts prior to 1775 appear to be safe. Those since that period were alledged to have been illegal, and therefore not recoverable but under the Honor of those who contracted them.

With regard to the Refugees, You will observe that something is done in favor of those now under the Protection of the British Army. But with regard to all others of that Description, I see nothing for them, except what You have in Canada, and the little Piece now added to Nova Scotia, between the original Boundary sent to You by Mr. Oswald, and that now obtained. The written Remonstrance, by a Letter from Mr. Oswald to the American Commissioners (No. 5)[6] was made in the view of having an authentic Proof that every Effort had been used, agreeably to my Instructions from Lord Shelburne, upon a Point wherein the National Honor is so deeply concerned. No. 6 is the rough Draft of a Letter which I also wrote upon the same Subject.[7] Neither of these Letters had been answered when I left Paris. But Mr. Oswald had seen the intended Answer to his Letter,[8] which was that the Refugees should have Compensation, provided Great Britain would compensate for all the Towns, Houses, Barns etc. destroyed during the War!

Upon the Return of a Messenger to Paris, with Your definitive Answer, if not very repugnant to the Terms now sent, the American Commissioners will, I doubt not, immediately sign the Treaty, so that You may have it in London before the Meeting of Parliament.

They would not stipulate for the quiet Evacuation of New York, on Account of their Treaty with France, which provides that America shall not make a separate Peace, or Truce, and they pretend to fear that their writing upon such a Point would be construed into a Proposition for a Truce. But they express themselves to be confident that Washington, upon Sight of this provisional Treaty, signed by them, will not obstruct the Evacuation.

I have the honor to be, with the greatest Respect, Sir, Your most obedient and most humble Servant.

H. STRACHEY

First Proposition: Alternative Boundaries Proposed by the American Commissioners

[7 November 1782]

From the North west angle of Nova Scotia vizt. That angle which is formed by a Line drawn due North from the Source of St. Croix River to the High Lands, along the said High Lands which divide those Rivers that empty themselves into the River St. Lawrence from those which fall into the Atlantic Ocean to the Northwesternmost head of Connecticut River; thence down along the middle of that River to the 45th Degree of North Latitude, from thence by a Line due West on said Latitude until it strikes the River Iroquois or Cataroquy, thence along the middle of said River into Lake Ontario through the middle of said Lake until it strikes the communication by water between that Lake and Lake Erie, thence along the middle of said communication into Lake Erie through the middle of said Lake until it arrives at the water communication between that Lake and Lake Huron, thence along the middle of said water communication into Lake Huron, thence through the middle of said Lake to the water communication between that Lake and Lake Superior, thence through Lake Superior Northward of the Isles Royal and Philipeaux to the Long Lake, thence through the middle of said Long Lake and the water communication between it and the Lake of the Woods, to the said Lake of the Woods, thence through the said Lake to the most northwestern point thereof, and from thence on a due western Course to the River Mississippi, thence by a Line to be drawn along the middle of the said River Mississippi until it shall intersect the northernmost part of the 31st Degree of North Latitude; South by a Line to be drawn due East from the determination of the Line lastmentioned in the Latitude of 31 Degrees North of the Equator to the middle of the River Apalachicola, or Catahouche, thence along the middle thereof to its junction with the Flint River, thence strait to the head of St. Mary's River, and thence down along the middle of St. Mary's River to the Atlantic Ocean; East by a Line to be drawn along the middle of the River St. Croix from it's mouth in the Bay of Fundy to it's Source, and from it's Source directly North to the aforesaid High Lands which divide the Rivers that fall into the Atlantic Ocean from those which fall into the River St. Lawrence; comprehending all Islands within twenty Leagues of any part of the Shores of the United States, and lying between Lines to be drawn due East from the points where the aforesaid Boundaries between

Nova Scotia on the one part and East Florida on the other shall respectively touch the Bay of Fundy and the Atlantic Ocean, excepting such Islands as now are, or heretofore have been, within the Limits of the said Province of Nova Scotia.

Henry Strachey: Observation on the Article of the Fishery

[7 November 1782]

3. That the People of the said United States shall continue to enjoy unmolested the Right of fishing <unmolested> on the Banks of Newfoundland, in the manner they have hitherto used, without Anchorage, but by drift.

Richard Oswald: Observations on the Article of the Fishery

[7 November 1782]

Since Mr. Adams Came here, the Commissioners, have taken more nottice of the <pro[posal]> refusal of admitting their having the priviledge of Drying in Newfoundland than I expected from what they told me at Settling the Plan of Treaty which was sent to England. But at last after a great deal of Conversation at different times on that Subject, It was agreed to be left out, upon Condition of their being allowed to dry upon any of the Unsettled parts of the Coast of Nova Scotia, when they happened to be so far from home as that their fish might run some risk of being Spoilt before they reached their own Shores.

Doctor Franklin said he believed it would be only on Such occasions that they would use <even> that priviledge, and even then it would be then only for a partial drying and Salting, so as to prevent the Fish Spoiling before they went home and delivered them to their Wives and Children to compleat and finish the Drying.

Also said. I observe as to *Catching Fish.* You mention only the Banks of Newfoundland. Why not all other places, and amongst others the Gulph of St. Lawrence? Are you afraid there is not Fish enough, Or that We should Catch too many; at the Same time that you know that we shall bring the greatest part of the Money we get for that Fish, to Great Britain to pay for your Manufactures? He agreed it might be proper not to have a mixture of their people with ours for Drying on Newfoundland, <He> But Supposed there would be no Inconveniency in throwing onshore their Fish for a few days on an Unsettled Beach, Bay or Harbour, on the Coast of Nova Scotia.

I am Sorry that I should have given occasion to so much trouble on this head by trusting to what was said by the Comm[issione]rs, as not being so positive in the matter but what they would give up the point, if objected to at home, and have now only to Submit it to Consideration, Whether it will not be proper to allow of Drying in Nova Scotia And also to let the Clause regarding the Catching of Fish be so expressed as <that> not to appear as if we're afraid of the Americans extending that branch of Commerce as far as they incline to pursue it, Since I really believe they will not like it, and that it will not be an easy matter to restrain them, if we should incline to do so.

R.O.

ALS in CO 5/8–3. Enclosures in FO 27/2: ADS of Oswald's observations on the fishery article; C of Strachey's observation on the fishery article; C of the American Commissioners' first proposition. Cs in FO 27/2, 95/511, and 97/157, and in MiU-C: Shelburne 70.

[1]Preliminary Articles: Second Draft, [4–7 Nov. 1782], above.

[2]See p. 271.

[3]First Proposition, herein.

[4]Strachey's article on the fishery, herein.

[5]Oswald's article on the fishery, herein.

[6]Above, [4 Nov. 1782], Strachey's draft for Oswald.

[7]Strachey to the American Commissioners, 5 Nov. 1782, above.

[8]Below, 7 Nov. 1782. The American Commissioners replied to Strachey on 6 November; see editorial note above, "Preliminary Articles: Second Draft," and n. 18.

RICHARD OSWALD TO Henry STRACHEY

Paris, Friday, 8 November 1782
Private

Dear Sir,

In hopes this will find you safe in England. I have to trouble you with the following Mem[oranda] after referring you to my Letter to the Secretary of State, which I suppose will come under your Observation.

Mr. Jay sent to me yesterday for a Copy of the proposed Treaty. I compared it with him, he kept one Copy. He was Singularly attentive to all the particulars and did not admit of the least alteration from the words of his own plan.

He Scored out of the Treaty the Seperate Article respecting W. Florida. But admitted it, in addition at the bottom as a Seperate Article. In so far you was right, and I was wrong in putting it into the Treaty.

In this Article, he also insisted that his own words should be replaced. Viz He had said that in case G[reat] B[ritain] at the conclusion of the present War Shall *be,* or be put in possession, We said, Shall *Recover* or be put in possession. He scored out the Word *recover* and put in the word *be* as above. This Seperate Article must therefor Stand as it was added only to the foot of your Copy and without the preamble as in the body of the Treaty of *Upon a further consideration of the just Limits, etc.*

Mr. Jay also struck out of the Treaty the Exception as to the Nova Scotia Islands, which I was surprised at, saying that if saved by the general principle of Sea Boundaries, there was no occasion for an Exception. I did not think it worth while to dwell upon that matter, since if any of those Islands are within 20 Leagues of the mouth of St. Croix River, he will surely not scruple to except them as pertinents of the Colony of Nova Scotia. Meantime the Exception must be left out of any Copy you send over, And I would also beg leave to add that from this Gentleman's precision, and attention to the Identity of these Copies in comparison with the original Drafts, I would advise that there should not be the least Alteration, not a single Word, different from the Drafts.

I was once thinking you might give the paper the dress of a little more formality as a Treaty, and I think you said you would change some of the Words, and put in better. In which you was Certainly right. But now I can assure you that if there is the least Alteration, if they cannot be replaced by Scratching, the whole must be wrote over again, besides disobliging these people.

After it is determined which of the two Districts of Territory shall be accepted of, you will no doubt have it inserted accordingly, in the body of the Treaty, exactly according to the first Draft. And you may at some time send over the other seperately. I find I have no Copy of the Description of the District of the First proposition, which goes round the Waters and Lakes. Although it should not be adapted, you may send it over.

I did not expect to find Mr. Jay so uncommonly Stiff and particular about these matters. Possibly the late Advices from America just received dated so late as a month ago, may have had some effect. However in case the Treaty is approved of at home and comes back without any alteration, I am perswaded the Commissioners will sign it immediately. The Mem[oranda] you left with me Viz.

1. Amnesty to be expressed as to Real, as well as personal property,

will be tried when we hear from home. I see it would be in vain now, perhaps not proper.

2. Destruction—to insert *by the fury of War,* the same as above.

3. Lawful Impediment—Lawful to be left out, the same as above.

4. A better Specification of the Currency in the payments of Debts the same as above

I send two packets of American Gazettes down to the 5th of last Month, directed to you, together with one of their New Pamphlets, which I have not read, but am told it is very strong Language.

Being in a hurry to dispatch the Messenger I have only to add that I am with Sincere regard Dear Sir Your most obedient humble Servant,

RICHARD OSWALD

Mr. Whitefoord gives his Compliments. He was to have sent you some things[1] by this Courier but he has been so close employed that he has not been able to go out about them and must defer them to the next opportunity.

ALS in FO 27/2. Oswald refers herein to his letter of 6–7 November to Townshend, above.

[1]"French Songs" originally appended as a footnote.

Richard Oswald to Thomas Townshend

Paris, 15 November 1782

Sir,

As Mr. Fitzherbert informs me he intends to dispatch a messenger to-night, I take the opportunity of referring to the letter which I had the honour of writing you on the 7th by the Courier Stayley, who set out on the 8th at three in the afternoon.

In that letter I made a full Report of my last conversation with the American Commissioners, as near to their own words as I could recollect them, which I thought it my Duty to do, however unpleasant they might appear to be. They principally turned on the Question regarding the Refugees and Loyalists, both as to Restitution and Compensation.

Since that time I had not seen any of those gentlemen, untill this morning; when I called on Mr. Jay and Mr. Adams separately, and sat with them a considerable time; trying to persuade them to take that

Matter again into consideration. But to no purpose. I had the same answers as I have always had, from each of them on that Subject, from the beginning of my Correspondence with them, Vizt. That it should never be said that they had agreed to any measures for the gratification of those who had been so instrumental in encouraging this War, and had so cruelly assisted in the prosecution of it; with many other Reflections, relative to their opinion of their Principles, Motives and Conduct as unpleasant as unnecessary to be here repeated. Adding, as they always have done, that if peace with Great Britain was not to be had on any other Terms, than their agreeing to those Provisions, the War must go on, although it should be for these seven years to come; and that neither they, nor their Congress had any Power in this Matter, notwithstanding, what to do for the Personal Safety, and the Effects of those Loyalists remaining with the Garrison of New York; and upon the whole, that things of the consequence proposed rests entirely with the States.

At the same time those two Commissioners owned that they were extremely desirous of Peace, and that the Treaty sent over may be agreed to. But if refused, they said they must wait for new Instructions from their Congress. That upon their report of such refusal to that Assembly, they would refer the Question in dispute to the States. It might take six Months severally to have them assembled; and perhaps six Months, or longer, to have Instructions on their Resolutions, from the Congress, Before which time, as the several Provinces will have made some progress in the liquidation of the unnecessary Destruction of private Property, they might expect to receive positive Orders to insist on reparation thereof, in their next instructions.

Both those Gentlemen told me today, that this Court had thought fit to take up the Question regarding the Loyalists, and become advocates for them; and Mr. Adams said that he had been sent for last Week to Versailles, and that Monsieur de Vergennes had talkt to him strongly in their favor, But that he paid no regard to his opinion or recommendation on the subject; and could guess at his motive for interfering as intended to prevent a speedy agreement with Great Britain, so as in the Interim they might bring forward their own Treaty, and those of their allies, to a more favorable Conclusion. The other Gentleman took notice also of the Circumstance, and gave the same account of his Opinion of the object of it. How far they are right, I don't pretend to say.

I at last proposed to those Gentlemen, that since they would not positively undertake for a Restitution or Compensation to the Refugees or Loyalists, that they would add a Clause to the Treaty, of Recommendation to the Congress in their favor in general, leaving it to them to discriminate according to Circumstances. Or that they, the Congress, should upon such Recommendation make one general Sweep of Acquittance, reserving the Right of certain Exceptions to themselves. This Expedient was proposed on Account of a few particular names which I had been often accustomed to hear at making applications on the Subject. But all to no purpose. At same time those Gentlemen owned they had an esteem and good-will towards many of those Parties, and would be glad to serve them as opportunities offered. But in either of those ways they could be of no use to them.

I then talked of the Evacuation of New York. Mr. Adams admitted that, without a due Precaution, there might be some cross accident in accomplishing it. However, he thought General Washington could have no Objection to receiving a Surrendry of the Place by Capitulation; to which their Treaty with France could not furnish any Objection; since by that Treaty, each nation was at liberty to prosecute the War in their own way. And so their General could do in that matter as he thought fit, and without consulting the General of the French Troops who was under his command.

Mr. Adams said, that by last Letters, they had now a well disciplined army of near 20 Thousand Men, including the French, who were about 4000, partly with General Washington, the rest in different Places.

He also said, and so did Mr. Jay, that their last advices from the Congress complained of Our Mode of evacuating the Garrison of Savannah, as if We had carried off in the way of booty, (they used that Word) a number of Negros[1] to be sold in the West Indies. I said it must have been Negros belonging to Loyalists who had retired with the Troops. And I was persuaded the Congress was misinformed. I hope it will prove so.

However it would appear that these Reports have so far gained ground amongst those People, that they are alarmed in Carolina, being apprehensive of something of that kind at the Evacuation of Charles Town, which, although surely without just reason, yet it is certain by Letters from Carolina just now received at Paris, the People there are apprehensive about some part of this kind of Property, which happens to be in the hands of Our Garrison. However unjust those Imputations may be, I think myself bound to initiate the Reports, since they come to me in such a way which does not admit of my suppressing them.

If New York is evacuated by Capitulation, every pretence to

Charges of this malicious kind will of course be prevented.

I have the honour to be Sir, Your most obedient humble Servant,

RICHARD OSWALD

C in FO 97/157. Cs in FO 27/2 and 95/511; omissions in Hale, *Franklin in France,* II, 182–85.

[1]See above, Oswald to Townshend, 6–7 Nov. 1782, and n. 3.

Vaughan's Second Mission to England

18 November 1782

Learning on 16 November that his government had rejected the articles which had been hammered out with the American Commissioners earlier in the month,[1] Richard Oswald urged JJ to go to England, because he "thought he could convince the Ministry." JJ declined, but Benjamin Vaughan, who had already considered returning to England to be near his wife at the birth of their first child, offered to make the trip.[2] Adams gave Vaughan a thorough briefing on the American position vis-à-vis the Loyalists.[3] Even earlier Vaughan had made known to Shelburne his displeasure at "the haughty spirit" of Strachey's mission, denouncing that "puny ignoble huckstering spirit, which comes from *other* hands." On critical issues like the Northeastern boundary Vaughan had done what he could to undermine the Cabinet's new emissary. On 1 November he had written Shelburne: "I should be grieved to hear that a little spot of cross, frosty land, which an Empress of Russia would give away at breakfast, should spoil a national accomodation."[4]

Vaughan left Paris at noon on 17 November,[5] ready to plead the American cause to Shelburne. The next morning at Calais he met Henry Strachey, who was returning from London. They discussed the problems of the American peace, but it is by no means clear that Strachey let Vaughan know how close the Cabinet was to reaching a decision on new instructions to the negotiators in Paris.[6] Vaughan reached London after Townshend had finished preparing Strachey's new instructions of 19 November,[7] stayed briefly, and got back to Paris on 27 November,[8] only four days after Strachey, delayed by illness, had re-joined his fellow negotiators.[9] Vaughan's second mission had come too late to have an impact on the British negotiating stance.

The letter that follows was written while Vaughan was on his way to England.

[1]See editorial note above, "Preliminary Articles: Second Draft."

[2]The Vaughans' daughter Harriet was born on 11 Nov. 1782.

[3]*AP,* III, 57–58 (16 Nov. 1782).

[4]Vaughan to Shelburne, 1 Nov. 1782. Tr in PPAmP: Vaughan and in MiU-C.

[5]*AP,* III, 58.

[6]Vaughan to Strachey, 18 Nov. 1782. ALS in DLC: Lamson Strachey, Tr in MiU-C.

[7]See editorial note above, "Preliminary Articles: Second Draft."

[8]*AP,* III, 77.

[9]The date of Strachey's arrival in Paris is given in Matthew Ridley's Diary. His illness is mentioned in Vaughan to Shelburne, 21 Nov. 1782, Tr in PPAmP: Vaughan and in MiU-C.

From Benjamin Vaughan

Calais, 18 November 1782

My dear sir,

I was not very easy on the noon when you *first* saw me; but I was still less so at *dinner,* to find there was no post. There was also no post the next day. Judge then my happiness, at finding Mr. Potter, with letters that contained a little girl which they called very beautiful; all but the upper lip which they said was like mine, and Mrs. Vaughan, as well as possible. I am not fond of shewing my concern in things, but I hope everything I meddle with, will not bear like ill marks of me.

I write this letter, however, not to be merry, but simply to hope that you will leave things open some short space longer. The person you have with you,[1] seems a very good tempered man; but I assure you we have at home, better natured statesmen, let him say as civil things as he will.

I have also to request your turning your thought to the imperfect powers of congress in foreign negotiations. By and by, you may negotiate on your own soil, or in some of the Western Islands; but, for some time to come you must negotiate in *Europe;* and, <added> to the necessary delay of a voyage, it is a very disadvantageous thing, to add the delay of geography, and waiting for assemblies meeting. *Internal* power may be very dangerous to increase, in the hands of congress, because it may alter your internal balance, but in foreign politics, you act externally and as a whole. If the colonies are inclined or averse to any particular point, that may come to issue in a negotiation, they may easily instruct their delegates previously; who may instruct the negotiators. Congress itself, as well as the separate assemblies, is a representative body however; and cannot be ignorant of the interests, and still less of the sentiments, of those who <represent> delegate them.

I own, I think it as important sometimes for the powers directing a negotiation, to be <as> speedy and secret in their exertions, as for those which are to direct an army. A measure in negotiation, may relate to the suppression of the use of armies; or, which is more in point, to the obtaining of a new ally, or pacifying an old enemy. In short, if ever America wants a supreme power over its several parts, it is, when it acts as a whole, and it never acts more as a whole, than when it settles with foreign powers.

I think farther, that the particular states, when they wish to take measures that relate to foreign affairs, ought at least to *advise,* upon the propriety of them with congress; who is to be supposed best informed in the scheme of foreign interests <and affairs>. I think you considered England as a foreign power, in every article, but two; I mean the refugees and English creditors; and there it would have been well to have left the matter to the interference of congress, as foreign, and not as domestick. I should almost think that even every *foreign* traitor, should be judged by a general power or a general assent; as that which may call for a common measure in the <end> consequence, ought to have a common consent in the course of it. I speak all this with deference; but as *amicus curiae;* and with a sense of ill-consequences that may attend this defect in your mode of confederation, both respecting your own interest and those of the powers who may have to deal with you.

But to return to private affairs. You wished I would get you a sword, in doing which I shall take a particular interest, but I beg you will inform my brother[2] of the price and fashion. I had much rather send you an *olive branch,* which I trust is more than a *summer* plant.

I know your time is now precious, and therefore I will not longer intrude; but I wish I could write the dispatches you are to send by the Washington Packet, which I observe you detain for the purpose. With my sincerest respects to Mrs. Jay, and my thanks for both your condescensions towards me, I have the honor to be, dear sir, your faithful and respectful friend and humble servant,

BENJN. VAUGHAN

ALS in CtY. Tr in NN: Bancroft: American IV, 268 1/2.
[1]Henry Strachey.
[2]Samuel Vaughan, Jr.

From Lady Juliana Penn

London, 23 November 1782

Sir,

You will be surprised that I take the Liberty of addressing you on my Affairs:[1] But the general Character of your Benevolence, still more confirmed to me by a Friend of mine now in the House with me encourages me to claim your Protection and Assistance in recovering my Rights, and those of an unfortunate Family.[2] They never have or could have done any thing to offend the State who have hitherto treated them with Rigor: But that rigor I trust may cease through your kind interposition. I Therefore conjure you Sir in the present Settlement of Affairs to interest yourself with that goodness and Philanthrophy which you are known to possess in so Emminent a degree, in the restoring us to our just Dues, and to that Happiness and Prosperity which the Descendants of William Penn have reason to expect: and cannot fail to experience if You will undertake Their Cause.

Certain that You will not refuse Your Protection, I already subscribe Myself Sir, Your Excellency's Much Obliged and Obedient Humble Servant,

JULIANA PENN

ALS.

[1]Lady Juliana Fermor (1729–1801), daughter of the Earl of Pomfret, married Thomas Penn (1702–75), son of the founder of Pennsylvania, in 1751. Upon the death of her husband, her three minor children inherited three-fourths of the Penn interest in the colony of Pennsylvania. An act of the Pennsylvania Assembly of 27 Nov. 1779 transferred the Penns' proprietary holdings to the commonwealth, leaving the family their private lands and "proprietary tenths" or manors. The same act appropriated £130,000 to compensate the Penns for their losses "in remembrance of the enterprising spirit of the founder and of the expectations and dependence of his descendants." Payments were to begin one year after the close of the Revolution. On 26 Oct. 1782 Shelburne informed Townshend that the King directed him "to take every step possible in favor of the Penn family." (Cited above in Townshend to Oswald, 26 Oct. 1782, source note.) Lady Juliana's eldest son John traveled to Paris in January 1783 to consult with the American Commissioners on the family's claims. Pennsylvania initiated payments to the Penn family in 1785; the family was further awarded an annual pension of £4,000 voted by Parliament in 1790 as compensation for their American losses. See Howard M. Jenkins, *The Family of William Penn, Founder of Pennsylvania: Ancestry and Descendants* (London, 1899), pp. 150–55.

[2]Lady Juliana's family present in Paris included her unmarried daughter Sophia Margaretta (1764–1847), her granddaughter Juliana Baker, her younger son Granville (1761–91), her late husband's nephew Richard (1735–1811), and her son-in-law William Baker.

FROM ROBERT R. LIVINGSTON

Philadelphia, 23 November 1782

Dear Sir,

I have before me your letters of the 25th and 28th June.[1] I congratulate you on your safe arrival at Paris, where I venture to hope your residence will on many accounts be more agreable than it was at Madrid. Nothing can be more agreable to us than your determination to write very frequently, since I am sorry to say that we have not yet been favored with such minute information on many points of importance as we have reason to expect. Both Doctor Franklin and yourself dwelth so much in generals in your last letters, that had it not been for a private letter of the Marquis to me,[2] Congress would have remained ignorant of points, which they have thought of sufficient importance to make them the foundation of some of those resolutions which are herewith transmitted to you. You need be under no apprehensions that Commissioners from the Court of Great Britain will be allowed to negotiate with Congress, their sentiments on this subject are sufficiently manifested in the resolutions that are sent to you and Doctor Franklin with this, and the case of Mr. Burgess which you will find in one of the papers of last week and in my letter to Doctor Franklin will afford you some evidence of the extreme caution of particular States on this head.[3]

That in the mass of our people there are a great number, who though resolved on independence prefer an alliance with England to one with France must be a mere speculative opinion which can be reduced to no kind of certainty. If we form our Judgement from acts of government we would suppose that no such sentiment prevailed. They all speak a different language, if from the declarations of individuals we must entertain the same opinion, since independence and the alliance with France connect themselves so closely together that we never speak of them separately. The mass of the people here are not so ignorant of the common principles of policy as to prefer an alliance with a nation whose recent pretentions and whose vicinity renders them natural Enemy's to that of a prince who has no claims upon them and no territory in their Neighbourhood; at least till the principles of his Government shall be changed and he gives evident proof of his Justice and moderation. I see but one source from which differences between us and France can ever arise. IF SPAIN SHOULD PERSIST IN HER WILD PRETENTIONS TO BOUNDLESS TERRITORY IN THIS COUNTRY AND BE SUPPORTED IN THOSE PRETENTIONS BY THE OTHER BRANCH OF THE HOUSE OF BOURBON SHE WILL SHARE IN THE RESENTMENTS AND JEALOUSIES THAT SUCH PRETENTIONS EXCITE. I LEARN FROM MR. Carmichael THAT THE COUNT[4] D'ARANDA'S POWERS ARE NOT YET EXPEDITED SO THAT AS FAR AS I CAN SEE THE FARCE OF NEGOTIATION IS THE SAME THOUGH THE SCENE AND THE PLAYERS ARE ALTERED.[5]

I think it unnecessary to repeat to you what I have already written to Doctor Franklin presuming that you communicate with freedom to each other. Mr. Jefferson will afford, I dare say, a very acceptable aid to your commission. I have not yet learnt from him whether he will take the duties upon him.[6]

WE CONTINUE TO BE AS MUCH DISTRESSED FOR MONEY AS EVER. TAXES COME IN VERY SLOWLY AND THE FIVE PER CENT DUTY WHICH WOULD PRODUCE A CONSIDERABLE REVENUE IS NOT COLLECTED BECAUSE RHODE ISLAND REFUSES TO PAY IT THOUGH EVERY OTHER STATE UNLESS IT BE GEORGIA FROM WHICH WE HAVE NOT HEARD HAVE PASSED LAWS FOR THAT PURPOSE.[7]

Mr. Barlow a poet of New England has requested me to transmit you his proposals for printing by Subscription a poem of which he is the author. I can give no character of the work but what you will get from the Specimen enclosed, which is all I have seen of it.[8] The enclosed resolution informs you of Mr. Boudinot's advancement to the Presidentship.[9] For other intelligence I refer you to my letter to Doctor Franklin, and the papers that accompany this.

I am Dear Sir with great Regard and Esteem your most obedient humble servant,

ROBERT R. LIVINGSTON

LS. Enclosure: Appointment of Boudinot as President, not located. Duplicate LS in JP; Dft in NHi: Robert R. Livingston; LbkC in PCC 118. For the Franklin-Morris cipher utilized herein, see above, Livingston to JJ, 8 Aug. 1782. The cipher passages have been deciphered by the editors herein; they do not appear in *RDC,* VI, 70–71, nor in *HPJ,* III, 2–3.

[1]For JJ to Livingston, 25 June 1782, see editorial note above, "The Status of the Peacemaking," n. 16. 28 June LbkCs in JP, CSmH, and PCC 110, II; *HPJ,* II, 317–19; *RDC,* V, 527–28.

[2]See Franklin to Livingston, 25, 28, 29 June 1782: *BFS,* VIII, 548–53, 555–58; *RDC,* V, 510–13, 525–26, 533–35. Probably Lafayette's letter of 25 June 1782 (*RDC,* V, 517–21), reporting that "the ministry in England are now deceiving the people with the hope that Sir Guy Carleton is going to operate a reconciliation." On 4 October a Congressional committee reported on JJ's letter of 25 June and Lafayette's of 25, 29 June (PCC 156). Thereupon Congress adopted a series of resolutions: (1) declaring that neither France nor the United States would conclude peace or truce "without the consent of the other"; (2) reaffirming America's intention to adhere to the alliance and to negotiate with Great Britain "in confidence and concert with his Most Christian Majesty"; (3) directing the States to "be vigilant" in guarding against British "emissaries and spies"; and (4) recommending to the States that British subjects coming from "any part of the British dominions" be barred from the U.S. during the war. *JCC,* XXIII, 637–39.

[3]Livingston's letter to Franklin of 21 Nov. 1782 cited the case of "Mr. Burgess, an English merchant [who] was not permitted to settle at Boston and obtain the rights of citizenship upon principles which must be alarming to England, as evidence of the respect paid to the resolutions of Congress." *RDC,* VI, 67.

[4]In the Dft of this letter Livingston wrote "Marquis," but the ciphered versions give Aranda's correct title.

[5]In his letter to Livingston of 12 June 1782, Carmichael had reported that in a conversation with Floridablanca and del Campo "they seemed to think the work of peace to be in a fair way. I have, however, some reason to suppose that neither their instructions to their ambassador at Paris for this object, nor those for him

to treat with Mr. Jay, are yet forwarded; and there are grounds to conjecture that this court would have retarded the negociation as much as possible had not the defeat of the Count de Grasse blasted their hopes of taking Jamaica." *RDC*, V, 489.

[6]On 12 November, Congress renewed Jefferson's appointment as a peace commissioner. Madison reported the feeling that the death of Jefferson's wife Martha on 6 Sept. 1782 might now make him more amenable to public office, while the improbability that Laurens would actually participate in the negotiations gave that appointment additional force. Jefferson's difficulties in procuring transportation abroad and his ultimate release by Congress from the assignment are recounted in his "Autobiography," *TJP*, VI, 210–11; Madison, "Notes of Debates," 12 Nov. 1782, *MP*, V, 268–70; JCC, XXIII, 720–21, 848.

[7]On 3 Feb. 1781, Congress urged the States to authorize a Congressional levy of a five percent impost. *JCC*, XIX, 112. By the date of this letter Rhode Island had rejected it, thereby ending the possibility of the unanimous consent deemed requisite under the Articles of Confederation. *Ibid.*, XXIII, 788–89; *LMCC*, VI, 542.

[8]Joel Barlow (1754–1812), of Connecticut, while an army chaplain journeyed to Philadelphia from West Point in the last week of October 1782 to seek subscriptions for the publication of his yet unfinished epic poem, "The Vision of Columbus," which was not published until 1787. See Theodore A. Zunder, *The Early Days of Joel Barlow, a Connecticut Wit* (New Haven, 1934), ch. VII.

[9]Elias Boudinot (1740–1821) of New Jersey was elected President of Congress on 4 Nov. 1782, succeeding John Hanson. *JCC*, XXIII, 708.

Henry Strachey's Remarks to the American Commissioners

[Paris], 25 November 1782

Since I was here last, I have seen, and conversed with, almost every one of the King's Council. They are unanimous in the desire of concluding the Peace. But they are also unanimous in declaring that they think You unreasonable in refusing a general Amnesty and Restoration of Property, to the Refugees. They are unanimous in declaring that those Two Points must be insisted upon, and that every Thing ought to be risqued, rather than submit to Terms highly dishonorable to the British Government. And I must add that those of His Majesty's Ministers, who have been the most zealous Advocates for the Independence of America, are the most forward (if there is the least difference) in condemning America for making a moment's hesitation upon these Points, which seem to affect equally the Honor, the Justice, and even the Policy of America, as of Great Britain.[1]

The Article of the Fishery is another Point. They were determined to resist the Proposition I carried over. They are apprehensive of future Quarels. To obviate which as much as possible, they have expunged that part of the Article, which proposed the Privilege of drying on Cape Sables, and upon the Shores of Nova Scotia, but have left to

You what is conceived will be amply sufficient for Your Accommodation.[2]

Objections were made to almost the whole of the Paper I carried from hence, as deficient in point of Form and Precision. The King's Ministers have therefore drawn out the Articles as they wish them to stand, and in Form similar to all other Treaties. They have left out several Preambles, as unnecessary, and unusual. The Point regarding the Debts, though somewhat altered in the Forms of Expression, is exactly as You put it, in respect to Substance. The Article of Independence, is adopted precisely in the Words dictated by Yourselves. The Boundaries, they are not satisfied with; and they hope upon a little more Consideration of the real Rights of the Crown, You will have no Objection to admit of the Extention of Nova Scotia to Penobscot. That is left open for amicable Discussion. But I will acknowledge, (depending upon your not taking Advantage of what I say) that they are not disposed to break off the Treaty absolutely, upon that Article.

The Restitution of the Property of the Loyalists, is the grand Point upon which a final Settlement depends. If the Treaty breaks off now, the whole Business must go loose, and take it's Chance in Parliament, where I am confident the warmest Friends of American Independence, will not support the Idea of the Confiscation of private Property.

Here is the Treaty[3] in such shape as Mr. Oswald can immediately sign—and the War is for ever, I hope, at an end. By this Treaty, You have your Independence confirmed, and in Your own identical mode of Expression. By this Treaty You acquire that vast Extent of Territory You have claimed. New York, with all your Artillery there, is ceded to You. You will consider well whether You will reject these great Objects for which You have so long and bravely fought, merely upon the Non-admission of a Demand the most humiliating and degrading to Great Britain, and clearly repugnant to the Honor, the Justice, and even the good Policy of America herself.

It is necessary I should apprise You, that in the Article of Restitution, the Words *Rights and Properties* are added to the Word *Estates,* in the view of securing the Proprietary Interests, derived from ancient and solemn Charters.[4]

Tr in NN: Bancroft: American. Endorsed: "25th November, 1782. As much as I could recollect of my opening to the Commissioners at Paris." Bancroft's endorsement: "The original of this paper is written and indorsed by the hand of Henry Strachey." This document prepared for the record represents Strachey's recollections of his remarks to the American Commissioners the morning of 25 November, when they met for the first time after Strachey's return from Britain two days earlier. These "opening remarks," delivered at Oswald's lodgings, summarized for the Americans the decisions of the British Cabinet on the draft treaty of 4 November. Much of the meeting was devoted to an Adams' exposition of American fishing rights. At the end of the meeting, Adams recounted, "Mr. Jay desired to know, whether Mr. Oswald had now Power to conclude and sign with Us?" When Strachey said that he had, "Mr. Jay desired to know if the Propositions now delivered Us were their Ultimatum. Strachey seemed loth to answer, but at last said, 'No.'—We agreed these were good Signs of Sincerity." *AP,* III, 74–75.

[1]See above, [4–7 Nov. 1782], "Preliminary Articles: Second Draft," n. 9, for the Cabinet's alternative proposals for treaty provisions on the Loyalists. Adams commented: "They every one of them, [in the Cabinet] unanimously condemned that [article] respecting the Tories, so that that unhappy Affair stuck as he foresaw and foretold that it would." *AP,* III, 72.

[2]Adams "could not help observing that the Ideas respecting the Fishery appeared to me to come piping hot from Versailles." Quoting the Treaty of Alliance with France and the Treaty of Utrecht, Adams discoursed learnedly and lengthily on the migratory patterns of the cod and haddock to rebut the Cabinet's objections. *Ibid.,* pp. 73–74.

[3]The "treaty" mentioned here is the proposed Cabinet draft, 11–15 November, cited in editorial note above, "Preliminary Articles: Second Draft," n. 19.

[4]The Cabinet draft, Art. V, stated: "It is agreed that Persons whose Estates Rights and Property's in America have been Confiscated at any time during the War shall meet with no Lawful Impediment to the Recovery of the Same." Other versions used either "Lands" or "Estates."

The Preliminary Articles Are Signed

30 November 1782

Once it appeared certain that peace negotiations with the United States were about to be concluded, the British government prorogued Parliament until 5 December "to give time," as Thomas Townshend explained, "to receive a final answer from the Powers with whom we are in Negotiation."[1] Fearful lest the reason for this action might be misunderstood in France, Grantham directed Alleyne Fitzherbert to explain the steps to Vergennes.[2] On the other hand, Shelburne assumed that JJ and his associates were less likely to react unfavorably.[3]

The two issues that agitated the negotiators until the very end were the Newfoundland fisheries and compensation for Loyalists. Townshend expressed London's concern when he instructed Oswald to make sure that the concession with respect to Newfoundland did not interfere with the King's rights or with privileges granted to the French.[4] In a letter written the following day, Shelburne explained to Oswald that England's attitude about both the fisheries and the Loyalists was prompted by a sincere desire to avoid future "dissention."[5] The American failure to respond to the refugee claims sorely troubled Vergennes, who ventured the hope that American intransigence would not endanger the peace.[6] There was in fact no possibility of compromise, as Benjamin Franklin made clear in a 26 November letter to Richard Oswald. "It is best for you to drop all mention of the Refugees," he advised, unless the British were willing to offer reimbursement for losses resulting from slaves who had been carried away and property that had been destroyed.[7]

The signing of the Preliminary Articles was a source of some satisfaction as well as relief to the British Commissioners. They did the best they could, and what they conceded, as Oswald wrote, resulted from "the Inflexibility of uncommon Circumstances."[8] Fitzherbert confessed "great pain" at having to agree to unattractive but inevitable peace conditions, but both he and Oswald praised Strachey for his "indefatigable" part.[9] Strachey, the key British figure in the final round of the Preliminaries, was delighted to be finished and on his way. "God forbid I should ever have a hand in another Peace,"[10] he wrote, and then took off from Paris.

Contrariwise, the mood of the American Commissioners was one of jubilation. JJ commented on their perfect harmony. "Mr. Adams was particularly useful respecting the eastern boundary," he wrote, "and Dr. Franklin's firmness and exertions on the subject of the Tories did us much service."[11]

Lastly, to Benjamin Vaughan, a self-propelled intermediary lacking formal credentials, who throughout had remained on more intimate terms with the Americans than with the British negotiators, the treaty-signing was peculiarly gratifying. He even penned a letter to Shelburne setting forth in parallel columns the initial claims of the Americans and the actual settlement laid down in the Preliminaries. Once the Preliminaries were signed, Vaughan sounded out Franklin about the latter's willingness to serve as the United States minister to the Court of St. James's. Should he decline, Vaughan volunteered the opinion that JJ would "do very well." "Mr. Jay," he informed Shelburne, "is good and manly; can respect and be respected, and has a wife of good sense, who can be received in the best companies, and be made an object of civilities and even of friendship."[12]

[1]Townshend to Oswald, 22 Nov. 1782, Dft and C in FO 27/2; LbkC in *ibid.,* 95/157.

[2]Grantham to Fitzherbert, 23 Nov. 1782, LbkC in FO 27/3.

[3]Shelburne to Oswald, 23 Nov. 1782, LbkCs in MiU-C: Shelburne 71 and in CO 5/8-3, C in 5/8.

[4]Townshend to Oswald, 22 Nov. 1782.

[5]Shelburne to Oswald, 23 Nov. 1782.

[6]Vergennes to Luzerne, 23 Nov. 1782, Dft in CP EU 22: 490–93.

[7]Franklin to Oswald, 26 Nov. 1782, Cs in NHi: Jay; in MiU-C: RGA; and in French in CP A 539: 45–50; partially in *RDC,* VI, 77–80; *BFS,* VIII, 621–27.

[8]Oswald to Shelburne, 30 Nov. 1782, ALS in MiU-C: Shelburne 71.

[9]Fitzherbert to Townshend, 30 Nov. 1782, ALS in FO 27/2; C in MiU-C: RGA, Add. Sydney, III, 18.

[10]Strachey to Nepean, 30 Nov. 1782, ALS in CO 5/8-3.

[11]JJ to Livingston, 12 Dec. 1782, LbkCs in JP and PCC 110, II; *RDC,* VI, 130; *HPJ,* III, 5-6. For further information about the final negotiations and the mood of the participants, see *Peacemakers,* pp. 372–82.

[12]Vaughan to Shelburne, 10 Dec. 1782, Tr in MiU-C: RGA: Vaughan; Massachusetts Hist. Soc., *Proceedings,* 2d ser. (1903), XVII, 426.

Preliminary Articles of Peace

Paris, 30 November 1782

Articles agreed upon, by and between Richard Oswald Esquire, the Commissioner of his Britannic Majesty, for treating of Peace with the Commissioners of the United States of America, in behalf of his said Majesty, on the one part; and John Adams, Benjamin Franklin, John Jay, and Henry Laurens, four of the Commissioners of the said States, for treating of Peace with the Commissioner of his said Majesty, on their Behalf, on the other part. To be inserted in, and to constitute the Treaty of Peace proposed to be concluded, between the Crown of Great Britain and the said United States; but which Treaty is not to be concluded, untill Terms of a Peace shall be agreed upon, between Great Britain and France; and his Britannic Majesty shall be ready to conclude such Treaty accordingly.

Whereas reciprocal Advantages, and mutual Convenience are found by Experience, to form the only permanent foundation of Peace and Friendship between States; It is agreed to form the Articles of the proposed Treaty, on such Principles of liberal Equity, and Reciprocity, as that partial Advantages, (those Seeds of Discord!) being excluded, such a beneficial and satisfactory Intercourse between the two Countries, may be establish'd, as to promise and secure to both perpetual Peace and Harmony.

Article 1st

His Britannic Majesty acknowledges the said United States, Viz: New Hampshire, Massachusetts Bay, Rhode Island and Providence Plantations, Connecticut, New York, New Jersey, Pennsylvania, Delaware, Maryland, Virginia, North Carolina, South Carolina and Georgia, to be free Sovereign and independent States; That he treats with them as such; And for himself, his Heirs and Successors, relinquishes all Claims to the Government, Propriety, and territorial Rights of the same, and every part thereof; and that all Disputes which might arise in future, on the Subject of the Boundaries of the said United States, may be prevented, It is hereby agreed and declared that the following are, and shall be their Boundaries Viz.

ARTICLE 2d

From the north west Angle of Nova Scotia, Viz: that Angle which is form'd by a Line drawn due north, from the Source of St. Croix River to the Highlands, along the said Highlands which divide those Rivers that empty themselves into the River St. Laurence, from those which fall into the Atlantic Ocean, to the northwesternmost Head of Connecticut River; thence down along the middle of that River to the 45th Degree of North Latitude; from thence by a Line due West on said Latitude, untill it strikes the River Iroquois, or Cataraquy; thence along the middle of said River into Lake Ontario; through the middle of said Lake, untill it strikes the Communication by Water between that Lake and Lake Erie; thence along the middle of said Communication into Lake Erie, through the middle of said Lake, untill it arrives at the Water Communication between that Lake and Lake Huron; thence along the middle of said water communication into the Lake Huron; thence through the middle of said Lake to the Water Communication between that Lake and Lake Superior; thence through Lake Superior northward of the Isles Royal & Phelipeaux, to the Long Lake; thence through the middle of said Long Lake, and the water Communication between it and the Lake of the Woods, to the said Lake of the Woods, thence through the said Lake to the most Northwestern point thereof, and from thence on a due west Course to the River Missisippi; thence by a Line to be drawn along the middle of the said River Missisippi, untill it shall intersect the northernmost part of the 31st Degree of North Latitude. South, by a Line to be drawn due East, from the Determination of the Line last mentioned, in the Latitude of 31 Degrees North of the Equator, to the middle of the River Apalachicola or Catahouche; thence along the middle thereof, to its junction with the Flint River; thence strait to the Head of St. Mary's River, and thence down along the middle of St. Mary's River to the Atlantic Ocean. East, by a Line to be drawn along the middle of the River St. Croix, from its Mouth in the Bay of Fundy to its Source; and from its Source directly North, to the aforesaid Highlands which divide the Rivers that fall into the Atlantic Ocean, from those which fall into the River St. Laurence; comprehending all Islands within twenty Leagues of any part of the Shores of the united States, and lying between Lines to be drawn due East from the points where the aforesaid Boundaries between Nova Scotia on the one part and East Florida on the other shall respectively touch the Bay of Fundy, and the Atlantic Ocean; excepting such Islands as now are, or heretofore have been within the Limits of the said Province of Nova Scotia.

ARTICLE 3[d]

It is agreed, that the People of the United States shall continue to enjoy unmolested the Right to take Fish of every kind on the Grand Bank, and on all the other Banks of Newfoundland; Also in the Gulph of St. Laurence, and at all other Places in the Sea where the Inhabitants of both Countries used at any time heretofore to fish. And also that the Inhabitants of the united States shall have Liberty to take Fish of every kind on such part of the Coast of Newfoundland, as British Fishermen shall use, (but not to dry or cure the same on that Island,) and also on the Coasts, Bays, and Creeks of all other of his Britannic Majesty's Dominions in America, and that the American Fishermen shall have Liberty to dry and cure Fish in any of the unsettled Bays Harbours and Creeks of Nova Scotia, Magdalen Islands, and Labrador, so long as the same shall remain unsettled; but so soon as the same or either of them shall be settled, it shall not be lawful for the said Fishermen to dry or cure Fish at such Settlement, without a previous Agreement for that purpose with the Inhabitants Proprietors or Possessors of the Ground.

ARTICLE 4th

It is agreed that Creditors on either side, shall meet with no lawful Impediment to the Recovery of the full value in Sterling Money of all bonâ fide Debts heretofore contracted.

ARTICLE 5th

It is agreed that the Congress shall earnestly recommend it to the Legislatures of the respective States, to provide for the Restitution of all Estates, Rights, and Properties which have been confiscated, belonging to real British Subjects; and also of the Estates Rights and Properties of Persons resident in Districts in the Possession of his Majesty's Arms; and who have not borne Arms against the said United States: And that Persons of any other Description shall have free Liberty to go to any part or parts of any of the thirteen United States, and therein to remain twelve months unmolested in their Endeavours to obtain the Restitution of such of their Estates, Rights and Properties as may have been confiscated; And that Congress shall also earnestly recommend to the several States a Reconsideration and Revision of all Acts or Laws regarding the premises, so as to render the said Laws or Acts perfectly consistent not only with Justice and Equity, but with that spirit of Conciliation which on the Return of the Blessings of Peace should universaly prevail. And that Congress shall also earnestly recommend to the several States, that the Estates Rights and Properties of such last mention'd Persons shall be restored to them; they refunding to any Persons who may be now in Possession the bonâ fide Price, (where any has been given,) which such Persons may have paid on purchasing any of the said Lands, Rights, or Properties since the Confiscation.

And it is agreed that all Persons who have any Interest in confiscated Lands, either by Debts, Marriage Settlements or otherwise, shall meet with no lawful Impediment in the prosecution of their just Rights.

ARTICLE 6:th

That there shall be no future Confiscations made, nor any prosecutions commenced against any Person or Persons, for or by reason of the Part which he or they may have taken in the present War, and that no person shall on that account suffer any future Loss or Damage either in his Person, Liberty or Property; and that those who may be in confinement on such charges, at the time of the Ratification of the Treaty in America, shall be immediately set at Liberty, and the Prosecutions so commenced be discontinued.

ARTICLE 7:th

There shall be a firm and perpetual Peace, between his Britannic Majesty and the said States, and between the Subjects of the one and the Citizens of the other, Wherefore all Hostilities both by Sea and Land shall then immediately cease: All Prisoners on both sides shall be set at Liberty, & his Britannic Majesty shall, with all convenient speed, & without causing any Destruction or carrying away any Negroes, or other Property of the American Inhabitants withdraw all his Armies Garrisons and Fleets from the said United States, and from every Port, Place, and Harbour within the same; leaving in all Fortifications the American Artillery that may be therein: And shall also order and cause all Archives, Records, Deeds and Papers belonging to any of the said States, or their Citizens, which in the Course of the War may have fallen into the hands of his Officers to be forthwith restored and delivered to the proper States & Persons to whom they belong.

ARTICLE 8:th

The Navigation of the River Mississippi from its Source to the Ocean, shall for ever remain free and open to the Subjects of Great Britain and the Citizens of the United States.

ARTICLE 9th

In case it should so happen that any Place or Territory belonging to Great Britain, or to the United States, should be conquered by the Arms of either, from the other, before the Arrival of these Articles in America, It is agreed that the same shall be restored, without Difficulty, and without requiring any Compensation.

Done at Paris, the thirtieth day of November, in the year One thousand Seven hundred Eighty Two

RICHARD OSWALD [Seal]
JOHN ADAMS [Seal]
B FRANKLIN [Seal]
JOHN JAY [Seal]
HENRY LAURENS [Seal]

Witness

The Words [and Henry Laurens][1] between the fifth and sixth Lines of the first Page; and the Words [or carrying away any Negroes, or other Property of the American Inhabitants] between the seventh and eighth Lines of the eighth Page, being first interlined

CALEB WHITEFOORD
Secretary to the British Commission.
W.T. FRANKLIN
Secy. to the American Commission

SEPARATE ARTICLE

It is hereby understood and agreed, that in case Great Britain at the Conclusion of the present War, shall recover, or be put in possession of West Florida, the Line of North Boundary between the said Province and the United States, shall be a Line drawn from the Mouth of the River Yassous where it unites with the Mississippi due East to the River Apalachicola.

Done at Paris the thirtieth day of November, in the year One thousand Seven hundred and Eighty Two.

Attest	RICHARD OSWALD [Seal]
CALEB WHITEFOORD	JOHN ADAMS [Seal]
Secy. to the British Commission	B FRANKLIN [Seal]
Attest	JOHN JAY [Seal]
W. T. FRANKLIN	HENRY LAURENS [Seal]
Secy. to the American Commission	

DS in DNA: RG 11, TS 102; Cs in PCC 85, 262–73; DLC: Franklin, ser.1, VIII, no. 26; MiU-C: RGA (Shelburne-American Peace); CP EU 22: 502–07; and in CP A 539: 68–78. See also Miller, *Treaties*, II, 96–107; *RDC*, VI, 96–100.

[1]The brackets appear in the Treaty.

How Two Foreign Ministers Responded to News of the Preliminaries

December 1782

When on the evening before the signing of the Preliminaries, Franklin wrote Vergennes informing him that the Preliminary Articles had been drawn up and expressing the "hope" that he would soon be able to send him a copy,[1] the news could not have come as a complete shock to France's foreign minister.[2] The Comte was pleased neither with the content of the Articles nor the clandestine manner of their negotiation. In his opinion, which his *premier commis* fully shared, America, by in effect leaving the war, had cut the ground from under France and Spain in their negotiations.[3] When Franklin called on Vergennes a few days later, the French minister let the Doctor "perceive that his proceeding in this abrupt signature to the articles had little in it, which could be agreeable to the King." Franklin "excused in the best manner he could, himself and his colleagues." At the same time he informed Vergennes that the American Commissioners planned to dispatch the Preliminary Articles to Congress and that arrangements were being made to secure a British passport for the vessel that would carry the provisional treaty terms. Vergennes cautioned that dispatching the terms at that time might raise unwarranted peace hopes in the United States,[4] but the Americans were not put off. Meeting at Laurens' on 11 December, the Commissioners agreed that JJ and Adams should draw up a joint letter to accompany the Preliminary Articles. JJ and Adams began their labors that very evening. The next day Adams made some additions to the draft, after which he took it to Laurens and then to Franklin for further modifications. The draft version printed below apparently represented the combined thinking of all four commissioners. While the greater part is in Adams' hand, JJ and Laurens each contributed a paragraph.

By the time the joint letter bearing the date of 14 December had been completed, the Commissioners had received the passport for Joshua Barney's ship *Washington*, which was to carry their dispatches to Congress. Franklin then told Vergennes of the ship's imminent departure, and even had the presumption to suggest that it might be well "to send part of the aids we have asked by this safe vessel." Shrewdly intimating how much the British would have liked to have seen an open break between the two allies, Franklin persuaded an indignant Vergennes that it was now too late to pull out. The *Washington* sailed with the Preliminary Articles—and the first installment of the last French loan of six million livres.[5]

If anything, the American Secretary for Foreign Affairs was even less charitable toward the Commissioners than his French counterpart. On 16 December Robert R. Livingston submitted to Congress JJ's brief note dated 28 September which clarified a reference to Oswald's second commission in Franklin's dispatch of two days earlier.[6] Livingston included in his letter of transmittal a quotation from JJ's private correspondence of 4 September hinting that difficulties had arisen in the Spanish-American negotiations.[7] Because the frigate *Danae* bearing October dispatches from France went aground in Chesapeake Bay, no further news reached Philadelphia until 22 December. The next day Congress heard JJ's letter of 13 October revealing a certain lack of confidence in French good will and Franklin's of the 14th manifesting an equal distrust of the British.[8] The letters seemed to suggest that the two Commissioners were at loggerheads. As James Madison put it, "although on a supposed intimacy and joined in the same commission, they the Ministers, wrote *separately,* and breathed opposite sentiments as to the views of France."[9] As we know now, the Commissioners were in basic agreement.

The most provocative passage in JJ's letter was his reference to the intercepted dispatch of Barbé-Marbois, France's secretary of legation at Philadelphia, with its boastfully indiscreet comment that Congress' instructions to its Commissioners left the King of France in effective control of America's peace negotiations, coupled with its sharp criticism of the fisheries' claims being advanced by the United States.[10] The release of the dispatch provoked both indignation at the letter's author[11] and denials as to its authenticity or as to the accuracy of the translation, denials made at that time and on and off for a century thereafter.[12] In fact, there is no longer any question that the letter was authentic and that Barbé-Marbois wrote it.[13]

Despite the fact that JJ himself had asked that his dispatch with the enclosure be kept "a profound secret" and cautioned that he did "not see how that is to be done if communicated to the Congress at large, among whom there always have been, and always will be, some unguarded members,"[14] Livingston laid the documents before Congress on 24 December. On that day, and again on 30 December, the issue of the French alliance and the instructions to the peace Commissioners were the subjects of a sharp debate. Abraham Clark of New Jersey, seconded by John Rutledge, moved to "revise the instructions relative to negotiations for peace, with a view to exempt the American Plenipotentiaries from the obligation to conform to the advice of France." Cooler heads prevailed. Clark's motion was postponed without a vote, with no record of it remaining in the official *Journals.*[15]

In turn, Madison now rallied the supporters of the French alliance in Congress, leaving Livingston to placate Luzerne. In conferences on 30 and 31 December the French Minister read to the Secretary for Foreign Affairs excerpts from Vergennes' dispatches dealing with the negotiations of the Peace

Preliminaries.[16] In response, Livingston promised to remind the American Commissioners of their instructions in *"a precise and clear manner but with delicacy,"* and he drew on the documents supplied by Luzerne to bolster a rebuke to JJ contained in a laboriously drafted letter of 4 January 1783, which he had commenced writing five days earlier.[17] Therein the Secretary questioned the basis of JJ's suspicions of the French court, which, he pointed out, his colleague Franklin did not share, and proceeded to defend France's negotiating stance. From the correspondence turned over to Livingston by Luzerne, the former could "discover nothing but an anxious desire for peace," which the French would withhold until America's independence was acknowledged. While questioning the authenticity of the Marbois letter on the fisheries, Livingston confessed that he was not suprised by its contents, since Marbois had "always endeavored to persuade us that our claim to the fisheries was not well founded." The Secretary contrasted Marbois' letter with the conduct of the French court as evidencing "the difference between a great politician and a little one." Finally, Livingston hinted that he would prefer hearing about the American negotiations directly rather than through Vergennes as intermediary.

JJ did not receive the Livingston rebuke until the end of May, six months after he and his colleagues had concluded the Preliminaries with the British. His reply was curt: "My letter by Captain Barney affords an answer to the greater part of your inquiries."[18] Indubitably, JJ felt the sting, and thereafter relations with this oldtime friend were never quite the same.

[1]Franklin to Vergennes, 29 Nov. 1782, *BFS,* VIII, 627; *RDC,* VI, 90.

[2]One of Vergennes' secret intelligence agents in London sent him a copy of a letter from the Home Secretary to the Bank of England reporting prematurely that peace Preliminaries would be signed by Great Britain and the United States on 23 November. Anonymous to Vergennes, 22 Nov. 1782, L in CP A. Previously, Adams had indiscreetly shown a draft of the Preliminaries—all except the Secret Article—to the duc de la Vauguyon, France's ambassador at The Hague.

[3]Rayneval blamed the news of the signing of the Preliminaries for provoking the equivalents demanded by Great Britain for Gibraltar. Rayneval to Vergennes, 25 Dec. 1782, CP A 539: 314–17.

[4]Vergennes to Luzerne, 19 Dec. 1782, Dft in CP EU 22: 562–63; translation in *RDC,* VI, 150–52; Morris, *Peacemakers,* pp. 383–84. The British passport is in DLC: Franklin VIII, 27.

[5]Franklin to Vergennes, 15 and 17 Dec. 1782, LS in CP EU 22: 538; *BFS,* VIII, 640–43; Miller, *Treaties,* 115–22; Morris, *Peacemakers,* pp. 383–84.

[6]Franklin to Livingston, 26 Sept. 1782, *BFS,* VIII, 602–03; *RDC,* V, 763–64. JJ to Livingston, 28 Sept. 1782, Dft in JP; LbkCs in PCC 110, II and in CSmH; *HPJ,* II, 348; *RDC,* V, 779. Livingston to Elias Boudinot, 16 Dec. 1782, Dft in NHi: Robert R. Livingston; *RDC,* VI, 141.

[7]JJ to Livingston, 4 Sept. 1782, above.

[8]JJ to Livingston, 13 Oct. 1782, LbkCs in PCC 110, II and in CSmH; *RDC,* V, 809, and *HPJ,* II, 348–49; Franklin to Livingston, 14 Oct. 1782, *RDC,* V, 811–12. These dispatches were also transmitted with Livingston to Boudinat, 22 Dec, 1782, *RDC,* VI, 159.

[9]*JCC,* XXIII, 870; *MP,* V, 436–39.

[10]Barbé-Marbois to Vergennes, 13 March 1782, deciphered translation with minor variations in *RDC,* V, 238–41, and *WJ,* I, 490–94.

[11]*JCC,* XXIII, 870.

[12]*Peacemakers,* pp. xii, 325; *RDC,* V, 241–42n.

[13]*Peacemakers,* pp. xii, 325.

[14]JJ to Livingston, 18 Sept. 1782, LbkC in PCC 110, II and in CSmH; *RDC,* V, 740; *HPJ,* 345–47.

[15]James Madison, "Notes of Debates," *JCC,* XXIII, 870, 872–74; *MP,* V, 436–39, 466–72.

[16]"The substance of a verbal communication made to the Secretary for Foreign Affairs by the Minister of France on the 30th and 31st of December, 1782," *RDC,* VI, 177–82; Luzerne to Vergennes, 30 Dec. 1782, CP EU 22: 605–13.

[17]Livingston to JJ, 4 Jan. 1783, ALS in JP; (a substantial variation of Dft, 30 Dec. 1782, in NHi: Robert R. Livingston, and of LbkC in Livingston's hand in PCC 118, pp. 384–97); *RDC,* VI, 177–80; *HPJ,* III, 14–19. Contradictions in dates and variations in the text raised problems for Wharton, *RDC,* VI, 173–76, which utilizes the LbkC version, while Sparks appears to have had access to the ALS, which is in *SDC,* IV, 525, under date of 4 Jan. 1783.

[18]JJ to Livingston, 1 June 1782, ALS in PCC 89, II, 472–73; Dft in JP; LbkC in PCC 110, II; *RDC,* VI, 464–65; and *HPJ,* III, 49–50.

JOHN ADAMS, BENJAMIN FRANKLIN, HENRY LAURENS, JOHN JAY TO ROBERT R. LIVINGSTON

Paris, 13 December 1782

Sir,

We have the Honour to congratulate Congress upon the Signature on the 30 of last month of <a preliminary Treaty> the Preliminaries of a Peace between the Crown of Great Britain and the United States of America, to be inserted in the definitive Treaty to be concluded between them So soon as the Terms between the Crowns of France and Great Britain Shall be agreed on. A Copy of the Articles is here inclosed, and We cannot but flatter ourselves, that they will appear to Congress, as they do to all of Us, to be consistent with the Honour and Interest of the United States, and We are persuaded Congress would be more fully of that opinion, if <it> they were apprised of all the Circumstances and Reasons which have influenced the Negotiation.

Although it is impossible for Us to go into that Detail, We think it necessary, nevertheless, to make a few Remarks on Such of the Articles as appear most to require Elucidation.

Remarks on Second Article, relative to the Boundaries.

The Court of Great Britain, insisted on retaining all the Territories comprehended within the Province of Quebec, by the Act of Parliament respecting it. They contended that Nova Scotia Should extend to the River Kinnebeck, and they claimed not only all the Lands in the

Western Country and on the Mississippi, which were not expressly included in our Charters and Governments, but also all-such Lands within <those Lines> them as remained ungranted by the King of Great Britain. It would be endless to enumerate all the Discussions and Arguments, on the Subject. We knew this Court and Spain to be against our Claims to the Western Country, and, having no Reason to think that Lines more favourable could ever have been obtained, We finally agreed to those described in this Article. Indeed they appear to leave Us little to complain of, and not much to desire. Congress will observe, that although our Northern Line is in a certain Part below the Latitude of forty five, yet in <another> others it extends <beyond> above it, <and> divides the Lake Superiour, and gives Us access to its Western and Southern Waters, from which a Line in that Latitude would have excluded Us.

Remarks on Article fourth respecting Creditors.

We had been informed that some of the States, had confiscated British Debts, but although each State has a right to bind its own Citizens, yet in our opinion, it appertains Solely to Congress in whom exclusively are vested the Right of making War and Peace, to pass Acts against the Subjects of a Power with which, the Confederacy may be at War. It therefore only remained for Us to consider, whether this Article is founded in Justice and good Policy. In our opinion no Acts of Government, could dissolve the Obligations of good Faith resulting from lawfull Contracts, between Individuals of the two Countries, prior to the War. We knew that some of the British Creditors were making Common Cause with the Refugees, and other Adversaries to our Independence. <*it was our Policy to render that Opposition as insignificant as possible, and it was easy to foresee that by satisfying these Creditors, they would be among the first to clamour for Peace and the Return of Commerce.*> Besides, Sacrificing private Justice to Reasons of State or political Convenience is always an odious measure, and the Purity of our Reputation in this respect in all foreign Commercial Countries is of infinitely more Importance to Us than all the Sums in question. It may also be remarked, that American and British Creditors are placed on an equal Footing.

We beg leave to add our Advice, that Congress should take Measures to obtain, as soon as possible an Account of the Losses Sustained and Cruelties suffered by the Citizens of the respective States of America, by Plunder, Burnings, Robberies and Exportation of Negroes, Plate and other Property, by the British Forces, and transmit them to Us, and preserve them for their own Use, as soon as possible. Should

Such an Account arrive before the Signature of the definitive Treaty, it may Serve as a Ground Work for demanding Satisfaction.[1]

Remarks on Articles 5 and 6 respecting Refugees.

These Articles were among the first discussed, and the last agreed to, and had not the Conclusion of <these Articles> this Buziness at the time of its Date been particularly important to the British <Ministry> Administration, <the Ideas which there prevail of British Honour> the Respect which both in London and Versailles, is Supposed to be due to the Honour, Dignity and Interests of Royalty, would probably have forever prevented our bringing this Article so near to the Views of Congress and the Sovereign Rights of the States as it now Stands. When it is considered that <the Sense of Honour in Great Britain and in the United States, were directly opposed to each other,> it was utterly impossible, to render this Article perfectly consistent both with American and British Ideas of Honour, We presume that the middle Line adopted by this Article, is as little unfavourable to the former, as any that could in Reason be expected.[2]

[*Following paragraph in JJ's hand.*]

As we had good Reason to believe that the Articles respecting the Boundaries, the Refugees and the Fisheries, did not correspond with the policy of this Court, we did not communicate the Preliminaries to the Minister until after they were Signed;[3] and we hope that these Considerations will excuse our having so far deviated from the Spirit of our Instructions. The Count de Vergennes on perusing the Articles appeared surprized[4] at their being so favorable to us.

[*Following paragraph in Laurens' hand.*]

To urge Congress to obtain the most ample Account of Losses sustained by the Citizens and respective States of America by Plunder, Robbery, burnings, exportation of Negroes etc. etc. by the British Troops and to a transmission as early as possible.[5]

Dft in MHi: Adams, reel 359, in the hand of John Adams except for one paragraph each by JJ and Henry Laurens, as indicated in the text. Endorsed by Adams: "rough draught of a common Letter." The LS version of this letter, dated 14 December, is signed by all four Commissioners (body of the letter in the hand of W. T. Franklin) is in PCC 85; LbkCs in PCC 106 and DLC: Franklin, ser. VIII, no. 29; *RDC,* VI, 131–33. Enclosed with the LS are Cs of the following: (1) Preliminary Articles—endorsed: "Provisional Articles with Britain, Duplicate"; (2) Oswald to American Commissioners, 4 Nov. 1782; (3) and (4) American Commissioners to Oswald and Strachey, and (5) Act of Parliament, 31 Oct. 1782.

[1]The LS version of Adams' paragraph on possible Patriot compensation was less pejorative in tone: "We beg leave to add our Advice that Copies be sent us of the Accounts directed to be taken by the different States, of the unnecessary Devastations and Sufferings sustained by them from the Enemy in the Course of the War. Should they arrive before the Signature of the definitive Treaty they might possibly answer very good purposes."

[2]At this point the LS version has this added paragraph: "As to the Separate Article, We beg leave to observe, that it was our Policy to render the Navigation of the River Mississippi so important to Britain, as that their Views might correspond with ours on that Subject. Their possessing the Country on the River, North of the Line from the Lake of the Woods, affords a Foundation for their claiming such Navigation: and as the Importance of West Florida to Britain was for the same Reason rather to be strengthened than otherwise, we thought it adviseable to allow them the Extent contained in the Separate Article, especially as before the War it had been annexed by Britain to W. Florida, and would operate as an additional Inducement to their joining with us in agreeing, that the Navigation of the River should forever remain open to both. The Map used in the Course of our Negotiations was Mitchells."

[3]At this point in the LS version the following phrase was added: "and not even then the Separate Article."

[4]The LS version includes at this point the phrase: "but not displeased."

[5]This entire paragraph was omitted in the final version.

To Robert R. Livingston

Paris, 14 December 1782
Private

Dear Sir,

From our Preliminaries and the King's Speech[1] the *present* Disposition and System of the british Court may in my opinion be collected. Although particular Circumstances constrained them to yield in[2] more than perhaps they wished, I still think they meant to make (what they thought would really be) a satisfactory peace with us. In the Continuance of this Disposition and System, too much Confidence ought not to be placed, for disappointed Violence and mortified ambition are certainly dangerous Foundations to build implicit Confidence upon; but I cannot forbear thinking that we ought not, in the common phrase, to throw cold water upon it, by improper Exultation, extravagant Demands, or illiberal publications. Should such a Temper appear it would be wise to discountenance it. It is our policy to be independent in the most extensive Sense, and to observe a proper Distance towards all nations, minding our own Business, and not interfering with or being influenced by the Views of any, further than they may respect us.

Some of my Colleagues flatter themselves with the Probability of obtaining Compensation for Damages.[3] I have no Objection to the Tryal,[4] but I confess I doubt its Success, for Britain has no money to spare, and will think the Confiscations should settle that account, for they do not expect that Retribution will be made to all.

Our affairs have a very promising Aspect, and a little prudence will secure us all that we can reasonably wish [or] expect.[5] The Boundaries between the States should be immediately settled, and all Causes of Discord between them removed. It would be imprudent to disband the army while a foreign one remains in the Country; and it would be equally unwise to permit americans to spill the Blood of our Friends in the Islands, for in all of them there are many who wish us well. (The sale of the *continental* Lands would if properly regulated and appropriated to that purpose, form a Fund on which we might borrow Money, especially if Foreigners could see good Reason to rely on our good Faith which, by being in certain Instances violated, has lost much of its Credit. I allude particularly to the Interest on Loan Office Certificates and the publications in our papers on that Subject, which do us Harm in Europe).

Present our affectionate Compliments to your Mother and to Mrs. Livingston. You say Nothing of your Daughter, which is not quite right considering the Interest I take in her Welfare. Mrs. Jay and her little one are well, which is more than I can say of myself.

Adieu. I am Dear Robert, your Friend

JOHN JAY

ALS in NHi: Robert R. Livingston, Dft in JP; incomplete in *WJ*, II, 109 *et seq.* and *RDC*, VI, 136–37.

[1]For the speech of George III at the opening of Parliament, 5 December, see *Parliamentary History*, XXIII, 203–07.

[2]"Yield us" in Dft.

[3]On 29 November Franklin had re-introduced the proposition of British indemnification of American patriots who had suffered confiscation or destruction of property by Royal forces during the war. *AP*, III, 80.

[4]"A further Tryal" in Dft.

[5]"Or" supplied by the editors; ALS torn here. "Reasonably expect" in Dft.

John Jay's Diary of the Peacemaking

Paris, 23 June–22 December 1782

Never a consistent diarist, JJ managed to record entries of events in which he participated on at least five scattered occasions. On the first, he recorded his activities during the crowded summer of '76 in bolstering the defenses of New York. The second covered the period 23 June to 22 December 1782 in Paris. The third treated his negotiations with Carmichael in March–April 1784. The fourth dealt with the years in which he rode circuit as Chief Justice of the United States Supreme Court, while the fifth covered medical treatment he received in May 1800 for a facial cyst.[1] Historically, the second cluster of entries is the most illuminating of the five and sheds important light on covert and controversial diplomacy.

To diplomatic historians, JJ's entries below under the date of 22 December 1782 are the most revealing and their authenticity was long contested. The principal involved was John Stuart, Viscount Mountstuart (1744–1814), the eldest son of the third Earl of Bute, George III's erstwhile intimate friend and the First Lord of the Treasury in the early years of his reign. While serving as the British envoy to Sardinia during the war years Mountstuart received permission from his government in the spring of 1780 to go to Geneva, pleading the "immense heats" of Turin and their effect on the health of Lady Mountstuart and his children. Since he had to travel through France, technically enemy country, in order to reach Geneva from Turin, he applied for a passport from the French minister at Turin. The application was granted, although the Comte de Vergennes expressed the hope that the Scotsman would not get involved in the factional quarrels that were tearing Geneva apart at this time.[2]

Had Vergennes known the purpose of Mountstuart's trip he never would have issued the passport. On arriving in Geneva, Mountstuart spent a good deal of time with his former tutor, an historian named Paul-Henri Mallet (1730–1807). Prior to Mountstuart's arrival Mallet had gone to Paris and had held extensive conversations with a fellow Gênevoise, Jacques Necker, the prestigious Director General of Finances in France, who headed a peace party and sought, behind Vergennes' back, to get France out of the war in order to facilitate balancing his budget. Mallet proposed to Necker that "some one province," say New England, be declared independent, "and the others obliged to return to their former allegiance." Necker was sympathetic.

Anxious to gain the limelight as a peacemaker, Mountstuart dashed off a dispatch reporting his personal conversations to the British Secretary of State for the Southern Department, Wills Hill, the Earl of Hillsborough (1718–93). There followed a long and detailed correspondence between Mountstuart in Turin and Mallet in Geneva. The former thought he was making progress until the blow fell. On 21 November 1780, Hillsborough wrote Mountstuart that he had laid his communications before the King, but that George III had expressed the view that any negotiations with France were out of the question so long as "she continues to abett and support Rebellion now raging in His Majesty's North American colonies," and certainly no attention could be paid to "proposals made or suggested" in the "unavowed and private manner" of Mountstuart's "Genevan friend." He was bluntly ordered not to pursue the matter further by a personal trip to Paris, nor to receive any proposals whatsoever from the French "if the Rebell Colonies are in any manner included."

Crushed by the response to his well-meaning efforts and further disheartened by the dismissal of Necker from office in the spring of 1781, Mountstuart licked his wounds and bided his time, trying in the spring of 1782, but without success, to insinuate himself once more in the role of mediator now that Lord North had been thrown out of office. Granted leave to return home, he reached Paris on 16 December 1782, after JJ and his colleagues had signed the Preliminaries but before France and Spain had completed their own preliminary negotiations. On 22 December he dined with Oswald. That same evening JJ made a social call on the British commissioner, and Oswald, as JJ recorded in his diary below,[3] read his American visitor the portion of Mountstuart's letterbook regarding his abortive Franco-Genevan negotiations.

In later years Edmond Charles Genêt (1763–1834), the one-time minister from France to the United States during the French Revolution, flatly denied that the events described therein had ever taken place.[4] He was wrong. He confused the time of the Mountstuart negotiations with the year 1782, when Necker was out of office, instead of 1780, when the banker was at the height of his power. Blandly asserting that Necker had never interfered in the concerns of the Department of Foreign Affairs, Genêt should have known that Necker would make doubly sure that no information of his covert diplomacy would leak either to Vergennes or his subordinates. At the time in question Genêt's father, Edmé Jacques Genêt, served as premier commis of the Bureau of Interpretation, passing on to Vergennes intelligence received from England and America. The elder Genêt held that post until September 1781, when, on his death, his precocious son succeeded him. In fact Edmond Genêt was in Vienna not Versailles in 1780.

Lord Mountstuart's letterbooks from Turin, now in the British Museum, as well as the Foreign Office Papers in the British Public Record Office, substantiate the account JJ entered in his diary of a covert proposal to dismember America.

[1]Notes on mission to Connecticut, 22–24 July [1776], in *JJ*, I, 300–01. Notes concerning William Carmichael, 27 March–19 April 1784, below. Circuit Court diary, 16 April 1790–4 Aug. 1792, AD in JP. Notes on the removal of a cyst, 6 May–20 June 1800, AD in private collection.

[2]For further details, see *Peacemakers,* pp. 99–104.

[3]JJ evidently prepared a memorandum on his talk with Oswald, which was endorsed "Mr. Oswalds account of an offer of France to England to divide U.S. between them. 1782." Endorsement in JP.

[4]DLC: Genêt, XLIV, reel 29, frames 025811–12.

John Jay: Diary of the Peacemaking

Paris, 23 June–22 December 1782

1782. 23 June. Arrived at Paris about noon. Spent the Afternoon at Passy with Doctor Franklin. He informed me of the State of the Negociation, and that he kept an exact Journal of it.[1]

24. Waited upon Mr. De Vergennes with the Doctor. The Count

read to us his Answer to the British minister.[2] Dined with the Doctor, and found Dr. Bancroft there.

25. Wrote to Count Aranda.

26. After Breakfast with the Doctor, met with Mr. Grenville on our Return. Recieved a Visit from Marquis la Fayette.

27. Recieved another visit from the Marquis. Went to Doctor Franklin at Passy this afternoon, where I found Mr. Jones and Mr. Paridizo[3] there. Made a visit this Evening to madame la Fayette.

28. Recieved a Letter of 27th Inst. from Count Aranda this Morning.

July 25. Visit from Mr. Benj. Vaughan, also Count Aranda.

26. Mr. Oswald and Mr. Whiteford[4] made me a visit; Mr. Oswald *seemed* desirous to know Mr. Vaughans Errand.

Oct. 1782. 12. Dined <with> at Dr. Franklins with Sir Edward Newenham,[5] his Lady, eldest Son, and two Daughters.

15. General du Portail[6] and Colonel Gouvion[7] set out for America. Gave the General Letters for Sec[retar]y Livingston, with which were inclosed others for Gov. Livingston, R. Morris, G. Morris, and Frederick Jay.[8]

16. Mr. Oswald recieved a Courier from London. Dined with Sir Edward.

17. Mr. Oswald sent me some English papers, but no other Communication. Sir Edward and Family spent this Evening here.

18. Dined with spanish Embassador,[9] a large Company, the Duke of Berwick and his Dutches, viscount le herrida,[11] etc., etc., etc. I took occasion to mention to the Embassador <with> Mr. Oswalds *new* Com[missio]n and my Regret that Spain should be later than Britain in acknow[ledgin]g our Independence. He said he had powers to treat with me *tres bellement* whenever I should be authorized to settle our Limits, which must be done previous to our Engagements. He asked whether I had mentioned that Matter to Congress. I told him I had. He said that when my further Instructions should [arrive] we might proceed etc.

Philip V. B. Livingston[12] arrived from Spa[in] where he had gone from England a Month or six Weeks before. He had seen my Brother Sir James in England, and removed the apprehensions I had been led to entertain of his having acted improperly. The Surmises against him appear by Mr. Livingston[s] account to be without Foundation.

19. Mr. Livingston breakfasted and dined with me. I carried him this morning to Dr. Franklin's. He doubts Lord Shelburns Sincerity.

Sir Edward and Family took their Leave of us; with many kind

Expressions etc. He gave me two magazines containing the Memoirs of himself and Family.

It *is said* there are great Commotions and expected Changes in the Cabinet here, and Joly Fleury[13] to go out.

Mr. F[leury] wrote to his Friends in Am[erica] that he was desired to stay here by Dr. Franklin and myself to assist in the Business of peace, and he desired his Correspondent to let such Ideas appear in the public papers. *I am sure* this Fact is ill founded; the Letter went by the ship which carried Duportail.

Mr. Fitzherbert rec[ieve]d a Courier from London.

20. Viscount le Herida and lady paid us their first visit. Mr. Fox[14] of Phi[ladelphi]a did the same.

I hear that Mr. Fleury at Council remarked that Mr. De Castres[15] had spent a great number of millions on the navy to little purpose, that Mr. Vergennes supported this assertion, and that De Castres carried the Matter so high as that one or other of those ministers would probably go out.

Do. Count de Vergennes speaking of the british Com[missione]rs here said, that unless they decided within ten Days or a Fortnight, they should not be permitted to stay here to keep up their Stocks and intrigue.

21 October 1782. Visited Mr. Oswald. He told me that he expected the Answer of his Court to the Articles, within a few Days, and as he had recommended them warmly, did not doubt of their being agreed to, that the last Courier had been sent on the following Business viz.

The Complaints against Rodney's Conduct at Statia[16] had been committed to the management of Mr. <De Castrie> Walpole[17] here, with Mr. De Castries, that De Castries had written to the English ministry that unless an order for Restitution was given within ten Days, he would direct Reprizals to be made at Granada. That Mr. Fitzherbert was charged to represent this Matter to Mr. Vergennes, who on seeing the Letter of Mr. De Castries expressed much Surprize.

He also told me that a Mr. Poultney[18] had within a few Days arrived here to place his Daughter (a rich Heiress) in a Convent, that Mr. Poultney in Confidence gave him the following curious anecdote vizt. "That in the latter part of last Winter or Beginning of last Spring there was an Englishman of Distinction here, who in Conversation with a Friend of Mr. Vergennes, expressed his Regret that the affairs of America would not be so arranged as to lead to Peace. The Friend mentioned this to Mr. Vergennes, who agreed to admit the Englishman to an Audience on the Subject. Accordingly the Englishman and this Friend waited upon the Minister, who in the Conference offered to divide America with Britain; and in Case the latter agreed to the partition that the Force of France and Britain should be used to reduce it to the obedience of the respective sovereigns. On parting the Minister said that in Case this offer should not be accepted, he reserved to himself the Right of denying all that he had said about it, that this offer was refused and that the Friend in a Letter to the Englishman had expressed his Regret on the Subject."

Mr. Oswald told me further that Mr. Poultney assured him that he recieved this Information from the Englishman's own mouth.

Mr. Oswald spoke handsomely of Mr. Poultney's Caracter. I advised him to trace the matter further, and if true, to get it properly authenticated, which he promised to do.

24 October. Mr. Oswald told me he had recieved a Courier last night. That our articles were under Consideration, and that Mr. Strachey, <Ld.> Mr. Townsend's Sec[retar]y, was on the way here to confer with us about them.

Mr. Oswald declined informing me of the particular Objections, but it was easy to percieve from his Conversation that they related to the back Lands, and he further said "he believed this Court had found means to put a Spoke in our Wheel": he told me that Fitzherbert had recieved an answer to the french Propositions, that the answer inadvertently gave away the Gum Trade, and that he had *in vain* desired him to postpone the Delivery of the Answer till he should apprize his Court of the Mistake, and give them an opportunity of correcting it. He consulted me on the possibility of keeping Mr. Stracheys coming a Secret. I told him it was not possible, and that it would be best to declare the Truth about it. vizt. that he was coming with Books and Papers relative to our Boundaries.

He also mentioned to me his having recieved several Letters from a Gentleman at St. Germains inviting him to go there and promising to communicate something of great Importance. He shewed me the last Letter. I advised him to go, especially as the Gent[leman] seemed to press it exceedingly.

Dined with Dr. Franklin. I found Mr. De Raynevalle there. Just <before> after Dinner, the Doctor informed me that Raynevalle had sent him word that he would dine with him to Day and would be glad to meet me there. I told the Doctor what I had heard from Oswald about Strachey, and that I thought it best not to say more to Rayneval than that we met with Difficulties, and that Oswald expected to recieve Instructions in a few Days.

We retired with Rayneval. He asked how Matters stood between us and Oswald. We told him that we could not agree about all our Boundaries. We mentioned the one between us and Nova Scotia. He asked what we demanded to the north. We answered that Canada should be reduced to its ancient Bounds. He then contested our Right to these back Lands, etc., etc.

He asked what we expected as to the Fisheries, we said the same Right we had formerly enjoyed. He contested the propriety of that Demand, adding some Strictures on the ambitious and Restless views of Mr. Adams, and intimated that we might be content with the Coast Fishery.

25 October. Had a long Conversation with Mr. Vaughan on the State of the Negociation. We agreed in all things.

26 October. Marquis Fayette called upon me. He had heard from Dr. Franklin that Shelburn was about sending his Sec[retar]y here. I explained this according to the advice I had given Mr. Oswald. He asked whether I thought New York would be evacuated. This was a leading Question, and I answered, No. He said General Washington had the taking of that place much at Heart and that he had often applied to the Ministers here for aid and that they seemed disinclined, and said that it was not worth while to form Expeditions for the taking of places which must necessarily be given up at a Peace.

He mentioned DEstaings going from hence to Spain, and probably thence to the West Indies, and that he was going with him. He also said that he would endeavour to turn that matter to our advantage and would correspond with General Washington on the Subject.

Mr. Adams arrived this Evening.

October 28, Monday. Mr. Adams was with me 3 Hours this morning. I mentioned to him the Progress and present State of our Negociation with Britain, my Conjectures as to the Views of France and Spain, and the Part which it appeared to me adviseable for me to act. He concurred with me in Sentiment on all these Points. He recounted the affairs of his Negociation in Holland and the Advice given him by the french Emb[assador] there. He spoke freely what he thought of Dr. Franklin. Being both of us engaged to dine with Mr. Allen of Boston,[19] we went there. He returned with me in the Evening which we spent in very interesting Communications to each other.

29. Mr. Oswald informed me that Mr. Strachey arrived Yesterday. He spoke of limiting our western Extent by a longitudinal Line on the

East of the Mississippi. I told him if that was insisted upon it was needless to talk of Peace, for that we never would Yield that point. He proposed to bring Mr. Strachey to see me. He did so.

Mr. Strachey came, and soon after Mr. Adams. Some loose Conversation ensued about the Refugees, English Debts, Drying Fish, etc. We are to meet him Tomorrow at 11 oClock at Mr. Oswalds.

Oswald told me in Confidence that his Court had not yet given an answer to the Spanish Propositions, and that they had offered to give Trinidad for Gibralter.

22 December 1782. Between 7 and 8 O'clock this Evening I visited Mr. Oswald. After some general Conversation he took occasion to say that Lord Mount Stuart the Son of Lord Bute had dined with him to Day, and that he had also seen his Brother Col. Stuart who had served the whole War in America. He spoke of the Colonel's aversion to the am[erican] War, and the Accounts he gave of the want of Discipline and Disorder which prevailed in the british army there, and the Depredations committed by them. He passed several Encomiums on the Colonel's Character, sometimes of the father and then of the Sons, and observing how unlike they were to what the Father was supposed to be, tho for his part he believed that more sins were laid upon his back than he had ever committed. He said that Lord Mountstuart execrated the American War, and had shewen him to day several Letters written by him at Turin (where he was Emb[assador] to Lord Hilsborough) on that Subject. Mr. Oswald asked me if I remembered what he had told me of Mr. Pultney's Information about the propositions of Count De Vergennes to Divide am[erica] with Britain. I told him I did. "Well," says [he], "the same kind of proposition was made to Lord Mountstuart." His Lordship brought with him here to Dinner his Letter Book which he did not chuse to leave with his Chargé D'Affairs and in it he shewed me his Letters written with his own Hand for he would not confide it to his Sec[retar]y, to Lord Hilsborough; and the first Letter was dated in the month of September 1780, from which it appears that a Mr. Mally who had formerly travelled with Lord Mountstuart, and is an honorary Professor at Geneva, and is employed to write the History of Hesse, etc., for which he recieves Annuities, a Man in short well known among Men of Letters, was employed by Mr. Neckar to make overtures to Lord Mountstuart about putting an End to the War by dividing Am[erica] between Britain and France, the latter to have the eastern part.

Mr. Oswald also says that Lord Mountstuart went to Geneva on the Occasion where he conversed with Mr. Mally and that his Lordship

22 Decr. 1782 Between 7 & 8 OC. this Evg I visited Mr Oswald — after some
general conversation he took occasion to say that Ld. Mount Stuart the
son of Ld Bute had dined with him E. Day, and that he had also seen
his Brother Col. Stuart who had served the whole War in America
he spoke of the Col.s aversion to the am. war, and the acct. he gave of
the want of Discipline & Disorder wh. prevailed in ye British army
there, & the Depredations committed by them — He passed several
Encomiums on the Coll.s Character, sometimes of the Father & then
of the Sons, & shewing how unlike they were to what the Father
was supposed to be, tho for his part he believed that more sins
were laid upon his Back than he had ever committed — He said
that Ld. Mountstuart execrated the american War, and had
shewn him to day several Letters written by him at Turin (where he was Emb.)
to Ld. Hillsborough on that Subject — Mr Oswald asked me if I
remembered what he had told me of Mr. Pulteney's Information abt. the
propositions of Ct. de Vergennes to divide am. with Britain — I told
him I did — well says he the same kind of proposition was made
to Ld. Mountstuart — "His Ld. brought with him here to Dinner his
Letter Book wh. he did not chuse to leave with his Chargé D'affaires
and in it he shewed me his Letters written with his own Hand for
he wd. not confide it to his Secy, to Ld. Hillsborough — and the first
Letter was dated in the month of Sept. 1780 from wh. it appears
that a Mr. ~~Mally~~ Mally who had formerly travelled w. Ld
Mountstuart, and is an honorary Professor at Geneva, and is
employed to write the History of Hesse &c. for wh. he receives
annuities, a Man in short well known among Men of letters
was employed by Mr. Necker to make overtures to Ld. Mountstuart
~~to~~ about putting an End to the War by dividing Am. between
Britain & France, the latter to have the eastern part —
Mr

Jay's Diary of the Peacemaking, 22 December 1782. *(Papers of John Jay. Rare Book and Manuscript Library, Columbia University)*

A British cartoonist views the Preliminary Peace. (*The British Museum*)

read to him out of his Letter Book some french Letters from this Mr. Mally to his Lordship on the Subject, after his Return to Turin. That this Correspondence of his Lordship with Lord Hillsborough contains a very curious and particular account of french Intrigues, particularly that Neckar wished for peace because his <Efforts> System could only raise money enough to provide for old Arrears and for current Expences, and were he obliged to sustain the Expence of the War he must break in upon it and perhaps be disgraced. It also mentioned the Intrigues to get de Sartine[20] out of the Marine Department, and Mr. Oswald says that the Overtures about am[erica] were conducted with a Variety of precautions for Secrecy, and with a Stipulation or Condition that both parties in Case they did not agree should be at Liberty to deny <what> all that passed. He told me that my Lord wrote strongly to Lord Hilsborough against the am[erican] War and that the latter in answer told Him it was a Subject out of his Line, and with which it was not proper for him to interfere. Lord Mountstuart was offended with the Minister for this and he brought his Letter book with him to Mr. Oswald to shew him the full State of the Matter. Mr. Oswald said that as he had told me the affair of Mr. Pultney he could [not] forbear mentioning this also, for it was a little strange that so extraordinary Matter should <be> come so circumstantial and correspondent, from two such different and unconnected Quarters. He desired me to consider this Communication as very confidential, adding that he could say more, but that it would not be proper for him at present to enter into a Detail of further particulars.

AD. Excerpts inaccurately reproduced in *WJ*, I, 136, 156–58, and, using the latter source, in *HPJ*, II, 311–12; III, 9–11, and in Frank Monaghan, ed., *The Diary of John Jay During the Peace Negotiations of 1782* (New Haven, 1934).

[1]For Franklin's "Journal," which he soon discontinued, see Introduction.

[2]For Vergennes' conversations with Grenville regarding the latter's powers and the British disposition to recognize the independence of the U.S., see Vergennes to Luzerne, 28 June 1782, C in CP EU 21: 336–44.

[3]Probably William Jones (1746–94), the renowned Oriental scholar, knighted 19 March 1783. John Paradise (1743–95), an Englishman born in Salonica, who married a Virginian and gained a reputation as a linguist and intimate of Dr. Samuel Johnson.

[4]Caleb Whitefoord (1734–1810), secretary to Oswald, wit, litterateur, connoisseur of the arts, and former London neighbor of Franklin. He attested to the signing of the Preliminary Articles.

[5]Sir Edward Newenham (1732–1814), member of the Irish Parliament for County Dublin, 1776–97, who was defiantly pro-American. Maurice R. O'Connell, *Irish Politics and Social Conflict in the Age of the American Revolution* (Philadelphia, 1965), pp. 25–35. SLJ sent Lady Newenham "a little canister of better Tea than can probably be found in the Shops of this City." 16 Oct. 1782. Dft in JP.

[6]Louis Le Bègue de Presle Duportail (1743–1802), *JJ,* I, 577n.

[7]Jean Baptiste Gouvion (1747–92), a French engineer and volunteer, who assisted Duportail in planning the West Point fortifications.

[8]See below for the following: JJ to Frederick Jay, 3 October (the only October letter to him extant), and three letters of JJ of 13 October, respectively, to Gouverneur Morris (above), Robert Morris, and William Livingston. In addition, JJ transmitted SLJ to William Livingston, 14 October, ALS and Dft in JP; SLJ to Mary White Morris, Dft in JP, 14 October; and 13 October, JJ to Robert R. Livingston, LbkCs in PCC 110, II and in CSmH; *RDC,* V, 809–10; *HPJ,* II, 348–49.

[9]For a description of the Conde de Aranda's residence at the Place Louis XV and its splendid vistas, see *AP,* III, 136, 137.

[10]Probably Charles Ferdinand Stuart-FitzJames (1752–87), but for the attainder of the line, 4th Duke of Berwick, also 4th Duke of Liria and Xerica, a gentleman of the Chamber to Charles III of Spain.

[11]Don Ignacio, Conde de la Heredia, Spanish ambassador at The Hague.

[12]Philip Van Brugh Livingston (1740–1810), uncle of SLJ.

[13]Jean-François Joly de Fleury (1718–1802) had replaced Necker as Minister of Finance on 24 May 1781.

[14]George Fox of Champlost, Philadelphia, to whom William Temple Franklin bequeathed the papers of Benjamin Franklin. *BFS,* VII, 328n.

[15]Charles Eugène Gabriel de La Croix, Marquis de Castries (1727–1801), head of France's Ministry of Marine, 1780–87.

[16]Admiral Rodney had taken swift reprisals against the residents of St. Eustatius on the British capture of that Dutch island. Piers Mackesy, *The War for America* (Cambridge, Mass., 1964), pp. 416–17.

[17]Thomas Walpole, the London banker and longtime western lands associate of Franklin, who had been assigned the task of negotiating with Castries concerning the claims of French settlers whose property on St. Eustatius had been seized by the British. See Fox to Walpole, 1 May 1782, FO 27/2.

[18]Sir William Pulteney (1729–1805), a member of Parliament from Shrewsbury, who had some years before made a secret peace proposal to Franklin. *Peacemakers,* pp. 110, 255, 359.

[19]Jeremiah Allen, a Boston merchant, one of the experts on the fisheries whom John Adams consulted when in Paris. *AP,* III, 83.

[20]Antoine Raymond Jean Gualbert Gabriel de Sartine, head of the Ministry of Marine, dismissed in October 1780 and replaced by Castries.

Paris Embraces the Jays

Despite an unusually rainy summer in 1782 and bouts of illness suffered by various family members throughout their stay, the Jays made a happy adjustment to life in Paris. From the start they enjoyed an active social life in contrast to the virtual isolation they had suffered in Spain. The Jays were quickly taken up in diplomatic circles, and the couple established an intimate relationship with the Lafayettes.[1] In addition to the Marquis, other former campaigners in America who extended hospitality to the Jays included the Comte d'Estaing, the Comte de Rochambeau, the Chevalier de Chastellux, and the Comte de Sarsfield.[2] This measure of acceptance by the aristocracy and officialdom of the host country brought the Jays into contact with the international diplomatic corps, including Aranda, the Baron de Walterstorff of Denmark, the Sardinian ambassador to France, and the Spanish ambassador to Naples.[3]

The group in which the Jays moved naturally included JJ's fellow peacemakers, both American and British, while John and his spouse formed part of a little American social circle, including Alice De Lancey Izard, Matthew Ridley, John Paul Jones, and Thomas Barclay. They made friends, too, with English men and women who were at the French capital for personal rather than official reasons, including Sir Edward Newenham, the political reformer and member of Parliament from Ireland, and Lady Juliana Penn and her family.[4]

Quickly Sally Jay established herself as a lady of fashion becoming her position.[5] Some years later, when William Temple Franklin's mistress sought to talk him out of marrying another, she pointed out to him the enormous expenditures incurred by fashionable ladies, especially the English ladies in Paris, and singled out the "amiable" Madame Jay as a prime example.[6] What Temple Franklin's mistress did not realize was that a considerable portion of the fabrics and dresses Sally Jay ordered was for her relatives back in the States, and that JJ's wife kept meticulous accounts of household and family expenses.[7]

[1]See, *e.g.,* SLJ to Noailles de Lafayette, 31 Oct. 1782, DftS in JP. In addition, there are numerous letters between JJ and Lafayette himself. *E.g.,* JJ to Lafayette, n.d. [March], 5, 16 April, 16 June 1782, DftS in JP; Lafayette to JJ, 16 June, 22 Sept., ALS in JP.

[2]D'Estaing to JJ, 2 July, 8 Oct. 1782, 15 Aug. 1783, ALS in JP. JJ to John Adams, March 1783, ALS in MHi: Adams, reel 359; Dft in JP. François Jean de Beauvoir, chevalier de Chastellux (1734–88), had been third in command of Rochambeau's forces in America. His *Travels in North America, in the Years 1780, 1781, and 1782* was to be published in Paris in 1786. Guy Claude, comte de Sarsfield, was a French military officer of Irish ancestry.

[3]SLJ to Catharine W. Livingston, 16 March 1783, Dft in JP; Walterstorff to JJ, n.d., 1783, ALS in JP; Sardinian Ambassador to JJ, 23 Aug. 1783, ALS in JP.

[4]Edward Newenham to JJ, 18 Oct. 1782, ALS in JP; Lady Newenham to SLJ, n.d., 1783, ALS (2) in JP; Lady Juliana Penn to SLJ, 1 April, Sept. 1783, ALS in JP; SLJ to Lady Juliana Penn, 8 Oct. 1783, Dft in JP.

[5]In Spain equally, SLJ exhibited a keen interest in women's fashions, mailing prints of Spanish dresses to Mary White Morris, one of her frequent correspondents. Mary White Morris to SLJ, 29 July 1781, ALS in JP.

[6]Blanchette (Mme. Joseph) Caillot to William Temple Franklin, 4 March 1787, ALS in CtY: Franklin.

[7]See, *e.g.,* SLJ to Catharine W. Livingston, Madrid, 22 July 1781, 21 Jan. 1782, DftS in JP; to Susannah French Livingston, 28 Aug. 1782, below. For items of clothing drygoods, and a watch and chain purchased by the Franklins for SLJ, see W. T. Franklin's account, 17 July 1781, AD in JP.

Alice De Lancey Izard to Sarah Livingston Jay

Tuesday, 2 July 1782

Dear Madam,

When I came home last evening I found a Letter from a friend of mine in London, which confirms the information I saw in the Newspapers with regard to your Brother,[1] and to Sir James Jay,[2] and add farther, that Sir James was arrived in London, and that he came over in the last Packet from New-York.

My Letter also mentions the Duel between Mr. Delany and Mr. Allen.[3] Mr. Delany has fallen a sacrifice, and has left a young, pretty Widow, without friends, or fortune. I am glad to hear that it is not Mr. Allen of Philadelphia, who was the cause of this misfortune, and is gone from Maryland.

I am very angry with myself for being so negligent as not to offer you my services with regard to Mantua makers, Milliners etc. I was going to do it several times yesterday, but was as often prevented by other conversations. I beg you will believe that I shall be extremely glad to be useful to you, in any way that you wish to employ me. This day will I hope convince you that your fever has entirely taken leave of you. I am Dear Madam, Your obedient Servant,

A. IZARD

Best Compliments to Mr. Jay.

ALS. Addressed: "Madame Jay, Hotel de la Chine, Rue neuve des Petits Champs, Paris." Endorsed. Alice De Lancey Izard, who stayed on in Paris after the departure of her husband for America, was the daughter of Peter De Lancey, with whose family JJ had been on intimate terms in America. Her brother James and her uncle Oliver were prominent Loyalists residing in England at that time. See also *JJ,* I, 631, 793.

[1]John Lawrence Livingston.

[2]See editorial note above, "Sir James Kicks Over the Traces."

[3]The Reverend Bennet Allen (c. 1737–c. 1814)—Lloyd Dulany (1742–82) duel, c. 18 June 1782, in London's Hyde Park climaxed a sixteen-year feud in which the politically ambitious Allen, a supporter of the Maryland proprietor, Frederick Calvert, 6th Lord Baltimore (1722–71), had opposed the policies and power of the influential Dulany family, comprising notably brothers Daniel Dulany the Younger (1722–97), Walter (1723–73), and half-brother Lloyd. For his attack in the *London Evening Post,* 29 Jan. 1779, on the politically ambiguous stand of the Dulanys in the current war, Allen was challenged by Lloyd. For fatally wounding Dulany, he was convicted of manslaughter, given a nominal fine, and sentenced to a brief prison term. Aubrey C. Land, *The Dulanys of Maryland* (Baltimore, 1955), esp. pp. 280–83; Josephine Fisher, "Bennet Allen, Fighting Parson," *Maryland Historical Magazine,* XXXVIII (1943), 299–322, and XXXIX (1944), 49–72.

FROM CATHARINE W. LIVINGSTON

Springestbury, 12 August 1782

My dear friend and brother,

I have been so elated this three days past with the prospect of Peace and the pleasing Idea of again embracing friends that ever were and will be dear to me, that I attempted but in vain to write to you and Sister. Now I fear I am doing it too late. Should it prove so I shall reproach myself for an omission I have never been guilty of before of permiting three vessels to leave this Port without a line from me, and particularly so as in all probability they would find you in Paris. Is my dear Sister with you? Your letter to the Chanceller on that subject leaves it doubtfull.[1] If she is remember me most affectionately to her, kiss her little dear Maria for me. Oh I long to fold it in my arms, to clasp her to my bosom, and bedew the dear innocence with tears of joy —but thank God that period is at hand. Remember your promise to your friends is binding, the time you fixed is at hand, and shall peace come without you, no I cannot admit the thought, it would not in that case by the blessed œra I expected.

I have seen Franks only a few moments, and that in a large circle could he but for a few minutes enter into my feelings, he would favor me with a visit at this place. I can make some allowance for him, his chagrin must be severe, as the Lady he left America engaged to was married the evening he arrived in this city.[2] I suppose you have heard of the Folly of the unfortunate Major Galvan, two pistols put an end to an existence that he could not endure because he was disappointed in his addresses to Mrs. Allen.[3] I have perused his affecting letters, wilt after his determination. They strongly mark him to have been possessed of all the sensibilities that adorn the human heart; but Love or disappointment had destined him their victim. I know no person stranger to sister, that took so much pleasure in reading her letters to me. He interested himself exceedingly in the perusal of them. Upon every arrival from France or Spain he waited on me to know if he might congratulate me on the hearing of or from your family, and in a very delicate and polite manner solicited the reading such sentences as I should not object to.

Mr. Vaughan[4] is gone to Virginia, to purchase if he can meet with an eligible situation an estate for his Fathers family. Mr. Morris has letters from that gentleman. He has taken a determination to quit his native country for a soil more free.

Should you meet with Mr. Ridley I shall take it as a particular favor if you will take that kind of notice of him that will be flattering to him. He is a man of worth; as such you will if acquainted with him esteem him. His attentions to me when he was in Philadelphia were delicate and agreeable. By the Nonsuch I have received a very friendly letter from him[5] accompanied with an exceeding genteel present. Be so obliging as to present him with my compliments. I shall do myself the pleasure of writing to him by an opportunity from Baltimore when I shall again trouble you with another scrawl. If at any time mine should be too long, in throwing them by you will be excused by my permission.

I have the pleasure to inform you that the first and last Parcels Mr. Johnston[6] shiped are arrived safe, the second number was taken at the Capes. I should not do Mr. Johnston justice did I not express myself obliged for the trouble he has taken in executing your commission. The things are hansome, and the best of their kind, and the three opportunities were the best that the Port of Nantz afforded. I regret exceedingly the ill fortune that has attended almost every thing you destined for your friends. I have been the most fortunate among them, and not I flatter myself the least grateful for the favors your generosity has confered upon me. To be ungrateful is I think to be very wicked. My ingrate B—[7] grieves me more than I can express, but the conviction of his error and a sincere repentance will I hope obtain a pardon.

Mr. Morris[8] has moved his family to his house in Market Street, a very elegant one it is, and will be furnished superb for an American house. He has two very hansome Chinese papers. One is in a different style from any we have seen here. It is in fifteen breaths. On each breath the ground work with different flower pots. From these ascend lofty trees of the different spices of their country. On the branches are a variety of birds, representing their native ones. Under the trees on the ground work are their watter fowl, and around the small shrubs and flowers a collection of butterflies in one branch on every tree, a fruit basket of different forms and curious workmanship filled with a representation of their fruits of every season. Of the fifteen trees the roots only are confined to one breath, the branches of each tree intermingle distinctly and when the breaths are joined, will form very broad trees. The coulor of the fruit and leaves of each tree differs, but the luxuriance and richness of the coulors is beyond description; to suit that paper they have White tabby painted in China. Mr. Morris has run up a building for a cold and warm bath. There is no conveniance indeed that [w]as not thought of; his ice house in the yard is a very great luxury as well as conveniance.

I wish it were in my power to fill up the rest of this paper with relations of your own family. It is some time since I have heard a word respecting them. Peter was well very lately. There is a good school at Brunswic Mama is anxious to put him to, it is a healthy place, and not far from her, but the family have heard that Mr. Benson intends fetching him to Poughkeepsie. I wish he would defer it till fall, that we might have your opinion. I believe I will write to him on the subject. I cannot see any end answered in taking him so far from our family. Should Peace succeed to our expectations, your brother will undoubtedly return to New York; Peggy will never let him rest till he does. I feel anxious for Peter and Nancy (in that case they will be much to be pitied), Nancy particularly. I have not heard any thing of Mrs. Munrow a long time. I am happy that Peter is so good a boy. I hope you will not be disappointed in him. Mrs. Morris is just come out. She says I am too late. I am so mortified that I can only add that I am your affectionate Sister.

AL. Addressed: "Honble His Excellency John Jay Esqr. Paris." Endorsed.

[1]JJ to Robert R. Livingston, 14 May 1782, ALS misdated 11 May, and Dft in JP; LbkC in CSmH and in PCC 110, II; Tr in PPamP: Force.

[2]David Franks to SLJ, 22 Sept. 1782, ALS in JP, wherein Franks mentioned his disappointment, without revealing the lady's name.

[3]French volunteer William Galvan (d. 1782) attained the rank of Major in the Continental Army in January 1780, served under Lafayette at Green Spring, in July 1781, and was Steuben's division inspector at Yorktown. Citing his "untoward and disobliging" behavior, Washington relieved Galvan on 24 Aug. 1781. Galvan's 24 July 1782 suicide note, addressed to "my dear friends" Lt. Col. Brockholst Livingston, Major Matthew Clarkson, and William Bingham, declared that "Love, in extinguishing in me every other passion, has disqualified me to follow any pursuit from which my country, my friends or my family might receive any advantage." *GWF,* XXII, 8–9. For Galvan's suicide note, see *Pennsylvania Mag. of Hist. and Biog.,* XXVI (1902), 407.

[4]John Vaughan.

[5]Letter not located.

[6]Joshua Johnson, American merchant at Nantes. See also *JJ,* I, 748.

[7]Henry Brockholst Livingston.

[8]Robert Morris.

Sarah Livingston Jay to Catharine W. Livingston

Paris, 14 August 1782

My dear sister,

I have regretted extremely the miscarriage of 8 of your letters which occasioned a space in the intelligence I had Received <dear

Kitty gave me reason for great regret, and for 5 months during which we received no letters from our friends appeared extremely tedious> of my friends of 5 months which solicitude magnifyed into an age.

The capture of the Jay and Lady Jay[1] must have prevented you likewise from hearing from us a very long time, expecially as I've not written to any of the family since I left Madrid which was on the 21st of May.

We did not arrive at Paris till the 23d of June and I was then so ill with the intermitting [fever] which I <had brought with from> catched at Bordeaux that I could scarcely quit my bed. No sooner had the bark succeeded in breaking it, than I was severely attacked by a disorder which from its very general influence <is> was called the influenza. The Physician told me that he had not seen any persons so severely attacked as Mr. Jay and myself. When that disorder abated my fever returned and its but 2 days since I've again left my bed. To compleat my distress my dear little babe as w[ell] as her Cousin[2] took the Hooping Cough on our Journey and the difficulty of struggling with that was increased by a fever which she caught from me and frequent fastings when I was too ill to suckle her. Since my arrival here I've met with a Clever Nurse for her but she is still ill though I hope now out of danger <travelling may be agreeable to young gentlemen but really tedious> especially with a family obliged to suffer many inconveniences <which rend diminishes the pleasures they might receive> which those who remain at home are exempt from.

The uncommon Coolness and frequent rains that has prevailed here this season has rendered it <the whole> very sickly. I was informed 3 weeks ago that the Lieutenant de Police had a return of 100 thousand sick persons in this City so that, you see our whole family (for a fortnight ago we had not one person well in it) are very fashionably disposed.

I wish I dared indulge myself in writing as long as it would be agreeable to me but my weakness prevails over my inclination. Give my [regards] to my dear Mrs. Morris. Her dear little boys are very well.[3] Mr. Jay saw them at Dr. Franklin's on Sunday. Tommy has no[t] had the Hooping Cough and therefore we have been obliged to mortify ourselves by not having them with us wh[en] Peter and the baby were so hard off. The next Holiday however we are to be favored with their Company and I feel an equal pleasure in the Expectation that I should were they my brothers. It gives me great pleasure to see how fond Mrs. Montgomery[4] is of them. They frequently spend their Holidays with her little son at her house. She is a very good hearted woman and I esteem her for the regard that I'm convinced she has for Mr. Morris's family. Mrs. Izard is very well; she lodges at the Hotel directly opposite to me and there seldom passes a day that we do not see each other.[5] Please to remember me to Mrs. Beache.[6] Tell her that her father is as well and as much beloved as ever. Present my Compliments to the Chevalier la Luzerne and Mr. Marbois. I've not seen any of their Connection yet. I enquired of the Marquis de la Fayette where the Chevalier's brother was but he thinks that he is not [in] town and has promised to enquire.

The Marchioness de la Fayette is a most amiable woman; <she will increase her family in the Course of next winter> she is confined to her house by indisposition, the consequence of an expected addition to her family.[7]

In the packet Mr. Vaughan had from me were letters for every one of the family not excepting master Peter. If Mr. V. could only reserve the Band Box. Master Peter has lost his Clothes which Mr. V took in his Chest. I'm very anxious about that Child I must own to you for time slips away unperceived at his age and if unimproved I think the detriment cannot be named. Do my dear Kitty let me know exactly whether [he] reads well and even condescend to let me know what he reads. I think some short agreeable History might be put in his hand and I could [wish] him to learn to spell very well that his opportunities for learning may increase [and] he may not be retarded in his progress.

Dft. Endorsed by JJ.

[1]For the *Jay,* an 18-gun Pennsylvania schooner, see *JJ,* I, 691. There were three other ships named *Jay,* a 12-gun Connecticut brigantine, commissioned 1 Feb. 1781; a 14-gun Connecticut brigantine, commissioned 6 Sept. 1781; and a 1-gun Connecticut boat, commissioned 20 May 1782. No references to the capture of the *Jay* or the *Lady Jay* have been located. Charles H. Lincoln, comp., *Naval Records of the American Revolution, 1775–1788* (Washington, D.C., 1906), pp. 357–58; see also George F. Emmons, *The Navy of the United States* (Washington, D.C., 1853), p. 147.

[2]Maria Jay and her cousin Peter Jay Munro.

[3]Thomas and Robert Morris, Jr.; see JJ to Matthew Ridley, 8 Jan. 1782, above.

[4]Dorcas Armitage Montgomery, widow of Philadelphia merchant Robert Montgomery (1743–70), and friend of the Bache family, who took her son Robert (b. 1770) to France in 1780 to be educated. *TJP,* X, 283; XIII, 165–66; *BFS,* VIII, 373.

[5]Alice De Lancey Izard remained abroad with her six children until 1783; Ralph Izard was then serving as a delegate to Congress from South Carolina.

[6]Sarah Franklin Bache; see *JJ,* I, 659.

[7]Adrienne de Noailles, the Marquise de Lafayette, was awaiting the birth of her fourth child, Virginia, born 17 Sept. 1782. The first child, a girl, had died. Surviving were Anastasie-Louise-Pauline (b. 1777), and George Washington (b. 1779). See below, SLJ to the Marquise de Lafayette, 31 Oct. 1782. M. MacDermot Crawford, *Madame de Lafayette and Her Family* (New York, 1907).

FROM FREDERICK JAY

Poughkeepsie, 15 August 1782
Triplicate

Dear Sir,

The preeceding is a fourth Copy of my last to you,[1] since which I have been favoured with yours of the 29th April[2] by Major Franks, who on his way to Philadelphia was kind enough to call upon me. The account he gave me of your Health and that of your Family were very pleasing to us all. May you and they long experience that great Blessing.

I was in great expectation to have had it in my power to have given you a full and Satisfactory account of our Fathers Estate, but from the present Situation of the times it is impossible. Mr. Benson and myself have taken an account of the Bonds and find them fall very short of what I expected, being not more (exclusive of Interest and Loan Office Certificates) than one half as much as was received from Mrs. Chambers.[3]

We have not as yet been able to collect in any monies due to the Estate, and it is very uncertain when we shall, as the greater part of the bonds are due from People in the power of the Enemy and very little dependance is to be made from the rents. However we shall do the best we can and endeavour to support the Family in as easy and comfortable a manner as circumstances will admit, hoping the time is near at hand when we shall again enjoy our former happy state.

Your son is still at Elizabeth Town. I would have fetched him some months ago, but the weather has been so exceeding warm that we did not think it prudent. Next month I shall go for him and you may be assured that he shall want for nothing. None of the Articles you have sent us ever came to hand except those mentioned in mine of the 20th April last. The silk you sent Peggy still remains at Elizabeth Town. She is much obliged to you for it.

Peters picture came Safe to hand, and if the Originals, mind, contains as much beauty (and I make no doubt it does) he must be handsome indeed. I've shewn it to several young Ladies, who all declare that they would rather die old Maids than not have a chance of getting this Young Beauty.

Peter enjoys good health, Nancy very indifferent. Mrs. Jay better than when we were at Fish Kill. *Gussy continues to behave well* and *remains* at *Kingston.* Mrs. M. lives in her own house in Albany—her going there was contrary to my advice and that of her Friends. Indeed it was a most imprudent step at this time.

Whether I shall remain here longer than the Fall will depend upon Circumstances. Was it not for Peter and Nancy I would move out of the State, as it is impossible for me to do any business here, especially as I have such a charge upon me. Whether I stay or not be easy about your son, I shall take care of him. Plato stays with me and behaves well. Your man Lewis is Peters A.D.C.[4] and is a pretty good Boy. Clarinda is sold and her sister Mary is for Sale; the other Mary boards with Zilpha at Fish Kill. Moll is with me and Susan[5] at Mr. William Van Wycks. I am, etc.,

FRED. JAY

ALS. Endorsed.

[1]Frederick Jay to JJ, 20 April 1782, above.

[2]JJ to Frederick Jay, 29 April 1782, Dft in JP.

[3]Anne Van Cortlandt Chambers bequeathed £ 4,300 to her nieces and nephews in her 1767 will, of which JJ, a co-executor, received £ 500. For the Chambers will, see New-York Hist. Soc., *Collections,* XXXII (1899), 168–70. See also *JJ,* I, 140–41.

[4]Aide-de-camp.

[5]All were Jay family slaves except Zilpha, who had been freed the preceding year.

Sarah Livingston Jay to Susannah French Livingston

Paris, 28 August 1782

My dear Mamma,

I had the pleasure of writing several letters to you and the rest of the family just before I left Madrid, but since my arrival here the indisposition of my family has prevented me from writing, except one letter to Kitty.[1] My dear little babe has been on the point of leaving me. Mr. Jay was at the same time very ill with the influenza, myself with the intermitting fever from which I've been but 9 days free, Peter had the hooping-cough and Abbe[2] was ill with the same epidemic disorder that Mr. Jay had; so that you see Mamma we were not in the most thriving way, nor in a situation that suggested the most agreeable ideas. At present thank God! we are all well.

I'm much pleased with France. It seems to be one of the favorite spots of Nature if we may judge of her disposition towards it by the enchanting prospects and fertile fields that perpetually engage the attention of a Traveller; but nothing pleased me more than the gaiety and industry of the inhabitants. I could not but remark their natural inclination for chearful objects displayed in their little flower gardens, for there is scarce a peasant's cottage without the appurtenance of a garden and many of them have little bowers that discovers a very pretty taste; in short such was the impression which their apparent content and good Humour made upon me that I became again reconciled to the lot of humanity, though some scenes in the preceding part of my Journey had almost disgusted me.

Today I have the pleasure of the Company of Mr. Morris's two sons, Mrs. Montgomery's son and one of Mrs. Izard's sons, and you can't imagine how happy I feel in seeing them.[3] It's true there could be an addition to the little society that would increase the pleasure I have in my little company of Americans and I sincerely wish my dear boy was with me, but have not resolution to send for him. I wish mamma you would be so good as to inquire what is the state of Jersey College at present and at what age the youngest that can be admitted at the Grammar school there must be.[4] Should any thing retard our return for any length of time it would be proper to consider in what manner the dear little fellow might profit most. Will you be so good as to give my love to him and tell him that I expect to be informed from his own pen how he liked the stuff I sent him by Mr. Vaughn for Spring clothes, and the buckles and buttons I ordered out for him from France before I left Spain.

Sister Susan is many letters in debt to me for I've not received one from her of a later date than October,[5] so that I quite long to hear from her, and shall thank her if she will when she writes to me enclose a lock of Peter's hair. I regret exceedingly the loss of a box sent out last fall for the two families, for had it arrived safe the contents of it would have contributed to their convenience. We have just heard that a Vessel has arrived safe to the south-ward in which was a box for Kitty with a pink lutestring negligee, 6 Eels[6] of Gauze and as much Catgut, 4 pair of embroidered silk shoes, 4 pair of silk stockings, 6 pair of white kid gloves and a suit of broad and narrow ribbon; but we have likewise had the mortification to hear of the capture of another vessel which contained a like parcel only differing in the Colour of the silk and ribbons. There has been still a third parcel shipped which we have not heard of since, but our frequent disappointments have discouraged us from risqueing any thing further until there is a peace concluded. When that will be God only knows.

Kitty I hope remains at Philadelphia, for I do not think it would be prudent for her to be at Elizabeth Town while that place is exposed to the encursions of the enemy, since an alarm from that quarter might dangerously affect her nerves. Indeed I should have possessed more tranquility of mind had all the family abandoned that seat for the present. But Mamma's ideas and mine differed on the subject and I wish the event may prove that I was too timid. I feared that other prudential motives might have induced Kitty to quit the situation I left her in and it was in order to prevent that necessity, that Mr. Jay desired Mr. Johnston[7] to send Kitty those little parcels. I wish some of them may have arrived in time.

Adieu my dear Mamma! God Almighty! bless you and protect the family. Remember me affectionately to my dear Papa, Susan, sister Linn, sister Watkins, William, Brockholst and Peter. Mr. Jay desires to be remembered to you and the rest of the family. Please to remember me to my old friends whenever you see them, though they are too numerous to admit of particular mention whenever I write, yet they never escape my memory, but on the contrary they possess my esteem as much as ever. I am my dear mamma, Your very affectionate daughter,

SARAH JAY

Remember me if you please to Hannah, and tell Bell I've not forgot her.

ALS. E in NcD: Charles Campbell Papers.

[1]SLJ to Catharine W. Livingston, 14 Aug. 1782, above.

[2]Abigail, the Jays' black servant; see *JJ,* I, 712.

[3]Thomas and Robert Morris, Jr., Robert Montgomery, and either Henry (1771–1826), Charles (1773–84), or George (1776–1828) Izard. Langdon Cheves, "Izard of South Carolina," *South Carolina Hist. and Geneal. Magazine,* II (1901), 216.

[4]The College of New Jersey, founded in 1746, maintained a preparatory grammar school since 1748. Thomas J. Wertenbaker, *Princeton, 1746–1890* (Princeton, 1946), p. 90.

[5]Susan Livingston to SLJ, 1 Oct. 1781, ALS in JP.

[6]The English ell was 45 inches.

[7]Joshua Johnson.

To Peter Van Schaack

Paris, 17 September 1782

Dear Sir,

Doctor Franklin sent me this morning your Letter of 11 August last.[1] I thank you for it. Aptitude to Change, in any Thing, never made a part of my Disposition, and I hope makes no part of my Character. In the Course of the present Troubles I have adhered to certain fixed Principles, and faithfully obeyed their Dictates, without regarding the

Consequences of such Conduct to my Friends, my Family or myself; all of whom, however dreadful the Thought, I have ever been ready to sacrifice, if necessary, to the public Objects in Contest.

Believe me, my Heart has nevertheless been on more than one occasion <really> afflicted by the Execution of what I thought, and still think was my Duty. I felt very sensibly for you and for others; but as Society can regard only the political Propriety of Men's Conduct, and not the moral Propriety of their Motives to it, I could only lament your unavoidably becoming classed with many whose morality was convenience, and whose Politicks changed with the aspect of public affairs.

My Regard for you, as a good old Friend, continued notwithstanding. God knows that Inclination never had a Share in any Proceedings of mine against you: from such "Thorns no man could expect to gather Grapes" and the only Consolation that can grow in their unkindly Shade, is a Consciousness of doing one's Duty, and the Reflection that as on the one Hand, I have uniformly preferred the public Weal to my Friends and <Relations> connections, so on the other I have never been urged by private Resentments to injure a single Individual.

Your Judgment, and consequently your Conscience differed from mine on a very important Question, but though as an independent American, I considered all who were not for us, and You among the Rest, as against us, yet be assured that John Jay did not cease to be a Friend to Peter Van Schaack.

No one can serve two Masters. Either Britain was right and America wrong; or America was right, and Britain wrong. They who thought Britain right were bound to support her, and America had a just claim to the Services of those who approved her cause. Hence it became our Duty to take one Side or the other, and no man is to be blamed for preferring the one which his Reason <though erroneous> recommended as the most just and virtuous.

Several of our Countrymen indeed left and took arms against us, not from any such principles, but from the most dishonorable of human motives. Their Conduct has been of a Piece with their Inducements, for they have far outstripped Savages in Perfidy and Cruelty—against these men every American must set his Face and steel his Heart. There are others of them, though not many, who I <verily> believe opposed us because they Thought they could not conscienciously go with us. To such of these as have behaved with Humanity I wish every Species of Prosperity that may consist with the good of my Country.

You see how naturally I slide into the Habit of writing as freely as

I used to speake to you. Ah my Friend! If ever I see New York again, I expect to meet with "the Shade of many a departed Joy." My Heart bleeds to think of it.

You mention my Brother. If after having made so much Bustle in and for America, he has (as is surmised) improperly made his Peace with Britain, I shall endeavour to forget that my Father had such a Son.

How is your Health? Where and how are your Children?[2] Whenever, as a private friend, it may be in my power to do good to either, tell me—While I have a Loaf, you and they may freely <cut and come again> partake of it. Don't let this Idea hurt you. If your Circumstances are easy, I rejoice. If not, let me take off some of their rougher Edges.

Mrs. Jay is obliged by your Remembrance, and presents you her compliments. The Health of us both is but delicate. Our little Girl has been very ill, but is now well.

My best wishes <will> always attend You, and be assured that notwithstanding any political Changes I remain, Dear Peter, Your affectionate Friend and Servant,

JOHN JAY

DftS. Endorsed by JJ: ". . . in ansr to 11 Augt. last." ALS not located. Eighth paragraph referring to Sir James omitted in *WJ*, I, 160–62, in *HPJ*, II, 343–45, and in Henry C. Van Schaack, *The Life of Peter Van Schaack, LL.D* (New York, 1842), pp. 301–03. For Peter Van Schaack, see *JJ*, I, 331–32.

[1]Letter not located; in *HPJ*, II, 327; *WJ*, I, 159–60; Van Schaack, *Life*, p. 301.

[2]Van Schaack's wife, Elizabeth Cruger Van Schaack, died in 1778 prior to her husband's departure for England. Their surviving children, Henry (d. 1797), Cornelius (b. 1766), and Elizabeth remained in the care of friends in Kinderhook. Van Schaack, *Life*, pp. 105, 305.

From David S. Franks

Philadelphia, 28 September 1782

I did myself the honor of writing to your Excellency a few days since[1] by the General Washington inclosing a Line for Mrs. Jay informing her of some things concerning the Family which I hope she will receive and that they will prove agreable to her.[2]

In my last I mentioned to you that we were here in great Tranquility. General Carleton has given orders to all the indian Parties to retire, from our frontier, in consequence of which an Expedition, planned by this Government against the Savages is laid aside.[3] Nigh

Charles Town they have had several skirmishes in one of which 'tis said the gallant Col. John Laurens (son of the President) is slain. The Report is generally believed and gives every one great uneasiness.[4]

I mentioned in my last that I had passed through Poughkeepsie on my way from Newbury Port to Philadelphia and that I found your family in perfect Health. I passed a night at Mr. F. Jays and delivered the Picture and other things intrusted to my Care.

Since I had the pleasure of seeing your Excellency I have experienced some adverse strokes which I could easily have dispensed with. The Lady whom I mentioned so often at San Ildefonso and Madrid I found married to another the very day I came to Philadelphia[5] and at the same time I was informed that I was left out of the Army of the United States, because I had no friend here who returned me to the Secretary at War as *on actual duty,* though the Conditions on which I went to Europe were, that I should retain my Commission and rank in the Army. I have memorialized Congress but am not certain I shall be readmitted.[6]

These circumstances make me wish once more to leave my native Country. If your Excellency thinks I can be of any service to you or can be employed without becoming a Burthen to you, I will, with the greatest alacrity, join you. I have applied to Mr. Livingston to use his influence to get me employed as a Consul abroad. He has promised that what he can do for me he will. I can't find out here, if Mr. Barkley[7] has the appointment of his own Deputies. Perhaps he has; if so I should be happy to serve under him and pray your Excellency would mention me to him. I must beg your Excellency's pardon for taking up so much of your Time on my own affairs. I wish I had something more interesting to write to you. I have few Friends and most of them out of Congress or absent.

I did not know of this opportunity so early as I could have wished or I would have sent you all the papers for some time past. By the next I will be careful to do it. When you have a moment to throw away I should be happy to have a Line from you. I pray my most respectful Compliments to Mrs. Jay and am with great Respect and Esteem, Your Excellency's most grateful humble Servant,

DAVID S. FRANKS

ALS. Endorsed. E in NN: Bancroft: American IV, 172.

[1]Letter not located.

[2]David S. Franks to SLJ, 22 Sept. 1782, ALS in JP.

[3]The Pennsylvania Assembly failed in its attempt to secure loans for financing expeditions to combat the intensified frontier warfare of 1782, and through

Congressional delegates requested that Washington "carry three expeditions into Indian country." A Congressional resolve of 13 Sept. 1782 to undertake such an expedition subject to Washington's approval was "declined" by the General on the basis of Sir Guy Carleton's personal assurance that present and future Indian activities would be confined to purely defensive operations. *Minutes of the Assembly of Pennsylvania,* 14 Aug. 1782; *JCC,* XXIII, 575; William Moore to General William Irvine, 4 Sept. 1782, and William Moore to William Maclay and William Montgomery, 26 Sept. 1782, *Pennsylvania Archives,* 1st ser., IX (1854), 630, 640; *GWF,* XXV, 198–99; L. S. Shimmell, *Border Warfare in Pennsylvania* (Harrisburg, 1901), pp. 133–39.

[4]John Laurens was killed in an engagement near Cheraw Creek, S. C. on 27 Aug. 1782. Wallace, *Laurens,* pp. 489–93.

[5]David Franks to SLJ, 22 Sept. 1782, and Catharine W. Livingston to JJ, 12 Aug. 1782, n. 2, above.

[6]On 31 Dec. 1781 Congress provided for the retirement as of 1 Jan. 1782 of all officers of the line below the rank of brigadier general, not belonging to the line of a particular state or to separate army corps. Citing his duties for the Superintendent of Finance, Franks petitioned for restoration of his commission. On 13 Sept. 1782 Franks' rank and pay were restored until his retirement 1 Jan. 1783. *JCC,* XXI, 1186–87; XXIII, 679–80; Franks' petition is in PCC 41, III, 268.

[7]Thomas Barclay (1728–93), U.S. consul-general in France, for whom see below, "Settling the Spanish Accounts," and n. 8.

To Frederick Jay

Paris, 3 October 1782

Dear Fady,

A Copy of your letter of the 8th of June last came to my hand yesterday and is the only one I've received from you of later date than the 1st of December last which arrived here on the 18th of last July.[1] You mention to have enclosed a triplicate of one you wrote me on the 20th of April, but it was not enclosed nor have I received either the original or any Copy of that letter. The Copy of our Father's Will and of Sir James's correspondance being the only papers that I found so enclosed.

I am perfectly satisfied with this Will and the Codicils annexed to it. I think with you that a division of the Real Estate must be postponed for the present. Whenever it may be done I am clear for Peter's taking the Farm at Rye and I desire you to assure him that I will enable him to do it in the manner that he shall think most easy and agreeable to himself. I hope you will continue to pay unceasing attention to every part of the Estate and, as I confide in your frugality, you may if necessary apply my share of the income to the maintenance of *yourself* and my *other brothers* and *sisters.*

When I mentioned to Mr. Benson my desire that our little Boy should remain at Poughkeepsie it was that his Grand Father might not be deprived of that consolation and not from an expectation that he would derive more advantages from his being there than in Jersey, both places being in that and many other respects nearly equal, for in both he had near and affectionate friends and relations, but as to his being placed at Goshen, I disapprove of it because he is as yet too young to be taken from under the eye and immediate care of his family. I hope you will receive this letter in time to prevent it; if not that you'll be so kind as immediately to fetch him back to Poughkeepsie and let him remain there with you for the winter. Before Spring you will probably receive particular directions from me on the subject.[2]

If a peace should take place it may be in our power to recieve the Legacies left by Mrs. Peloquin. I have not seen her will, but supposing it to be what we heard it was, I think I should be furnished with proper powers of attorney to receive yours etc.[3]

You say nothing of the Health of the Family. God grant that they may all be and continue well.

I wrote to You by Major Franks, and sent by him Peters Picture for my Father.[4] Nothing had I then heard of his having been long confined to his bed, much less of having exchanged this world for a better.

I find he has given Plato to me. He doubtless lives with you. Tell him I shall remember and reward his attachment to my Father by making his Life as easy and happy as may depend upon me. Zilpha and Mary may also entertain the same Expectations. Comfort all the old servants by letting them percieve that though they have lost a kind and indulgent Master, yet that his children remember their Services and will not permit the Evening of their Lives to be resolved in Distress. If New York should be evacuated and Claas remain there, treat him kindly for his Mothers Sake.

We have sent you many Things to a very considerable amount for the use of the Family but I understand that the greater part have been lost.

We are all pretty well. Our best wishes always attend you all. Tell Peter and Nancy to keep up their Spirits, to take care of their Health, and by that Means join with you in compensating by a happy Meeting on my Return for the Pain occasioned by our long Separation. Remember us to all our Friends and believe me to be Dear Fœdy, Your affectionate Brother.

Dft. The first half of the letter is in the hand of SLJ, the latter part is in JJ's hand.

[1]Frederick Jay to JJ, 8 June 1781, not located; 1 Dec. 1781, in JP.

[2]Hereinafter the letter is in JJ's hand.

[3]Marianne Peloquin of Bristol was the first cousin of JJ's father, Peter Jay. For the lengthy litigation concerning the Jay's claim on her estate, see the editorial note below, "An American in England." For Marianne Peloquin, see *JJ,* I, 39.

[4]JJ to Peter Jay, [29] April 1782, above.

To William Livingston

Paris, 13 October 1782

Dear Sir,

Caty writes me[1] that you honor our little Boy with a constant correspondence,[2] and that he improves (as indeed most others might do) by your Letters, and that he still promises to be good for something. This is agreable news, and I thank you for the share you have in giving occasion to it. We were for two months in a State of painful Suspence respecting Maria. Sally caught a fever at Bordeaux; from thence here she nourished the Child[3] only at Intervals, and we were obliged to make boiled bread and water a Substitute for milk. On our arrival here we got a nurse, and that nurse after a few Days left her. Another *safe* one was hard to be found, and we weaned her. She pined away daily, and at Length became seriously ill. Accident brought us acquainted with an honest poor Woman in the Neighbourhood, who had a Child near of Maria's age. We took her into the House, and though Maria has been weaned near a month she immediately took the Breast, and by slow Degrees recovered.

Both Sally and myself have had a great Share of Sickness since we left Spain. She is now in tolerable Health. For my part, I am at present neither very well nor very sick, and though in good Spirits, have but little Strength, and am never free from a pain in my Breast.

This is a very fine Country, almost as much so as our own, but not quite. Art has done more for this; nature more for ours. I am told they have fine Fruit here, and I believe it, for there is abundance and great Variety of every kind, but I have not seen any that was good, for I have not seen any that was ripe. The Summer was so remarkably cool and rainy, that a wit being asked, What News? answered, "that the Winter had come to spend the Summer at Paris," and another of the same Gentlemen being asked, whether he had ever seen such a Summer before said "Yes, last Winter." I am dear Sir, Your very affectionate Servant,

JOHN JAY

ALS in MHi: William Livingston. Endorsed.
[1]Letter not located.
[2]See above, Peter Augustus Jay to SLJ, 18 July 1781, and n. 4.
[3]Eight-month-old Maria Jay.

To Robert Morris

Paris, 13 October 1782

My Dear Sir,

<Amidst> Wherever and however occupied, I remember my friends and always find my own Satisfaction promoted, when I have Reason to think that I am conducing to theirs. This has led me to make your Sons[1] the Subject of this Letter. It is an interesting one to you, and therefore not indifferent to me.

On my arrival here I found them placed in a Pension at Passy. My Nephew and Daughter were ill with a hooping Cough, and lest your Sons should catch it, we denied ourselves the pleasure of having them with us till after that obstacle had ceased. I have frequently seen them at Doctor Franklins as well as at my own House. They had promised to dine with us every Wednesday but Mr. Ridley prolonged it to every other Wednesday. They are fine Boys and appear to possess a full Share of natural Talents. I am told that they have made a Progress in French proportionate to the Time they have been learning it. Of this I am not an adequate Judge myself, and therefore must depend on the Judgment of Others. The Pension at which they are has been so far well enough but I think with Mr. Ridley that a better is to be wished for, and to be sought. He is at present making the necessary Inquiries, and I have every Reason to believe that the Trust you have reposed in him will be conscientiously and faithfully executed.

Mr. Ridley finds it difficult to decide on the Expediency of carrying them to Geneva, and from what I have heard, I think he has Reason to entertain Doubts on that Head; as I have no materials to judge from but the Report of others, and those perhaps not altogether well founded, it is difficult for me to form a decided opinion on the Subject. I can only say that I have heard more against than for it.

My opinion may perhaps seem singular and the more so as it

cannot be properly explained in the Compass of a Letter. I think the Youth of every *free*, civilized Country should if possible be educated in it, and not permitted to travel out of it till age has made them so cool and firm as to retain their national and moral Impressions. Connections formed at School and College <are important> have much influence and are to be watched even at that Period. If judiciously formed they will often endure and be advantageous through Life. American Youth may possibly form proper and perhaps useful friendships in European Seminaries but I think not so *probably*, as among their Fellow Citizens with whom they are to grow up, whom it will be useful for them to *Know* and early be known to, and with whom they are to be engaged in the Business of active Life, and under the Eye and Direction of Parents whose advice and authority, and Example are frequently of more worth than the hireling Professors particularly <on> in the Subjects of Religion, Morality, Virtue, and Prudence.

The fine and some of the useful arts may doubtless be better acquired in Europe than in America, and so may the living European Languages; but when I consider that a competent knowledge even of these may be gained in our Country, and that <religion, morality> almost all of the more substantial and truely valuable acquirements may in my opinion with more facility and certainty be attained there than here, I do not hesitate to prefer an American Education.

I fear that the Ideas which my Countrymen in general concieve of Europe are in many respects rather too high. If we should ever meet again you shall know my sentiments very fully on this Head.

But your Sons are here, and What is to be done? Mr. Ridley is about doing what I think with him is the best thing that at present can be done, vizt., to put them in one of the best pensions that can be found, and to give them the advantages of such extra Tutors as may be requisite.

Perhaps further Information may place Geneva in a more favorable Light. You shall have <further> frequent Letters from me on this Subject, and while I remain here, you may be assured of my constant attention to these promising Boys. Be pleased to present our Compliments and best wishes to Mrs. Morris. I am, dear Sir, with sincere Esteem and Regard Your Affectionate friend and Servant.

Dft. Endorsed by JJ. LS, in the hand of SLJ, advertised by Paul C. Richards Autographs. Omissions in *WJ*, II, 350–52, and in *HPJ*, II, 103–05.

[1]Thomas and Robert Morris, Jr. For Robert Morris' views on education, see his 3 Jan. 1783 letter to JJ, below.

Sarah Livingston Jay to Mary White Morris

Paris, 14 November 1782

With what pleasure my dear madam do I take up my pen as a medium of or substitute for a conversation with you; by admitting no other idea to rob me of your image, I enjoy, at least for the moment the most pleasing delusion. Yesterday your little sons by passing their holiday with me made me very happy. Robert so exceedingly resembles Mr. Morris that I feel for him a respect mingled with my love; though at the same time I regret his distance from his father's example and counsil. When (as it sometimes happens) among our little Americans that my decision is referred to respecting matters of right and wrong, I always request Robert's opinion; and when he hesitates, I ask him what he thinks would be his Father's sentiments upon such occasions, to which he generally replys very justly; and I remark to him the certainty of his acting with propriety while he imitates so worthy an example. Tommy (who is likewise a fine boy) told me that his last letters mentioned Hetty's and Maria's illness.[1] I hope they are now quite recovered as well as my dear Kitty. Will you embrace them for me?

If during my stay in Paris it is in my power to serve you, nothing my dear Mrs. Morris can give me greater pleasure than receiving your commands. At present the prevailing fashions are very decent and very plain. The gowns most worne are the robes à l'Angloise which are exactly like the Italian habits that were in fashion in America at the time I left it. The sultana, resembling the long polinese is also à la mode, but as it is not expected that it will long remain so, every body makes them of slight silk. There is so great a variety of hats, Caps, cuffs etc. that it is impossible to describe them. I forgot to mention that the robe à l'Angloise if trimmed either with the same or with gauze is dress, but if intirely untrimmed must be worn with an apron and is undress: negligees are very little in vogue: fans of 8 or 10 sous are almost the only ones in use.

At the Marquis de la Fayette's table I had the pleasure of hearing you my dear Mrs. Morris mentioned the other day as well as Mr. Morris in terms to me the most grateful imaginable. The Marchioness is a most amiable woman; she expressed her inclination to see America in very flattering terms, and I could not forbear assuring her that if she ever honored us by a visit, she would find that her Character there had already prepared the Americans to receive her in a manner, that would convince her that the Marquis, though much esteemed, was not the only one of his Family that they respected.

The Queen has lately returned to Versailles after a residence of 8 or 10 weeks at Passey. While there, I used sometimes to have the pleasure of seeing her at the Plays. She is so handsome and her manners are so engaging, that almost forgetful of republican principles, I was ever ready while in her presence to declare her born to be a Queen. There are however many traits in her character worthy of imitation even by republicans, and I cannot but admire her resolution to superintend the education of Madame Royale her daughter,[2] to whom she has alotted chambers adjoining her own, and persists in refusing to name a Governatete for her. The Duchess of Polniac is named for that office to the Dauphin.[3]

I have just been interrupted by a visit from the Princess Mazarin, who informed me that the Count d'Artois would be here in 8 or 10 days hence, and the Prince her husband soon after. So I conjecture the seige of Gibralter is to be abandoned.

I have had so many interruptions since I've been writing this short letter that I must entreat you will impute some of the blunders with which it is filled to that cause.

Please to present Mr. Jay's and my Compliments to Mr. and Mrs. White,[4] Mr. Morris, the Chevalier la Luzerne, Mr. Marbois and Mr. Holker.[5] Mr. Jay likewise desires me to assure you that his esteem for you is not less than that with which I have the honor to be, my dear madam, Yours sincerely,

SA. JAY

ALS in CSmH. Dft in JP.

[1]The Morrises' daughters, Esther (Hetty) (b. 1774) and Maria (b. 1779).

[2]Marie Antoinette's daughter, Princess Marie Thérèse Charlotte, afterwards Duchesse d'Angoulême, then four years old.

[3]Yolande Martine Gabrielle de Polastron, Duchesse de Polignac, succeeded the Princess de Rohan-Gemenée as *gouvernante des Enfants de France* in 1782.

[4]Mary White Morris' brother, William White (1748–1836), and his wife, Mary Harrison White (d. 1797). White, a 1765 graduate of the College of Philadelphia, was ordained both a deacon in 1770 and a priest in 1772 in London. Returning to America in 1772, he would become rector of Christ Church, Philadelphia, chaplain to Congress, and later, first Protestant Episcopal bishop of the diocese of Pennsylvania.

[5]French entrepreneur John Holker, Jr. arrived in America in 1778 as Agent for the Royal Marine and Inspector General of Trade and Manufactures of France, to become as well a partner of Robert Morris and others in private ventures. Appointed 25 June 1780 French Consul General for Pennsylvania, Delaware, New Jersey, and

New York, he resigned that post 3 Oct. 1781 in compliance with French law prohibiting French officials from engaging in trade. *RMP,* I, 30; *JCC,* XI, 713; Marquis de Chastellux, *Travels in North America in the Years 1780, 1781, and 1782,* trans. and ed. by Howard C. Rice, Jr. (Chapel Hill, 1963), I, 330–32; Clarence L. Ver Steeg, *Robert Morris, Revolutionary Financier* (Philadelphia, 1954), pp. 32–34, 161.

III

AMERICA AND THE GENERAL PEACE

America and the General Peace

Although not directly involved in the negotiations between Great Britain, on the one side, and the Bourbon partners, along with the United Provinces, on the other, the American Commissioners had ample reason for concern about the maneuvers that preceded the settlement.[1] The discussions among the European powers impinged at times on American interests. Spain was concerned lest the United States be allotted territory bordering on the Mississippi, both banks of which she sought to control, and her ally, France, concurred with her in seeking to curb America's territorial appetite. In turn, France wished to share with England exclusive rights to the fisheries, and deplored America's assertions of rights off the Grand Bank and Nova Scotia. Both allies recognized the mutual peril to which they might be exposed should America by a quick peace quit the war.

All along a major setback to a speedy settlement had been Spain's insistence on recovering Gibraltar, a demand unsupported by her weak military posture and further undermined by the collapse of the Allied siege of that fortress. To exercise maximum control over these negotiations Vergennes dispatched Rayneval to England on a series of missions, starting on 7 September 1782. Rayneval persuaded his superior of Shelburne's basic moderation and peaceable intentions. Thereupon Vergennes brought immense pressure upon the Conde de Aranda, Spain's plenipotentiary in Paris, and his chief, Floridablanca, to offer some equivalent for Gibraltar.[2] Convinced that everything depended on this issue, Vergennes sent Rayneval back to England for further talks.[3]

By the time Rayneval reached London on 20 November, he discovered that the adverse military news about Gibraltar, along with the impending peace settlement with the United States, had made the British conscious of their strengthened bargaining position. The result was a tougher negotiating stance. After considering the new stepped-up equivalents demanded by Great Britain, Rayneval and Shelburne drew up a draft treaty outlining the alternatives, and the British Cabinet accepted it after heated debate. In sum, Spain would concede as equivalents for Gibraltar, Puerto Rico or Guadeloupe with Dominica, or Martinique with St. Lucia. To accept this resolution of the issue France would have to be prepared to sacrifice one of its own islands, receiving Spanish

A GENERAL PEACE.

NEW-YORK, March 25, 1783.

LATE laſt Night, an EXPRESS from New-Jerſey, brought the following Account.

THAT on Sunday laſt, the Twenty-Third Inſtant, a Veſſel arrived at Philadelphia, in Thirty-five Days from Cadiz, with *Diſpatches* to the *Continental Congreſs*, informing them, that on Monday the Twentieth Day of January, the PRELIMINARIES to

A GENERAL PEACE,

Between *Great-Britain, France, Spain, Holland,* and the *United States of America,* were SIGNED at Paris, by all the Commiſſioners from thoſe Powers; in conſequence of which, Hoſtilities, by Sea and Land, were to *ceaſe* in Europe, on Wedneſday the Twentieth Day of February; and in America, on Thurſday the Twentieth Day of March, in the preſent Year One Thouſand Seven Hundred and Eighty-Three.

THIS very *important* Intelligence was laſt Night announced by the Firing of Cannon, and great Rejoicings at Elizabeth-Town.---Reſpecting the Particulars of this truly intereſting Event no more are yet received, but they are hourly expected.

Publiſhed by* James Rivington, *Printer to the King's Moſt Excellent Majeſty.

Santo Domingo in return, an exchange that France found uncongenial.[4] Everything now pointed to pressure on Spain to drop its demand for Gibraltar. To give France time, Shelburne persuaded the Cabinet to prorogue Parliament until 5 December, a move which Rayneval hailed as "the most daring and decisive action that this Minister could have taken in the present state of affairs and in view of his personal situation," because, as the British minister had confided to the French undersecretary, unless France could persuade Spain to accept a reasonable settlement before Parliament reconvened, his ministry would fall.[5]

When Rayneval returned to London on 2 December, accompanied by Vergennes' son, he discovered that the British public was aroused over the rumors of the loss of Gibraltar and that Shelburne, to appease his Cabinet, felt impelled to revise his demands upwards for equivalents to include Guadeloupe, the Bahamas, Trinidad, and Minorca.[6] Now anxious more than ever to control the Allied side of the negotiations and to bring about a quick peace while a conciliatory negotiator was still at the helm in England, Vergennes decided to force Spain to abandon its demand for the Rock.[7] On 11 December the British Cabinet rejected France's proffered equivalents, and made a new counter-offer: the Floridas and Minorca would go to Spain, Dominica and the Bahamas would be restored, and the rights of British subjects to cut logwood in Honduras would be recognized.[8] Rayneval's letter urging acceptance of these altered terms reached Versailles on 15 December, prompting a meeting between Aranda and Vergennes the following morning. Aranda, who believed that Spain should give primary consideration to maintaining its empire in America and viewed the new proposals as promoting that end, dropped the demand for Gibraltar and accepted Shelburne's terms.[9] Aranda's courageous decision was taken on his own initiative and in defiance of instructions from his government.[10]

Before the Preliminaries were signed odds and ends remained to be tidied up, but only one issue outstanding directly concerned America—that was the fisheries. The British assigned certain coasts in Newfoundland to the French fishermen and returned the islands of Saint Pierre and Miquelon. Vergennes sought to have a clause inserted explicitly protecting French fishermen from the Americans, whose fishing rights or liberties secured in their own Preliminaries sorely discomfited him. The French minister warned Fitzherbert that "they will crowd into the areas reserved for us and deprive us of exercising the greatest part of our fishing right." All that he could obtain from the British in his own Preliminaries was an oral undertaking to prevent encroachments on the fisheries "of the subjects of France during the temporary exercise which is accorded them on the coast of the island of Newfoundland." Neither the Preliminaries nor the Definitive Treaty incorporated such a provision, however.[11]

Other concessions or equivalents did not touch on the United States. In the final settlement England exchanged the island of Tobago for Dominica, yielded Senegal, and allowed France a diminished concession in India without conceding her a political foothold.[12] Spain kept the two Floridas and Minorca while granting certain rights to England's logwood cutters in the Gulf of Mexico. Great Britain retained Gibraltar and regained the Bahamas and certain West Indian islands captured from her by the Allies. The terms of peace between Great Britain and the United Provinces were not settled until May 1784, when the Dutch were forced to agree to a humiliating peace. Vergennes persuaded the British to return Trincomalee to the Dutch in exchange for Negapatan, a minor port south of Madras which had fallen into British hands, but the Dutch had to concede to the British the right of free navigation of the Moluccas.[13]

On 20 January 1783, Vergennes, Aranda, and Fitzherbert met at Versailles and signed the French and Spanish Preliminaries of Peace. The United States was represented at the signing by Benjamin Franklin and John Adams. Absent were JJ traveling in Normandy[14] and Laurens at Bath for his health.[15] After witnessing the signatures of the ministers of the three courts, the Americans signed the British declaration of cessation of arms. A month later, at the request of the British government, they reciprocated with a declaration of their own, for which see JJ's draft, below.[16]

[1]These negotiations are treated in detail in *Peacemakers,* pp. 398–408.

[2]Vergennes to Montmorin, 13 Oct. 1782, CP E 609: 83–84; Montmorin to Vergennes, 17 Oct. 1782, *ibid.,* pp. 103–05. See also Response of the Court of France to the Note of the Court of London, 4 Aug. 1782, DS in FO 27/3, C in MiU-C: Shelburne 71; also Propositions of Spain to England, addressed by Aranda to Fitzherbert, 6 Oct. 1782, cited above, Oswald to Townshend, 7 Oct. 1782, in n. 3. See also Grantham to Fitzherbert, 21 Oct. 1782, LbkC in FO 27/2.

[3]Vergennes to Montmorin, 12 Nov. 1782, LbkC in CP E 609: 207–12; Vergennes to Aranda, 14 Nov. 1782, LbkC in *ibid.,* pp. 227–28; Shelburne to Rayneval, 13 Nov. 1782, Dft in MiU-C: Shelburne 71, and Fitzherbert to Grantham, 15 Nov. 1782, FO 27/3.

[4]For an account of the new British position and counter-proposals, see Rayneval to Vergennes, 21 Nov. 1782, CP A 539: 3–7. Vergennes found Shelburne's new demands "neither moderate nor discreet." Vergennes to Montmorin, 26 Nov. 1782, CP E 609: 282–85.

[5]Rayneval to Vergennes, 27 Nov. 1782, CP A 539: 54–57.

[6]Rayneval to Vergennes, 4 Dec. 1782 (3 letters), L and 2 ALS in *ibid.,* pp. 135–43, 145–46, 153–54.

[7]*Ibid.,* pp. 135–46.

[8]Grantham to Fitzherbert, 11 Dec. 1782, Tr in MiU-C and in FO 27/3.

[9]Rayneval to Vergennes, 12 Dec. 1782, CP A 539: 220–22; Vergennes to Montmorin, 17, 18 Dec. 1782. CP E 609: 386–89, 418; Aranda to Floridablanca, 18 Dec. 1782, AHN Estado: leg. 4215, exp. 3, no. 2355, p. 24.

[10]Montmorin to Vergennes, 28 Dec. 1782, CP E 609: 449–55. See also *Peacemakers,* pp. 406–08, and documents cited.

[11]For the allocation of the Newfoundland coast between England and France for purposes of fishing and for other fishing privileges granted the French, see Preliminary Articles, sects. 3, 4, 6, F. G. Davenport and C. O. Paullin, *European Treaties Bearing on the History of the United States and Its Dependencies* (Washington, 1937), p. 147; final treaty, *ibid.,* p. 153. For Vergennes' insistence on exclusive fishing rights, see Vergennes to Rayneval, 15, 18 Jan. 1783, CP A 450: 161–183, 200–04.

[12]Davenport and Paullin, *Treaties,* IV, 152–54, 158–61.
[13]See *Peacemakers,* pp. 408–09, and documents cited.
[14]See below, Matthew Ridley's Journal, 7–23 Jan. 1783.
[15]*Peacemakers,* p. 409.
[16]The British proclamation was published as a broadside in London and New York. DNA: Treaty Ser., no. 103. Both declarations are in French and English. The American Declaration was agreed to unanimously by Congress on 11 April 1783, issued as a circular letter to the governors of the States the next day, and transmitted to Sir Guy Carleton, commander of the British forces in New York. Miller, *Treaties,* II, 108–10; *JCC,* XXV, 984–85; *RDC,* VI, 367–68.

From Gouverneur Morris

Philadelphia, 1 January 1783

Dear Jay,

I have received your Letter of the thirteenth of October from Paris. I am daily convinced of the Necessity of writing principally in Cypher because It will among other things tend eventually to give one's Letters a safe Passage when it shall have been found that impertinent or designing Curiosity exercises her Talents in vain.

That Part of your Letter to me in Cypher I have communicated only to Mr. Morris and Mr. Livingston, to them and to them only for Reasons which will be obvious to you. Your Letters to Congress (FOR SUCH I CALL THOSE YOU WRITE TO THE MINISTER OF FOREIGN AFFAIRS) are what they ought to be and have the Effect you would wish. (YOU SHOULD REMEMBER HOWEVER THAT THE BACK LANDS ARE AS IMPORTANT IN THE EYES OF SOME AS THE FISHERIES IN THOSE OF OTHERS.) Men are forgetful and therefore it will be well by timely Declarations of your Sentiments to recall your Conduct while in Congress. You and I differ about the Western Country, etc., but you and your Sovereign are of the same Opinion.

Gen. McDougall, Col. Brooks of the Massachusetts and Col. Ogden of the Jersey Line are now here with a Petition to Congress from the Army for Pay.[1] The Army are now disciplined and their wants as to food and Cloathing are relieved but they are not paid. Their back Accounts are not settled. If settled the Ballances are not secured by competent funds. No Provision is made for the Half-Pay promised them. Some Persons and indeed some States pretend to dispute their Claim to it. (THE ARMY HAVE SWORDS IN THEIR HANDS. YOU KNOW ENOUGH OF THE HISTORY OF MANKIND TO KNOW MUCH MORE THAN I HAVE SAID AND POSSIBLY MUCH MORE THAN THEY THEMSELVES YET THINK OF.) I will add however that I am glad to see Things in their present Train. Depend on it good will arise from the Situation to which we are hastening. And this you may rely on that my Efforts will not be wanting. I pledge myself to you on the present occasion and ALTHOUGH I THINK IT PROBABLE THAT MUCH OF CONVULSION WILL ENSUE, YET IT MUST TERMINATE IN GIVING TO GOVERNMENT THAT POWER WITHOUT WHICH GOVERNMENT IS BUT A NAME. GOVERNMENT IN AMERICA IS NOT POSSESSED OF IT (BUT THE PEOPLE ARE WELL PREPARED. WEARIED WITH THE WAR, THEIR ACQUIESCENCE MAY BE DEPENDED ON WITH ABSOLUTE CERTAINTY AND YOU AND I, MY FRIEND, KNOW BY EXPERIENCE THAT WHEN A FEW MEN OF SENSE AND SPIRIT GET TOGETHER AND DECLARE THAT THEY ARE THE AUTHORITY, SUCH FEW AS ARE OF A DIFFERENT OPINION MAY EASILY BE CONVINCED OF THEIR MISTAKE BY THAT POWERFUL ARGUMENT THE HALTER. IT IS, HOWEVER, A MOST MELANCHOLY CONSIDERATION THAT A PEOPLE SHOULD REQUIRE SO MUCH OF EXPERIENCE BEFORE THEY WILL BE WISE. IT IS STILL MORE PAINFUL TO THINK THAT THIS EXPERIENCE IS ALWAYS BOUGHT SO DEAR. ON THE WISDOM OF THE PRESENT MOMENT DEPENDS MORE THAN IS EASILY IMAGINED, AND WHEN I LOOK ROUND FOR THE ACTORS ———LET US CHANGE THE SUBJECT.)

Accept my sincere Wishes that the Year now commencing may prove to you and yours the kind Dispensor of every human felicity. Present me on the occasion to Mrs. Jay affectionately. All your friends are well and rejoice that you are in a situation so essential to America as that which you now hold. (SOME PERSONS HAVE HINTED TO ME THAT YOU ARE TOO SUSPICIOUS. I THINK THEY ARE MUCH MISTAKEN.) The observation, if it proceeds from the Heart, shews only that they are not so well acquainted with human Nature as you are. Go on my good friend, continue to merit the Esteem of all good men and give to Envy her favorite food. When you are tired of Europe and have completed your Business there, I will invite you in Shenstone's[2] Language:

"Come, Come, my friend, with Taste, with Genius blest,
E'er Age impair thee and e'er Gold allure."

Adieu. Yours,

GOUV. MORRIS

DftS, with cipher passages indicated by parentheses, in NNC: Gouverneur Morris. Endorsed by Morris. RC in cipher in *ibid.* ALS, with ciphered and deciphered passages later obliterated, in JP, endorsed by JJ: ". . . Recd. 17 Feb. 83." With deletions and "corrections" in Jared Sparks, ed., *The Life of Gouverneur Morris with Selections from His Correspondence and Miscellaneous Papers* (3 vols., Boston, 1832), I, 248–49.

[1]The officers of the main army encamped at Newburgh dispatched Major General Alexander McDougall, Colonels Matthias Ogden (1755–91), and John Brooke (1752–1825) to Philadelphia to present to Congress a memorial demanding provision for the back pay due the officers and men and some assurance that the promises of half-pay pension for officers on retirement would be kept. The three-man delegation arrived in Philadelphia 29 December and presented the memorial on 6 January. *LMCC,* VI, 570; *JCC,* XXIV, 95n. The memorial is in *ibid.,* pp. 291–92. This letter buttresses the circumstantial evidence cited by one investigator to implicate Gouverneur Morris

as a principal in the "conspiracy." See Richard H. Kohn, "The Inside History of the Newburgh Conspiracy," *WMQ*, XXVII (1970), 193n., and *Eagle and Sword: The Federalists and the Creation of the Military Establishment, 1783–1802* (New York, 1975), pp. 21, 23 *passim*.

[2]William Shenstone (1714–63), English poet.

Matthew Ridley's Journal

[7–23 January 1783]

7 January. Mr. Jay and myself set off from Paris. Slept at Magny.[1]

Wednesday, January 8. Got to Rouen, put up at Hotel Vatel.

Thursday, January 9. Mr. Holker[2] and Mr. Garvey called on us. Dined at Mr. Holkers.

Friday, January 10. Mr. Garvey, Mr. Fontenay and several others dined with us at Mr. Holkers. Fixed for a Jaunt to Havre de Grace to set out to morrow. Went in the Morning to Breakfast with Young Mrs. Holker[3] and went also to the Hale.

Saturday, January 11. Set out with Mr. Jay, Mr. Holker and Mr. Garvey for Havre. Slept at Bolbec, a Capital manufacturing Town for Linen, passed thro Yvetot another capital place for Linens, checks etc.

Sunday, January 12. Got to Havre. Dined at Mr. Ferays. Continual Rain. No walking.

Monday, January 13. Dined at Mr. Lalanne. Mr. Limosin called and pressed us much to dine with him to morrow but we told him we could not as we were to set out. He staid the Evening with us and has promised me some dimensions of Iron in bars that will suit the Havre Market.

Tuesday, January 14th. Still rain. Walk out to See the port but the Weather so bad could not stay. Set out on our return for Rouen. Lay at Bolbec.

Wednesday, January 15. Heavey Rain. Got to Rouen about 5 OClock in the Evening.

Thursday, January 16. Some Company to dine with us at Mr. Holkers.

Friday, January 17. Dined at Mr. Garveys.

Saturday, January 18. Dined at Mr. L. Quesnels.[4]

Sunday, January 19. Dined in the Family way.

Monday, January 20. Received Letters advising the arrival of Vessels at L'Orient. Also advised from Paris that the preliminary Articles of Peace were agreed to the 18th, were to be read over the 19th and signed the 20th. The Dutch from their Tardiness have not got their Affairs settled for the present.

Dined at Young Mrs. Holkers. Mr. Jay was to have dined there but being much indisposed could not go. Found him bravely in the Evening. My Letters from America mention the resignation of Mr. Livingston as Minister for Foreign Affairs.[5] Not known who will succeed.

Tuesday, January 21st. Dined at Mr. Quesnels.

Wednesday, January 22d. Set out on our way to Paris.

Thursday, January 23d. Arrived at Paris about 5 OClock in the Evening. Found all well.

AD in MHi: Ridley.

[1]Magney-en-Vexin, a village half way between Paris and Rouen.

[2]John Holker, Sr. (1719–86), a cloth manufacturer at Rouen who held the post of *Inspecteur Général des Manufactures du Royaume.* André Remond, *John Holker, manufacturier et grand fonctionnaire en France au XVIIIe siècle, 1719–1786* (Paris, 1946).

[3]Elisabeth Julie Quesnel, the wife of John Holker, Jr., for whom see above, SLJ to Mary White Morris, 17 Nov. 1782, and n. 5. See also Kathryn Sullivan, *Maryland and France, 1774–1789* (Philadelphia, 1936), pp. 46–47, 58–64.

[4]Probably Louis Quesnel, of the Rouen mercantile family, a relation of Mrs. John Holker, Jr..

[5]See below, Livingston to JJ, 1 May 1783.

To Benjamin Franklin

Paris, 26 January 1783

Sir,

It having been suspected that I concurred in the appointment of your Grandson to the Place of Secretary to the American Commission for peace, at your Instance, I think it right thus unsollicited to put it in your power to correct that mistake.

Your general Character, the opinion I had long entertained of your Services to our Country, and the friendly attention and aid with which you had constantly favored me, <during the whole Course of my Residence> after my arrival in Spain, impressed me with a Desire of manifesting both my Esteem and Attachment[1] by stronger Evidence than Professions. That Desire extended my Regard[2] for you to your Grandson. He was then indeed a Stranger to me, but the Terms in which you expressed to Congress your <approbation of his Conduct and Character left> opinion of his being qualified for another place of equal Importance were so full and satisfactory as to leave me no Room to doubt of his being qualified for the one abovementioned.

<My opinion of you convinced me that you would not hazard an ill-grounded Recommendation and therefore> <I was persuaded> I was therefore happy to assure you in one of the first Letters I afterwards wrote you from Spain,[3] that in Case a Secretary to our Commission for peace should become necessary, and the appointment be left to us, I should take that opportunity of evincing my Regard for you by nominating him or words to that Effect. What I then wrote was the spontaneous Suggestion of my own mind, unsollicited, and I believe unexpected by you.

When I came here on the Business of that Commission, I brought with me the same Intentions and should always have considered myself engaged by Honor as well as Inclination to <have> fulfill<ed those Expectations> them; unless I had found myself <decieved> mistaken in the opinion I had imbibed of that young Gentleman's Character and Qualifications <for the place in Question> but that not being the Case, I found myself <not only> at Liberty <but also desirous> to indulge my wishes and to be as good as my word—for I expressly declare that your Grandson is in my opinion qualified for the place in Question, for that if he had not been no Consideration whatever would have prevailed upon me to propose or join in his appointment. This explicit and unreserved State of Facts is due to you, to him, and to Justice; and you have my Consent to <publish, give Copies of, or> make <such other> any use of it that you may think proper.[4]

I have the Honor to be Sir with great Respect and Regard Your obliged and obedient Servant

JOHN JAY

DftS. An earlier Dft, designated "Dft A," is also in JP. Variances between the two are noted below. C in NHi: Robert R. Livingston. LbkC in DLC: Franklin VIII, 44–45; *RDC,* VI, 231; *SDC,* IV, 73–74. This letter was prompted by a difference of opinion between Laurens and John Adams as to the propriety of the commission issued by JJ and Franklin 1 Oct. 1782, above, naming Franklin's grandson, William Temple Franklin, secretary to the peace commission. Laurens had seen and approved the commission on 10 January, and declared that young Franklin had "acted with propriety as secretary to the commission from the time of my arrival here." *RDC,* V, 789–90. Adams, on the contrary, considered himself "directly affronted in this affair." As the sole peace commissioner originally, he felt that Franklin should have consulted him before extracting a promise from JJ when the latter was in Madrid. He also felt that John Thaxter, Jr. (1755–91), Abigail Adams' cousin, who had come to Europe as Adams' private secretary, "had a better right" to the post. *AP,* III, 102–03. Ridley had filled Adams in on the background of the appointment. *Ibid.,* p. 38. Adams gave belated but grudging approval. *Boston Patriot,* 10 Aug. 1811.

[1]"Gratitude" in Dft A.

[2]"Turned my attention to" in Dft A.

[3]See above, JJ to Franklin, 30 Jan. 1782.

[4]"Prudent and proper" in Dft A.

To John Vaughan

Paris, 15 February 1783

Dear Sir,

The only letter I have had the Pleasure of recieving from you is dated the 3rd of November last.[1] I regret the Miscarriage of the others, as well because they were from you, as because they doubtless contained Information which either on domestic or public accounts, and perhaps on both, was interesting.

Your elder Brother has spent much Time here, I need not add, *usefully;* he is at present in England. Your younger Brother is here still and well.[2] An acquaintance with those Gentlemen is among the agreable Circumstances I have met with in this Country. They both possess my cordial Esteem and good wishes, and I shall be happy to number them with my fellow Citizens.

Accept my thanks for the Intelligence contained in your Letter; it was more circumstantial and satisfactory than what I recieved from my other Correspondents. You seem pleased with America, and I am glad of it. It affords ample Field to a Mind turned like Yours to Observation; I find you are cultivating it, and already begin to reap.

I congratulate you on the Peace. I hope America will not think the Terms very exceptionable; all things considered, we certainly have Reason to think they were not to be refused.

A Treaty of Commerce has lately been concluded with Sweden,[3] and other Nations will probably follow the Example of that Kingdom. Much remains to be done; it is often less difficult to acquire, than to preserve and enjoy.

England has yet to make Peace with the turbulent Spirit of Faction; the Minister it is thought has a precarious as well as uneasy Seat.

Mr. Dickenson has Talents and good Intentions, and I think it will not be his Fault if Pensylvania does not derive Advantages from his administration.[4] Parties must be expected in Republics, and provided the People are well informed, their Errors are seldom of very long Duration. News Papers will sometimes be licentious, but they had better be so than in the contrary extreme.

I am still an Invalid; a little Excursion lately made into Normandy has by giving me Exercise and a Change of Air, been of some Use to me. Mrs. Jay is tolerably well; she is obliged by your Attention, and presents you her best Compliments. My best Wishes attend you.

I am Dear Sir, your obedient Servant,

JOHN JAY

ALS in PPAmP. Dft in JP.

[1]John Vaughan to JJ, 3 Nov. 1782, ALS in JP; E in NN: Bancroft: American.

[2]Benjamin Vaughan and Samuel Vaughan, Jr.

[3]The Swedish-American Treaty of Amity and Commerce was concluded by Franklin and the Swedish plenipotentiary, Count Gustav Philip Creutz some time in January 1783. (JJ and John Adams had made Creutz's acquaintance on 19 Nov. 1782, *AP*, III, 62). Over the next two months the treaty underwent minor changes in wording and finally received the date of 3 April although it was not finished until the middle of that month. See Amandus Johnson, *Swedish Contributions to American Freedom, 1776–1783* (2 vols., Philadelphia, 1953–57), I, ch. X *passim.* For the treaty, see Miller, *Treaties,* II, 123–49.

[4]In the elections of 1782 the Republicans ousted their radical Constitutionalist opponents from control. John Dickinson, returning to Pennsylvania politics, was elected to the Supreme Executive Council, and on 7 November, elected President of the Executive Council over his opponent James Potter. Robert L. Brunhouse, *The Counter-Revolution in Pennsylvania, 1776–1790* (Harrisburg, 1942), chs. IV, V *passim.* For Dickinson, see also *JJ*, I, 148–51, 364, 366–67 and n., 581.

Resolving Differences Over Passports

[Paris, 1–3 February 1783]

Having considered his mission complete with the signing of the Preliminaries, Oswald returned to England. Alleyne Fitzherbert persuaded the American Commissioners that his powers to treat with France also permitted him to conduct business with them in the absence of a commissioner to the Americans. Toward the end of January, Fitzherbert conferred with Franklin on the renewal of "reciprocal intercourse . . . whether by commerce or otherwise" between Britain and her former colonies. Discussions with the French, Spanish, and Americans resulted in tentative agreements to exchange passports with the British for merchant vessels.[1]

It was perhaps natural that Franklin, who had not only issued but printed passports during the Revolution, should proceed to draw up a passport in much the same form as he had used hitherto.[2] However, JJ and Adams objected to the passport he prepared for this occasion, which was to read as follows:

"To all Captains or Commanders of Ships of War or Privateers, belonging to the United States of America, or Citizens of the same, Greeting.

"We the Underwritten, Ministers Plenipotentiary from the Congress of the said States to the Court of France do hereby in their Name, strictly charge and require of you, as we do likewise pray and desire the officers and Ministers of all Princes and Powers in Amity with the said States, to permit and suffer the *Merchant* Vessel called the commanded by belonging to Great Britain to sail to any of the Ports thereof to any Port or Place, whatsoever, *except those of the said States* in North America, *together with the Merchandize wherewith she may be laden,* without any Let, Hindrance or Molestation whatsoever, but on the contrary affording, the said Vessel, all such Aid and

Assistance as may be necessary. Given at Paris, the First Day of February 1783."[3]

After conferring with Fitzherbert on 1 February, JJ wrote Adams the note below. The next day Adams invited his fellow commissioners to a meeting on the 3rd to discuss "the Passports to be given to and received from the British Minister" and "Preparations for the Signature of the definitive Treaty."[4] It was at the meeting of 3 February that Adams showed Franklin and JJ his "First Sketch of a Definitive Treaty, made Feb. 1 1783."[5]

At this meeting the Americans agreed on a new form for the passports, to be issued jointly by the three named Commissioners then present in Paris. Franklin apparently did not object strenuously to this change, but another modification met stiff opposition on his part. Fitzherbert noted that Franklin "chicaned to the very last upon the business of the Passports, and finally moved for the inserting in them this odious and ungracious Clause, 'that they should not be considered as Protections for *any Ships bound to Ports in North America.*' This motion was founded upon the Prohibitory Acts passed by Great Britain which he affects to consider as still in force, but he was overruled in it by his Colleagues without any Instance from me."[6] The new passport agreed upon that day read as follows:

"We John Adams, Benjamin Franklin, and John Jay, three of the Ministers Plenipotentiaries of the United States of America, for making Peace with Great Britain, To all Captains or Commanders of ships of War privateers or armed Vessels belonging to the said States or to either of them, or to any of the Citizens of the same And to all others whom these Presents may Concern, send Greeting.

"Whereas Peace and Amity is agreed upon between the said United States and his Britannic Majesty, and a suspension of Hostilities to take place at different periods in different Places hath also been agreed upon by their respective Plenipotentiaries. And whereas it hath been further agreed by the said Plenipotentiaries, to exchange Passports for Merchant Vessels, to the End that such as shall be provided with them shall be exempted from Capture although found in Latitudes at a Time prior to the taking Place of the said suspension of Hostilities therein. Now therefore know ye Commander now lying at the Port of and bound from thence to And we do earnestly enjoin upon and recommend to you to let and suffer the said Vessel to pass unmolested to her destined Port, and if need be, to afford her all such succor and Aid as Circumstances and Humanity may require.

"Given under our Hands and Seals at Paris on the day of in the Year of our Lord 1783."[7]

By 9 February the printing of the French, Spanish, and American passports was completed, and Fitzherbert forwarded them to England, with the understanding that none would be used until a similar number of British passports had been dispatched to Paris. Fitzherbert received the British passports on 18 February and completed the exchange with the American commissioners.[8]

[1]Fitzherbert to Grantham, 25 Jan. 1783, ALS in FO 27/5, 239–41; 27/2, 317–19.
[2]See *The Passports Printed by Benjamin Franklin at His Passy Press.*
[3]DS in hand of William Temple Franklin in MHi: Adams, reel 360.
[4]Adams to Franklin, 2 Feb. 1783, DLC: Franklin.
[5]MHi: Adams, reel 360.
[6]Fitzherbert to Grantham, 9 Feb. 1783, FO 27/5, 354–55.
[7]Wording from printed form, signed by three commissioners, in PPAmP: Franklin.
[8]Fitzherbert to Grantham, 9, 20 Feb. 1783, ALS in FO 27/5, 352–53, 415–16; Fitzherbert to American Commissioners, 18 Feb. 1783, ALS in MHi: Adams, reel 360.

To John Adams

Paris, 1 February 1783

Mr. Fitzherbert has just been with me. He will give passports for American merchantmen, on our doing the like for British ones. He informed me that Doctor Franklin is preparing a number of these Passports, in his own name. As this Business appears to both of us to appertain rather to the American Commissioners for peace, than to the residentiary minister at this or any other Court; would it not be proper to apprize the Doctor of our Sentiments, before the passports he is now making out shall be delivered?

Yours etc.

JOHN JAY

ALS in MHi: Adams, reel 360.

The United States' Declaration of the Cessation of Hostilities

20 February 1783

The King's "Proclamation declaring the cessation of arms,"[1] issued 14 February, reached Fitzherbert four days later. Thereupon he dispatched the long-awaited British passports,[2] remarking in an accompanying note that the step was taken in expectation of reciprocal action by the Americans.[3] The latter agreed to give Fitzherbert "an authentic Act, declaring their adoption of the said Epocha," for transmittal to London by the next messenger.[4] The "authentic Act" was drafted by Adams, then revised by JJ. The Commissioners styled their "Act" a "Declaration," but, like that of George III, it was actually a proclamation of the declaration agreed to in January, and is found below, preceded by a covering letter drafted by JJ, the latter reflecting the Americans' growing concern over trade relations.[5]

[1] *RDC*, VI, 251–52.

[2] See editorial note above, "Resolving Differences Over Passports," 13 Feb. 1783.

[3] ALS in MHi: Adams, reel 360; *RDC*, VI, 255.

[4] Fitzherbert to Grantham, 20 Feb. 1783, LS in FO 27/5, 415–16. He had requested the passports of Grantham on 3 February, the date when he exchanged ratifications with Vergennes. *Ibid.*, pp. 317–19.

[5] By the time the British passports had arrived, many American ships, particularly Virginia vessels laden with tobacco, had reached Europe anticipating the reopening of trade. On the assumption that both parties accepted the principle of reciprocal trade, the American Commissioners were hopeful that the vessels could enter English ports free of tonnage and aliens' duty. Fitzherbert, unauthorized to respond, sought advice from the home authorities. Fitzherbert to Grantham, 22 Feb. 1783, LS in FO 27/6, 3–7.

American Commissioners to Alleyne Fitzherbert

Paris, [*c.* 20 February 1783]

Sir,

We have recieved the Letter which you did us the Honor to write on the 18th Inst. together with the Passports mentioned in it.[1]

His Britannic Majesty's Proclamation of the 14th Instant has our entire Approbation, and we have the Honor of transmitting to you, herewith enclosed, a Declaration perfectly correspondent with it.

It appears to us important to both Countries that a System be speedily adopted to regulate the Commerce between them; and it gives us pleasure to inform you that we are authorized to form one, on <the most liberal> Principles so liberal, as the British Merchants shall enjoy in America and her Ports and Waters, the same Immunities and Priviledges with her own; provided that a similar Indulgence be allowed to those of our Country, in common with British merchants in general.

We presume that such a System will on consideration appear most convenient to both; <but if it should not, we shall be ready to frame one on narrower Principles of Reciprocity.> if so, we shall be ready to include it in the definitive Treaty.

We flatter ourselves that this overture will be considered as a Mark of our Attention to the Principles adopted in the Preamble of our Preliminaries, and of our Desire to render the commercial Intercourse between us free from Embarrassing and partial Restrictions.

We have the Honor to be with great Regard and Esteem Sir Your most obedient and very humble Servants.

Dft in JJ's hand in MHi: Adams, reel 360. Endorsed by Adams: ". . . Sketch of a Letter to Mr. Fitzherbert." Enclosed was the draft of "A Declaration of the Cessation of Arms," immediately below.

[1]Fitzherbert to American Commissioners, 18 Feb. 1783, ALS in MHi: Adams, reel 360; *RDC*, VI, 255.

By the Ministers Plenipotentiary of the United States of America for Making Peace with Great Britain, a Declaration of the Cessation of Arms, as Well by Sea as Land, Agreed upon Between His Majesty the King of Great Britain and the United States of America.

Paris, 20 February 1783

Whereas Preliminary Articles were Signed at Paris, on the Thirtieth Day of November last, between, the Plenipotentiar*ies* of his Said Majesty the King of Great Britain, <and the Ministers Plenipotentiar*ies* of> [1] the Said States to be inserted in, and to constitute the Treaty of Peace <proposed> to be concluded, *between* his Said Majesty and the said United States, when Terms of Peace Should be agreed upon between his Said Majesty, and his most Christian Majesty. And Whereas Preliminaries for restoring Peace between his Said Majesty the King of Great Britain, and his most Christian Majesty, were Signed at Versailles, on the Twentieth Day of January last, by the respective Ministers of their Said Majesties. And whereas Preliminaries for restoring Peace, between his Said Majesty the King of Great Britain, and his Majesty the King of Spain were also Signed at Versailles on the Twentyeth Day of January last between the Ministers of his Majesty the King of Great Britain and his Said Majesty the King of Spain.[2] And Whereas for putting an End to the Calamity of War as Soon and as far as possible, it hath been agreed, between, the King of Great Britain, his most Christian Majesty, the King of Spain, the States General of the United Provinces and the United States of America, as follows, that is to Say:

That such Vessells and Effects as Should be taken in the Channel and in the North Seas, after the Space of Twelve Days, to be computed from the Ratification of the Said Preliminary Articles, Should be restored on all Sides. That the Term Should be one Month, from the Channel and the North Seas as far as the Canary Islands inclusively whether in the ocean or the Mediterranean, Two Months from the Said Canary Islands as far as the Equinoctial Line or Equator, and lastly Five Months in all other Parts of the World, without any Exception, or any other more particular Description of Time or Place.

And Whereas the Ratifications of the Said Preliminary Articles, between his Said Majesty the King of Great Britain, and his most Christian Majesty, in due Form, were exchanged by their Ministers, on the Third Day of this instant February, From which Day the Several Terms <of> abovementioned of Twelve Days, of one Month, of two Months and of Five Months, are to be computed, relative to all British, and American Subjects, Vessells and Goods.[3]

Now Therefore We, the Ministers Plenipotentiary, from the United States of America for making Peace with Great Britain, do <*hereby*> notify <the Same> to all[4] the *People* and Citizens <Inhabitants and Subjects> of the Said United States of America <and We do, in the Name and by the Authority of the Said States declare that it is their Will and Pleasure, and their Order and Injunction to all Officers> <both at Land and Sea, and to all other their Citizens and Subjects whatsoever> *that Hostilities <against> on their part against his Britannick Majesty both by Sea and Land, are to cease at the Expiration of the Terms herein before specified therefor, and which Terms are to be <issues> computed from the 3 Day of February inst. And we do in the Name and <Behalf> by the Authority of the said United States accordingly warn and injoin all their officers and Citizens <whom it may con[cern]>* to forbear all Acts of Hostility, <either by Sea or Land,> whatever either by Land or or by Sea, against his Said Majesty the King of Great Britain, <his Vassalls> or *his* Subjects, <from and after the respective Times abovementioned, to be computed from the Said third Day of February instant, and> under the Penalty of incurring <their> the highest Displeasure of the *Said United* States.

<Done> Given at Paris, the Twentyeth Day of February, in the Year of our Lord one Thousand Seven hundred and Eighty Three, *under our Hands and Seals.*[5]

Dft, in the hand of Adams, with JJ's corrections indicated in italics hereinabove, in MHi: Adams, reel 360. Endorsed by Adams: "Declaration of 20 Feb. 1783 of the Armistice and computation of the Terms from 3 Feb. 1783." D, in the hand of Adams and signed by himself, Franklin, and JJ, in *ibid.* Endorsed by Adams: "Declaration of an Armistice, made by the American Ministers on the 20. Feb. 1783." LbkC in PPAmP: Franklin; *RDC,* VI, 257–58; *SDC,* X, 127–29.

[1]"And of" in the final version. *RDC,* VI, 257–58.

[2]"By their respective Ministers" in the final version.

[3]"Effects" in final version.

[4]"Twentieth" in final text.

[5]The final text bears the signatures of Adams, Franklin, and JJ, with their seals affixed, countersigned by Fitzherbert.

FROM MONTMORIN

Madrid, 22 February 1783

I do not believe, Sir, that I can send you my compliments on the peace by a more appropriate voice or one that would be more agreeable to you than that of the marquis de la fayette.[1] He is your friend, your adopted compatriot, and will be counted by posterity among the numbers who contributed most to the great revolution in which you were one of the principal actors and which the peace has just concluded.

I will not speak to you of the dispositions of Spain. M. de la fayette will tell you better than I what he saw of them. He leaves from here pleased with what was shown to him, and I hope that you will see it too.[2] I would be quite truly satisfied to see harmony and a good understanding reign between Spain and the United States of America. I shall be quite happy if I can contribute to it in some way; you know my feelings for your country. They are and will always be the same.

M. de la fayette is going to leave for paris this very instant and leaves me only time enough to assure you of a perfect and true attachment with which I have the honor to be, Sir, your very humble and obedient servant

LE CTE. DE MONTMORIN

Permit Mme. Jay to find here the assurance of my respect.

ALS in French, trans. by the editors. A note in English was added by Bourgoing: "Dear Sir, I hope you will permit me to join my compliments to those of my chief. You know we have but one soul, and this identity is no where more sensible than in all what concerns your country and your person. Pray present my respects to Mistress Jay. We are not selfish and injust enough to wish you return soon in our city. It would be prefer [sic] too much our interests to yours."

[1]See editorial note below, "Lafayette, Jay's Self-Appointed 'Political Aide-de-Camp,' Takes on the Spaniards," and letters thereto.

[2]*Ibid.*

TO JOHN DICKINSON

Paris, 11 March 1783

Mr. Penn,[1] the Heir and Descendant of the Founder of Pensylvania, promises to present to you my Congratulations on your Election to the Place of chief magistrate in it: an Event from which the Common Wealth will I am persuaded derive very essential advantages.

This Gentleman's present Prospects differ from his former Expectations; but it is a Difference which must recommend him to the attentions of those who think and feel with the Justice and Delicacy you do. I make no apology for this Letter. Your urbanity and Sensibility render it unnecessary.

I have the Honor to be with great Esteem and Respect, Your Excellency's most obedient and very humble Servant,

JOHN JAY

ALS in PHi: Logan, XII, 34. Endorsed by JJ: ". . . His Excellency John Dickensen Esquire, President of Pennsylvania." On the previous day JJ wrote a letter to Robert Morris, also introducing John Penn, and adding: "The Manner in which Mr. Penn's family has been affected by the American Revolution need not be explained to you. I am not a Pennsylvanian and therefore forbear discussing that Subject. I will only observe that I have no reason to believe that this family has done us Injury, and that I wish the ultimate Decision for your Commonwealth may leave them no just cause to complain." Dft in JP; variations in *HPJ,* III, 34.

[1]For John Penn, see note to Lady Juliana Penn to JJ, 23 Nov. 1782, above.

Sir James' New Role: Self-Appointed Negotiator in Paris

Having worn out his welcome in England,[1] Sir James took off for The Hague, whence he reached Paris in early December of 1782, his head buzzing with schemes. First, he approached the Marquis de Castries to sell a naval invention to the French which the British had declined buying.[2] With characteristic presumption, he then used this proffer to establish his credentials as a patriotic American, and called upon the Comte de Vergennes no less to vouch for him back in the States.[3] Next he sought a direct contact with the Comte to discuss his scheme for a commercial monopoly, exploiting his brother's prestige to help clinch the deal.[4]

According to one undocumented account, JJ, possessed as he was of a strict sense of propriety and wishing nothing less than to be indebted to the Comte while negotiations were still continuing, confronted his brother and gave him a dressing down.[5] To the contrary, JJ's own letters indicated that while in Paris Sir James gave his brother a wide berth, and this despite the fact that JJ had interceded with Franklin to obtain James' discharge as a prisoner on parole in an exchange with a British officer.[6]

Failing a face-to-face conference with France's foreign minister, Sir James contacted intermediaries in the Foreign Office. Among them was Edmond Charles Genêt, premier commis of the Bureau of Interpretation. According to Genêt's recollections, obviously colored by later incidents—by Chief Justice

Jay's denunciation of minister Genêt for meddling in America's domestic politics, compounded by the Frenchman's distaste for the treaty JJ made with the British in 1794—Sir James engaged in some indiscreet babbling. "I heard him frequently affirm that John had always been opposed to the Independence of the United States," Genêt quoted Sir James as having told him, Sir James adding that JJ "hated France as much as his ancestors who were Huguenots, and that if he could he would procure a reconciliation between England and her old colonies in America and baffle all the expectations of France by an alliance between the two countries," amounting virtually to a "reunion."[7] Such twisted and malicious comments on Sir James' part were calculated to intensify suspicions the French already nurtured about JJ's independent course as a negotiator.

Capitalizing on the virtual stalemate in the trade negotiations between America and England, Sir James pressed his grandiose trade monopoly project upon the French Foreign Office in the spring of 1783.[8] He now proposed that, instead of granting credits to French business firms to trade with America, the French government extend long-term credits to a few selected American commercial houses, hinting that a firm of his own (not even existing on paper) be among the select number. Such an arrangement, Sir James argued, would make it possible for the French to compete in the States with the formidable Tory-British connection. This and similar proposals he discussed with the newly-appointed Controller General, Henri-François d'Ormessson, who sent along a memorandum about the conversation to the Foreign Minister.[9] Months elapsed, but nothing materialized.

While Sir James was carrying on these negotiations with the French government behind his brother's back, he was seeking to entice Dutch businessmen into establishing trade outlets throughout America, a project not unlike the monopolistic scheme he was offering France. He had undoubtedly raised the subject with his friend Charles William Dumas while at The Hague, and continued to pursue it in correspondence with Dumas from Paris.[10] Hence, Sir James' piteous pleas to Vergennes that he had lost a fortune while awaiting a response from Versailles were typically disingenuous.[11]

Discouraged by his lack of progress on the Continent, Sir James returned to London by early October of '83. It is worth noting that his unauthorized trade proposals to the French ran completely counter to his brother's trade ideas. JJ was opposed to encouraging the importation into the United States of French luxury products.[12] As events turned out, neither Vergennes nor Sir James could be given credit for blocking a trade agreement between the United States and England, against which powerful forces in the latter country were to be quickly mobilized.

[1]See Townshend to Oswald, 11 Oct. 1782, above.

[2]See above, Shelburne to Townshend, n.d., June–July 1782, and Sir James Jay to Townshend, 9 July 1782.

[3]Sir James to Vergennes, 25 Jan. 178[3], below. There is no record to show that

Vergennes acted on Sir James' plea. While in Holland Sir James had procured a letter of introduction to Vergennes from the Duc de la Vauguyon. Vauguyon to Vergennes, 12 June 1782, CP H 548, and cited below, in Sir James Jay to Vergennes, 28 Sept. 1783.

[4]Sir James to Genêt, *c.* 15 May 1783, below.

[5]Monaghan, *Jay,* p. 215.

[6]Franklin's discharge of Captain Dundas on parole, 25 Nov. 1782, FO 97/157.

[7]Edmond Genêt, "Memorandum for My Memoirs," in DLC: Genêt, XLIV, reel 29, frames 025811–12.

[8]Sir James to Vergennes: "Observations and Proposals Concerning Commerce Between France and the U.S.A." (*c.* 20 May 1783), below.

[9]Henri-François de Paule Le Fèvre d'Ormesson (1751–1807) had been named Controller General of Finance by Louis XVI on 30 March 1783, a post he held until 3 November of that year, when he was replaced by Calonne. D'Ormesson to Vergennes, 23 May 1783. CP EU: 24.

[10]See Dumas to Sir James Jay, 4 Feb., 13 March, 21 Aug., 23 Sept., 3 Oct. 1783, AC in French in Algemeen Rijksarchief, The Hague: C. W. F. Dumas.

[11]See below, Sir James to Vergennes, 28 Sept. 1783.

[12]JJ to Gouverneur Morris, 24 Sept. 1783, Dft in JP, *HPJ,* III, 82–85; and Morris to JJ, 10 Jan. 1784, below.

Thomas Townshend to Richard Oswald

Whitehall, 11 October 1782

Sir,

I was upon the point of sending off a Messenger with a Dispatch for you when your Packet of Letters dated the 5, 7 and 8 inst. arrived by <Magg> Ogg with the Draught of the Treaty. I shall now delay for a few days the sending that Dispatch in which it will be necessary for me to make some alterations.

A meeting of the King's Confidential Servants is Summoned to deliberate upon the Contents of the Papers which I had the pleasure of receiving from you to day. I shall write to you again as soon as their Opinion is taken, and will transmit it to you at the same time every thing which I shall have collected on the subject of the Boundaries.

I think it necessary to acquaint You, that Sir James Jay has been here some months, and talks now of going over to Holland to Negotiate his Exchange for Colonel Tarleton or some other Field Officer. He is in great disgust with us all, and I can hardly think for any other reason, than because he has not been kept here at a considerable Expence, to which I am at a loss to know how he is intitled; Otherwise he has been treated with common Civility, which is all an indifferent man has a right to.

If he goes over to Holland, I suspect he is desirous to do ill Offices. I mention this to You because You may possibly hear more of him and be able to prevent his Executing any ill designs if he has such.

I am with great Regard etc.

T. TOWNSHEND

Dft in FO 27/2. Endorsed. C in FO 95/511; LbkCs in 97/157 and in MiU-C: Shelburne 70.

Sir James Jay to Vergennes

Versailles, 25 January 178[3]

Sir,

As it is certain that the Measures I proposed would be highly injurious to any of the Powers at War against whom they should be put in execution; As they are Measures that could be executed by England as well as by France; As I hastned into France to communicate them here, and offered to risque my person in the execution of them, I submit it to Your Excellency whether you may not with great propriety write to Monsieur la Luzerne to the following effect, and direct him to communicate the paragraph to the President and Members of Congress, and likewise to the Governor of the State of New York, vizt.

That having heard that some doubts had been raised in America of Sir James Jay's attachment to his Country, you think it but an act of Justice to have it made known to the Members of Congress and other friends in America, that you have had great and decided proofs of his zeal for the interest of America and the Common Cause. And if the war had continued, he would have rendered them essential services.

I have the honour to be, with great respect, Your Excellency's Most Obedient and Very humble Servant.

LE CHEVALIER JAY

ALS in CP EU 23: 12–13. Endorsed erroneously: "M. Jay, 1778, 25 Janvier." Under 25 Jan. [1782] in Stevens, *Facsimiles,* XXIV, no. 2015.

Sir James Jay to Edmond Charles Genêt

Paris, Thursday, [c. 15 May 1783]

Dear Sir,

I have had a conversation with Mons. A and I have a pleasure in telling you, what I know you will be glad to hear, that I am much more satisfied with him than I was before. It now begins to look as if our Machine would be set in motion.

I intend to be in Versailles about 1 or 2 o'Clock to morrow. The two inclosed short papers are intended for Mons. D.C.[1] It is thought that it would be proper, if a noble friend of yours should be in Versailles to-morrow, or another particular circumstances should happen, that the papers should be then delivered, and it is for that reason that I send them to you know [sic] in hopes that you may find an opportunity of getting them translated by the time I arrive. I shall explain the matter further when I see you. In the mean while, I remain, with great regard, Yours.

JAMES JAY

ALS in DLC: Genêt, XIX, 5674. Addressed: ". . . Mr. Genet, Jamaica South."

[1]Probably Charles Eugène Gabriel de la Croix, Marquis de Castries, the French Minister of Marine.

Sir James Jay to Vergennes: Observations and Proposals Concerning Commerce Between France and the United States of America

[Paris, 20 May 1783]

The English used to give the Merchants in America long Credit, in order that they might have sufficient time to sell the goods imported from England, receive the money from the Retailers, and obtain suitable Articles of Merchandize or Bills of Exchange, to remit to England in payment of the goods.

The Trade between the two Countries were carried on in the following manner. The American Merchant imported goods from London and other places in England, and sold them on Credit to the Retailers. The Retailers sold them in detail, some part, tho but a small one, for ready money; some they exchanged for produce; some they sold on Credit, and those were often paid for in produce instead of money. Those Articles of produce, the Retailer would either give to the Merchant in payment, or would turn into Cash, as he found it most advantageous to himself, or as it happened to suit the Merchant to receive the one or the other.

In a Trade which was thus carried on upon Credit in all its branches, in a Country where there was a scarcity of money, and where it required much time to turn produce into Cash; it is obvious that a variety of circumstances might occasion delays in the circle of payments, which would ultimately affect the Merchant, and occasion a delay in his remittances.

The American Merchants not having sufficient Capitals to carry on an extensive Trade on their own stock, obtained goods on Credit from their Correspondents in England. The wealth of the English Merchants, their Credit and Resources, enabled them to give that credit, and to prolong it occasionally. They found their advantage in so doing, in the increased sale of their goods; and experienced the truth of that maxim in Commerce, that it is more advantageous to sell a great quantity at a moderate profit, than a small quantity at a more considerable profit.

The Merchants in France are neither accustomed nor able to give such Credit; and consequently every American who wishes to form commercial connexions with France, will find in that one circumstance alone, not to mention some others, sufficient reason to decline going deep into the french Trade.

It has been said that Government, sensible of this impediment to Trade, wish to remove it; and to that end have determined to support some Houses in France, in order to enable them to give the like Credit to the Americans that the English have done and will do again.

This idea is a good one; but much will depend on the choice of the persons who are to be thus supported. A man who has been accustomed to get all he can on every thing he does, will not easily pursue a plan of doing a great deal at a small profit on each transaction.

But tho supporting some Houses in France in order that they may give longer Credit to the American Merchants, [it] is in fact an indirect or intermediate method of establishing a longer Credit between the French Manufacturer and the American Merchant. The great object to France, is to sell as much of her Manufactures and Products in America as she possibly can; and on that self evident principle, it is worth considering, whether, as matters are circumstanced, it will not greatly conduce to that end to support some native Houses in America.

Supposing there were no obstacles in the way, it must be sometime before the Houses in France can establish such Connexions in America as will induce American Merchants to send over Commissions to them for goods. It must be sometime before they will be prepared with sufficient Magazines to furnish complete assortments of goods with the advantages which the English Merchants do. But if these Houses in France are to be supported in sending goods on their own account to America, where is the difference, to the Kingdom, between supporting them, and giving similar support to some American Houses who are disposed to trade in french goods? There is no difference except that the latter will occasion a greater importation and sale of french goods. It may therefore be proper to consider, whether it will not be for the interest of the french trade in general, to give the like facilities and encouragements to some American Houses, in order to spread the Manufactures and Produce of France, and to establish subordinate connections in the french Line of Commerce. For it is an indisputable Truth that when Merchants and Retailers of goods have formed their Connexions and have got into a Line of Trade, that such connexions are not easily to be dissolved nor diminished. The Merchants in England, and their Tory friends in America, will do every thing in their power to reestablish old connexions in America; and to make new ones in all the United States. If they should be beforehand with the french Merchants and the friends of France in establishing connexions in America, they will gain a great advantage: for in this Case, as in war, it is often easier to prevent an Enemy from gaining an advantageous ground, than to dispossess them of it. A Competition after such an Event, will be carried on under great disadvantages, whereas if proper Exertions were to be made at present, those difficulties would be easily prevented.

The Writer, for his own part, is sensible of the discouragements alluded to in some of the preceeding observations: and for that reason thinks it would be imprudent for him, in the present state of things, to form connexions and do business on Credit, in the ordinary way it is done in this Country. It is in the power of Government to remove those discouragements by only affording an equal support to that which it is proposed to give to some Houses in France: and it is on that head, that he wishes to know the same of Government, that he may take his Measures accordingly.

AD enclosed in Vergennes to D'Ormesson, 21 May 1783, in CP EU 24: 220–25; C in CtY.

SIR JAMES JAY TO VERGENNES

Versailles, 28 September 1783
at the Renommeé, Rue St. Francois

Sir,

It is useless to observe to a man of your experience and civility that there comes a time when it is necessary to bring an affair to a conclusion; and that in making these requests to bring it about, one is not lacking in delicacy. But permit me, Sir, to assure you that I am no more eager to obtain the former than I am concerned to avoid the latter.

Persuaded as I was that the plan of subsidizing the American houses was to be adopted, and in the confidence that I placed on the explicit promise I was given of such support, I have declined to make other connections. I have been guided by these considerations from month to month, until two seasons have been lost for transacting such business, on the frequent occasions when I was in contact with other countries, and a thousand louis in commissions beyond my expenses in France. With a little reflection you will recognize, Sir, that the circumstances render it necessary for me to know very soon if I am to receive such support, or not.

The politeness and friendship with which you tendered me your services when I had the honor of sending you the letter of M. le Duc de Vauguyon prompt me at this late time to speak to you on the above subject. I beg you, then, to speak to M. D'Ormesson about this business, and to inform me of the time of this conversation so that I can respond to any question that you may be disposed to put to me on that subject. The concerns in which you are involved do not allow me to be sure of your response, although I believe that you would consent to my request. Moreover, in order not to be mistaken I spoke of the business to M. de Rayneval and told him that, if you would wish to grant me this favor, and if I could learn by Tuesday noon I would defer my departure for London and would await the result of the conference. He wrote me in turn. His letter has given me ground to believe that I would not be mistaken if with your assent I arranged to return here. I pointed out to him in my reply that M. D'Ormesson ought to be here Friday morning, and that I would meanwhile remain nearby. I mentioned also that I would stay until Saturday noon in order that you and M. D'Ormesson might choose the most suitable hour to talk about this business while I would be here within reach to explain such difficulties as might occur, because I imagine that neither you nor M. D'Ormesson have been adequately instructed in this subject. I begged M. Rayneval to communicate to you what I wrote him. But partly from accident on the one hand and a little forgetfulness on the other, one has failed to do so. To avoid such oversights for the present I am addressing myself at this time to you yourself.

The business at hand is very simple. I rest entirely in your hands. M. D'Ormesson will not leave here until Wednesday. If you could devote a few minutes of your time to speak with him of this business before his departure, and should you judge my presence necessary, I will be honored to be at your command should you let me know the moment. But on the other hand, if there is nothing more to do, you would render me a particular favor if you would have the kindness to let me know. If you would stop to consider the commitment that I have already undertaken in maintaining the promises and appearances of which I have spoken; when you consider that a greater loss of time could cause still another loss of an entire season, and all the disadvantages that could ensue from it, I flatter myself that you will not deny me this information; and that you will not think that, in asking this favor, I am lacking in the profound respect with which I have the honor of being, Sir, Your humble and most obedient servant,

JAMES JAY

ALS in French, translated by the editors, in CP EU 25: 329–30. Endorsed: ". . . request to comply with the promise made to him to support the plan to subsidize the American firms."

Lafayette, Jay's Self-Appointed "Political Aide-de-Camp," Takes on the Spaniards

[21 November 1782–20 February 1783]

Following the victory at Yorktown, Lafayette, having obtained permission from Congress, sailed for France at the end of December 1781. Congress instructed Secretary Livingston to notify Franklin that he was to employ Lafayette "in accelerating the supplies to be obtained from France."[1] The Marquis expanded his limited role, and was in frequent and close attendance at the conferences of the American Commissioners with Oswald during the fall of '82, acting in liaison with the French court.

Once the American Commissioners believed that they were on the verge of concluding a Preliminary Treaty with the British, they found less than a compelling need for the presence of Lafayette. Consequently, they were not disposed to deter the Marquis from accepting a commission to command the land forces in a Franco-Spanish expedition that d'Estaing was to lead against the British West Indies.[2] Lafayette delayed his departure for Brest until late November, wishing first to secure from the Americans an authorization for his departure. At a meeting with the Commissioners at Passy on 23 November, the Marquis produced a letter he had written Vergennes the day before[3] urging "instantaneous succor" for the United States and another addressed to the Americans and printed below. Neither document pleased the Commissioners. The letter to Vergennes, outlining American finances and stating the need for further French aid "nettled F[ranklin] as it seemed an Attempt to take to himself the Merit of obtaining the Loan if one should be procured."[4] Lafayette's letter to the Commissioners of the 21st, below, with its claim that he had been "detained" in Europe by JJ and Franklin "upon Political Accounts" irked both Commissioners, since it had been at the Marquis' own request that they had asked Congress to permit him to remain in France.[5]

Adams found his colleagues' irritation contagious, for his diary entry for 23 November contained this acid analysis of Lafayette's character: "This unlimited Ambition will obstruct his Rise. He grasps at all civil, political and military, and would be thought the Unum necessarium in every Thing. He has so much real Merit, such Family Supports, and so much favour at Court, that he need not recur to Artifice."[6] Accordingly, on the same day that the Marquise de Lafayette solicited JJ on her husband's behalf for a written authorization for his leave, the three Commissioners formally accommodated Lafayette in a letter releasing him from any diplomatic duties.[7]

Arrived at Cádiz, Lafayette was impatient at the fleet's delay and bored by idleness. He now pressed Vergennes for permission to use his presence in Spain to secure Spanish money for his adopted country, while being careful to communicate his new self-assumed role to his good friend JJ.[8] In turn, Carmichael welcomed Lafayette's assistance, which the latter, fervently hoping to secure Spain's formal recognition of the United States, rendered with his customary élan.[9]

Once Spain and France signed the Preliminaries with England on 20 January 1783, the armada assembled at Cádiz was broken up. Lafayette first made his peace with the Comte de Montmorin, Adrienne's uncle, who could not help having been affected by the prevailing gossip concerning the war hero's liaisons. Montmorin, a consummate diplomat, proved exceptionally helpful in the Marquis' dealings with the Spanish court.[10] Wearing the uniform and sword of an American major-general, Lafayette was graciously received at the Pardo by Charles III, who, the Frenchman reported, had "odd notions" about the American Revolution and its threat to the Spanish colonies.[11] In a series of meetings with Floridablanca, Lafayette drew from a reluctant First Minister an agreement to "abide for the present" by the Florida boundary fixed in the Separate Article, to accept Carmichael's credentials before the Marquis left Spain, and to present the Secretary of the American Mission to the King as soon as JJ could be informed and had signified his approval. That last qualification was dispensed with, however, as events moved too rapidly to await word from Paris. Floridablanca invited Carmichael to a dinner he was giving in Madrid for the ambassadorial corps, a function which Lafayette also attended.[12] The sudden haste to accept Carmichael was prompted at least as much out of fear that the much disliked Señor Jay would return to Madrid as by diplomatic necessities. As Montmorin later put it, JJ's manner had caused the Spaniards to bristle, while Carmichael's popularity in Spain made him an appropriate replacement for the absent peacemaker. Should Franklin be replaced, Montmorin counselled Vergennes, try to have JJ take over at Versailles, but keep him out of Spain.[13]

The Marquis, who considered himself JJ's "political aide-de-camp,"[14] rendered a full account of his mission. As JJ had foretold,[15] he secured no money, but merely elicited a promise on the part of the Spaniards to consider anew the territorial disputes with the United States. One tangible result was Carmichael's formal presentation at the Court as chargé d'affaires of the United States on 22 August.[16] What Lafayette's mission did prove was that Charles III and his Principal Minister could be persuaded to make an important concession to a highly placed aristocrat, a favor which they disdained bestowing upon commoners from a revolutionary republic. When on the fifth or sixth of March Lafayette visited JJ,[17] he apparently turned over to him an aide-mémoire, which he refers to in his 2 March letter to Secretary Livingston. That document is no longer found in JP.

[1]*JCC,* XXI, 1134–36 (23 Nov. 1781).

[2]Spain was unenthusiastic about D'Estaing's self-nomination. Vergennes to Montmorin, CP E 609: 464–65.

[3]Lafayette to Vergennes, 22 Nov. 1782, *RDC,* VI, 67–70.

[4]*AP,* III, 71.

[5]Franklin to Livingston, 25 June 1782, *RDC,* V, 510–13; JJ to Livingston, 25 June, see n. 16 of editorial note, "The Status of the Peacemaking," above. See also Louis Gottschalk, *Lafayette and the Close of the American Revolution* (Chicago, 1942), pp. 381–86.

[6]*AP,* III, 71.

[7]Noailles de Lafayette to JJ, 27 Nov.; JJ's reply, 28 Nov. 1782, both below. The American Commissioners to Lafayette, [27 Nov. 1782], below.

[8]Lafayette to JJ, 26 Dec. 1782, below; to Vergennes, 1 Jan. 1783, CP EU 23: 48; to Livingston, 5 Feb. 1783, *RDC,* VI, 238–39.

[9]Carmichael to Livingston, 21 Feb. 1783, *RDC,* VI, 259; Lafayette to Carmichael, 20 Jan. 1783, below, which was intended as much for the Spanish authorities as for Carmichael.

[10]Lafayette to JJ, 15 Feb. 1783, below.

[11]Lafayette to Livingston, 2 March 1783, *RDC,* VI, 268.

[12]Lafayette to Floridablanca, 19 Feb; Floridablanca to Lafayette, 22 Feb. 1783, PCC 175; Lafayette to Vergennes, 18 February, to Livingston, 2, 13 March; Montmorin to Vergennes, 18 Feb. 1783, CP E 610: 246–61; *RDC,* VI, 268–69, 294.

[13]Montmorin to Vergennes, 18 May 1783, CP E 610: 483–84.

[14]Lafayette to JJ, p. 518; to Livingston, 2 March 1783, *RDC,* VI, 269.

[15]See JJ to Lafayette, 19 Jan. 1783, below.

[16]See Carmichael to JJ, 23 Aug, 1783, below. Montmorin to Vergennes, 23 Aug. 1783, CP E 611: 159.

[17]See JJ to Lafayette, [5] March, below. While Lafayette informed Vergennes of the conciliatory disposition of Spain toward the U.S., Montmorin was more realistic about the likelihood of Spain's abandoning her long-standing policy of trade monopoly toward her colonies. Vergennes to Montmorin, 1 March, 1 April; Montmorin to Vergennes, 5 April 1783. CP E 610: 283, 392, 407–13.

Lafayette to Franklin, Adams, and Jay

Paris, 21 November 1782

Gentlemen,

Since the Early Period when I Had the Happiness to Be Adopted Among the Sons of America I ever Made it My Point to do that which I thought Would prove Useful to Her Cause or Agreeable to Her Citizens. After We Had Long Stood By ourselves, France did join in our Quarrell, and so Soon as Count d'Estaing's departure Made My presence Unnecessary, I Had a Permission to Return to France, Where, among things, I Endeavoured to impress this Court with the propriety to Send a Naval force, and an auxiliary Army to serve under the orders of General Washington. The plan of a descent in England Lengthened My negotiation,[1] the Succour was at Last Sent and Arrived at a Critical Period. It prevented Evil, But did not produce Any great immediate Good Untill that Naval Superiority which Had been promised was sent to co-operate With us, and Helped us in the Capture of Cornwallis.

This Event ended the Campaign in Virginia, and the Army I Had Commanded was of Course Separated. Congress gave me Leave to go to France and to Return at Such time as I should think proper. I had it in command to Make some Representations at this Court, and the General's particular instructions were By all Means to Bring a Naval and Land Assistance to Operate in our America.

Count de Grasse's defeat Having Ruined our plans, I now was despairing to fulfill the Intention of Congress and the Orders of my General, when it was proposed to me to Serve in the Army under the direction of Count d'Estaing. This Has Appeared to me the only Way I had to serve my Views. I Had the Honor to Consult you About it, and Upon Your Approbation of the measure, I consented to accompany Count d'Estaing in His Expeditions, provided it was in my Capacity and Ever Under the Uniform of an American officer, who Being for a time Borrowed from the United States Will obey the first order or take the first Opportunity to Rejoin His Colours.

Had I not been detained by you, Gentlemen, upon Political Accounts which you Have Been Pleased to Communicate to Congress, I would long ago Have Returned to America. But I was with you of Opinion that my Presence Might Be Useful, and Since it Appears Matters are not Ripe for a Treaty, My first Wish is Now to Return to America with such force as May Expell the Enemy from the United States, serve the Views of Congress, and Assist your Political Opinions. When or How this May Be Offered I am not yet Able to determine or I would not be at Liberty to Mention. But, However certain I have been of your Opinion, I think it a Mark of Respect to Congress not to Depart untill I have Your official Approbation of the Measure.

With the Highest Respect, I have the Honor to be, Gentlemen, Your Obedient Humble Servant,

(signed) LAFAYETTE

Tr in NN: Bancroft: American IV, 278 1/2.

[1]For Lafayette's role in the ill-fated cross-Channel invasion project of 1779, see *Peacemakers*, pp. 28, 35–36, 42.

From Noailles de Lafayette

Paris, Wednesday, 27 November 1782

I wish, Sir, I could have had the honor of seeing you yesterday, since M. De la Fayette, before departing, left me several messages for you. But since your affairs prevented you from giving me the pleasure of delivering them myself, I take the course of writing to you since the mail for Brest leaves today.

M. De la Fayette asked me to tell you that according to the conversation with M. Bancroft he did not feel obliged to put off his departure, M. Bancroft having told him that that was your opinion. He told me afterwards that should you have to write to him, he begged you to be good enough to give me your letter, advising me only if your intention was to have it sent by mail that is to run the risk of its being unsealed and read en route, or else to send it by a safe and secret way that he indicated to me. It would perhaps arrive a little later, but certainly before he sails.

I await your reply, Sir, and I do not plan to seal my letter for Brest before receiving yours. Your good wishes for M. De la Fayette convinces me that you appreciate what my sorrow must be at this moment. So I would be delighted to have the honor of seeing you if your affairs permit it. You also know, I trust, Sir, how tenderly I share the sentiments of M. De la Fayette, to render justice to all those matters with which I have the honor of being, Sir, your very humble and very obedient servant,

NOAILLES DE LA FAYETTE

Permit me, I beg you, to extend my fond regards to Madame Jay. I believe her too sensitive and she shows me too much kindness for me not to be assured that she would wish to share my sorrow.

ALS in French, trans. by the editors. Endorsed.

JOHN JAY, JOHN ADAMS, AND BENJAMIN FRANKLIN TO LAFAYETTE

[Paris, 27 November 1782]

Sir,

We have recieved the Letter you did us the Honor to write on the 25th[1] Inst.

Our Country has had early and repeated Proofs both of your Readiness and abilities to do her Service. The Prospect of an inactive Campaign in america, induced us to adopt the opinion, that you might be more useful here than there, especially in Case the Negotiation for peace on the Part of France and England, should <be> <(as there was Reason to hope)> be committed to your management, for Your Knowledge of our affairs, and attachment to our Interests, might have been very advantageous to us on such an occasion. But as an opportunity now offers of your being instrumental in producing a Co-operation, which would probably put a glorious and speedy Termination to the War in america, we for our part, perfectly approve of your going with Count D'Estaing in the manner proposed.

We have the Honor to be etc.

Dft in hand of JJ. Endorsed by JJ: "Dr. of joint Letter to Marqs. Fayette. App[rize]d verb[ally]." Dated 28 Nov. 1782 in *RDC*, VI, 89.

[1]Error for 21st. See letter of that date, above.

TO NOAILLES DE LAFAYETTE

[Paris, 28 November 1782]

Madam,

<Mr. Jay is> I am exceedingly mortified <by the> at <having been> <Yesterday> being obliged to deny <him> my self the Honor of waiting upon <the Marchioness de la Fayette> Yesterday; <for he was> having been engaged with Gentlemen on public Business the whole Day and Evening.[1]

The Letter which the Marquis expected from the american commissioners was sent to him yesterday, and <Mr. Jay> I will devote <the first> my first Leisure Hour <he has> to writing to <the Marquis> him again.

<Mr. Jay> My attachment to the Marquis will always <induce> lead <him> me to seek Opportunities of manifesting it, and <he> I regret the Pain which his Departure must occasion <by

occasion> to the affectionate Sensibility of so amiable a Lady. Remember nevertheless Madam that he is gone to give you new proofs of his deserving you, and to <gather Laurels> <add to> <More Laurels gather fresh Laurels> bring fresh Laurels to a House long accustomed to expect and to merit them.

<Mr. Jay will feel> I shall feel unhappy until <he> I shall have the Honor of recieving your Commands, and I shall endeavour some Time to Day to breake away from my Colleagues, and to assure you in Person, of the perfect Respect and Esteem with which I have the Honor to be.

Dft. Endorsed: ". . . To Marchons. Fayette, in ansr. to 27 Nov. 1782."

[1]On the 27th JJ was tied up with Oswald, Franklin, and Adams most of the afternoon and evening, and dined with Adams. *AP*, III, 78.

FROM LAFAYETTE

Cadiz, 26 December 1782

Dear Sir,

My Letters to Doctor Franklin Have Hitherto Acquainted you With Every thing that Related to Me. I Have Been With the Convoy As far as Cape St. Mary, and then I came in a frigat to this Port. On My Way I have dispatched a Vessel to General Washington, and Have Communicated Particulars of our Situation, as well as Proposals for Military Operations.[1]

The Convoy I came With is Coming in, a Good Number of French and Spanish Ships are getting Ready, the French Division at Gibralter is going to Embark, so that We intend to Sail With a powerful Reinforcement. On my Arrival at this Place, I Have Been told that our American Preliminaries are Agreed Upon, for which I Heartily Rejoice With You, But Am Sorry to Hear that My Lord Shelburne Has Not Been Candid with the French.[2] Should He Think that America May Forget Treaties, he will Be Much Disappointed. This May Be for the United States a New Opportunity to Shine in Their Political Character. In Case it Becomes Necessary to Go on With Military Operations, I very much Hope They will Be Successful.

In the first Moments I Saw Count d'Estaing He Asked for my Opinion Upon the Present Political Situation of our Affairs. It Appears that the Spanish Court, and Count de Montmorin Himself Wanted Him to take those Informations. My Answer Was that America Had Made Treaties, and Would Stand By them, That Her Steadiness was Equal to Her Spirit, But that Unless they Give Monney, No Efforts Can Be

Expected. Upon this Monney Affair, I am very Urging. Count d'Estaing Has Wrote to Count de Montmorin a private letter Which is to Be Laid Before the Spanish Court. I Have wrote one to Carmichael By Post Which is to Be Opened by Count de Florida Blanca. I Have So far Conquered My Hatred to Count O'Reilly as to Speak freely With Him Upon this Matter. I do not Much Expect from the Attempt; but As No American plenipotentiary was Committed, As Limits and Every Political idea was out of the Way, I Have thought there was not Amiss in seizing the present Opportunity to tempt them into an offer to Send us Monney from the Havanna. I do not Believe it Will Succeed, But there is No Harm in the Trial.

You Will Greatly oblige me, My dear Sir, to keep me Acquainted With Everything that is interesting to America. My Heart is in it, You Know, and your Communications Will be Very Well come. I live with Mr. Harrison[3] and Am Very Happy in His Acquaintance. But Your Letter Had Better Be Sent to Madame de Lafayette With a Particular Recommendation.

Be pleased to Remember me Most Affectionately to Mr. Franklin, Mr. Adams, and Mr. Laurens, and to let them know Any thing in this letter that Appears Worth Communicating. My Best Compliments Wait Upon Doctor Bancroft.

I Request, My Dear Sir, You Will Be So kind as to Present My Best Respects to Mrs. Jay and to Receive the Hearty Assurance of the High and Affectionate Regard I Have the Honor to Be With Dear Sir Your obedient Humble Servant,

LAFAYETTE

ALS. Endorsed: ". . . Recd. 18 Jan. 1783. Incomplete and erroneous in *HPJ,* III, 11–12.

[1]See Lafayette to Franklin, 4, 6 (ALS in PPAmP: Franklin XXVI) Dec. 1782, Hale, *Franklin,* II, 231–32; 8 Dec., *RDC,* VI, 120. Lafayette to Washington, 4 Dec. 1782, Louis Gottschalk, ed., *The Letters of Lafayette to Washington* (New York, 1944), pp. 257–58.

[2]Apparently a criticism of Shelburne for not keeping France informed of the negotiations with America. However, the British did seek to reassure Rayneval that the fishing rights granted the Americans did not pose a future conflict in the area that was being set aside for the French fisheries, while being careful not to disclose the secret article. Rayneval to Vergennes, 4 Dec. 1782, CP A 539: 168.

[3]Richard Harrison.

To Lafayette

Rouen, 19 January 1783

Dear Sir,

Accept my thanks for your obliging Letter of the 26 December last, which the Marchioness was so kind as to send me Yesterday. I congratulate you on your safe arrival at Cadiz, and you have my best wishes that the same good Fortune you have hitherto experienced, may continue to attend you.

The State of my Health making a Change of Air, and exercise advisable, I left Paris ten Days ago on an Excursion into Normandy. Hence I suppose it has happened that I have neither heard of nor seen your Letters to Dr. Franklin.

If I am not mistaken a Copy of the American preliminaries has been sent to Spain; and I flatter myself that Count de Montmorin will think them perfectly consistent with our Engagements to our allies. It appears to me singular that any Doubts should be entertained of American good Faith; for as it has been tried and remains inviolate they cannot easily be explained on Principles honorable to those who entertain them. America has so often repeated and reiterated her Professions and Assurances of Regard to the Treaty alluded to, that I hope she will not impair her Dignity by making any more of them, but leave the continued uprightness of her Conduct to inspire that Confidence which it seems she does not yet possess, although she has always merited.[1]

Our warmest acknowledgments are due to you for the Zeal you manifest to serve America at all Times and in all places, but Sir I have little Expectation that your Plan of a Spanish Loan will succeed. I Confess that I am far from being anxious about it. In my opinion America can with no Propriety accept Favors from Spain < and for my own part I would rather borrow money to repay what we have recieved from her, than submit to pick up any Crums that may fall from her Table >.

My absence from Paris has deprived me of the means of Information, and therefore I cannot at present gratify either your wishes or my own on that Head. God knows whether or no we shall have peace—a variety of contradictory Reports daily reach me, but they deserve little Credit. It is again said that Charlestown is Evacuated. That may be. It is also said the Enemy have left New York, but I adhere to my former Opinion, and do not believe a word of it.[2] Mrs. Jay writes me[3] that Mr. Oswald is gone to London, but for what Purpose I am ignorant. Thus my dear Sir are we held in a State of Suspence which nothing but Time can remove. I propose to return next week to Paris and shall then write to you again.

Adieu. I am witn perfect Respect and Esteem, Dear Sir, Your most obedient Servant.

Dft in RAWC. Endorsed by JJ. *HPJ,* III, 25–26, does not include material deleted in the Dft.

[1]On 2 Jan. 1783 a formal declaration was drafted in French at Versailles to be made by the American Commissioners affirming their adherence to the French alliance; a final version bore the date of 20 Jan. 1783, "done at Passy," and was apparently intended to accompany the Declaration of the Cessation of Hostilities which the Americans issued on the occasion of the signing of the Franco-Spanish Preliminaries with Great Britain. (See 20 Feb. 1783, above). Whether Franklin was involved cannot now be ascertained. A fair inference of the attitude of the American Commissioners can be drawn from JJ's remarks in this letter. Evidently JJ's colleagues concurred, for the unsigned draft still reposes in the Quai d'Orsay. See Declaration of the American Commissioners, Cs in French, 2 and 20 Jan. 1783, in CP EU 23: 14–15, 70–71. That JJ had no thought that the Preliminaries constituted a "separate peace" was explicitly asserted by him in a letter to Stephen Sayre, 15 Dec. 1782, Dft in JP; *HPJ,* III, 25.

[2]Charleston was evacuated on 14 Dec. 1782; New York, on 25 Nov. 1783.

[3]SLJ to JJ, 17 Jan. 1783, below.

Lafayette to William Carmichael

Cadiz, 20 January 178[3][1]

Dear Sir,

Your letter of the 14th[2] has this day come to hand. The occasion of it I lament, but it becomes my duty to answer.

From an early period I had the happiness to rank among the Foremost in the American Revolution. In the affection and confidence of the People, I am proud to say, I have a great share. Congress honors me so far as to direct I am to be consulted by their European Ministers; which circumstances I do not mention out of Vanity, but only to shew that in giving my Opinion I am called upon by dictates of Honor and duty which it becomes me to obey.

The measure being right, it is beneath me to wait for a private Opportunity. Public concerns have a great weight with me but nothing upon Earth can intimidate me into Selfish considerations. To my Opinion you are entitled, and I offer it with the Freedom of a heart that ever shall be independent.

To France you owe a great deal; to others you owe nothing. As a Frenchman, whose heart is glowing with patriotism, I enjoy the part France has acted, and the connection she has made. As an American I acknowledge the obligation and in that I think true Dignity consists, but dignity forbade our sending abroad Political forlorn Hopes, and I ever objected to the condescention; the more so, as a French Alliance had secured their Allies to you and because America is more likely to receive advances than to need throwing herself at other People's head.

The particulars of the Negociation with Spain I do not dwell upon. In my Opinion, they were wrong, but I may be mistaken. Certain it is that an exchange of Ministers ought to have been, and now an exchange of powers must be upon an equal footing. What England has done is nothing, either to the Right or to the Mode. The Right consisted in the People's will; the Mode depends upon a consciousness of American dignity. But if Spain has hitherto declined to acknowledge what the Elder Branch of Bourbon thought honorable to declare, yet will it be too strange that England ranks before her in the date and the benefits of the acknowledgement.

There are more powers than you know of, who are making advances to America. Some of them I have personally recieved; but you easily guess that no treaty would be so pleasing as the one with Spain. The three natural Enemies of Britain should be strongly united. The French Alliance is everlasting, but such a treaty between the Friends of France is a new tie of confidence and affection. The Spaniards are slow in their motions but strong in their attachments. From a regard to them, but still more out of regard to France, we must have more patience with them than with any other Nation in Europe.

It has hitherto been kind not to help Spain in exposing the weak side of her policy; so that when England is encouraged by a want of Union in her Enemies, no part of the faults be laid upon the United States.

But peace is likely to be made, and how then can the man who advised against your going at all, propose your remaining at a Court where you are not decently treated? Congress, I hope, and through them the whole nation, do not intend their Dignity to be trifled with; and for my part I have no inclination to betray the confidence of the American People. I expect we are going to have peace, and I expect Spain is going to act by you with propriety. But should they hesitate to treat you as a public Servant of the United States, then, however disagreeable is the task, Mr. Carmichael had better go to Paris, where France may stand a Mediator, and through that Generous and Common Friend we may come to the wished for connection with the Court of Spain.

With an high regard and sincere affection I have the honor to be Dear Sir, Your Obedient Humble Servant.

C. With omissions in *RDC*, VI, 222–23.

[1]Misdated; should read "1783."

[3]Not located, but mentioned by Lafayette in following letter.

FROM LAFAYETTE

Madrid, 15 February 1783

Dear Sir,

I am Happy in this private Opportunity to write to You, and Have long Wanted Safe Means to do it Confidentially. The Same Reason, I suppose, Has prevented My Hearing from You to this Moment. But as I am just Arrived at Madrid, and the Gentleman Who Carries this is just Setting out I shall only Write a few Lines.

My feelings on the Occasion of a General Peace are Better known to You than I Could Express them. They are Consistent With My Zeal for Our Cause, and My love to America, and More I Cannot Say.

On My leaving Paris I Had Great Hopes of our plans. On My Arriving at Cadiz, I found they Had Succeeded Beihond [sic] My Expectations. Nay, Besides the More Advantageous Cooperation With America, particulars of which I will Relate, I Had Some Hopes Monney Might be Got for that Purpose. Upon this I wrote to Mr. Carmichael. I Had the Honor to Give You an Account of My Conduct and ideas on the Occasion, But Your Answer Has Not Come to Hand.[1]

Upon the Prospect of a Peace, I Had a Letter from Mr. Carmichael Wherein He Entreats My Advice upon His future Conduct. He Had No letters from Paris. My Advice Being Asked for, I Gave it in a letter, a Copy of Which I Enclose, and Sent it By post for the Perusal of the Court of Spain and probably of the Court of Versailles with Spanish Constructions Upon it.[2]

I am told El Campo on His journey to Paris is instructed to Settle Matters with You, and I wish it at last May Be Upon a proper footing.[3]

I Had determined Upon Going to America, But Had A letter from Mr. Carmichael Wherein He Entreats My Coming to Madrid, and Says I May Be Useful in Reasoning with this Ministry. I Gave up My favorite Plan, and Contenting Myself With Sending a letter to Congress,[4] I Have Posted of[f] to Madrid Where Now I am and Had only a Short Conference with the french Ambassador, and an other with Mr. Carmichael Whose ideas, I am Happy to find, Coincide With Mine on the line We ought to follow. In the few days I Remain Here I Would Wish 1st to induce this Ministry to Give El Campo liberal Instructions, 2dly to See that the American Charge d'Affaires Be Officially Received, 3dly to Advise their Proposing to You a loan of Monney. My Expectations are very small, But I Have Been invited Here. The little I can do I must Exert to the Utmost. Whatever disposition I find them in, I Will Hasten to Paris, and Give You Every Intelligence I Can Collect. I look Upon Myself as Your Political Aid de Camp. If I may Any How Serve America, I am Happy and satisfied.

At all Events, When My Advice is Asked for, No Court, No Country, No Consideration Can Induce Me to Advise a thing that is not Consistent With the dignity of the United States.

By the Month of June I Intend taking up Again My Plan of a Voyage to America. Until that time I Have Nothing to do, and towards <start> the First of March, I will offer Myself to You With Spanish Intelligence, and a Great Zeal to do Any thing that May Serve the Public.

I Beg My Best Respects to Be Presented to Your Colleagues. I do not write to them, and in this letter They May See What You think worth Communicating. My Most Respectful Compliments Wait Upon Mrs. Jay. I Have Hardly time Enough left to write a line to Mde. de Lafayette, and in Great Haste Subscribe Myself Most Respectfully and Affectionately Yours,

LAFAYETTE

P.S. Mr. Littlepage Having Been pleased to Come into My family for the Expedition, I Have Advised Him to Go with me on My journey to Paris. His Voyage to America is But little differed [sic] and it May prove Agreable to Him to know the Best part of france.

ALS. Endorsed: "... Recd. 28 Feb. 1783." Enclosure: Lafayette to William Carmichael, 20 Jan. 178[3], immediately above.

[1]See above, Lafayette to JJ, 26 Dec. 1782, and JJ's reply of 19 Jan. 1783.

[2]Immediately above.

[3]Bernardo del Campo had been named Spain's provisional envoy to Great Britain. Del Campo journeyed to London by way of Paris, bringing further instructions relating to the peace negotiations. Danvila y Collado, *Reinado de Carlos III,* V, 389–94.

[4]Lafayette to the President of Congress (Boudinot), 5 Feb. 1783. ALS and duplicate LS in PCC 156, pp. 312–14, 332–35; *RDC,* VI, 237–38.

To Lafayette

Paris, Wednesday Noon, [5] March 1783

Mr. Jay presents his <respec[tful]> sincere Congratulations to the Marquis de la Fayette on his safe Return to Paris, and is much obliged by his Intention of visiting him this Evening or To morrow morning. As Mr. Jay is engaged <to dine, and> to pass this Evening abroad, he must be deprived of the Honor of the Marquis visit until Tomorrow, when he will be very happy to see <the Marquis> him. He begs his respectful Compliments to the Marchioness, in whose Joy on this occasion both he and Mrs. Jay sincerely partake.

Dft. Endorsed.

Congress Debates the Commissioners' Conduct

12–25 March 1783

The packet *Washington* reached Philadelphia on 12 March with the Commissioners' joint letter of 13 December and the Preliminary Treaty of 30 November 1782. For four days the Congress read and debated the dispatches and treaty text. While it was agreed that the terms obtained were "on the whole extremely liberal," the "separate and secret manner" in which the American Commissioners had conducted their negotiations with the British, along with the separate secret article, prompted some rather severe remarks on the part of the Gallican faction, remarks notably directed against JJ.[1] Sharing Congress' critical views, Livingston asked that body on 18 March for directions in drafting a reply to the American Commissioners. He requested instructions on three points: (1) He wanted to be instructed to provide the French with a copy of the secret article; (2) to be authorized to inform the American Commissioners why Congress had him reveal that article, while requesting them to accept the northern boundary of West Florida described in that article regardless of which nation held that area at the end of the war; and, finally, (3) he requested a Congressional ruling that the Preliminary Articles were not to become effective until Great Britain concluded its peace treaty with France.[2]

Congress referred Livingston's three resolutions to a five-man committee (Abraham Clark, Nathaniel Gorham, Alexander Hamilton, John Rutledge, James Wilson).[3] In its report of 21 March, largely reflecting the ideas of one of the committeemen, Alexander Hamilton, and the comments of Richard Peters of Pennsylvania made in open debate on the 19th, the committee recommended that the Commissioners be thanked for their "zeal and firmness," but instructed to communicate the provisions of the secret article to the French court and, if possible, exclude that article from the treaty with Britain. If the article could not be omitted, then the boundaries outlined therein were to apply to whatever power should receive West Florida in the peace settlement. Finally, Livingston was to inform the Commissioners of Congress' regret that the Preliminary Articles had not been "communicated to the Court of France before they were signed."[4]

The sharp debate continued through Monday, the 24th, without agreement being reached before adjournment. Meantime, on the previous day word reached Philadelphia of the signing of the Preliminary Treaties between Britain and the co-belligerents on 20 January. Congress did not meet on the 25th, and on that day Livingston, despairing of obtaining "any express decision" from that body, wrote the letter below.

[1]Madison, "Notes of Debates, 12–15 Mar. 1783, *MP,* VI, 328–33; *JCC,* XXV, 924–26.

[2]Livingston to President of Congress (Boudinot), 18 Mar. 1783. LS in PCC 110, II, 41–53; *RDC,* VI, 313–16.

[3]*JCC,* XXV, 936; *MP,* VI, 357–69.

[4]*MP,* VI, 375–78; *JCC,* XXV, 714–15.

Robert R. Livingston to the American Commissioners

Philadelphia, 25 March 1783

Gentlemen,

I am now to acknowledge the favor of your joint letter by the Washington,[1] together with a copy of the preliminary articles; both were laid before Congress. The articles have met with their warmest approbation and have been generally seen by the people in the most favorable point of view.

The steadiness manifested in not treating without an express acknowledgment of your independence previous to a treaty is approved, and it is not doubted but it accelerated that declaration. The boundaries are as extensive as we have a right to expect, and we have nothing to complain of with respect to the fisheries. My sentiments as to English debts you have in a former letter.[2] No honest Man could wish to withhold them. A little forbearance in British creditors till people have recovered in part from the losses sustained by the war will be necessary to render this article palatable, and indeed to secure more effectually the debt. The article relative to the loyalists is not quite so accurately expressed as I could wish it to have been. What, for instance, is intended by *real British subjects?* It is clear to me that it will operate nothing in their favor in any State in the Union, but as you made no secret of this to the British commissioners, they will have nothing to charge you with; and indeed, the whole clause seems rather to have been inserted to appease the clamor of these poor wretches than to satisfy their wants. Britain would have discovered more candor and magnanimity in paying to them three months' expense of the war establishment, which would have been an ample compensation for all their losses and left no germ of dissatisfaction to bud and bloom and ripen into discontents here. Another mad administration may think the noncompliance of the Legislatures with the recommendations of Congress on this subject a sufficient cause for giving themselves and us new troubles. You, however, were perfectly right in agreeing to the article—the folly was theirs, who did not either insist upon more or give up this <nothing>.

But, gentlemen, though the issue of your treaty has been successful, though I am satisfied that we are much indebted to your firmness and perseverance, to your accurate knowledge of our situation and of our wants for this success, yet I feel no little pain at the <extreme> distrust <you have> manifested in the management of it; particularly in signing the treaty without communicating it to the court of Versailles till after the signature, and in concealing the separate article from it even when signed. I have examined, with the most minute attention, all the reasons assigned in your several letters to justify these suspicions. I confess they do not appear to strike me so forcibly as they have done you; and it gives me pain that the character for candor and fidelity to its engagements which should always characterize a great people should have been impeached <by them> thereby. The concealment was, in my opinion, absolutely unnecessary; for, had the court of France disapproved the terms you had made after they had been agreed upon, they <certainly> could not have acted so absurdly as to counteract you at that late day, and thereby put themselves <so far> in the power of an enemy who would certainly betray them and perhaps justify you in making <a separate peace> terms for yourselves.

The secret article is no otherwise important than as it carries in it the seeds of enmity to the court of Spain, and shows a marked preference for an open enemy. It would, in my opinion, have been much better to have fixed on the same boundaries for West Florida, into whatever hands it fell, without showing any preference, or rendering concealment necessary; since all the arguments in favor of the cession to England would then have operated with equal force, and nothing have been lost by it; for there can be no doubt that, whether Florida shall at the close of the war be ceded to England or to Spain, it will be ceded as it *was held* by Britain. The separate article is not, I suppose, by this time a secret in Europe; it can hardly be considered as such in America. The treaty was sent out to the General, with this article annexed, by Sir Guy Carleton, without the smallest injunction of secrecy.[3] So that, I dare say, it has been pretty generally read at headquarters. Congress still conceal it here. I feel for the embarrassment explanations on this subject must subject you to, when this secret is known to your allies.

I intended to have submitted this letter to Congress, so that you might have had their views upon this subject, but I find there is not the least prospect of obtaining any direction upon it in time to send by this conveyance, if at all. I leave you to collect their sentiments, as far as I know them, from the following state of their proceedings: After your joint and separate letters and the journals had be[en] submitted to them by me, and had been read, they were referred back to me to report, when I wrote them the enclosed letter No. 1. When the letter was taken into consideration the motions No. 2, No. 3, [and] No. 4, were made and debated a whole day, after which the letter and motions were committed, and a report brought in, No. 5. This was under consideration two days, when the arrival of a vessel from Cadiz, with letters from the Count Destaing and the Marquis De Lafayette, containing accounts that preliminaries were signed, induced many members to think it would be improper to proceed in the report, and in that state it remains without any express decision.[4] From this you will draw your own inferences.

I make no apologys for the part I have taken in this business. I am satisfied you < r own integrity > will readily acquit me for having discharged what I conceived my duty, upon such a view of things as you presented to me. In declaring my sentiments freely, I invite you to treat me with equal candor in your Letters, and, in sending original papers, I guard against misrepresentations that might give you pain. Upon the whole, I have the pleasure of assuring you that the services you have rendered your country in bringing this business to a happy issue are very gratefully received by your Country, however we may differ in sentiments about the mode of doing it.

I am sorry that the extreame negligence of the different States has prevented, and will probably long prevent, my being able to send you a state of the < ravages > injury done to real property, and the number of slaves destroyed and carried off by the British troops and their allies, though no pains have been or shall be wanting on my part to urge them to it.[5] I have the honor to be, gentlemen, With very great respect and esteem, Your Most Obedient Humble Servant.

LbkC in PCC 118. Endorsed: ". . . To the Honorable John Adams, Benjamin Franklyn, John Jay, Henry Lawrance, Ministers plenipotentiary for concluding a peace, etc." Dft in NN: Livingston Family Papers: Robert R. Livingston. Cs in MHi: Dana and Adams, reel 360; Lbk version in *RDC,* VI, 338–40.

[1]For the Commissioners' joint letter of 13 Dec. 1782, see above.

[2]See Livingston to Franklin, 6 Jan. 1783 (*RDC,* VI, 198–200), wherein he stated: "English debts have not, that I know of, been forfeited, unless it be in one State,

and I should be extremely sorry to see so little integrity in my countrymen as to render the idea of withholding them a general one; however, it would be well to say nothing about them, if it can conveniently be done."

[3]On 13 March, Carleton and Digby dispatched to Washington a copy of the treaty with a request that he should forward it to Congress "in the most speedy manner." Washington's dispatch enclosing a copy of the Carleton-Digby letter and the enclosed treaty was read in Congress, 24 March. Carleton and Digby to Washington, 19 March 1783, DLC: Washington 4, reel 90; Washington to President of Congress (Boudinot), 21 March 1783, in PCC 152, XI, 179, with endorsement indicating date of receipt; *GWF,* XXVI, 249.

[4]The enclosures were: No. 1, Livingston to the President of Congress, 18 March 1783; No. 2, Hugh Williamson's motion of 19 March; No. 3, Richard Peters' motion of the same date; No. 4, Hamilton's motion of the same date; and No. 5, the committee report of 21–22 March, dealing with the three earlier documents. Enclosure Cs with their numbers in MHi: Adams, reel 360, following Livingston's letter of 25 March.

[5]See Livingston's Circular letters to the Governors of 12 Nov. 1781, 12 Sept. 1782, and 18 March 1783, and his letter to Governor Trumbull, 22 Jan. 1782. LbkCs in PCC 119; *RDC,* IV, 839; V, 123, 720; VI, 326. According to a marginal note in the Foreign Affairs Domestic Letterbook, only Connecticut had returned the required statistics by March 1783. PCC 118, note to letter of 18 March.

To Matthew Ridley

Paris, 28 March 1783

I well remember that you consulted me, I think in August and September last, about the Propriety of sending to America a Supply of Arms and Cloathing for the State of Maryland. Although it had then become somewhat probable that another Campaign would be prevented by a Peace, yet it was not certain; and I was clearly of Opinion that even the fairest Prospect of it, ought not to relax our Preparations for war, but on the contrary that they ought to be continued with unremitted Vigor to the very signing of the Treaty. I therefore advised you in the most explicit Terms to send out the Supplies in Question, and was happy to find that you had procured the Means of doing it.

With sincere Esteem and Regard I am, Dear Sir, Your most obedient and very humble Servant,

JOHN JAY

ALS in MHi: Ridley.

To John Adams

Sunday, 10 O'Clock, n.d. [March 1783]

On calling this Moment for my Man Manuel to comb me, I am told he is gone to shew my Nephew the Fair. I fear they will have so many fine Things and Raree Shows to see and admire, that my Head will remain in *Statu quo* till afternoon, and consequently our intended Visit to Count Sarsfield be postponed. Thus does Tyrant Custom sometimes hold us by a *Hair,* and thus do ridiculous Fashions make us dependent on Valets, and the Lord knows who. Adieu my Dear Sir, yours sincerely,

J. Jay

ALS in MHi: Adams, reel 359, undated; Dft in JP is endorsed by JJ: "To Mr. Adams, March 1783."

To Montmorin

Paris, 3 April 1783

As the Letter you did me the Honor to write by Marquis d[e la] Fayette makes no mention of some long Letters from me to you and the Chevalier, I am convinced that they have miscarried.[1] I should sooner have thought so if the Channel through which they were sent had not been such as to render such accidents very rare and improbable.

It seems too that you have heard nothing from me about the Peace. This must appear no less singular to you than it would to me if I had not heretofore experienced many similar mortifications from the Post office.

The Conversation I have had with the Marquis was very interesting. He carries his Zeal for America where ever he goes. When we meet I will repeat some of the civil things he said of you.

We have not had a Line from Congress since the arrival of the Preliminaries in America. The Councils of Britain still continue deranged. When the definitive Treaties will be signed is uncertain. It is said that witnesses to the Ex[ecutio]n of them are requested from Vienna and Petersborough.

I shall be very glad to see you here, for in my opinion your Talents may be as useful at Versailles as at Madrid.

I shall request the Favor of the Countess de Montmorin to give this Letter a place with her Dispatches. I have the honor to be with great

Respect and Attachment Your Excellencys Most obedient and very humble Servant.

Dft.

[1]Montmorin's letter of 22 Feb. 1783 is above. Only a Dft of an early letter, 26 June 1782, of JJ's to Montmorin is extant in JP (ALS in CP E 608: 405–06), as is a Dft of JJ to Bourgoing, 26 Sept. 1782 (E in NN: Bancroft: American IV, 171).

To George Washington

Paris, 6 April 1783

Dear Sir,

It is most certain that the Letters alluded to in your Excellency's of the 18 October last (which with sundry post Marks was sent to my Brother) have all miscarried.[1] The Sea, or the Enemy, or the unceasing and jealous attention of the French and Spanish Governments to American Letters and papers may in this as in many other Instances have been unkind to me.

I think the Motto of *si recte facies* on one of the continental Bills may be changed for *recte fecisti.*[2] You have saved your Country, and lived to see her blessed with Liberty and peace. As an American I present you my thanks, and as a friend my Congratulations.

Notwithstanding the favorable Aspect of our affairs, I doubt the Propriety of disbanding the army until all the foreign forces in our Country shall be removed from it. The Experience of ages recommends Caution on this Head.

It is very evident to me that the encreasing Power of America is a serious object of Jealousy to France and Spain as well as Britain. I verily believe they will secretly endeavour to foment Divisions among us,[3] and I think it highly expedient that we should proceed to settle the Boundaries of such of the States as have Disputes about them, and endeavour to secure the Continuance of Harmony and Union by carefully removing such Causes of Dissention as may from Time to Time arise. I write thus freely, from a persuasion that this Letter will go safe. Mr. Mason[4] of Virginia will be the Bearer of it.

Mrs. Jay speakes of your Happiness and rejoices in it. We both request the favor of you to make our Compliments and Congratulations to Mrs. Washington. There are many here who expect to see you in Europe, but I think they don't know You.

With constant and perfect Esteem and Regard I have the Honor to be, Dear Sir, Your most obedient and very humble Servant,

JOHN JAY

ALS in DLC: Washington, vol. 218, p. 132. Dft in JP.

[1]Washington's letter of 18 Oct. 1782 contained this comment: "Not having received from your Excellency, during the last Winter or summer, the acknowledgment of any Letters, except of my public Dispatches of October last, I apprehend that some private Letters which I have had the pleasure of addressing to you since that time, have miscarried." *GWF,* XXV, 274–75.

[2]JJ proposes changing the phrase "If you do right" (Horace, *Epistles* 1.1.59–60) to "You have done well."

[3]An asterisk later added by Jared Sparks, who noted at the bottom of the page: "Mr. Jay is a man of suspicions."

[4]George Mason, Jr. (1753–96), eldest son of George Mason of Gunston Hall, who went to Europe in 1779 when poor health forced him to resign from military service. Kate Mason Rowland, *The Life of George Mason, 1725–92* [New York, 1964), I, 293, 314, 320. As late as 13 June, JJ wrote Washington that Mason was carrying a letter from him. ALS in DLC: Washington, vol. 22, p. 36 (sentence omitted from *HPJ,* III, 50, and *WJ,* II, 119).

To Elias Boudinot

Passy, 11 June 1783
private

Dear Sir,

You will I hope recieve this Letter from the Hands of Doctor Bancroft,[1] whom I take the Liberty of recommending as well as introducing to your Excellency. I have had the Pleasure of being intimately acquainted with this Gentleman, for this Year past, and assure you[2] that in the Course of it, he has to my Knowledge been a useful and zealous friend to America. His long Residence in this Country, and his acquaintance with[3] our Affairs in Europe from the Beginning of the War, enable him to afford you much interesting Information.

I have within a few Days past recieved a Letter from your Nephew[4] at Madeira, desiring to be appointed Consul there by the American Minister here, until Congress shall be pleased to pass some Resolution on the Subject. I enclose a Copy of that Letter and of my answer to it.

When I consider the Circumstances under which our Ancestors settled in America, and recollect what I have heard of the Friendship which subsisted between them, I find myself heartily[5] disposed to serve this young Gentleman, and to act a Part towards him which I am sure would have been exceedingly agreable to my Parents, who always expressed the most friendly Sentiments of the Families from which his Father descended.

I have the Honor to be with great Esteem and Regard, Dear Sir, Your most obedient and humble Servant,

JOHN JAY

FROM JOHN MARSDEN PINTARD

Madeira, 19 April 1783

Sir,

Having been directed by my worthy Uncle Elias Boudinot Esq. (now President of Congress) to appeal in Behalf of and render every assistance to Americans who by the Fortune of War, were brought to this Place, I accordingly on every occasion, when any of my unfortunate Countrymen were brought in here, assisted them, not only with my advice but likewise my Purse; particularly in the Case of Capt. Stewart belonging to Baltimore in Maryland, who was taken and put on Shore here, together with his whole Crew consisting of 12 Men, who applyed to the french Consul at this Place to support them, and procure them a Passage to Lisbon, but he told them he could not do any thing of the Kind unless they entered into the french Service; which Proposition as much surprized me as Capt. Stewart. I then told him not to make himself uneasy that I would support him and his Men while they were here, and would undertake to procure them a Passage to Lisbon, which I accordingly did; altho very much thwarted by the English Consul at this Place, who I must say behaved with a Degree of Venom on this occasion, which ought and I hope will be remembered by every honest american, who may have occasion to view the Particulars of this Transaction.[6] I wrote to the President and to Mr. Boudinot and to his Exc[ellenc]y Mr. Franklin, to which Letters I have as yet received no answers but am in daily Expectation of receiving them; together with the appointment of Consul from the United States of America at this Place which my good uncle Mr. Boudinot in his last Letter dated the 15th of November last informs me that he will apply for, and he has not the least doubt that it will be obtained for me.

The Friendship which has always subsisted between the two Families flatters me that I will have your Excellencys Influence in this affair. Provided there could not be a Consul appointed by Congress at this Place until an Alliance or Treaty of Commerce should take place between the United States and Portugal, I most earnestly request the Favor of your Excellency in Conjunction with your Brother Commissioners, to appoint me acting Consul at this Island of Madeira, until that Treaty or alliance should take Place, when I have almost a Certainty of that appointment from Congress. From an application made me a few Days ago by the Captain of an American Vessel, who came in here in his Way from Nantes to America, to procure for him his necessary Papers and Clearances, which it is the Duty of a Consul to do, his Excellency the Governor of this Island was pleased to nominate me Consul for the Time being, which office I am now executing according to the best of my Abilities, and hope that Congress will think fit to give me that appointment, and of which I make but little doubt as I flatter myself that your Excellency's Interest, together with that of my Friends in America, will be more than sufficient to obtain that office, especially if I am so happy as to be honored with that appointment from the Commissioners to Europe which doubtless your Influence with them will easily obtain.

Your Excellency will doubtless, before you have read thus far ask yourself who it is that is writing to you in this intimate Stile. But the Friendship which formerly subsisted between the two Families flatters me that you will not be displeased with the Freedom I have taken when I acquaint you that it is the Son of Mr. Lewis Pintard formerly of New York. If I am so happy as to be honored with a Line from you on this Subject, you'll please to direct for me to the Care of Messrs. John Searle and Co. Madeira; and in the interim I remain etc.

(signed) JOHN MARSDEN PINTARD

To John Marsden Pintard

Answer
Paris, 7 June 1783

Sir,

Your Favor of the 19th April last reached me a few Days ago. It gives me Pleasure to find that you are informed of the Friendship which formerly subsisted between our Families, and you rightly suppose that I will be influenced by it.

The American Ministers in Europe are not authorized either severally or jointly, to appoint a Consul; and consequently I cannot have the Satisfaction of fulfilling your Expectations on that Head. It is probable however that your Application to Congress will prove successful, especially if supported by your uncle, whose Recommendation will derive no less Weight from his private than from his public Character. The Part which your Father has acted during the War must also have a favorable Effect. He deserves well of his Country, and his Children will experience the Benefit of it, while they follow his Example. I will write to your Uncle on the Subject. Be assured of my Disposition to maintain and continue the ancient Friendship between our Families by rendering to your's every Service in my Power. Place me therefore on the List of your Friends and Correspondents, and whenever you think I may be useful to you, let me know it.

I am Sir with sincere Regard etc.,

J. J.

ALS in DLC: Elias Boudinot, II. Endorsed by Boudinot: ". . . His Excy John Jay Esq 11 June 1783 recommending Dr. Bancroft and enclosing Copy of J. M. Pintards Letter." Enclosures: John Marsden Pintard to JJ, 19 April 1783, C in JJ's hand, and JJ to Pintard, 7 June 1783, ACS.

[1]JJ wrote similarly to Robert Morris, 10 June 1783, Dft in JP. For Bancroft's duplicity, see *JJ* I, 330n.

[2]"With great truth" deleted in Dft.

[3]"With the conduct of" deleted in Dft.

[4]John Marsden Pintard, son of Lewis (1732–1818) and Susanna Stockton Pintard (1742–72), claimed relation to Elias Boudinot through the marriage of his mother's sister, Hannah Stockton, to Boudinot. Like the Jays, the Boudinots and the Pintards were descendants of Huguenot refugees. For the Pintard family, see "Letters from John Pintard to His Daughter," New-York Hist. Soc., *Collections* (4 vols., 1940–41), I, ix–xii. Pintard's father was a prominent New York merchant and a principal importer of Madeira wines for some years after the Revolution. Young Pintard was appointed by Congress to serve as commercial agent in Madeira on 31 Oct. 1783. *JCC,* XXV, 779–80. He became consul in 1790.

[5]"Thoroughly" deleted in Dft.

[6]For this incident see *JCC,* XXV, 771 *et seq.*

From Robert R. Livingston

Philadelphia, 1 May 1783

Dear Sir,

Your public and private Letters have remained long unanswered, owing to the stagnation of commerce here on the prospect of peace, and the delay occasioned by Mr. Jefferson's disappointment who was charged with both for you.[1] I have now before me your Letters of the 13th August (which Mr. Wright did not deliver till about a fortnight ago) and the 7th and 14th December. I immediatly wrote to your brother, inclosed your Letter to him and informed him and Benson of your directions with respect to money matters.[2] I received no answer to my letter, but Benson who is now here tells me that they have at present no need of it or I should have advanced the money, though the late resolution of Congress of which a copy will be sent you makes your salaries payable here only in bills.

I informed you of the arrangements made with Mr. Morris for the payment of your salary commencing the 1st of January 1782 which was the more agreeable to me as it gave you an advantage in the exchange which as you will see by the accounts that have been sent was not inconsiderable. But Doctor Franklin having objected to this mode of payment which made the salaries depend upon the fluctuations of the exchange, Congress in conformity to his opinion passed the resolution for fixing it at 5 livres 5 sous the dollar and made it retrospect to the first of January 1782.[3] A deduction has accordingly been made out of the quarter's salary due the 1st of April equal to all the advantage made by the exchange. The ballance will be remitted you, unless upon further conversation with Benson he should be of opinion that it may be wanted for the uses you mention and chuse to retain it. You say Doctor Franklin has paid you to July last. But as my accounts are opened with our ministers on the first of January I wish you would to avoid perplexing them settle with Mr. Franklin, and repay him out of the bills in his hands for your use all that he advanced from the first of January 1782. This will simplity his accounts and mine, and stop bills which in one instance I have been so imprudent as to endorse. Your receipt then will close my accounts.

I was extremly affected by those parts of your Letter[4] which relate to your family as they convinced me that neither time nor the intrigues and pleasures of courts had altered the tender sentiments which you formerly felt for those among us that shared your esteem. I drew from them very pleasing inferences as to the duration of our friendship. I have great satisfaction in assuring you that your family on this side the atlantic are well and as far as I can learn at their ease. Nothing in my power shall be wanting to render them more, when I return home, which will I believe be in the course of a few weeks.

You have been informed of my resignation last winter. At the pressing instances of Congress I have been prevailed upon to remain in office till the 1 Monday in May, when they are to proceed to an election.[5] Who my successor will be I know not. The return of peace renders it unnecessary to make further sacrafices of fortune, time, and ease, to the public. I hope by the blessing of God to repair in some measure the waste of these which the war has occasioned, and to live the rest of my life for my friends, my family and myself. Duane and Scott[6] have made a rascally attempt during my absence to injure me in the state (but have not been able to succeed) where I happily stand too well to be shaken by them.

I am sorrey to hear of your indisposition, and that of your family. I hope your jaunt to Normandy has reestablished your health. I thank you for your kind inquiries with respect to my girl; she is considered here as an uncommon fine one and now happily paired by another that promises to be every way her equal to whom I mean to take the liberty of making you god father, unless your love to the established Church (which was always a predominant passion)[7] should have reconciled you to that of the country in which you now are, and determined you not to yield that good office to a heretic.

For news and politicks I refer you to my public Letters. You will find by them that I differ some what with you on some important points,[8] in which, however, I candidly confess to you, that you have more people here who coincide with you in opinion than I would wish, since I have serious apprehensions that we shall e'er long be guilty of "the sin which is worse than the sin of witchcraft."

Mr. Adams has written a long letter to Congress which he has thought proper to address to the president and not to me In which he shews the necessity of sending a minister to Great Britain, describes the character of the person who ought to go, reasons very skilfully against his being able to dance, speak french, or keep a mistress, and concludes with recommending Mr. Dana *or you* "if Congress can do such injustice as to pass *him* by." The Committee called upon me last night to confer on the subject of this letter. I will venture to pronounce that it will not procure Mr. Adams a mission to Great Britain.[9]

Remember me in the most affectionate terms to Mrs. Jay and convey my love in a kiss to my little god daughter. And believe me my Dear friend when I assure you that I am yours with the most unalterable attatchment,

R. R. L.

ALS. Dft in NHi: Robert R. Livingston. E of Dft version in NN: Bancroft: American.

[1]Jefferson delayed his departure, first, because Congress had declined to ask the British for a safe conduct across the sea for him; and, secondly, because bad weather held up his sailing from Baltimore. On 1 April Congress formally released him from his appointment; whereupon he wrote JJ that he would not need lodgings in Paris. Jefferson to JJ, 11 April 1783, ALS in RAWC; Dft in DLC: Jefferson, IX, 1521; *TJP,* VI, 260–61; *HPJ,* III, 40; *WJ,* I, 170–71; Dumas Malone, *Jefferson, The Virginian* (Boston, 1948), pp. 399, 400.

[2]See above, JJ's letters to Livingston, 13 Aug., 7, 14 Dec. 1782. JJ's letter to his brother Frederick of 7 December, below, was enclosed in his dispatch to Livingston of the same date, also below.

[3]The resolution of Congress of 7 March 1783 was made retroactive to 1 Jan. 1783, *JCC,* XXIV, 175–76. For Franklin's protest of 14 Oct. 1782, see *RDC,* V, 811–12. For Livingston's explanation of the mode of payment adopted that year, see Livingston to JJ, 9 May 1782, *RDC,* V, 407.

[4]JJ's letter of 14 Dec. 1782, above.

[5]Livingston's letter of resignation was written 2 Dec. 1782. *RDC,* VI, 100–01. With Livingston's consent, Congress deferred until May the date when a new Secretary would be chosen. *JCC,* XXIII, 759, 819, 823–24.

[6]For months a faction in New York headed by James Duane, John Morin Scott, and Judge John Sloss Hobart had been trying to remove Livingston as chancellor on the ground that he could not hold two offices at the same time. Backed by Governor Clinton, Livingston retained the chancellorship while yielding the Secretaryship. See correspondence in NHi: Robert R. Livingston, cited by Dangerfield, *Livingston,* p. 177n.

[7]In the Dft version the passage reads: "which was always very prevalent, has cured you of your antient prejudices and should have reconciled you . . ." For Livingston's second daughter, see below, JJ to Livingston, 19 July 1783, and n. 17.

[8]See above, Livingston to American Commissioners, 25 March 1783.

[9]In the Dft version this sentence reads: "It is an extraordinary composition and will if I am not much mistaken defeat the purpose for which it was intended." Adams' letter of 5 Feb. 1783 (*JAW,* VIII, 33–40; *RDC,* VI, 242–47) was read in Congress 28 April, and the following day was referred to a committee composed of Alexander Hamilton, Oliver Ellsworth, and John Rutledge. Their report, submitted 1 May, was confined to the points Adams raised concerning the negotiation of a commercial treaty with Great Britain and ignored his suggestions for the appointment of a minister to that country. *JCC,* XXIV, 320–21. In concluding his letter, Adams had written: ". . . if I had the honor to give my vote in Congress for a minister to the court of Great Britain, provided that injustice must be finally done to him who was the first object of his country's choice, such have been the activity, intelligence, and fortitude of Mr. Jay . . . that I should think of no other object of my choice than that gentleman." *RDC,* VI, 246–47. Although Wharton prints Adams' letter as having been addressed to Livingston, the LS in PCC 84, IV, 339–48, is addressed to the President of Congress.

From Robert Morris

Office of Finance, Philadelphia, 12 May 1783

Sir,

The Bills drawn by Congress in their Necessities, press very heavily upon me; and one of the greatest among many Evils attending them is the Confusion in which they have involved the Affairs of my Department. I have never yet been able to learn how many of these Bills have been paid nor how many remain due; neither am I without my fears that some of them have received double Payment.

To bring at length some little Degree of Order into this Chaos after waiting till now for fuller light and Information, I write on the Subject to Mr. Barclay[1] who will have the honor to deliver this Letter and I send him a Copy of the enclosed Account. I have directed him to consult with your Excellency and obtain an Account of the Bills which have been paid and to transmit me an Account both of those and of such as remain due and to take Measures with you for Payment of the latter so as to prevent double Payments which I seriously apprehend. The enclosed will inform you that the Bills which are gone forward drawn on you amount to three hundred and eighty four thousand four hundred and forty four Dollars.

Let me intreat you Sir to forward these Views as much as possible for you will I am sure be Sensible how necessary it is for me to know the exact State of our pecuniary Affairs lest on the one Hand I should risque the public Credit by an Excess of Drafts or on the other leave their Monies unemployed while they experience severe Distress from the Want.

I am Sir with perfect Respect your Excellency's Most obedient and humble Servant,

R. M.

LbkC in DLC: Robert Morris, Official Letterbook, II.

[1]In the same letterbook is Morris to Barclay of this date, wherein Morris expatiates at greater length on his plan for arranging the payment of the bills drawn on the American ministers in Europe, since repayment of these bills was proving a severe drain on anticipated funds from the French loans of 1782 and 1783. He instructed Barclay to consult the American Commissioners, enclosed an account from the Treasury of bills drawn on them, and requested Barclay to obtain "an Account of the Payment made on them as well as those still due" and to take measures to have them paid by drafts on M. Grand. No copy of the account sent to Barclay with this letter has been located. The accounts which Barclay later prepared of the bills drawn on JJ in Spain are found in DNA: RG 39, Foreign Ledger of Public Agents in Europe, I, 196. For further correspondence on Morris' plans to re-arrange payment of such bills, see his letters to Adams and Franklin of 12 May and to Grand of 9 May 1783, all in DLC: Morris Lbk.

From William Livingston

Burlington, 21 May 1783

Dear Sir,

I embrace the opportunity of Doctor Wearings[1] going to France (a young Gentleman belonging to South Carolina and Strongly recommended to me by President Boudinot) to send you a line, which I hope you will never receive, provided the non reception of it is owing to your having left Paris for America, when it arrives in France.

The Treaty is universally applauded; and the American Commissioners who were concerned in making it, have rendered themselves very popular by it. The Whigs in this State are however extremely opposed to admitting the refugees amongst us, and I am apprehensive of some difficulty on that account. There is still a greater difficulty that we have to Struggle with. Too many of Strong professional Whigs now openly show what I have long suspected them of, that they love their money better than their liberty by their Scandalous aversion to pay the necessary taxes. If this reaches you in Europe, I hope I shall hear from you as soon as possible.

I am Sir, Your most humble servant,

WIL. LIVINGSTON

ALS.

[1]Probably Dr. Richard Waring (1760–1814), son of John Beamor Waring. Joseph I. Waring, "Waring Family," *South Carolina Hist. and Geneal. Mag.*, XXIV (1923), 81–100.

From Gouverneur Morris

Philadelphia, 30 May 1783

Dear Jay,

My Time will not permit any Thing more at this Time than to assure you of my Affection and to pray you will present me most warmly to Mrs. Jay and your little ones. Believe me I take a sincere Interest in all which may concern them. I could not if I would say any Thing on Politics worthy of Attention. All your friends here are well, myself among the Number. Adieu, always believe me very sincerely Yours,

GOUV. MORRIS

P.S. In the Talk of future ministerial Arrangements my Sentiment has been to fix you at Versailles in Preference either to London or Madrid; for this I have numerous Reasons not worthy of Repetition in the present Moment.[1]

ALS. Endorsed by JJ: ". . . recd. 1 July by Capt. Barney; answered 17 July by ditto."

[1]The reference is to the discussions concerning a peacetime diplomatic establishment which the news of the Preliminaries had touched off in Congress, along with the letters of Adams, Dana, Franklin, and Laurens requesting permission to return home. PCC 80, II; *RDC,* VI, 106, 110–14. On 1 April Boudinot observed that Congress, "oppressed by the ill timed parsimony of the States," was considering "reducing their Ministers in Europe." Boudinot to James Searle, D.C: Boudinot. In May a Congressional committee submitted a "Report on Peace Arrangements for the Department of Foreign Affairs." *HP,* III, 351–53; *MP,* 44, 67; *JCC,* XXV, 965, 967.

From Robert Morris

Philadelphia, 31 May 1783

Dear Sir,

I have none of your Letters to answer; the receipt of those which you formerly honored me with afforded me very great satisfaction, which I mention as an inducement for you to write more. We are told that your Health is injured and that you have been traveling to try whether change of air and Exercise will restore it. Wishes rarely produce any effect but I cannot restrain mine. They are offered with sincerity for the restoration and continuance of Good Health, and for the perpetual Happiness of you and yours. Governeur Morris heard a few days since that you are going back to Spain, and telling this a little abruptly to Kitty Livingston affected her Spirits so much that she has not recovered herself perfectly to this hour; that worthy Girl is most truly Her Sister's and your *Friend*.

Governeur is very sincerely attached to you. I know it for I know him thoroughly; he is this Morning set off for New York and will be gone about a Fortnight. He leaves me encumbered with more difficulties than any one man ought to encounter. I have made an effort to get clear of this troublesome and dangerous office but as yet I am not permitted to retire. On the Contrary, I must of necessity encrease my Engagements to a degree that renders it entirely uncertain when I shall have it in my Power to see them discharged.[1] If you can obtain me aid, for Heavens sake, or rather for the sake of our Country, do it.

The Blessings of Peace flow in upon us Spontaneously, but it requires the full exercise of more Virtue and good Sense than has yet appeared in our Councils to secure the Continuance of them. Providence has been Wonderfully kind and if Faith is acceptable in Heaven, we must be favourites as we place our whole Trust in Providence and do nothing for ourselves. You will Learn from the Public Prints, the Journals of Congress, the Letters of Mr. Livingston etc. every thing worth knowing and, as I can ill spare my own Time, I will not take up yours with repetitions. Congress Complain that they do not hear often enough from any of their Ministers abroad.

I am most sincerely, Dear Sir, Your affectionate Friend, and obedient Servant

ROBT. MORRIS

LS. Endorsed by JJ: ". . . recd. 1 July 1783 by Capt. Barney; answered 20 Instant by Ditto."

[1]Morris' letter of resignation as Superintendent of Finance was dated 24 Jan. 1783, but he agreed to remain in office for a limited time after 31 May. *RDC*, VI, 228–29, 405–06.

Negotiating a Trade Treaty

1 June 1783

In his first draft of the Preliminary Treaty JJ had included an article calling for commercial reciprocity between Great Britain and the United States,[1] a provision later deleted because of objections from the British Cabinet. It had been understood, however, especially in view of Shelburne's own advocacy of liberalized trade, that a commercial agreement would soon be negotiated, and the preamble to the Provisional Articles promises that the principle of reciprocity would be incorporated in the final treaty. Both sides in the negotiations had assumed that Shelburne's liberal trade views would prevail, views shared by a number of influential English merchants, by the West India planters, and by a small but vocal group of Americans in London.[2] In short, conditions seemed highly propitious when, in December of 1782, JJ and Franklin stated that the time had come to work out the details of "a mutual agreement to repeal all such laws as are now in force in both countries for preventing all reciprocal intercourse between them. . . ."[3]

JJ and Franklin had acted in anticipation of receiving instructions from Congress to negotiate a trade treaty. These instructions were not adopted by Congress until the winter of '82 and the following spring, by which time Adams, Franklin and JJ (or any one of them) were authorized to enter into commercial stipulations with Great Britain to obtain for Americans direct trade with "all parts of the British dominions and possessions" in "like manner" as "all parts of the United States may be open to British subjects." Prudently, Congress granted the three Commissioners discretionary powers to waive insistence on a commercial agreement should difficulties intervene.[4] In fact, such instructions did not reach Franklin until early September, but after the Definitive Treaty had been signed.[5] Later that year Congress authorized its ministers plenipotentiary abroad to negotiate trade treaties with European powers generally.[6]

Eager as Shelburne may have been to effect an immediate liberalization of commerce, he recognized the soundness of the counsel of John Pownall, his adviser on trade matters, that it would be necessary for Parliament to pass special enabling legislation.[7] A bill proposed in Shelburne's administration and introduced by young William Pitt (1759–1806), Chancellor of the Exchequer, would have temporarily admitted to the ports of Great Britain and her possessions in the New World American goods in American bottoms on the same terms as British goods in British bottoms.[8] Weeks of heated debate followed its introduction on 7 March 1783, continuing after the Shelburne ministry had fallen. The shipping interests, led by William Eden, launched a well-organized campaign in opposition. Eden had quickly come under the influence of a sensationally successful new book, *Observations on the Commerce of the American*

States, from the pen of Lord Sheffield. A staunch advocate of continuing the Navigation Laws, Sheffield, drawing upon a battery of statistics, argued that the Americans should be treated as foreigners and excluded from the trade they had enjoyed as colonials. Thereby British shipping could gain at American expense and America made to pay for the war. The Parliamentary debate revealed that a majority in both houses took a renewal of American trade for granted and considered Congress too impotent to retaliate.[9]

When in April the Fox-North coalition took over the reins of government, Oswald was replaced in Paris by David Hartley (c. 1730–1813), scientist, political economist, and pro-American member of Parliament. Hartley was charged by Fox with negotiating a reciprocity agreement to be incorporated in the peace treaty. It was reputed, so Laurens told JJ, that Hartley would propose dual citizenship as well as reciprocal trade. On the sticky issue of citizenship JJ felt that an instruction from Congress was needed. While favoring the proposal as a temporary expedient, he cautioned that the Americans "should avoid being either too forward or too coy," and confessed his lack of faith in "any Court in Europe," the British included.[10]

Having approved Eden's amendment to the Shelburne bill giving regulatory power to the King in Council,[11] the new ministry was in a strong position to negotiate a mutually acceptable commercial arrangement. However, the free trade movement had lost momentum. Unaware of the changed attitude in London or at the least blind to its implications, Hartley plunged enthusiastically into what he expected would be a swift and successful negotiation. On 29 April he sent Fox three articles that he and the American Commissioners had drawn up that morning,[12] the first of which called for the establishment of reciprocal trade between the two nations as soon as Britain's armed forces had quit the United States.[13] In that dispatch and in two others written a day later,[14] Hartley urged Fox to inaugurate the new commercial policy even before the withdrawal of troops. The Ministry could enter with confidence into a prompt arrangement with the Americans, who, he argued, "have no Sentiments of hostility, nor any desire to injure, or to affront any part of the British nation. . . ."

Hartley's euphoric belief that London would consent to the three articles[15] was shattered by the receipt of a stinging rebuke from Fox. It was not intended, Hartley was told, to allow American ships entry into British ports with any cargoes that British vessels could bring, but only to permit them entry with American goods.[16] The Foreign Secretary enclosed a copy of an Order in Council issued on 14 May, which allowed unmanufactured American goods to come into England in British or American ships. This Order in Council was followed on 6 June by another permitting free importation into Britain of indigo and naval stores, and of tobacco on payment of the "Old Subsidy," the five per cent ad valorem of colonial days.[17] While the American Commissioners considered these Orders as evidence of Britain's liberal disposition, they were understandably perturbed that neither had a word to say about items *manufactured* in the United States.[18]

Undeterred by this setback, Hartley vigorously defended his position to his superior while concurrently seeking common ground that would satisfy both parties.[19] To work out a compromise between the American insistence on free trade and his own government's restrictive policies, Hartley suggested on 21 May that both nations might agree to a temporary revival of their prewar trade relationship.[20] Since the Americans exhibited no inclination to consider the proposition until Hartley had been authorized to act on it,[21] the British negotiator, in a private letter of 23 May, sharply rebuked his superior for undercutting "every disposition of peace" professed by the Americans and warned that unless the British adopted a liberal line the negotiations would collapse. "As surely as the rights of Mankind have been established by the American War," he affirmed, "so surely will all the acts of Navigation of the world perish and be buried among occult Qualities."[22]

Hartley's enthusiasm seems to have been communicated to the American Commissioners. On 1 June both JJ and Adams prepared draft trade conventions. JJ's would have barred British subjects from exporting slaves to America, "It being the Intention of the said States intirely to prohibit the Importation thereof," and would have liberated trade between America and Ireland from prewar restrictions.[23] Adams proposed a temporary convention whereby the citizens of the United States could import into, or export from, any British dominion in American ships any goods which had been so imported or exported by the American colonists before the start of the war, paying the same duties and charges as British subjects, and extending reciprocal privileges to the latter.[24] Hartley, in turn, similarly favored reciprocity, while denying Americans the right of direct trade between the British West Indies and Great Britain.[25]

Further exchanges between Hartley and Fox got nowhere, as the latter now felt it advisable to defer a trade agreement until after the Definitive Treaty.[26] It was increasingly evident that only a full Parliamentary inquiry could bring about any substantial reinterpretation of the Navigation Laws.

An order in Council of 2 July proved a shattering blow to any lingering expectations Hartley and the Americans may still have shared. It closed the British West Indies to American ships and sailors and barred entry of all American goods into the West Indies except for an enumerated list that did not include such significant items as fish, cured meats, and dairy products.[27] The Order in Council completely foreclosed any possibility of an agreement to liberalize trade and presaged a decade of intense controversy between the two nations.[28]

[1]See above, Preliminary Articles, First Draft, 8 Oct. 1782, and n. 3.

[2]*Peacemakers,* p. 429.

[3]Franklin is thus reported in Fitzherbert to Grantham, 25 Jan. 1783, FO 27/5. Two months earlier Franklin had expressed regret that the reciprocal trade article

had been omitted from the Preliminary Treaty. Vaughan to Shelburne, 7 Dec. 1782, LbkC in PPAmP: Vaughan. Soon JJ and Franklin were hinting about the desirability of including such a clause in the Definitive Treaty. Vaughan to Shelburne, 26 Dec. 1782, Tr in MiU-C. Not long thereafter Oswald claimed to have put a stop to a proposal by Vaughan to draw up with JJ a treaty of commerce between the two nations. Oswald to Shelburne, 8 Jan. 1783, MiU-C: Shelburne 71: 225–27.

[4]Livingston to Franklin, 31 Dec. 1782 (in Cipher) in PPAmP: Franklin; *JCC, XXIII,* 38; XXIV, 320–21 (1 May 1783); DLC: Franklin, VIII, 83.

[5]John Adams to President of Congress (Boudinot), 8 Sept. 1783, *RDC,* V, 683.

[6]Such treaties to be of 15-year duration and to require Congressional approval. *JCC,* XXV, 753–54 (29 Oct. 1783).

[7]Almost immediately after recommending alterations in the statutes, Pownall cautioned that working out specific commercial concessions might best be deferred until a U.S. diplomatic representative took up residence in England. He saw no need to delay the enabling legislation, however, and submitted a draft of the proposed statute early in February. Pownall to Shelburne, 30 Jan., 2, 7 Feb. 1783, ALS in MiU-C: Shelburne 72, 471–86, 487–501, 503–13.

[8]In forwarding a copy of the bill to Paris, Grantham urged that it be shown to the Americans to reassure them of British interest. Grantham to Fitzherbert, 5 March 1783, Dft in FO 27/6, 25–28. Word came back promptly of the favorable reaction of the Americans and of their assertion of power to grant Great Britain reciprocal benefits. Vaughan was particularly desirous of opening the British West Indian trade to the Americans. Vaughan to Shelburne, 6, 7, 14 March 1783, Tr in PPAmP: Vaughan. See also Vincent T. Harlow, *The Founding of the Second British Empire, 1763–1793* (2 vols., New York, 1952), I, ch. 9; A. L. Burt, *The United States, Great Britain, and British North America* (New York, 1940), pp. 55–59.

[9]Both JJ and Franklin spoke out against Parliament's short-sighted action and held out the prospect of a retaliatory American navigation act. JJ to Vaughan, 28 March 1783, C in Peter Jay Munro's hand in JP; *HPJ,* III, 34–38, *RDC,* VI, 349–50; *WJ,* II, 114–16. See also *Peacemakers,* p. 430. The *Observations* of John Baker Holroyd, 1st Earl of Sheffield (1735–1821), was first published in 1783.

[10]JJ to Livingston, 22 April 1783, ALS in PCC 89, II, 464–66; LbkCs in JP and PCC 110, III; *RDC,* VI, 388–90; *HPJ,* III, 42–44; *SDC,* VIII, 224–26; *WJ,* I, 171–73.

[11]Hartley's instructions to draft a reciprocal trade treaty encouraged JJ to write optimistically to Philadelphia. Fox to Hartley, 10 April 1783, FO 4/2, 3–8 and MiU-C: RGA. The C in MiU-C: Hartley I, does not include the last paragraph, which was written as a separate letter. JJ to Livingston, 11 April 1783, PCC 89, II, 460; Dft in JP; *RDC,* VI, 368; *HPJ,* III, 41–42. George III confirmed Hartley's instructions in a dispatch to the latter of 18 April 1783, ALS in MiU-C: Hartley I. Notification that Parliament had given temporary control over commerce to the King in Council was sent to Paris the day the bill passed. ALS in MiU-C: Hartley I; Dft in FO 4/2, 19–20.

[12]ALS in FO 4/2, 23–38; C in CP EU 24: 168–79; *RDC,* VI, 396–97.

[13]ALS in *ibid.;* C in MiU-C: Hartley I.

[14]ALS in FO 4/2.

[15]Hartley to Fox, 3 May 1783, ALS in FO 4/2, 43–44. By contrast, Franklin was less sanguine. Franklin to Vergennes, 5 May 1783, CP EU 24: 168–79; *BFS,* IX, 38.

[16]Fox to Hartley, 15 May 1783, Dft in FO 4/2, 47–50; Tr in MiU-C.

[17]*Acts of the Privy Council of England, Colonial Series,* ed. by W. L. Grant and James Munro (6 vols., Hereford, 1908–12), V, 527–32; *RDC,* VI, 428–29.

[18]*Peacemakers,* p. 431.

[19]Hartley to Fox, 20 May 1783, FO 4/2, 55–60.

[20]David Hartley, Observations and Propositions, 21 May 1783, D in NHi: Jay; *RDC,* VI, 443–44. Hartley's Proposed Articles of Agreement, delivered by him to the

American Ministers for their Consideration, 21 May 1783, C in NHi: Jay; *RDC*, VI, 442.

[21]Hartley to Fox, 22 May 1783, in FO 4/2, 61–72; C in MiU-C: Hartley I. American Commissioners to Elias Boudinot, 10 Sept. 1783, LS in PCC 85, reel 114, pp. 370–85, 398–411; *RDC*, VI, 687–91.

[22]Hartley to Fox, 23 May (private), 2, 5 June 1783 (private), LbkCs in MiU-C: Hartley I.

[23]JJ's draft of a Temporary Trade Agreement, 1 June 1783, for which see below.

[24]*RDC*, VI, 460.

[25]*Ibid.*, pp. 465–69.

[26]Fox to Hartley, 10 June 1783, FO 4/2, 88–94, LbkC in MiU-C: Hartley I; Hartley to American Commissioners, 14 June 1783, *ibid.*; *RDC*, VI, 483–87; Harlow, *Second British Empire*, I, 472–74; Hartley to Fox, 20 June 1783, FO 4/2, 95–110. For Fox's attitude, see Reid, *Charles James Fox*, pp. 174–76.

[27]*Acts of the Privy Council, Colonial Series*, V, 530. The reactions of Hartley and the Americans are described in Hartley to Fox, 17, 24 July 1783, FO 4/2, 127–30, 135–36.

[28]After signing the Definitive Treaty, Hartley drew up a schedule of articles on trade remaining for consideration, 1 Nov. 1783. MiU-C: Hartley I; FO 4/2. JJ had already anticipated the difficulties ahead, which he attributed to "the partial politics" prevailing in the British Cabinet. JJ to Vaughan, 13 Sept. 1783, Dft in JP.

John Jay: Draft Treaty of Commerce with England

[Paris, n.d., 1 June 1783]

Whereas a Variety of Circumstances and Considerations oppose the forming at Present a Permanent Treaty of Commerce between the Imperial Crown of Great Britain and the United States of America, And whereas it is expedient that a Commercial Interest should be without Delay opened and Regulated between the Kingdom and Territories of Great Britain and the said States by a temporary Convention, Therefore

It is agreed that for a Term of   from the Date hereof

Provided that the Subjects of his Britannic Majesty shall not have any Right or Claim under this Convention to carry or import into the said States any Slaves from any Part of the World, It being the Intention of the said States intirely to prohibit the Importation thereof.[1]

And whereas Questions may arise respecting the Operation of this Convention on Ireland, It is agreed that it shall not be construed to restrain that Kingdom from accepting from and granting to, the said States further and more extensive Commercial Privilege than that Ireland and the British American Colonies enjoyed with respect to each other before the late War.[2]

And whereas this Convention is dictated by Temporary Convenience, and the Discussion of Questions respecting Reciprocity has in forming of it been avoided, therefore it is agreed that no Arguments shall be drawn from it for or against any Propositions or Claims which either Party may make in treating of and framing the proposed future Treaty of Commerce.

LbkC in DLC: Franklin, ser. 1, VIII, 162–63.

[1]On JJ's willingness to act on this sensitive issue without explicit instructions, see Introduction.

[2]The Navigation Acts of 1663 and 1671 imposed restraints on trade between Ireland and the American colonies. See Lawrence A. Harper, *The English Navigation Laws* (New York, 1939), pp. 161, 162, 246.

To George Clinton

Passy, 12 June 1783

Dear Sir,

It would give me great Pleasure to be certain that this Letter will be delivered to you at your Home in the City of New York, but it is even doubtful whether orders to evacuate it have as yet been dispatched. What Motives enduce this Delay can only be conjectured; perhaps it may be designed by some of the British Cabinet to stimulate our doing more for the Tories than they otherwise expect. For my own part I think we should cautiously avoid saying or doing any thing about or concerning their Pretensions until every British Soldier shall be removed. It would ill become us to take that Matter under Consideration with a Rod over our Heads, and it would be much more agreable to my Feelings to see our remaining houses burnt, than be *driven* into that or any other Measure. Whatever we may do for the Tories should flow and appear to flow spontaneously from our Justice, Benevolence and Humanity, and neither be nor seem to be expressed from us by the weight of external Influence on our Hopes or Fears.

Doctor Bancroft who goes from hence to England, and from there probably in a Packet to New York, will be the Bearer of this Letter. This Gentleman has been useful to his Country and friendly to me, and I recommend him to you as one whom I esteem and by whom I have been obliged.

I am dear Sir with great Regard and Esteem, Your most obedient Servant.

P.S. 13 June 1783: Mr. Hartley this Moment informed me that orders to evacuate the United States were actually sent to the British Commander in Chief at New York.[1]

Dft.

[1]Fox's dispatch to Hartley of 10 June 1783 (MiU-C: Hartley I; LbkC in FO 4/2, 88–94) informed him of the King's orders "for the speedy and complete evacuation of all the Territories" of the U.S., with instructions to communicate this order to the American Commissioners.

To Peter Van Schaack

Passy, 16 June 1783

Dear Sir,

I have recieved your favor of the 30th Ulto. Your affectionate answer to my Letter of the 17th September last reached me about a month afer its Date.[1] The Prospect I then and long afterwards had of being able to visit England, where the Death of a Relative[2] gave me some private Business to transact, induced me from Time to Time to postpone writing to you. It so happened however that my continuing at Paris remained expedient and whether and when I shall see London is still doubtful.

The Report you have heard respecting my future Destination is not justified by any Intelligence I have of the Designs of Congress on that Subject; and therefore the Jaunt you have in Contemplation should not be suspended on that account.[3] I assure you most frankly and sincerely that it will always give me Pleasure to see you; our meeting shall be that of old friends, and as our Intercourse in that capacity may and will be innocent, I shall neither impose upon myself nor upon you any Restraints which Rectitude and Integrity will dispense with. To America I shall continue a faithful servant, and to you a faithful friend. Should these characters clash I shall as heretofore prefer the former, but where and while they do not, let us as in the Days of our Youth indulge the Effusions of Friendship, without Reserve and without Disguise.

Benson[4] is an honest Man and loves you. <It grieved him to act a part that wounded You, but he Devoted himself to < <his Country and to> > what he thought < <his Interest, made many other Considerations> > submit his Duty, and steadily followed where it pointed the way without being deterred by the thorns that> I approve the advice he gave you; it exactly corresponds with my own Sentiments.

The Disorder in your Eyes afflicts me. It merits and I hope engages your greatest Care and Attention. At all Events, be resigned, and remember that many will rejoice in the End for the Days wherein they have seen adversity. <It is a harsh Preceptor, and it has been yours.

Tuition ceases when the End is obtained. May this be your Case.>

Mrs. Jay joins me in presenting to you our best wishes. I am dear Peter Your affectionate Friend.

Dft. Variant version in Van Schaack, *Life,* pp. 307–08.

[1]Van Schaack's reply to JJ's letter above of 17 Sept. 1782, dated 15 Oct. 1782, and his letter of 30 May 1783 are in *ibid.,* pp. 303–07.

[2]See editorial note below, "An American in England."

[3]In his 30 May letter, Van Schaack had remarked: "Fame says you are to be the ambassador at this court, and this had induced me to suspend a jaunt I have determined to take to Paris, by the way of Holland."

[4]In that same letter Van Schaack reported: "I have a letter from my brother [Henry Van Schaack] of the 16th April. Our old friend Benson was then at New-York, upon a requisition to Sir Guy Carleton, to contract his lines to the island of New-York. I fear this business will create some contention. God forbid! Every American, of whatever description, must wish to prevent any ill blood, and as much as possible to cultivate a 'spirit of conciliation.'"

To Philip Livingston

Passy, 28 June 1783

Dear Sir,

Your favor of the 7th Inst.[1] was delivered to me three Days ago. I am happy to hear that your Tour has contributed to the Reestablishment of your Health. I should have written to you frequently, if I had known where to direct my Letters. The one you mention to have written to me came safe to Hand.

Some months have elapsed since any of the american Ministers here have recieved either official or private Letters from Philadelphia which contain interesting Intelligence of any kind.

The Report you have heard of Spain's ceding to France the Territory you mention is I believe groundless. The Intentions of Congress respecting Settlements on the Mississippi we at present are entirely ignorant of; nor am I possessed of any Information which can influence or direct either your or my Judgment on the Question you state. Were I a Landholder in W. Florida, I certainly would present a Memorial to the Spanish Court to obtain Permission to make the most of it. There are Englishmen who hold Lands in France, etc. I think the Landholders in Florida should unite in this application, and appoint agents to manage it.

Mrs. Jay presents her affectionate Compliments to you. I am Dear Sir with great Regards yours sincerely,

J. J.

DftS.

[1]On 7 June Philip Livingston, writing from Milan (ALS in JP), had presumptuously sought information from JJ on the disposition of West Florida, which, Livingston had heard, Spain had ceded to France, along with Louisiana. As a large patentee in West Florida, he solicited private advice on the steps he should take vis-à-vis Spain, France, or the U.S., should Congress move to protect American settlements on the Mississippi. JJ's noncommittal reply was what might have been expected from a proper and prudent diplomat. See also below, JJ to Frederick Jay, 7 Dec. 1783, n. 5. In his letter of the 7th, Livingston mentions his of 22 Feb. 1783 to JJ, ALS in JP.

From Philip Schuyler

Albany, 1 July 1783

My Dear Sir,

Although our correspondance has ceased for some time, and probably occasioned by incidents, not in our power to command, yet my affection and esteem for you have not suffered the least diminution, nor has my gratitude for your generous intervention in the day of my distresss when It was criminal in the eyes of a misguided multitude to be my friend.

The provisional treaty with Britain affords perfect satisfaction, to the informed, and those whose passions do not lead their Judgement, and to the honest. There are however fools and knaves who condemn the sixth article, who think the fifth too favorable for the Tories, and who fault the line of boundary. The former characters however, a circumstance not very common, lead a vast majority.

Peace my Dear Sir was become indispensibly necessary. An unaccountable inattention to the public weal prevailed, an injurious Jealousy of the power of Congress had more or less pervaded every State, public confidence had sunk, with public credit, and a train of absurd and despicable politics was pursuing, which must inevitably have ended in our ruin, had not the conduct of the enemy been equally ridiculous, and unaccountably pussilanimous.

The greater part of our Army is disbanded. They are returned to their different States, exclaiming at the ingratitude of their fellow citizens. Indeed they have too, too much reason.

Mr. Carter,[1] my son in law, will have the honor of delivering you this. He and Colonel Wadsworth have furnished the supplies for the French army, and have acquitted themselves with great propriety, and to the entire satisfaction of the French commander and chief, and the other officers. They go to sollicit a discharge of the bills which have been drawn in their favor. It is probable that by your intervention their business may be much expedited. Will You permit me to intreat Your Attention to them and to their concerns.

Since you left America two of my daughters have married. Colonel Hamilton has Betsy and Mr. Stephen Van Renselaer has Peggy.[2]

My health is so much impaired, that it is become absolutely necesary, in order to pass the remainder of my days with tolerable satisfaction, that I should retire from public life, and retreat to my Saratoga hobby-horse, where I hope some day to have the pleasure of embracing you, unless you should consent to remain in Europe.

Please to make my best respects acceptable to Your Lady. I am Dear Sir with great truth and Sincerity, Your Excellency's Affectionate and Obedient Servant,

P. SCHUYLER

ALS in RAWC. Endorsed by JJ: "answered 16 September 1783."

[1]Schuyler's son-in-law, John Barker Church, alias "John Carter," had formed in 1780 a partnership with Jeremiah Wadsworth, the former Commissary General, and amassed a fortune from army contracts. A substantial part of the assets of Carter & Wadsworth was tied up in bills of exchange which they had received in payment for supplies to the French naval and military forces in America. By an *arrêt* of March 1783, the French government imposed a one-year moratorium on the payment of these bills. Church and Wadsworth sailed to France to seek payment of these obligations. See John Platt, "Jeremiah Wadsworth" (Ph.D. diss., Columbia University), pp,. 22–50; see also *JJ*, I, 596.

[2]Elizabeth Schuyler (1757–1854) and Alexander Hamilton were married 14 Dec. 1780. Margaret Schuyler (1758–1801) and Stephen Van Rensselaer (1764–1839), the eighth Patroon of Rensselaerwyck, were married 6 June 1783. Cuyler Reynolds, ed. *Family History of Southern New York*, I, 6–10; III, 1379.

To Gouverneur Morris

Passy, 17 July 1783

Dear Morris,

I have recieved <your> two Letters from you, one of the 29 April by Col. Ogden, the other of 30 May by Capt. Barney.[1] I am glad to see the Colonel and shall readily do him any Service in my power, as well on account of your Recommendation as his own merit.

By this Time I suppose there is much canvassing for foreign appointments. I thank you for thinking of me. But as I mean to return in the Spring, your arrangement so far as it respects me must be altered. Upon this point I am decided, and <I> beg of you to tell my Friends so.

Orders are gone to evacuate New York. The present british ministry are duped I believe by an opinion of our <Dissension> not having

Decision and Energy sufficient to regulate our Trade so as to retaliate their Restrictions. Our ports were opened too soon. Let us however be temperate as well as firm.

Our Friend Morris I suspect is not a Favorite of this Court. They say he treats them as his Cashier. They refuse absolutely to supply more money. Marbois writes <much> tittle Tattle, and I believe does mischief. Congress certainly should remove to some interior Town, and they should send a minister forthwith to England. The french Emb[assador] at Petersburgh[2] has thrown cold Water on Danas <Reception> being recieved before a peace. <This I regard> <The Policy of this court> The ministers of this Court are <Desciples> qualified to act the part of Proteus. The Nation <however is> I think is <basically> really with us, and the King <is> seems to be well <intentioned> disposed.

Mrs. Jay presents you her Compliments. Sir James is here yet, why I dont know.

Adieu. Yours sincerely.

Dft. Endorsed; ". . . in ansr. to 29 Ap. and 30 May last; by the Washington, Cap. Barney." *HPJ,* III, 52–54, omits next to the last paragraph.

[1]29 April 1783 letter not located; 30 May 1783, above. Col. Matthias Ogden of the New Jersey Line received leave from Congress for a private business trip. Ogden to George Washington, 14 April 1783. DLC: Washington 4. He returned to America later that year. Ogden to President of Congress, PCC 78, XVII, 361.

[2]Charles Olivier de Saint-Georges, Marquis de Vérac.

American Commissioners to David Hartley

Passy, 17 July 1783

Sir,

We have the honour to inform you that we have just received from Congress, their Ratification in due Form of the Provisional Articles of the 30th of November 1782, and we are ready to exchange Ratifications with his Britannic Majesty's Minister as soon as may be.[1]

By the Same Articles it is Stipulated that his Britannic Majesty shall with all convenient Speed, and without causing any Destruction or carrying away any Negroes or other Property of the American Inhabitants withdraw all his Armies, Garrisons and Fleets from the United States and from every Port, Place and Harbour within the Same.

But, by Intelligence lately received from America, and by the enclosed Copies of Letters and Conferences between General Washington and Sir Guy Carleton it appears that a considerable Number of Negroes belonging to the Citizens of the United States, have been carried off from New-York contrary to the express Stipulation contained in the said Article.[2]

We have received from Congress their Instructions to <remonstrate upon this Violation of the Treaty, and to take such Measures for obtaining Reparation as the Nature of the Case will admit.> *represent this Matter to you, and to request that speedy and effectual Measures be taken to render that Justice to the parties interested which the true Intent and meaning of the Article in Question plainly dictates.* (No. 1)[3]

We do ourselves the honour of making these Communications to you Sir, that you may transmit <it> them and the Papers accompanying <it> them to your Court, and inform us of their Answer.

We have the honour to be, Sir, Your most obedient and most humble Servants.

JOHN ADAMS

DftS, body of letter in hand of W. T. Franklin, signed only by Adams, in MHi: Adams, reel 361. JJ's corrections are indicated in italics. See also *RDC,* VI, 556–57.

[1]Congress after debate, provisionally ratified the Preliminary Treaty on 15 April 1783. *JCC,* XXIV, 242.

[2]On 15 April 1783 Congress instructed Washington to make proper arrangements with General Carleton for taking over the posts and recovering "negroes and other property of the United States in the possession of the British forces, or any subjects of or adherents to his said Britannic Majesty," a well as to arrange for freeing "all land prisoners." *Ibid.,* XXIV, 242–43. Following a meeting between Washington and Carleton on 5 May, Livingston informed the American Commissioners that the British were continuing to violate the 7th article of the treaty by "sending off the slaves under pretence that the proclamations had set them free, as if a British general had, either by their laws or those of nations, a right of proclamation to deprive any man whatever of his property." Livingston to the American Commissioners, 28 May 1783. *RDC,* VI, 453.

[3]JJ's proposed insert, immediately below.

John Jay: Article for Inclusion in American Commissioners to David Hartley

Passy, 17 July 1783

No. 1.

We are also instructed to represent to you, that <so> many of the british Debtors in america have in the Course of the War Sustained such considerable and heavy Losses by the Operation of the british arms in that Country, <as at present to be> that a great Number of them <are> have been rendered incapable of immediately satisfying those Debts; <and to> we refer it to the Justice and Equity of Great Britain so far to amend the Article on that Subject as that <the> no Execution shall be issued <to> on a Judgment to be obtained in any such Case but after the Expiration of three Years from the Date of the definitive Treaty of peace. Congress also think it reasonable that <only> such part of the Interest which may have accrued <on any such> on such Debts during the war shall not be <demand[ed]> payable, because as all Intercourse between the two Countries had during that period become impracticable as well as improper, it does not appear just that Individuals in america should pay for Delays in payment which were occasioned by the civil and military measures of Great Britain. <We> In our opinion the Interest of the Creditors as well as the Debtors requires that some Tenderness be shewn to the latter, and that they should be allowed a little Time to acquire <those> the means of discharging Debts which <at present> in many Instances exceed the whole amount of their property.

Follows No. 2.[1]

Dft in MHi: Adams, reel 361. Nos. 1 and 2 in hand of W. T. Franklin. JJ's insertions are indicated in italics.

[1]Adams proposed the following insertion, marked "No. 2" by W. T. Franklin: "As it is necessary to ascertain an Epocha, for the Restitutions and Evacuations to be made *we propose that* it is agreed, that his Britannic Majesty, shall cause to be evacuated the Posts of New York, Penobscot, <Niagra, Detroit, Mihilimackinac> and their Dependencies, with all other Posts and Places in Possession of His Majestys Arms, within the United States in the Space of three Months after the Signature of this definitive Treaty, or Sooner if possible, excepting those Ports contiguous to the water Line, mentioned in the fourth Proposition, and these shall be evacuated, when Congress shall give the Notice therein mentioned."

The Commissioners Defend the Treaty

18–19 July 1783

Secretary Livingston did not conceal his displeasure at the methods used by the American Commissioners in negotiating the Preliminary Articles. His outspoken letter of 25 March 1783 was followed by a dispatch of 21 April announcing Congress' ratification of these Articles.[1] In this second letter Livingston, while refraining from further comments on the departure by the Commissioners from their instructions, took issue with certain ambiguous phrases in the treaty as well as with the Declaration of the Cessation of Arms.

The Commissioners waited more than two months for official word of the

American reaction to the treaty. On 15 June Adams received a letter from Livingston of 14 April, briefly informing him that "Congress, the day before yesterday, agreed to ratify the Provisional Articles as such, and to release their prisoners, in which the British took the lead."[2] Not until 3 July, however, did the Commissioners see Livingston's lengthy dispatches of March and April.

The Commissioners met at Passy that evening to read and consider these letters. That no joint action was taken at that time may be accounted for on two scores. Henry Laurens, having departed the preceding month for England, was appealed to by Franklin to "return as soon as possible," but received the request too late to reach Paris before the Commissioners finally acted. Furthermore, the dispatches delivered on 3 July by Captain Barney were only duplicate copies of the public letters. Prudence might have dictated postponing a reply until the originals reached Paris with Colonel Ogden's arrival on 12 July.[3]

Meantime, the irrepressible Adams could not contain his anger. On 5 July he wrote Robert Morris: "if any man blames us, I wish him no other punishment than to have, if that were possible, just such another peace to negotiate, exactly in our situation." To Livingston he claimed that "your dispatches, sir, are not well adopted to give spirits to a melancholy man or to cure one sick with fever." Indeed, Adams wrote the Secretary three letters in as many days defending himself and his colleagues and denouncing French policy.[4]

Precisely when the Commissioners took up the task of drawing up a joint reply to Livingston's strictures is not known. Since the "Commencement of the Letter to Mr. Livingston . . ." (Document I below) mentions Barney's arrival but not Ogden's, it seems likely that drafting began as soon as the duplicate dispatches were received on 3 July.

It also seems likely that JJ was the author of most of the letter as finally agreed upon (Document III below). Only a copy of the "Commencement" draft has been found, and this copy includes the portion "concluded to be left out" as the result of Franklin's "Observations" (Document II below). The "Commencement" outlines four points to be covered in the Commissioners' reply. Franklin's "Observations" resulted in the omission of the arguments relating to the first two. The final version below of the joint reply, in the hand of William Temple Franklin, dated 18 July, includes arguments relating to the third and fourth points of JJ's draft, and to the separate and secret article. It is signed by Adams, Franklin, and JJ. Since it was JJ who had insisted on removing this article from the body of the treaty and placing it separately at the end, it seems highly probable that it was he who formulated the Commissioners' defense of their action on this point.[5] Laurens, who had many months before temporized on the issue of the need for treating separately from the French,[6] had some time earlier in July prepared a draft beginning of a letter which was much more deferential toward the French court and the alliance than either JJ's or the final letter.[7] However, before the letter was finally agreed to, Laurens had left Paris and was not around to sign it. It should be added that on 22 July Franklin hastened to reassure Livingston that he did not share the suspicions of Versailles harbored by JJ and Adams.[8] JJ's private letter to Livingston of 19 July (Document IV, below) includes all the remarks which Franklin persuaded the Commissioners to omit from the joint public dispatch.

Before the joint dispatch of 18 July reached the United States Livingston had quit the post of Secretary for Foreign Affairs and could no longer reply to the Commissioners in an official capacity. Still, he might have been expected to say something further in his private correspondence with JJ. However, the Chancellor's letters to JJ for the remaining period, 1783–84, are curiously silent on this topic.[9]

[1]Livingston to the Commissioners, 2 April 1783, *RDC,* VI, 386–87. For Congressional ratification of the Preliminaries on 15 April 1783, see *JCC,* XXIV, 243–51.

[2]Livingston to John Adams, 14 April 1783; Adams to Livingston, 16 June 1783, *RDC,* VI, 374–76, 488–91; *JAW,* VIII, 54–55, 70–73.

[3]Franklin to Laurens, 6 July 1783; Laurens to Franklin, 17 July 1783; Adams to Livingston, 13 July 1783, *RDC,* VI, 516, 538–40, 555, *JAW,* VIII, 95–97.

[4]Adams to Robert Morris, 5 July 1783; to Livingston, 9, 10, 11 July 1783. *RDC,* VI, 515, 529–34, 535–36; *JAW,* VIII, 81–83, 86–91, 93–95.

[5]See editorial note above, "Jay Draws Up the Preliminary Articles," 2 Oct. 1782.

[6]Laurens to Livingston, 24 Dec. 1782. *RDC,* V, 165.

[7]Passy, c. July 1783 in MHi: Adams, reel 103, pp. 225–27.

[8]Franklin to Livingston, 22 July 1783, *BFS,* IX, 59–75, at pp. 60–61. Ridley was incorrect about Laurens' having signed the joint letter, but right on the mark about the Carolinian's avowed confidence in the French Court. Diary, July 1783, MHi: Ridley.

[9]See below, Livingston to JJ, 29 Nov. 1783, and 25 Jan. 1784; *Peacemakers,* pp. 444–45.

[Document I]

To Robert R. Livingston: Draft

"Commencement of the Letter to Mr. Livingston as 1st drawn up by Mr. Jay, But concluded to be left out."

[Passy, 18 July 1783]

Sir,

We have had the honor of receiving by Capt. Barney your two Letters of the 21 and 25 April last,[1] with the Papers referred to in them.

We are happy to find that the provisional Articles have been approved and ratified by Congress; and we regret that the Manner, in which that Business was conducted, does not coincide with your Ideas of Propriety.

Your Doubts on that Head appear to have arisen from the following Circumstances.

1. That we entertained and were influenced by Distrusts and Sus-

picions, which do not seem to you to have been altogether well founded.

2. That we signed the Articles, without previously communicating them to this Court.

3. That we consented to a separate article, which you consider, as not being very important in itself, and as offensive to Spain.

4. That we kept, and still keep, that article a secret.[2]

With respect to the first, your Doubts appear to us some what singular. In our Negociation with the British Commissioner, it was essential to insist on; and, if possible, to obtain his Consent to four important Concessions, viz.

1. That Britain should treat with us as being what we were, viz. an independent People.

The French Minister thought this Demand Premature, and that it ought to arise from, and not precede the Treaty.

2. That Britain should agree to the Extent of Boundary we claimed.

The French Minister thought the Demand extravagant in itself, and as militating against certain Views of Spain, which he was disposed to favour.

3. That Britain should admit our Right in common to the Fishery.

The French Minister thought this Demand too extensive.

4. That Britain should not insist on our reinstating the Tories.

The French Minister argued, that they ought to be reinstated.

Was it unnatural for us, Sir, to conclude from these Facts; that the French Minister was opposed to our succeeding on these four great Points, in the Extent we wished? For it appeared evident, that his Plan of a Treaty for us, was far from being such an one, as America would have preferred; and, as we disapproved of his model, we thought it imprudent to give him an Opportunity of moulding our Treaty by it.

Whether the Minister was influenced by what he really thought would be best for France, is a Question, which, however easy, or however difficult, to decide, is not very important to the Point under Consideration. Whatever his motives may have been, certain it is, that they were such as militated against our System; and as in private Life, it is deemed imprudent to admit opponents to full Confidence, so, in public affairs, the like Caution seems equally proper.

But, admitting the force of this Reasoning, why, when the Articles were compleated, did we not communicate them to the French Minister, before we proceeded to sign them? For the following Resons, Sir!

As Lord Shelburne had excited expectations of his beng able to put a speedy Termination to the War, it became necessary for him, either to realize those Expectations, or to quit his Place. The Parliament having met, while his Negociations with us were pending, he found it expedient, to adjourn it for a short Term, in Hopes of then meeting it with all the Advantage, which he might naturally expect, from a favorable Issue of the Negociation. Hence it was his Interest to draw it to a close before that Adjournment expired; and to obtain that End, both he and his Commissioner prevailed upon themselves to yield certain points, on which they would, probably, have been otherwise more tenacious. Nay we have, and then had, good Reason to believe that the Latitude allowed by the British Cabinet for the Exercise of Discretion, was exceeded on that Occasion.

You need not be reminded, Sir; that the King of G[reat] Britain had pledged himself in Mr. Oswald's Commission to confirm and ratify, *Not* what Mr. Oswald should *verbally agree to,* but what he should *formally sign his name and affix his Seal to.*[3]

Had we communicated the Articles, when ready for signing to the French Minister, he doubtless would have complimented us on the Terms of them; but at the same time he would have insisted on our postponing the Signature of them, until the Articles, then preparing between France, Spain and Britain, should also be ready for signing, He having often intimated to us, that we should all sign at the same Time and Place.

This would have exposed us to a disagreable Dilemma.

Had we agreed to postpone signing the Articles, the British Cabinet, might, and probably would, have taken Advantage of it. They might have insisted that, as the Articles were *Res infecta,*[4] and as they had not authorized Mr. Oswald to accede to certain matters inserted in them, they did not conceive themselves bound in honor or justice to adopt Mr. Oswald opinions, or permit him to sign and seal, as their Commissioner, a Number of Articles, which they did not approve. The whole Business would thereby have been set afloat again; and the Minister of France would have had an Opportunity, at least, of approving the objections of the British Cabinet, and of advising us to recede from Demands, which in his Opinion, were immoderate, and some of which were too inconsistant with the Views and Claims of Spain to meet with his Concurrence.

If, on the other hand, we had refused to postpone the signing, and supposing that no other ill consequence would have resulted, yet certainly, such refusal would have been more offensive to the French Minister, than our doing it without his Knowledge, and consequently without his Opposition. Our withholding from [him] the Knowledge of these articles, until after they were signed was no Breach of our Treaty with France, and, therefore, could not afford her any Ground of Complaint against the United States. It was indeed a Departure from the Line of Conduct precribed by our Instructions; but we apprehend that Congress marked out that Line for their own Sakes, and not for the Sake of France. They directed us to ask and be directed by the advice of the French Minister because they supposed it would be for the Interest of America to receive and be governed by it. It was a Favor she asked from France, and not a Favor that she promised to, and we withheld from, France. Congress, therefore, alone have a Right to complain of the Departure. As to the Confidence which ought to subsist between Allies, we have only to remark, that as the French Minister did not think proper to consult us about his Articles, our giving him as little Trouble about ours, was perfectly equal and reciprocal.

LbkC in MHi: Adams, reel 103, p. 219–24, Endorsed: "... Commencement of the Letter to Mr. Livingston as 1st drawn up by Mr. Jay, But concluded to be left out." LbkC in DLC: Franklin VIII, 207–11. Incomplete in Hale, *Franklin in France,* II, 200–01.

[1]The references are to Livingston's dispatches dated 25 March, above, and 21 April 1783 (*RDC,* VI, 386–87).

[2]Items 3 and 4 omitted from JJ's private letter to Livingston of 19 July, below.

[3]See Oswald's revised commission, dated 21 Sept. 1782, above.

[4]"A subject not concluded."

[Document II]
BENJAMIN FRANKLIN'S OBSERVATIONS ON JAY'S DRAFT

[Passy, 18 July 1783]

Mr. F. Submits it to the Consideration of Mr. Jay whether it may be adviseable to forbear at present the Justification of ourselves respecting the Signature of the Preliminaries because:

That matter is at present quiet here.

No Letter sent to the Congress is ever kept secret.

The Justification contains some charges of unfavourable Disposition in the Ministers here towards us, that will give offence and will be denied.

Our Situation is still critical with respect to the two Nations and the most perfect good Understanding should be maintained with this.

The Congress do not call upon us for an Account of our Conduct or its Justification. They have not by any Resolution blamed us. What Censure we have received is only the private Opinion of Mr. Livingston.

Mr. Laurens is not here, who is concerned with us.

Will it be attended with any Inconvenience if that part of the Letter which relates to the Signature be reserved to a future Occasion.

LbkC in DLC: Franklin VIII, 212: "Mr. Franklin's Observations on Mr. Jay's first Draft of a Letter to Mr. Livingston which occasioned the foregoing part to be left out." LbkC in MHi: Adams, reel 103, pp. 224–25. Hale, *Franklin in France,* II, 201–02, with omissions.

[Document III]
JOHN ADAMS, BENJAMIN FRANKLIN, AND JOHN JAY TO ROBERT R. LIVINGSTON

Passy, 18 July 1783

Sir,

We had the honour of receiving by Capt. Barney your two Letters of the 25th March and 21st April, with the Papers referred to in them.

We are happy to find that the Provisional Articles have been approved and ratified by Congress, and we regret that the Manner in which that Business was conducted, does not coincide with your Ideas of Propriety. We are persuaded however that this is principally owing to your being necessarily unacquainted with a Number of Circumstances, known to us who are on the Spot, and which will be particularly explained to you hereafter, and, we trust, to your Satisfaction and that of the Congress.

Your Doubts respecting the Separate Article we think are capable of being removed, but as a full State of the Reasons and Circumstances which prompted that Measure would be very prolix, we Shall content ourselves with giving you general Outlines.

Mr. Oswald was desirous to cover as much of the Eastern Shores of the Missisippi with British Claims as possible and for this purpose we were told a great deal about the ancient Bounds of Canada, Louisiana, etc., etc. The British Court who had probably not yet adopted the idea of relinquishing the Floridas, seemed desirous of annexing as much Territory to them as possible, even up to the mouth of the Ohio. Mr. Oswald adhered strongly to that Object as well to render the British Countries there of sufficient Extent to be (as he expressed it) worth keeping and protecting: as to afford a convenient Retreat to the Tories for whom it would be difficult otherwise to provide; and, among other Arguments he finally urged his being willing to yield to our Demands to the East, North, and West, as a further Reason for our gratifying him on the Point in Question. He also produced the Commission of Governor Johnson extending the Bounds of his Government of W. Florida up to the

River Yassou and contended for that Extent as a Matter of Right upon various Principles which however we did not admit.[1]

We were of Opinion that the Country in Contest was of great Value, both on Account of its natural Fertility, and of its Position, it being in our Opinion the Interest of America to extend as far down towards the Mouth of the Missisippi as we possibly could. We also thought it advisable to impress Britain with a strong Sense of the Importance of the Navigation of that River, to their future Commerce on the interior Waters from the Mouth of the River St. Lawrence to that of the Missisippi, and thereby render that Court averse to any Stipulations with Spain to relinquish it. These two objects militated against each other; because to inhance the Value of the Navigation was also to inhance the Value of the Countries contiguous to it, and thereby disincline Britain to the Dereliction of them. We thought therefore that the surest Way to reconcile and obtain both Objects would be a Composition beneficial to both Parties. We therefore proposed that Britain should withdraw her Pretensions to all the Country above the Yassous and that we would cede all below it to her in Case she should have the Floridas at the End of the War, and at all Events that she should have a Right to navigate the River throughout its whole extent. This proposition was accepted and we agreed to insert the contingent Part of it in a separate Article for the express purpose of keeping it secret for the Present. That Article ought not therefore to be considered as a mere Matter of Favor to Britain, but as the Result of a bargain in which that article was a *"quid pro quo."* It was in our Opinion both necessary and justifiable to keep this Article secret. The Negotiations between Spain France and Britain were then in full Vigour, and embarrassed by a Variety of clashing Demands. The Publication of this Article would have irritated Spain, and retarded if not have prevented her coming to an Agreement with Britain. Had we mentioned it to the French Minister, he must have not only informed Spain of it, but also been obliged to act a Part respecting it that would probably have been disagreeable to America, and he certainly has reason to rejoice that our Silence saved him that delicate and disagreeable task. This was an article in which France had not the smallest Interest, nor is there any-thing in her Treaty with us that restrains us from making what Bargain we pleased with Britain about those or any other Lands, without rendering Account of such Transaction to her or any other Power whatever. The same Observation applies with still greater Force to Spain, and neither Justice or Honor forbid us to dispose as we pleased of our own Lands, without her Knowledge or consent. Spain at that very time extended her Pretensions and Claims of Dominion not only over the Tract in Question, but over the Vast Region lying between the Floridas and Lake Superior; and this Court was also at that very Time soothing and nursing of those Pretensions by a proposed conciliatory Line for Splitting the Difference. Suppose, therefore, we had offered this Tract to Spain in case She retained the Floridas, should we even have had Thanks for it? or would it have abated the Chagrin she experienced from being disappointed in her extravagant and improper Designs on that whole country? we think not.

We perfectly concur with you in Sentiment, Sir, *"that honesty is the best policy."* but until it be shown that we have trespassed on the Rights of any Man or Body of men, you must excuse our thinking that this Remark as applied to our Proceedings was unnecessary.

Should any Explanations either with France or Spain become necessary on this Subject, we hope and expect to meet with no Embarrassments. We shall neither amuse them nor perplex ourselves with ostensible and flimsy Excuses, but tell them plainly that as it was not our Duty to give them the Information, we considered ourselves at Liberty to withhold it, and we shall remind the French Minister that he has more Reason to be pleased than displeased with our Silence. Since we have assumed a place in the Political System of the World let us move like a Primary and not like a Secondary Planet.

We are persuaded, sir, that your Remarks on these Subjects resulted from real Opinion, and were made with Candor and Sincerity. The Best Men will view Objects of this Kind in different Lights even when Standing on the same Ground: and it is not to be wondered at that we who are on the Spot and have the whole Transaction under our Eyes should see many Parts of it in a stronger Point of Light than Persons at a Distance, who can only view it through the dull Medium of Representation.

It would give us great Pain if any-thing we have written or now write respecting this Court should be construed to impeach the Friendship of the King and Nation for us. We also believe that the Minister is so far our Friend, and is disposed so far to do us Good Offices, as may correspond with, and be dictated by his System of Policy for Promoting the Power, Riches, and Glory of France. God forbid that we should ever sacrifice our Faith, our gratitude, or our Honour to any Consideration of Convenience; and may he also forbid that we should ever be unmindful of the Dignity and independent Spirit which should always characterize a free and generous people.

We shall immediately propose an Article to be inserted in the

Definitive Treaty for postponing the Payment of British Debts for the Time mentioned by Congress.[2]

There are, no doubt, certain ambiguities in our Articles, but it is not to be wondered at when it is considered how exceedingly averse Britain was to Expressions which explicitly wounded the Tories, and how disinclined we were to use any that should amount to absolute Stipulations in their Favour.

The Words for restoring the Property of *real British subjects* were well understood and explained between us not to mean or comprehend American refugees. Mr. Oswald and Mr. Fitzherbert know this to have been the Case, and will readily confess and admit it. This mode of Expression was preferred by them as a more delicate Mode of excluding those Refugees, and of making a proper Distinction between them and the Subjects of Britain whose only *particular* Interest in America consisted in holding lands or property there.

The[3] Article, vizt., where it declares that no *future confiscations* shall be made, etc., ought to have fixed the time with greater Accuracy. We think the most fair and true Construction is, that it relates to the Date of the Cessation of Hostilities. That is the Time when Peace in Fact took Place, in consequence of Prior informal though binding contracts to terminate the War. We consider the Definitive Treaties as only giving the Dress of Form to those Contracts, and not as constituting the Obligation of them. Had the Cessation of Hostilities been the Effect of a Truce and consequently nothing more than a temporary Suspension of War, another Construction would have been the true one.

We are Officially assured by Mr. Hartley that positive Orders for the Evacuation of New York have been despatched, and that no avoidable Delay will retard that Event. Had we proposed to fix a Time for it, the British Commissioner would have contended that it should be a Time posterior to the Date of the definitive Treaty, and that would have been probably more disadvantageous to us than as that Article now stands.

We are surprised to hear that any Doubts have arisen in America respecting the time when the Cessation of hostilities took Place there. It most certainly took Place at the expiration of one Month after the Date of that Declaration in all Parts of the World, whether by Land or Sea, that lay North of the Latitude of the Canaries.

The Ships afterwards taken from us in the more Northerly Latitudes ought to be reclaimed and given up: We shall apply to Mr. Hartley on this Subject, and also on that of the Transportation of Negroes from New York contrary to the Words and Intention of the Provisional Articles.

With great Esteem, we have the honour to be, Sir, Your most obedient and most humble Servants.

JOHN ADAMS
B. FRANKLIN
JOHN JAY

LS in hand of W. T. Franklin in MHi: Adams, reel 103, pp. 211–18; PCC 85, pp. 300–12; LbkCs in DLC: Franklin VII, 200–07 and in PCC 106; E in MHi: Cranch. Variations in text in *RDC,* VI, 566–70.

[1]"the King not being authorized in our opinion to extend or contract the bounds of the colonies at present" appears in *RDC* version.

[2]See above JJ: Article for Inclusion in American Commissioners to Hartley, 17 July 1783.

[3]"sixth" in *RDC* version.

[Document IV]
TO ROBERT R. LIVINGSTON

Passy, 19 July 1783

Dear Robert,

Our Dispatches by Barney must be ready the Day after Tomorrow. The many Letters I have written and have still to write by him, together with Conferences, Company etc. keep me fully[1] employed. You will therefore excuse my not descending so much to particulars as both of us indeed might wish.

As little that passes in Congress is kept entirely secret, we think it prudent at least to postpone giving you a more minute Detail than you have already recieved of the Reasons which induced Us to sign the provisional articles without previously communicating them to the french minister. For your private Satisfaction however I will make a few Remarks on that Subject. Your Doubts respecting the Propriety of our Conduct in that Instance appear to have arisen from the following Circumstances vizt.

1. That we entertained and were influenced by Distrusts and Suspicions which do not seem to You to have been altogether well founded.

2. That we signed the Articles without previously communicating them to this court.

With Respect to the *first:* In our negociation with the british Com[missione]r it was essential to insist on, and if possible obtain his Consent to four important Concessions.

1. That Britain should treat with us as being what we were, vizt. an independent people. The french minister thought this Demand premature, and that it ought to arise from, and not precede the Treaty.

2. That Britain should agree to the Extent of Boundary we claimed. The french minister thought our Demand on that Head extravagant in themselves, and as militating against certain Views of Spain which he was disposed to favor.

3. That Britain should admit our Right in Common to the Fishery. The french minister thought this Demand too extensive.

4. That Britain should not insist on our reinstating the Tories. The french minister argued that they ought to be reinstated.

Was it unnatural for us to conclude from these Facts that the french minister was opposed to our succeeding on these four great points, in the Extent we wished? It appeared evident that his plan of a Treaty for america, was far from being such as america would have preferred; and as we disapproved of his model, we thought it imprudent to give him an opportunity of moulding our Treaty by it.

Whether the Minister was influenced by what he really thought best for us, or by what he really thought best for France, is a Question which however easy or difficult to decide, is not very important to the Point under Consideration. Whatever his motives may have been, certain it is that they were such as opposed our System; and as in private Life it is deemed imprudent to admit opponents to full Confidence,[2] especially respecting the very Matters in Competition, so in public affairs the like Caution seems equally proper.

Secondly—But admitting the Force of this Reasoning, why, when the articles were compleated, did we not communicate them to the French Minister, *before* we proceeded to sign them? for the following Reasons—

The Expectations excited in England by Lord Shelbourn's Friends, that he would put a speedy Period to the war, made it necessary for him either to realize those Expectations, or prepare to quit[3] his Place. The Parliament being to meet before his Negociations with us were concluded, he found it expedient to adjourn it for a short Term, in Hopes of their meeting it with all the advantage that might be expected from a favorable Issue of the Negociation. Hence it was his Interest to draw it to a Close before that adjournment should expire; and to obtain that End both he and his Commissioner became less tenacious on certain Points than they would otherwise have been. Nay we have, and then had, good Reason to believe that the Latitude allowed by the British Cabinet for the Exercise of Discretion was exceeded on that occasion.

I must now remind you that the King of G<reat> Britain had pledged himself, in Mr. Oswald's Commission, to confirm and ratify *not* what Mr. Oswald should *verbally* agree to, but what he should *formally sign his name and affix his Seal to.*

Had we communicated the articles when ready for signing to the French Minister, he doubtless would have complimented us on the Terms of them, but at the same Time he would have insisted on our postponing the Signature until the articles then preparing between France Spain and Britain should also be ready for signing, he having often intimated to us that we should all sign at the same Time and Place. This would have exposed us to a disagreeable Dilemma.

Had we agreed to postpone signing the articles, the British Cabinet might and probably[4] would have[5] taken advantage of it. They might (if better prospects had offered) have insisted that the articles were still *Res infecta.*[6] That Mr. Oswald had exceeded the Limits of his Instructions, and for both these Reasons that they concieved themselves still at Liberty to dissent from his Opinions, and to forbid his executing a Set of Articles they could not approve of. It is true that this might not have happened, but it is equally true that it might, and therefore it was a Risque of too great Importance to run. The whole Business would in that Case have been set afloat again, and the Minister of France would have had an opportunity at least of approving the objections of the British Court, and of advising us to recede from Demands which in his opinion were immoderate, and too inconsistent with the claims of Spain to meet with his Concurrence.

If on the other Hand, we had contrary to his advice and Request, refused to postpone the signing, it is natural to suppose that such Refusal would have given more offence to the French Minister than our doing it without consulting him at all about the Matter.

Our withholding from him the Knowledge of these articles until after they were signed, was no violation of our Treaty with France, and therefore she has no Room for Complaint, on that Principle, against the United States.

Congress had indeed made and published a Resolution not to make peace but in Confidence and in Concurrence with France. So far as this Resolution declares against a *separate* peace, it has been incontestably observed, and admitting that the words in Confidence and in Concurrence with France, mean that we should mention to the French Minister and consult with him about every Step of our Proceedings, yet it is most certain that it was founded on a mutual Understanding that France would patronize our Demands and assist us in obtaining the

Objects of them. France therefore by discouraging our claims ceased to be entitled to the Degree of Confidence respecting them which was specified in the Resolution. It may be said that France must admit the Reasonableness of our Claims, before we could properly expect that she should promote them. She knew what were our Claims before the Negociation commenced, though she could only conjecture what Reception they would meet with from Britain. If she thought our Claims extravagant, she may be excusable for not countenancing them in their full extent; but then we ought also to be excused for not giving her the full Confidence on those Subjects which was promised on the implied Condition of her supporting them.

But Congress positively instructed us to do nothing without the advice and Consent of the French Minister, and we have departed from that Line of Conduct. This is also true, but then I apprehend that Congress marked out that Line of Conduct for their own Sake, and not for the Sake of France. The object of that Instruction was the supposed Interest of America, and not of France; and we were directed to ask the advice of the French Minister, because it was thought advantageous to our Country that we should recieve and be governed by it. Congress *only* therefore have a Right to complain of our Departure from the Line of that Instruction.

If it be urged that Confidence ought to subsist between Allies, I have only to remark that as the French Minister did not consult us about his articles, nor make us any Communications about them, our giving him as little Trouble about our's did not violate any Principle of Reciprocity.

Our joint Letter to You by Captain Barney[7] contains an Explanation of our Conduct respecting the separate article.

I proceed now to your obliging letter of the 1st May, for which I sincerely Thank You.

This will probably find you at Claremont. I consider your Resignation as more reconcileable to your Plan and views of Happiness,[8] than to the public Good. The War may indeed be ended, but other Difficulties of a serious Nature remain; and require all the address and wisdom of our best men to manage.

As Benson informed You that my Family had no present occasion for Supplies from me, I am more easy on that Head than I have been. I have some fear however that they may rather have been influenced to decline my offers, by Delicacy with Respect to me, than by the Ease of their Circumstances. I wish you would take an opportunity of talking freely with my Brother Peter on this subject, Assure him that it would distress me greatly were he or indeed any of the Family to experience Embarrassments in my Power to obviate. He may share with me to the last shilling, and so may Nancy, about whom until within a Day or two I had been very uneasy. Tell them and Fœdy that I mean if God pleases, to return next Spring, and that one of the greatest Pleasures of my Life will be that of rendering it subservient to their Ease and Welfare. I write to Fœdy by this Opportunity and authorize him to draw upon me for £150 York money to be divided between the three.[9] If on conversing with Peter you should find that more would be convenient to him, be pleased to supply it, and draw upon me for the amount at thirty Days Sight.

I intend in my next to send You a State of my private account with the public. I have not Time now to prepare it.

What you mention of the Conduct of two certain Gentlemen with Respect to You, does not surprize me. I know them both.[10]

I have lately heard of Mr. Kissam's Death. It affected me much. He was a virtuous and agreable Man, and I owed him many Obligations. His Children are now orphans. I am God-father to one of his Sons, named Samuel after his uncle a very worthy Friend of ours, for whom I had a great Regard, and who I hear is also dead. When you go to New York pray make some Inquiries about that unfortunate Family, and let me know the Result. I have lately recieved a Letter from one of the Sons, who it seems is at Edinburgh, and who before the War, was a promising Boy. When I see New York I expect to meet the Shades of many a departed Joy.[11]

Thinking of Mr. Kissam's Familty, calls to my Mind the Fate of the Tories. As far as I can learn, the general opinion in Europe is that they have Reason to complain, and that our Country ought to manifest Magnanimity with Respect to them. Europe neither knows nor can be made to believe what inhuman barbarous wretches the greater Part of them have been, and therefore is disposed to pity them more than they deserve.

I hope for my Part that the States will adopt some Principle for deciding on their Cases—and that it will be such an one as, by being perfectly consistent with Justice and Humanity, may meet with the approbation not only of disinterested[12] Nations at present, but also[13] of dispassionate Posterity hereafter. My opinion would be, *to pardon all, except the faithless and the cruel,* and publicly to declare that by this Rule they should be judged and treated. Indiscriminate Severity would be wrong as well as unbecoming; nor ought any Man to be marked out for Vengeance, because as King James said, he would make a *bonny*

Traitor.[14] In short, I think that the *faithless and the cruel* should be banished forever, and their Estates confiscated. It is just and reasonable. As to the Residue, who have either upon Principle openly and fairly opposed us, or who from Timidity have fled from the Storm, and remained inoffensive; let us[15] not punish the first for behaving like men, nor be extremely severe to the latter because Nature had made them like Women.

I send you a Box of plaistor Copies of Medals. If Mrs. Livingston will permit you to keep so many mistresses, reserve the Ladies for Yourself, and give the Philosophers and Poets to Edward.

Now for our Girls. I congratulate you on the Health of the first, the Birth of the Second, and the promising appearance of both. I will chearfully be Godfather to the latter.[16] What is her name?[17]

Our little one is doing well, and will have a Brother or Sister next month. If People in Heaven see what is going on here below, my ancestors must derive Pleasure from comparing the Circumstances attending the Expulsion of some of them from this Country, with those under which my Family will be encreased in it.

Since my Removal to this place, where the air is remarkably good, the pain in my Breast has abated, and I have now no Fever.

Mrs. Jay is tolerably well. Assure Mrs. Livingston and our other Friends with you, of our Regard.

I am Dear Robert, Your affectionate Friend,

JOHN JAY

ALS in NHi: Robert R. Livingston. Endorsed by Livingston. Dft in PPInd; Tr in NN: Bancroft LIV, 440; incomplete in *WJ,* I, 174–81.

1"Tightly" in Dft.

2"Transaction" in Dft.

3"Expose himself to popular odium and the Hazard of" in Dft.

4"(In Case a prospect of doing better had offered)" in Dft.

5"Either prevailed upon themselves or been prevailed into" in Dft.

6"A subject not concluded."

7The joint letter of 18 July 1783, above.

8"Private Interest" in Dft.

9See JJ to Frederick Jay, 18 July 1783, under "Transatlantic Bonds," below.

10See above, Livingston to JJ, 1 May 1783, referring to James Duane and John Morin Scott.

11Benjamin Kissam, Sr., died in 1782. Benjamin Kissam, Jr. (1759–1803), who received his M.D. at Edinburgh in 1783, served as Professor of Medicine at Columbia College, 1785–92. The earliest letter from Dr. Kissam to JJ which has been located is dated 3 Dec. 1783, ALS *in JP.* For Kissam, Sr., see *JJ,* I, 52 *et seq.*

12"Dispassionate" in Dft.

13"With disinterested and cool thinking" in Dft.

14"The Plunder is not a justifiable Object of Punishment" in Dft.

15"Forgive" in Dft.

[16]"While you Live, and a father to her in Case you should leave her Infancy which God forbid" in Dft.

[17]Livingston's younger daughter was christened Margaret Maria (1783–1818).

To William Livingston

Passy, 19 July 1783

Dear Sir,

On the 1st Instant I had the Pleasure of recieving your Favor of the 21 May last,[1] but have neither seen nor heard any Thing of Doctor Wearing whom you mention as the Bearer of it. Should he come this Way, I shall certainly pay him all the Attention which you or President Boudinot could wish.

I am happy to hear that the provisional articles meet with general approbation. The Tories will doubtless <give Trouble> cause some Difficulty but that they have always done, and as this <is the last> will probably be last Time <that the Refugees will plague us,> we must <keep our Temper and Patience> make the best of it. A universal indiscriminating Condemnation and Expulsion of those People <will> would not redound to our Honour, because <it would thus nearly resemble an Effort of blind> so harsh a Measure <could only result hasty> would partake more of Vengeance, <ever to be ascribed to that considerate Regard to Justice and Humanity which [h] is> than of Justice. For my part I wish that all except the *faithless and the cruel* may be forgiven—that Exception <will include but> would indeed extend to very few, but even if it applied to the Case of one <or two> only, that one ought in my Opinion to be <pardoned> saved.

<A Letter said to be written in New York and published in an English paper mentions your having been at New York, and that you there said "a Gallows ought to be erected in every street to hang the Tories on.">

The Reluctance with which the States in general pay the necessary Taxes is much to be regretted. It injures both their Reputation and Interest abroad as well as at Home, and tends to cherish the Hopes and Speculations of those who wish we may <always be> become and remain an unimportant divided People. The Rising power of America is a serious object of Apprehension to more than one Nation, and every Event that may retard it will <give them> be agreable to them. A continental national Spirit should therefore pervade our Country, and Congress should be enabled by a Grant of the necessary powers, to regulate the Commerce and general Concerns of the Confederacy, and we should remember that to be constantly prepared for War is the only Way to have Peace. The Swiss on the one Hand and the Dutch on the other bear Testimony to the Truth of this Remark.

The General and the Army have by their late Moderation done themselves infinite Honor, and it is to be hoped that the States will not only be just but generous to those brave and virtuous Citizens. America is at present held in a very respectable point of View, but as the Eyes of the World is upon her, the Continuance of that Consideration will depend on the Dignity and wisdom of her conduct.

I mean to return next Spring. My Health is some what better. Sally will increase our Family next Month. I am Dear Sir, Your affectionate and humble Servant.

Dft. Endorsed by JJ. JJ's deletions not included in abridged version in *WJ,* II, 121, or in *HPJ,* III, 54–55.

[1]See above.

To Robert Morris

Passy, 20 July 1783

Dear Sir,

By Captain Barney I was favored with yours of the 31st May. By this Time I hope you will have recieved several Letters from me which were then on the way. Want of Health has long made much writing painful to me, so that my Letters in general are short.

My Jaunt to Normandy did me some Service, but less than I expected. The pure air of this Place has been useful to me. The pain in my breast is abated and I have had no fever since I came here, which was about six weeks ago.

Mr. Barclay having called upon me for my Accounts I have written to Mr. Carmichael to come here with the Books and Papers.[1] As yet I have not recieved his answer. Before I left Spain I requested him to make out a State of them and to send it to you. I am anxious to have this matter settled.

I hear Kitty is about to return to Elizabeth Town, and I am sorry her Health continues so delicate. I believe every word that you tell me about her and indeed about any body else, for in no one's Sincerity do I repose more Confidence than in yours.

Gouverneur is happy in your Esteem; it adds to mine for him. I have long been attached to him, and sincerely wish that our Friendship instead of being diminished may continue to gain Strength with Time. Your intended Resignation alarmed me, and would have been followed with ill Consequences to our affairs. I rejoice that you continue in Office, and by no Means Regret that it will be less in your power than Inclination to retire soon. I am well aware of the Difficulties you will continue to experience. Every man so circumstanced must expect them. Your office is neither an easy nor a pleasant one to execute, but it is elevated and important and therefore Envy, with her inseparable Companion Injustice, will not cease to plague you. Remember however that Triumphs do not precede Victory, and that Victory is seldom found in the smooth Paths of Peace and Tranquility. Your Enemies would be happy to drive you to resign, and in my opinion both your Interest and that of our Country oppose your gratifying them. <Sully[2] had also his Difficulties, but had he turned his back upon them, the name of Sully would not have been so illustrious as it is.> You have Health Fortune Talents and Fortitude, and you have Children too. Each of these Circumstances recommend Perseverance.

As to money, this Court will afford you no further Supplies. The Minister has said it was easy to be a Financier, and draw Bills, when others provided the Funds to pay them. At another Time he intimated that his Court was not treated with a proper Degree of Delicacy on that Subject and said "that you treated them as your Cashier." A french officer from america who is a friend of yours told me that La Luzerne and Marbois were not pleased with the Manner of your application to them about Money Matters. I mention these Facts because it may be useful for you to know them.

The Loan in Holland goes on, and from that Quarter your Bills must be saved if at all. Mr. Adams set out for amsterdam the Day before Yesterday, and will push on that Business. If the Dutch began to draw Benefit from our Trade they would lend more chearfully.

The British Ministry have not yet authorized Mr. Hartly to consent to any thing as to Commerce. They amuse him and us and decieve themselves. I told him yesterday that they would find us like a Globe —not to be overset. They wish to be the only Carriers between their Islands and other Countries, and though they are apprized of our Right to regulate our Trade as we please, yet I suspect they flatter themselves that the Different States possess too little of a national or continental Spirit ever to agree in any one National System. I think they will find themselves mistaken.

Young Bache[3] came here two Days ago from Geneva and left your Sons in good Health. My former Letters inform you that I was satisfied with their Situation there and that Mr. Ridley Conduct in that Business way is in my opinion both judicious and meritorious.

What is to be done with the Bills to which the Papers herewith enclosed relate?

Mrs. Jay is writing to Mrs. Morris. Be pleased to present my Compliments to her and believe me to be Dear Sir your affectionate Friend.

Dft. Paragraphs 3, 4, 5 11 of the Dft omitted from *HPJ*, III, 64–66, and *RDC*, VI, 577–78.

[1]See JJ to Carmichael, 1 July 1783. Dft in JP, and see "Settling the Spanish Accounts," below.

[2]Maximilien de Béthune, duc de Sully (1560–1614), financial superintendent under Henry IV of France.

[3]Benjamin Franklin Bache (1769–98), son of Sarah Franklin Bache, had accompanied his grandfather to Europe.

Lafayette to the American Commissioners

Chavaniac, 22 July 1783

Gentlemen,

Having Been Honoured With Letters from Congress, it Becomes my duty to Consult You Upon a point Which they Have particularly Recommended: In the late preliminaries no time is Mentionned for the American Merchants paying their English debts, a Matter of Great Moment to our Merchants who Require at least three or four Years to Accomplish the Business. Upon the Receipt of the Letter, I Have Adressed Count de Vergennes and Represented to Him How important a favorable decision on this point would Be to the french trade. Having the Uneasiness of our American Merchants on that affair, I Cannot Help Partaking of it, and Would Consider it as a Great favor to Be Acquainted With the present Situation of things, and With the farther Measures You Might think proper for me to Undertake.[1]

The General Satisfaction Which arose from the terms of peace, is a Matter of justice to You, Gentlemen, that Affords Me a Most Unfeigned pleasure. Give me leave to present You With the Assurances of an Affectionate Respect. I Have the Honour to Be With Your obedient Humble Servant,

LAFAYETTE

ALS in MHi: Adams, reel 361. Endorsed by Adams.

[1]In a private letter to Lafayette of 12 April 1783, Elias Boudinot reported: "The Terms of Peace give universal Satisfaction except that no Time is mentioned for the American Merchants paying their English Debts. Having the greatest parts of their Estates in the publick Funds, and having suffered greatly by the Depreciation

of the money, Inevitable ruin must be their Portion if they have not three or four years to Accomplish the Business. This is a matter of very considerable Consequence to which I hope our Ministers will pay attention in the definitive Treaty. This should also be an object with France, as if not remedied, will throw our Merchants too absolutely in the hands of the English Creditors. Shall I ask your attention to this subject . . ." J. J. Boudinot, ed., *The Life, Public Services, Addresses and Letters of Elias Boudinot* (2 vols., Boston, 1896), I, 315–17. The Commissioners had already, in their letter to Hartley of 17 July 1783, above, suggested that the article on debts in the Definitive Treaty be amended to delay execution on a judgment of an American debt to a British creditor for three years from the date of the treaty. Their modification was not incorporated in the Definitive Treaty. No reply from the American Commissioners to Lafayette's letter has been found.

From Gouverneur Morris

Philadelphia, 25 July 1783

Dear Jay,

This Letter will be delivered to you by Messrs. Wadsworth and Carter who are on their way to Paris. I think you know them both. Carter is married to the Daughter of our friend Schuyler; Wadsworth the Commissary General of the American Army. I think you are well acquainted with him. I could not omit so favorable an opportunity to assure you of the Continuance of my Existence and what amounts to the same Thing my friendship and Esteem. By a Letter of Recommendation which you wrote in favor of Mr. Grigby[1] I see clearly that your Health was (then at least) mending. I hope it is perfectly restored and that among many Cares and some Pleasures you will find a moment in which to tell me so. I very frequently write to you but very seldom hear from you. My Letters indeed are not worth much for they are in general careless things just penned from the Heart without attention or Method or any Thing to recommend them but the Confidence with which they throw themselves on your Indulgence.

We hear the definitive Treaty has arrived at New York but we have not seen it, nor is New York yet evacuated or like to be so in any very short Period. Congress are sitting at Princeton; of their movements and of every other public Thing Wadsworth will give you full Information.[2]

Remember me affectionately to Mrs. Jay. Tell her that not long since I saw her Son who is really a very fine Boy and if he were thrown from under the Wings of Grandmamma etc., and obliged to shift and shuffle for himself would get rid of an inconvenient Bashfulness which now hangs about him. But with it and just as he is I repeat to you again that he is a very fine Boy and although Beauty is but a slender accomplishment yet it is worth Something especially when as in the present Case it anounces Candor and Ingenuousness of Disposition.

Adieu, beleive me affectionately yours,

GOUV. MORRIS

ALS. Endorsed: ". . . Ansd. 24 Sepr. 1783."

[1]A Dft of JJ's letter of introduction for Joshua Grigby to Robert Morris of 8 April 1783 is in JP. Grigby, a young man of "considerable property," had been recommended to JJ by Benjamin Vaughan.

[2]This is a veiled reference to the mutinous behavior of soldiers furloughed by Congress before a final settlement of their accounts had been made. A threatening assembly of soldiers outside the State House in Philadelphia, where the Congress and the Supreme Executive Council of Pennsylvania were separately meeting, persuaded Congress to move to Princeton, where the delegates convened from 30 June to 4 Nov. 1783. See Varnum L. Collins, *The Continental Congress at Princeton* (Princeton, 1908), ch. II *passim.*

To John Adams

Passy, 26 July 1783

Dear Sir,

I hope I may by this Time congratulate You on your safe arrival, and happy meeting with your Son at Amsterdam.[1] Mr. Laurens is here, and in better Health than I have heretofore seen him since he left America. His Stay will probably be short, for his Permission to return creates Doubts in his mind as to the Propriety of his continuing to act with us, unless by our particular Request; and Mr. Hartley has as yet no answer from his Court. Mr. Laurens talks of returning this Fall.

As this Letter may be inspected before it reaches you, it will not be very interesting. The Draft of a Treaty with Denmarck is prepared, and will be sent I beleive with Barney.[2] I've not seen it. Mr. Laurens thinks a change in the British Ministry probable, but of whom the next will be formed is uncertain. We have had no accounts from America since you left us, except certain Paragraphs in English news papers which you have doubtless seen.

I consider your Loan as in some degree our *Spes altera,*[3] and hope you will be able to render it at least equal to our present Exigences. You would derive Honor, and our Country advantage from it.

Should any thing worth communicating occur, you shall hear

from me again. Present my Compliments to your Son, and believe me to be with great Esteem and Regard, Dear Sir Your most obedient Servant,

JOHN JAY

ALS in MHi: Adams, reel 360. Addressed: "His Excellency John Adams Esquire."

[1]Adams left Paris 19 July for the United Provinces. Adams to Livingston, 18 July 1783, *JAW,* VIII, 107–09; *RDC,* VI, 560–62. John Quincy Adams, journeying from Russia, had arrived in Amsterdam on 21 April 1783. *AP,* III, 108.

[2]In his letter to Livingston of 22 July 1783, Franklin enclosed a "project of a treaty" proposed by the Danish government (*BFS,* IX, 59–73; *RDC,* VI, 580–88). This "project" was the revised version of one Franklin had submitted. Congress took no action on the treaty until April 1784, when directions were given for resumption of negotiations. Only in 1826 was a treaty of amity and commerce finally concluded with Denmark. For the Danish "Counterproject," see *ibid.,* pp. 519–27.

[3]"Second hope," Vergil, *Aeneid* 12.168.

FROM ROBERT MORRIS

Philadelphia, 26 July 1783

Dear Sir,

Mr. Darby and Mr. Grigby have severally delivered your introductory letters of the 8th of April and I flatter myself that they will think themselves obliged to you. They are very deserving young Gentlemen and make an agreable addition to our Circle of Society. This however will be of short duration as their own pursuits will very soon seperate us. Mr. and Mrs. Carter, and Col. Wadsworth will soon add to the American Circle in Paris. They are too well known to Mrs. Jay and yourself to need recommendation from me. Kitty Livingston has left us about a Month. She is at Elizabeth Town and very well and I am told all the Family are so. Mrs. Morris always thinks and speaks of Mrs. Jay and yourself, through that Medium of esteem and respect which You never fail to impress so strongly on Your Friends and Acquaintance.

My situation as a Public Man is distressing. I am Cursed with that worst of all political Sins, Poverty. My engagements and Anticipations for the Public amount to a Million of Dollars; it racks my utmost invention to keep pace with the demands, but hitherto I have been able to preserve that Credit which kept our affairs alive untill you had the opportunity of Concluding a Glorious Peace, and now a little exertion on the part of the States would enable me to make payment and quit the Service with reputation. The want of that exertion may ruin the Public credit and involve the Country in New Convulsions.

I hope my Dear Friend that you and our other Ministers, will be able to procure me some further assistance from France and Holland; it is as important at this as it has been at any other Period, but less will do. Our Government is yet too Weak, bad Men have too much sway, there are evils afloat which can only be avoided or cured by wise and honest Measures, assisted by the lenient hand of time.

I am ever, my Dear Sir, Your Affectionate humble servant

ROBT. MORRIS

ALS.

To William Bingham

Passy, 29 July 1783

Dear Sir,

I have been favored with your obliging Letter of the 10th Instant, and sincerely congratulate You and Mrs. Bingham on your safe arrival.[1] A tour through parts of Europe cannot fail of being agreable to her and your having made it before will enable you to render it particularly so. We flatter ourselves with having the Pleasure of seeing you here, and of enjoying much interesting Conversation on a Variety of Subjects.

The Washington had a short passage, but brought us little news, except a Report that many European Goods were cheaper at Philadelphia than here, and that the Price of American productions had risen very considerably. A Year will be necessary for our Commerce so to regulate itself as to afford those engaged in it certain Principles for Calculation.

As to a Treaty of Commerce with Britain, it seems doubtful as yet whether that Cabinet has adopted any fixed Plan or System of Policy with Respect to America.

Their proclamation respecting the Trade between us and their Islands will be found to be impol[it]ic as well as ill timed.[2] It is in vain to reason with those who listen only to the Dictates of their Passions and their feelings. An American Navigation act will be more convincing and persuasive than the best Speeches of Mr. Pitt or any other eloquent and patriotic member of either House. Britain may try the Experiment and adopt a partial monopolizing System of Commerce, but it will injure her, not *us;* provided we are wise. We have the World before us, and a navigation act on the principle conducting our Commerce on the Footing of the most exact reciprocity with all Nations, will tend more to increase than diminish our power. While we can undersell other nations the British Islands will buy from us though at neutral ports and the Charge of two Freights instead of one. Canada and Nova Scotia are s[ai]d to be able to supply the Islands. This will prove a Bubble, those who blow it up may perhaps get something by it.

I hope to hear often from you. Remember however that Letters by the post are liable to Inspection. Present our best Compliments to Mrs. Bingham and believe me to be, Dear Sir, Your affectionate Friend and Servant.

Dft.

[1]The Binghams sailed for England in May 1783, reaching Gravesend in early July. Margaret L. Brown, "Mr. and Mrs. William Bingham of Philadelphia," *Pennsylvania Mag. of Hist. and Biog.*, LXI (1937), 288–89.

[2]Royal proclamation of 2 July 1783, restricting trade between the U.S. and the British West Indies to British-built and -owned ships. *RDC*, VI, 541.

From Joshua Johnson

London, 22 August 1783

Dear Sir,

I am much honored with your favor of the 9 Instant[1] which reached me in course of Post. You will have seen a full Account of the Revolt at Philadelphia and the removial of Congress from thence to Prince Town. In their taking the latter step I think that they are perfectly right, for I have been told that they have not been treated well in Philadelphia, besides your observations are Just; two such Bodys do not agree very well, and always introduce party and discord.

Mr. Williams' stoppage[2] has given me an infinite deal of uneasiness, particularly so on Account of his Family; as for the rest of our Countrymen in France I immagine that they will find it hard work to keep from sinking. Doctor Bancroft has taken his Passage in the Commerce, Capt. Truxton, who left the Downs on the 13 Instant. Your Letter for Maderia is forwarded.

As an American and one who loves his Country I cannot bear to see her Insulted without doing every thing I can to prevent it. I therefore hold it my duty to inform you, that a Certain Mr. George Moore of this City has dispatched the Ship George Capt. Scott or Capt. Christall with Convicks for Baltimore; in order to evade any Suspicion she has cleared for Novascotia, but the Broker informs me her destination is for Baltimore. This Mr. Moore is Brother to Mr. Phillip Moore of Philadelphia and a Mr. Moore late a Partner of Mr. Williams. Capt. Truxton told me that he saw a Letter from Mr. Salmon of Baltimore to George Moore recommending this Scheme. If you see this business in the same light I do I doubt not but you will represent it immediatly to Congress and the Govenor and Council of Maryland.[3] I shall also write them by the first Ships going to warn them against such dirty practices. Some other Vessells are gone or agoing with what is called Indented Servants but which may be a mear cover. I expect the Nonsuch every day and which I hope may give me occasion of writing you again.

Should you determine on paying this Country a Visit, I hope that you will believe me when I assure you that Mrs. J. and myself shall be happy to see you and your Lady to whom pray make our Compliments acceptable and believe me with sincerity my, Dear Sir, Your most Obliged Humble Servant,

JOSHUA JOHNSON

P.S. You will oblige me by using my Name cautiously for this reason I am amongst a People that may make my residence unpleasant.

Mr. Bingham is gone to Paris; if you are intimate with him you will oblige me by mentioning me to him, for this reasoning: I think Americans ought at present to hold together.

I this Instant see in Lloyd's List that they have altered the Name of the Ship from the George to the Swift; she Sailed from Gravesend the 21 Instant.

ALS.

[1]Letter not located.

[2]See Ridley to Wallace, Davidson, and Johnson, 3 Aug. 1783, reporting that Jonathan Williams had defaulted. MHi: Ridley.

[3]A week later Matthew Ridley wrote Governor William Paca of Maryland similarly notifying him of the shipment of convicts by the Moores, "said to be for Nova Scotia but . . . destined under colour of Indentures for Baltimore," and adding: "I have no doubt that you may be on your Guard against such practices, for I have no doubt as the Idea hath been once started but Endeavours may be used by Indentures or otherways to introduce all the Felons from England or Ireland or elsewhere amongst us." Immediately on receipt of Ridley's letter, Paca apprised the Maryland Assembly of the "Fraudulent Plan." Ridley to Governor of Maryland, 12 Sept. 1783. MHi: Ridley; *Maryland Archives,* XLVIII, 484. For later protests against British convict dumping in the United States, including JJ's recommendation as Secretary for Foreign Affairs and his representation to the British Foreign Office, see *JCC,* XXIV, 494, 528–30 (1788); R. B. Morris, *Government and and Labor in Early America* (New York, 1946), p. 327.

From William Carmichael

San Ildefonso, 23 August 1783

Sir,

I have the honor to inform your Exc[ellenc]y that I was presented yesterday to the King and this day to the Prince and Princess of the Asturias[1] as Chargé d'affaires[2] of the United States of America. I have every reason to be satisfied with my reception as also with the Conduct of his Exc[ellenc]y the Conde de F. Blanca on this occasion.

If your Exc[ellenc]y hath received any recent instructions from Congress relative to the Mission here which you think may contribute to the interests of our Country I make no doubt that you will take a safe opportunity of conveying copies of them to me Should not circumstances permit your early return to Spain.

With respectful compliments to your Lady, I have the honor to be, Your Excellencys Obedient and Most Humble Servant.

WM. CARMICHAEL

ALS.

[1]See *JJ,* I, 743n. for the Prince, the future King Charles IV. His wife, María Luisa Teresa de Parma (1751–1819), was also his first cousin.

[2]Carmichael was left as chargé in Spain after JJ's departure. For Lafayette's role, see editorial note above, "Lafayette, Jay's Self-appointed 'Political Aide-de-Camp,' Takes on the Spaniards."

American Commissioners to Henry Laurens

[Paris, c. 24 August 1783]

We have recieved your Letter of the 9 August[1] Instant and entirely approve of the Packets having proceeded on her Voyage immediately on your leaving her. We fear however that our consenting to your Proposition of going over to England in her, caused you more Trouble than convenience; especially as it deprived you of your carriage at a time when you had a Journey to make.

We have perused the notes of your Conversation with Mr. Fox, and although in general we approve it, yet candor obliges us to remark, that you seem to have somewhat mistaken our Sentiments on your Proposal to speak to Mr. Fox about the Reception of an American minister by the British Court.

Britain having acknowledged the sovereignty of the United States, and treated with us as with an independent nation, it followed as a natural consequence that they would recieve our minister. Mr. Hartley's official Communication to us on that subject, was in the most explicit Terms. No Doubts could remain on that Head. In conversing with us on this Subject, and about this communication, you observed that there was a wide Difference between a Ministers being ceremoniously and formally recieved, and his being received and treated in a cordial friendly manner, that we were not as yet accurately informed of the Intention of the British Cabinet on the latter point, and that you thought it would be expedient to ascertain it in a Conversation with Mr. Fox. With this Sentiment we coincided; and you promised to inform us of the Result.

The British Court prefer forming a definitive Treaty of the provisional articles, without any alterations or additions. We wish with you that certain matters in them could have been more accurately adjusted, but as at the Time of signing them, you made no Objections to any of the articles or Expressions, we presume you then thought as we did, that they were in the best State that, all things considered, it was in our power to put them.

Dft in NHi: Jay. Endorsed by JJ: ". . . Dr. Answer to Mr. Laurens's Letter of 9 August 1783."

[1]Laurens had taken off for England, arriving there on 10 June, and heading for Bath. Laurens to the American Commissioners, 17 June 1783, *RDC,* VI, 493. Writing from London on 9 August, Laurens detailed for the American Commissioners his lengthy conversation with Charles James Fox on 5 August. Laurens asked Fox whether an American minister would be acceptable at the British court. "Most undoubtedly, sir," Fox replied. *Ibid.,* pp. 637–40.

FROM EDWARD BANCROFT

[London, c. August 1783]

My Dear Friend,

I have long delayed doing myself the honor of writing to you, partly, because, in truth, since my arrival here, very little has occurred worthy of Communication. I have however watched and taken some pain to discover the views of ministers here respecting our Country, and I am sorry to have learned within these two or three days, from an infallible Source, that this Government is now much more unfavourably disposed towards us than we imagined when I was with you. Indeed I believe that there has been since, and that very lately, a Considerable Change in the Sentiments of Ministers respecting what Concerns us and perhaps the Knowledge of the late riot at Philadelphia, and of disorder of our Finances may have very much Contributed to the Change and have seen them think us of little or no importance. Our navigation to the British West indies is I believe at an end; at least I am sure it is determined on here to adhere to the Terms and System of the late Proclamation so long as the Act under which it was issued remains in Force; and I am well assured that it is the disposition and intention of Ministers to endeavour to engage Parliament the next session to adopt and establish that System permanently.

I have suggested to one of them the danger of a Retaliation on our part and was answered "that this might happen, but that we could not retaliate in that way but from resentment, and to our own injury; that by such retaliation we should deprive ourselves of the best and indeed only way of disposing of a great part of our Produce, to the *destruction* of *our Agriculture,* that by injuring ourselves in this way we might indeed deprive the British Planter of the means of Supplying themselves so Cheaply as formerly and engage them to Clamour in our favor; that Gov[ernmen]t expect they will Clamour, but are determined not to Sacrifice the Essential Intrests of the State to the partial Intrests of West India Planters. That allowing American vessels admission to the British Islands would in reality be to allow the vessels of all other nations to come there under the Cover of American Names "and *13 Stripes"* and that unless the Westindia Colonies Can be made a means of increase to the British Navigation, Great Britain had better let them become independant like the United States and thus rid herself of the trouble and expence of Defending them in war, and from the Disadvantage of Purchasing and using only *their* Sugar at a Price which no other Nation in Europe would pay for it. That the people of America, being now an independant Nation, are unreasonable in expecting Priviledges which Great Britain never granted to any independent Nation whatever, and at the same time offering Great Britain not the smallest indulgence in return. That the British Government is ready to favour the United States as far as may consist with the intrests of Great Britain, but can not sacrafice those intrests without some equivalent advantages, etc. etc."

If one could suppose that these are not *yet* the Prevailing Sentiments of this Ministry, I am persuaded (from the course from which they came) that they will soon become such; and that we are not likely soon to be very Closely connected here. Indeed I understand the expectation of any commercial Treaty whatever this year is now laid aside, and with regard to the definitive Treaty with us, *it is to be* only a

Transcript of the Provisional articles under a new name.

You will be pleased to Communicate the foregoing to Dr. Franklin, and make what other use of it you may think prudent, but do not let any one but the Doctor know that any part of it comes from me. The Evacuation of New York will not take place until late in the fall, and then the Army will only remove to Halifax where Sir Guy Carlton will remain and Establish his Quarters this Winter. Governor Wentworth formerly of New Hampshire is restored to, and gone to Execute his office of Surveyor General of the Woods in Nova Scotia and Lord Storment is gone to Scotland and has left Lord North his substitute as President of Council. He, Lord Storment, is most likely to become a favorite and put himself at the Head of what are called the Kings Friends; who however can never long be a ruling Party here. Mr. Fox and Lord North seem to know that their existence as Ministers depends on their supporting each other and therefore are not likely to quarrel.

I am just setting out for the Downs where I expect to embark tomorrow. Make my respectful Compliments to Mrs. Jay, Dr. Franklin, Mr. Grand, and other Friends, and believe me with the utmost Sincerity and gratitude, My Dear Sir, your most affectionate and Devoted Humble Servant,

EDW. BANCROFT

P.S. What was insinuated to us about Mr. Oswalds intention of procuring payment of an old demand on Gov[ernmen]t *as his Reward,* was not true as I learn. He conducted himself with great delicacy on that Subject and never mentioned it whilst his friend was in Power least some improper imputation should be made.

ALS in Private Collection, Philadelphia. Addressed: "To the Honble John Jay Esqr., Minister Plenipotentiary of the United States, etc., etc., at Passy near Paris." Endorsed: ". . . Without date; Recd. 22 Augt. 1783, by Mr. Ths. Barclay, Esqr."

Signing the Definitive Treaty

3 September 1783

According to Fitzherbert's account to his own government, JJ and Adams were reconciled as early as February, 1783, to have the Preliminary Articles adopted as the Definitive Treaty with but few verbal changes based on the French treaty text. It was Franklin, the British diplomat reported, who was holding out for reparation by the British for damages inflicted in America.[1] Fitzherbert's report hardly takes into account the strenuous efforts of all the American Commissioners to secure reciprocal trade advantages.

In fact, down almost to the very last minute both sides sought to incorporate substantial changes. As late as 6 August the Americans and Hartley were locked in debate over certain substantive and verbal alterations. For example, the Americans wanted to include in Article IV a provision, drafted by JJ above, whereby the British government would agree to instruct its courts to postpone execution on judgment debts for three years from the date of the treaty, such judgments not to include interest during the period of the war. Had that provision been incorporated much of the postwar controversy which raged down to the adoption of the Jay Treaty in 1794 might have been obviated. As regards the provisions in Article V concerning restitution for confiscated estates, it was proposed that a balance sheet be struck by British adherents and citizens of the United States, an old Franklin notion. In the eighth article the Americans pressed to incorporate free navigation not only for the Mississippi but also for the St. Lawrence River. It was sought, apparently by the British, to make the release of prisoners in Article IX dependent upon their satisfying any debts contracted during their captivity. The Americans tried (Article X) to incorporate a provision pledging Great Britain to interpose in favor of the United States with the Barbary States, and another (Article XI) allowing merchants nine months' time to leave the enemy country. The latter article betrayed the hand of Franklin in the proposal that all those "who labor for the common subsistence or benefit of mankind" were not to be molested in time of war. Two other Franklin notions would have outlawed privateering and ended the term "contraband" (Article XII). A Hartley proposal would have entitled citizens of either country to own property in the other or acquire such under the laws of inheritance (Article XIII). In addition, the British tried to have a provision inserted (Article XVII), ostensibly to protect the Indians, permitting their own armed forces to remain in the forts then occupied contiguous to the water line until Congress gave them notice to evacuate, while the Americans, most likely JJ, sought a pledge that England would evacuate all places within the United States within three months after signing the Treaty (Article XVIII).[2] In addition and behind Hartley's back, the Duke of Manchester, the newly appointed British ambassador at Paris, had hinted to Vergennes that, in light of the prospective friction which emigration southward from Georgia might create, it would be well to set up a buffer zone between Spanish Florida and the United States. Vergennes, however, was not encouraging.[3]

None of these intriguing propositions were incorporated in the final treaty, nor were proposals of the Canadian fur merchants, Tories, and British creditors.[4] In fact, the negotiators settled on the identical treaty they had drawn up almost a year before, with two exceptions. A new preamble, which Hartley attributed to Adams,[5] was substituted for the more succinct one in the Preliminary Treaty, and, of course, the separate article about Florida was dropped.

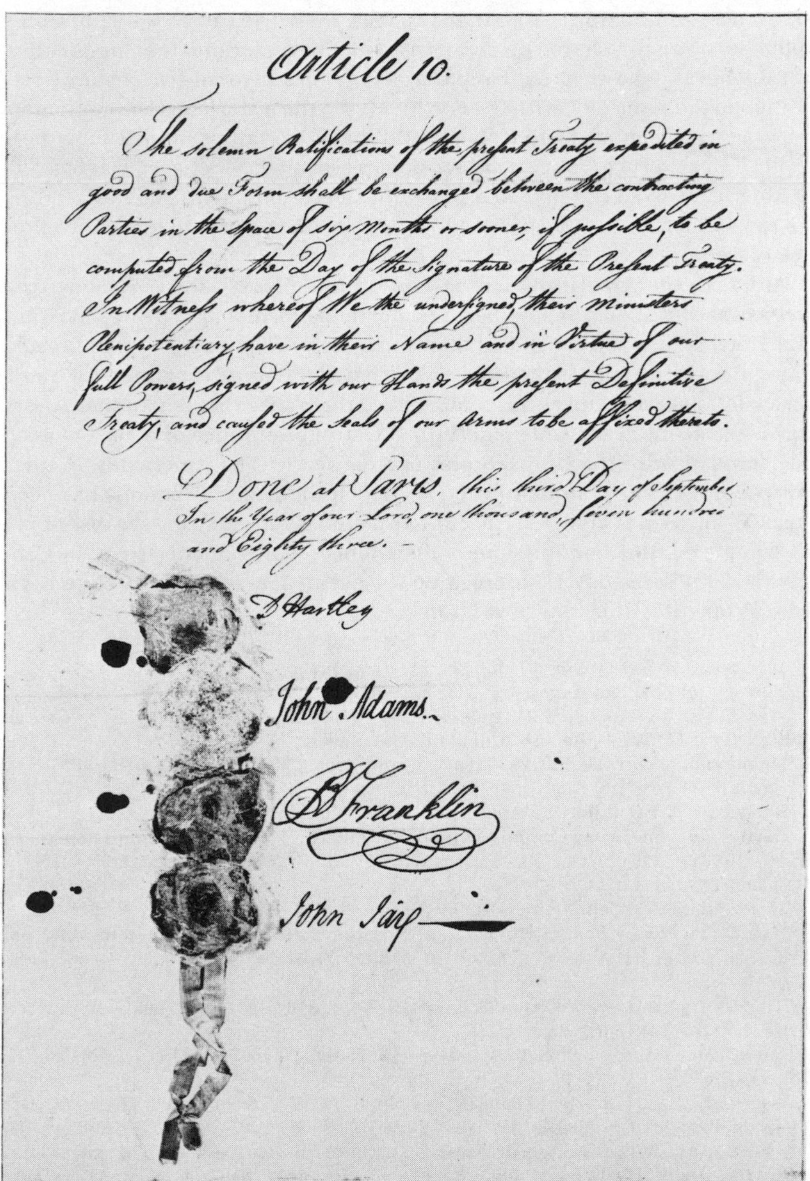

Article 10.

The solemn Ratification of the present Treaty expedited in good and due Form shall be exchanged between the contracting Parties in the Space of six Months or sooner, if possible, to be computed from the Day of the Signature of the present Treaty. In Witness whereof We the undersigned their Ministers Plenipotentiary have in their Name and in Virtue of our full Powers, signed with our Hands the present Definitive Treaty, and caused the Seals of our Arms to be affixed thereto.

Done at Paris, this third Day of September In the Year of our Lord, one thousand, seven hundred and Eighty three. —

D Hartley

John Adams.

B Franklin

John Jay

Final Page of the Definitive Treaty, 3 September 1783. *(Department of State Archives, Washington, D.C.)*

Hartley's instructions stipulated that the ceremony of the signing was to take place in Paris. This seemed to pose a possible difficulty, since Great Britain, France, and Spain had arranged to sign their treaties at Versailles on 3 September. Franklin shared his concern about this unanticipated complication with Rayneval, who reported back that Vergennes favored two separate formalities on the same day, with the one involving the American Commissioners occurring early enough so that they could reach Versailles in time to witness the other closing rites.[6] The exchange of correspondence between Hartley and the Americans fixed the time and place for the signing, with Hartley sending off a special note to his "Dear friend" Franklin, urging him to make the effort to be present.[7]

Although the Americans feared last minute delays,[8] the ceremony took place as scheduled on 3 September. The participants met at Hartley's lodgings at the Hôtel d'York and concluded their business by 10:30 A.M., JJ, Franklin, and Adams signing for the United States.[9] A congratulatory exchange followed. Hartley felicited the Americans and assured them that "his Britannic majesty and his confidential servants entertain the strongest desire of a cordial good understanding with the United States of America."[10] The Americans, in turn, rejoiced with Hartley "in that event, by which the Ruler of nations has been graciously pleased to give peace to our two countries."[11] As soon as transcribing was completed, the Commissioners dispatched copies of the treaty to Congress.[12] On the same day JJ summed up the events succinctly: "If we are not a happy People it will be our own Fault."[13]

[1]Fitzherbert to Grantham, 9 Feb. 1783, FO 27/5, 354–55.

[2]Hartley to Fox, 26 Aug. 1783, FO 4/2, 161–89.

[3]Manchester to Fox, 13 July 1783, British Museum: Add. MSS., 47661–3. George Montagu (1737–88) was the 4th Duke of Manchester.

[4]Memorandum for Definitive Treaty (June 1783), MiU-C: Hartley II, 28.

[5]Hartley to Fox, 26 Aug. 1783, FO 4/2, 161–89.

[6]Rayneval to Franklin, 29 Aug. 1783, *RDC,* VI, 662.

[7]Hartley to American Commissioners, 29 August; American Commissioners to Hartley, 30 Aug. 1783, *RDC,* VI, 662–63, Hartley to Franklin, 2 Sept. 1783, ALS in PHi; photocopy in MiU-C.

[8]JJ to Adams, 2 Sept. 1783, Dft in JP.

[9]Hartley to Fox, 3 Sept. 1783, FO 4/2. For the ceremony, see *Peacemakers,* pp. 435–36. The Definitive Treaty is found in Miller, *Treaties,* pp. 151–57; *Peacemakers,* pp. 462–65.

[10]Hartley to American Commissioners, 4 Sept. 1783, FO 4/2; LbkC in MiU-C: Hartley III; *RDC,* VI, 673–74.

[11]American Commissioners to Hartley, 5 Sept. 1783, LbkC in MiU-C: Hartley III; *RDC,* VI, 677.

[12]See, *e.g.,* JJ to Charles Thomson, 12 Sept. 1783, ALS in DLC: Thomson; Dft in hand of Peter Jay Munro in JP; New-York Hist. Soc., *Collections* (1878), I, 175–76; *RDC,* VI, 694–95. John Thaxter, Jr., was dispatched to Congress bearing an official copy of the treaty. He reached Philadelphia 22 Nov. 1783. See Adams to JJ, 13 Feb. 1784, below.

[13]JJ to Robert Morris, 12 Sept. 1783, Dft in hand of Peter Jay Munro in JP; *HPJ,* III, 77–78.

FROM VERGENNES

Versailles, 28 August 1783

M. De Vergennes begs M. Jay, minister plenipotentiary of the United States of America, to do him the honor of dining at his residence at Versailles next Wednesday, 3 September.

C in French. See also *HPJ*, III, 72.

SARAH LIVINGSTON JAY:
A TOAST TO AMERICA AND HER FRIENDS

Paris, [after 3 September 1783]

1 The United States of America, may they be perpetual
2 The Congress
3 The King and Nation of France
4 General Washington and the American Army
5 The United Netherlands and all other free States in the world
6 His Catholic Majesty and all other Princes and Powers who have manifested Friendship to America
7 The Memory of the Patriots who have fallen for their Country —May kindness be shown to their Widows and Children
8 The French Officers and Army who served in America
9 Gratitude to our Friends and Moderation to our Enemies
10 May all our Citizens be Soldiers, and all our Soldiers Citizens
11 Concord, Wisdom and Firmness to all American Councils
12 May our Country be always prepared for War, but disposed to Peace
13 Liberty and Happiness to all Mankind.

AD. SLJ had planned "a Ball when peace is concluded." See SLJ to Catharine W. Livingston, 14 Dec. 1782, below.

TO WILLIAM CARMICHAEL

Passy, 5 September 1783

Sir,

The definitive Treaties were signed the Day before Yesterday. Our's is in the Words of the provisional articles. We are so employed in preparing Dispatches for America that at present I can only acknowledge the Reciept of your Letter of the 23d <Augt> ult. and congratulate you on the Event which is the Subject of it.

I am Sir your most obedient <humble> servant,

J. J.

P.S. My last to you was <dated> of the 22d August 1783.[1]

Dft. Endorsed in JJ's hand: ". . . To Mr. Carmichael, 5 Sept. 1783. In answer to 23 Aug. 1783."

[1]See editorial note below, "Settling the Spanish Accounts," and n. 15.

From Henry Laurens

London, 5 September 1783

Dear Sir,

Upon my late arrival at Bath or a few days after, I received your Letter of the 8th July and the day before yesterday just as I was leaving that place I was honored by receipt of another of the 24th Ultimo.[1] I thank you for both. Had Mr. Barclay delivered my dispatch of the 9th August before your last date, certainly you would have told me so. I have however some hope a Copy which I sent under Cover to Doctor Franklin the 27th[2] reached you before you signed the Definitive. I had no anxiety, because it was not essential, to be present at that Ceremony, but should it be composed of the Provisional without alteration I shall rather rejoice at having been absent.

Doctor Franklin will have informed you of my intended return to France and of the affecting Cause,[3] but I shall not begin my Journey till the 10th Instant. Should you be on your way to this Kingdom I wish we may rencontre. If we miss, you will find a Packet directed to you in the hands of Mr. Oswald. No doubts you have seen Mr. Jening's "Candor of Henry Laurens Esq?" I think I have demonstrated the propriety of his Title Page and that "Mr. Edmund Jenings" is one of the weakest and wickedest of Men. I am sorry he has wounded the Gentleman he calls his benevolent friend.[4]

You say Mrs. Jay is recovering slowly. The little Girl is well. Whence I infer you have two little Girls and wish you great joy and perfect reestablishment of the good Lady's health. If my Daughter was present I am sure she would most heartily join. Harry does. His Sister is with a friend a Mile or two from hence.[5]

I have the honor to be, Sir, Your Obedient humble Servant,

HENRY LAURENS

ALS. Endorsed by JJ: ". . . Recieved 10 September."

[1]Neither letter has been located.

[2]Laurens to American Commissioners, 9 Aug. 1783, for which see above, American Commissioners to Laurens, [c. 24 Aug. 1783], n. 1.

[3]At the point of embarking for America, for which he had received permission from Congress (Laurens to Livingston, 27 June 1783, *RDC,* VI, 507), Laurens learned that his brother James was dying in Vigan, France.

[4]Edmund Jenings (1731–1819), an English-educated Marylander and confidant of John Adams, who spent most of the war years at Brussels and elsewhere on the Continent, quarreled with Henry Laurens about the publication of an anonymous letter late in 1782, in which Laurens was cautioned by John Adams against possible misconduct. Laurens believed Jenings to be its author, and the resultant pamphlet war failed to settle the mystery of authorship. Cf. *RDC,* VI, 285n. with *AP,* II, 356n. Wallace, *Laurens,* p. 417. For the suspect role of Jenings as a double agent, ostensibly serving the American cause while working for the British, see James H. Hutson, ed., *Letters from a Distinguished American: Twelve Essays by John Adams on Foreign Policy, 1780* (Washington, D.C., 1978).

[5]The references are to Laurens' devoted daughter Martha (1759–1811) and to Henry Laurens, Jr. (1763–1821), his only surviving son. Wallace, *Laurens,* pp. 414–16.

To Joshua Johnson

Passy, 5 September 1783

Dear Sir,

I have been favored with Yours of the 22 Ult. The Day before Yesterday, the definitive Treaties were signed. Our's is in the words of the provisional Articles, so that commercial Regulations remain yet to be formed.

The account you give me respecting a certain Scheme shall be transmitted and I hope Care will be taken to put a Stop to such practices for the future. I think and feel exactly as you do on that Subject.[1]

Mr. Bingham I hear is in Holland. When he arrives here I shall remember your Request.

Be pleased to present our Compliments to Mrs. Johnson. I am, Dear Sir, your most obedient Servant.

Dft.

[1]The reference is to the dumping in America of British convict servants, to which Johnson had alerted JJ on 22 August above.

From Benjamin Franklin

Passy, 10 September 1783

Sir,

I have received a letter from a very respectable person in America containing the following words vizt.

"It is confidently reported, propagated and believed by some among us, that the Court of France was at bottom against our obtaining the Fishery and Territory in that great Extent in which both are secured to us by the Treaty; that our Ministers at that Court favoured, or did not oppose this Design against us, and that it was entirely owing to the Firmness, Sagacity and Disinterestedness of Mr. Adams, with whom Mr. Jay united, that we have obtained these important Advantages."[1]

It is not my Purpose to dispute any Share of the Honour of that Treaty which the Friends of my Colleagues may be disposed to give them; but having now spent Fifty Years of my Life in public Offices and Trusts, and having still one Ambition left, that of carrying the Character of Fidelty at least, to the Grave with me, I cannot allow that I was behind any of them in Zeal and Faithfulness. I therefore think that I ought not to suffer an Accusation, which falls little short of Treason to my Country, to pass without notice, when the means of effectual Vindication are at hand. You, Sir was a Witness of my Conduct in that Affair. To you and my other Colleagues I appeal by sending to each a similar Letter with this, and I have no doubt of your Readiness to do a Brother Commissioner Justice, by Certificates that will entirely destroy the Effect of that Accusation.

I have the honour to be, with much esteem, Sir, Your Most Obedient and Most humble Servant.

B. FRANKLIN

LS. Endorsed: ". . . answered 11 Inst." Tr in MH: Sparks. Variations in *RDC,* VI, 686 and n.; *BFS,* IX, 91–93.

[1]This extract is from a letter written by Dr. Samuel Cooper of Boston under date of 5 May 1783. *BFS,* IX, 91–92n.

To Benjamin Franklin

Passy, 11 September 1783

I have been favored with your Letter of Yesterday, and will answer it explicitly.

I <have never been witness to any action or Conversation of yours which indicated a Reluctance> have no Reason whatever to believe that you was averse to our obtaining the full Extent of Boundary and Fishery secured to us by the Treaty. Your Conduct respecting them throughout the Negociation indicated a strong and <evident> steady attachment to both those objects, in my opinion and promoted the attainment of them.

I remember that in a Conversation which Mr. de Rayneval, the first Secretary of Count De Vergennes, had with you and me, in the Summer of 1782, you contended for our full Right to the Fishery, and argued it on various Principles.

Your Letters to me when in Spain, considered our Territory as extending to the Missisippi, and expressed your opinion against ceding the Navigation of that River, in very strong and pointed Terms.[1]

In short Sir: I do not recollect the least Difference in Sentiment between us respecting the Boundaries or Fisheries. On the contrary, we were unanimous and united in adhering to, and insisting on them. Nor did I ever percieve the least Disposition in either of us, to recede from our Claims, or be satisfied with less than we obtained.

I have the Honor to be with great Respect and Esteem, Sir, Your most obedient and very humble Servant.[2]

Dft. Without Dft deletions in *HPJ,* III, 73–74.

[1]See Franklin to JJ, 2 Oct. 1780, 27 Jan. 1781, *BFS,* VII, 142–45, 200–02.

[2]For John Adams' more grudging response to Franklin of 13 Sept. 1783, see *RDC,* VI, 696–97. On this incident, see also *Peacemakers,* p. 445.

To William Livingston

Passy, 12 September 1783

Dear <Robt.>[1] Sir,

My last Letter[2] informed you that on the 13th Ult. Mrs. Jay was delivered of a Daughter. <Whom> We have called her Ann. Sally is pretty well recovered. <but> The Child has a violent Cold. Maria <has also had a cold but is now> is very well. We hope next Summer to present these little Girls to You, for I assure you we look forward with Impatience to the Day when we shall embark for America. Peter I suppose continues with you. We hope to hear that he speaks more plain, and improves in Strength both of body and mind.

A Monsieur Montgolfier has invented Globes which he fills with inflammable air so much lighter than <the> common air as that they rise above the Clouds with great Velocity and are capable of carrying up with them a very considerable weight. The enclosed Prints represent the ascent and Fall of the first that was exhibited at Paris. This Invention is considered as very important, and further Improvements will probably render it useful in various Respects.[3]

The enclosed is the seed of a flowering Shrub. I am, Dear Sir, with affectionate Regard, Your most obedient Servant.

P.S. Mr. Thaxter who carries the definitive Treaty is the Bearer of this, and I recommend him to your friendly attention. He is a very deserving young Gentleman.

Dft. Endorsed by JJ.

[1]On the same day JJ did address a letter to Robert R. Livingston, ALS in NHi: R. R. Livingston; Dft in JP; E in NN: Bancroft: American; *RDC,* VI, 695–96; *HPJ,* III, 78–80; *WJ,* II, 127–28.

[2]Letter not located.

[3]The Montgolfier brothers, Jacques Étienne (1745–99) and Joseph Michel (1740–1810), launched the first successful unmanned hot air balloon on 5 June 1783 at Annonay near Lyons. JJ's reference, however, is to the first successful balloon ascent in Paris on 27 Aug. 1783. The balloon, constructed by the brothers Robert under the direction of physicist Jacques Alexandre César Charles (1746–1823), reached a height of 3,000 feet and traveled 15 miles.

To Egbert Benson

Passy, 12 September 1783

My Good Friend,

Is it not almost Time for me to expect a Letter from you? The one enclosing Letters of Attorney was the last <of yours that have reached me>.[1]

Mrs. Jay gave me another Daughter last Month, and you are <its> her godfather. I hope next Summer to introduce her to you.

Do <my dear Friend> tell me something about my Family; I have not heard of them since May last.

I am preparing Dispatches to Congress (to accompany the definitive Treaty which is in the Terms of the provisional articles) and therefore cannot write long Letters.

Your irregular and violent popular Proceedings and Resolutions against the Tories[2] hurt us in Europe. We are puzzled to answer the Question, how it happens that if there be settled Governments in America the people of every Town and District should take upon themselves to Legislate. <In short> The People of America must either govern themselves according to their respective Constitutions and the Confederation, or relinquish all Pretensions to the Respect of other Nations. The News Papers in Europe are filled with Exagerated accounts of the Want of Moderation, Union, Order and Government which they say prevails in our Country.

I hope our affairs will soon assume <a more promising> a different aspect. The Waves will run high for some time after a Storm. These Matters give me more Regret than surprize, but I do not wonder at their appearing very extraordinary in these Countries where the Tone of Government is high.

We have the <strongest> fullest assurances that New York will be evacuated without Delay. I am impatient for that Event. Our Remonstrances to the british Minister on that Subject have been strong and frequent.

I am Dear Benson your affectionate Friend.

Dft. *HPJ,* III, 74–75, lacks Dft deletions.

[1]See above, Benson to JJ, 25 April 1783.

[2]Among the anti-Tory laws enacted by the New York State legislature was the notorious Trespass Act of 17 March 1783 (*Laws of N.Y., 6th sess., 1783,* p. 283), enabling those who had fled from the enemy to sue for trespass to their real or personal property during their absence, depriving defendants of the right to plead in justification any military order or command of the enemy for the occupation or destruction of the property, and providing that such suits could be finally determined in any inferior court. A wave of litigation followed. R. B. Morris, ed., *Select Cases of the Mayor's Court of New York City, 1674–1784* (Washington, D.C., 1935), pp. 57–59. For the operation of the New York Confiscation and Citation Acts, see Julius Goebel, Jr., *The Law Practice of Alexander Hamilton* (2 vols., New York, 1964–69), I, 224–281.

Lafayette to Sarah Livingston Jay

Wensday Morning, [September 1783]

Marquis de Lafayette Most Respectfull Compliments Wait Upon Mrs. Jay, and Will Have the Honor to Wait Upon Her to the French Play House, But is Sorry to find the play to Be Acted is a New and a Very Indifferent One, Which, What is the Worse, Has not yet been printed. On Saturday We Have *Phèdre,* a Celebrated piece of Racine, and if that is More Convenient, the Same Arrangement that Was to take place to day, will Subsist for Saturday in Every point. And in the Mean While, the M[arqui]s de Lafayette Would propose Mr. and Mrs. Jay's Going on Friday Next to the Opera House, Where a Celebrated piece *Castor et pollux*[1] is to be Acted, and Where He Has got a Box.

He begs Mr. and Mrs. Jay Will please to Honor Him with their

Orders, and will Be Happy to Hear they Both and the little Child are in Good Health.

AL. Endorsed by JJ: ". . . Sepr. 1783."

[1]This lyric tragedy by Pierre Joseph Bernard, with music by Rameau, was a part of the general repertory of the theater of the Académie royale de musique et de danse, performed at the time of this invitation at L'Opéra, located in the salle of the Porte-Saint Martin. P. L. Jacob, [Paul Lacroix], ed., *Bibliothèque Dramatique de Monsieur de Soleinne* (Paris, 1844), III, 99, 106.

Transatlantic Bonds

With the return of peace the Jays became a focal point for visits by fellow Americans now going abroad for reasons of business, pleasure, or education. The Jays kept their families at home posted on personal affairs, including the addition of a daughter, and their families, in turn, notably Governor Livingston, reported on the education and welfare of young Peter Augustus Jay. In correspondence with friends and relatives Jay made a point of urging that the new nation adopt a program of constitutional and legal stability along with sound fiscal policies.

To Robert R. Livingston

Paris, 7 December 1782

Dear Sir,

On the 18 July last Dr. Franklin paid me nine Months Salary due on that Day. I have not taken up any Money on the Bills sent by you on that account, because until the 18 October another quarter did not become due.[1] I mentioned this more at large in a former Letter, and desired you to pay a Sum of Money to Mr. Benson for the use of my Family at Poughkeepsie. I fear this Situation is not easy, and therefore I must beg the Favor of you to pay to my Brother Frederick out of your Rents in our State, the Sum of fifty pounds York Money every three Months, and re-imburse yourself by deducting it from each quarters Salary which you will recieve for me from Mr. Morris. I am uneasy on this Subject, but it gives me Consolation to reflect that your Friendship for me will lead you to undertake this Trouble and that without Delay. The enclosed Letter to my Brother[2] mentions this Matter, be pleased to forward it, and believe me to be with warm and sincere attachment, Your Friend,

JOHN JAY

our Preliminaries were signed last Saturday, and go to you by Capt. Barney.

ALS in NHi: R. R. Livingston. Addressed: *"(To be sunk in Case of Capture),* The Honable Robt. R. Livingston, Esqr., Secretary for foreign affairs, etc. Philadelphia." Endorsed: ". . . private." DftS in JP.

[1]JJ to Robert R. Livingston, 13 Aug. 1782, above.

[2]See letter immediately below.

To Frederick Jay

Paris, 7 December 1782

Dear Fœdy,

<My> The last Letter I have recieved from you is dated the 8 June last.[1] Major Franks writes me[2] that he passed a night with you at Poghkeepsie in his way to Philadelphia and that you were all well. God grant that you may continue so.

By some American papers I percieve that the Interest due on Loan Office Certificates has not been duly paid. I know how this must affect the Family, and therefore in my Letter to Mr. Livingston which is to cover this, I have desired him to pay you fifty pounds York money out of each quarters salary for which he is <to send me> from time to Time to send me Bills. This money is to be at the Disposition of Peter, Nancy and yourself <for> towards the Subsistence of the Family, in which I also include Mrs. M. *and Augustus* to both of whom I am persuaded your care and attention will be properly extended.

Sally and our little Girl are well. I am but so so. Peter is in perfect Health. He lives in an academy and dines with us every Sunday and sometimes oftner.[3]

Sir James is in Holland and has written to me.[4] Ph. Vb. Livingston[5] assures me that Sir James has been grossly misrepresented for that his Conduct since his arrival has been that of a warm American. We join in the best wishes for you all. I am, Dear Fœdy, your affectionate Brother,

J. J.

DftS. Endorsed by JJ. ALS not located.

[1]Letter not located.

[2]David S. Franks to JJ, 28 Sept. 1782, above.

[3]Probably the private boarding schools of M. Le Coeur, or of Pechigny, both located in Passy. John Quincy Adams, Jesse Deane, and Benjamin Franklin Bache attended Le Coeur's school in 1778; in 1780, John Quincy and Charles Adams attended Pechigny's school. *AP,* II, 271, 301, 434.

[4]Letter not located.

[5]SLJ's first cousin, Philip Livingston (1740–1810), eldest son of Peter Van Brugh Livingston, who was then touring Europe. Known as "Gentleman Phil" from his polished manners, Livingston had been the private secretary to Sir Henry Moore, Governor of New York from 1765–69. Edwin B. Livingston, *The Livingstons of Livingston Manor* (New York, 1910), p. 8.

SARAH LIVINGSTON JAY TO CATHARINE W. LIVINGSTON

Paris, 14 December 1782

I wrote to you my dearest sister the other day,[1] but as Captain Barney still waits dispatches from Doctor Franklin I must again trouble you though nothing new has occurred at least of a domestic nature. Our public affairs indeed wear a different aspect. Let us my dear Kitty rejoice together and bless God! for the prospect of approaching Peace. I already begin to enjoy in imagination some delightful scenes. Oh! Kitty perhaps the time draws near when we shall fold each other to our bosoms, and when our Domestic felicity shall again be compleat.

Cousin Phill. Livingston set out from Paris yesterday with young Mr. Curson[2] for Marseilles, wither they go for Amusement; they are both very well. Among all the pleasures which Paris affords (and they are not few) none of them gratify me like the frequent opportunity of seeing my Countrymen. At present you would be surprised to see what a Circle we form when collected. We have received an agreeable addition to our society by the arrival of Mrs. Ridley[3] the day before yesterday. Mrs. Price[4] and Mrs. Montgomery have the suit of rooms over my head in this same Hotel, and Mrs. Izard lives directly opposite and has two daughters that are grown up.[5] There are three days in the week that we take tea and play Cards at each others houses, besides meeting upon other occasions. I was telling young Franklin[6] the other day that he must aid me in contriving a Ball when Peace is concluded.

I fear my dear you begin to think that the idea of amusements is the only one that I attend to, and to convince you that that would be a mistake, I assure you I regret nothing more than the omission of a Chaplain to the Doctors appointments. All the foreign Ministers have one and I think it would be particularly useful here as there are always a great number of Americans at Paris and having no public worship, they seek amusements, but you know how much easier it is to contract bad habits than to quit them. Besides there are likewise some young Americans here for their Education and it really distresses me that they should be brought up without any idea of religion. Being unprejudiced they see the absurdity of many things taught in their school, but they have none to direct them aright.[7]

Remember me my dear sister to Mama, Susan, sister Linn, sister Watkins, William and Peter. When you write again let me hear from Hannah and tell me whether Mama remains at Eliz[abeth] Town and whether Papa has been re-elected.[8] Peter writes me no more letters. Adieu my lovely sister. Spare no attention to your health, remember it is absolutely necessary to the happiness of your affectionate.

SA. JAY

ALS. Addressed: "Miss Kitty W[ilhel]m[ina] Livingston, at the Honble Robert Morris's Esqr., Philadelphia." Endorsed in an unidentified hand.

[1]Letter not located.

[2]Samuel Curzon was then touring Europe on the proceeds of an inheritance from an uncle. See also *JJ,* I, 209. Jacob Hall Pleasants, *The Curzon Family of New York and Baltimore, and Their English Descent* (Baltimore, 1919), p. 42.

[3]Matthew Ridley was reunited with his wife Anne Richardson Ridley and their son Essex (1776–96) at Calais on 7 Dec. 1782. Married in England in 1775, Anne Ridley remained in that country throughout the war years, and visited SLJ on 14 Dec. 1782, two days after her arrival in Paris. Matthew Ridley "Journal," 7, 12 and 14 Dec. 1782 in MHi: Ridley.

[4]Mrs. James Price, the wife of an English merchant who lived in Montreal before the Revolution. James Price sailed for France in the summer of 1781 for a "considerable stay," offering his services to Congress while he remained abroad. Price's letter is in PCC 78, XVIII, 403. See also *JJ,* I, 259.

[5]Margaret (1768–1824) and Charlotte (1770–92), the two eldest daughters of Ralph and Alice De Lancey Izard. Langdon Cheves, "Izard of South Carolina," South Carolina *Hist. and Geneal. Magazine* II (1901), 216–17.

[6]William Temple Franklin.

[7]SLJ did not appear sensitive to the concept of separation of church and state, already being articulated in America.

[8]William Livingston was reelected again and again, serving continuously as New Jersey's governor from 1776 to 1790.

From Robert Morris

Philadelphia, 3 January 1783

Dear Sir,

You have not heard from me so often as you had a right to expect. I lament but cannot help it. Constant employment puts it out of my Power to do many things I wish to do and *that* of writing to my Friends is amongst the Number. My private letters however cannot be of much consequence and you must accept the *Will* for the *Deed.*

General Du Portail delivered me your very obliging letter of the 13th October.[1] It manifests that Degree of Friendship which your well known Sincerity had taught me to depend upon. I was convinced, my

Dear Sir, that the moment you approached near to my Boys, your care and attention would be extended to them. They will feel the Benefit of your Councils and they will be gratefull or I am much mistaken.

It would create an useless expence of yours and my own time to detail the reasons which induced me to send them to Europe. Perhaps some circumstances have already occurred to cause Regret, but at the time the Resolution was taken, our Seminaries were in Confusion, the Teachers of Language and Science had all engaged in the Army or were enrolled amongst its followers, as Deputy Quarter Masters, Deputy Commissaries, Clerks etc. I was fearful the Period for Instruction might pass without a Possibility of Communicating it in this Country. The Phrenzy is now over and the different Classes of Citizens have returned or are returning to their Proper Stations in Civil Society. However Two of my Boys are in Europe and being there they must be instructed in all those things which they ought to learn. The Place where this can best be done I submitted to Doctor Franklin and Mr. Ridley, for altho Geneva was originally intended, yet if any objections against that Place exist, I had no such predilection for it, as to make a Point of their being placed there.[2] I would wish to avoid all unnecessary expence but I do not desire to save one farthing of money as a deduction from the Learning of my Children. The more they cost me the less I shall give them but Instruction at this Age is of infinitely more consequence than the Money it Costs can be hereafter. Upon these principles I wish them without Regard to expence to be placed where they can acquire the most perfect Education. From what Mr. Ridley says I fear Doctor Franklin has found it Troublesome to interfere. Permit me, my Dear Friend, to add you to the Number of my Boys Guardians in Europe. Indeed you have anticipated my wishes in this Respect by the flattering assurance of "your constant attention to these promising Boys while you remain there."[3] A promise from such Characters as yours operates like a Voluntary Tax, the Payment of which is inevitable, therefore I have only to vest in you a share of the Parental authority and my Children will reap the Benefit. Mr. Ridley will be happy in consulting your opinions as I shall in depending on them. My acknowledgements shall be made hereafter.

I think these Children have tractable dispositions, that the Groundwork was laid for good morals and wish them to acquire as much knowledge and as many accomplishments as possible. At the Period when an eager pursuit of pleasurable objects may be likely to run away with them, I think of bringing them Home, even If I should be obliged to give them another Tour in Europe afterwards. I have

Two Sons[4] here who shall have the best Instruction to be obtained in this Country and hereafter we may Contrast them with each other and determine which has the advantage. Your letter of the 13th October I plead as my Appology for this and all other trouble I may give you, on this (to me) very interesting Subject.

I cannot take time at present to enter on any political discussions. But you must allow me to declare my perfect Satisfaction in and approbation of your Conduct in Europe. All who have had the opportunity of knowing what it has been are struck with admiration at your patience under Difficulties and your firmness in rising superiour to them. Go on my Friend, you deserve and will receive the Gratitude of your Country. History will hand down your plaudit to Posterity. The men of the present Day who are generally least grateful to their Co[n]temporaries, esteem it an Honor to be of your acquaintance.

I am Sorry to hear that Mrs. Jay and yourself have been indisposed but I hope you are recovered and partaking the enjoyments of this Season with the Gay, Sprightly Inhabitants of Versailles and Paris. My best wishes ever attend you. Mrs. Morris bears the warmest attachment to Mrs. Jay and yourself. She is very well and very Merry. Kitty Livingston has been Plagued with Intermittants throughout the Fall, but she now looks charmingly and a certain Young Gentleman of this City is of my opinion.

Our Friend Governeur writes you Political letters,[5] but as he tells you nothing of himself it is just that I tell you, how industrious, how useful he is. His talents and abilities you know they are all faithfully and disinterestedly applied to the Service of His Country. I could do nothing without him and our joint labours do but just keep the wheels in Motion.

With Sincere attachment, I am My Dear Sir, Your Friend and humble Servant,[6]

ROB. MORRIS

LS. Endorsed: ". . . Recd 17 Feby 83." Paragraphs 2 through 4 omitted in *WJ,* II, 110–11, and in *HPJ,* III, 13.

[1]JJ to Robert Morris, 13 Oct. 1782, above.

[2]See below, JJ to Catharine W. Livingston, 1 July 1783, n. 8.

[3]See above, JJ to Matthew Ridley, 8 Jan. 1782, and JJ to Robert Morris, 25 April 1782.

[4]William White (1772–98) and Charles (b. 1777) Morris.

[5]Gouverneur Morris to JJ, 6 Aug. 1782 and 1 Jan. 1783, above.

[6]This sentence is in the hand of Robert Morris.

FROM WILLIAM LIVINGSTON

Elizabeth Town, 8 January 1783
(Duplicate)

Sir,

I have just now received your Letter of the 14th October.[1] Next to your being here, I rejoice at your being in France, as I presume that if Madrid can please a Spaniard it is as much as can be expected.

I hope that my little grand daughter is by this time recruited from her tedious Journey, and thrives on the salubrious milk generated by lawful matrimony. As to Master Peter, all the pains the family takes with him, carry with them their own reward: *labor ipso voluptas.*[2] He is one of the most sagacious boys of his age that ever I met with; and has almost every fable of Aesop and Gay at his fingers' end.[3]

I always had an aversion to venturing any political news across the ocean. This aversion has been not a little encreased by observing the imprudence of others, in writing to their friends in Europe whatever comes into their heads concerning the state of our affairs without considering that it was at least five to one that their unguarded effusions escaped falling into the hands of the enemy. Having therefore not settled my cypher with you (which I have often regretted) I dare not venture any thing on that subject, on which I could otherwise tell you something of no inconsiderable moment. Be assured that we shall be glad to hear from you and Mrs. Jay, as often as possible.

As poor Brockholst lost his whole collection of garden seeds by his capture, I shall be much obliged to you for the seeds of any such vegetables in which the French gardens excell ours, as well as for those of any pretty flowering shrubs that are not to be found amongst us. This, you will say, is an odd commission for an Ambassador, but as Mr. Oswald will probably lead you through many thorny paths, it may be well enough to amuse yourself sometimes with collecting a few flowers that you may accidentally meet with during the Journey. I am, Dear Sir, your most humble Servant,

WIL. LIVINGSTON

ALS. Addressed: "A Monsieur John Jay, chez Grand Hotel D'Orleans, A Paris." Endorsed: ". . . ansd. 21 May 1783, it was recd. same Day."

[1]Probably SLJ to William Livingston, 14 Oct. 1782, above.

[2]"Work itself is a pleasure."

[3]Aesop's *Fables* were available in American editions in 1762. Poet and dramatist John Gay (1685–1732) authored two series of *Fables,* published in 1727 and 1738. Since the first American edition of Gay's *Fables* did not appear until 1794, Peter Jay must

have been reading one of the numerous eighteenth-century English editions. See also, Peter Augustus Jay to SLJ, 18 July 1781, n. 1, above. Evans, 9049, 27034.

William Livingston to Sarah Livingston Jay

Elizabeth Town, 8 January 1783
(Quadruplicate)

My dear Mrs. Jay,

I received your Letter of the 15th October[1] on my way to this place where I had not been since the beginning of October last. It is the first letter I have had from you since your arrival in France.[2] I am glad to hear you was recovered from your indisposition; and wish I could felicitate Mr. Jay on the like fortunate event respecting himself.

I long to see you both, and my dear little french grand-daughter Maria. My sweet little Peter is now standing at my elbow; and as you desire me to tell you what I think of him I will give you my Opinion with the greatest impartiality. He is really and without flattery one of the handsomest boys in the whole country and exceedingly sprightly and active, of a very quick apprehension and an exceeding good memory. Of late he is as fond of his books as can be wished, and he reads well for a boy of his age. I think that he has lost but very little by his not having been at school since he left Poughkeesie. However we were determined to comply with his father's request as to sending him thither again, and should have resigned him into the hands of his Uncle Fady whenever he had called for him for that purpose whatever mortification our parting with him might have cost us. But Mr. Benson's Sentiments upon that subject (which I am told have been transmitted to Mr. Jay)[3] will I hope reconcile you to his being still with his grand Mama Livingston, who notwithstanding her great fondness for him, is far from spoiling him, as there is really not a boy in the Country more orderly or under better command than Master Peter.

We had some thoughts last Fall of putting him to school in this Town; but considering the expence of boarding and how little more he would learn by that means than at Home, we concluded to defer it till Spring, when he can foot it from Home with his Basket containing his dinner, and need not return till after the second school, which I think will greatly contribute to his health and strength by the due quantity of excersise it will afford him. Mr. Jay's directions in the interim shall however be the rule of our conduct respecting him. He has lost much of his bashfulness, and begins to go to and converse with strangers with considerable freedom. I am sorry that he still retains his bad pronunciation of some words occasioned by his not being able to pronounce the G and C, substituting the *D* for the former and the T for the latter. Gold for instance he calls *Doold* and Come *tome.* But I hope this will soon wear off, as most of my children were long puzzled with the pronunciation of certain letters of the Alphabet which they afterwards articulated as well as others.

A few days ago a number of transports arrived at New York from Charles Town in consequence of the evacuation of that Garrison.[4] I long earnestly for their leaving New York that I may again be able to live with my family which labours under many inconveniencies on account of my absence from it, as I do in my turn for being obliged to live at a distance from them.[5] I long exceedingly to see you and Mr. Jay in safety over that Element which has been so fatal to mine. I am, your affectionate Father,

WIL. LIVINGSTON

P.S. Peter does not yet learn to write, but I enclose you a specimen of his Genius for imitation in that way.[6] [*We have n*]ot received your Letter with [*your acco*]unt of the Pyrenees.[7]

ALS. Addressed: "Mrs. Sarah Jay."

[1]Probably SLJ to William Livingston, 14 Oct. 1782, above.

[2]No letters from SLJ to William Livingston between 24 June 1781, above, and 14 Oct. 1782 have been located.

[3]No letters from Egbert Benson to JJ between 27 Nov. 1781, ALS in JP, and 25 April 1783, below, have been located.

[4]Charleston had been evacuated by the British on 14 Dec. 1782.

[5]Livingston's reference to his intermittent residence in the state capital of Trenton.

[6]Enclosure not located.

[7]Letter not located.

From Sarah Livingston Jay

Paris, 17 January 1783

My dear Mr. Jay,

I had just sent for paper etc. to write to you when your letter of the 13th January was handed me. I hope before this you have received mine by Mr. Johnston,[1] who persisted in his resolution of following you, though I told him that you would probably have left Rouen before he would arrive there. You have my thanks my dear for both your kind letters.[2] I am sorry that your health has received so little benefit as yet from your journey. My hopes of service were so very sanguine that that consideration almost banished the dread of a separation. My disappointment will even exceed my former hopes if your absence is not compensated for by additional health. I believe your sleep and mine have fled together, perhaps to drown the cares of some less happy persons, for my waking hours are not painful ones.

Mrs. Ridley, her cousin[3] and son drank tea with me last Evening. She is not well, but as the cause of her illness is a natural one, there is less reason to regret it.[4]

Yesterday at 3 o'Clock Mr. Whitford waited upon me to desire me to inform you that a fine bay horse of Lord Mount Stuart's[5] which you have seen (but not the unsound one) is to be disposed of at present for 40 Guineas with saddle and bridle etc., for 36 guineas without. Mr. Whitford wishes to know as soon as possible whether you would choose to make the purchase. Did I tell you Mr. Oswald was going to England?[6] He went last Wednesday afternoon after calling upon me for my commands and requesting to be remembered to you. I've received a letter for you from the Marquis de la Fayette, who is at Cadiz, but am ignorant whether you would wish to have it forwarded.[7] The expectations of a Peace seem to be again revived but on what foundation I can't tell. I suppose you have heard that Captain Hill[8] has brought some Prizes in to L'Orient and left a few American privateers amidst a fleet of Merchantmen consisting of twenty sail and without a convoy so that it is supposed they will have their choice.

The family are all very well and the servants conduct themselves to a *charm*. Our Neighbours are very friendly and we pass our time very sociably ensemble. Maria runs about in a kind of go-cart and continues as fond of me as ever. Adieu my dear Mr. Jay, believe me to be most, Affectionately yours,

SA. JAY

ALS. Addressed: "A Monsieur Jay, Chez Monsr. Holker, Chevalier de L'Ordre Royale et Militaire de St. Louis, Rouene." Endorsed. Errors in *HPJ*, III, 22–23.

[1]JJ's letter not located. SLJ to JJ, 11 Jan. 1783, ALS and DftS in JP.

[2]For 9 Jan. 1783, see *HPJ*, III, 20.

[3]John Hunt.

[4]Mrs. Ridley was pregnant.

[5]For Caleb Whiteford and Lord Mountstuart, see the editorial note above, "John Jay's Diary of the Peacemaking."

[6]The new ministry of William Henry Cavendish Bentinck (1738–1809), the third Duke of Portland, moved swiftly to replace Oswald by naming David Hartley to conclude the peace with America. It was Henry Laurens who first broke the news to Oswald. Oswald to Caleb Whitefoord, London, 16 Feb. 1783, W. A. S. Hewins, comp., *Whitefoord Papers* (Oxford, 1898), p. 185.

[7]Lafayette to JJ, 26 Dec. 1782, above.
[8]Probably Captain Hugh Hill of the 20-gun privateer *Cicero*.

FROM SARAH LIVINGSTON JAY

Paris, 17 January 1783

My dearest Mr. Jay,

This morning directly after your letter was sent to the Post-Office I had the honor of a visit from the Marchioness de la Fayette, who came to enquire whether I still had the letter from the Marquis. She was greatly relieved upon finding that I had not entrusted it with the Post, and this Evening while I was sitting with Mrs. Ridley the Marchioness came in to make a visit, and finding me there, told me she had sent to my house for the letter and was distressed that I was not <there> at home, for that she had already written you a letter and had a safe conveyance by which to send it at 10 o'Clock to night, upon which finding it then to be 1/2 past eight I took leave of her and Mrs. Ridley to write you these few lines by her servant who is attending in the antichamber. As Mrs. Ridley has Company she can't make use of this opportunity to write to Mr. Ridley but requests that you will inform him that she has received his letters of the 14th and 16th, and likewise that she has received a letter from England to night by which she finds that Mr. Ridley's mother is very well.

Adieu my best beloved! Continue to ride on horse-back and use every possible means for the restoration of your health that I may soon have the pleasure of assuring with what sincerely I am, your very affectionate wife

SA. JAY

ALS. Addressed: "A Son Excellence Monsieur Jay, Chez Monsieur Holker Chevalier de L'Ordre Royale et Militaire de St. Louis, Rouenne."

TO SARAH LIVINGSTON JAY

Rouen, 18 January 1783

My dear Sally,

A little Letter I wrote you this morning,[1] contained a promise of another by Tomorrow Post, and to perform it I am now retired to my Room.

I fear your Expectations respecting the speedy Recovery of my Health are too sanguine. As I lost it by almost imperceptible Degrees, the Restoration of it will doubtless be gradual, and I shall think myself happy if I regain it on those Terms. If my Endeavours succeed, I shall be grateful; if not, I shall be resigned. I hope you will always consider these matters in their true Points of View, and not permit vain Hopes or causeless Fears to distress either you or me. The more easy and happy you are, the more I shall be so also, and consequently the better prospects we shall both have of future Health. I am better than when I left you, though not much. The weather has been and still is very unfavorable, but it must change soon, and thank God it cannot change for the worse.

If the Letter from the Marquis came by the Post, that is, if there are post Marks on the cover, send it to me, if not, keep it till I return, and observe the same Rule as to all other Letters you may recieve for me.

This Town is daily amused with contradictory Reports respecting Peace. They are anxious about it, and with Reason, for the uncertainty of its taking Place, holds Commerce suspended, and injures the mercantile Interest greatly. I am pleased with this City and the people of it. They are industrious and hospitable. Their manufactures are very considerable and very proper for our Country, with whom they will certainly have a great Trade unless it be fettered and embarrassed with superfluous Regulations and ill-judged Restrictions. I suspect the Trade of this Country stands in need of Revision very generally.

Present my Comp[limen]ts and best wishes to Mrs. Ridley and your neighbours. I am glad the Servants behave well, they shall be rewarded for it. Kiss our little Girl for me, and believe me to be, My dear Sally, Your very affectionate Husband,

JOHN JAY

ALS. Incomplete in *HPJ,* III, 23–24.
[1]Not located.

FROM FREDERICK JAY

Poughkeepsie, 26 January 1783
(Copy)

Dear Sir,

Inclosed you have copy of my last to you under the 15th August.[1] You perhaps may be surprised, as you have often been, at my not writing you more frequent, but when you are informed that my Silence was owing to indisposition and to no other cause, I flatter myself you'll think it a sufficient apology. On the 1st Sep[tember] a Fever seized me, which continued with little intermissions until late in December. It reduced me greatly, and had such an affect on my Sight that I could neither read, write or at times even see. I am now thank God much better, though far from well, which I attribute to a journey I took to Elizabeth Town on a visit to your son, and leaving off the use of all medicine. To my late illness it is owing that your Son remained at Eliz[abeth] Town, and was not put to school at Goshen as was intended, and which would in my opinion have been to his advantage, though I am happy that our plan was not carried into execution, as by your letter of the 3rd October,[2] which came to hand a few days since, and is the only one received Since your residence at Paris, you disapprove of the measure. I have brought him with me to spend the remaining part of the season at this place, and I shall give him all the instruction in my power. He is in perfect health, would read well did he speak plain, is a good boy, has the beauty of his Mother in every aspect. In the spring he will return to his friends in Jersey.

In regard to the Bristol Legacies, I can only at present say, that Mr. Mathew Couper[3] of New York did in the month of November at the request of the Executors of Mrs. Peloquin, advertize that *they* were ready to pay off the Legacies due to ones Family, saving them particularly for proper discharges being given. I wrote to Mr. Couper on the subject, who informs me that he had wrote to Mr. James Daltera[4] one of the Executors, to know if monies drawn by the Claimants would be paid, in which case he would take my Draughts and pay the money which would suit my present purpose much better than getting it another way. Should I not receive a letter soon from Mr. Couper, I shall send you the necessary Papers.

The old servants are provided for in as comfortable a manner as they could wish, or is in our power. Plato is with me, and should New York be evacuated and Claus remain there I shall take care of him.

Of the many articles you mention to have sent for the use of the Family no more have arrived than what is mentioned at foot, and all of inferior Quality, which makes the loss much greater, I would advise you not to order any more, the risque is great and the expence of transportation very high.

I am much obliged to you for your kindness in offering me a part of your share of the income of the Estate. Be assured that the Estate in its present Situation will afford but little assistance to any of us, and I see no prospect, at least very little, of a favorable change.[5]

I cannot on any consideration remain here longer than the Spring.

My interest has already suffered too much. It has now become necessary to pay some attention to myself. Whether I shall settle in Boston or Philadelphia or either will depend entirely on circumstances. Be that as it may. I shall continue to give the Family as much of my assistance as possible.

The Family are all pretty well. Nancy has frequent and severe turns of her old Complaints. I think her in a poor way. Gussy is at Kingston and behaves well. Mrs. Munro is still in Albany.[6] Peter [is] very well.

I am greatly surprised that you have neither received the Original or any copy of mine of the 20th April last.[7] How it happened that it was not inclosed in mine of June last[8] I can't conceive. You have herein inclosed another Copy.

List of Articles received for the use of the Family: 1 Bale of blankets, 2 ps.[9] blk. Cloth, 2 Do. Baize, 1 Do. Oznabrigs, 30 Bushells Salt; received in 1781 and 1782. 2 ps. coarse Linen, 1 Bale Blankets, 6 1/2 oz. Silk, 1/4 Do. thread; received in January, 1783. 6 pair stockings, 2 blk. Handker[chief]s, Silk for Mrs. Jay.

Remaining in Philadelphia 6 ps. Linen, 2 ps. hand[kerchief]s, and some thread and Silk. Twenty four Blankets, not worth transportation, sold in Phi[ladelphi]a for £ 28-10, out of which have paid the freight of Goods by the Favourite and Nonsuch £ 18-1, which leaves a ballance due to you of £ 10-09, which B[a]l[an]ce, I have received and passed to your Credit.

The Family join me in our best wishes for your health and that of Mrs. Jay and the Child. I am with sincere affection, Yours,

FRED. JAY

ACS. Addressed: "His Excellency John Jay Esquire, at Paris." Endorsed: ". . . enclosing Copies of 20 Ap. and 18 Augt. 1783, Rcd. July 1783 via England."

[1]Frederick Jay to JJ, 15 Aug. 1782, above.

[2]JJ to Frederick Jay, 3 Oct. 1782, above.

[3]Matthew Couper, a sea captain and merchant. Frederick Jay to JJ, 10 Jan. and 27 April 1784, ALS in JP.

[4]Bristol merchant James Daltera (1729–1801), master in the Society of Merchant Venturers, and partner in the firm of Daltera and Roche. W. E. Minchinton, ed., *The Trade of Bristol in the Eighteenth Century,* XX (Bristol, 1957), 63.

[5]See JJ to Frederick Jay, 3 Oct. 1782, and "The Estate of Peter Jay," above.

[6]Frederick Jay to JJ, 15 Aug. 1782, above.

[7]Frederick Jay to JJ, 20 April 1782, above.

[8]Frederick Jay to JJ, June 1782, not located.

[9]Abbreviation for "piece," a length of material varying from 10 to 28 yards. Simmonds, *Dictionary of Trade* (London, 1858).

Patience Lovell Wright to John Adams and John Jay

8 March 1783
London, Wax Work, Pall-mall

Dear Sirs, Contrymen,

I may venture to write to you as whatever is useful to human Nature Cannot but be Pleasing. As nothing in the world is So useful and beneficial as Government founded on Comon Equity and prudance, so nothing is So Delights my mind as the Contemplation of the Happiness of having a Part in the well Regulated Comunity. Their is Such a Charm in good order and Stedy Descipline that the world in all futer ages will admire and Read the History of our Days with the highest pleasure. America has Excited other Nations in Elivation and greatness of mind, with a Zeal to Contribut to the Preservation of the priveledges of Nature and general felicity. We now Send you a Copy of our thoughts on the Subject of *taxes, Comon Law,* etc. My perticuler friends and aquaintance all Joyne in the good wishes and Send me Some Hints to be forwared to your Govenours in the Diferent States. When King Solomon Built the temple he Receivd presents from all Parts and accepted Presents of all Kinds from the People. So in like manner you wise men will take our materials as Coming from honest well ment Zeal to serve the grand Cause of our Contry. You will Rejoyce that in the Contry of your Enimies you have all the wise all the good in all Dinomenaturs with you in heart and Soul Ready to assist in any thing in their Power.

The most extrordinary treetment the Kings Friends has meet from *him* and the *Junto* has opened the minds and understandings of all Partis. Now good will Come out of Evil, and the *Good* Politicks of America Sound fourth to all the admiring World. Give us permission to lay our small mite before you. Public men must Expect Empertenent letters and visits. I wish much the pleasure of Seeing Mr. Adams and Mr. Jay and other worthy Contrymen now in Europe. My Intention is to make a Colection of their Busts in wax work to present to the State House in City Philadelphia for a monument of their glory and my *own* good Judgment.

I hope the thought will meet with you approbation and Incouragment. Women are faithful Friends and in all great Revolutions in Church and State have done wonders. The Honour already of the Friendship of our worthy heros, your Coleagues Doctor Franklin and

Mr. Lawrance, Marques Delefiatt etc. will lay the Foundation of my Intended Plann.

May I meet with your Friendship and deserve your Esteem is, amongst the higist [*sic*] Wishs of honored gentlmen, your faithfull humble Servant,

PATIENCE WRIGHT

Per favor Mr. Lawrance.[1]

ALS. Addressed: "Messrs. Adams, Jay, Commissioners for America, etc. etc. etc., at Paris." Endorsed by JJ. Patience Lovell Wright, the wax modeler, who, while in England during the Revolutionary War, acted as a spy for the Americans. She was the mother of the artist Joseph Wright. See below, JJ to Robert R. Livingston, 4 Sept. 1782, n. 1. Groce and Wallace, *New-York Historical Society's Dictionary of Artists in America,* p. 705.

[1]Henry Laurens.

To Frederick Jay

Paris, 6 April 1783

Why my dear Brother will you not write to me?[1] Why thus deprive me of the Consolation of hearing of those for whom I have <the most> so much <of my> Regard and affection? It is hard, and it is unaccountable. Not a single Line from you this whole Winter. My Friends at Philadelphia do not mention <their> having recieved one Letter from you to be forwarded to me. I am sure you have no reason to think I have forgotten, or that I neglect you.

I congratulate you on the Peace. In my opinion Peter with your and Mr. Benson's assistance should take early measures for having the Farm at Rye valued, and I advise him to take it at the valuation.[2] That being done he should prepare to remove to and repair it, and tell him that <during my absence he may depend on recieving from me at least one hundred and fifty pounds per Year, and more if necessary.> I will from Time to Time supply him with what he may want. I advise him <on removing there> to hire a good overseer and to pay him liberal wages. The only way to get a good Man will be to pay him well. If the House stands, let him patch it up for the present. Nancy, I take it for granted will be with him <and if Polly> can hire <some sensib[le]> and I advise them to hire a clever middle aged Woman <can be had and should be hired> to live with them. I doubt whether it would be convenient for him to remove to Rye before next Spring. He will then have the Summer before him to raise the Farms a little out of its Ruins before Winter. At any Rate I think it would not be <best> prudent to remove before New York is evacuated.

If the House will admit of it, I think <John Strang>[3] might find it convenient to take a Room in it. That situation would do for his Business, and the convenience of having so good a Man in the Family would compensate for the additional Trouble it would occasion. I recommend it only for consideration, for with the little Information I have I cannot decide on the <propriety> Expedience of it.

It appears to me that Peter should for the first Year or two content himself with as little stock and tilling as possible, and encrease it as he gets up his Fences. The wood being destroyed stones will be his only fencing stuff, and they make but slow and expensive work. But he must not be discouraged by either Circumstance, for the first Patience and perseverance will afford a Remedy, and I will try to make the latter as easy to him as possible. By abstaining from all expensive amusements and avoidable superfluities I shall be able to <help> give him some help.

You I suppose will return to New York. Pray let me know your Views and Intentions. I will zealously second them, and do my best to serve you all. Let me know what Money you have recieved <on my account> from me through Mr. Livingston's hands. Your silence afflicts me exceedingly. James is here but has not visited us. Remember me affectionately to Peter and Nancy and Mrs. Jay. I am your affectionate Brother.

Dft. Endorsed: ". . . by Mr. Redford." ALS (not located) enclosed open in JJ to Egbert Benson, 6 April 1783, ALS in PHi: Dreer; DftS in JP.

[1]See Frederick Jay to JJ, 26 Jan. 1783, above.

[2]JJ's blind brother Peter, who inherited his father's farm at Rye. See above, "The Estate of Peter Jay."

[3]John Strang, JJ's former law clerk. See *JJ,* I, 145.

From Egbert Benson

Philadelphia, 25 April 1783

You doubtless my Friend will be surprized to receive a Letter from Me dated at this Place. I am here on an Errand from the State to the Delegates, too extensive to be the Subject of a Letter, and not proper to be entrusted to Paper.[1]

I sincerely congratulate You on a Peace. It is almost a Consummation of all my Wishes, and gives general Satisfaction here. A few Years of Wisdom and Virtue are requisite to secure to Us *all* the Happiness which ought to result from it.

With this You will receive Letters of Attorney from Your Brothers and Sister to receive their Legacies, and also a Certificate of Your being one of Your Father's Executors to enable You to receive the Legacy left to him.[2] I found myself exceedingly at a Loss as to the Mode of authenticating these Papers. Our Friend the Governor[3] would chearfully have given Us something like an Exemplification under the Great Seal, but an Objection arose, and I think it was well founded, that nothing could be exemplified unless it was Matter of *Record.* It is only by a Construction of our Act of Assembly that a Letter of Attorney under which *Lands* are conveyed can be recorded, but the Case of *personal* Interests cannot be brought within the Provisions of the Act. I had our entire Copy of Your Father's Will with the Codicils made out, and intended to have sent it to You certified under the Seal of the Court of Probates, but found the Copy exceedingly bulky, and very expensive and inconvenient in Conveyance, and it occurred to Me that as an Executor You could *separately* release a Debt, and therefore supposed, unless Mrs. Peloquin's Executors meant to be captious, that they would pay You the Legacies if You produced *reasonable* Evidence that You was authorized to receive them, and I should imagine the Privy Seal of the State will carry with it a sufficient Degree of Authenticity for that purpose.

Peter, Nancy, Frederick and Mrs. Jay are well, and I beleive will remain at Poughkeepsie til late in the fall even admitting the British Troops should leave the Southern parts of the State soon. Your little Boy is in Health and has been with Us at Poughkeepsie for some time, though I beleive that at present he is on a Visit to his Relatives at Elizabeth Town.

I have a great deal to *say* to You, but dare not *write* it. To communicate satisfactorily, I must lay open the Conduct of Individuals. This can only be safely done in one of those confidential Conversations which We have so often had, and which I most ardently wish We may soon have again. My best Regards to Mrs. Jay. Yours sincerely,

EGBT. BENSON

ALS. Addressed: "John Jay Esqur." Endorsed: ". . . ansd. 10 July 1783 by Capt. Barney," for which see *HPJ*, III, 51.

[1]Benson was charged with informing the New York delegates in Congress of his recent interview with Sir Guy Carleton at Governor Clinton's behest. The subject was the evacuation of New York City. Benson was rightly convinced that Carleton was stalling and "that he only intends to save appearances to negotiate and by

that means to effect a Delay." Benson to Governor Clinton, 17 April 1783, *PPGC*, VIII, 140–44. See also Clinton to Alexander Hamilton and William Floyd, 16 April 1783, *ibid.*, pp. 139–40.

[2]Enclosures not located.

[3]Governor George Clinton.

To William Livingston

Paris, 21 May 1783

Dear Sir,

It was not until this Morning that your obliging letter of the 8th January last reached me.[1] I thank you for it sincerely, and regret that its arriving so late in the Season will render it useless to send you an assortement of Seeds for this Spring. You may expect them in the Fall and they shall be fresh and of this Year's Growth.

Your accounts of my Boy are flattering, and so is your affectionate Attention to him. Mr. Benson rightly understood the Reason of my desiring that he might be carried to Fishkill. When that Reason ceased I preferred his returning to, and remaining with his Grandmama, and wrote so to my Brother, but the Letter it seems did not reach him in Time.[2] When Peter returns to you, which will probably be this month be pleased to take the Direction of him.

Your little grand Daughter, as well as her Parents, has had her Share of Trouble and Sickness. She is now well and Thrives finely. My Health has been Injured by the Heats of Spain, and since my arrival here I have not had Leisure to attend properly to it. Mrs. Jay has lost some of her Complaints by our change of Situation, though She is not yet strong and hearty.

As to Politics, I can add little to what you must have already heard on that Subject, especially as it would not be expedient to write freely unless in Cypher. I hope our Countrymen will not delay to secure and encrease the Blessings of Peace, by wise Regulations and Establishments. The Boundaries of the different States should be immediately settled, and every Cause of Dissention provided against, as far as possible. Our public Credit requires Appreciation, and the sooner that work is begun the better. Hard things are said of us on that Head. Mr. Morris's Letters to Congress have occasioned much Speculation. I wish he may not have resigned.[3]

I cannot conclude this Letter without congratulating you most sincerely on the Termination of your long Exile from Liberty Hall, and on the happy Period put by the Peace, to the Snares and Dangers which beset you during the war. Indeed every American must enjoy the present Moment. I confess I do in a great degree and with great Thankfulness, but as our happiness is erected on the Tombs, and Distress of so many of our virtuous Countrymen, there is a Solemnity in its aspect which will not permit me to say with Horace *"nunc est bibendum, nunc pede libero Pulsanda tellus."*[4] May God continue to bless and preserve you. I am, Dear Sir, your affectionate and humble Servant,

JOHN JAY

ALS in MHi: Livingston, II. Endorsed. Dft, in the hand of Peter Jay Munro, in JP.
[1]William Livingston to JJ, 8 Jan. 1783, above.
[2]JJ to Frederick Jay, 3 Oct. 1782, above.
[3]See Robert Morris to JJ, 31 May 1783, n. 1, above.
[4]"Now to drink and trip it on the light fantastic toe." Horace, *Odes* 1.37.1–2.

To CATHARINE W. LIVINGSTON

Passy, 1 July 1783

Dear Kitty,

Your's by Col. Cambray,[1] dated the 28 January last, was delivered to us by that Gentleman about a fortnight ago, and though several Vessels have since arrived, the only American Letter I have yet recieved by them is from Mr. Benson.[2]

I am surprized that no Letter from me has reached you since the arrival of Major Franks. I have written not only several but many[3]; but I have been so used to Disappointments of this Kind during the war, that they give me less Chagrin than formerly, especially as the Restoration of Peace affords more various, more frequent and more safe conveyances than we have had since I left you.

We have been for this month past in this Village, in apartments for which we are indebted to the friendly attention of Dr. Franklin. My Health was such as to render the air and confinement of a large City, during the Summer months, improper for me. I have already experienced Benefit from the Change, for though not well I am better. Mrs. Jay promises us a welcome Guest next month.[4] Maria is greatly altered for the better. She grows finely, but she suffers too much from her Teeth to be enoculated with Safety.

Sir James is still here, but has not been near us, a strange whim! Why he stays and what are his views, I cannot even guess.[5]

Peters Trip to Poughkeepsie was unexpected, and, I think, unnecessary. I have written to Fœdy and your Father on the Subject,[6] and it is my opinion that he should remain with the Family at Eliz[abeth] Town, and under their Direction until my Return, which I pray God may not be unnecessarily delayed. Your Sentiments on this Head correspond with my own. Long and faithfully have I served my Country, and it would be cruel longer to neglect the concerns of my Family. My Happiness is bound up with theirs and never can be separated. I long for Leisure and Rest. Indeed, unless I obtain it, premature old age, if old age at all, must be my Lott.

Mrs. Izard will probably be at Ph[iladelphi]a before this Letter, and carrys with her some fine Children. She sailed from Bordeaux.

I have lately recieved a Letter from your Cousin Ph. V. B. Livingston.[7] He was at Milan the 7 June, in much better Health than when he left us last Winter, though he did not appear to have much to complain of then.

Mr. Ridley and his Family are here and well. He lately left the Morris' at Geneva in good Health and well placed.[8] He deserves well of them. Mr. Hunt, a Relation of Mr. Ridley, will be the Bearer of this Letter.

Mr. Morris's Letter occasioned much Speculation on this Side of the Water, and I presume much discussion on yours. I shall consider his Resignation as a public misfortune. Whether that Event takes place or not, assure him of my constant Esteem, Regard and attachment, and accept the same assurance from Your affectionate Friend,

JOHN JAY

ALS in MHi: Ridley Papers. Addressed: "Miss Kitty W. Livingston, To the Care of the Hon'ble Robt. Morris, Philadelphia."

[1]French volunteer Louis Antoine Jean Baptiste Cambray, Chevalier de Digney (1751–1822), served as a lieutenant colonel in Duportail's corps of engineers, and was breveted colonel on 2 May 1783. André Lasseray, *Les Français sous treize étoiles* (2 vols., Paris, 1935), I, 139–40.

[2]Catharine W. Livingston to JJ, 28 January, AL in JP, and Egbert Benson to JJ, 25 April 1783, above.

[3]Only two of JJ's 1782 letters to Catharine have been located: 21 January, above, and 13 December, ALS in MHi: Ridley.

[4]SLJ was then eight months pregnant.

[5]See editorial note "Sir James' New Role: Self-Appointed Negotiator in Paris," above.

[6]JJ to William Livingston, 21 May 1783, above; JJ to Frederick Jay, not located. For Peter Augustus Jay's stay in Poughkeepsie, see Egbert Benson to JJ, 25 April 1783, above. For JJ's further instructions to his brother, see below, 18 July 1783.

[7]Cited in JJ to Philip Livingston, 28 June 1783, above.

[8]On 19 May 1783, Matthew Ridley left Paris for Geneva with his two charges, Thomas and Robert Morris, Jr., and their newly engaged tutor, Nicolas Jean Hugou de Bassville (1753–93). The Morris boys and their tutor remained in Geneva, while Ridley returned to Paris on 1 June 1783. Hugou de Bassville, a native of Abbeville,

was to acquire a reputation as a journalist, and an envoy of the French Republic, who met his death at the hands of a Roman mob. His assassination was to provide a long-standing grievance of the Republic against the Papacy. See Frédéric Masson's *Les Diplomates de la révolution: Hugou de Bassville à Rome; Bernadotte à Vienne* (Paris, 1883).

To Frederick Jay

Passy, 18 July 1783

Dear Fœdy,

The last Letter from you which has reached me is dated the 26 January last. It accounted for your prior Silence in a manner which gave me much anxiety. It was the first Intimation we had recieved of your Illness.[1] Sickness has long been a Guest in our Family, and I fear will continue too familiar with us. I much approve of your taking but little or no medicine. By Temperance Exercise and attention to Diet I was formerly restored to a tolerable Degree of Health after <a Fever had for two years brought me very low> haveing been much reduced by a Fever which did not quit me except at Intervals for two Years. I believe your Constitution to be a good one and if you nurse it, that is, if you observe and avoid what ever you find injurious to it, it <will> may last a great while. To these Observances I owe what Health I have, and which though far from considerable affords me a Share of Chearfulness and Spirits without which Life would be a Burden. I shall be with you if God spares my Life next Spring. You may rely upon this.

Poor Nancys Illness gives me great Concern.[2] God grant that her Health may be re-established and that we yet may be so happy as to spend many good Days together. Peters continuing in good Health affords me much Consolation. If we meet again nothing but Death shall separate me from him.

I have recieved from Mr. Benson your Letters of Attorney, and I shall take the first opportunity that offers of compleating that Business.[3] Accept my Thanks for your kind attention to my little Boy. I hope he will live to be sensible of your affection and to return it. In my opinion, he had better remain at Eliz[abeth] Town until affairs become so settled as that a regular plan for his Education can be formed and executed. On my Return that will be my first Care.

In a former Letter to you[4] I advised Peter to have the Farm at Rye valued and to take it at the Valuation. Nothing in my power shall be wanting to make that and every other affair in which he is interested easy to him. I have also written on this Subject to Mr. Benson.[5] I am anxious to know your views and Intentions in order that I may second and promote them. Sir James is here, but he does not come near us, and I am ignorant why he stays and what he is doing. Peter Munro has written to his Father but recieved no answer.[6] Kitty Livingston has sent me a sensible judicious Letter which you wrote her about Mrs. M.[7] I am persuaded that you acted right on that occasion, and you shall have my support.

You may expect to have another Nephew or niece next month. I shall send you the earliest advice of that Event. Orders have been sent for the Evacuation of New York, and hope it will soon be compleated.

We hear that <merchandize is> dry Goods are cheaper with you than here so that altho Peace gives me an opportunity of sending you articles of that kind without much Risque, I decline it for that Reason. If you want money for Family use I can and am ready to supply you. You may draw at thirty Days Sight for 150 pounds <your> York money. Divide it equally between you Peter and Nancy <equally> and tell me if more be necessary. While I have, none of you shall want. Sally thinks Peggy should have answered her Letter. Remember us affectionately to her and to all the Family. Present our Compliments to the Van Wycks and our other Friends. I am, Dear Fœdy, Your affectionate Brother,

JOHN JAY

P.S. We are in better Health than usual. The pain in my Breast has abated. Peter is very well.

DftS. Endorsed: ". . . in ansr. 26 Jany. last."

[1]Frederick Jay to JJ, 26 Jan. 1783, above.

[2]*Ibid.*

[3]Egbert Benson to JJ, 25 April 1783, above.

[4]JJ to Frederick Jay, 6 April 1783, above.

[5]JJ to Egbert Benson, 6 April 1783, cited in source note of preceding letter.

[6]No letters from Peter Jay Munro to his father, the Rev. Harry Munro, have been located.

[7]Eve Jay Munro. Catharine W. Livingston's letter and the enclosed letter from Frederick Jay have not been located.

Sarah Livingston Jay to William Livingston

Passy, 18 July 1783

My dear Papa,

I had the pleasure of receiving your favor of the 8th of January some time in May, and that of the 21st of May, the 2nd of July,[1] and sincerely thank you for those instances of your remembrance. You was very obliging my dear sir to be so minute in your account of my son, and I have reason to hope from the example as well as precepts of those who have been so kind as to watch over his education that you have not flattered me. Though really but for that circumstance I should have been a little apprehensive that the pleasing description flowed rather from the partiallity than the judgement of his indulgent grandfather. If any thing could have encreased my desire to return to America, my wish to see the dear little fellow and to evince my gratitude to his friends would have been the motives. If you should think of any thing not to be easily procured in America, that would facilitate the prosecution of his studies, and will be so good as to acquaint me what it is, I'll endeavor to procure it here and bring it with me. Or if there is any thing, beside the garden-seeds, which you, my dear sir, are desirous of having from Europe you cannot flatter me more than by letting me know what it is that I may have the pleasure of being the bearer of it. Mr. Grand,[2] who has a well chosen collection of Fruits, Flowers and shrubs in his garden has promised Mr. Jay that he will order his gardener to preserve seeds of the choicest Fruits etc. which he has, and we will not fail sending them out in time to be sown next spring. But don't promise yourself much from them, for really the fruits I have tasted in Europe bear no comparison to those with which I've been so often regaled from your garden, excepting only the melons and grapes in Spain. The last year it's true, the season was unfavorable to the fruits in France, and I have not yet had an opportunity of judging of the peaches and pears this year, which ought to be fine if ever they are for the summer is confessedly a fine one, but the earlier fruits have still maintained their inferiority to ours.

Can you, my dear sir, account for the backwardness of speech in my children? Peter indeed may alledge the want of his mother's example, but what excuse can be found out for Maria, who is a great deal with me, and is very active *except* with her tongue? Mr. Jay imputes her not yet talking to the confusion of tongues she has heard since her birth, since she must learn two or three words to express each individual thing she would speak of, and candor obliges me to confess that I'm of that opinion, for to do her justice she does not seem to want inclination.

I am a subscriber for a little work intitled L'Ami des Enfans par M. Berquin,[3] of which we receive a volume the first of every month, and could Peter read french I would send them to him as they were published, for I really think they merit the title the Author has chosen for them, as in those little volumes the excellence of virtue and the depravity of vice is contrasted by the examples of Children of amiable and unamiable characters in so natural and easy a manner as cannot fail to impress the tender and uncorrupted minds of children with proper dispositions. Perhaps when I return if you have leisure, and think any of the tales may be useful to my children, you will be so obliging as to assist me in translating some of them into english for their use.

Adieu my dear Papa! May you long enjoy in health and independance the well earned reward of your truly patriotic conduct, and live to see your children's children following your example.

As the packets from France and England will begin to Sail in September for New York, I hope the intelligence between friends will be more frequent than formerly, and if indisposition does not prevent me from writing, you shall not Papa have reason to complain of the silence of his dutiful and affectionate daughter,

SA. JAY

ALS. Endorsed by the recipient and also in an unidentified hand. DftS in JP.

[1]William Livingston to SLJ, 8 Jan. 1783, above; 21 May 1783, not located.

[2]The Jays' neighbor, Parisian banker Ferdinand Grand, whose country residence was near the Hôtel de Valentinois in Passy. *AP,* II, 303.

[3]Arnaud Berquin's (1750–91) popular *L'Ami des enfants,* honored by the French Academy in 1784 as the "most useful" publication of the year, was translated into several languages and first published in America in an English translation in 1786. Evans, 19504, 19505.

To Catharine W. Livingston

Passy, 20 July 1783

Dear Kitty,

I have now your kind Letter of the 24 May last,[1] before me. I sincerely thank You for it. It is a little singular that so few Letters from us have reached You, especially as several of them have been written since the Cessation of Hostilities.

Mrs. Izard is on the way to Philadelphia. The Departure of the Vessel in which she expected to sail disappointed her exceedingly, and occasioned much Embarrassment and Expence. Few Ladies are capable of managing better under such Circumstances. She deserves Credit for Prudence as well as Talents. If you should see her (as it is probable you will either at Philadelphia or in her way to New York) present our best Compliments to her.

Your Letter by Mr. Vaughan came safe to Hand.[2] Franks, I hear, is making money. If that be true, he will, I am persuaded think of me, though I confess the Circumstance you mention does not argue more Delicacy than Punctuality.[3]

There are some parts of your Letter on which I could make interesting Remarks, and I should not hesitate to be very particular, could I be sure that this Letter will reach you uninspected, but your Removal from Philadelphia[4] renders this the more uncertain, and I think it most prudent not to run any Risque.

If God preserves my Life and hears my Prayers we shall see each other next June or July, and then my dear Cate we will exchange much interesting Information. During the Course of the late Revolution, many have been put to a Variety of Trials, and I think I can better estimate the value both of Men and Things than I should otherwise have been able to do. It is to be lamented, however, that although Experience generally adds to our Prudence, it often diminishes our Happiness, at least so far as respects this World.[5] My future Situation will excite but little Envy, and, as I shall stand in Nobody's way,[6] I shall cease to be exposed to those little Tricks and Machinations which though rarely ever fatal to honest and prudent men, always cause a certain Degree of Trouble and Indignation.

Mr. Morris it seems has postponed his Resignation,[7] and I rejoice at it. That Resolution is fortunate for the public, and in my opinion conducive to his Reputation. He has his Enemies it is true, and so all men so circumstanced ever have had and ever will have.

Farewell my good and faithful Friend. Believe me to be with the most sincere Esteem and Regard, Your affectionate Brother,

JOHN JAY

ALS in MHi: Ridley. Addressed: "Miss Kitty W. Livingston." Endorsed. Dft in JP; paragraphs 2 through 4 omitted in *HPJ*, III, 67.

[1]Letter not located.

[2]Letter not located.

[3]The report seemed to be belied by Franks' strenuous, but unsuccessful, efforts to secure an appointment as a consul in a European port. See below, Charles Thomson to JJ, 15 Jan. 1784, also PCC 79, III, 267.

[4]SLJ to Mary White Morris, 17 July 1783, ALS in CSmH.

[5]JJ deleted the following phrase from the Dft in JP: "As my views, and expectations are very limited, I flatter myself with being seldom disquieted with vain Hopes or causeless Fears."

[6]JJ deleted the following phrase from the Dft: "Nobody will think it worth while to spread Snares on my Paths or invidiously wound my Reputation."

[7]See above, Robert Morris to JJ, 3 May 1783, n. 2.

To Frederick Jay

Passy, 26 August 1783

Dear Fœdy,

I wrote to you the 14th Instant informing you that Sally had the Day before been delivered a Girl.[1] It gives me Pleasure to be able to acquaint you that the mother is doing well, and that her Daughter is in perfect Health. She is <this day> to be baptized this morning by the name of Anne. I wish we could as easily give her the Virtues as the name of our amiable Sister. We shall take the Liberty of <considering> making Mrs. Jay one of the Sponsors. Miss Penn and our Friend Egbert Benson are to be the others.[2] Make our affectionate Compliments to Mrs. Jay and tell her that we hope to have the Satisfaction of presenting her God Daughter to her next Summer.

A Duplicate of your Letter of the 26 January last (including Copies of others viz. 20 April and 15 August 1782[3]) which came to Hand three weeks ago by the way of England was sealed with the old <Family> Seal of the Family Arms which belonged to our great grandfather.[4] The Impression was not very fair, but whether that was owing to the Seals not having been perfectly clean, or to any other Cause I cannot tell. I wish to have a Seal engraved exactly like it and You would oblige me greatly, <therefore> if you would be so good as to send me some good Impressions of it enclosed in several Letters by different Conveyances. In order that the Impressions may be the Fairer, take a little warm Suds and a *soft* Brush and clean the Seal well before You use it.

I replied on the 18th Ult. by Capt. Barney, to your Letter of the 26 January last which enclosed copies of two former ones and which is the last I have had the Pleasure to recieve from you.[5] I wish to hear from you exceedingly, and as we may write by the way of England as well as by the way of France, we might by a little attention often recieve Letters from each other. My Health is better than it has been, though not yet re-established. With sincere and great Regard for you and all the Family, I am Dear Fœdy, Your very affectionate Brother.

I hear Sir James is still at Paris. Peter Jay Munro is very well.

Dft. Endorsed.

[1]Ann Jay was born on 13 August. On 26 Aug. 1783 JJ also wrote Catharine W. Livingston announcing the birth of the Jays' daughter, ALS in MHi; Dft in JP. JJ's 14 August letters to his brother and to William Livingston are not located.

[2]Sophia Penn was one of Ann Jay's godmothers. Lady Juliana Penn and her

son Grenville were proxy godparents for Margaret Barclay Jay and Egbert Benson. See SLJ to Susannah French Livingston, 12 Sept. 1783, ALS in JP.

[3]Frederick Jay to JJ, 20 April and 15 Aug. 1782, above, and 26 Jan. 1783, below.

[4]Pierre Jay, *JJ,* I, 29.

[5]JJ to Frederick Jay, 18 July, and Frederick Jay to JJ, 26 Jan. 1783, above.

(John Jay Homestead, Bedford, New York)

IV

CLOSING MONTHS ABROAD

An American in England

The Definitive Peace settled, JJ could now contemplate a long-deferred trip to England to collect a legacy left by the Peloquin family and to take the cure at Bath for a variety of ailments. His correspondence had for many months contained references to his poor health, but official duties prevented his departure from Paris until 9 October. Traveling by way of Calais and Dover, he reached London on the 14th. By coincidence two of the other three American peace negotiators also crossed the Channel during the period of JJ's stay in England, their collective, if unofficial, presence provoking some raised eyebrows back in the States.[1]

JJ had planned originally to go on to Bristol and then to Bath after a week or ten days in the capital, but illness detained him in London, at the same time curtailing his social life. In London JJ stayed at the Cavendish Square residence of the William Binghams. There he received some old friends and renewed former acquaintances, notably among the small but articulate knot of American merchants who were promoting a program for the liberalizing of trade between Great Britain and the new nation. Among them were Elkanah Watson (1758–1842), the Rhode Islander whose trading firm in Nantes had established a London branch, and Joshua Johnson, who had also arrived from Nantes to take up residence in Cooper's Row.

JJ's social contacts were not confined to the American colony, however. He spent time with Benjamin Vaughan and Richard Oswald, and may have paid at least one visit to Shelburne at Bowood Park. He also had the opportunity to discriminate among erstwhile friends who were now in exile. JJ felt free to receive those New York Loyalists whose public behavior since coming to England had been circumspect and to be entertained by them in turn. Contrariwise, he was reluctant to acknowledge other New York refugees reputed to have circulated "infamous Lies" against the United States or whose conduct during the war had rendered them unacceptable to patriotic Americans. Thus, while he received the Reverend John Vardill and Lieutenant Colonel James De Lancey when they visited him at the Binghams, he declined to return their calls. He made no effort to see the Oliver De Lancey family and snubbed William Bayard, Senior, when he passed him on the street.[2]

JJ's decisions about whether or not to renew old friendships were dictated by his sense of what was in the national interest, and he did not relish having to turn his back on former close associates. Silas Deane is perhaps the outstanding example. Deane tried unsuccessfully to contact JJ late in November of 1783, and again two months later. JJ's stiff reply of 23 February 1784 from Paris was a final rebuke. Therein he found himself under "the cruel necessity" of failing to acknowledge Deane's card left at the Binghams as well as a letter. His comment was crushing:

> But I love my country and my honour better than my friends, and even my family, and am ready to part with them all whenever it would be improper to retain them. You are either exceedingly injured, or you are no friend to America, and while doubts remain on that point, all connection between us must be suspended. I wished to hear what you might have to say on that head, and should have named a time and place for an interview, had not an insurmountable obstacle intervened to prevent it. I was told by more than one, on whose information I thought I could rely, that you recieved visits from, and was on terms of familiarity with General Arnold. Every American who gives his hand to that man, in my opinion, pollutes it.[3]

Men whom JJ was not eager to see in London included two members of his own family. He did receive Peter Jay Munro's father, the Reverend Harry Munro, at Bingham's residence, but they fell into an argument, parted on bad terms, and never laid eyes on each other again. JJ avoided a similar encounter with Sir James.

Poor health aside, JJ managed to visit the main sites of London. By permission of George III JJ, in the company of John Adams, was given a conducted tour of Buckingham Palace by the renowned American historical painter Benjamin West (1738–1820), a number of whose works were hanging on the palace walls. Three days later, on 11 November, JJ joined Adams as an auditor of the King's speech at the House of Lords.[4] In addition, he attended a performance at the Drury Lane Theatre and a meeting of the Royal Society. He must have found congenial company during his evening at the Club of Honest Whigs, where he met its president, Dr. Richard Price (1723–91), the nonconformist minister, author, and friend of American independence. Even though he had still not shaken off his persistent sore throat, he finally headed for Bath, arriving there on 27 November. Thence he made two trips to Bristol, one briefly in mid-December, another at greater length as the new year began.

JJ's Bristol visit was prompted by the desire to collect the legacy left to himself, his brothers and sisters, and his father by Marianne Peloquin. The Peloquin estate proved a legal thicket for executors, legatees, and attorneys alike. Her original will of 27 April 1768 was followed by eleven codicils. The will disposed of various real estate holdings to a number of named legatees of Bristol, and set up a trust fund to be administered by the Mayor and Aldermen of Bristol in the amount of £19,000, the income from which was to be divided among religious and charitable institutions and a group of thirty-eight poor men and women of Bristol. By her first codicil, bearing the same date as the will, she left Peter Jay £1,000, Sir James Jay £500, and three other New Yorkers —JJ's aunt, Françoise Jay Van Cortlandt,[5] £1000, and cousins James Van Cortlandt, £500, and Augustus Van Horne £500. In a later codicil (No. 5), dated 19 November 1769, all the living children of Peter Jay were also named as legatees, as follows: Augustus Jay, £100; Eve Munro, £500; Anna Maricka, £500, and Peter, John, and Frederick, £500 each. In the seventh codicil, dated 5 December 1772, new trustees were named, to wit—Josiah Tucker, Dean of Gloucester, a prolific writer of tracts and an opponent of the war with America, Robert Hale, and Chester Willoughby, while Dr. Archibald Drummond replaced Isaac Picquenit, originally designated.

The effort to settle the Peloquin estate involved JJ in protracted and irritating negotations in Bristol. The sticking points, as the Peloquin executors saw it, were (1) the possibility that JJ's father had pre-deceased Mrs. Peloquin, thereby causing that particular bequest to lapse; and (2) the need to prove Peter Jay's will bequeathing his estate to his own children (a copy of Peter's will and JJ's proffered bond being deemed insufficient). Dr. Archibald Drummond, as Jay reported, entertained "so many scruples about *legal evidence* and imaginary contingencies" that a frustrated JJ started back to London on 9 January.[6] Thereafter his friends Peter Van Schaack and Benjamin Vaughan represented the Jays in England until the matter was at length concluded.[7]

The affidavits in dispute were submitted to Attorney General Lloyd Kenyon (1732–1802) for his opinion. That official was prepared to waive the requirement that legal papers issued in America bear stamps, impliedly conceding that the Stamp Act of 1765 no longer had validity in the ex-colonies (!), but he insisted that stamped receipts be required for moneys issued in England. As regards Peter's will, the opinion insisted on *"legal"* proof, ruling out affidavits from America as inadequate "till remedied by treaty or law."[8] To compound the difficulties, Sir James, then in England, entered a caveat against his brother's receiving the money due the family until he himself was paid a fourth part of the £1000 bequeathed to his deceased parent. At length, and shortly before JJ sailed for America, he was able to write Frederick that the Peloquin executors had agreed to recognize the power of attorney and pay the legacies.[9]

Meantime, JJ had started back to London on 9 January, and after spending a few weeks more in the capital, reached Dover on 22 January, crossed the Channel to Calais, and was reunited with his family toward the end of the month.

Of the letters below relating to the period of JJ's English sojourn, the choicest are those between the traveler and his wife whom he had left behind. The fullest correspondence between John and Sarah Livingston Jay for any four-month period of their marriage, they reveal the abiding affection and concern for family which ever marked the relations between the pair.

[1]See James Monroe to Benjamin Harrison, 14 Feb. 1784, *LMCC,* VII, 442; Jefferson to Madison, 20 Feb. 1784, *TJP,* VI, 544–551, at p. 546: "Messrs. Adams and Jay have paid a visit

to the court of London unordered and uninvited. Their reception has been forbidding."

[2]See below, JJ to Egbert Benson, 15, 16, 18 Dec. 1783. For some of the Loyalist exiles, see also Mary Beth Norton, *The British-Americans* (Boston, 1972).

[3]JJ to Silas Deane, 23 Feb. 1784. *HPJ,* III, 114–16; *Deane Papers,* V, 280–81.

[4]*AP,* III, 150n.

[5]On the death of Françoise Jay Van Cortlandt, her daughter, Eva Van Cortlandt White (1737–1836), claimed her share through her husband Henry White, who was in England prosecuting the claim at the same time as JJ. See also *JJ,* I, 30, 101.

[6]JJ to Peter Van Schaack, 5 Jan. and 8 Jan. 1784, in JP; to Frederick Jay, 22 Jan. 1784. Another executor, Josiah Tucker, appeared to JJ to be "fair and reasonable, though perplexed."

[7]For the role of Benjamin Vaughan and Shelburne's Secretary to the Treasury Thomas Orde (1746–1807) as intermediaries with the Attorney General, see Vaughan to JJ, 20 and 30 Jan. 1784, both ALS in JP.

[8]Copy of opinion enclosed in Benjamin Vaughan to JJ, 8 March 1784, ALS in JP; recopied and enclosed in JJ to Frederick Jay, 9 March 1784, for which DftS is in JP without enclosure.

[9]JJ to Frederick Jay, 27 April 1784, below.

From Sarah Livingston Jay

Passy, Wednesday Evening, 15 October 1783

My dear Mr. Jay,

Mr. Ridley tells me that a gentleman who is going to England on fryday, will call at Autueil to-morrow to take his commands. I've therefore advised Peter to write this Evening, and am myself too happy in hearing of the opportunity, to defer 'till to-morrow the pleasure of telling you that myself and little family are perfectly well. The day after you left us,[1] having occasion to go into your room, Maria saw the door open and with her usual glee when going to see you, she came running into the room, when all on a sudden disappointment succeeded expectation and her little head drooped. I catched her in my arms and while embracing her thought her still dearer to me for the sympathy I found between her feelings and my own. My little Ann still continues to thrive. Ben[2] has been quite recovered ever since Sunday, and you may banish all apprehensions of Maria's having catched the disorder since there is no appearance of it.

Mr. Adams called upon me this morning to let me know that he shall set out for England next monday and you may rely upon my profitting of that opportunity as well as every other that offers of telling you how we all do, and if we continue as well as we are at present, I am happy to think the satisfaction you'll derive from that circumstance will more than compensate for the time you bestow in reading my letters.

I hope by this time you've arrived in London without meeting with any material interruption, and that your health will be so much benefited by your journey that you will not be obliged to prolong your stay beyond what you proposed: for I can assure you upon my word, that I find a deficiency, a vacancy, a something wanting since your absence that even surpasses what I expected. Do not however fear that I encourage unpleasant ideas, the reverse being the case, for I flatter myself that this little excursion will re-establish your health, and in that expectation have really enjoyed the fine weather we have lately been favored with.

Present my Compliments to any of our friends that you may see, and believe me to be, my dearest, best of friends, most sincerely and affectionately Yours,

SA. JAY

Our friend Mrs. Ridley is better.

ALS. DftS in JP.

[1]For JJ's departure from Passy and arrival in London, see JJ to SLJ, 15 October, and JJ to Catharine W. Livingston, 20 Oct. 1783, both ALS in JP.

[2]Benoit, a family slave. See *JJ,* I, 702.

FROM PETER JAY MUNRO

Passy, 16 October 1783

Dear Sir,

As some American Gentlemen are going from here to London, I have taken the Liberty of troubleing them with a few lines for you.

I hope you have had a Pleasant Journey, and that you have arrived at London, in better health and without having had an opportunity of trying Perrin's courage.[1] We are continually awondering. One wonder's whether you travelled all Night? another when you got to Calais? when you sailed? whether you was Sea sick? how you like England? etc. etc. If I was to tell you them all I would in reality make a *wonderful* of it. Ever since your Departure, our Conversation at the Breakfast table has been begun by "I wonder Mr. Jay is now?" or by some other, I have already mentioned. Do not fear to put an end to our conversation by answering the above Questions for we have a fresh set all ready.

Mr. Mongolfier has sent up a Globe tied to a Rope, and two men with it, they tried to fill it with Smoke while in the air, and Succeeded. Then these new Navigators instead of *spare Masts, spare Sails, Cord-*

age etc. etc. will take with them a supply of *Straw, Old Shoes, Rabbits Skins* and *other animal Substances.*[2]

Our house is not yet ready, nor will it be in some Days. My aunt talks of removing next week, but for my part I don't think we shall be settled there before <next week> the first of November. Several Persons have been to look at the House since we have taken it.[3]

My aunt is in good health and so is Nancy. Maria has been a little unwell, and is still very Pale. Mr. Adams will set out for England Monday. Sir James I believe is gone,[4] for the 9th Instant he sent here for a Passport, and Mr. Gregson, whom we saw last night at Mrs. Mongomery's, informed us that he was to set off that morning. When you see my father remember me to him.

I am Dear Sir, Your Dutiful Nephew,

PETER JAY MUNRO

P.S. Benoit is cured.

ALS in NNMus: Jay.

[1]Probably a variation of "perrosin," a concoction of pine resin in wine, used medically, to pass water. *Oxford English Dict.*

[2]The first manned balloon ascension occurred on 15 Oct. 1783, when Pilâtre de Rozier (1756–85) piloted a Montgolfier balloon to a height of 80 feet, remaining airborne for 4 minutes, 25 seconds. Altitude and airborne time were quickly surpassed. Faujas de Saint-Ford, *Description des expériences aérostatiques de MM. de Montgolfier* (2 vols., Paris, 1784), I, 268–77; II, 4.

[3]See below, SLJ to JJ, 6 Nov. 1783, and n. 1.

[4]Sir James arrived in England 26 October.

To Sarah Livingston Jay

London, Harley Street Number 30, 26 October 1783

My dear Sally,

I have had the Pleasure of recieving your Letters of the 15 and 17th Instant,[1] and thank You for them. Since my arrival here I have written twice to You. One of those Letters informed You of my having been taken ill of a Dysentery, and of my being then far recovered.[2] All Remains of that Disorder are now removed, and I find myself as well as when I left You. I have consulted Doctor Warren[3] (the Physician who attended me during my late Sickness, and who is at the Head of his Profession here) about the Pain in my Breast, and the Propriety of taking the Bath waters for it. He tells me that Pain does not arise from the Lungs, that the waters of Bath may be safely used, but that although I may expect some good from them, yet that Exercise and

Relaxation from all Business which requires much Thought and application, can alone compleat the Cure.

The Duration of my absence will be entirely regulated by the object which occasioned it, vizt., the Recovery of my Health. If that was out of Question, I should immediately return, for I assure you the Charms neither of this Country, nor indeed of any other, are <not> sufficiently powerful to detain me from You.

On my arrival here I took private Lodgings. Mr. Bingham and Mr. Vaughan insisted on my going with them. The former reminded me of his Invitation when at Paris, and of my not having refused to accept it. The latter pressed me in the most friendly Manner to take a Room with him. Mr. Bingham's Invitation being prior and Mrs. Vaughan being ready to lay in,[4] I removed to Mr. Bingham's. I fear our friend Vaughan is not quite pleased.

Lord Shelbourne has sent me an Invitation to pass some Days with him at his Country House. I think it is situated between this and Bath, so that the acceptance of this Invitation will be convenient as well as agreable.

Mr. and Mrs. Ricketts[5] are here. They dine with us Tomorrow so that my next will probably tell you more about them.

Mr. H. White purposes to send his eldest Son[6] (whom he has educated at Hamburgh, but who is now here) to France, in order to perfect him in the Language. He expects to go to St. Quintins through paris, and will probably set out from here with me. He is about twenty Years old, and a well looking young man. His Stay at Paris will be only for a few Days, and all things considered, I think it best that he should pass them with us.

Don't be in too great a Hurry to remove to your House unless it should be in order to recieve You. Your Residence in it will not be comfortable, at least for some Time. The first or second Week in November would be early enough.

Does Maria begin to talk yet? Mrs. Bingham has a little Girl of twenty months that prattles cleverly.[7] I hope Nancy is not too much for You. Unless your appetite continues you should cease to nurse her.

My Compliments to our Friends. I am my dear Sally, Your very affectionate Husband,

JOHN JAY

P.S. It turns out that Mr. Carter[8] was driven by Bankrupcy to America. His true name was *Church,* which (the better to conceal himself) he changed for *Carter.* The Fortune he has made enables him to settle with his Creditors, and assume his former name. I hear he has done both. He has a rich Uncle to whom he has also reconciled himself. Perhaps you had better appear ignorant of this affair till you hear more about it. Read this postscript to Doctor Franklin.

ALS.

[1]SLJ to JJ, 17 Oct. 1783, ALS in JP.

[2]JJ to SLJ, 15 Oct. 1783, ALS in JP, contains news of his arrival; his 18 Oct. 1783 letter, DftS in JP, reports his bouts with dysentery.

[3]Cambridge-educated Dr. Richard Warren (1731–97) became Physician in Ordinary to King George III in 1763. William Munk, *The Roll of the Royal College of Physicians of London* (3 vols., London, 1878), II, 242–47.

[4]The Vaughans were expecting their second child, Sarah, who was born on 28 Feb. 1784.

[5]SLJ's first cousin Sarah Livingston Ricketts (1755–1825), daughter of Peter Van Brugh Livingston, and her husband Captain James Ricketts (1753–1824), of the 60th Regiment of Royal Americans. Edwin B. Livingston, *The Livingstons of Livingston Manor* (New York, 1910), pp. 549–50.

[6]Henry White (*JJ*, I, 101), Loyalist husband of JJ's first cousin Eva Van Cortlandt White, sailed for England with their son John in 1783, leaving his wife behind in New York City. Lorenzo Sabine, *Biographical Sketches of Loyalists of the American Revolution* (2 vols., New York, 1864), II, 417–18.

[7]Ann Louisa Bingham, born on 6 Jan. 1782.

[8]See also above, Philip Schuyler to JJ, 1 July 1783.

To Peter Jay Munro

London, 26 October 1783
Harley Street No. 30

Dear Peter,

I have recieved and am pleased with your Letter of the 16 Instant. It is well written as to Matter and Stile, and tolerably as to hand writing and spelling, in both of which however, there is still Room for Improvement.

You will learn from my Letters to your Aunt, that I have been sick, and that I am recovered. As you say nothing of your own Health, I presume it is good, and you have my best wishes that it may continue so. Inform me from Time to Time how Your Aunt and the Children do.

Your Remarks on Mongolfier's supplying his Globe with Smoke while in the air, are just.[1] Have you heard whether the men who ascended with it made any Experiments on the State of the air etc.?

Sir James I am told is here, but I have not seen him. Nor have I seen or heard from your Father, to whom my arrival must be known through the Channel of the News Papers. Mr. H. White tells me, he has written Letters to Mr. V[an] Horne,[2] etc. and to your Mother, in which he refuses to let the Bristol Legacy be applied to her use. When we meet, I will tell you more of this Matter.

Present my Compliments to Mr. W. Franklin, Mr. Le Motte and your Friend Benjamin.[3] I am Dear Peter, Your affectionate Uncle,

JOHN JAY

P.S. I recieved the enclosed Letter for You, from Mr. White who brought it from N[ew] York.[4]

ALS in NNMus: Jay.

[1]See above, Peter Jay Munro to JJ, 16 Oct. 1783.

[2]JJ's cousin Augustus Van Horne (*JJ,* I, 101). No letters from Henry White to Van Horne or Eve Jay Munro have been located.

[3]Le Motte was apparently Peter Jay Munro's tutor; Benjamin was Benjamin Franklin Bache. Before leaving America, JJ had assumed personal responsibility for the education of his nephew, Peter. JJ to Eve Jay Munro, 29 Sept. 1779, ALS in collection of Charles Wheeler, Bethesda, Md.

[4]Enclosure not located.

To Sarah Livingston Jay

London, 28 October 1783,
Harley Street Number 30

My dear Sally,

My last to you was dated the 26 Inst. and committed to the Care of Col. Wadsworth[1] who set out for Paris this Morning. As it enclosed one for Peter I omit writing to him at present.

Yesterday Mr. Adams delivered to me your Favor of the 19 Inst.[2] enclosing Locks of your own and our Children's Hair, which I shall endeavour to have wrought in the best Manner. As yet I have seen so little of London that I can form but a very imperfect Judgment of it.

I was last Evening at the Drury Lane Theatre, where the celebrated Mrs. Siddons[3] displayed her Talents in the Character of Belvidera, to which she did ample Justice. The House is neat and well lighted, but not so magnificent as those at Paris. Capt. and Mrs. Rickets dined with us Yesterday. She is very little altered since you saw her. She has one Child but I have not seen it.[4]

Mrs. Foy[5] is married to Col. Carlton, the Brother of the General. Her Sister Betsey shortly afterwards went to America with much less than half the Beauty she brought from thence. H. Cruger married his Housekeeper,[6] and is now at New York. Betsey Johnson I hear is here, but I have not seen her. She is the Wife of some Gentleman (I do not remember his Name) whom she found at New York a Year or two ago.[7]

On coming Home this Evening I found a Card from Major General Maunsel. I shall return his Visit, and the more readily as his Connection with Watkin's Father may enable him to give some Information respecting him and his.[8]

A Visitor has just come in. I must therefore postpone adding any thing except that I am, My Dear Sally, Your very affectionate Husband,

JOHN JAY

P.S. Mr. Van Schaack who is just entered desires me to present his best Compliments to you.

ALS.

[1]Soon after his trip to Paris in the summer of 1783, Jeremiah Wadsworth went to England and Ireland, where he invested his remaining credit balance in merchandise, which he later disposed of in America at a considerable profit. John Platt, "Jeremiah Wadsworth: Federalist Entrepreneur" (unpub. Ph.D. dissertation, Columbia University, 1955), pp. 24, 49, 54–57.

[2]SLJ to JJ, 19 Oct. 1783, ALS in JP; *AP*, III, 149.

[3]On 27 Oct. 1783 the Drury Lane Theatre presented Thomas Otway's (1652–85) tragedy, *Venice Preserved*, featuring the acclaimed Sarah Kemble Siddons (1755–1831). *Gentleman's Magazine* (London, 1783), p. 956.

[4]Maria Eliza Ricketts (b. 1783).

[5]Hannah Van Horne Foy, daughter of John Van Horne of Somerset County, N.J., and SLJ's second cousin, was the widow of Captain Edward Foy of the Royal Artillery. Her second husband, whom she married in London in 1753, was Lieutenant-Colonel Thomas Carleton (1735–1817), Sir Guy Carleton's brother, and shortly to be named governor of the newly created province of New Brunswick.

[6]Henry Cruger (1739–1827), son of New York merchant Henry Cruger (1707–80), attended King's College for three years, withdrawing in 1757 to set up as a merchant in Bristol. A leader of the radical movement in England, he represented Bristol in Parliament in 1774 and 1784, and was mayor of that city in 1781. Returning to the U.S. in 1790, Cruger was elected to the N.Y. State Senate in 1792. His second wife was Elizabeth Blair (d. 1790). Lewis Namier and John Brooke, *The House of Commons, 1754–1790* (3 vols., New York, 1964), II, 280–82.

[7]Elizabeth Johnson and William Sharp received a marriage license in New York on 1 July 1782. *Names of Persons for whom Marriage Licenes were Issued by the Secretary of the Province of New York* (Albany, 1860), p. 205.

[8]Major General John Maunsell (1724–95), an Irish-born British army officer, married Elizabeth Stillwell Wraxall, the widow of Captain Peter Wraxall, in 1763. Mrs. Maunsell's younger sister, Lydia Stillwell, wife of John Watkyn Watkins, Sr., was the mother-in-law of SLJ's sister, Judith Livingston (Mrs. John W.) Watkins, Jr. Before the Revolution the Maunsell and Watkins families owned neighboring estates on Harlem Heights in New York. Both Maunsell and Watkins Senior spent the Revolution in England. Charles A. Maunsell, *History of the Family of Maunsell* (2 vols., London, 1917–20) and John E. Stillwell, *Stillwell Genealogy* (4 vols., 1929–31), vol. II. See also JJ, I, 561.

From Elias Boudinot

Princeton, 1 November 1783
(Private)

Sir,

I was honored by your several private favours, recommending Mr. Vaughan and some other Gentlemen, to whom I have endeavoured to pay every civility in my power, also one enclosing my Nephew's Letter from Madeira, for which I am much obliged to you.[1] Congress has thought proper to appoint him their Commercial Agent at that Island.[2] He is a deserving young American, who I doubt not will do honor to his appointment. If you can be of any Service to him, I shall take it as a particular favour done to me.

I have the honor of enclosing a copy of the Acts of Congress relating to yourself individually, the authenticated copies of which I transmit in a set of instructions to the Commissioners jointly by this opportunity.[3] Congress did not think it just or honorable to alter or abridge your Salary while absent at Bath for your Health, and therefore have passed only a simple permission for your going to Bath for the reestablishment of your former vigour.

We are still in this Town, but on the 6th instant Congress mean to adjourn to Annapolis[4] having determined at present to have two places of residence, or Fœderal Towns, one near the fall of Potomack, the other near the falls of Delaware.[5]

I send the News Papers to the Commissioners which will let you into the general state of things.

Capt. Jones,[6] the Bearer of this, can also give you much general Information.

I carefully forwarded your Letters to the North River.

I have the Honor to be, with the most sincere regard and esteem, Sir, Your most obedient and very humble Servant,

ELIAS BOUDINOT

ALS in PPInd. Endorsed: "Recd 8 Decr. 1783." Dft in DLC: Boudinot. J. J. Boudinot, ed., *The Life, Public Services, Addresses and Letters of Elias Boudinot* (2 vols., Boston, 1896), II, 15–16, incorrectly dates this letter 5 Nov. 1783; error repeated in excerpt in *LMCC*, VII, 369. This letter was included in a packet from Boudinot to the American Commissioners; see below, John Adams to JJ, 7 Dec. 1783, n. 1.

[1]See above, JJ to Elias Boudinot, 11 June 1783.

[2]On 31 Oct. 1783, John Marsden Pintard was named commercial agent "to assist the merchants and other citizens of these United States, trading to the Island of Madeira and Porto Santo." *JCC*, XXV, 780.

[3]Instructions to the American Commissioners, 29 Oct. 1783 (*JCC*, XXV, 754–57; *RDC*, VI, 717–19), authorized entering into commercial treaties with the Emperor of Germany and other European powers, expressed Congress' reluctance to join the League of Armed Neutrality, urged speedy conclusion of the treaty with Great Britain, authorized JJ to order Carmichael to repair to Paris to settle accounts, and granted JJ leave to go to Bath for his health.

[4]The original authorized date of adjournment (12 November) was moved back seven days, but, lacking a quorum, Congress did not reconvene until 13 December. *JCC*, XXV, 714, 802, 807, 809; Edmund C. Burnett, *The Continental Congress* (New York, 1941), pp. 584–87, 590. Meantime, on 29 October, Boudinot announced his decision to retire from public life. Five days later Thomas Mifflin was elected President of Congress, and, in his absence, Daniel Carroll (1730–96) of Maryland was elected chairman.

[5]This resolution for an alternate residence of Congress was adopted 21 Oct. 1783. *JCC*, XXV, 654–60, 664–68, 714.

[6]On 1 Nov. 1783, Congress resolved that Captain John Paul Jones be recommended to Franklin "as agent, to solicit . . . for payment and satisfaction to the officers and crews for all prizes taken in Europe under his command." Jones sailed with Joshua Barney on the *General Washington* on 10 Nov. 1783. *JCC*, XXV, 787–88. Hulbert Footner, *Sailor of Fortune: The Life and Adventures of Commodore Barney* (New York, 1940), p. 148.

From Benjamin Vaughan

[London], 3 November 1783

My Dear sir,

I shall not sett off till tomorrow afternoon, by which time you may be better. If I should hear nothing further from you, I shall without fail deliver your message at Bowood Park,[1] which is near Calne in Wiltshire, on one of the two roads to Bath.

I shall certainly, if living and well, be back before Tuesday, to get you and Mr. Bingham, and Mr. Adams and Son,[2] into the House of Lords on the 11th instant.

Lord Shelburne in the letter you saw,[3] says that he shall be very happy to shew the American Commissioners every mark of regard in his power, in their public or private characters; that he looks upon the interest of the two countries to be still the same; and considers any distraction which arises in America, as essentially affecting Great Britain. This is over and above the former letter.

Mrs. Vaughan is so languid and exhausted, that it will be out of her power to receive Mrs. Bingham, till she is better or I am returned, which I beg you would take the trouble to signify to Mr. and Mrs. Bingham with our best regards.

I am, my dear sir, Your faithful and affectionate,

BENJN. VAUGHAN

ALS.
[1]Shelburne's country estate.
[2]John Quincy Adams.
[3]Letter not located.

From Robert Morris

Philadelphia, 4 November 1783

Dear Sir,

Since the date of my last letter, I have received several of yours dated the <10th of March, 21st of April, 21st of May, 10th of June and> 20th of July.[1] The first of these was delivered by Mr. Penn, a Young Gentleman whose Fate I lamented long before I saw him. I had always opposed both in my public and private character those unjust measures which have deprived him of so considerable a share of his Patrimony, and we always feel ourselves disposed to befriend in every instance those whose cause we have espoused in any one; so that you will readily believe that your Recommendation of him had its full weight. His Mother is said to be a fine Woman and I am glad Mrs. Jay and yourself had so good an opportunity of knowing her well. It is a great misfortune to this Family that they are of a make so little calculated for the Turbulence of the times. They are mild tempered very open and Honest, wish well to Mankind and would not injure the most insignificant of Gods Creatures. They feel their injuries a little but know not how to seek Redress. I will Serve them in any thing that consistently I can.[2]

In your letter of the 21st April you desire me to write to Mr. Carmichael for your Accounts. This has been rendered unnecessary by one Article of the instructions of Congress to you on that point, besides which I expect that Mr. Carmichael has before this time complied with your own request, made in consequence of Mr. Barclays application. This was the proper channell, for he alone being authorized to settle the European accounts, it would be of no use to send them here untill passed by him.[3]

Your letter of the 21st May recommends Mr. Vaughan and that of the 10th June Doctor Bancroft. To these Gentlemen I shew a full proportion of the attention which my numerous engagements will permit me to devote in that way. Mr. Vaughan has brought a large Family and I thought him wrong to remove at his time of Life from amongst old acquaintance and Friends into a New World. However I hope he will not be disapointed in his Sanguine expectations of superiour happiness here. I think Doctor Bancroft has merited Rewards from this Country which he will never get. I esteem him much. I like his manners and understanding. It seems to me that both will wear well and grow better upon use and acquaintance.

I hear your Health is mended since the date of your last letter of the 20th July, and rejoice at it. Your distant Friends suffer irreparable injury if you are indisposed to write. Those who write so well should write often, and even your short letters say so much in so few Words that it is impossible not to wish for them if longer ones cannot be had.

I acknowledge the Force of all your observations on my intended Resignation and know the necessity of perseverance so long as there is a prospect of being usefull, but you must also acknowledge that it is folly in the extreme to Continue in the drudgery of Office after you see clearly that the public cannot be benefitted, your own affairs suffering, your Feelings daily wounded and your Expectation endangered by the Malice and misrepresentation of envious and designing Men. During the War I was determined to go through with the work I had undertaken and although my Resignation was made before the Signing of the Provisional Treaty was known, yet I made no hesitation to declare to a Committee of Congress that if the War lasted, I would continue. The War however ceased. Congress feared to dismiss their army without some Pay. They had not Money and could only make payment by paper Anticipation and Even this could not be effected without my assistance. I was urged to Continue and forced into that Anticipation. The Army were dispersed and since their departure the Men who urged these measures most and who are eternally at War with Honour and Integrity, have been continually employed in devising measures to prevent my being able to fulfill my engagements, in hopes of effecting my Ruin in case of failure. I must however in justice to the Majority of Congress which has ever been composed of Honest Men declare that the Faction I allude to is but inconsiderable in numbers, <but> although they make themselves of some Consequence by their assiduity, you know the Lees etc. I should disregard these men totally if I found a disposition in the Several Legislatures to support National Faith, credit and Character, but unhappily there is at present a total inattention on their parts. I am however persuaded that sooner or later the Good Sense of America will prevail and that our Governments will be <executed> entrusted in the hands of Men whose principles will lead them to do justice and whose understandings will teach the Value of National Credit. This may be too long in coming to pass, at least for me and therefore you may rest assured that I quit all public Employ the Moment my engagements are fulfilled.

The Court of France having refused the last sum asked, I do not wish to trouble them Farther. I am not sensible of having at any time made an improper application, either as to *Substance or Manner.* Those who are solicited in such cases, are in the situation to make whatever objections they find Convenient. I wish however that the Ministers in France were Sensible of one Truth, which is, That my administration either saved them a great deal of Money or a great deal of disgrace, for if I had not undertaken it when I did, they must either have advanced Ten times the amount I received, or have deserted America after having undertaken her Cause, and perhaps have been obliged to subscribe to very indifferent terms of Peace for themselves.

It is happy for me that the Loan in Holland stepped in to our Relief after the Refusal of the Court to grant the moderate Sum of Three Million of Livres as the Concluding point. This Refusal was Ill timed and Impolitic, I could shew resentment with some effect if I were so disposed, but so far from it, I retain a gratefull Remembrance of past favours and make a point to promote the Commercial intercourse between France and this Country. I must also shew my sense of the Obligations conferred on us by the Hollanders.[4]

We hear that the Definitive Treaty is signed. I long to see it, for you may depend that unless some new articles are added respecting our Intercourse with the British West Indies, it will be both a Work of difficulty and time to carry Measures that will justify your Opinion of us.

I thank you for the kind sentiments which you express of me in several parts of your letters. I will endeavour to deserve them. Accept my thanks also for what you write respecting Mr. Ridley and my Boys. I shall never forget his care of and attention to them. I think they are now put in the way of acquiring an Education that will justify the plan I have pursued. My other Boys[5] shall have the best instructions this Country affords and at a future day if we live, a Comparison may be drawn.

I saw Governor Livingston two days since at Prince Town. He is very well and rather fatter than formerly. He told me the Family were all well except Kitty who is recovering from an Illness she has lately sustained. I think she has much more of Sickness than she ought and infinitely more than she deserves. I will not say any thing to you on the late Acts of Congress for fixing two places of permanent Residence etc. least I should not preserve that decorum which is due from the Servant to the Sovereign.[6]

Your reasons for protesting the bills are not Solid. It is the only instance I ever met in which I could Controvert any Reasons on which you founded your Conduct. I am paying those bills with 20 per Cent. Damages.[7]

I do not know whether Gouverneur writes to you by this opportunity, you must Cherish his Friendship. It is worth possessing.[8] He has more virtue than he shews and more Consistency than any body believes. He values you exceedingly and hereafter you will be very usefull to each other. Mrs. Morris will write to Mrs. Jay and say for herself what she has to say, though I don't believe she will tell her as she does every body else the high estimation in which she holds Mrs. Jay and yourself. Permit me also my Worthy Friend to assure you both of the Sincerity of that affection with which I profess myself, Your most obedient and humble Servant,

ROBT. MORRIS

ALS. CS in JP; endorsed: "... ansd. 25 Feb. 1784." *WJ*, II, 134–37, and *HPJ*, III, 93–95, omit much of the letter, including Morris' rebuke, all of which was crossed out in the MS. by William Jay.

[1]JJ to Robert Morris, 10 March and 20 July 1783, above; 21 April and 10 June 1783, both Dfts in JP; 21 May 1783, recommending Samuel Vaughan, Sr., not located.

[2]For the Penn family's proprietary problems, see above, Lady Juliana Penn to JJ, 23 Nov. 1782, n. 1.

[3]See below, editorial note, "Settling the Spanish Accounts."

[4]On the Dutch and French loans, see *RDC*, VI, 595, 752–26; *JCC*, XXV, 589n., 792–93; *JAW*, VIII, 154–55.

[5]Charles and William White Morris.

[6]See above, Elias Boudinot to JJ, 1 Nov. 1783, n. 5.

[7]For the protested bills endorsed by John Chevalier to Robert Morris, see above, JJ to Morris, 20 July 1783, and also JJ to John Frederick Perregaux, 12 Nov. 1782, Dft in JP. On 4 March 1783, Morris instructed Carmichael to pay these bills with damages amounting to $2,700, and to reimburse himself through Ferdinand Grand. Morris to Carmichael, 4 March 1783, *RDC*, VI, 271.

[8]Gouverneur Morris's short note to JJ of 7 Nov. 1783, ALS in JP, is to "assure you of the continuance of my Love."

From Sarah Livingston Jay

Chaillot,[1] 6 November 1783

My dear Mr. Jay,

This Evening Mr. and Miss Laurens[2] favored me with their Company, and as they set out tomorrow for England I could not suffer them to go without a little token of my remembrance, and that they might be ennabled to give you an account of your little girls I sent for them down, and was not a little flattered by Miss Maria's behaviour. She does not yet speak, but she improves in her health and looks. Louisson[3] still continues to take great care of the Children and is quite delighted with her new situation. As the weather is very fine she walks with <the children> them on the terrace and I rarely omit giving them a ride.

Every body that sees the house now is surprised it has so long remained unoccupied. It is so gay, so lively, that I am sure you'll be pleased with it. Yesterday the windows were open in my Cabinet while I was dressing and it was even then too warm. Dr. Franklin and his Grandsons and Mr. and Mrs. Cayo, and the Miss Walpoles[4] drank tea with me likewise this Evening and they all approve your Choice. As the sky is very clear and the moon shines very bright we were tempted to walk from the Salloon upon the terrace and while the Company were admiring my situation, my imagination was retracing the pleasing Evenings that you and I have passed together in contemplating the mild and gentle rays of the moon. Should the whether be less pleasant when you return I shall be mortified.

It is with regret that I'm obliged to quit subjects that afford pleasing ideas, for one that I fear has already given you pain, but as Mr. Franklin tells me that he has informed you of Abbe's leaving Passy,[5] my further silence about it instead of preventing anxiety would only appear misterious. I fancy her extreme jealousy of Louisson added to the inticements of an English washerwoman who promised to pay her if she would assist her in washing, was the cause of that mis-step. She had for some time treated Louisson so uncivilly that she had told me that were it in my power to dismiss Abbe, and I still chose to keep her, she should be obliged to leave me, but that as she found that Abbe was impertinent to me, she must bear it likewise. Immediately upon finding that Abbe was gone with her Cloaths Mr. Franklin wrote to the Lieutenant of the Police who had her taken up (at that washer woman's) and put in a house of confinement. Four days after Peter went to see her as if without my knowledge, and advised her to let him solicit my permission for her return, but she replied that instead of desiring that, she would run-away again were I to send for her, and that she would remain where she was 'till your return, or 'till she might be sent to America instead of returning home to be laughed at and work too. As she inquired about the family, Peter told her that the Children were well and that my Cook seemed a Clever woman. She said she hoped I was Content since she was gone for that I was intirely governed by Louisson.

Today Peter called again, telling her that, as he had come to Paris to pay some visits, he could not forbear calling to see if she was more reasonable, but she remained still obstinate. Dr. Franklin thinks I ought not to take notice of her for 15 or 20 days; but I'm so afraid of her suffering from the Cold that I think it better that Peter should call now and then as if by accident that she may not suffer after her repentance. Pray don't let this affair make you uneasy. The irregularity of her Conduct for some time past has made me expect the step she has taken.

When you return bring me if you please 2 Doz. Knives and a silver tea-pot and tea-bowl.

Mr. Poussin[6] has been very dilatory indeed. We have not yet half the Kitchin furniture, but I hope after a few more messages he'll think fit to comply with his engagement.

I believe I did not tell you that 2 or 3 weeks ago I dined with Mr. Pitt[7] at the Marquis de la Fayette's.

You can't imagine how much I'm obliged to you for your frequent letters. I wish it was in my power to make you as agreeable returns, but you are so good that you'll take the will for the deed and be content with the assurance of the sincere regard of Your affectionate Wife,

SARAH JAY

ALS. Endorsed: ". . . recd. 22 ansd. 23d."

[1]The Jays moved from Passy to Chaillot in early November. SLJ's 22 November letter to her sister explained that since JJ's departure for England "I'm removed to a very pretty new house between Passy and Paris that I'm sure he will be pleased with, for the sun shines upon it all the day, which at this season is very agreable and it has a pleasant terrace where the children can take the air." SLJ to Catharine W. Livingston, 22 Nov. 1783, ALS in MHi: Livingston. SLJ's first letter from Chaillot is dated 4 Nov. 1783, and it is to JJ, ALS in JP.

[2]Henry Laurens, Sr., and his daughter Martha had just returned from the south of France where they visited Laurens' dying brother, James. See above, Henry Laurens to JJ, 5 Sept. 1783.

[3]Louisson was the Jay childrens' nurse.

[4]Thomas Walpole's daughters Catherine and Elizabeth.

[5]William Temple Franklin to JJ, 27 Oct. 1783, not located. For JJ's acknowledgment of this letter, see below, JJ to William Temple Franklin, 11 Nov. 1783.

[6]Apparently the Jays' Chaillot agent.

[7]Out of office at the moment, Pitt became prime minister in December.

From Catharine W. Livingston

Elizabeth Town, 9 November [17]83

Your letter my dear Sir announcing the birth of your little girl reached us ten days ago: the one to Pappa on the same subject has not yet been received.[1]

I think I may put in a claim now for my little god daughter. Had she not had a sister I should not have had the presumption to propose your commiting her to any care till her education requires another situation. We flatter ourselves that Sister will spend next Summer with us. Clear, wholesome air, will be absolutely necessary for her and her Infants, after a Sea voyage. I hope that your attention to your private concerns will not deprive you of being here, or this family the pleasure of your company. The coolest room this house affords shall be prepared for your reception, that Mama has determined since she first knew of your returning. I shall endeavor to keep my horse in good order, that you and Sister may enjoy one of the pleasantest and most beneficial modes of exercise, I have found it such. I brought with me last June from Philadelphia one of Duke Lauzerns riding horses, and a new saddle, and continue in the practice of riding on horseback.

The last accounts of your health are more favorable than those for some preceeding Months, and I rejoice at it. A Voyage and your native air will, I do not doubt confirm it. Sister will be more at ease and experience fewer difficulties among her friends.

It was impossible for any person unless nearly allied to be more anxious for Mrs. Izards arrival than myself, but how deficient that Lady's in benevolence when contrasted with my dear Mrs. Morris.[2] My friend solicited me to come to Phi[ladelphia] with a view to indulge me with the pleasure of conversing with a Lady who had lately enjoyed yours and Sisters society, but that Lady tho twice in this Village nearly twenty four hours each time, neither waited on any of us or informed us of her being there. Mr. Izard with whom I am personally acquainted I cannot excuse for not sending for me, to him I often expressed the great desires I had to see Mrs. Izard before I left Phi[ladelph]ia. My brother[3] waited on her in that City, and I would have requested Pappa to have given Mr. Izard an invitation to bring his family here, had not my brother and Major Clarkson assured me that they had no intention to move Northward and Mrs. Morris's letter confirmed their assertion.[4]

Your brother Fr[ederick] left us this morning. He took with him our little favorite, with a promise to return him in a few days. Peter and Nancy are about moving to Rye. Fady had not heard whether they had left Poughkeepsie. Peter in the course of the summer made several visits to his place at Rye. Mrs. Munro is at Albany, I think. I am not certain, what reply your brother made to my enquiries, his stay here was very short. He lives in the lower part of Mrs. Whites House, talks of getting a house in the Spring. It is said that Mrs. White solicited him to take possession as a protection to her family, as many apprehend that the evacuation will be succeeded by riots, the people in that State being ripe for everything destructive to the loyalists. We have had a hint from some of our acquaintances that they intend us a visit at that time. It will give me pleasure to afford an asylum, should it be necessary, but it will be a shame to the authority of their government if Treatys do not protect the parties concerned but there has been already shameful violations.

I do not wonder that they should say hard things of us in Europe, we deserve it all, and will more I fear. The assembly of this State are convened, we have not yet heard if Pappa is re-elected tho we are told there will not any one be named in opposition to him.[5]

As soon as you determine your Port to arrive at in America, inform me of it. I do not think I shall leave home till about the time you are expected, I will then greet your arrival.

Mrs. Turnbull[6] has solicited Mama to let me spend this winter with her. Mama has refused, alledging the delicacy of my health. I did intend last month to have paid Aunt Clarkson[7] a visit, but such an October I believe was never before known. It was one continued serious [sic] of bad and stormy weather.

To morrow I am going with a Party to the falls.[8] My only inducement to the jaunt at this season is to pay Sister Watkins a visit, I have not seen her since her confinement. Mr. Watkins looks very ill. I fear he is not long for this world. His father has left him handsome if he knew how to improve it, but very unfortunately for himself and family he is an extreme helpless Man. His Mother sails in a short time to dispose of her property in Wales. She and her children except Jack are indifferently provided for, Mr. Watkins estate having suffered materially in the War.

I suppose you at this time in England, where Major Upham[9] promises himself the pleasure of seeing you. He is an aid to the Commander and Chief, a Native of New England and formerly a Lawyer in one of those States. His humane and benevolent conduct to his Countrymen, has preserved the esteem that his deserting his Country never would have lost him. I shall also commit to that gentlemans care a Packet for Sister which he is either to deliver to you or forward to France by a Private conveyance.

That health may be restored to you, you to your friends, is the Sincere wish of.

C. W. L.

ALS.

[1]JJ to Catharine W. Livingston, 26 Aug. 1783, ALS in MHi: Ridley; Dft in JP; JJ to William Livingston, not located.

[2]For Alice De Lancey Izard's departure from Europe, see above JJ to Catharine W. Livingston, 20 July 1783.

[3]Henry Brockholst Livingston.

[4]Letter not located.

[5]Livingston was continuously reelected governor, serving until his death in 1790.

[6]William Turnbull's first wife.

[7]Elizabeth French Clarkson (1722–1808); see *JJ*, I, 451.

[8]Passaic Falls.

[9]Loyalist Joshua Upham (1741–1808), a Harvard graduate and a member of the Massachusetts bar, served as a colonel in the King's Dragoons. After the Revolution he settled in New Brunswick. Sabine, *Loyalists,* II, 372–73; Norton, *The British-Americans,* pp. 240–41.

To William Temple Franklin

London, 11 November 1783
(Copy)

Dear Sir,

Accept my Thanks for your obliging Letter of the 27 Ult.[1] which I should have answered last post, but was then much indisposed. Unfortunately I have not had a well Day since my arrival for I had no sooner recovered of a Dysentery, than a sore Throat succeeded.

I suspect that Abby's Elopement was not resolved upon in a sober moment. It was a measure for which I cannot concieve of a Motive. I had promised to manumit her on our Return to America, provided she behaved properly in the mean Time. Amidst her Faults, she has several good Qualities, and I wish to see her happy and contented on [her] own account as well as our's. Have you heard any Tidings of her? I presume you have, as I do not apprehend it possible for her to elude the Vigilance of the Police. She should be punished, though not vigourously. Too much Indulgence and improper Company have injured her. It is a Pity.

Is there any thing that I can do for you or your good Grandfather while I stay here. If there is, tell me. With my best Compliments to him, I am Dear Sir, Your affectionate and humble Servant,

JOHN JAY

ALS in PPAmP: Franklin CV, 150. Addressed: "Wm. T. Franklin Esqr., Secty to his Excellency Doctr. Franklin Minister Plenip of the United States of America, Passy, near Paris." Endorsed.

[1]Letter not located.

FROM SARAH LIVINGSTON JAY

Chaillot, 12 November 1783

My Dear Mr. Jay,

Last Sunday evening your letter of the 4th inst. enclosing one from Susan[1] was handed me at Dr. Franklin's, and the same evening I received another from Susan dated the 19th of July,[2] in which she mentions Peter's having recovered from the measles. You are perfectly right in disapproving Peter's leaving Mama for frivolous visits, and I am much obliged to her for withholding her consent.

I regret exceedingly those succeeding attacks which have prevented your journey to Bath, but hope before this that the inflamation of your throat has ceeded to prudent measures, but do not suppose that you will leave London 'till after you have seen the Ceremony that will attend the Prince of Wales's first taking his Seat in the house of Lords.[3]

I hope the weather is fine in England for we have had a most enchanting Autumn here. You'll be pleased with our situation when you return, for which I most ardently long, though I would not have you leave England until you have given it a fair tryal.

From one of Susan's letters it appears that brother Peter was already at Rye in July, and I can easily figure to myself the zeal with which he is endeavoring to restore order to the house and farm with the double expectation of immediate convenience and the hopes of procuring an agreeable surprise for you. This instant Ben has brought in a letter from Mr. Adams for Peter and one from you dated the 7th for me.[4] I thank you my dear for the repeated marks of your attention, and assure you, that if you do not hear as frequently from me it must be owing to the miscarriage of my letters, not to negligence since I have written 6 or 7 times at least.

Peter and the Children are very well, as well as myself. Maria's constitution seems to have regained it's former strength and my little Nancy is a perfect Cherub, without making the least allowance for the partiallity of a mother. Apropos, I am very much pleased with the plan you have designed for my bracelet and should it be well executed would entirely answer my wishes.

Yesterday morning Madame Cayo and myself accompanied by Mr. F.,[5] Peter and Ben, breakfasted with Major Monchfort[6] at the Invalides[7] and he was so polite as to attend us through the different appartments and explained to us the various designs in the Dome, which is really a most magnificant piece of architecture. The Major told me that when the Emperor[8] visited it, he inquired of his Guide (who was ignorant of his Rank) whether the Door in the Dome might not be opened, but was answered that it was only opened when the fete Dieu was celebrated, upon which the Emperor demanded if it was not opened when the King came there? You may judge of the Emperor's surprise upon being told that the King had never been, for he immediately declared that he would desire him to come, and by that expression discovered his real rank upon which the man offered to open the Door but the Emperor would not permit him.

Our friends at Auteul and Passy are much as you left them and desire to be remembered to you. Please to present my Compliments of Congratulation to Mr. and Mrs. Vaughan and remember me to Mr. and Mrs. Bingham. Mr. and Mrs. Carter propose going to England in January. Mrs. Price[9] arrived in Paris last Saturday and the next day she and her husband called upon me and invited Peter and me to dine with them on Monday which we accordingly did.

Have you received any letters yet in answer to those written by Barney?[10] Adieu my dear Mr. Jay. May Heaven soon restore you to Health and Me. Yours affectionately,

SA. JAY

Have I reminded you that when you return we shall have occasion for some plain English Knives. This Evening Count Montmorin called upon me, and desired his Compliments to you.

ALS. DftS in JP.

[1]JJ to SLJ, 4 November, and Susannah Livingston to SLJ, 6 Oct. 1783, not located.

[2]Not located.

[3]The Prince of Wales (1762–1830), later George IV, took his seat in the House of Lords when Parliament opened on 11 November.

[4]JJ to SLJ, 7 Nov. 1783, not located. John Quincy Adams to Peter Jay Munro, not located; and see Peter Jay Munro to JJ, 12 Nov. 1783, DftS in NNMus: Jay.

[5]William Temple Franklin.

[6]Comte Jules de Montfort, a French volunteer in the American forces (beginning March 1777), who rose to major in the Pulaski Legion in April 1778, resigning January 1779. *JCC,* X, 364; XIII, 239.

[7]Hôtel des Invalides, built 1671–76 by Libéral Briant as a veterans' hospital. Behind it is the church, Dômes des Invalides, the masterpiece of Jules Hardouin-Mansart.

[8]Joseph II, whose sister was Marie Antoinette.

[9]Mr. and Mrs. James Price.

[10]See below, JJ to SLJ, 29 Nov. 1783, n. 4.

To Sarah Livingston Jay

London, 14 November 1783

My dear Sally,

However my Letters may be short and unentertaining, you will I am sure give me Credit for Punctuality, especially if you recieve as many from the Post Office as I send to it. The last I had the Pleasure of recieving from You was dated the 4th Instant. As Mr. Johnson lives at the Distance of three miles from me, I think it would be best to direct your Letters to me at Mr. Binghams No. 30, Harley Street. I dined with Mr. Johnson Yesterday in Company with many of our Countrymen. Mr. and Mrs. Johnson[1] present their Compliments to you and offer to execute any Commissions with which you may at any Time find it convenient to charge them. They are prettily settled here and seem to be both happy and hospitable.

I have Invitations to pass some time in the Country with Mr. Baker and Mr. Penn,[2] but am too anxious to be with you again, to avail myself of the Civilities of those and many other Gentlemen of this Country. I was Yesterday at the Royal Society[3] and afterwards spent the Evening with the Club *of honest Whigs,*[4] at the Head of which is the celebrated Doctor Price.[5] Their first Toast was their absent Member Dr. Franklin of whom they spoke with Great Respect and affection.

America has many excellent Friends in England, and I may also say, many implacable Enemies. This People is immersed in Pleasure, and yet very far from being happy. A Stranger finds among them much to commend and much to blame. Nothing has as yet exceeded my Expectations, and I shall probably return to America fully persuaded that Europe collectively considered <has> is far less estimable than America.

My Throat continues exactly the same. I shall probably set out for Bath on Wednesday next. Remember me to all our Friends. I long to be with You. God bless you my Dear Wife. I am your very affectionate Husband,

JOHN JAY

P.S. Littlepage is here, for what purpose I know not.

ALS.

[1]Joshua and Catherine Nuth Johnson.

[2]William Baker and Richard Penn.

[3]Founded in London in 1660 and granted a royal charter in 1662, the Royal Society

is Great Britain's oldest scientific organization. The Society conducted extensive overseas correspondence, and between 1663 and 1783 elected 53 fellows from the British North American colonies. Margery Purter, *The Royal Society: Concept and Creation* (Cambridge, Mass., 1967), pp. 235–38; Raymond P. Stearns, *Science in the British Colonies of America* (Urbana, Ill., 1970), pp. 106–14.

[4]One of the many informal London supper clubs of the time and noted for its liberal politics, including among its members the Unitarian clergyman and chemist Dr. Joseph Priestley (1733–1804), scientist and inventor John Canton (1718–72), Benjamin Franklin, and Dr. Richard Price. Verner W. Crane, "The Club of Honest Whigs: Friends of Science and Liberty," *WMQ*, XXIII (1966), 210–33.

[5]Dr. Richard Price (1723–91), dissenting minister, author of moral and political tracts, including *Observations on the Nature of Civil Liberty, The Principles of Government, and the Justice and Policy of the War with America* (1776). See Henri Laboucheix, *Richard Price* (Paris, 1970).

FROM SARAH LIVINGSTON JAY

Chaillot, 18 November 1783

My dear Mr. Jay,

Last Saturday I was so happy as to receive your kind letter of the 10th and 11th instant.[1] From the number, I perceive that not one has miscarried. I hope before this you've received a letter from me that was intended for the post, though by mistake detained too long, which Dr. De Butte has promised Peter to take charge of. In my letter, favored by Mr. Laurens, you have Abbe's history. She still remains where she then was. Peter offered her permission to return if she would behave well, but she refused to accept it, saying she was very happy where she was for that she had nothing to do. Her being at Passy where she had so little occupation has been of great disservice to her.

I went yesterday to enquire Mrs. Ridley's Health, and Arthur returned with information that Mrs. Ridley had been so ill the preceeding night that they thought she would have expired before Morning.[2] I am not easy about your sore throat, it continues too long. Are you very careful of it? I am just interrupted by a visit from Colonels Wadsworth and Carter. Colonel Wadsworth was troubled with a sore throat in England he tells me, and has not yet got rid of it. Mrs. Carter has not yet increased her family.[3]

Today, and two or three days past, we have had windy, rainy weather and the Chimneys have smoked very much. Would you believe that I receive as much pleasure from the stormy weather as I did from the fine? It proceeds from the regret I had during the fine weather that you did not participate [in] it, and the hope I now have that the sun will again revisit our mansion at your return.

I am glad that Lady Julianna will soon be in London. Pray make my best Compliments to her, and tell her that I never think of her and her family without regretting their absence.[4] The first part of our acquaintance passed in the interchange of ceremonious visits and soon after I learnt the value of her social ones. Fortune was so cruel as to deprive me of them.

Dr. Franklin charges me to present you his Compliments whenever I write you, but forbids my telling you how much pains he takes to excite my jealousy at your stay. The other evening at Passy he produced several pieces of steel, the one he supposed you at Chaillot, which being placed near another piece which was to represent me, it was attracted by that and presently united, but when drawn of[f] from me and nearer another piece which the Doctor called an English Lady, behold! the same effect. The Company enjoyed it much and urged me to revenge, but all could not shake my confidence in my beloved friend. The Doctor has just sent me word that he will drink tea with me this Evening notwithstanding the storm. Mr. Grand accepts readily your proposals.[5]

The Children and myself enjoy perfect health, and I hope it will not be long before my dear Mr. Jay will be able in person to make the same declaration of himself to his ever affectionate Wife,

SA. JAY

ALS. Addressed: "His Excellency John Jay Esquir., to the Care of Mr. Joshua Johnson Mercht., Great Tower Hill, London." Endorsed: ". . . ansd. 29 Do."

[1]JJ to SLJ, 10 November, also contains his 11 November letter. ALS in JP.

[2]Matthew and Ann Ridley's second son, Lucius Lloyd, was born on 24 Sept. 1783. Mrs. Ridley fell ill about a fortnight after the child's birth. Matthew Ridley Journal, 24 Sept. 1783 and 21 Jan. 1784, in MHi: Ridley.

[3]The Churches were awaiting the birth of their third child.

[4]JJ's 11 November letter to SLJ mentions that "Lady Juliana will be here on Thursday next."

[5]Not located.

To Sarah Livingston Jay

London, 18 November 1783

Dear Sally,

The last of your Letters which has reached me is dated the 4 Inst. The Post which arrived to Day has I hope brought others for me, but if he has I shall not recieve them till the morning.

My former Letters inform you that a sore Throat has for some Time past detained me here.[1] Lady Juliana Penn tells me that her Son had one of the same kind for ten weeks. As I may just as well take the medicines ordered for me, at Bath as here, I am determined to set out for that Place in a few Days. Indeed the only Medicine I take is Jesuits Bark. Mr. Chace,[2] who sends you his Compliments, talks of going with me. I recieved a Letter Yesterday from one of the Executors at Bristol,[3] from which I percieve that I shall meet with no Trouble in settling Matters there. I am exceedingly anxious to be with you, so much so that I am sure the Pleasure of telling you so, would conduce more to my Health than a long stay at Bath. Besides, the Season advances, and with it the Glooms of this Climate, which in this month is particularly unpleasant.

Mr. Munro[4] was with me Yesterday, and is to see me again Tomorrow. He says much. What he intends to do, I have not yet understood. When I return, you shall have a full Detail of Particulars. Letters from New York dated in October, assign the fifth or sixth of December as the Time when the Evacuation is to be compleated.[5] I wish it may then take place. There are surmises that it may be postponed till Spring, which would be cruel and irritating.

My Compliments to our Friends. I am my Dear Sally, Most sincerely and affectionately yours,

JOHN JAY

P. S. Mr. and Mrs. Fitch and Mrs. Grant,[6] who sail in a few Days for Jamaica present their Compliments to You, and so do Mr. and Mrs. Vaughan, Mr. and Mrs. Bingham, etc. etc.

ALS.

[1]JJ to SLJ, 10 and 11 November, ALS in JP; SLJ to JJ, 4 Nov. 1783, not located.

[2]Samuel Chase arrived in London, 7 September, as agent of the Maryland General Assembly to redeem Bank of England stock purchased before the Revolution, but release of which was blocked by the trustee James Russell, claiming compensation for property confiscated by the state of Maryland during the war. The issue was still unsettled when Chase left England in August 1784. Jacob M. Price, "The Maryland Bank Stock Case: British American Financial and Political Relations Before and After the American Revolution," in Aubrey C. Land, Louis Carr, and Edward C. Papenfuse, eds., *Law, Society, and Politics in Early Maryland* (Baltimore, 1977), pp. 8–11, 15; see also Morris L. Radoff, *Calendar of Maryland State Papers, No. 2, The Bank Stock Papers* (Annapolis, 1947), pp. xiv–xxv, 1. For Samuel Chase, see *JJ,* I, 233.

[3]Letter not located.

[4]For the Reverend Harry Munro, see editorial note above, "An American in England."

[5]For the evacuation of New York City, see below, Robert Morris to JJ, 27 Nov. 1783, n. 1.

[6]West India merchant Eliphalet Fitch, his wife, and Mrs. Grant, a relative, met Catharine W. Livingston in Philadelphia in 1774, and saw the Jays in Paris in June 1783. John Adams identified Fitch as "a native of Boston, [who] holds the office of Receiver General, I think in Jamaica." Fitch had returned to England before sailing for Jamaica. SLJ to Catharine W. Livingston, 11 June 1783, DftS in JP; *AP*, III, 134.

From Peter Jay Munro

Chaillot, 20 November 1783

Dear Uncle,

Young Mr. Adams has informed me, that he never saw you look so well as you do at Present. I am glad to hear it. Though I long for your arrival I hope you will not return before you are quite rid of all your Complaints. My aunt says the same. Is the Inflamation in your Throat of the same kind as that which gave you so much Pain and trouble some years ago? As you say nothing of England in any of your letters, we expect you will tell us a great Deal at your return.

Aunt Jay and the Children are well. Nancy is but little trouble to her mamma. Before I conclude I must tell you a Punn, made upon you and Mr. Fox. I saw it in the Courier de l'Europe.[1] Perhaps you Have heard of it. A London wit hearing that you and Mr. Fox had had a Conference; "Bon, dit il, nous voila donc revenus au tems d'Esope, où les *Quadrupedes* et les *Oiseaux* avoient le don de la Parole."[2]

When you see my Father remember me to him, and beleive me to be, Dear Uncle, Your Dutiful Nephew,

P. J. MUNRO

P.S. I have been so unfortunate as to break my Pen-knife, and I would be very much obliged to my Uncle If he would bring me another. Mrs. Ridley is very ill. Mrs. Price is arrived.

ALS. Addressed: "His Excellency John Jay Esqr. at Mr. Bingham's, Harley Street, No. 30, London." Endorsed: ". . . ansd. 6 Decr. 1783, Recd. 5 Dec. 1783." DftS in NNMus.

[1]*Courier de l'Europe*, a French language newspaper published in both London and Boulogne by Samuel Swinton, a secret agent of the British Admiralty. The French permitted its circulation in France because of its substantial coverage of the American Revolutionary War. *Peacemakers*, p. 138; see also, Louis Eugène Hatin, *Bibliographie historique et critique de la presse périodique française* (Paris, 1866), p. 74.

[2]"Fine!," he said, "here we are back in the time of Aesop, when quadrupeds and birds had the gift of speech."

To Sarah Livingston Jay

London, 23 November 1783
Harley Street No. 30

My dear Sally,

I wrote to you by the last Post, and also by Mr. Barry,[1] who set out for Paris Yesterday. Those Letters express my concern at your Silence, and therefore will perhaps excite some unpleasant Emotions. Mr. Laurens gave me your kind and agreable Letter of the 6th Instant Yesterday. I sincerely thank You for it. Mr. Laurens was detained above a Week at Calais waiting for proper weather etc. Similar obstacles have probably deprived me of the Pleasure of recieving other Letters from you. I cannot omit mentioning this Circumstance, and informing you that I will forbear all further Conjectures on the Subject until I hear from You.

It gives me great Satisfaction to hear that you are so well pleased with your House etc. I am anxious to participate with you in the Comforts you mention. Sun Shine is a Rarity here, and "the Light of wax Candles" is a poor Substitute for it. Is it not strange that Maria should not speake yet. Mrs. Bingham's Little girl of the same age prattles not a little.

I am much displeased with Abbys Conduct. I think with the Doctor that it would be best to suspend all attention to her for some Time. I hope she is separated from Wine and improper Company, and that, without being indulged in the Conveniencies, she has all the Necessaries of Life. If so, Sobriety <and> Solitude and want of Employment will render her Temper more obedient to Reason. I am glad the other Servants behave well. I shall not forget your orders, and will readily execute any others you may favor me with.

My Throat continues a little inflamed. The next Letter you will recieve from me, will be dated at Bath, where my Stay shall not be a moment longer than the object of my going there may require. I am really home Sick, and find few Things more unpleasant than absence from my Family. A Smile from you and the Caresses of our little ones are worth more to me Than all the Pleasures of this Town.

Mr. and Mrs. Bingham, to whose very friendly attention I am much indebted, present their Compliments to You. Remember me to Peter, and our Friends at Passy and Auteuil. I am my dear Sally, Your very affectionate,

JOHN JAY

ALS.

[1]John Barry (1745–1803), naval officer, commanding the *Alliance.* Lincoln, comp., *Naval Records of the American Revolution,* p. 199.

From William Livingston

Trenton, 24 November 1783

Dear Sir,

Since my letter to Mrs. Jay of the 20th instant, I find myself favoured with yours of the 12th September[1] by Mr. Thaxter who is the bearer of the definitive Treaty. *Finis coronat opus.*[2] The British have first and last given us a *desp[er]ate* deal of trouble, but who would have thought not long since that we should so soon have rose superior to it, and with so much glory? You are not an ambitious man, but I think it must be flattering to the most unambitious to hear the Members of Congress ascribe to you such particular merit in the Treaty with Great Britain.[3] Many of them have been very unreserved to us on that Subject in conversation.

I have written to Sally particularly as to Master Peter, and therefore refer you to that letter as to what respects my dear and only grandson.[4]

I thank you for the seeds of the flowering Shrub.

I wish you great joy in the birth of Anne, and ardently long to see my two little grand daughters as well as their parents on this side the Atlantic. God preserve you from such a dreadful passage on your return, as you had in going. I am, dear Sir, Your most humble Servant,

WIL. LIVINGSTON

ALS. Addressed: "The Honble. John Jay Esqr., Plenipotentiary from the United States to the Court of France, at Passy, near Paris." Endorsed.

[1]William Livingston to SLJ, 20 November, not located; JJ to William Livingston, 12 Sept. 1783, above.

[2]"The end crowns the work."

[3]For the Definitive Treaty, see above, JJ to Charles Thomson, 12 Sept. 1783, n. 1.

[4]William Livingston to SLJ, 8 Jan. 1783, above.

From Sarah Livingston Jay

Chaillot, 27 November 1783

My Dear Mr. Jay,

I had not received a letter from you of a later date than the 14th inst. until last evening, when your two letters of the 18th and 21st were handed me; but if my anxiety at your silence was banished, my mortification was increased, as I found you had reason to suppose me inattentive. I wrote you on the 12th, and Doctor DeButts took charge of the letter, and on the 20th I sent Lewis with another to the post-office, but I hope you have received them both by this time.[1] I am delighted to find you begin to wish your return and can answer that a sister-sentiment has long since found a place in my own breast: but since you are absent, rather prolong your stay as long as may be necessary for your health than by returning too soon leave occasion to regret not having given the waters of Bath a sufficient tryal.

You'll find by my other letters that my little family was perfectly well when I wrote, and heaven be praised! We still continue so. The weather here is really delightful, and now that we are a little settled I should like to inoculate the Children, if you approve of it. The famous Inoculator, Dr. Sutton[2] is here; so that if upon reflection you think it would be proper let me know.

The Coachman's wife was brought abed of twins the day before yesterday, and as he is anxious to see her I can't detain him, but will write you a longer letter to morrow. Good night my Love.

Peter's letter is not yet ready, so that I've time to tell you that a Globe of Montgolfiers went up the other day from the Muette with two persons in a <Globe> gallery that was fixed to it. After the rope that detained it was cut it asscended three thousand feet high, and the gentlemen that was attached to it, observing at one time that it descended rather too rapidly, threw into it a little more straw, and then it again mounted, by which means they remained in the air 'till they had gone from the place from whence they set out to Paris, passed over the whole City, and concluding they had stayed as long as the experiment required, suffered themselves to descend gradually near the Boulevards, without having expended more than a third part of the straw they had provided.[3] Next Saturday Monsieur Charles will entertain the public with a like experiment of a Globe filled with inflammable Air. Don't you begin to think of taking your passage next Spring in a Ballon?

God bless you.

AL. DftS in JP.

[1]Neither JJ to SLJ, 21 Nov. 1783, nor SLJ to JJ, 20 Nov. 1783 have been located.

[2]The British physician Daniel Sutton (c. 1735–1819) significantly altered the method of smallpox inoculation in 1763 by using fresh serum from a smallpox blister, drawn before its maturation, injected only by a superficial puncture of the skin

and not through the widely used methods of a long incision or deep cuts. Sutton's treatment included keeping the patient as cool as possible and limited to a diet of vegetables and citrus fruits. John N. Force, "Daniel Sutton and the Revival of Variolation," *Univ. of California Publications in Public Health* (Berkeley, 1931), I, 323–35; David Van Zwanenberg, "The Suttons and the Business of Inoculation," *Medical History* (London, 1978), pp. 71–82.

[3]On 21 Nov. 1783 Pilâtre de Rozier and the Marquis d'Arlandes (1742–1809), piloted a hot air Montgolfier balloon to a height of 3,000 feet, remaining aloft for twenty minutes, and traveling five miles. Among the signers of the official deposition of the event was Benjamin Franklin. Saint-Ford, *Expériences aérostiques,* II, 19–22. For the English translation of this deposition, see *The Annual Register* (London, 1783), XXVI, 70–71.

From Robert Morris

Philadelphia, 27 November 1783
(Copy)

My Dear Sir,

I Congratulate you on the signing of the Definitive Treaty and on the evacuation of New York which took place on Tuesday.[1] Our Friend Gouverneur Morris is there. He has been gone about 18 Days and I expect him back very soon. He will then give you the Detail and inform you of such things as you may wish to know respecting any of your particular Friends.

I agree with the Sentiments expressed in your letter of the 12th September. Treaties of Commerce are dangerous rather than other wise, and if all Governments were to agree that Commerce should be as free as Air I believe they would then place it on the most advantageous footing for every Country and for all mankind. The restrictions which Great Britain is aiming at will in the end work for our Good, if we can work good out of any thing, which in the present State of things seems doubtful. If Great Britain persists in refusing admittance to our Ships in their Islands, they will probably have great cause to repent for I shall not be surprized to see a general Prohibition to the admittance of theirs into our Ports, and if such a measure is once adopted they may find it very difficult to obtain any alteration and in that Case, the advantages of carrying will be much against them. Should the court of France pursue the same Policy we shall fall in with the Dutch and probably have more Connections in Commerce with them than with any other People.

I have received the prints of the Rise and fall of the *Ballon.* Pray cannot they contrive to send Passengers with a Man to steer the course, so as to make them the means of conveyance for Dispatches from one Country to another or must they only be sent for intelligence to the Moon and Clouds.

Congress are now collecting at Annapolis but I think will not make a House untill towards the end of next week. General Mifflin accepts the presidents chair.[2]

We are dismissing the remains of our Army and getting rid of expence so that I hope to see the end of my engagements before next May, but I doubt whether it will be in my power to observe that punctuality in performing them which I wish and have constantly aimed at.

I rejoice at the encrease of your family because I consider it as an encrease of happiness to Mrs. Jay and yourself. Mrs. Morris and myself beg to be affectionately Remembered to her. Our Boys and their Tutor Monsieur Basseville have given us great satisfaction by their last letters and I think they are in a good way.

I am sending some Ships to China[3] in order to encourage others in the adventurous pursuits of Commerce and I wish to see a foundation laid for an American Navy. I am Dear Sir, Your Affectionate Friend and Humble Servant,

ROBT. MORRIS

CS. Endorsed: "... Recd. 7 Ap 1784." Major omissions in *WJ,* II, 138–39; *HPJ,* III, 96–97; and *RDC,* VI, 735.

[1]Under the direction of Sir Guy Carleton, the British evacuation of New York City was completed on 25 Nov. 1783, with the removal of approximately 6,000 troops and 7,000 Loyalist civilians. The formal administration of New York City was assumed by the Council for the Southern District, created in 1779 by the New York State Legislature. Henry P. Johnston, "Evacuation of New York by the British, 1783," *Harper's Magazine,* LXVII, (Nov., 1883), 909–23; James Riker, *Evacuation Day, 1783* (New York, 1883). For the Council for the Southern District, see *Laws of the State of New York, 1778–1781,* 3d Sess. (New York, 1782), pp. 96–97.

[2]For Mifflin's election, see above, Elias Boudinot to JJ, 1 Nov. 1783, n. 4.

[3]The *Empress of China* did not sail until February 1784.

To Sarah Livingston Jay

Bath,[1] 29 November 1783

My Dear Sally,

Your kind Letters of the 12 and 18 November which are the last I have recieved gave me great Pleasure. The apprehensions excited by the Lapse of three long weeks without a Line from You, were painful, and formed a strong Contrast to the agreable Emotions occasioned by these chearful and affectionate Letters. Accept my thanks for them, and be assured that I shall be happy in Proportion as I have Reason to think you so.

The English call this an uncommon fine autumn. It would not be commended in America.

You mention Letters from Susan.[2] What does she say of our Boy? Where is Caty? Have you no Letters from her?[3] The late Vessels from America have not brought me a Line. My Letters perhaps have been sent to the Post Office and gone on to France. I have no answer to the Letters by Barney.[4] When you see Count de Montmorin present my Compliments to him.

I am sorry to hear that Mrs. Ridley continues so ill. Could not the Physician of St. Germains be prevailed upon to attend her, and would not that Place be better for her than Autieul?

My sore Throat has abated a little, tho but very little. I impute it to the Climate, and I hope soon to quit the former with the latter. Lady Juliana told me it *first* appeared here about twenty years ago.

It gives me Pleasure to hear our Friend the Doctor is in such good Spirits. Tho his magnets love Society, they are nevertheless true to the Pole, and in that I hope to resemble them. Make my Compliments to him and the young Doctor. Believe me I am as anxious to return, as you can be to see me. This has been a long Separation. May it soon and happily terminate. God bless and preserve you my Dear Wife. I am yours affectionately,

JOHN JAY

Kiss our dear little Girls for me. Notwithstanding my being here, direct your Letters for me to the care of Wm. Bingham Esquire, Harley Street No. 30 London.

ALS.

[1]JJ probably left London on the 24th. He arrived at Bath on 27 November. See above, JJ to SLJ, 23 November; JJ to Peter Jay Munro, 29 Nov. 1783, ALS in NNMus: Jay.

[2]See above, SLJ to JJ, 12 Nov. 1783.

[3]See above, Catharine W. Livingston to SLJ, 9 Nov. 1783.

[4]Joshua Barney arrived in Paris on 3 July, returning to Philadelphia at the end of September 1783. Footner, *Sailor of Fortune,* pp. 144–47. JJ's letters sent by Barney during the latter's stay in Paris include JJ to Charles Thomson, 19 July; to Robert R. Livingston, 19 July; and to Robert Morris, 20 July 1783. For the replies to these letters, see Charles Thomson to JJ, 26 September, Dft in DLC: Charles Thomson; Robert Morris to JJ, 4 Nov. 1783, above; and Robert R. Livingston to JJ, 29 November, immediately below.

FROM ROBERT R. LIVINGSTON

New York, 29 November 1783

Dear John,

I am two letters in your debt[1] and am conscious that I shall make an ill return for them in offering you this product of a midnight hour after a day spent in the fatigue of business and ceremony that our present situation exacts. But having just been informed by Mr. Plat[2] that he sails tomorrow morning I can not permit him to go without offering you my congratulations on an event to which you have so greatly contributed to bring about, the evacuation of this City by the British on Tuesday last.

Our enemies are hardly more astonished than we ourselves and than you will [be] when you hear that we have been five days in town without the smallest disturbance, that the most obnoxious Royalists that had sufficient confidence in our clemency to them have not met with the least insult. Their shops were opened the day after we came in, and Rivington himself goes on as usual. His State of New York gazette is as well received as if he never had been printer to the Kings most excellent majesty.[3] So that your friends in Europe will find their apprehentions ill founded, and that the race of Tories will not after all be totally extinct in America. Perhaps with good training, and by crossing the breed frequently (as they are very tame) they may be rendered useful animals in a few generations.

On the receipt of your Letter I went down to your brother. Had two long siting[s] with him, conversed freely with him about his situation and told him of your directions relative to him and his sister.[4] He expressed a strong sense of your tenderness for them and promised when ever their occasions should render it necessary that he would draw upon me. He is now at Rie with your sister Nancy who tho not perfectly does not appear to me to be in such a situation as to give you much cause of uneasiness. I am not with out hopes that her native air may reestablish her health.

I have seen Fady and his wife within this two days. They have a part of Hary Whites house in which Mrs. White remains and will I believe remain this winter undisturbed. He has entered upon business. As I have scolded him [for] his neglect to write I hope you will learn some things from him that I can not enlarge upon.

I thank you for your prints of the air balls,[5] But wish to have some fuller account of their composition and the use proposed to be made of them. As an aieriel architect I can not but be curious about the first castles in the air that promise to <be attended> have some stable use.

Receive my congratulations on the birth of your daughter and make my compliments to Mrs. Jay on the occasion.[6]

I had hardly finished the last line when I was alarmed by a very loud rumbling noise accompanied by a quick tremulous motion of the earth. The family are too much alarmed to permit me to add more. Adieu.

R. R. LIVINGSTON

P.S. 30th. We have two small tremours in the course of the night and accompanied with the same kind of noise though not louder than very distant thunder. I shall answer your Letters more at large by the packet.

ALS. Endorsed: ". . . Recd. 11 Ap. 1784. DftS in NHi: Robert R. Livingston. Substantial omissions in *WJ*, II, 139–40, in *HPJ*, III, 98–99, and in *RDC*, V, 735–36.

[1]For JJ to Livingston, 19 July 1783, see above. In his letter to Livingston, 12 Sept. 1783, JJ urged adherence to "exact Reciprocity with all nations" to exert pressure on the British for a trade treaty. Dft and ALS in JP; *HPJ*, III, 78–80; *RDC*, VI, 695–96.

[2]Jeremiah Platt (1744–94), a New York City merchant and partner in the firm of Broome and Platt. Walter Barrett, *The Old Merchants of New York City* (4 vols., New York, 1885), IV, 212.

[3]James Rivington, the detested arch-Tory printer, had by the latter part of the war engaged in espionage for the Patriots, a fact that was never revealed to the readers of his newspaper. He remained in New York City after the British evacuation, changing the name of his newspaper from *The Royal American Gazette* to *Rivington's New-York Gazette and Universal Advertiser*, with the issue of 22 Nov. 1783. Bowing to public animosity, he suspended publication 31 Dec. 1783. Catherine S. Crary, "The Tory and the Spy: The Double Life of James Rivington," *WMQ*, 3d ser., XVI (1959), 61–62.

[4]For JJ's directions to his brother Peter and sister Anna Maricka, see above JJ to Livingston, 19 July 1783.

[5]JJ's prints of the balloon ascensions enclosed in his letter of 12 Sept. 1783 have not been located, but see Illustration section.

[6]At this point in the DftS, Livingston deleted his original closing and substituted: "I had hardly finished the last line when my table was shaken by a pretty smart shock of an earthquake accompanied with a very loud noise like the rumbling of thunder at no great distance. The noise continued about 8 seconds with a quick tremulous motion. My mother and sisters are all in my room and very much alarmed. Downstairs you will easily believe it. It is impossible to add anything more. Adieu. P.S. You shall hear from me by the packet which sails in a few days. In every circumstance and situation be assured my dear John of my unalterable friendship."

See also report in *The Independent Journal or, The General Advertiser* [New York], 1 Dec. 1783.

FROM SARAH LIVINGSTON JAY

Chaillot, 30 November 1783

My dear Mr. Jay,

Your two letters of the 21st and one of the 23d inst. have given me a degree of mortification that would be difficult for any one unacquainted with strong attachments to conceive. I flattered myself that not only Mr. Laurens had long since arrived in London, but also that you had received my letters of the 12th and 18th, and that those of the 20th and 27th would not have left a sufficient interval in your intelligence to have occasioned uneasiness. Did I not still hope that some of those little messengers of tenderness were from time to time arriving with evidence of my attention, I should be inconsolable, for really I would rather you should think me dying than suppose me indifferent where your pleasure is concerned. If the Post did not go early tomorrow I should defer writing 'till the morning, for what with the too apparent, though half concealed doubts of my attention which your letters betray, and Mr. Franklin's telling me that you write him that you have not enjoyed one day's health since you left France,[1] I am so dejected that I can scarcely know what I say. Pardon me, my Love. I fear you are not candid and that while you amuse me with accounts of a sore throat you are more seriously indisposed. Kind heaven! Avert my fears.

I'll endeavor to divert my uneasiness by re-perusing the latter part of your last letter.

You ask me if it is not strange that Maria does not yet begin to speak? I think it is and regret it, for there is something vastly amusing in observing the young ideas as they begin to shoot. The Children are both perfectly well at present, and if they continue so until your return, I'll answer for their recompensing you for any pleasure's you'll leave behind. I don't know whether it's good policy to tell you so often what a sweet little babe my Nancy is, but really I love to anticipate your pleasure. You never saw a little creature more fond than Maria is of her sister, and I often find a trickling tear stealing down my face while regarding her caresses. Whether from a regret that you do not participate [in] that pleasure or from what other cause I leave you to decide, but certain I am there is a luxury in the sensation that I would not exchange for any other but the pleasure of seeing you.

Tomorrow Monsieur Charles will entertain the public with the sight of a very large Globe which is to ascend from the Tuilleries, with a kind of Carr attached to it in which two persons will sit.[2] As I can see it as well from the terrace as the Garden I'll inclose my ticket which may serve to give you an idea of it.[3] Peter is writing to you and will, I suppose, give you further accounts of it as well as of the Procession at Paris when the Declaration of Peace was proclaimed there.[4]

For my own part I should be delighted to contribute to your amusement, but to tell the truth my uneasiness has made me more stupid than ever. Take care of your health, banish anxiety and believe me to be my dearest Life, Your very affectionate

SA. JAY

ALS. Addressed: "His Excellency John Jay Esqr. at Wm. Bingham's Esqr., Harley Street No. 30, London. Endorsed: ". . . and. 8 Decr. No. 17." Dft in JP.

[1]Letter not located.

[2]In the second ascension over the Tuileries on 1 Dec. 1783, Jacques Caesar Charles and Monsieur Robert piloted their hydrogen balloon to a height of 250 ft. Saint-Ford, *Expériences aérostatiques,* II, 39–44; *Annual Register,* XXVI (1783), 71–75. See also, SLJ to JJ, 2 December, AL in JP, and Peter Jay Munro to JJ, 2 Dec. 1783, DftS in NNMus: Jay.

[3]Enclosure not located.

[4]The public proclamation followed the exchange of Declarations of the Kings of England and France, 3 Sept. 1783, CP A 544: 71.

William Livingston to Peter Augustus Jay

Trenton, 6 December 1783

My dear little sweet lovely sugar-plumb darling, Peter Jay,

Grand Papa has received your Letter of the 30th of November,[1] and is very glad indeed to find that you have improved so much in your writing. Continue to be industrious my dear little fellow, and be sure to write a Copy every day, and then Papa and Mamma when they return will be surprised to find what a pretty hand you write, and they will love you ten times more for it.

I hope I shall soon have another letter from you and am Your affectionate Grand Father,

WIL. LIVINGSTON

ALS. Endorsed in an unidentified hand: ". . . A letter from Grandpapa, 6 December 1783."

[1]Letter not located.

From John Adams

London, 7 December 1783

Dear Sir,

The night before last, Commodore Jones arrived, with Dispatches from Congress.[1] Two Packets were directed to the Ministers, and one larger one to Dr. Franklin. The two first I opened. One of them contained nothing but News Papers. The other contained, a private Letter from the President and a Sett of Instructions to the Ministers for Peace. These I copied, and Sent on the Originals to Passy, together with the Packet to Dr. Franklin, unopened.

If it is found to contain a Communication to Us, In conformity to the Resolution of the first of last May the Doctor will inform Us by the first Post if not by Express.[2]

In the meantime, I wish to consult with you, if it were possible upon our new Instructions, which chalk out some new Business for Us. I would send you a Copy of them, if I were not afraid of ministerial Curiosity. Mr. Bingham makes me think you will be soon here.

I inclose herewith a Letter from the President to you and another to Mr. Laurens, which I must beg the Favour of you to deliver to him, as I dont know his Address.[3]

Mifflin is the new President, and Congress have adjourned to Anapolis, and are to Set after sometime, one Year, at George Town upon Potomack and one year on the Delaware. Colonel Ogden had arrived with the News of the Signature of the definitive Treaty,[4] but Thaxter had not in the first Week in November.[5]

Barneys destination is Havre de Grace, and his orders are positive to Sail in three Weeks, for Philadelphia.

Mr. Morris has drawn So many Bills upon my Bankers in Amsterdam, that a Number have been protested for Non Acceptance.[6] So that if Mr. Grand cannot assist in preventing the Protest for Non Payment, the Catastrophe must now come. This you will not mention at present. With great Esteem, I am yours,

JOHN ADAMS

ALS. Endorsed: ". . . recd, 8 Decr 1783, ans. 9 Decr. 1783."

[1]For these instructions, see above Elias Boudinot to JJ, 1 Nov. 1783, no. 3. In addition to the private letter to JJ above, the packet contained Boudinot's private letters to the other three Commissioners. *LMCC,* VII, 361–62; *RDC,* VI, 719–20; *JAW,* IX, 153–54; Boudinot, ed., *Life,* II, 7–8, 10–11.

[2]See editorial note, "Negotiating a Trade Treaty," above.

[3]Elias Boudinot to JJ, 1 Nov. 1783, above, for Laurens' letter, see p.662.

[4]On 31 October Colonel Ogden informed Congress of the signing of the Definitive Treaty. Elias Boudinot to the American Commissioners, 27 October and 1 Nov. 1783, *LMCC,* VII, 356–57; *RDC,* VI, 720.

[5]On 22 November John Thaxter delivered the Definitive Treaty to President Mifflin at Philadelphia. The latter, since Congress was not then sitting, sent a circular letter to the governors of New Hampshire, Connecticut, New York, New Jersey, and Delaware, and to General Washington announcing the receipt of the treaty. *LMCC,* VII, 376–77.

[6]See *AP,* III, 151–52; see also Ferguson, *Power of the Purse,* pp. 128–29.

Sarah Livingston Jay to William Temple Franklin

[Chaillot], Sunday noon [7 December] 1783

Mrs. Jay present[s] her Comp[limen]ts to Mr. Franklin and takes the liberty of requesting him to write a few lines to Mr. Le Noir,[1] desiring permission for Abbe to quit the place of Confinement where she now is immediately, as [she] is very ill and extremely desirous to return and Mrs. Jay fears a delay may be dangerous. If Mr. Franklin has leisure at present to write, the Servant will wait for the letter in order to carry it to the Lieutenant de Police.

Mrs. Jay flatters herself that nothing has intervened to prevent Mr. Franklin and his Grand father and Cousin from honoring her with their Company this Evening.

AL in PPAmP: Franklin CVIII, 58. Addressed: "Mr. Franklin, Passy."

[1]Jean-Charles Pierre Le Noir (1732–1807), lieutenant of the Paris police, deeply involved both in the surveillance of foreigners and in espionage operations. See *Peacemakers,* p. 142n.

From Peter Jay Munro

Chaillot, 7 December 1783

Dear Uncle,

No change has happened in the Family since my Last[1] except the return of Abegail. While she <remained> was Confined in the Common Prison together with numbers worse than herself she grew daily more hardened, but a disorder she is subject caused her removal to the infirmery. <It so happened that I went to see her the day after but was not admited. The coachman was> There not finding any of her lewd companions, and seeing no one but the nurse and apothecary's man she had sufficient time for reflection, which she so well improved that the Day before yesterday I found [her] extremely penitent and desirous to return. My aunt complied with her request and I brought her home last night.[2]

When we told you in our last letter that Mr. Charles ascend[ed] 1500 toises[3] we spoke within bounds, it appears by a letter he published since that he was 1524 toises from the earth. He went in 35 minutes a League and an half by land, but he assures the public it was more than 3 in the air. The next day after having emptied and folded the globe which had not received the least damage he return[ed] to Paris with those who had followed him.

It is 14 Days since the date of your last. I am Dear uncle, your affectionate nephew,

P. JAY MUNRO

DftS in NNMus: Jay.

[1]Peter Jay Munro to JJ, 4 Dec. 1783, DftS in NNMus: Jay.

[2]Abbe's expenses in jail amounted to 60 livres, which William Temple Franklin laid out for the Jays. SLJ: account of money paid Mr. Franklin, 19 Dec. 1783, AD in JP.

[3]Fathoms.

FROM SARAH LIVINGSTON JAY

Chaillot, 7 December 1783

My Dear Mr. Jay,

As I have <written> wrote you three letters last week,[1] <I've> and having now nothing new to tell you, <and therefore could> I might say <only> with the school boys, that this is to let you know that I am well, hoping you are so likewise. Did I not feel so anxious about your health as to render fear more prevalent than hope, you will not be surprised at my uneasiness, when I tell you that 14 days have elapsed since the date of your last letter,[2] and that at length the evening of this long day has arrived without the wished-for lines which the post usually brings me of a sunday Evening. Perhaps the wind has been contrary to my wishes. I'll endeavor at least to flatter myself <at least> that indisposition has not been the reason of my not hearing.

On Fryday, Peter called to see Abbe. She begged he would solicit leave for her return. As I feared she would not receive benefit from the society she had, I granted her request, and <she appears> <I> am glad to find her penitent and desirous to efface by her future Conduct the reproach her late mistress has merited.

The Children are well and Peter I suppose will tell you that he is, for he is writing to you.

The Countess d'Artois <is now writing> has lost her only daughter and I really feel for her, for she is a princess of an amiable character and vastly fond of her Children.[3]

Let me hear from you soon, for suspense is painful to your affectionate Wife

SA. JAY

DftS.

[1]SLJ to JJ, 30 November, above; 2 December, AL, and 4 Dec. 1783, ALS in JP.

[2]JJ to SLJ, 23 Nov. 1783, above, which was received on 30 November; see Peter Jay Munro to JJ, 30 Nov. 1783, DftS in NNMus.

[3]Charles-Philippe d'Artois and his wife Marie-Thérèse de Savoie lost their only surviving child, Sophie (b. 1776) on 5 Dec. 1783.

To Sarah Livingston Jay

Bath, 8 December 1783

My dear Sally,

I have this moment recieved your agreable and aff[ectiona]te Letters of the 27 and 30 November and greatly regret that the anxiety to hear from you expressed in some of mine gave you Concern. It is evident that the long Interval in which I recieved no Letters from you, was occasioned by unavoidable accidents, and the number I have since been favored with shew your attention as well as excite my Gratitude.

It gives me very sincere Pleasure to hear that you and the Children are well. God grant you and they may continue so. The civil Things (if I may use that Expression) which you say of Nancy raises my Curiosity as well as affords me Pleasure. It is a pleasing Subject.

I entirely approve of you having them both inoculated by Dr. Sutton. We may not have such another opportunity, and I think it ought not to be neglected. I fear the Coachman thinks his Wife too bountiful. How hard it is that such interesting Blessings should be marred by straightened Circumstances! Make him some Present on the occasion. He is a good Fellow and will thank you for it.

Three Times have I been interrupted since I began this Letter, and I find I must defer to another opportunity, the saying all I meant to tell you by this, but as there is nothing very important or pressing in the Matter, you will be no great Loser by the Omission. I thank you for the Print you enclosed, and the account you give me of Montgolfier's Experiment. I wrote to you and to Peter last post.[1] Remember me to him and to our Friends at Passy and Autieul. Adieu my Dear Wife. Yours affectionately,

JOHN JAY

ALS.

[1]JJ to SLJ, 7 December, and JJ to Peter Jay Munro, 8 Dec. 1783, not located.

From Patience Lovell Wright

London, 8 December 1783

Esteemd Sir,

I have the pleasure of Resiving letter from my Friends in America that inform me that my Son is apointed by Congress to Paint a likeness and also moddel in Clay a Busto of General Washington, and he is to Send by the next Ship (that Sails from Philadelphia) Copys of those likenesses for his *mother* in London for to be done in wax. I have long wishd for that honour and now feal greatful for my life being Spaird to See this hapy day. I wish for nothing more then to finish the portrites in wax Bustos of all you worthy *heros* that have done honour to themselves and to their Contry by their *Wisdom,* their *valor* and good *Counsell.* They under God have Saved my Contry. Amongst the first Stands the Busto of a Jay, Lewarance, Adams, Franklin, Morris and General Washington full length for *Posterity.*

The New buildings now to be erected for Congress and Publick Use will be done at the *time* and <nere by> on the Spot of my Werk nere my Fathers Inheritance. I also wish a Corner of the building may be allotted for those Bustos that my work may be their Ready, for the diferent artists to *Copy by,* in *marbel* or *Brange* [sic] for the diferent States. As when time and a more Convenent opertunity may make it proper to Erect these Publick testimonies of the Publick gratitude of My Contry to those great and truly Honourd Characters, then will Mrs. Wrights Likeness in wax, taken from them when Living, and done at the desire of their Contry, be a Lasting honour to *her* and a honour to that age and Contry, and give pleasure to Strangers and be useful to Posterity.

I hope in a few weeks to See the Copys from America and desire that my honourable Contrymen that are now in England may Encourage me in so proper a Work.

I am Dear Sir your faithful Friend and very humble Servant.

PATIENCE WRIGHT

This Comes by Mr. Langburn.

ALS. Addressed: "The Honorable Jay Esqr. at Bath." Endorsed: ". . . Recd. 23 Inst."

To John Adams

Bath, 9 December 1783
South Parade No. 5

Dear Sir,

Last night I recieved your obliging Favor of the 7 Inst. and the Letters mentioned to be enclosed with it. The one for Mr. Laurens was immediately sent to his Lodgings.

The Circumstances you mention are interesting, and will afford matter for Deliberation and Comments when we meet. My Return to London will depend on one of two Things vizt., on being satisfied that I am to expect little or no Benefit from the Waters, or (in Case of their being useful) on my having reaped all the advantage they can afford me. They have I think done me some, but as yet not much good. My Physician tells me more Time is necessary.

I perfectly approve of your not having sent me Copies of any *private* Papers, which is probably of the less Importance as our Commission is not yet come to either of our Hands; though perhaps it may, as you observe, be enclosed in the Packet directed to Doctor Franklin. My Letters make no mention of it.

From what I heard you say at London I had flattered myself that you intended soon to visit this Place. It is worth your seeing, and you would find it agreable. Be pleased to make my Compliments to your Son, and believe me to be Your Friend and Servant,

JOHN JAY

ALS in MHi: Adams. Addressed: "His Excelly. John Adams Esqr., minister plenipotentiary from the United States of America, etc., at Mr. Stockdales, Bookseller, Piccadilly, London." Endorsed. DftS in JP.

From Sarah Livingston Jay

Chaillot, 11 December 1783

My dear Mr. Jay,

The arrival of several posts without any letters from you, as seventeen days had elapsed since the date of your last,[1] had in spite of my endeavors to the contrary dejected my spirits. Not that I thought you negligent, but because I feared some accident had prevented your writing. But last evening your letter of the 29th Ult. restored the tranquility of my mind, which had indeed been likewise interrupted by another cause. Will it be necessary before I relate the other reason for my anxiety to ask your forgiveness for the measure I adopted without attending your approbation. The tenderness of your friendship for me, will I know make you jealous of my having any cause for anxiety concealed from your knowledge and participation and it is on that score alone I fear your displeasure.

You may recollect my dear, that in one of my letters I requested your opinion about the inoculation of our Children.[2] After I had written, upon more mature reflection, I concluded I already knew your sentiments sufficiently to Authorise my having the operation performed if Mr. Sutton should think it advisable, and that by attending the event without letting you know it, I should spare you a degree of solicitude that would be unavoidable and perhaps retard the recovery of your health. I therefore the next day sent for the Doctor, and finding him very sanguin about the success of it, I immediately prepared myself and children according to his directions, and a day or two after he inoculated them. For 8 days after, they were both so well that I could with great sincerity assure you of their health every time I wrote, and last Sunday evening after I had finished my letter Louisa came into the parlour to let me know that she feared my little one was going into convulsions. She looked so terrifyed that Peter catched the alarm, and you may suppose I did not remain insensible, but recollecting your fortitude upon a former distressing occasion I endeavoured to imitate it and desiring them to be calm, I took the babe in my lap and made Louisa hold a bason of luke warm water in which we bathed her feet about a quarter of an hour, sitting in a current of air, after which I walked with her in the dining room, the windows and doors being open, but the Child well covered except her head, 'till midnight, when her fever was exceedingly abated and she fell into a sweet sleep that continued untill morning, when we observed that several pustules had made their appearance. In the morning when the Doctor visited me he assured me that all danger was then over, and that the measures I had taken prevented her from having convulsions. Fortunately Maria's simptoms did not appear untill the next evening, and then after a very smart fever the small pox discovered itself, since which they have been bravely, and to-day quite gay and well. Sunday or Monday the Doctor will give them medicine to carry off the humors and he begs me to assure you that they are quite recovered.

When shall I receive such charming tidings from you as that you likewise are perfectly recovered? You have stated your return upon such a footing, that much as I long to see you, I dare not yet wish

<your return> it. <Yet> Doctor Franklin tells me that while he was in England he rarely saw an American there but what was troubled with a sore throat sometime after his arrival, and therefore should you not receive that benefit from Bath which we hoped I think with you that you'll get rid of the sore throat by leaving England.

There was nothing new in Susan's letter[3] but what I told you that Peter was recovered from the Measles. Caty is at Eliz[abeth] Town, but I've no letters from her. Peter tells me that Paul Jones is arrived, but I do not know whether we have letters by him, nor from whence he sailed.

I told you, I think, that Abbe had returned: She has a violent Cold. As I've prevailed upon her to remain in bed, I hope she'll recover in a week or two. As I have not slept for several nights on account of the Children I hope I shall to night rest well, for they are both in a sweet sleep. Be assured my dear Mr. Jay that I enjoy my health perfectly and that I am most sincerely and affectionately yours,

SA. JAY

Mrs. Carter was brought a-bed of a daughter last Sunday and she and the infant are both very well.[4]

ALS. Addressed: "His Excellency John Jay Esqr. at Wm. Bingham's Esqr., Harley Street No. 30, London." Endorsed: ". . . and. 26 Inst. incd. to Dr. Franklin."

[1]Probably JJ to SLJ, 23 November, above, which she received on 30 November; see Peter Jay Munro to JJ, 30 Nov. 1783, DftS in NNMus: Jay.

[2]See above, SLJ to JJ, 27 Nov. 1783.

[3]Susan Livingston to SLJ, 6 Oct. 1783, not located.

[4]Catherine Church was born 7 Dec. 1783.

William Livingston to Peter Augustus Jay

Trenton, 12 December 1783

My dear Peter Jay,

I have already sent you an answer to your dear little letter,[1] but to encourage you the more to send me another, I write this. Pray my little darling, send me another letter as soon as possible.

I hear that when you was in the Church in New York and the Minister prayed for King George, that you shook your head, as much as to say that you did not like it. It was right in those people to pray for their king, because he is *their* king; but you not thinking of that, and being a good Whig, have got great honour by shaking your head, and grand papa is always pleased when his dear little Peter gets honour.

Pray stick close to your writing, and if you do, you will soon be fit to be Grand pappa's Secretary. Tell grand mamma that I advanced the Servant whom I sent her, three dollars which must be deducted from his wages. And tell Aunt Sukey and Aunt Caty that I hope they will spare no pains to teach you to write a good hand. I am my dear P., your affectionate Grand father,

WIL. LIVINGSTON

ALS.

[1]Peter Augustus Jay to William Livingston, 30 Nov. 1783, not located.

To Egbert Benson

Bristol, 15, 16, 18 December 1783

Dear Benson,

I arrived here from Bath Yesterday afternoon, for the Purpose of settling affairs with the Executors of Mrs. Peloquin. As I have not yet seen those Gentlemen, I cannot at present say any Thing on that Subject.

Sometime ago I recieved from Frederick an Instrument of writing appointing Persons to appraise the Farm at Rye.[1] I executed it, and sent it to Sir James, that he might do the like, and requested him either to forward it to New York, or return it to me for that Purpose. He wrote me in answer that he would be at New York near as soon as a Letter could get there, and that he would take it with him.[2] Inform Peter of these Circumstances, and that I advise him to take the Farm at the Valuation. In that Case I think it might not be amiss for him to execute and have recorded, an Instrument of writing, reciting the Clause in the will on that Subject; reciting the nomination of the appraisors, reciting their appraisement (which two latter Papers should also be recorded) and declaring his acceptance of the Premises at the Sum therein specified. If there be anything which he would chuse to have sent from these Countries, I will readily execute his Orders. I doubt not but his Legacy will be immediately paid, and I wish to recieve his Directions as to the Disposition of it. At all Events in case money should be convenient to him, you or Frederick may draw upon me for his use to the amount of three hundred pounds York money at ten Days Sight. He need not fear Interest; I shall charge him none. I hope before the Ship sails which is to carry this Letter, that it will be in my Power to write positively as to the Success of my Journey here.

If my old mare is alive, I must beg of you and my Brothers to take very good care of her. I mean that she should be well fed, and live Idle unless my Brother Peter should chuse to use her. If it should be necessary to advance money to recover her, I am content you should do so, even to the amount of double her Value. Draw upon me for what may be necessary for this Purpose. I hear her Colt was delivered to you for me by Col. DeLancey; let it not be sold. Billy Van Wyck was at the Expence of the getting that Colt, and of keeping the Mare some months, and had she not been stolen, and he thereby prevented from performing his part of the Bargain, the Colt would have been his. At any Rate I ought and am willing to make him a reasonable allowance for those Expences.

Having been very well assured that the Conduct of Judge Ludlow, Mr. Watts, H. White and Peter V. Schaack had been perfectly unexceptionable, and that they had not associated with the abominable Tory Club in London (which filled the public papers with the most infamous Lies against us) I recieved and returned their Visits.[3] Vardil also made me a visit, but I never returned it.[4] Reports of Cruelties exercised by my old friend James DeLancey of West Chester have also kept us asunder.[5] I wish those Reports may prove as groundless, as he says they are. He paid me a visit but I did not return it. He was an honest Friend to me, and I sincerely lament the Circumstances which prevent my taking him by the Hand as cordially as ever. I have not seen any of General DeLancey's Family. I once met Billy Bayard[6] in the Street, but we passed each other as perfect Strangers.

Shortly after my arrival in London I was taken very ill of a Dysentery and after that with a sore throat. I am now thank God in tolerable Health. The Waters of Bath have done me some good.

Bristol, 16 December 1783

Mr. Daltera was with me this morning. On perusing the Letters of Attorney etc., he observed that it did not appear from any of the Papers when my Father died, which was very important, because in Case he had not survived Mrs. Peloquin, the Legacy she left him would have lapsed. He also asked whether there was any Person in England who could prove the Hand writing of either of the Parties or witnesses to the Letters of Attorney. He proposed to go with me to her Sollicitors and to leave the papers with him to report on them, which was immediately done. Finding that evidence of the Time of my Fathers Death would be required, I wrote this Evening to Mr. V. Schaack and requested him to collect and reduce into the form of affidavits whatever circumstantial Evidence Mr. White or Col. DeLancey or other Americans in London might be able to give respecting it.[7]

December 18, 1783

I met Mr. Daltera this morning at the Sollicitors. I told him that Mr. Van Schaack could prove your Hand, and it was agreed [that the] Letters of Attorney should be immediately sent to London for that Purpose. Nothing further can be done till we hear from Mr. Van Schaack, and I shall set out immediately for Bath and remain there until his answer arrives.[8]

I am Dear Benson, Your affectionate Friend,

JOHN JAY

ALS in PHi: Society. DftS in JP.

[1]Document not located, but originally included in Frederick Jay to JJ, 2 Oct. 1783, ALS in JP.

[2]Not located.

[3]George Duncan Ludlow (1734–1808) was a justice of the New York Supreme Court of Judicature. John Watts, Jr. (1749–1836) was the last Recorder of New York City under British rule. For Henry White, see *JJ*, I, 101 n. 3. For the sale of the forfeited estates of all three and the settlement of their claims by the British government, see Harry B. Yoshpe, *The Disposition of Loyalist Estates in the Southern District of New York* (New York, 1939), pp. 121–33, 200, 208. Peter Van Schaack's property, "not being confiscated," he claimed merely £170 for loss of profession, but the claim was disallowed "for want of satisfactory proof of loss." *Ibid.*, p. 207.

[4]In the DftS JJ wrote: "I <recieved him coldly> . . . <He asked me whether he could safely return to>."

[5]The DftS continues: "<I sincerely loved him>."

[6]Loyalist William Bayard, Sr., who sailed for England in 1783. For his schedule of losses and award, see Yoshpe, *Loyalist Estates*, p. 189; also *JJ*, I, 486.

[7]On 1, 5 Jan. 1784 JJ acknowledged receiving from Van Schaack the affidavit he requested. ALS in NN: Emmett and in PHi: Conarroe, IX, 19.

[8]JJ to Van Schaack, 21 Dec. 1783, ALS in CtY.

To Sarah Livingston Jay

Bath, 20 December 1783

My dear Sally,

My last mentioned my Return from Bristol, and the Obstacles which retard my compleating the Business which called me there.[1] No Letters from you have since reached me, but as I make it a general Rule to write twice a week it will be as little my Fault as yours if we do not hear often from each other.

At Length my dear Sally it is in my Power to assure you that I am much better than I was. I have no Pain in my Breast and my appetite is good. My Throat indeed continues obstinate but not painful. The Moment I can get that Bristol Business dispatched I shall set out for France. I often anticipate in Imagination the Pleasure of finding myself in the midst of my little Family and exchanging with them a Variety of little anecdotes which have happened during our Separation. I am tired of being away from you, and happy shall we be if we all meet in good Health and Spirits. Let me intreat you to be careful of your Health and not to permit Care or Anxiety of any kind to injure it. In two of my late Letters[2] I approved of your inoculating our little Girls if Dr. Sutton and you knew of no objections to it. I mention it again, in Case those Letters may not have come to Hand. Take Care that Nancy does not grow too much for you. On the least Appearance of it I must insist either that you wean her, or get a Nurse for her.

Tell Peter I am pleased with his Letters and will tell him so myself one of these Days, for at present a Vessel being about to sail soon for New York from Bristol obliges me to write a Number of Letters.

The Messrs. and Miss Laurens present their Compliments to you. In a Letter I recieved from Mr. Chase[3] he does the same.

God bless you my dear Wife. I am your affectionate Husband,

JOHN JAY

ALS.

[1]JJ to SLJ, 19 Dec. 1783, not located.

[2]JJ to SLJ, 8 December above and 10 December, ALS in JP.

[3]Samuel Chase to JJ, 16 Dec. 1783, ALS in JP.

To Benjamin Franklin

Bath, 26 December 1783

Dear Sir,

Since we parted I have been so much and so long indisposed as that (except short letters to Mrs. Jay) I have denied myself the Pleasure of writing to my Friends. The Kindness you have shewn us both, has nevertheless not been forgotten, nor has my Disposition to acknowledge and be influenced by it in the least abated.

We have lately had a Report here that you was very ill with the Stone, and some have said that you intended to seek Relief from an operation.[1] This Report has alarmed your Friends, and I am anxious to know how far it may be well founded. It would give me sincere Satisfaction to have it contradicted under your own Hand.

I decline saying any thing about politics, for obvious Reasons. The public Papers afford you the Means of forming a Judgment of them especially as your long Experience and knowledge of this Country enable you to see further than ordinary observers.

There are many in this Country who speake of you with great Respect. The honest Whig Club drink your Health very affectionately. There are others who like you as little as the Eagle did the Cat, and probably for the same Reasons. When we meet we will talk these Matters over with less Reserve than I can write. Present my affectionate Compliments to your two Grandsons, and believe me to be with great Esteem and Regard, Dear Sir, Your obliged and obedient Servant,

JOHN JAY

P. S. As we have yet no News of Mr. Thaxter's arrival, would it not be well to send over Copies of the Treaty?

ALS in PPAmP: Franklin XXX, 155. Addressed: "His Excellency Doctr. Franklin, Minister plenipotentiary from the United States of America at the Court of France, Passy." Endorsed by William Temple Franklin. Postscript omitted in *BFB,* X, 233. Dft in JP. Endorsed: ". . . cov[erin]g one for Mrs. Jay (no. 22)."

[1]In his 6 Jan. 1784 reply, Franklin wrote: "It is true, as you have heard, that I have the stone, but not that I have had thoughts of being cut for it. It is as yet very tolerable." *BFB,* X, 260; *BFS,* IX, 150–52.

To Sarah Livingston Jay

Bath, 26 December 1783

My dear Sally,

The number of this Letter will convince you that the long Interval in which you recieved no Letters from me, is to be ascribed to causes not in my Power to obviate. Your Favors of the 11 and 14th Inst. were delivered to me Yesterday, together with two from Peter, to whom I already owed two Letters.[1]

My approbation of your Proposal to inoculate the Children, was conveyed in three different Letters.[2] I commend your Fortitude and rejoice with you in the Success of it. I am indeed happy and thankful that they are both recovered. I lament Abbys Death.[3] It would have given me great Pleasure to have restored her in Health to our own Country. I am persuaded of your attention to her, and think with you, that her being at Home, and well taken Care of, are Circumstances of Consolation. The Situation of the Family during their Illness must have pressed hard upon you, and though the Recovery of our dear little Girls doubtless gave new Vigour to your Spirits, yet I fear they have been too much agitated by the variety as well as Degree of Emotions which you have lately experienced. That Consideration makes me extremely anxious to be with you, and were it not for the Bristol Business (to finish which I wait for Papers to be sent me from London by Mr. Van Schaack) I would set out for France Tomorrow morning.

Let me entreat you my dear Sally to continue tranquil and composed. Amuse yourself a little by seeing your Friends at their Houses and at yours. I need not remind you that People passing through this World are not to expect to have *all* the way strewed with Roses. Let us be grateful for Blessings and resigned to adverse Incidents.

I shall write to Mr. Johnson on the Subject of a Maid such as you mentioned.[4] My Absence shall not be a Moment longer than may be unavoidable. My Health mends, and if with you would mend faster.

God bless and preserve you and our little ones. My Love to Peter, and Compliments of the Season to the Doctor and our other Friends. I am my Dear Sally, Your affectionate Husband,

JOHN JAY

P.S. As my Letters were directed to you at Chaillot, perhaps the penny post, not knowing your Houses, may have left them in the post office. Let Peter make Inquiry for them there.

ALS. Received on 6 January, as mentioned in Peter Jay Munro to JJ, 6 Jan. 1784, DftS in NNMus: Jay.

[1]Peter Jay Munro to JJ, 11 and 14 Dec. 1783, both DftS in NNMus. SLJ to JJ, 14 Dec. 1783, not located.

[2]JJ to SLJ, 8, 20 Dec. 1783, above, and 10 Dec. 1783, ALS in JP.

[3]The news was conveyed in SLJ to JJ, 14 December. Peter Jay Munro, in his of the same date to JJ, noted: "in my last I mentioned abby's return but must now refer you to my aunt's letter for an account of her."

[4]SLJ's request for assistance in acquiring a maid was probably contained in her letter of 14 December. No letter on this subject from JJ to Joshua Johnson has been located.

From Catharine W. Livingston

Elizabeth Town, 30 December 1783

Permit me, my dear Sir, to wish you and Sister, the Compliments of the season, and to assure you that no one more sincerely wishes the ensueing year may be propitious to your every wish than your friend who has now the pleasure of writing to you.

The Church disputes far from subsideing, rage with more violence than ever. The Whigs finding the *Moreans* or in plain English the Tories the strongest party, are determined to petition the Legeslature for their interposition. They will never stop short of depriveing Mr. Moore of the Rectorship, in which though I am no Churchwoman I think they are perfectly right. They ought indeed to go further. They should silence Mr. Moore altogether. I am no friend to persecution, but I think in the present criticle situation of their City the Tories will have no reason to complain if we do nothing more than prevent their holding any Office which may give them influence, until they can consent, to lay aside their hankering after the flesh pots of Britain.[1]

Yesterday opened the Election for their City Members, a very contested one was expected. I am sorry to hear that some Men bid fair to succeed who are very unequal to the task of Legislation.[2]

The danceing Assembly met with great opposition, some from Religious, or others from Politicle motives opposed it, but the *Loyal* Managers, (Augustus Van Courtland and Daniel Ludlow) resigning, and expunging some of their rules appeased the populace and they have carryed them into execution.[3] A private Ball at the Chancellors, another at Uncle P. V. B. Livingston's in Compliment to his Excellency General Washington, (as he quartered there) are all I have heard of.

Your friend Dr. Bancroft spent some time with us going and returning from New York. Mr. Holker introduced him and has assured us that the Doctor had not had for several years so agreeable a relaxation from Politicks. When I last heard from Philadelphia that gentleman was prepareing to sail for Charles Town, but the weather seting in very severe shortly after it is probable has detained him. The Doctor did not leave us without a promise to repeat his visit in the Spring. I shall consider his doing it a mark of his approbation of the reception we gave him. A more agreeable visitor we could not have entertained, as he gave us a more particular account respecting your health and family than any we have received since your residence in France. I believe I mentioned in a former letter that we had not the pleasure of seeing Mrs. Izard. And Colonel Ogden, if I may judge from his remissness, must make another Voyage to Europe to be instructed in good breeding.

Mr. Robert Morris I hear seems determined to quit the first of next May; then G[ouverneur] M[orris] will, I suppose, return to his *Mammy.*

We have never been so at a loss to tell where you are as at present not having received any letters of a later date than August. Are Mr. and Mrs. Ridley in Paris or London, the Doctor and Mr. Holker differed on that subject. If it be not premature will you wish them joy for me. I wrote to Mrs. Ridley the same time I writ to Sister and intended it to go from Phila[delphia] that you should hear from us before the Arrival of Sir Guy. Sisters letter I detained to go with Major Upham at his particular request. Mr. Holker thought proper to bring back the letter and send it in the LOrient Packet, which must have occasioned its very late arrival.

The Legislature of this State having risen we are hourly expecting my Father home. By the enclosed letter you will see its determined that Master Peter stays with us this Winter. He is very ambitious to write equal to his Aunt Susan his instructer. This morning, as I was looking over him, I read his copy for the day—*Commend virtuous deeds.* I must do more than that, says he, I must imitate them. He has read Robinson Crusoe and Don Quixote. He is now reading Nature Delineated[4] and is exceedingly pleased with the natural History they contain. He begins the exercise of the day and closes the same with reading a few Chapters in the Bible. He has learnt many of the hymns in the book you sent him and frequently expresses a great desire to see you and his Mamma. He enjoys good health and is often complimented with having his Mamma's complextion. It is indeed sun and frost proof. His under teeth are like Sally's, the upper ones that have made their appearance are rather larger, they are perfectly white, but foul the soonest of any I ever saw. As we have paid attention to drawing the decayed and those that were in the way, they have every chance of being sound and well cut.

Your brother Fady and Mrs. Jay are well. Nancy and Peter I suppose as much so as usual or I should have heard to the contrary. In the spring I intend to pay them a visit. Would this Winter if it were practicable and I were sure it would be convenient to them. Kiss Sally and your sweet babes for me, and I'll pay you with interest when we have the pleasure of meeting. Mamma, Susan and Peter unite with me in Love to Sister and you. Your Affectionate Friend and Sister,

C. W. L.

ALS. Endorsed: ". . . Recd 1 Apr 1784." Enclosure not located. Omissions in *HPJ,* III, 101–03.

[1]When arch-Loyalist Charles Inglis resigned the rectorship of Trinity Church on 1 Nov. 1783, Trinity's Loyalist Corporation replaced him with assistant minister Benjamin Moore (1748–1816). The self-authorized "Whig Episcopalian" faction, led by Robert R. Livingston and James Duane, failed to force Moore's resignation and

therefore petitioned the Council for the Southern District for his removal. The Council vested temporary control of the Church, pending legislative action by New York State, in the hands of nine trustees including Duane, William Duer, and Lewis Morris. Early in February the trustees appointed as rector Samuel Provoost (1742–1815), assistant minister of Trinity Church from 1766 to 1771, who had resigned because of Trinity's growing Loyalist congregation. Although refusing to acknowledge the legality of Provoost's appointment, Moore resigned on 7 February. On 17 April 1784 the New York State legislature passed "An Act for making such Alterations in the Charter of the Corporation of Trinity Church as to render it more conformable to the Constitution of the State." The new vestry elected Provoost rector on 22 April 1784, in effect separating Trinity Church from English control and making it a unit of the Church in America in communion with the Church of England. Morgan Dix, *et al., A History of the Parish of Trinity Church in the City of New York* (6 vols., New York, 1898–1962), II, 1–25, 245–54; *Laws of the State of New York* (2 vols., New York, 1789), I, 128–31. For Charles Inglis and Lewis Morris, see *JJ,* I, 86 and 173, respectively.

[2]From 29 December to 5 Jan. 1784 the city's electors chose representatives to the State Assembly and Senate. For Robert R. Livingston's comments on the election results, see his 25 Jan. 1784 letter to JJ, below. Sidney I. Pomerantz, *New York: An American City, 1783–1803* (New York, 1938), pp. 26, 29.

[3]On 3 Dec. 1783 *Rivington's New-York Gazette* carried a notice for a meeting "to take into Consideration the Propriety of establishing a Dancing Assembly," signed by the Assembly's managers Augustus Van Cortlandt, Nicholas Fish (1758–1833), Lewis Scott, and Henry Brockholst Livingston. The managers postponed the opening of the Assembly from 18 December until the 23rd in order to be "fully prepared." An unsigned article in the 22 December *Independent Journal or the General Advertiser* promised that "the greatest care had been taken to exclude every character, whose admission could possibly give a pang to a real Whig." *Rivington's New-York Gazette,* 3, 13, and 17 Dec. 1783. For the Dancing Assembly prior to the Revolution, see *JJ,* I, 116. For Daniel Ludlow, see *JJ,* I, 114.

[4]Noel Antoine Pluche's (1688–1761) *Nature Delineated: being a new translation of those universally admired philosophical conversations, entitled, Spectacle de la Nature, compiled originally for the rational amusement of young noblemen* (4 vols., London, 1739), and numerous other English editions translated from his *Spectacle de la Nature* (Paris, 1732).

FROM PETER JAY MUNRO

Chaillot, 4 January 1784

Dear uncle,

A few minutes ago we had satisfaction of receiving your letter of the 22 ult.[1] We are mortified that your business detains you so long from us, but rejoice to find your health has mended since your arrival at Bath. My aunt is very well and is at present writing to you. Children enjoy exceeding good health. Nancy is remarkably quiet. By this time you must have received our letters mentioning Abbigail's Death. She never kept the Servants in such awe as since her Death. Her *Friend* Ben[2] dares not stir without a Candle. C'est elle! follows the least noise that is heard. One was terribly frightened at seeing herself in the Glass

(I think with reason); the Snow falling off the house set another aroaring, shook his bed exceedingly and I am not sure but what it caused it geting a wetting also. What is worse we can not persuade them it was not a Spirit. Daily, or rather nightly, some thing happens which frightens them, and sets us a laughing.

I am, Dear uncle, Your affectionate nephew,

PETER JAY MUNRO

DftS in NNMus: Jay.

[1]JJ to SLJ, 22 Dec. 1783, ALS in Rendell coll.

[2]For JJ's conditional manumission of Benoit, see below 21 March 1784.

FROM GOUVERNEUR MORRIS

Philadelphia, 10 January 1784

Dear Jay,

I write to acknowledge your Letter of the twenty fourth of September.[1] Being uncertain where you are, and consequently what Course this Letter may take, and thro what Hands it will pass, I shall not say so much as I otherwise might. I will direct to the care of Doctor Franklin.

Your Attachment to America when removed from it, is the old Story of Travellers; but when it comes from one in whose Feelings we feel an Interest, decies repetita placebit.[2] Of your Health you speak despondingly, yet say your Spirits are good. Believe me, my Friend, good Spirits will both make and preserve good Health. I mean to extend this Observation generally but not universally. Whatever Lott besides us I wish you at least one happy year, and I hope that Heaven will do you the Justice to grant a long Succession of them. Make my good Wishes acceptable to Mrs. Jay, and present me tenderly to your Children.

I was lately in New York, and have the Pleasure to tell you that all your friends were well. Things there are now in that kind of Ferment which was rationally to have been expected; and I think the superior Advantages of our Constitution will now appear in the Repressing of those turbulent Spirits who wish for Confusion, because that in the regular order of things they can only fill a subordinate Sphere.

This Country has never yet been known to Europe, and God knows whether it ever will be so. To England, it is less known than to any other part in Europe, because they constantly view it thro a Medium either of Prejudice or of Faction. True it is that the general Government wants Energy, and equally true it is that this Want will eventually be supplied. A national Spirit is the natural Result of national Existence, and altho some of the present Generation may feel colonial Oppositions of Opinion, that Generation will die away and give Place to a Race of Americans. On this Occasion, as on others, Great Britain is our best Friend, and by seizing the critical Moment when we were about to divide, she has shewn clearly the dreadful Consequences of Division. You will find that the States are coming into Resolutions on the Subject of Commerce, which if they had been proposed by Congress on the plain Reason of the Thing, would have been rejected with Resentment and perhaps contempt.

With Respect to our Taste for Luxury, do not grieve about it. Luxury is not so bad a Thing as it is often supposed to be, and if it were, still we must follow the Course of Things and turn to Advantage what exists since we have not the Power either to annihilate or create. The very Defenition of Luxury is as difficult as the Suppression of it, and if I were to declare my serious Opinion, it is that there is a lesser Proportion of Whores and Rogues in Coaches than out of them. If I am mistaken, I shall say, with the poor roman Catholic, it is a pleasing Error, for my intimate Acquaintance lies among those who ride in Coaches.

Do not condemn us till you see us. Do not ask the British to take off their foolish Restrictions. Let them alone and they will be obliged to do it of themselves. While the present Regulation exists it does us more of political Good, than it can possibly do of commercial Evil.

Adieu. Believe me always Yours,

GOUV. MORRIS

ALS in RAWC. Endorsed: ". . . by Col. Harmar Recd. 1 Ap 1784." DftS in NNC: Gouverneur Morris.

[1]JJ's letter of 24 Sept. 1783, Dft in JP; omissions in *WJ*, 130–32 and in *HPJ*, III, 82–85. Therein JJ expresses his affection for America, urges enlarging the powers of the Confederation, injecting vigor into state governments, along with the prompt settlement of boundary disputes and the promotion of union, and indicates some concern about reports abroad of the spread of luxury in Philadelphia.

[2]"Though ten times repeated, it will continue to please."

Last Days in France

Social pleasantries aside, the Jays were understandably eager to get home as soon as they properly could, staying in France only until peace was concluded and the Spanish accounts settled. It was Congress rather than the British government that held up ratification of the Definitive Treaty. By mid-December the delegates from only seven states had made their appearance at Annapolis, the nation's temporary capital, whereas the assent of nine states was required for ratification under the Articles of Confederation. Finally on 14 January 1784 delegates from two other states took their seats, and Congress proceeded at once to vote unanimous ratification. It still was necessary to transmit the ratification to Paris in compliance with the terms of the treaty, and only a bare six weeks remained to meet the treaty's deadline. Three different agents were entrusted with copies of the ratification. All were delayed by accidents of weather. Colonel Joseph Harmar reached Paris first, arriving the end of March, and just ahead of Colonel David Franks, who reached London the next day. Technically, the ratification had come too late, but the British Ministry waived the point, and on the twelfth of May Franklin and Jay for the United States and Hartley for Great Britain amicably exchanged ratifications in Paris.[1]

The settlement of the Spanish accounts, both public and private, depended upon the cooperation and personal presence in Paris of Carmichael. The Jay-Carmichael relationship continued to be so tense and the negotiations so protracted that the subject merits a separate account.[2] Financial affairs finally straightened out, the Jays left Paris on 16 May, and sailed from Dover 1 June on the *Edward,* Captain Coupar.

[1]Morris, *Peacemakers,* pp. 447–48.
[2]See editorial note below, "Settling the Spanish Accounts."

From Charles Thomson

Annapolis, 14 January 1784

Dear Sir,

I received your favour by Mr. Thaxter with the prints enclosed.[1] We are at a loss what to think of this new invention, or what the curious will make of it if real. Time must determine whether it is only for the amusement of Children or may be improved to useful purposes.

I sincerely congratulate you on the return of peace, and it is my most ardent prayer that the U.S. may improve the Opportunity now afforded of becoming a happy people. The treaty was this day ratified being the first day we have had nine states since the last of October.[2]

The ratification is forwarded by Col. J. Harmar the bearer whom I beg leave to recommend to your particular attention and civility.

Mrs. T.[3] desires to be remembered to Mrs. Jay, to whom you will please to make my most respectful compliments. I am with sincere esteem and regard, Your Most Obedient and most humble Servant

CHAS. THOMSON

ALS. Addressed: "The honble. John Jay Minister plenipotentiary of the United States at Paris." Endorsed: ". . . by Col. Harmar, ansd 7 Ap. 1784." C in DLC: Charles Thomson. *HPJ,* III, 105–06, omits opening paragraph.

[1]JJ to Charles Thomson, 12 Sept. 1783, Dft in JP in the hand of Peter Jay Munro; ALS in DLC: Charles Thomson; *HPJ,* III, 76–77; *RDC,* VI, 694–95; New-York Hist. Soc., *Collections,* I (1879), 175–76. The prints evidently illustrated the balloon ascension.

[2]The unanimous resolution to ratify is in *JCC,* XXVI, 23.

[3]Hannah Harrison Thomson.

From Charles Thomson

Annapolis, 15 January 1784

Dear Sir,

Though I am sensible that Lieut. Col. D. S. Franks, who is the bearer of this needs no introduction or recommendation to you, yet I cannot suffer him to go without a line from me. He is intrusted with a triplicate Ratification of the definitive treaty, which passed yesterday, the first time we have had nine states represented since October last, and which was done with the unanimous consent not only of every state but of every member in Congress. The proclamation[1] and recommendation[2] of which he carries copies passed also with a like unanimous Consent, so that I have strong hopes the treaty will be carried into full effect, and that when the passions of the people are cooled a spirit of conciliation will prevail. But considering what many have suffered, whose feelings are still alive and whose wounds are not yet closed and considering that our new established governments have not attained their full tone and vigour, it can hardly be expected that people will in a moment forget what is past and suddenly return to an interchange of friendly offices with those, whom for years past they have considered as their most bitter enemies.

My apprehensions are greatest from your state where the people have suffered most, and yet there is such a spirit and vigour in that government, that I trust matters will be conducted with prudence and moderation. We have had no delegates from that state since the first

Monday in November, occasioned as I am informed by a law of the state which prevented the meeting of the Assembly till the city was evacuated. However as the Assembly is now met we expect delegates will soon be sent.[3]

There has been a scene for six months past over which I would wish to draw a veil. I may perhaps have an opportunity of explaining myself farther. However the prospect begins to brighten and as I love to indulge a hope which corresponds with my fond wishes I flatter myself that prudence and good sense will prevail.

Mrs. Thomson desires to be affectionately remembered to Mrs. Jay, to whom you will please to present my Compliments.

I wrote to you yesterday by Col. Harmar who was immediately dispatched with a ratification of the treaty by the Packet from New York. He carried with him a duplicate to be forwarded by Mr. Morris.

I am with sincere esteem and affection, Dear Sir, Your obedient and humble Servant,

CHAS. THOMSON

ALS. Addressed: "Honble John Jay, minister plenipoty. of the United States of America, Paris. Favoured by Col. D. S. Franks." Endorsed: ". . . Recd. 12 Ap 1784 by Co. Franks." C in DLC: Charles Thomson. Omissions in *HPJ,* III, 106–07, and *LMCC,* VII, 417.

[1]The 14 January Proclamation affirmed the passage of the Definitive Treaty and called upon the States to observe its terms. See also below, Franklin and JJ to Hartley, 31 March 1784. *JCC,* XXVI, 29–30.

[2]Pursuant to the fifth article of the Definitive Treaty, the 14 January "recommendation" to the state legislatures, unanimously resolved by Congress, urged the restoration of Loyalist estates confiscated between 30 Nov. 1782 and 14 Jan. 1783. *JCC,* XXVI, 30–31.

[3]On 3 Feb. 1784, the New York State Senate and Assembly elected Charles De Witt, John Lansing, Jr., Walter Livingston, Alexander McDougall, and Ephraim Paine (1730–85) as delegates to the Continental Congress. Paine was the first to attend on 25 March, but neither McDougall nor Lansing attended in 1784. *JCC,* XXVI, 165–67. For Walter Livingston, see *JJ,* I, 186.

From Robert R. Livingston

New York, 25 January 1784

Dear John,

Your brother is just returned from Rie and informs me that he left Peter and Nancy there in health and as well situated as they could expect though not quite as well as they could wish the delay of the season having prevented their making <the> many necessary repairs.

We are all in great expectations of the fulfilment of your promise and hope to embrace you in the spring. The quiet which I mentioned to have prevailed here when I last wrote you[1] has met with few interruptions accept [sic] that Rivington has been beat by N. Cruger[2] and intimidated by the committee of Mechanicks so as to be induced to stop his press. The impudence of the tories have in some instances given a handle to the warm whigs to attack them. Our extreme moderation gave them confidence, and not content with protection they sought for power, particularly in filling up the vacancy in the vestry with violent Royalists and appointing Mr. Moore, whose conduct has been extremely reprehensible, Rector of Trinity Church <and continuing> about 10 Days before we came in and continuing him in spite of the earnest request of the whig members. This ended in a petition to the Legislature, who upon a presumption that the charter was suspended with the other laws of the state during the government of the british in the City, made void this election and vested the temporalities of the church in nine trustees till the charter could be reorganized, for which purpose a law is now before them.[4]

Our parties at present consist of three kinds: the Tories who still hope for power under the Idea that all remembrance of what has passed should be lost, though they omit no occasion to shew their attachment to Britain and their aversion to our government. The warm and hotheaded whigs who are for the expulsion of all tories from the <government> State and who would wish even to render the more moderate whigs suspected in order to preserve in their own hands all the powers of Government. The third are those who wish at present to suppress all violences, to soften the rigorous laws with respect to the tories by degrees, as they see their party broken and the remembrance of their past misdeeds obliterated; who are unwilling to injure them either in their persons or property or to banish them from that social intercourse which may by degrees wear down mutual prejudices. But who at the same time think it improper to loose immediately all distinction between the virtuous Citizen that has done his duty <of the Community> at the expence of every thing he holds dear. And those that have preferred their personal interests to those of the community, who would wish not to shock the feelings of the first by obliging them to submit to the last, but who would rather that this distinction should be found in the sentiments of the people than that it should be marked out by the Laws.

Certain disqualifications in the election Law passed before the evacuation have given those that are supposed to be the second of these parties the appointment of representatives for this district.

They are Lamb, Sears, Willet, Hughes, Van Zandt, Rutgers, Harpur, Stag.[5] However I am not without hopes from the weight of the characters which form the third party that they will prevent those violences which the second may meditate and support a respect for the laws which indeed I must do <them> all parties the justice to say they profess and that they have yet by no act contradicted that profession.

You will receive with this a ratification of the treaty. Congress are now convened at Annapolis.[6] The object of general politics which most ingages our attention at present is the West India trade which we consider as of the utmost moment. The several states are about to empower Congress to restrict the commerce of Britain till she opens that trade to us.[7]

This is a short sketch of our general and particular politicks which I should not have thought is worth while to trouble you with <but that it might> had I not imagined that every thing here must be interesting to you if you realy mean to execute your plan of returning so soon to us. I have particular reasons for wishing that return had been hastened since I want your aid in a very interesting suit that I have commenced against Hoffman[8] and in a dispute which has unhappily arisen between me and the uper Manor in both of which your advice would be of singular use to me even if (as I suppose) you should not return to the bar.

The number of real estates that are daily selling here belonging to persons that are about to leave the state together with confiscated property which will be sold in the spring, the scarcity of money and the high price of bills open a great field for speculation if a man had such credit in Europe as to be enabled to draw about 6 or 8000 £ on six weeks sight. I wish as you are upon the spot that you would endeavour to establish such a credit for me upon some good house <either in England or Holland>. I will allow six per cent for the Money, and give real security to any agent that may be appointed here to take it for so much as I shall draw. If this can not be done in England it may be easily done in Holland on your representation of the security. I have also thought that at this critical moment Lady Warrens (now Colonel Skinners estate) might be purchased on good terms if you think so and chuse to be concerned.[9] I wish you to make it on our joint account taking up money in England to pay for it provided it does not exceed £ 6000 Sterling. Coll. Skinner purchased it at 5000, since which it has suffered greatly by the destruction of all the wood, etc., and if I mistake not he will be compelled by <some> good round taxes to part with it.[10]

Business and politicks have already extended this Letter to such an unreasonable length that I dare not hazard another nearer my heart than others but must at this time confine all it dictates to simple assurances of the sincere and inviolable friendship with which I am, Dear John, unalterably Your's.

Dft in NHi: Robert R. Livingston. Endorsed by Livingston. ALS in JP, endorsed by JJ: ". . . Recd. 12 Ap 1784 by Col. Franks." E in NN: Bancroft: American. Substantial omissions in *WJ*, II, 145–46, and in *HPJ*, III, 108–09, owing to deletions by William Jay. The ALS is a shorter and more temperate version of the Dft, with the exception noted.

[1]See above, Livingston to JJ, 29 Nov. 1783.

[2]New York and West India merchant Nicholas Cruger (1743–1800), son of Henry Cruger, Sr.; see *JJ*, I, 81, 101.

[3]Rivington and Cruger are not mentioned in the ALS.

[4]For Trinity Church, see above, Catharine W. Livingston to JJ, 30 Dec. 1783, n. 1.

[5]Elected to represent the City and County of New York in the 7th session of the State Assembly, convened 21 January, were: Robert Harpur, John Lamb, Isaac Sears, Peter Van Zandt (1730–1812), John Stagg (1732–1803), William Malcolm, Henry Rutgers (1745–1830), Henry Hughes, and Marinus Willett. For Harpur, Malcolm, and Willett, see *JJ*, I, 432, 623, and 245, respectively.

[6]In the ALS, much more condemnatory of Congress, Livingston speaks of "their curious resolution to have two places of residence, of which they are by this time ashamed and tired."

[7]See the editorial note above, "Negotiating a Trade Treaty."

[8]In the October 1784 term of the Supreme Court held at Albany, Livingston brought an action of ejectment against Zachariah Hoffman. The dispute, which goes back to 1744, concerned certain lands on the southern boundary of Livingston's estate, Clermont. Livingston acted as his own attorney, while Hoffman was represented by Egbert Benson, Alexander Hamilton, and Aaron Ogden (d. 1839). Livingston won his suit, and Hamilton later lost his motion for a new trial. The matter was eventually settled by a compromise. Dangerfield, *Livingston,* pp. 183–84, 480n. For Ogden, see also *JJ*, I, 687.

[9]The vast colonial and European land holdings of Admiral Sir Peter Warren (1703–52), were inherited by his wife Susannah De Lancey Warren (1707–71), who entrusted the management of her New York City property to her brother Oliver De Lancey. Livingston's reference is to Warren's 300-acre Greenwich Village estate, which upon Lady Warren's death was inherited by her daughters and managed jointly by her brother and her sons-in-law Colonel William Skinner (d. 1780), Major-General Charles Fitzroy (1737–97), and Willoughby Bertie, Earl of Abingdon (1740–99). One of the few estates of a Loyalist absentee landlord to remain intact throughout the Revolution, the Warren properties in New York City and Cortlandt were divided among Fitzroy, Abingdon, and Colonel Skinner's daughter, Susanna Maria Skinner (1744–1821). Julian Gwyn, *The Enterprising Admiral* (Montreal, 1974), pp. 36, 47, 64–68.

[10]The ALS includes the postscript: "Since writing the above I am more doubtful whether Lady Warren's estate would turn out a good purchase at the rate I mention. I could only therefore wish you to inquire at What it may be got."

Settling the Spanish Accounts

28 January–15 May 1784

Not knowing when he left Madrid in May of 1782 whether or not he could return after completing his assignment in Paris, JJ decided to keep for the time being the rented home his family had been occupying. He departed for France before either his personal accounts in Spain or those of the government could be settled, leaving such matters in the charge of William Carmichael, Secretary of the mission. These settlements dragged out for some two years, during which time JJ kept prodding Carmichael for an accounting. A peremptory, and even sarcastic, tone crept into JJ's letters, with Carmichael adopting in response an air of injured innocence and chilly courtesy.

Initially, Carmichael was directed to sublease the house and to dispose of JJ's four mules, but enjoined from taking any other action without specific instructions.[1] Meanwhile there had been dishearteningly little progress in settling the accounts. Just as JJ was leaving Spain it was learned that Carbarrús' banking house had failed to distinguish properly between American government funds entrusted to its care and JJ's personal funds.[2] When Cabarrús pressed for prompt settlement, Carmichael advised him that, until the records were disentangled, that would be impossible.[3] Seemingly, it would have been to Cabarrús' advantage to get this accomplished quickly, but more urgent matters kept claiming his attention and that of his staff. As weeks went by, Carmichael was forced to report periodically to JJ that he had not yet received a corrected version of the two separate accounts.[4]

Absent a complete accounting by the Spanish banker, Carmichael sought to reconstruct all past transactions, but toward the end of July of 1782, he conceded that his calculations were "as exact as it could be" without having Cabarrús' figures or "having carefully Compared his receipts with the Charges made to his Debits." Finally, on 19 August Carmichael was able to write his superior that he had received Cabarrús' revised figures.[5] Transmitting JJ's private account, he informed JJ that he intended to retain the public one until he could verify its accuracy, and to do this he needed Cabarrús' receipts in JJ's hands. In his reply of 9 October below, JJ confessed that he could be of no help since all of his banking transactions with Cabarrús had been made through Carmichael. When months went by without further clarification from the Secretary of the mission, JJ on 30 January 1783 dispatched a chilly letter demanding satisfactory data about both accounts.[6]

Failing to obtain what he considered proper cooperation from Carmichael, JJ first turned to Robert Morris, requesting that the public account be sent to Philadelphia.[7] Then, when he learned that Thomas Barclay, the vice-consul to France, had been appointed commissioner to examine and settle the accounts of all American officials in Europe,[8] he recognized the necessity of having

Carmichael come to Paris with all his records in order to explain his bookkeeping not only to the official examiner's satisfaction but to JJ's as well. On 1 June 1783, JJ urged Congress to issue instructions to that effect,[9] but even before waiting for a reply from America he went ahead and on his own authority ordered Carmichael to the French capital.[10]

Carmichael's answer was respectful but unresponsive.[11] The accounts, he conceded, did deserve early attention, but he felt obliged to stay in Spain until directed by Congress to go elsewhere. Unwilling to rely entirely on his own judgment, he had talked with Montmorin, who agreed with him completely and who was writing separately to explain his reasoning. Montmorin's letter to JJ reached Paris before Carmichael's did,[12] prompting JJ to suspect that his assistant was evading him while using the French ambassador to fight his battles. JJ's rebuke of 14 August is printed below. Carmichael replied, respectfully but stiffly, that their ideas of duty differed and that he still declined to come.[13] Montmorin received JJ's politely phrased acknowledgment, which lacked its customary warmth.[14]

JJ now had second thoughts. On 22 August he sent off a more conciliatory letter to Carmichael, in which he suggested that Barclay might be induced to conduct the audit in Spain.[15] In turn, Carmichael expressed his appreciation of JJ's increased understanding of his position and added that his reluctance to leave had been attributable to preparations related to his forthcoming presentation to the royal family.[16] For the time being JJ was content to let the matter rest, but on learning early the next year that he had Congress' backing, he renewed his request that Carmichael deliver the accounts both to Barclay and himself in Paris. Unwilling to disobey Congress, Carmichael reported that he would shortly leave but that in the meantime he found it necessary to explain his trip to a suspicious Floridablanca.[17]

Satisfied that he himself was never returning to Spain, JJ had on 20 September 1783 directed his assistant to give up the house, pay the rent due, and dismiss the porter.[18] According to local custom, JJ had been forced to purchase some equipment that went with the house, such as attached looking glasses and the wallpaper, and the cost of these was to be passed along to the next tenant. Most of the furniture had been obtained from a dealer who had guaranteed to buy it back at three-quarters of the original price, an option Carmichael was to exercise unless he wished to buy some or all of the pieces himself. Other miscellaneous furniture and equipment was to be sold, except for the portraits of famous Americans, which were to be given to the Abbé O'Ryan, and the liquor, which Carmichael was to accept as a gift. On receipt of these instructions, Carmichael sent word that he had begun taking inventory and would resell to the dealer only if he could not get a better price elsewhere.[19] JJ's concern, however, was about quick liquidation rather than the total sum realized, as he indicated in his letter of 28 January, 1784, below.

At long last Carmichael journeyed to Paris in March 1784 for the express purpose of settling the accounts.[20] Nonetheless, as appears from Jay's Notes below, he did little or nothing about them until pressured by JJ, who reminded Carmichael that his dilatory conduct was holding up the departure of the Jays for America and that he should bring the public accounts to Barclay who was now back in Paris.[21]

JJ experienced less delay in obtaining his own financial statement,[22] but he was so displeased by what he found therein that he was prompted to write Carmichael a nine-page letter itemizing his complaints.[23] Instead of accepting the wines and liquors as a present, Carmichael had entered them as a debt owed to JJ and then recorded the identical amount as a charge against JJ for "Sundry Expenses attending sales," a procedure that JJ found unspecific and unsatisfactory. Furthermore, Carmichael should have obtained receipts from Lewis Littlepage for moneys advanced him, he failed to account for several pieces of furniture, and some of his figures did not balance.

Worst of all, JJ complained, Carmichael had badly mishandled the cash advances he was supposed to have been making to the wife of Manuel Egusquiza, a servant of the Jays who had accompanied them to Paris. These advances were to be deducted from Manuel's wages when his employment terminated. Although explicitly requested to inform JJ what he had advanced Manuel's wife,[24] Carmichael never did report the amount he dispensed. When JJ turned to his servant's wife, she answered that Carmichael denied having instructions to pay her anything, but she said that he had kindly lent her some of his own money, which Manuel was to repay when he returned home.[25] She also said that Carmichael did not want SLJ to learn about these transactions "to avoid Questions," adding that he was "scandalized" about something unspecified that SLJ had done to Manuel. On the basis of this communication, which must have been unsettling to one already disposed to regard Carmichael with something less than complete enthusiasm, JJ paid his departing servant in full.[26] When JJ now learned that the mission's Secretary had advanced Manuel's wife a sum exceeding what her husband had earned in France and that this amount had been entered as a debt owed by him to Carmichael, his reaction was predictable, and his letter reflected his state of mind.[27]

Receiving no reply to this letter, JJ sent off a two-sentence note, written in the third person and dated "May 1784," demanding to know when he would receive an answer to his previous letter and when they would meet to conclude their business.[28] Carmichael finally showed up in answer to this summons, and the private account was settled at Paris on 12 May.[29] The antagonists compromised on the sums paid Manuel's wife; JJ had objected to the figure of 1,200 reals in the preliminary accounting, but now agreed to pay two-thirds of that amount.

JJ's public accounts were turned over to Barclay on 14–15 May, and, most important, included an itemized list of loans advanced JJ by the Spanish government.[30] When Alexander Hamilton became Secretary of the Tresury he accepted this total of $174,011, to which was added interest calculated at five per cent from the date of the loan, amounting to an additional $99,007.89. This combined total of $273,018.89, was paid to the Spanish government by William Short, the American minister to The Hague, during his sojourn in Spain in 1793.[31]

A few moments remained between JJ and Carmichael. The latter, in an effort at reconciliation, talked frankly with his superior. Carmichael denounced Littlepage for having played a double game and given the impression that JJ had left his ward in Madrid "to be a spy upon him and given him a cypher to enable him to convey his advice more safely and securely." JJ assured Carmichael that this was "a most impudent falsehood," a denial the former was obliged to assert publicly when Littlepage on his return to the States would revive the charges.[32]

[1]Carmichael had a prospect for the house but none for the mules. Carmichael to JJ, 28 May 178[2], 8 June, 9, 23–24 July 1782, all ALS in JP. On 3 August JJ wrote that he decided to retain possession of the house temporarily, but to dispose of the mules at any price and dismiss the mulekeeper and all other servants except the porter. JJ to Carmichael, 3 Aug. 1782, DftS in JP. By 18 October Carmichael could report that he had been able to dispose of three of the mules, but the fourth, having gone lame, was unsalable. Carmichael to JJ, 19, 21 Aug., 18 Oct. 1782, all ALS in JP.

[2]Cabarrús and Lelannes to JJ, 18 May 1782; Carmichael to JJ, 20 May 1782, all ALS in JP.

[3]Carmichael to JJ, 28 May 1782.

[4]Carmichael to JJ, 8 June, 3 July, 23 July 1782, all ALS in JP. An interim statement from Cabarrús, dated 25 June 1782, also in JP, admitted to an error of omission but did nothing to clarify the situation.

[5]Carmichael to JJ, 19 Aug. 1782, ALS in JP.

[6]JJ to Carmichael, 30 Jan. 1783, Dft in JP.

[7]JJ to Robert Morris, 21 April 1783, Dft in JP.

[8]*JCC,* XXIII, 728–30 (18 Nov. 1782).

[9]JJ to Robert R. Livingston, 1 June 1783, ALS in PCC 89, II: 472–73; Dft in JP; LbKCs in PCC 110, III, and in JP.

[10]JJ to Carmichael, 1 July 1783, Dft in JP.

[11]Carmichael to JJ, 1 Sept. 1783, ALS in JP.

[12]Montmorin to JJ, 31 July 1783, ALS in JP.

[13]Carmichael to JJ, 1 Sept. 1783, ALS in JP.

[14]JJ to Montmorin, 14 Aug. 1783, Dft in JP.

[15]JJ to Carmichael, 22 Aug. 1783, Dft in JP.

[16]Carmichael to JJ, 28 Sept. 1783, ALS in JP.

[17]Carmichael to JJ, 16 Feb. 1784, ALS in JP.

[18]JJ to Carmichael, 20 Sept. 1783, DftS in JP.

[19]Carmichael to JJ, 12 Oct. 1783, ALS in JP.

[20]Carmichael to JJ, 12 Mar. 1784, ALS in JP, indicates that the Secretary had left Madrid on 3 March, reached Bayonne on 11 March, and expected to be in Paris shortly thereafter, actually arriving on 27 March. See below, "Jay's Paris Notes Concerning William Carmichael"; also JJ to Charles Thomson, 7 April 1784, *HPJ,* III, 123.

[21]JJ to Carmichael, 11, 19 April 1784, Dfts in JP.

[22]Papers relating to the settlement of JJ's personal account were enclosed in Carmichael to JJ, 15 April 1784, ALS in JP.

[23]JJ to Carmichael, 24 April 1784, Dft in JP.

[24]See JJ to Carmichael, 9 Oct. 1782, below.

[25]Señora Egusquiza to Señor Manuel Egusquiza, 16 Oct. 1782, E in Spanish in JP. JJ quoted this letter in its entirety in Spanish and then translated it into English in JJ to Carmichael, 24 April 1784, Dft in JP.

[26]Signed receipt for wages [2 April 1782], ADS in JP.

[27]JJ to Carmichael, 24 April 1784, n. 25.

[28]JJ to Carmichael, [6] May 1784, Dft in JP.

[29]Carmichael to JJ, 12 May 1784, ALS in JP.

[30]See above, Spanish loans obtained by JJ, [1 Jan. 1781–21 March 1782], and editorial note, "Issues in Negotiation." The accounts are in DNA: 11828, RG 39, Foreign Ledger of Public Agents in Europe, I, 132, 181, 188, 189, 192–97.

[31]An additional $74,087 was paid by the Secretary of the Treasury in satisfaction of advances made during the American Revolution to Oliver Pollock at New Orleans (*JJ*, I, 717). See Bemis, *Pinckney's Treaty*, pp. 325–334. An additional sum of $397,230 advanced by Spain to the United States was considered a subsidy.

[32]See *Letters, Being the Whole of the Correspondence Between the Honorable John Jay, Esq. and Mr. Lewis Littlepage* (Eleazar Oswald, ed., New York, 1786), pp. 41–42.

To William Carmichael

Hotel etc.,[1] Paris, 9 October 1782

Sir,

Your Favors of the 19 and 21 August are now before me.[2] In the former you say, *"I recieved Mr. Cabarrus's accounts stated I apprehend in the Manner you directed. This Change obliges me once more to compare them with the Bills of Exchange paid etc."* As I have never given Mr. Cabarrus any Directions about <stating> his accounts but through You, I can give you no new Information on that Subject, nor have I any Idea of the *Change* you speake of.

Doctor Franklin is desirous of having the <copies of the> accounts of the Bills,[3] which I desired you to make out for him before I left <you> Madrid. The sooner all these money matters are settled the better, for as they have all passed through your Hands, they could not (in case any accident should happen to you) be so easily liquidated by any Body else.

I shall be ready to settle Mr. Cabarrus's private account with me, whenever he shall authorize any person here on his Behalf to do it.

Be pleased also to send me your private account with me for as we are all Mortal, the sooner these kind of matters are settled the better.

Your Letter of the 21 August mentions your having paid Mr. Littlepage "a Quarters Salary," and you add, *"If this advance is Contrary to your Excellencys Intentions, I will place it to my own account."* You acknowledge the Reciept of my Letter of the 3d August. It contained the following paragraph, viz: "Mr. Littlepage writes me that *(agreable to my Consent,)* he had applied to and recieved from you sixty Dollars." I presume you did not attend to this Circumstance, or you could not have supposed it possible for me to accept your offer of placing that advance *to your own account.*

We have nothing new except a Report not yet confirmed that Madras is taken.[4] God grant it may be true. It is also said that the French have lost a 74 gun Ship off the Harbour of Boston,[5] and that Sir Samuel Hood had arrived on the American Coast with a Fleet superior to that of our allies.[6] <This is bad news.>

We are at present in tolerable, tho not very good, Health, but this is a good Climate and an agreable Place, and as <our> we are <always> in good Spirits and comfortably situated I flatter myself that Health will again be added to the number of our Blessings.

I fear my Mules and Servants have given you <a good Deal of> much Trouble. I hope the former are sold and none of the latter except the Porter retained. I wish to know how much you have paid to Manuels Wife (who is welcome to stay in the House) for otherwise I shall be at a Loss <to know how to> in settling with him.

Doctor Franklin has been much indisposed but is getting better.

I am Sir, Your most obedient and humble Servant.

Dft. Endorsed by JJ: ". . . in ansr to 19 and 21 Augt."

[1]Hôtel de la Chine at the Palais Royal.

[2]William Carmichael to JJ, 19 (enclosing JJ's account with Cabarrús) and 21 Aug. 1782, both ALS in JP.

[3]The bills drawn upon JJ by the Congress which Franklin had accepted for payment. See also Foreign Ledger of Public Agents in Europe, I, D in DNA: RG 39.

[4]The British South India presidency of Madras was unsuccessfully attacked by the French throughout 1782.

[5]On 9 Aug. 1782 the 74-gun French warship *Le Magnifique* sunk in Boston harbor after striking a submerged rock. On 3 September Congress voted to give the U.S. warship *America* to the French as compensation for their lost vessel. *JCC,* XXIII, 543.

[6]Under the command of Admiral Hugh Pigot (c. 1721–92) and Lord Admiral Samuel Hood (1724–1816), the British fleet anchored in New York harbor on 5 Sept. 1782 awaiting military action by de Vaudreuil. Pigot sailed on 24 October and Hood on 22 November without incident. James, *The British Navy in Adversity,* pp. 360–61.

To William Carmichael

Passy, 14 August 1783

Sir,

I have this moment recieved a Letter from His Excellency the Count de Montmorin,[1] in which he mentions your having communicated to him my Letter to you of the [———][2] ult. and also favors me with his Sentiments on the Subject of it. As that Letter was written by me in a public Capacity, to you in a public Capacity, and on public Business, I indulged the Expectation of recieving an answer to it from You.

When public Servants are officially called upon to settle their accounts, I think the ordinary current Business of their appointments must so far give way to that object, as may be necessary to the <occasion> <attainment> accomplishment of it. As the accounts in Question have been kept by you, as they have been increased since my absence, and as they should be brought here together with the original Vouchers and Documents in the safest Manner, I am still of Opinion that you should bring them here without Delay, and join with me in attending their Settlement.

Whatever may be your Determination, permit me to desire you to inform me of it explicitly by the Return of the Post.

I am, Sir, Your most obedient and humble Servant.

Dft.

[1]Montmorin to JJ, 31 July 1783, ALS in JP.

[2]Left blank in manuscript. The letter referred to is JJ to Carmichael, 1 July 1783, Dft in JP.

To William Carmichael

Paris, 28 January 1784

Sir,

Your letter of the 12th October[1] was delivered to me in England at a time when I was so ill, as to write only to Mrs. Jay. That Circumstance and the Constant Expectation of receiving the Letter you intended to write when the Appraisement you was making of my Effects should be finished, but which I have not yet received, are the Causes which have delayed my writing to you since. It is not necessary that I should enter into Particulars, because they may be more conveniently discussed when we meet. I subjoin to this Letter a Copy of the Resolution of Congress I lately received Dated the 1st October last, which obviates your former Objections to leaving Spain, and it is in pursuance of it that I now desire you to come here without Delay, and to bring with you all the Books, vouchers and Papers necessary to make a final and complete Settlement of the Accounts of public money which have passed through our Hands. I have no reason to think that the Interest of the United States will be injured by your Absence from Madrid for the Space of time necessary for the Purpose in question or that it will be attended with any other Inconveniences than such as would probably attend your Absence at any future Period.

If when you receive this Letter any of my Effects which I <have> requested You to sell should be undisposed of, you will oblige me greatly by causing them to be sold immediately to the highest Bidder for ready money, so that on your coming here, we may also be able to liquidate and Settle our private account. The Readiness with which you undertook to do that Business for me merits and has my Acknowledgments. Let not an apprehension of my sustaining Loss by the Instant Sale of those Effects restrain you from Turning them immediately into as much money as they will fetch, for I would rather submit to that loss then <to> leave any thing behind me of a private or indeed of a public nature unsettled, which may in the least depend upon me to adjust.

I wish you a safe and pleasant Journey, and am, Sir, Your most obedient and very humble Servant.

(signed) JOHN JAY

"In Congress, October 1st 1783. Resolved that Mr. Jay be authorized to direct Mr. Carmichael to repair to Paris should Mr. Jay be of opinion that the Interest of the United States at the Court of Madrid may not be injured by Mr. Carmichaels absence, and that he bring with him the Books and vouchers necessary to make a final and complete Settlement of the accounts of public money which have passed through the Hands of Mr. Jay himself and that Mr. Barclay attend Mr. Jay and Mr. Carmichael to adjust those accounts."

The aforegoing is a true Copy of the Extract sent me by President Boudinot in a letter of 1st Nov[embe]r last.

(signed) JOHN JAY

C in hand of Peter Jay Munro. Endorsed: "... In Ansr. to 12 Octr. last." Two other Dfts also in JP.

[1]See editorial note above, "Settling the Spanish Accounts."

Jay's Paris Notes Concerning William Carmichael

[Paris, 27 March–19 April 1784]

Mr. Carmichael was 9 days going from Madrid to Bayonne, from whence he wrote to me on 12 March and arrived at Paris 27 March 1784.

Mr. Barclay arrived Sunday, 11 April 1784. I gave notice of it same Day to Mr. Carmichael.

Monday, 12 April, Mr. Carmichael called on me in his way to Passy where he dines; is to see Barclay and call in the Evening.

Tuesday, 13 April, informed Mr. C. that Barclay and I had agreed that the accounts should be sent to his House, as he might work at them in our absence, and call for us as Difficulties might arise. Mr. C. promised to send the first part of them Tomorrow.

Wednesday, 14 April, this Evening Mr. C. was here, had not sent the accounts, promised to send them Tomorrow.

Friday, 16 April, recieved private accounts in Letter dated 15 Inst.

Saturday, 17 April, Mr. Barclay says, Mr. C. had not yet given him any accounts, alledging that the sending them to B[arclay's] House had made a new arrangement of them necessary. Would send them this Evening.

Sunday, 18 April, Mr. Barclay informed me this Evening that he had not yet recieved any accounts from Carmichael.

Monday morning, 19 April, wrote to Mr. C. on the Subject.

AD. JJ's letters of 11 and 19 April and Carmichael's of 15 April are cited in editorial note, above.

To John Adams

Chaillot, 6 February 1784

Dear Sir,

Dr. Franklin informs me, that in your Passage from England to Holland, you experienced many more difficulties than are common even at this rigid Season.[1] Mine from Dover to Calais, was far from being short or pleasant. Neptune however was less uncivil to me than to You. Neither of us have enjoyed much of his Favor, but I will forgive him with all my Heart, if he will let me pass once more in Safety through his Dominions. When, my Friend, shall we find ourselves by our own firesides, enjoying the Liberty and Security, for which we have suffered so many anxious Hours!

I presume that the state of affairs in Holland are by this Time in as good a State as you can put them; and therefore I think the objects stated in the papers you shewed me at Bath, render it proper that you should again give us the pleasure of your Company here.

My best Compliments to your Son. With sincere Esteem and Regard. I am, Dear Sir, Your Friend and Servant,

JOHN JAY

ALS in MHi: Adams XLV, 126. Dft in JP. Addressed: "His Excellency John Adams Esquire." Dft in JP.

[1]For Adams' rough passage from England to Holland, 5–8 Jan. 1784, and the ensuing overland journey to The Hague, see *AP,* III, 152.

FROM JOHN BARD

New York, 7 February 178[4]

Dear Sir,

Your very Obliging letter of the 23 of May[1] has come to my hands. I Thank you Sir for your kind and Friendly attention to me, which I shall always think of with Pleasure.

My Family has made two moves, First from hydepark to Belle Vale, and from thence to New York where we have been settled about three months, and where I think it Probable I shall remain the remainder of my life. These changes have been more in obedience to the taste and Inclynation of my Family than my own, which has ever been greatly Delighted with the amusements and Improvements of the country, which you have been most obligingly attentive to Gratify me in. Though I am moved to Town, It will allways give me great Pleasure to receive any Curious Uropian [sic] Productions, Especially from your hands.

I have long thoug[ht] with you that we have aboundant reason to be Satisfyed with our own Country, which is now Thank God rendered more Hapy by the reestablishment of Peace, which your Leabours have had so great a share in Promoteing, and which has rendered you so Justly Dear to your Country.

You Kindly complain my Dear Sir of not mentioning the state of health of my own Family, to whome you have given so many proofs of Friendship and respect. I wish I could give you a more agreeable account of them in this respect. In my own Family my Two Daughters have been very Ill of a very Dangerous and Contagious disease which began in my Sons[2] Family and by which he has lost three very fine children.[3] This Desease which has been an Epedemical Eruptive fever, attended with an Inflamation and Ulceration of the throat, has been very General and Fatal in this City. My Daughters have recovered, but these accidents have thrown both our Familys into much Distress.

I do very Earnestly hope your removal from Spain, and change of air and climate has perfectly restored your and Mrs. Jays health, to whome we all present our best Wishes. I am Dear Sir, Your affectionate Friend, and Humble Servant,

JOHN BARD

ALS, misdated "1783," endorsed: ". . . 7 Feb 1783—shd be 84, Recd. 1 Ap. 1784 by Col. Harmar."

Dr. John Bard (1716–99) practiced medicine in Philadelphia until 1746, when on the advice of Franklin he moved to New York City where he established a flourishing practice. A Loyalist, Bard retired to his Hyde Park farm in 1778, resuming his practice in New York City in 1783. He was reputed to be the first American physician to take part in a systematic dissection for the purpose of instruction and the first to report a case of extra-uterine pregnancy. John McVickar, *A Domestic Narrative of the Life of Samuel Bard* (New York, 1882), p. 7.

[1]Letter not located.

[2]Bard's son Samuel (M.D., Edinburgh, 1765) was a founder and faculty member of King's College Medical School which opened in 1767. A Loyalist, he was the only pre-Revolutionary faculty member to resume teaching duties when the Medical School was reestablished in 1785. Humphrey, *From King's College to Columbia,* pp. 242–48, 262; see also John Langstaff, *Doctor Bard of Hyde Park* (New York, 1942).

[3]Samuel Bard's three daughters, Sarah, Harriet, and Mary, succumbed to the scarlet fever and measles epidemics that swept New York City in the summer of 1783. Langstaff, *Doctor Bard,* p. 140; McVickar, *Samuel Bard,* p. 115.

From John Adams

The Hague, 13 February 1784

Dear Sir,

I have received a Letter from Mr. Gerry, at Philadelphia 23 Nov.[1] Thaxter arrived there the night before. I presume he has written by Mr. Reed,[2] and that his Letter is gone to You, as he probably addressed his Letter to Us all.

Mr. Morris has drawn afresh by this Vessell. Let me beg of you and the Doctor, to advise him to Stop his Hand. If I can possibly save those already drawn, which however I still despair of, it will be upon Terms so enormously avaricious, that it will raise a tremendous Clamour in

America. It is ruinous to borrow money in Europe upon such Terms but it will be more ruinous, to let the Bills go back.

I think I could not justify going to Paris, while the Fate of these Bills is depending. You will be so good as to go on with the Doctor in Execution of the last Instructions. If there is any Point, upon which you wish for my Opinion, I will give it you, with Pleasure, at any time, by Letter. Has Mr. Laurens declined acting? How is the Doctor's Health? And how is Mrs. Ridley?[3] If a Commission Should come to us all to treat with England, as it will be a thorny Work and likely to produce Discontents and Clamours, it is not my Intention to withdraw my Shoulders from any Part of the Burthen. You will pardon me for suggesting, that We ought to obtain if We can from every Power We treat with, an Article that American Produce imported into their Ports in American Bottoms, Shall pay no more duties then if imported in Vessels of the subjects of those Powers.

My Situation is very disagreable. It is not for me to judge of the Propriety of the draughts. I am only in a ministerial Capacity, and ought to procure the Money if possible, upon any Terms within my Instructions, but to be obliged to go to the Utmost Extent of them, when I know that Such Numbers will blame me for it, because they won't believe the necessity of it, is unpleasant.

There is a Despotism in this Country in the Government of Loans as absolute as that of the grand Senior. Five or Six People have all the Money under their Command, and they are as avaricious as any Jews in Jews Quarter. This Country revenges itself in this Way, upon the Powers of Europe for the Insults it receives from them in Wars and Negotiations.

Mr. Gerry desires his Respects And affection to you, in very strong and high terms; thinks the Removal of Congress has strengthened the Union, and that the British Proclamations, have had the Same Effect. My Respects to your good Family, and believe me, yours most Sincerely,

JOHN ADAMS

Will Denmark stipulate, that both her Islands in the West Indies shall be free Ports to Us?[4]

ALS. Endorsed.

[1]Elbridge Gerry's 18-page letter to Adams (MHi: Adams, reel 361) eulogizes JJ ("I consider it as an act of Justice, with a meretorious Washington and Green, to rank those that are equally so in my Mind, an Adams and Jay") and stresses JJ's loyalty to Adams: "Mr. Jay is very friendly to you, having written a Letter highly in your Favour to Congress, recommending you as Minister to the Court of London,

and declared his Refusal if the Office is offered to him." (JJ to Robert R. Livingston, 30 May 1783, duplicate and triplicate ALS in PCC 89, II, 468, 486; LbkCs in JP, PCC 110, III; *RDC*, VI 457–58). Condemning a Congressional bloc, whose "oligarchical influence" in Philadelphia, he felt, would be diluted by the new proposal to erect two "federal towns" for the Congress, Gerry advised Adams "to communicate what you think expedient to Mr. Jay and Mr. Dana, of the preceding Scroll."

[2]Joseph Reed had accompanied the Reverend John Witherspoon on an ill-fated European fund-raising mission for the College of New Jersey. John F. Roche, *Joseph Reed: A Moderate in the American Revolution* (New York, 1968), pp. 213–15. See also *JJ*, I, 562.

[3]Henry Laurens was in England to recover a personal claim of 2,800 from the British Treasury. For Anne Ridley, see JJ to Robert Morris, 25 Feb. 1784, below.

[4]A reference to the two largest, St. Croix and St. Thomas.

To Elbridge Gerry

Paris, 19 February 1784

Dear Sir,

It was not until last week that your Favor of the 24 November last reached me.[1] I am glad to find it dated at Philadelphia, as that Circumstance leads me to suppose you was again serving our Country in Congress. It is of the last Importance that our federal Head should constantly <possess both confidence and power> be a wise one, and that every art to diminish its Respectability should be fruitless.

A Report prevails that Connecticut will not acquiesce in the late Decision of her Controversey with Pennsylvania. <Our enemies> They who fear our <becoming> being a united and consequently a <great> formidable people (and I can hardly tell you who do not fear it) rejoice at this <news> Intelligence.[2] Some of our best Friends think the order of Cincinnatus will eventually <split> divide us into two mighty factions <and that our officers in solliciting the permission> <to permit>. The permission of the King of France for his officers to <wear that Badge> be of <seem to admit that the> that order was asked but the like Compliment was <due to them> not paid to our own Sovereign. The King has consented without having requested the opinion of Congress on the Subject, that I can learn.[3] We wish to receive a Ratification of the Treaty of peace, and I <sincerely> hope that every article in it will be scrupulously adhered to on our Part.

Mrs. Jay presents her Compliments to You. With sincere Regard and Esteem, I am Dear Sir [your] most obedient servant.

P.S. Mr. Adams is in Holland, trying to save Mr. Morris's Bills.

Dft. Endorsed by JJ: ". . . in ansr to 24 Novr. last."

[1]Not located.

[2]A congressional court of arbitration instituted August 1782 to determine disputes over Wyoming lands, located in Pennsylvania but settled by Connecticut adventurers, sat at Trenton from 12 November to 30 Dec. 1782, and on 2 January unanimously upheld Pennsylvania's jurisdiction. The attempt to dispossess the Connecticut claimants led to bloodshed, with the issue not finally settled in Pennsylvania's favor until 1790. *JCC,* XXIV, 6–32; *LMCC,* XI, 368, 376–77. See also Julian P. Boyd, *The Susquehannah Company: Connecticut's Experiment in Expansion* (New Haven, 1935).

[3]The Society of the Cincinnati accepted all French officers of the rank of colonel or above who had served in America. When Major Pierre Charles L'Enfant sailed for France in the fall of 1783, he brought a letter from Washington to Lafayette requesting the Marquis to superintend the organization of a French branch of the Society. Royal permission was granted 18 Dec. 1783. Edgar E. Hume, *Lafayette and the Society of the Cincinnati* (Baltimore, 1934), pp. 1–11. Apprehensive of military power in the postwar era, Gerry quickly established himself as a leader in New England in countering the rise of the Society. George A. Billias, *Elbridge Gerry: Founding Father and Republican Statesman* (New York, 1976), pp. 100 *passim.* For other opponents both in America and in France, see [Aedanus Burke], *Considerations on the Society or Order of Cincinnati* (Charleston, 1783); H. G. R. de Mirabeau, *Considérations sur l'order de Cincinnatus, ou imitation d'un pamphlet anglo-américain* (London, 1784).

To William Bingham

Chaillot near Paris, 22 February 1784

Dear Sir,

Two Days ago I met with the 78 and 79 numbers of a periodical Publication printed in London and to be had at Elmsly's Bookseller in the Strand, Entitled "Annales politiques, civiles, et litteraires du Dix-Huitième Siecle" par Monsieur Linguet, who I believe is the same writer that has published <some> Strictures on the Bastile.[1]

The <singular> asperity with which this Gentleman handles American affairs is <so> very remarkable <that I cannot forbear>.[2] His Remarks on the Case of the Loyalists, the paper money etc. <look more like> bear no marks of Impartiality nor even of Candor.

I think our Friends and Countrymen would do well to read this work, not so much perhaps on account of its intrinsic Importance, <but as> as on account of its affording a Clue which with others, may serve to lead us to the politics of more consequential Men. As you are a man of observation as well as Leisure, It would not be money ill bestowed to subscribe for this work. It is *finely* if not truely written, and contains many entertaining and some Instructive Pages.

Mrs. Jay presents her best Compliments to Mrs. Bingham and you. We hope the Charms of London will not detain you from us longer than bad Weather and bad Roads may render it necessary. We shall endeavour to get away by May, and I should be mortified to set out <not before> without having had the Pleasure of again assuring you in Person of the affectionate <Esteem and> Regard and Esteem with which I am, Dear Sir, Your friend and servant.

P.S. I take the Liberty of enclosing a Letter for our friend Stuart.[3]

Dft. Endorsed by JJ.

[1]Simon Nicolas Henri Linguet (1736–94), a French journalist and attorney, whose attacks on fellow members of his profession led to his expulsion from the French bar and exile in 1775. In London Linguet began publishing *Annales politiques, civiles et littéraires du dix-huitième siècle* in 1777. Permitted to return to France in 1780, Linguet almost immediately alienated the Court and was kept in the Bastille for two years. Upon his release he returned to England, where he resumed publication of the *Annales* in 1783. His attacks upon American policy appeared in issues of the *Annales* in late 1783. *"Loyalists proscrits en Amérique"* and *"Amérique: Papier monnaie evanoui: Congrès en suite. Système de finance"* are in *Annales,* X, 332–41 and 353–70. Darlene Levy, "Simon Linguet's Sociological System: The Exhortation to Patience and an Invitation to Revolution," *Studies in Voltaire in the Eighteenth Century,* LXX (1970), 219–93.

[2]The rest of the phrase is indecipherable.

[3]See immediately below, JJ to Gilbert Stuart, 22 Feb. 1784.

To Gilbert Stuart[1]

Chaillot, 22 February 1784

Sir,

In the Price I paid you for my Picture and the Copy <to be paid> <made> of it for Mr. Bingham, I find <on Recoll> <that> no Provision was made for the Frame of the latter. To supply that omission I now <therefore enclose> subjoin an order in your Favor on Messrs. Smith, Wright and Gray for five Guineas. In the choice of the Frame be pleased to discover and be directed by Mr. Binghams Fancy.

If I can be of <any> use to You here, or elsewhere, command me.

I am Sir Your most obedient <and very humble> Servant.

To Messrs. Smith, Wright, and Gray[2]

Chaillot, near Paris, 22 February 1784

Messrs. Smith, Wright and Gray

Be pleased to pay to Mr. Gilbert Stuart on order five Guineas, and place the same to the account of Your humble Servant.

Dft in DeWint: Joseph Downs Manuscript coll. Endorsed by JJ.
[1](1755–1828), American portrait painter for whom JJ sat during his London visit.
[2]A banking firm on London's Lombard Street, also used by Benjamin Franklin.

To David Hartley

Chaillot, near Paris, 22 February 1784

Dear Sir,

In whatever Point of Light our two Countries may in future view each other, or whatever System of Politics may prevail in either, I <always> shall continue to consider you as one <to whom> who merits my Esteem as a public Man, and my acknowledgments as a Friend. I regret my leaving England without having <seen> had an opportunity of bidding you farewell, and the more so as it is not probable that we shall again see each other. It is my Intention to embark for America in the Spring, and the present complexion of affairs affords little Room to expect <either> that public Business will in the mean Time either call you here or me to London. I thank you most sincerely for the kind attentions with which you favored me when in England; and shall be happy in every opportunity of giving you better Evidence than Professions of the Sense I entertain of them.

In the Haste with which I left Bath I inadvertently omitted to leave the usual Fee <which I think is a Guinea> at the Kings pump Room. As you frequently go there permit me to beg the Favor of you to supply this omission, and to apologize for it. I still remain indebted to You for the Sword and Candlesticks. Not knowing what they amount to nor what the usual Fee to the pump Room is I cannot give you an order on my Banker for the exact Sum, but I subjoin one to the Extent of ten Guineas, of which you will be pleased to recieve whatever may be due.

<I beg the Favor of You> Be so obliging as to present my best Compliments to your Brother, and to let me know whether your Sister has recovered.[1] With real Regard and Esteem I am, Dear Sir, Your obliged and obedient Servant.

To Messrs. Smith, Wright, and Gray

Chaillot, near Passy, 22 February 1782

Be pleased to pay to David Hartley Esquire on order ten Guineas, or as much less as he shall call for.

J. J.

Dft in RAWC. Endorsed by JJ. C in MiU-C: Hartley.

[1]Hartley's half-sister Mary and half-brother Winchcombe Henry Hartley (c. 1740–94), M.P. and, like David, an opponent of the North ministry.

To Robert Morris

Paris, 25 February 1784

My good Friend,

Your Favor of the 4 November[1] last found me in England, where though I suffered much sickness, I left the Pain in my Breast, but a sore throat I caught there, still remains obstinate and troublesome.

The Resolution of Congress of 1st October last did not reach me until in December on my Return here last Month, I wrote in Pursuance of it, to Mr. Carmichael to come here without Delay, with the Books and Vouchers. I daily expect to hear from him, and shall be happy to see that Business settled, before I embark, which I hope will be in April, but from or to what Port, and in what Vessel, is as yet uncertain.

I enclose herewith,[2] a State of the account of my Salary, from which you will percieve that a considerable Ballance remained due in October last, and which is the more interesting, by Reason of advances made on sundry occasions for public purposes, of which regular accounts shall also be sent You.

There is no Doubt but that you have had much to struggle with, and will have more. Difficulties must continue inseparable from your office for some Time yet, and they will be the means either of increasing or diminishing your Reputation. In my opinion you must go on. Success generally attends Talents and Perseverance, and those Thorns will in due Season probably bear Flowers if not Fruit.

There are Parts of your Letter on which, though I concur with you in Sentiment, I forbear to make Remarks, because this may not pass to you uninspected. I hope we shall meet in the Course of a few months, and then Reserve will cease to be necessary.

Our Friend Ridley has lost his wife.[3] He feels it sensibly, and I sincerely pity him. He is now at Rouen. He lately shewed me Letters from the Boys. They were well, and doing well.

What you say of Gouv[erneu]r accords with my opinion of him. I have never broken the Bands of Friendship in my Life, nor when broken, have I ever been anxious to mend them. Mine with him will I hope last as long as we do; for though my Sentiments of Mankind in general are less favorable than formerly, my affection for certain Individuals is as warm and cordial as ever. Mr. Ridley carried a Letter to Rouen from me to him.[4]

Mrs. Jay presents her affectionate Compliments to you and Mrs. Morris, to whom we join in sincerely wishing all the Happiness with which amiable merit should be ever blessed. Tell Gouv[erneu]r I long to take him by the Hand, And believe me to be, my Dear Sir, with constant Attachment, Your affectionate Friend and Servant,

JOHN JAY

ALS. Dft in JP. Endorsed. Paragraphs three and six omitted in *WJ,* II, 150–51, and in *HPJ,* III, 115–17.

[1]Robert Morris to JJ, 4 Nov. 1783, above.

[2]Enclosure not located.

[3]Anne Ridley died on 21 Jan. 1784, predeceased by her infant son Lucius, who died on the 8th. Matthew Ridley to John Adams, 10 Feb 1784, in MHi: Adams, reel 362.

[4]JJ to Gouverneur Morris, 10 Feb. 1784, DftS in JP. Omissions in *WJ,* II, 146–48, and in *HPJ,* III, 109–12.

From Richard Oswald

London, 27 February 1784

Dear Sir,

Having had occasion lately to call upon Mr. Stephens,[1] Secretary of the Admiralty, he told me he had received a Letter from you,[2] in relation to Certain American Prisoners who had gone on board Some of the King's Ships to the East Indies, and desiring that they might be ordered to England.

Mr. Stephens begged his Compliments and wished to know whether he can have the names of those Men, which he said would be convenient, since in case of a general or publick Order, there might be mistakes in the claims of some of the People not so well entitled to a discharge.

I told Mr. Stephens that I doubted of your being possessed of the names of those American Seamen, but that under the direction of a particular or private Order, it might be easy to make the necessary discrimination. He seemed to be of the same opinion, and yet wished the question might be askt. Upon the return to which he said the necessary Orders would be dispatched to that Country.

I hope and Sincerely wish that this may find you in the Same State of good health as when you left this Country, and that Mrs. Jay is also well. I beg my best respects to her, and also to my worthy Friend Doctor

Franklin. Wishing also he would let us know when we are to have the honour of a Visit from him, a question often askt, but which I have not the pleasure of being able to answer. I have the honour to be with Sincere regard and esteem, Dear Sir, Your most obedient humble Servant,

RICHARD OSWALD

I beg my Compliments to young Mr. Franklin. As Mr. Stephens is desirous of an Answer as Soon as possible, your Sending it to me will be obliging.

ALS in RAWC. Endorsed: ". . . ansd. 5 March 1784," for which see below.

[1]Sir Philip Stephens (1725–1809), who had been serving since 1763 as undersecretary of the admiralty. During the American Revolution he administered an international intelligence-gathering operation. Francis P. Renaut, *Le Secret service de l'amirauté britannique, 1776–1783* (Paris, 1936).

[2]See below, JJ to Oswald, 5 March 1784.

From David Hartley

London, 2 March 1784

My Dear Sir,

I return you my best thanks for your much esteemed favour of the 22d of February last and particularly for those very friendly sentiments which you are so good as to express towards me. I assure you that similar sentiments are most sincerely reciprocal on my part. Your public and private conduct has impressed me with unalterable Esteem for you as a public and private friend. I shall be very sorry to be deprived of any opportunity of seeing [you] before your departure for America but I am in hopes that your ratifications may arrive time enough to give me an opportunity of exchanging the British ratifications with you personally as well as with our other friends. The real pleasure that it would give me to see you again before your departure is an additional motive of anxiety to me to wish the speedy arrival of the American ratification. Upon the earliest notice of such arrival I shall immediately apply for the dispatch of our ratification. If I should not have the good fortune to see you again I hope you will always think of me as eternally and unalterably attached to the principles of renewing and establishing the most intimate connexions of amity, intercourse and alliance between our two Countries.

I presume that the Subject of American intercourse will soon be resumed in Parliament as the term of the present act approaches to its expiration. The resumption of this subject in Parliament will probably give ground for some specific negotiation. You know my sentiments already.

As to the little matters of money which you mention in your letter I will take and settle them. I thank you for your enquiries concerning my Sister. She continues much in the same way as when you were at Bath—that is to say, as we hope in a fair way of final recovery though very slowly. My Brother is very well and returns you thanks for your obliging remembrance of him. He joins with me in sincere good wishes to yourself and family, and to the renovation of all those ties of consanguinity and friendship which have for ages been interwoven between our two Countries. I am, Dear Sir, your very sincere and obliged friend,

D. HARTLEY

P.S. I beg my particular compliments and good wishes may be expressed for me to Mrs. Jay, and for all her present and future family connexions and concerns in life, and to our old venerable friend—Moses.[1]

ALS in RAWC. Endorsed: "... Recd. 8 March 1784." C in MiU-C: Hartley IV, and in NHi: Misc. Mss.: Hartley.

[1]"Moses" was the British code name for Banjamin Franklin. See Cecil B. Currey, *Code Number 72: Ben Franklin, Patriot or Spy?* (Englewood Cliffs, N.J., 1972), p. 12.

To Richard Oswald

Chaillot near Paris, 5 March 1784

Dear Sir,

Had your Favor of the 27th Ult. been delivered to me a little sooner, an answer to it might have gone by <this> to Days post, but that not having been the Case, this Letter will remain some Days in the Office.

I am much obliged to you for communicating what passed between you and Mr. Stephens respecting the Letter he suppos<ed>es to have <recieved> been from me. The fact is, that I <have> never had the Honor of writing to that Gentleman on any Subject whatsoever.

As to the American Prisoners who may be on Board of British Ships of war, or otherwise confined either in "the East Indies" or in other Parts of the world, it never appeared to me necessary that particular applications should be made for their Release, because I presumed that at the Conclusion of the War, proper orders would be immediately given for liberating them agreable to the articles of Peace. The Difficulty of distinguishing Americans from Englishmen, existed on both Sides. The united States have nevertheless made the Discrimination and discharged all these Prisoners. It is probable that some <English> British Subjects taking advantage of their speaking the same Language may <call themselves> personate American prisoners and thereby elude their Engagements, but <certain that> though that Inconvenience is almost inevitable, <being inseparable from the Case, cannot possibly be avoided, nor it cannot however> yet it cannot be very important in time of peace when Seamen are plenty. However that may be, Justice and Humanity dictate that liberal and effectual Measures be taken to execute this part of the Treaty; and I am persuaded that both Considerations will have their due Degree of Influence in drawing the <that> Business to a speedy and satisfactory Conclusion.

With Respect to the Names or Descriptions of the Americans alluded to, I am <ig[norant]> entirely uninformed nor do I think it easy or indeed practicable to obtain full and accurate Intelligence on the Subject. <Records must be had to> Personal Examinations and the Evidence which may attend or arise out of each Case <will> would <in my opinion> probably be sufficient to determine the merits of the far greater part of them; and as to <rest it may> those which might remain doubtful it would be better to <let> risque the Escape of some disguised Englishmen, than the unjust Detention of <Men> Americans entitled to a Discharge.

Our friend Dr. Franklin is recovering from a slight <fit> attack of the Gout. I expect to see him to morrow, and shall not omit mentioning your kind Inquiries respecting him. His visiting England appears to me doubtful. It is a Country in which he has many Friends as well as many Enemies, and I believe he is as desirous of seeing some of the former as he is indifferent about the Generality of the latter.

Mrs. Jay and my little family are well and she presents her best Compliments to you. We are preparing to set out <for America> in the Course of 6 or 8 Weeks for New York where it will always give me pleasure to hear of your welfare, and (if in my power) <of being> to be useful to You. Be pleased to make my Compliments to Mrs. Oswald, your Nephew[1] and Mr. Whitford. With the best Wishes and with the most <great Esteem and Regard> sincere Regard and Esteem, I am, Dear Sir, Your most obedient Servant.

Dft. Endorsed by JJ: ". . . in ansr to 27 Ult."

[1]Probably John Anderson, who with his uncle had posted bail for Henry Laurens upon his release from the Tower of London on 31 Dec. 1781. Henry Laurens, "A Narrative of the Capture of Henry Laurens," South Carolina Hist. Soc., *Collections,* I (1857), 60.

From William Bingham

London, 10 March 1784

Dear Sir,

I received your agreable Letter of the 22nd November[1] and exceedingly regret your <Speedy> Intention of Speedily departing for America, more especially as it will deprive Mrs. Bingham and myself of the pleasure of personally assuring Mrs. Jay and you of our affectionate Regards.

We shall leave England in the Beginning of May, and Shall take Holland in our Route to Spa, where we intend to remain about two Months, and expect to be in Paris about September.

I Sincerely wish you every possible Happiness, and that agreable Reception in America, which your assiduous and Successfull Endeavors in the public Service, So amply merit.

It is not only in the periodical Publication that you allude to, that the Affairs of America are treated with Partiality and Prejudice. The People at large are unfavorable to our Interests, and cannot assume a Sufficient Degree of Magnanimity, to forgive the Injuries they have Sustained, from a Pursual of the American War. However, Administration Seems at present more disposed to listen to just and equitable Terms of Commercial Intercourse with the United States, than when you were here. The Distresses of the Islands, in Consequence of the unwise Measures of Government, have occasioned warm Petitions to be presented, requesting an immediate Change of System, as essential to their Salvation. The vigorous Steps of Retaliation, pursuing by the States, have likewise assisted in bringing them to Reason. Maryland has passed a Law imposing Such heavy Duties on the Entry and Clearance of British Shipping in her Ports, as to operate as a Prohibition, which deprives the Country of a most valuable Branch of Commerce.[2] I hope the other States will follow the Example, which will Soon convince this Kingdom, of the Infatuation of their present Conduct.

Two contending Factions in the House of Commons, have for Some Time past occasioned a total Suspension of all the efficient Powers of Government. The Ministry have at length gained Some little

Advantage, but the Power and Influence of both Parties are So nearly ballanced, that without an Union, this Country must continue to exhibit a Scene of great Anarchy and Confusion. And the Views and Principles of the respective Leaders, are So very dissimilar, that I do not See, how they can coalesce, and at the Same Time preserve their Honor, or their Reputation for Consistency of Conduct.

If I can render you any Services in this Place, you know with what Freedom you may lay your Commands on me, and with what pleasure I Shall execute them. I am with great Regard, Dear Sir, Your affectionate Friend and obedient humble servant,

WM. BINGHAM

P.S. Our Lottery Ticket No. 2989 has unfortunately proved a Blank.

ALS. Addressed: "Son Excellence, Jean Jay, Chaillot, pres de Paris." Added in an unidentified hand: "Hôtel d'hauche." Endorsed: ". . . recd 13 May 1784."

[1]A slip of the pen for JJ's 22 Feb. 1784 letter, above.

[2]In December 1783 the Maryland legislature imposed a duty of five shillings per ton on British vessels using Maryland ports and a two percent ad valorem duty on British goods imported on British ships. W. S. Jenkins, ed., *Records of the States of the U.S.A., Laws of Maryland, 3 Nov.–26 Dec. 1783,* ch. XXIX (Washington, D.C., 1949).

FROM LEWIS LITTLEPAGE

Paris, Rue d'Artois, 16 March 1784

Sir,

Having, in the hurry of closing some letters from London to my Uncle, transmitted the original state of the account *between your Excellency and myself,* I must entreat you to take the trouble of making out a summary of the amount without delay; as it is possible I *may be enabled to settle it before your departure.*

I, at the same time, take the liberty to observe, that all efforts on my part for that object, are dictated by my private sentiments of delicacy, rather than any actual *obligation* upon me for sums advanced to me during my minority upon the credit of my Guardian, and which were discontinued as soon as subsequent circumstances seemed to *invalidate his order,* and place me in a more immediate state of *personal responsibility.*

Be pleased to inform me what measures you have ulteriorly taken for your re-imbursement in America, and the result of them. I have the honor to be with perfect respect, Your Excellency's most obedient and most humble servant,

L. LITTLEPAGE

ALS. Addressed: "Á Son Excellence Monsieur Jay, Ministre Plenitre. des etats unis au pres de S.M.C. à Paris." Endorsed: ". . . ansd. immediately."

To Lewis Littlepage

Chaillot, 16 March 1784

Mr. Jay presents his Compliments to Mr. Littlepage, and agreable to the Request contained in his Letter of this Day, sends him enclosed a Copy of the account of Monies paid by Mr. Jay to and for Mr. Littlepage as settled 6 July 1783[1], and informs him that Mr. Jay has not taken any measures for his Reimbursement in America.

Dft. Endorsed: ". . . In ansr to his of same Date." ALS not located.
[1]Enclosure not located.

JJ: Conditional Manumission of Benoit

Chaillot, 21 March 1784

To all to whom these Presents shall come or may concern, I John Jay <Esq. formerly> of the City of New York in America, Esqr. <but> but now residing at Chaillot near Paris in France Send Greeting. Whereas in the month of December in the Year 1779 I purchased at Martinico a Negroe Boy named Benoit who has ever since been with me, And whereas the Children of Men are by Nature equally free, and cannot without Injustice be either reduced to, or held in Slavery, And whereas it is therefore right, that after the said Benoit shall have served me until the Value of his Services <shall> amount to a moderate Compensation for the money expended for him, he should be manumitted. And whereas his <faithful> Services for three Years more would in my opinion be sufficient for that Purpose, Now Know Ye that if the said Benoit shall continue to serve me with a common and reasonable Degree of Fidelity for three Years from the Date hereof he shall <be from and after the Expiration of that Term be> ever afterwards be a Free Man, And I do <accordingly> for myself, my Heirs, Ex[ecuto]rs and adm[inistrato]rs consent, agree and declare that all my Right and Title to the said Benoit shall then cease, determine and become absolutely null and void, and that he shall thenceforth be as free to all Intents and Purposes as if he had never been a Slave. In witness whereof I have hereunto set my Hand and Seal at Chaillot the 21 Day of March in the Year of our Lord 1784.

Sealed and delivered in the Presence of.

Dft. Endorsed. Deletions in *WJ*, I, 230.

From Benjamin Franklin

Passy, 30 March 1784

Dear Sir,

Yesterday late in the Evening arrived here an Express from Congress with the Definitive Treaty ratified, which I enclose with the Resolutions, Proclamation, and the President's Letter. The Congress anxious that the Ratification should arrive within the Term stipulated, dispatched it seems three Expresses, by different Vessels, with authenticated Copies. This came by the French Pacquet Boat: Major Franks sailed before, with another, in a Ship for London. As the Term is long since expired, and I have already sent to Mr. Hartley the Excuses for the Delay,[1] and as Major Franks may probably be arrived in London, and have delivered his Copy to Mr. Laurens and the Post going on Thursday, I hardly think it necessary to send an Express on the Occasion to London, but shall be glad of your Advice, and to consult with you on the Steps to be taken for the Exchange, in Case Mr. Laurens has not already made it, which I wish he may, as it will save Trouble.

All the News I learnt from Col. Harmar who brought the Dispatch, is that the Winter has been uncommonly severe in America, that the Pacquet Boat was long detained in New York by the Ice, and that one which sailed from hence in October, was lost on Long Island going in, some of the People and Passengers saved though much frozen, others froze to death. With great Esteem, I am, Your most obedient humble Servant,

B. FRANKLIN

The Post has the Mail with all the common Letters and the Dispatches for the Court. Our Express is a Day before him. I have received no private Letters from any of my Friends.

ALS. Endorsed.

[1]Franklin to Hartley, 11 March 1784, LbkC in DLC: Franklin.

Benjamin Franklin and John Jay to David Hartley

Passy, 31 March 1784

Sir,

We have now the Pleasure of acquainting you, that the Ratification of the Definitive Treaty is arrived here by an Express from Congress. You have already been informed that the Severity of the Winter in America, which hindered Travelling had occasioned a delay in the assembling of the States. As soon as a sufficient Number were got together, the Treaty was taken into Consideration, and the Ratification passed unanimously. Inclosed you have Copies of the Proclamation issued on the Occasion, and of the Recommendatory Resolution. The Messenger was detained at New York near a Month, by the Ice which prevented the Packet-Boat's sailing, otherwise he would probably have been here in February. We are now ready to exchange the Ratifications with you, whenever it shall be convenient to you.

With great and sincere Esteem we have the honour to be, Sir, your Excellency's most obedient and most humble Servants,

B. FRANKLIN
JOHN JAY

C in MiU-C: Hartley. Enclosures: 14 Jan. 1784 Congressional Proclamation, enjoining strict compliance with the Definitive Treaty and Congressional resolution of the same date recommending to the States the restitution of confiscated estates, for which see *JCC,* XXVI, 29–31.

To Henry Laurens

Chaillot, near Paris, 5 April 1784

Dear Sir,

A Letter in Secretary Thompson's Hand writing directed to the American Ministers for Peace, and hinting the Expediency of an Article for extending the Term assigned by the Treaty for the Exchange of Ratifications, arrived last Month and was communicated to me by Dr. Franklin.[1] Shortly afterwards we were both confined, he by the Gout and I by the Rheumatism. At the first subsequent visit I paid him he informed me, that not being able to see me he had written a Letter requesting you to negociate for such an article.[2] I approved of the Measure, and now mention these Circumstances to account for my not having joined in the Letter.

Col. Harmar last Week brought us the American Ratification and thereupon <we wrote a joint Letter to> the Doctor agreed to prepare

Letters on the occasion to you and Mr. Hartley. He sent me the Latter, and I signed it.[3] <He after Consideration he thought it best that> He has written <a private Letter> to Mr. Adams on that Subject and I presume has done the same to You.[4] These Informalities do not Strike me as of any Importance, for provided Business be done, I am content that the Trouble arising from Forms should be avoided. The Doctor I am sure means nothing else. I think it best notwithstanding that these Matters should be explained.

It would give me Pleasure to hear that your Health is re-established. That of myself and Family continues delicate, the youngest Child being far from well and Mrs. Jay frequently indisposed. My english sore Throat <continues> is still obstinate. We should by this time have been on the Road to one of the Ports to embark for America, but the late arrival of Mr. Carmichael whom I expected sooner, with the public Accounts, and the absence of Mr. Barclay who is to settle them, detain me.

Be pleased to present our best Compliments to Miss and Mr. Laurens. With great Respect and <Esteem> Regard I have the Honor to be, Sir, your most obedient and very humble Servant.

Dft. Endorsed by JJ: ". . . To His Excy. H. Laurens Esq., 5 Ap. 1784."

[1]Charles Thomson's 5 Jan. 1784 letter to the Commissioners is in *JCC,* XXVI, 8.

[2]Franklin to Laurens, 12 March 1784, *BFB,* X, 292–94; *BFS,* IX, 178–81.

[3]See immediately above, letter of 31 March 1784.

[4]Franklin to Adams, 31 March 1784, ALS in MHi: Adams, reel 363; *BFS,* IX, 190. Franklin to Laurens, 31 March 1784, LbkC in DLC: Franklin.

To John Adams

Chaillot, near Paris, 8 April 1784

Dear Sir,

I thank You for your obliging Letter of the 2d Instant[1] and congratulate you on the Recovery of your Health, as well as on the Success of your Measures for preserving our Credit, for which you certainly merit the Acknowledgment of the United States in general, and of their Financier in particular.

It seems to me that this Climate would be at least as propitious to your Health as that of Holland, and therefore if nothing remains to be done there, I think your Presence here would be seasonable.

Our Dispatches by Col. Harmar are such, that I think others must soon follow, and I wish you may be here when they arrive. Those Dispatches are silent on several Subjects, on which Congress will not in my Opinion, leave us long uninformed of their Sentiments.

Little is at present on the Carpet, and that little but little advanced. If you was here it would probably be sooner ripened. To write by the post, is to write to others as well as to You.

Carmichael is at Length arrived with the public accounts, but Mr. Barclay who is to settle them, is still absent though daily expected. As soon as they are settled I shall embark for America, and I should greatly regret leaving Europe without some previous Conversation with You.

The mention made of me by your Correspondents is consolatory, and it is kind in you to communicate it. My best compliments to your Son, and with great and sincere Esteem and attachment I am, Dear Sir, Your Friend and Servant,

JOHN JAY

ALS in MHi: Adams, XLV, 127. Dft in JP. Addressed: "His Excellency John Adams Esq." Endorsed.

[1]Adams to JJ, 2 April 1784, ALS in JP; LbkC in MHi: Adams, reel 107; *WJ*, II, 153, and *HPJ*, III, 120. Therein Adams informed JJ: "The money for the payment of Mr. Morris's bills is happily secured, but we were a long time in bringing the loan to bear."

To Peter Augustus Jay

Chaillot, near Paris, 8 April 1784

My dear Boy,

Your Aunt informs me that you are learning to write,[1] and has sent me <a Sample> one of your Copies which <pleases me> is very well done. I hope you <who> will have so far advanced, <as to be able to read> by the time that this Letter arrives, as to be able to read it. She also tells me that you love your Books, and <take great pains to improve yourself.> that you daily read in the Bible and have learned <som[e]> by Heart some Hymns in the Book I sent you. These Accounts give me great pleasure, and I love you <the more> for being such a good Boy. The Bible is the best of all Books, for it is the word of God, and teaches us the way to be happy in this world and in the <other> next. Continue therefore to read it, and to regulate your Life by its precepts.

I hope it will please God to bring us all together this Summer, and then I will assist you in your Studies. I sent you from London some maps, of which your aunts will teach you the use. Your mama is very anxious to see you and assures you of her affection. Your Sister Maria is very well, and Nancy <begins to recover> who has been above two months <in a bad way> very sickly and declining, begins to recover. They are charming little Girls and I am sure you will be pleased with them.

God bless and preserve you my dear Son. <Study in earnest when you study, and play in earnest when you play. Do nothing by Halves.>

I am your very affectionate Father.

J. J.

DftS. Endorsed by JJ. Enclosure not located.

[1]See above, Catharine W. Livingston to JJ, 30 Dec. 1783.

From Henry Laurens

Bath, 11 April 1784

Dear Sir

I am this morning honored by receipt of your favor of the 5th Instant and return thanks for the Contents.

Doctor Franklin had in due course advised me of Mr. Secretary Thomson's Letter apologizing for the delay of the Ratification and also of the subsequent arrival of that and other Papers from Congress in the hands of Colonel Harmar, adding his expectation of duplicates by Major Franks, in both Cases speaking as in your joint sentiments.

In the first instance I proposed to Mr. Hartley who happened to be at Bath, a convention for extending the stipulated term for Exchange, at the same time requesting if the formality could be safely dispensed with, the Ministers accordance should be signified to me in writing. Mr. Hartley went to London, applied to Lord Caermarthen[1] and transmitted to me the following intimation: "It is not thought necessary on the part of Great Britain to enter into any formal Convention for the prolongation of the term in which the Ratifications of the definitive Treaty were to be exchanged as the delay in American appears to have arisen merely in consequence of the inclemency of the Season."[2]

In the second Case, upon receipt of Dr. Franklin's Letter I writ to Mr. Hartley in the words of a subjoined Copy and also writ to the Master of the Pennsylvania Coffee House desiring him to inform Major Franks upon his appearance that I had lodged a Letter for him in that Gentleman's hands.[3]

Mr. Hartley's answer in due course should have been with me to day but it has not appeared and as I am informed Major Franks arrived in London on Wednesday last and went onward for Paris the next day, 'tis not improbable Mr. Hartley accompanied or soon followed him, there's somewhat of an inducement to the journey.[4]

Ill health my Dear Sir, is almost Ill every worldly thing. I sympathize with you, if you are determined to cross the Atlantic. I wish the Sea Air and change of Climate may have such good effects upon your self Mrs. Jay and the Children as I hope to experience from the same step. I went to London the middle of January determined upon taking a Passage for America to Sail in March, continued there seven Weeks without a day of health, returned to Bath about three Weeks ago and have been constantly confined to the House. To day I feel something like amendment. If it continues three or four days I shall go to London on the late errand hoping to embark very soon after Mr. Harry returns from France.

Miss Laurens is at Church but I may safely unite her Compliments and Best wishes to Mr. and Mrs. Jay and to the little folk with my own because I often hear her say she loves them. With great Respect and Regard, I have the honor to be, Dear Sir, Your Obedient humble Servant,

HENRY LAURENS

ALS in RAWC. Endorsed: ". . . Recd 18 Ap 1784." Enclosure: Laurens to David Hartley, 7 April 1784, CS.

[1]Francis Osborne, Marquis of Carmarthen (1751–99), was appointed Secretary of State for Foreign Affairs by William Pitt in December 1783.

[2]Franklin to Laurens, 12 March 1784, *BFS*, IX, 178–81. Hartley to Laurens, 26 March 1784, *RDC*, VI, 789–90.

[3]Laurens' letter to the Master of the Pennsylvania Coffee House has not been located. In his enclosed 7 April letter to Hartley, Laurens had written: "I have this moment intelligence from Dr. Franklin of the arrival of a Messenger from Congress with Ratification of the definitive Treaty, which the Doctor says, 'A duplicate is sent via London by Major Franks who probably is arrived by this time. If Mr. Hartley should not have an intimation to come to Paris upon the occasion it will be very agreeable to us, meaning Mr. Jay and himself, that you who are equally impowered should finish this business.'

"I take the liberty of troubling you with a Letter to Major Franks under a flying Seal, if it be most agreeable to you to make the necessary Exchange on this side of the Water I will do myself the honor of waiting upon you on the first intimation of that Gentlemans arrival unless it should be altogether convenient to you on a visit to your dear friend here to conclude work at Bath."

[4]Hartley left London on 17 April but did not reach Paris until the end of the month due to "unavoidable delays on the road." Hartley to Carmarthen, 30 April 1784, FO 4/2; Laurens to Thomas Mifflin, 24 April 1784, RDC, VI, 795–97.

Jay and Franklin Reminisce

As the feverish place of diplomatic negotiations slackened, JJ and Franklin had numerous chats in which they exchanged reminiscences. A pioneer oral historian with a keen ear for gossip, JJ contemporaneously recorded some of the old Doctor's wonderful anecdotes, but in the following fragmentary record he begins with an account of an interview he himself had with a ship's captain he first met in the summer of 1780, and with whom he enjoyed another encounter in the spring of the following year. The recorded conversations with Franklin began on 19 July 1783, when the Jays were living under Franklin's roof at Passy, and continued in the course of visits between the Jays, on the one hand, and Franklin and his grandson, William Temple Franklin, on the other. The conversations took place either at Passy or at Chaillot, to which SLJ had removed her household during the months when JJ was in England. The last recorded Franklin item was in March of 1784 following JJ's return to France, while two conversations that JJ had with other visitors are recorded in April of that year, some six weeks before he and his family embarked for America.

John Jay and Benjamin Franklin Reminisce

[Paris], 19 July 1783–17 April 1784

1 April 1781. Rutherford Cook,[1] born in the City of New York, carried when a Child to New Haven, of or near which place his mother was a Native and Sister to the Mother of Gen. Arnold[2] was brought up to the sea. Lately a Master of a Vessel called the True Blue from Boston and one of the Captors of the Dover Cutter in which he had sailed from England, told me that Arnold was born at Norwich in Connecticut, his Father a merchant who left about five or six hundred pounds among his Children, which were Benedict and a Sister.[3] The General was brought up an apothecary under Dr. Lothrop of [———].[4] That with Slight Recommendations he went to England, spent what little he had, but returned with goods on Credit to the Amount of 5000£ Sterling which he sold and spent the Money for so that in an after Composition with Mr. Lintot[5] of N. York on the part of his Creditors they lost 3400£ Sterling, That he afterwards settled at New Haven and was concerned in the West India Trade, that in one voyage he was concerned jointly with Mr. Babcock and went Supercargo. It consisted chiefly of Horses. His orders were to go to an English Island where he was to prefer

selling his Horses at 20£ a Head than Risque going to a French Island where am[erican] vessels had been often seized. He nevertheless went to Guadaloupe, sold his Horses for double the Sum, but accounted only for twenty pounds for each. He used to tell Cook that his Grandfather was the first Governor of Rhode Island,[6] and that an Estate in England belonging to his Family would probably fall to him. It was inherited, and that Arnold refused on this account to be married by a presbyterian Minister lest his Children should on such an Event be embarrassed by it, and was married by a Justice of the peace to his first wife who was a Daughter of [———] at [———].[7]

Cook sailed several Years in his Employ.

19 July 1783. Dr. Franklin told me that not long after the elder Lewis Morris[8] (who was once chief Justice of N. York) came to the Government of New Jersey, he involved himself in a Dispute with the assembly of that Province. The Doctor (who was then a printer in Ph[iladelphi]a) went to Burlington while the assembly was sitting there, and were engaged in the Dispute with their Governor. The House had referred his message to a Committee, consisting of some of their principal Members. Jos. Cooper was one of them. But tho they were Men of good understanding and respectable, yet there was not one among them capable of writing a proper answer to the Message, and Cooper who was acquainted with the Doctor prevailed upon him to undertake it. He did and went thro the Business much to their Satisfaction. In Consideration of the Aid he gave them in that way and afterwards, they made him their Printer.[9] (This shews the then State of Literature in Jersey).

Robert Hunter Morris,[10] the Son of the former, and who for about a Year was Governor of Pennsylvania, the Doctor knew very well. It seems that the Doctor was at New York on His way to Boston when Morris arrived there from England. He asked the Doctor many Questions about Pennsylvania, about the Temper of the People, and whether he thought it difficult for him to pass his Time agreeable among Them. The Doctor told him nothing would be more easy if he avoided Disputes with the Assembly, but replied he laughingly, *why would you have me deprive myself of one of my greatest pleasures.* He was fond of disputing and thought he had Talents for it. However added he I will take your advice. On Franklin's Return from Boston to Ph[iladelphi]a he found the Governor and assembly in warm altercations. The Doctor was a member of the assembly, and was appointed to Draw up their answers. Morris after having sent a Message to the assembly, met Samuel Rhodes[11] and asked him what he thought of it.

Rhodes said he thought it very smart. Ah, said Morris, I thought so too when I had finished it, but tomorrow we shall see Benj. Franklin's answer and then I suspect we shall both change our minds. Altho he knew that Franklin conducted the Dispute against him, yet they were always good Friends, and frequently dined together, etc. When the Doctor's Son[12] was many Years afterwards made Governor of Jersey, and was going to take upon him the Government, Morris came to meet him on the Road, and behaved kindly and in a friendly Manner. He was a very good natured Man, had Talents and Learning but his Imagination was too strong and he was not deep in any Thing.

The elder Lewis Morris was brought up by an Uncle. When young he was very wild. His uncle sent him to the W. Indies with a Vessel and Cargo, which he spent. On his Return he married. His uncle observed to him on that occasion "that now when he wanted every thing he got himself a wife."[13] He replied that now he did not want every thing. His uncle asked him what it was that he did not want. He answered that *now he did not want a wife.* Dr. Franklin was told this by some of Morris's Cotemporaries.

19 July 1783. Dr. Franklin says he was very well and long acquainted with Andrew Hamilton[14] the Lawyer, who distinguished himself on Zengers Tryal at New York. He was a Scotchman who came <very> young into Pennsylvania, some said he came a Servant. Mr. Brooke who in those Days was an old Man told Dr. Franklin that he had seen Hamilton who then lived at Lewis Town studying the Law in an Osnabrigs Shirt and Trowsers, that he observed him often, and that from his great application he predicted that he would one Day make a Figure in that Profession. He was a man of exceeding good Talents and ready Elocution.

William Allen[15] then one of the most wealthy Men in Pen[nsylvani]a and afterwards Chief Justice, married Hamilton's Daughter. That event gave Hamilton more weight and Consideration. He practiced generously, and took no Fees in the Cause of Zenger. The City of New York presented him with the Freedom of the City in a gold Box with handsome Inscriptions.[16]

He left a good Estate, made by laying out his Money as he acquired it in both Lotts and Lands which rose daily in Value.

His Son[17] was afterwards Governor of Pennsylvania, sustained a good Character, had a decent share of Talents but not much improved.

Sep. 1783. Dr. Franklin lived at Ph[ildelphi]a in the Neighbourhood of Mr. Boudinot the Father of Elias Boudinot[18] the present President of Congress. The father was a Silver Smith who had come from N.

19 July 1783 Dr. Franklin says he was very well and long acquainted with Andw. Hamilton the Lawyer who distinguished himself on Zengers Tryal at New York. He was a Scotchman who came ~~very~~ young into Pen-sylvania, some said he came a Servant – Mr Brooke who in those Days was an old Man told Dr. Franklin that he had seen Hamilton who then lived at Lewis Town studying the Law in an Osnabrigs Shirt and Trowsers, that he observed him often, and that from his great application he predicted that he wd. one Day make a figure in that Profession – He was a man of exceeding good Talents & ready Elocution –

Wm. Allen then one of the most wealthy Men in Pena. & afterwards Ch. Justice – married Hamilton's Daughter – that Event gave Hamilton more weight & Consideration – he practiced generously, & took no Fees in the Cause of Zenger, the City of New York presented him with the Freedom of the City in a Gold Box with handsome Inscriptions –

~~his~~ He left a good Estate, made by laying out his Money as he acquired it in Lotts & Lands wh. rose daily in Value –

His Son was afterwards Gov. of Pensylva. – sustained a good Character, had a decent Share of Talents but not much improved –

John Jay's Oral History of Franklin's Reminiscences. *(Papers of John Jay. Rare Book and Manuscript Library, Columbia University)*

York to settle at Ph[ildelphi]a, a man much devoted to Whitfield,[19] by whom his son was baptized *Elias* after the Prophet of that name. Dr. Franklin remembers Elias coming to his father's Door with half a Water Melon and a Spoon in his Hand. Several neighboring Boys gathered round in hopes of sharing in the Melon. Elias observed their Intention, but told them as they came up, that those who asked should receive nothing, and went on eating his Melon. The others imagining he meant to share with them, and fearing to ask lest they should as he threatened be refused, silently waited his Motions. He went on however eating his Melon, and finished it. He was 8 or 9 year old. He had a sister who was a sensible girl, she wrote verses and had Wit. Mr. Stockton of Princeton married her,[20] and took Elias into his office and taught him Law, which he practiced at Eliz[abeth] Town until the War, with the Reputation of Integrity and fairness.

Ap. 1784. Mr. T. Walpole told me that David Hartley was the Son of an eminent Physician at Bath.

March 1784. Doctor Franklin, who has lived long and much with Quakers, tells me that he thinks the far greater part of them approve of defensive tho not of offensive War. In the Course of the War which ended in 1748 It was thought necessary to erect a Battery at Ph[ildelphi]a and a Lottery was made to defray part of the Expence. At that Time the Doctor was of a fire Company of thirty Members, twenty two of whom were Quakers. They had sixty pounds of public or Company Stock, and the Doctor proposed to lay it out in Lottery Tickets. It was their Custom in all Money Matters to give Notice or make the Motion a Week before its Determination. When the Doctor moved his Proposition, Anthony Morris a Quaker member opposed it strenously, observing that the Friends could not apply Money to Purposes of war and that if the Doctor persisted in this motion, it would be the means of breaking up the Company. The Doctor observed that the Minority must be bound by the Majority, and as the greater part of the Company were Quakers it would be in their power to decide as they pleased.

When the Day for the Determination came, Anthony Morris was the only Quaker who appeared. The Doctor observing that Circumstances pressed for the Vote, Morris said he expected that other members would soon come in, and begged that the Vote might be deferred for an Hour. While that matter was in agitation, the Waiter called him out, telling him that two Men below Stairs wanted to speake to him. He found they were two Quaker members of the Company. They told him they came from six or seven others who were in a House next Door but one. They came to inquire whether he was strong enough to carry his Motion; if not, that on being sent for, they could attend and vote with him. But they wished to avoid it if possible lest they should give offence to certain of the Friends who were more scrupulous on that Head. The Doctor returned and agreed to Anthony Morris's Request for another Hour. The Hour elapsed and not a single Quaker appeared. The Question was then put and carried.[21]

While Governor Thomas[22] was Governor of Pennsylvania shortly after the taking of Louisbourgh by an armament from Boston, advice came to Ph[ildelphi]a that the Garrison was in great want of Gun powder. Governor Thomas communicated it to the Assembly and wanted them to afford Supplies. The Quaker Majority in the Assembly would not consent to supply any Gun Powder. But they granted three thousand pounds to be laid out in Flour, Wheat or other *Grain* for the use of the Garrison. Governor Thomas said that by *other Grain* was meant Gun powder. He laid the money out accordingly and nothing was said about it.

March 1784. Doctor Franklin told me that the Quaker Morris Family of Ph[ildelphi]a are descended from Anthony Morris,[23] a Quaker who came here from England about the beginning of this Century. It was said among the old People, that he was a natural Son of a Spanish Embassador in England. The Doctor says he always thought he looked a little like a Spaniard. He was an industrious money gathering Man, as well as a rigid Quaker. He once found a friend of his reading a large Book. What, says he, *art thee reading that Book? Why a man might* earn forty Shillings in the Time necessary to read it through.

Dr. Franklin says he knew the Father and Grandfather of W. Bingham[24] the continental agent at Martinico. The Grandfather was a Sadler, the Father a merchant.

17 Ap. 1784. Mr. Mckennin one of the Council of Antigua, told me that Valentine Morris,[25] Governor of that Island told him, he had a Copy of Mr. Bingham's Letter Book. Mr. Bingham was then at Martinico.[26]

AD.

[1]For an earlier talk of JJ with Captain Cook, see *JJ, I,* 807. Rutherford Cook was a first cousin of Benedict Arnold.

[2]Benedict Arnold was the son of Benedict and Hannah Waterman King Arnold.

[3]Hannah Arnold.

[4]Doctors Daniel and Joshua Lothrop operated a drugstore in Norwich.

[5]Bernard Lintot, a New York merchant, and counsel to Arnold's London creditors.

[6]Benedict Arnold served variously as governor of Rhode Island, 1662–63, 1669–72, 1677–78. American Historical Association, *Annual Report* (1906), II, 331–332.

[7]Arnold's first wife was Hannah Mansfield, the daughter of Samuel Mansfield,

sheriff of New Haven. They were married 22 February 1767.

[8]Lewis Morris (1671–1746), chief justice of New York (1715–33) and governor of New Jersey, 1738–46. For his son, Robert Hunter Morris, see below.

[9]The events alluded to transpired in April 1745, when the New Jersey Assembly replied to a critical and abusive message of Governor Morris. See "Papers of Lewis Morris, 1738–46," New Jersey Historical Society, *Collections* IV (1852), 237, 277–278; Thomas F. Gordon, *The History of New Jersey* (Trenton, 1834), pp. 101–103. Samuel Cooper was a member of the New Jersey Assembly. "Autobiography," *BFS,* I, 294, 295.

[10]Robert Hunter Morris (c. 1700–64), chief justice of New Jersey and governor of Pennsylvania, 1754–56, was Lewis Morris's second son. His conversation with Franklin is also reported in "Autobiography," *BFS,* I, 389–390.

[11]Samuel Rhoads (1711–84). a member of the Pennsylvania Assembly, mayor of Philadelphia, and a Franklin associate in various civic and philanthropic activities.

[12]William Franklin.

[13]On 3 Nov. 1691 Lewis Morris married Isabella, daughter of James Graham, attorney-general of New York.

[14]Andrew Hamilton (d. 1741), whose origin is obscure, married Anne (Brown) Preeson, a wealthy Maryland widow, and became a prominent Philadelphia lawyer, most celebrated for his defense of John Peter Zenger, the New York printer, in 1735.

[15]William Allen (1704–80) married Margaret, daughter of Andrew Hamilton, in 1734.

[16]John Peter Zenger (1697–1746), whose *New-York Weekly Journal* aroused the wrath of the province's royal officials. See Livingston Rutherfurd, *John Peter Zenger: His Press, His Trial, and a Bibliography of Zenger Imprints; Also a Reprint of the First Edition of the Trial* (New York, 1904).

[17]James Hamilton (c. 1710–83), lieutenant-governor of Pennsylvania (1748–50, 1759–63), and acting governor, 1771–73, who played a neutralist role in the American Revolution.

[18]Elias Boudinot III (1706–70), the silversmith, was the father of Elias Boudinot IV, commissary general of prisoners and president of Congress, 4 Nov. 1782–3 Nov. 1783.

[19]George Whitefield (1715–70), the noted evangelist.

[20]Annis Boudinot married Richard Stockton, the Signer, whose sister Hannah married Elias Boudinot IV.

[21]For Franklin's lottery project, see *Pennsylvania Gazette,* 12 Dec. 1747, in *Papers of Benjamin Franklin,* ed. by Leonard W. Labaree *et al.,* eds., *The Papers of Benjamin Franklin* (New Haven, 1959–   ), III, 220–224, 229–231, 288–299. The incident is also recounted in Franklin's "Autobiography," *BFS,* I, 364–366.

[22]George Thomas (c. 1695–1774), who was involved in bitter quarrels with the Pennsylvania Assembly over appropriations for defense both at the time of the War of Jenkins' Ear and again when France entered the war in 1744.

[23]Anthony Morris (1654–1721), Quaker leader, removed from England to Burlington, West Jersey, in 1683, and three years later to Philadelphia. The genealogists list him as the son of Anthony and Elizabeth (Senior) Morris. R. C. Moon, *The Morris Family of Philadelphia* (5 vols., 1898–1909).

[24]William Bingham was the son of William and Mary (Stamper) Bingham. His paternal grandfather was James Bingham, a Philadelphia saddler; his father branched out from saddlery to commerce, trading extensively in the West Indies. Robert C. Alberts, *The Golden Voyage: The Life and Times of William Bingham, 1752–1804* (Boston, 1969), pp. 10, 11; also *JJ,* I, 548n.

[25]William Mackinnen, member of the Antigua Council, 1764–98, and considered a friend of America; Valentine Morris named lieutenant-governor of Antigua in 1772

and governor of St. Vincent, 1772–79. Vere L. Oliver, *The History of the Island of Antigua* (3 vols., London, 1849–99), II, 226, 273.

[26]Verso are fragmentary JJ diary entries beginning 11–19 April 1784, for which see above, p. 690.

FROM JOHN ADAMS

Hague, 20 April 1784

Dear Sir,

I am extreamly Sorry, to read in your Letter of the 8th that you think of embarking for America. Let me beg of you to reconsider that Project. If you persist in it, I shall repent of having written for my Family and wish I had it in my Power to go there too.

The Committee to whom the Dispatches by Thaxter were referred have reported that a Commission be sent to the 3 named in the Resolution of the 1 of May last, to treat with all the maritime Powers, who may wish to treat, and I Suppose Such a Commission will Soon arrive.[1] As soon as I know of its arrival, I will Sett off, for Paris.

I have received a Letter, under a Cover, which you knew of. The Writer desires to be remembered to you, your Lady, and to Mr. Carmichael. Dana is, as I Suppose, a Member of Congress, and now at Anapolis.[2]

If you should be decided to return home, which I hope you are not, I beg to know about what Time you expect to leave Paris, for I should regret as much as you, the Loss of an Opportunity to converse with you before you go. With great and Sincere Esteem, Yours,

JOHN ADAMS

ALS. Addressed: "Á Son Excellence Monsieur John Jay, Ministre Plénipotentiaire des États Unis de l'Amerique, à Chaillot, près Paris, France." Endorsed: ". . . Recd. 26, and. 27 Ap. 1784."

[1]A committe composed of Elbridge Gerry, Thomas Jefferson, and Hugh Williamson, named on 15 Dec. 1783 to report on letters from various ministers abroad, delivered its report five days later. It recommended that Congress issue a commission which would enable the American ministers to negotiate treaties of amity and commerce with European nations. These recommendations, however, were not adopted until May 1784. *JCC,* XXV, 813, 821–28; XXVII, 368–72.

[2]Adams' reference is to a letter from Elbridge Gerry, in which Gerry wrote: ". . . Mr. Dana is arrived and requested to attend Congress. I have suggested to some of my Friends the good policy of appointing him to a Seat in Congress, and to him the advantages to be at this Time expected from the Measure, and I flatter myself, it will be adopted." Gerry closed by presenting "my best Respects to Mr. Jay his Lady and Mr. Carmichael, if in Paris." Dana was elected to Congress in February 1784, replacing James Sullivan. Elbridge Gerry to John Adams, 14 Jan. 1784, ALS in MHi: Adams, reel 362; *LMCC,* VII, 413.

FROM WILLIAM TEMPLE FRANKLIN

Sunday, [25 April 1784]

My dear Sir,

I waited Yesterday on Madame Le Brun,[1] and made her the Proposition of painting Mrs. Jay, but notwithstanding all the Arguements I made use of to engage her to undertake it, she could not be prevailed with. It being impossible, as she informed me, for her to do it in time, having already commenced seven Portraits, and One Historical Pieçe, for which she is much pressed. She added she was sorry, it so happened, as it would have given her Pleasure to have painted Mrs. Jay, whom she well remembers to have seen. I asked her who she could recommend, that would do it well. She mentioned the same Painter I already spoke to you about, viz. M. Roslin,[2] who lives [at] Gallerie du Louvre. He has great Merit, and I don't doubt will undertake it immediately.

I am Dear Sir, Your obliged and grateful humble Servant,

W. T. FRANKLIN

ALS. Endorsed.

[1]French portrait painter Marie Louise Elisabeth Vigée-Lebrun (1755–1842), remembered for her portraits of Marie Antoinette.

[2]The Swedish portrait painter Alexandre Roslin (c. 1718–93), of great vogue in Paris in his day.

TO JOHN ADAMS

Chaillot, near Paris, 27 April 1784

Dear Sir,

Your Favor of the 20th Instant arrived last Evening. It is not in pursuance of a recent or hasty Resolution, that I am preparing to return. It has been long taken and maturely considered. The public accounts still detain me, for though always kept by Mr. Carmichael, I do not chuse to leave them unsettled behind me. When that Obstacle ceases, which I expect will be very soon, I shall leave Paris. I daily expect answers to Letters by which I desired a Friend in London to enquire and inform me about a New York Vessel there.[1] It is probable I may go in her, if not, I must look out for some other opportunity. There are accounts of Barney's arrival.[2] Perhaps he may be sent back with the Papers you mention. If so, we may soon see him, and in that Case I would return with him.

The coming of your Family will be a great Consolation to you and them.[3] May you have a speedy and happy meeting. I wish they had made you a visit immediately on the Return of Peace, and in this wish Mrs. Jay sincerely joins. Would it be very inconvenient to you to come to Paris? I cannot propose that you should leave any thing undone, which ought to be done, but if there be no Objection of that Sort, a Trip to Paris would not be an unpleasant Excursion. Who knows but that you might meet the Commission here. If not, you will certainly meet a cordial Welcome from, Dear Sir, Your Friend and Servant,

JOHN JAY

Mr. Hartley is daily expected. My Compliments to your Son. Just as I began to fold up this Letter a Gent[leman] told me that he saw Mr. Hartley this morning at Dr. Franklin's.

AL in MHi: Adams, XLV, 128. Dft in JP. Endorsed.

[1]JJ's 13 April 1784 to Joshua Johnson, DftS in JP, inquires whether Johnson would check with Captain Coupar to ascertain the time of his sailing and to request him to pick up the Jays at Dover to avoid their traveling to London. Johnson's reply has not been located.

[2]Lieutenant Joshua Barney returned to the U.S. the first week in March 1784, but owing to the high cost of needed repairs, his ship, *George Washington,* was ordered by Congress to be sold at auction. *JCC,* XXVI, 210.

[3]As early as September 1783, Adams urged his wife Abigail (1744–1813) and their daughter Abigail (1765–1813) to join him in Europe, but they did not arrive until August 1784. *AP,* III, 156n.

To Frederick Jay

Chaillot, near Paris, 27 April 1784

Dear Fœdy,

Mr. P. Van Schaack informs me by a Letter dated the 12 Inst.[1] at Bristol that Mrs. Peloquin's Executors "have at length agreed to recognize the Powers of Attorney and to pay the Legacies." The one however to our father they will not pay until his will be proved and Letters of Administration taken out in England.

I have desired Mr. Johnson of London to talk with Capt. Coupar about taking us in at Dover, but not <yet> having recieved an answer I cannot tell you precisely when or in what Vessel we shall sail. I fear it will be late before we set out.

Mrs. Allaire, the wife of Mr. Peter Allaire[2] of New York, will be the bearer of this. I found her here in <very> a distressed Situation. I have lent her thirty Guineas and given her a Credit with Mr. Nesbit at L'Orient for her <the> Passage money and Subsistence while there. Mention this *only* to her Husband who I flatter myself will readily re-imburse this money by paying to You.

We are all tolerably well except little Nancy who suffers from teething and bad Cold.

Your last Letter is dated 7 February.[3] My Love to all the family. I hope Peter will not refuse the farm at least <until after> before I arrive <for I have much to say to him on that and other subjects>.

I am Dear Fœdy your affectionate Brother,

J. J.

DftS. Endorsed by JJ: ". . . by Mrs. Allaire." ALS not located.

[1]Letter not located.

[2]Rebecca Allaire was the wife of Peter Allaire (1740–1820), a New York merchant of Huguenot stock. The latter's involvement in double espionage in France resulted in his being thrown into the Bastille on 15 Feb. 1780 at Franklin's behest and detained until the French fleet sailed from Brest for America on 2 May. Released 24 May, he was expelled from France. In May 1783 Allaire left Ostend for America, after placing his wife and infant child in a convent at Armentières. When her funds ran out, Mrs. Allaire went to Paris, where, desperate and on the verge of suicide, she contacted SLJ. On JJ's return from England, he generously advanced the funds herein described. Frantz Funck-Brentano, *Les Lettres de cachet à Paris, étude suivie d'une liste des prisonniers de la Bastille, 1659–1789* (Paris, 1903), p. 405; M. Truffe to Benjamin Franklin, 21 Jan., 9 March 1784. PPAmP: Franklin. For his later espionage activities, see *TJP,* XVII, 91n.

[3]Not located.

To Vergennes

Chaillot, 4 May 1784

Sir,

Intending to set out in the course of next week on my Return to America I request the honor of your Excellency to give me such a Passport for my Family and Baggage as is usually granted in similar Cases.

I have the Honor to be with great Respect, Your Excellencys most obedient and very humble Servant.

Dft. Endorsed: ". . . sent to W. T. Franklin."

To Vergennes

Chaillot, 8 May 1784

Sir,

I have recieved and thank your Excellency for the Passport inclosed in your obliging Letter of the 5 Instant,[1] and have now the honor of transmitting the account necessary to compleat the order respecting my Baggage.

There is a New York Vessel at London, in which I have engaged a passage. The Captain offers to take us on board at Dover, but to avoid Embarrassments at the Custom House there, I have proposed to him to call for us at Calais, or any other neighbouring port on this Coast, which he may prefer. Until his answer arrives I shall not be able to designate precisely the port of our Embarkation though I <think> am persuaded it will be Calais.

I propose to myself the Honor of calling in a few Days for your Excellency's <orders> Commands. In the mean time permit me to assure you of the Respect and Consideration with which I have the Honor to be your Excellency's most obedient and most humble Servant.

Dft. Endorsed: ". . . in ansr. to 5 Inst."

[1]Letter not located.

To Lafayette

Chaillot, 8 May 1784

<My> Dear Sir,

I was surprized to see you pass in your Carriage two Days ago, having understood that you was gone to the Country.

Tell me when you will be at Home. I want to call upon you and talk over two or three matters. Will Tomorrow morning suit You?[1]

I have found a New York Ship that will take us on board at Dover, <and so that you will no longer be exposed to the Inconveniences which your polite offer to taking us with you might have exposed you>. My sense however of your obliging offer to take us with you remains the Same. I shall never think of France without recollecting your friendly Attention to Americans and American affairs. Our best <compliments> wishes to your amiable Lady. I am Dear Sir your <affectionate> obedient and affectionate Servant,

J. J.

DftS. Endorsed by JJ.

[1]Lafayette replied: "I have been Rambling about these past days, My dear Sir, and Came in last Evening when I received your kind letter. I am sorry to loose the Opportunity of a Voyage with You, and would Have been most Happy in your and Mrs. Jay's Compagny. Being obliged to go out this Morning on Appointments, I would Be afraid not to Have as long a time to spend with you as I might wish. Therefore Beg leave to propose Your Breakfasting to Morrow with me When We May be free from Visits and Have a longer Chat upon our public and private affairs. Should it However be inconvenient I will to day call upon or wait for you at any Moment you please to determine." Lafayette to JJ, 9 May 1784, ALS in CtY.

From John Adams

The Hague, 11 May 1784

Dear Sir,

Your favour of the 27 April is before me. I wish very Sincerely that my family had made a Visit to me, or I to them on the Conclusion of the Peace. The two Ladies will be affectionate Friends, I dare answer for it, if they should ever meet.

There are Things constantly to be done here, but if there were not, it would be impossible for me, to come to Paris at present, without arranging affairs for the whole Year. My Friend Mr. Dumas, in whose Care I could Safely leave this House has purchased another into which he is about to enter which will oblige me if I leave this at all, to take another Family into it, and where to find one, worthy of the Trust I know not.

The whole affair of a Commission, and of all arrangements are So uncertain that I conclude upon the whole to wait here with Patience untill I know what to depend upon. When the Arrangements arrive, I shall then be able to determine what to do. At present I am all in the dark. If you go I think it is proper you should take with you, the Ratification of the Treaty, and I most Sincerely wish you, a prosperous Voyage, and all Happiness forever.

Your Sincere Friend and very humble Servant,

JOHN ADAMS

ALS. Endorsed. Addressed to "His Excellency Mr. Jay." LbkC in MHi: Adams, reel 107.

ACKNOWLEDGMENTS

The preparation and editing of this volume have been made possible by the generous support of the National Historical Publications and Records Commission and the National Endowment for the Humanities. By special grants the Rockefeller Foundation underwrote the cost of calendaring the photocopy collection of diplomatic archives, which supplements the Jay manuscripts and which has been heavily levied upon to document the years of John Jay abroad. That Foundation is providing additional support for the concluding volumes.

The staff of the Jay Papers has continued to enjoy the cooperation of a considerable company of librarians and archivists here and abroad, and, above all, of the dedicated staff of the Columbia University Libraries, whose Rare Book and Manuscript Library which houses the Jay Papers is headed by Mr. Kenneth A. Lohf.

The initial volume appropriately paid tribute to the revolving staff of scholars who have served the Jay Papers. Special mention again must be made of Dr. Mary-Jo Kline, presently editor of The Papers of Aaron Burr, whose contribution extended beyond that initial volume and whose fine intelligence was enlisted in resolving some of the tortuous problems posed by an exploration of diplomatic documents. In addition, this volume has benefited substantially by the research and editorial skills of Dr. Floyd M. Shumway and the Misses Elaine G. Brown, Janet F. Asteroff, and Deborah Lerner, while foreign language questions have frequently been put to Mr. Curtis Wolcott Church and Professor Madeleine de Gogorza Fletcher, both of Columbia University, and to Linda Chivian Levitz and Jesús Velasco. Grateful acknowledgment is due Mrs. Mary Vaughan Marvin of Hallowell, Maine, and Mrs. Helen G. Matthew, Sweet Briar, Virginia, for leads in unearthing Benjamin Vaughan correspondence, and to Lino S. Lipinsky de Orlov, Curator of the John Jay Homestead, Bedford, New York, whose ripe scholarship on all matters concerning the Jay family places the editors once more in his debt. Frequent levies have been made on the time and knowledge of the editorial staffs of the various statesmen series currently in process of publication, with special thanks due to Mrs. Claude-Ann Lopez of the Papers of Benjamin Franklin. Corona Machemer and William B. Monroe of Harper & Row provided invaluable editorial assistance.

The sources of all documents published herein which do not form a part of the Papers of John Jay in the Columbia University Libraries are indicated in the respective source notes and permission to publish these papers is gratefully acknowledged. Material from the Royal Library at Windsor Castle is published with the gracious permission of Her Majesty Queen Elizabeth II. Transcripts of Crown-copyright records in the Public Record Office appear by permission of the Controller of H.M. Stationery Office.

INDEX